Biblical

and

Theological Essays

Selections from the Detroit Baptist Seminary Journal
1996–2000

D1615796

Biblical

and

Theological

Essays

Selections from the Detroit Baptist Seminary Journal
1996–2000

William W. Combs, Th.D.
Editor

BMH Books
Winona Lake, Indiana
www.bmhbooks.com

Biblical and Theological Essays
Selections from the Detroit Baptist Seminary Journal: 1996–2000

Copyright © 2010 by
Detroit Baptist Theological Seminary

Published by BMH Books
P.O. Box 544, Winona Lake, IN 46590 USA
www.bmhbooks.com

ISBN 978-0-88469-263-8
RELIGION / Biblical Studies / General

Printed in the United States of America

Contents

Part 3: Historical Studies

Part 4: Ministry Studies

Preface

Detroit Baptist Theological Seminary is now more than thirty years old, having begun in the fall of 1976. Located in Allen Park, Michigan, a suburb in the metro-Detroit area, DBTS has, for all those years, been dedicated to the task of training men for the gospel ministry. Graduates from the seminary now serve in local churches in the USA as well as on the foreign field. Others have gone on to teach on the college and seminary level.

In 1996 it was decided that the seminary would begin an academic theological journal to advance the scholarly discussion of issues important to the faculty and administration of DBTS. The first issue of the *Detroit Baptist Seminary Journal* appeared in the spring of that year and has been published annually since then. *DBSJ* is abstracted in *New Testament Abstracts, Old Testament Abstracts,* and *Religious and Theological Abstracts. DBSJ* is indexed in the *Christian Periodical Index* and the *ATLA Religion Database®.*

The articles included in this anthology cover the first five years of the *Journal.* They represent a range of issues, including textual, biblical and theological, historical, and ministry studies. We believe they are well worth reading today. We trust they will be of help to students, pastors, and scholars alike in furthering their understanding of the Word of God and thus advancing the cause of Christ in our day.

William W. Combs
Editor

Contributors

All contributors are members of the faculty of Detroit Baptist Theological Seminary.

William W. Combs, Academic Dean and Professor of New Testament

R. Bruce Compton, Professor of Biblical Languages and Exposition

David M. Doran, President and Professor of Practical Theology

Robert V. McCabe, Professor of Old Testament

Rolland D. McCune, Professor of Systematic Theology

Gerald L. Priest, Professor of Historical Theology

Mark A. Snoeberger, Assistant Professor of Systematic Theology and Director of Library Services

Part 1:

Textual Studies

ERASMUS AND THE TEXTUS RECEPTUS[1]

William W. Combs

This first issue of the Journal is dedicated to Dr. William R. Rice, the founder of Detroit Baptist Theological Seminary. Like most fundamentalists in this century, Dr. Rice has always used the King James Version in his public ministry. He often consulted other versions and commonly suggested alternative or improved translations from the pulpit. He never made an issue of Greek texts and English translations. Yet today there is a growing debate in fundamentalism regarding English translations of the Scripture and the texts behind them, especially the NT Greek text. One area of dispute involves the Greek Textus Receptus. For those who may be new to this controversy, Textus Receptus is a Latin term that means "Received Text." The name itself comes from an edition of the Greek NT produced by Bonaventura and Abraham Elzevir (or Elzevier). The Elzevirs printed seven editions of the Greek NT between 1624 and 1678.[2] Their second edition (1633) has this sentence in the preface: "Textum ergo habes, nunc ab omnibus receptum, in quo nihil immutatum aut corruptum damus" (Therefore you [dear reader] have the text now received by all, in which we give nothing changed or corrupted).[3] From this statement (Textum…receptum) comes the term Textus Receptus or TR, which today is commonly applied to all editions of the Greek NT before the Elzevir's, beginning with Erasmus' in 1516.

Numerous individuals who identify themselves with fundamentalism are now arguing that the TR is to be equated with the text of the original manuscripts of the NT. For example, D. A. Waite says:

---

[1] This article appeared in the Spring 1996 issue of *DBSJ*, vol. 1, pp. 35–53.

[2] J. Harold Greenlee, *An Introduction to New Testament Textual Criticism,* 2nd ed. (Peabody, MA: Hendrickson, 1995), p. 65. Unlike the editions of Erasmus, Estienne, and Beza before them, the Elzevirs were not editors of the editions attributed to them, only the printers. The 1633 edition was edited by Jeremias Hoelzlin, Professor of Greek at Leiden. See Henk J. de Jonge, "Jeremias Hoelzlin: Editor of the 'Textus Receptus' Printed by the Elzeviers Leiden 1633," *Miscellanea Neotestamentica* 1 (1978): 105–28. De Jonge also notes that Abraham and Bonaventura were not brothers, as is frequently repeated, but that Abraham was the nephew of Bonaventura (p. 125, n. 48).

[3] Bruce Metzger aptly calls this an advertising blurb (*The Text of the New Testament,* 3rd ed. [New York: Oxford University Press, 1992], p. 106). The preface to the 1633 edition was written by Daniel Heinsius (de Jonge, "Jeremias Hoelzlin," p. 125).

It is my own personal conviction and belief, after studying this subject since 1971, that the words of the Received Greek and Masoretic Hebrew texts that underlie the King James Bible are the very words which God has preserved down through the centuries, being the exact words of the originals themselves. As such, I believe they are inspired words.[4]

That the TR, which underlies the KJV, could be thought to be "the exact words of the originals themselves" would seem to be far-fetched, to say the least, to anyone familiar with the history of the TR. But possibly, that is part of the problem; some who hold the TR position may not be adequately informed about the position they champion. This article will seek to shed some light on this subject by bringing forth the well-established facts about the history of the TR.

ERASMUS' BACKGROUND

The origins of the TR go back to the Roman Catholic priest and Christian humanist Desiderius Erasmus of Rotterdam, who lived from 1466 to 1536.[5] He was the second illegitimate son of a priest named Gerhard, and Margaret, a physician's daughter.[6] His early education was at a school in Gouda and then under the Brethren of the Common Life at Deventer. After his father and mother both died of the plague, Erasmus was sent to another Brethren school at Bois-le-Duc and was eventually persuaded to enter the Augustinian monastery at Steyn. After five years, in 1492, he was ordained a priest.[7] The very next year Erasmus was able to escape the secluded life by becoming secretary to the bishop of Cambrai. Erasmus had hopes of accompanying the bishop to Italy, but the trip never materialized. In 1495 he received permission from the bishop to travel to France to study for his doctorate in theology at the University of Paris.

---

[4] *Defending the King James Bible* (Collingswood, NJ: Bible For Today Publishers, 1992), pp. 48–49.

[5] It is not clear if Erasmus was born in 1466 or as late as 1469, since his own statements appear contradictory. See, e.g., Roland H. Bainton, *Erasmus of Christendom* (New York: Scribner's, 1969), p. 7; and Albert Rabil, Jr., *Erasmus and the New Testament* (reprint of 1972 ed.; Lanham, MD: University Press of America, 1993), pp. 2–3, n. 3.

[6] Erasmus had an older brother named Peter.

[7] John C. Olin, "Introduction: Erasmus, a Biographical Sketch," in *Christian Humanism and the Reformation: Selected Writings of Erasmus,* ed. John C. Colin, 3rd ed. (New York: Fordham University Press, 1987), p. 3; Rabil, *Erasmus,* p. 5.

ERASMUS' KNOWLEDGE OF GREEK

The language of educated persons in the sixteenth century was Latin, "the language in which Erasmus thought, spoke and wrote."[8] It was truly the *lingua franca* of Europe. Because of this Erasmus was able to visit countries such as England, socialize with important people, and even teach at Cambridge, though he could not speak English. But Erasmus was also born into a time when there was a renewed interest in learning the original languages of Scripture (Hebrew and Greek), and he shared that passion for Greek. In his early years at Deventer and his later studies at the monastery at Steyn, Erasmus apparently learned no more than the letters of the Greek alphabet and the meaning of some individual words.[9] While at the University of Paris, he took up the study of Greek in greater earnest. What he learned seems to have come from his own personal study with the help of a few friends.

Erasmus left Paris in 1499, without having finished his doctorate, in order to visit England. He stayed for eight months and made a number of important friendships, including Thomas More and John Colet. During this time Erasmus dedicated himself to the mastery of Greek, and upon his return to Paris, he began to study it with greater determination.[10] About the importance of Greek, he wrote:

> Latin scholarship, however elaborate, is maimed and reduced by half without Greek. For whereas we Latins have but a few small streams, a few muddy pools, the Greeks possess crystal-clear springs and rivers that run with gold. I can see what utter madness it is even to put a finger on that part of theology which is specially concerned with the mysteries of the faith unless one is furnished with the equipment of Greek as well, since the translators of Scripture, in their scrupulous manner of construing the text, offer such literal versions of Greek idioms that no one ignorant of that language could grasp even the primary, or, as our own theologians call it, literal, meaning.[11]

---

[8] Edwin M. Yamauchi, "Erasmus' Contribution to New Testament Scholarship," *Fides et Historia* 19 (October 1987): 7. Léon-E. Halkin observes that at the age of fourteen "Erasmus was speaking Latin as a living language" (*Erasmus: A Critical Biography,* trans. John Tonkin [Cambridge, MA: Blackwell Publishers, 1993], p. 2).

[9] Erika Rummel, *Erasmus as a Translator of the Classics* (Toronto: University of Toronto Press, 1985), p. 5.

[10] B. Hall, "Erasmus: Biblical Scholar and Reformer," in *Erasmus,* ed. T. A. Dorey (Albuquerque: University of New Mexico Press, 1970), pp. 89–90; Bainton, *Erasmus,* p. 59; Rummel, *Erasmus as a Translator,* pp. 11–12.

[11] Epistle 149. The translation is from *The Correspondence of Erasmus,* vol. 2 in the *Collected Works of Erasmus*, trans. R. A. B. Mynors and D. F. S. Thomson (Toronto: University of Toronto Press, 1975), p. 25, hereafter cited as CWE.

Erasmus returned to England in 1505 to prepare for his doctorate at Cambridge. However, he did not stay in England, because the very next year he was given the opportunity to visit Italy. In Italy he could perfect his Greek since many Greeks were teaching Greek there. They had fled after the fall of Constantinople in 1453. Erasmus' first stop in Italy was in Turin, where he received his doctorate in theology. He traveled throughout Italy and spent some time in the home of the famous Venetian scholar-printer Aldus Manutius. Aldus had gathered around him a group of Italian and Greek scholars who ate, slept, and worked together, while pledging themselves to speak only Greek. Here in Venice and during his entire three years in Italy, Erasmus was able to perfect his Greek.

In 1509 Erasmus returned to England and had mastered Greek so well that in 1511 he was invited to teach the language at Cambridge University. Erasmus left England in 1514 for Basel to join forces with the printer Johann Froben. Together they began to publish a number of important works, including his Latin-Greek NT in 1516.

ANNOTATIONES ON THE NEW TESTAMENT

In the summer of 1504, while he was working at the library of the abbey of Parc, near Louvain, Erasmus discovered a manuscript by the Italian humanist Lorenzo Valla (1407–57). He published it a year later under the title *Adnotationes in Novum Testamentum.*[12] Valla's purpose was to evaluate the Vulgate as a translation of the Greek New Testament, and his work consisted of a compilation of annotations on the Vulgate in light of Greek manuscripts.

> Valla attempted to patch up the Latin scriptures and render them a more faithful reflection of the Greek. Thus he presented in his work for the most part a "collatio," a comparison of the Latin Vulgate with the Greek New Testament. He set for himself a straightforward scholarly task: the evaluation of the Vulgate as a translation of the Greek New Testament. In carrying out his task he found many passages, he said, vitiated by unlearned or negligent copyists; others he found corrupted by conscious alteration on the part of audacious scribes; still others he found inaccurately translated from the Greek. In his "collatio," then, Valla annotated these passages in order to offer Latin Christians the clearest possible understanding of the New Testament.[13]

---

[12] For a discussion of Valla's work, see Jerry H. Bentley, *Humanists and Holy Writ* (Princeton, NJ: Princeton University Press, 1983), chapter 2.

[13] Ibid., pp. 35–36.

Valla's work had a profound influence upon Erasmus, so much so "that he devoted much of his career to the task of developing, refining, and extending Valla's methods."[14] Like Valla, Erasmus was convinced that the Vulgate New Testament had many deficiencies that could only be corrected by appeal to the Greek New Testament. But that viewpoint was not well received in Erasmus' day.

> The Greek original was regarded as the biased authority of schismatical, if not heterodox, Greeks: to use their Greek original was to favour their dangerous opinions. Again it was assumed that the making of the Vulgate Latin version had been guided by inspiration of the Holy Spirit; it had been sanctified by eleven hundred years of use in the Latin Church; and it was most intimately related to the most sacred traditions of worship, piety and doctrine. Many thought that to turn aside to the Greek was not only unnecessary, it would begin the dissolution of the Catholic authority.[15]

In addition, many medieval scholars, beginning in the twelfth century, had even begun to teach that the Latin Scriptures were more reliable than the Greek.[16]

Six months after discovering Valla's *Adnotationes,* Erasmus wrote to John Colet in December of 1504 saying that he was going to devote the rest of his life to the study of Scripture.[17] Erasmus made his second trip to England in 1505, and until recently, most scholars believed that it was about this time Erasmus began working on his own Latin translation of the NT, his first effort into the field of biblical studies since being inspired by Valla's work.[18] This belief was based on some manuscripts containing Erasmus' Latin NT translation and the Latin Vulgate in parallel columns. These manuscripts, two dated 1509 and one 1506, incorrectly led scholars

---

[14] Ibid., p. 69.

[15] Hall, "Erasmus," p. 85.

[16] This was based on a misunderstanding of Jerome's prologue to the Pentateuch (Bentley, *Humanists and Holy Writ,* p. 16).

[17] Epistle 181, CWE 2:86.

[18] P. S. Allen, *Erasmus: Lectures and Wayfaring Sketches* (Oxford: At the Clarendon Press, 1934, pp. 67–68; Rabil, *Erasmus,* pp. 61, 92. Allen and (apparently) Rabil (p. 67) say that Erasmus produced a translation of the entire NT before he left England. Others have suggested that he only began the work at this time. See C. C. Tarelli, "Erasmus's Manuscripts of the Gospels," *Journal of Theological Studies* 44 (1943): 160; Eileen Bloch, "Erasmus and the Froben Press: The Making of an Editor," *Library Quarterly* 35 (April 1965): 115–16; Henk J. de Jonge, *"Novum Testamentum a Nobis Versum:* The Essence of Erasmus' Edition of the New Testament," *Journal of Theological Studies* 35 (October 1984): 402 and "The Character of Erasmus' Translation of the New Testament as Reflected in His Translation of Hebrews 9," *Journal of Medieval and Renaissance Studies* 14 (1984): 83; Yamauchi, "Erasmus' Contributions," pp. 8–9.

to believe that Erasmus was working on his Latin translation ten years before its publication. However, Andrew J. Brown has now demonstrated conclusively that these dates apply only to the Vulgate text contained in them, and that Erasmus' translation was added to these manuscripts in the 1520s.[19] Rummel notes:

> The theory that Erasmus had begun work on a translation before 1506 was, however, at odds with his own testimony, for he consistently claimed that the idea of adding a translation to his New Testament edition occurred to him only when the project was already well advanced. In polemics against Edward Lee, Johannes Sutor, and Frans Titelmans, Erasmus declared that the plan was conceived by friends when the publication was already in progress. He claimed that it had not been his own intention to add a new translation—scholarly friends had urged him to do so—and insisted that nothing had been further from his mind at first. He described the circumstances surrounding the publication of the translation in similar terms in a letter to Budé: "When the work was already due to be published, certain people encouraged me to change the Vulgate text" (Ep 421:50–2). In 1533 he repeated this version of events: "When I had first come to Basel I had not even thought about translating the New Testament—I had merely noted down some brief explanatory notes and had decided to be content with that" (Allen Ep 2758:12–14).[20]

Erasmus' first endeavor into NT studies was not his Latin translation, but his *Annotationes* on the NT, which was eventually published in 1516 as part of his Latin-Greek NT. Similar to Valla's *Adnotationes,* "in their original form, the *Annotations* were predominantly a philological commentary, recording and discussing variant readings and commenting on passages in the Vulgate that were in Erasmus' opinion either obscurely or incorrectly rendered."[21] When he began working on these annotations is not certain, but by the time of his stay at Cambridge (1511–14), his letters indicate considerable progress. There he was able to compare the Vulgate against certain Greek and Latin manuscripts. In a letter dated July 8, 1514, Erasmus tells a friend: "After collation of Greek and other ancient manuscripts, I have emended the whole New Testament, and I have annotated

---

[19] Andrew J. Brown, "Date of Erasmus' Latin Translation of the New Testament," *Transactions of the Cambridge Biographical Society* 8-4 (1984): 351–80.

[20] Erika Rummel, *Erasmus' Annotations on the New Testament* (Toronto: University of Toronto Press, 1986), pp. 20–21. Interestingly, before Brown's study was published, Rummel also believed that Erasmus started his Latin translation as early as 1506. See her *Erasmus as a Translator of the Classics,* p. 89.

[21] Ibid., p. vii.

over a thousand passages, not without benefit to theologians."[22] In a later letter to Johannes Reuchlin, he notes: "I have written annotations on the entire New Testament."[23] It was the desire to publish these annotations that ultimately led to Erasmus' Latin-Greek NT.

THE COMPLUTENSIAN POLYGLOT

Actually, the first *printed* Greek NT was produced under the auspices of Cardinal Francisco Ximenes de Cisneros of Spain at the university he built in Alcalá.[24] The Greek NT was printed in 1514 as volume 5 of a larger work called the Complutensian Polyglot (Alcalá was called Complutum in Latin).[25] It was not until 1520 that permission was obtained from Pope Leo X to *publish* the work, though it seems not to have circulated until 1522.[26] The Complutensian Polyglot was actually a complete Bible in six volumes. The OT had the Hebrew, Latin Vulgate, and Greek Septuagint texts in parallel columns, and in the NT, the Latin Vulgate and Greek in parallel columns. Only 600 copies of the Complutensian Polyglot were ever printed. Because of its expense, its influence was limited in comparison to the more popular editions of Erasmus.

PUBLICATION OF THE NEW TESTAMENT

Erasmus came to Basel to meet Froben in August of 1514. He carried with him a number of works. Beatus Rhenanus, an employee of Froben, wrote a letter to a friend in September in which he reported: "Erasmus of Rotterdam, a great scholar, has arrived in Basel most recently, weighed down with good books, among which are the following: Jerome revised, the complete works of Seneca revised, copious notes on the New Testament, a book of similes, a large number of translations from Plutarch, the Adages...."[27] It seems clear that when Erasmus came to Basel in 1514, his intention was to publish his annotations accompanied only by the Latin Vulgate.[28] But it is not certain that Erasmus originally planned for Froben

---

[22] Epistle 296, CWE 2:300.

[23] Epistle 300, CWE 3:7.

[24] For an excellent discussion of the Complutensian New Testament and the facts surrounding its publication, see Bentley, *Humanists and Holy Writ,* pp. 70–111.

[25] Metzger, *Text of the New Testament,* p. 96.

[26] Allen reports that was when a copy reached Erasmus at Basil *(Erasmus,* p. 144).

[27] Cited by Rummel, *Erasmus' Annotations,* p. 23.

[28] Brown, "Date of Erasmus' Latin Translation," p. 374; Rummel, *Erasmus' Annotations,* p. 23.

to do the work—rather intending that project for Aldus.[29] But Aldus died in February of 1515, and by the summer of 1515 Erasmus and Froben had reached an agreement.

During this time plans were made to include the actual text of the Greek NT, probably at the instigation of the printer. Many scholars believe that Froben had heard of the imminent publication of the Complutensian Polyglot and wanted to publish his own edition of the Greek NT first in order to reap the anticipated financial rewards.[30] In later years Erasmus implied that he had been pressured into undertaking it: "At that point Johann Froben—of blessed memory—took advantage of my being accommodating."[31] Because Erasmus had not intended to print a Greek text when he came to Basel, he now had to rely on Greek manuscripts locally available.[32]

Reluctantly, Erasmus also agreed to substitute his own Latin translation for the Vulgate. Because it was done hastily, his 1516 Latin translation retains much of the Vulgate wording and "represents a much less comprehensive revision than Erasmus' later editions.... After 1516 when he had more leisure, he undertook the thorough-going revision which was printed in the second edition of 1519."[33]

The actual printing began in August of 1515. The work was carried on at a frantic pace, involving two presses, and was completed by March of 1516. In June of 1516 Erasmus wrote to a friend: "At last I have escaped from the workhouse in Basel, where I have got through six years work in eight months."[34] Erasmus himself confessed that the first edition was "thrown together rather than edited."[35] There were numerous

---

[29] Rabil, *Erasmus,* p. 90; Hall, "Erasmus," p. 95.

[30] See e.g., Rummel, *Erasmus'* Annotations, p. 23. Allen doubts this was the motivation of Froben (*Erasmus,* pp. 44–45).

[31] Epistle 2758, cited by Rummel, *Erasmus'* Annotations, p. 23.

[32] The Greek manuscripts used by Erasmus will be discussed below.

[33] Brown, "Date of Erasmus' Latin Translation," p. 374. Based on his study of Hebrews 9, Henk J. de Jonge estimates that Erasmus' Latin translation owes sixty percent of its text to the Vulgate, even in its final 1535 (5th) edition. He notes: "It is clear that, in the chapter under consideration, Erasmus' translation is not an independent version, but a revision of the Vg. with the aid of Greek manuscripts" ("The Character of Erasmus' translation of the New Testament as Reflected in His Translation of Hebrews 9," *Journal of Medieval and Renaissance Studies* 14 [1984]: 82).

[34] Epistle 411, CWE 3:290.

[35] "praecipitatum verius quam aeditum," Epistle 402. The Latin text is from P. S. Allen, H. M. Allen, and H. W. Garrod, eds., *Opus epistolarum Des. Erasmi Roterodami,* 12 vols. (Oxford 1906–58), 2:226, hereafter cited as Allen *EE.*

typographical errors. F. H. A. Scrivener complained: "Erasmus' first edition is in that respect the most faulty book I know."[36]

Though the Complutensian Polyglot was *printed* in 1514, Erasmus' Greek NT of 1516 was the first one to be *published*. It was, as has been noted, a Latin-Greek edition, which he called *Novum Instrumentum*. Years later, in 1527, Erasmus explained that he "chose the word *Instrumentum* in the title because it conveyed better than *Testamentum* the idea of a decision put down in writing: *testamentum* could also mean an agreement without a written record."[37] The more than one thousand pages of *Novum Instrumentum* contain three main parts: the Greek text, Erasmus' Latin translation, and his *Annotationes in Novum Testamentum*. The latter, as we have noted, were his explanatory remarks. Erasmus felt they were essential in order to explain and defend his Latin translation according to its Greek base.[38] The Greek and Latin texts are set out in parallel columns with *Annotationes* following on separate pages. To forestall criticism Erasmus prefaced the text of the NT with a number of apologetic writings. These included a letter addressed to the Reader, a dedication to Pope Leo X, an appeal to study Scripture *(Paraclesis)*, a program of theological studies *(Methodus)*, and a defense of his work *(Apologia)*.[39]

PURPOSE OF THE *NOVUM INSTRUMENTUM*

It is a common misconception that Erasmus' main purpose behind the *Novum Instrumentum* was to produce a Greek NT. Erasmus' work is commonly described as the "first publication of the Greek text of the NT."[40] De Jonge has shown that "Erasmus and his contemporaries regarded the *Novum Instrumentum* and its later editions in the first place as the presentation

---

[36] *A Plain Introduction to the Criticism of the New Testament,* 2nd ed. (London: Deighton, Bell, and Co., 1874), p. 383.

[37] de Jonge, *"Novum Testamentum a Nobis Versum,"* p. 396, n. 5. Erasmus' explanation is found in Epistle 1858, Allen *EE* 7:140.

[38] For a full discussion of the *Annotationes,* see Jerry H. Bentley, "Erasmus' *Annotationes in Novum Testamentum* and the Textual Criticism of the Gospels," *Archiv für Reformationsgeschichte* 67 (1976): 33–53 and Rummel, *Erasmus'* Annotations.

[39] Erika Rummel, "An Open Letter to Boorish Critics: Erasmus' *Capita argumentorum contra morosos quosdam ac indoctos,"* *Journal of Theological Studies* 39 (October 1988): 438.

[40] E.g., L. D. Reynolds and N. G. Wilson, *Scribes and Scholars,* 3rd ed. (Oxford, Clarendon Press, 1991), p. 160. Similarly, see Greenlee, *Textual Criticism,* p. 63; and David A. Black, *New Testament Textual Criticism* (Grand Rapids: Baker, 1994), p. 29.

of the NT in a new Latin form, and not as an edition of the Greek text."[41] The primary purpose of Erasmus was to publish his annotations along with his Latin translation. The Greek text was only there for the purpose of confirming the Latin translation. This is easily demonstrated.[42]

First, the title under which Erasmus published his work includes these words, *Novum Instrumentum...recognitum et emendatum,* which means "The New Testament...revised and improved." These words must refer to Erasmus' Latin translation, not to any Greek text, since there was not at that time a printed edition of the Greek NT in circulation that could be "revised and improved." "They mean: here you have a NT, obviously in the language in which it was current, Latin, but in improved revised form, i.e., no longer in the generally current Vulgate version."[43] The title offers no evidence at all that the *Novum Instrumentum* contains an edition of the Greek text.

Second, in his dedication to Pope Leo X, Erasmus says:

> I perceived that that teaching which is our salvation was to be had in a much purer and more lively form if sought at the fountain-head and drawn from the actual sources than from pools and runnels. And so I have revised the whole New Testament (as they call it) against the standard of the Greek original. ...I have added annotations of my own, in order in the first place to show the reader what changes I have made, and why; second, to disentangle and explain anything that may be complicated, ambiguous, or obscure.[44]

In Erasmus' own words, then, what he offers is his new translation based on the Greek. In addition, he has included his explanatory remarks *(Annotationes),* which were to justify the new translation's deviations from the Vulgate. In all of this, Erasmus gives not a hint that he is also offering an edition of the Greek text.

Third, numerous statements in the *Apologia* clearly demonstrate that what Erasmus was defending was not the Greek text, but his new Latin translation. At one point he says the "Greek text has been 'added' (!) so that the reader can convince himself that the Latin translation does not contain any rash innovations, but is solidly based."[45] This is not to say that the Greek text was not important, but clearly it was subordinate to the

---

[41] *"Novum Testamentum a Nobis Versum,"* pp. 395ff.

[42] The following points are taken from de Jonge, *"Novum Testamentum a Nobis Versum."* For a similar viewpoint, see also Rummel, *Erasmus'* Annotations, pp. 23–26; Halkin, *Erasmus,* pp. 104–105; Hall, "Erasmus," pp. 94–96.

[43] de Jonge, *"Novum Testamentum a Nobis Versum,"* p. 396.

[44] Epistle 384, CWE 3:222–23.

[45] de Jonge, *"Novum Testamentum a Nobis Versum,"* p. 400.

Latin translation. Erasmus was concerned about the Greek text only to the extent that it proved his Latin translation was not plucked out of thin air. That he was not primarily interested in the Greek text is clear from the fact that he never brought out a separate edition of just the Greek text, in spite of the fact he was encouraged to do so.[46]

SOURCES FOR THE *NOVUM INSTRUMENTUM*

Seven manuscripts were used by Erasmus in Basel to compile the Greek text that was printed alongside his Latin translation.[47]

1. Codex 1[eap], a minuscule containing the entire NT except for Revelation, dated to about the 12th century.
2. Codex 1[r], a minuscule containing the book of Revelation except for the last 6 verses (Rev 22:16–21), dated to the 12th century.
3. Codex 2[e], a minuscule containing the Gospels, dated to the 12th century.
4. Codex 2[ap], a minuscule containing Acts and the Epistles, dated to the 12th century or later.
5. Codex 4[ap], a minuscule containing Acts and the Epistles, dated to the 15th century.
6. Codex 7[p], a minuscule containing the Pauline Epistles, dated to the 11th century.
7. Codex 817, a minuscule containing the Gospels, dated to the 15th century.

All of these were the property of the Dominican Library in Basel except for 2[ap], which was obtained from the family of Johann Amerbach of Basel.[48] Manuscripts 1[eap] and 1[r] had been borrowed from the Dominicans by Johannes Reuchlin. Erasmus borrowed them from Reuchlin.

Thus Erasmus had three manuscripts of the Gospels and Acts; four manuscripts of the Pauline Epistles; and only one manuscript of Revelation.[49] However, the main sources for his text were Codices 2[e] and

---

[46] Epistle 352, CWE 3:172–73. See also de Jonge, *"Novum Testamentum a Nobis Versum,"* p. 401.

[47] Cornelis Augustijn, *Erasmus: His Life, Works, and Influence,* trans. J. C. Grayson (Toronto: University of Toronto Press, 1991), p. 93; Brown, "Date of Erasmus' Latin Translation," p. 364; de Jonge, *"Novum Testamentum a Nobis Versum,"* p. 404; Yamauchi, "Erasmus' Contributions," pp. 10–11; Bentley, *Humanists and Holy Writ,* pp. 127–32

[48] Brown, "Date of Erasmus' Latin Translation," pp. 364–5. Amerbach (c. 1445–1513) was the first humanist printer in Basel and Froben's predecessor and teacher. See Bloch, "Erasmus and the Froben Press," p. 112.

[49] Clinton Branine (*The History of Bible Families and the English Bible* [Greenwood, IN: Heritage Baptist University, n.d.], p. 12) makes the fantastic claim that Erasmus used 2nd century manuscripts of the Gospels, Acts, and Epistles, and 5th century manuscripts of the Gospels.

2ap.[50] Erasmus did not compile his own Greek text from the manuscripts at his disposal, few as they were; instead, Codices 2e and 2ap themselves served as the printer's copy for all the NT except Revelation. They still contain Erasmus' corrections written between the lines of the text and occasionally in the margins, which came from the other four manuscripts, though he made little use of some of them.[51] A comparison between the manuscripts used by the printer and the printed text indicates that the printer did not accept every correction that Erasmus proposed, and that the printer made some revisions not authorized by Erasmus.[52]

For the book of Revelation, Erasmus had only one manuscript (1r). Since the text of Revelation was imbedded in a commentary by Andreas of Caesarea and thus difficult for the printer to read, Erasmus had a fresh copy made. The copyist himself misread the original at places, and thus a number of errors were introduced into Erasmus' printed text.[53] For example, in Revelation 17:4 Codex 1r and all other Greek manuscripts have the word ἀκάθαρτα ("impure"), but Erasmus' text reads ἀκαθάρτητος, a word unknown in Greek literature. In a similar fashion, the words καὶ παρέσται ("and is to come") in 17:8 were misread as καίπερ ἔστιν ("and yet is").[54] These and other errors produced by the scribe who made the copy of Revelation for the printer are still to be found in modern editions of the TR, such as the widely used version published by the Trinitarian Bible Society.[55]

Because Codex 1r was missing its last page and thus the last six verses of Revelation (22:16–21), Erasmus retranslated these verses from the

---

[50] K. W. Clark, "Observations on the Erasmian Notes in Codex 2," *Texte und Untersuchungen* 73 (1959): 749–56; Bentley, *Humanists and Holy Writ*, p. 127. Tarelli ("Erasmus's Manuscripts of the Gospels," pp. 159ff.) suggests that Erasmus may have also consulted Codex E, which was also the property of the Dominicans at Basel, but, as Bentley has shown (*Humanists and Holy Writ*, pp. 129–30), the evidence points in the opposite direction.

[51] Clark, "Observations on the Erasmian Notes in Codex 2," p. 751; Bo Reicke, "Erasmus und die neutestamentliche Textgeschichte," *Theologische Zeitschrift* 22 (July–August 1966): 259.

[52] Clark, "Observations on the Erasmian Notes in Codex 2," p. 755.

[53] Rummel, *Erasmus' Annotations*, p. 38. Some of these errors can conveniently be found in Frederick H. Scrivener, *A Plain Introduction to the Criticism of the New Testament*, pp. 382–83, n. 2.

[54] The marginal note in the old *Scofield Reference Bible* corrects this error (p. 1346).

[55] Η ΚΑΙΝΗ ΔΙΑΘΗΚΗ. This version is subtitled *The New Testament: The Greek Text Underlying the English Authorised Version of 1611*. My copy is not dated, though it was published in 1976. See Andrew J. Brown, *The Word of God Among All Nations: A Brief History of the Trinitarian Bible Society, 1831–1981* (London: Trinitarian Bible Society, 1981), p. 130.

Latin Vulgate, and he honestly admitted in the *Annotationes* that he had done so.[56] But again, this produced, by my count, twenty errors in his Greek NT that are still in the TR today.[57] They have no Greek manuscript support whatsoever.[58]

In other parts of the NT Erasmus occasionally introduced into the Greek text material taken from the Latin Vulgate where he thought his Greek manuscripts were defective. For example, in Acts 9:6 the words τρέμων τε καὶ θαμβῶν εἶπε, κύριε, τί με θέλεις ποιῆσαι καὶ ὁ κύριος πρὸς αὐτόν ("And he trembling and astonished said, Lord, what wilt thou have me to do? And the Lord said unto him") were inserted by Erasmus at this point because they were in the Vulgate. He frankly admitted in his *Annotationes* that he took the words from the parallel passage in Acts 26:14. Though still found in the TR, the words have absolutely no Greek manuscript support.

With so few manuscripts from which to establish his Greek text, Erasmus was bound to adopt a reading that would ultimately, in light of future manuscript discoveries, prove to be in error. This is especially true in the book of Revelation where Erasmus had only one manuscript. Since no two manuscripts agree exactly, it is essential that manuscripts be compared to determine where the errors lie. But since that was not possible in Erasmus' case, his text in Revelation is limited by the accuracy of his one manuscript. An example of this problem can be seen in Revelation 20:12. Following Codex 1[r], the text of Erasmus and the TR read ἑστῶτας ἐνώπιον τοῦ θεοῦ ("standing before God"). However, all other Greek manuscripts read ἑστῶτας ἐνώπιον τοῦ θρόνου ("standing before the throne").[59]

[56] Rummel, *Erasmus'* Annotations, p. 193, n. 15.

[57] v. 16: insertion of τοῦ before Δαυίδ and ὀρθρινός instead of πρωϊνός; v. 17: aorist tense ἔλθε twice instead of the present ἔρχου, aorist tense ἐλθέτω instead of the present ἐρχέσθω, insertion of καί after ἐρχέσθω, present tense λαμβανέτω instead of the aorist λαβέτω, and insertion of τό before ὕδωρ; v. 18: συμμαρτύρομαι γάρ instead of μαρτυρῶ ἐγώ, present tense ἐπιτιθῇ instead of the aorist ἐπιθῇ, πρὸς ταῦτα instead of ἐπ᾽ αὐτά, and omission of τῷ before the last occurrence of βιβλίῳ; v. 19: present tense ἀφαιρῇ instead of the aorist ἀφέλῃ, omission of τοῦ before the first occurrence of βιβλίου, ἀφαιρήσει instead of ἀφελεῖ, βιβλίου instead of τοῦ ξύλου, insertion of καί before τῶν γεγραμμένων, and omission of τῷ before the last occurrence of βιβλίῳ; v. 21: insertion of ἡμῶν before ᾽Ιησοῦ and insertion of ὑμῶν after πάντων. See Scrivener, *A Plain Introduction to the Criticism of the New Testament*, p. 382, n. 2; Metzger, *Text of the New Testament*, p. 100, n. 1.

[58] Scrivener, *A Plain Introduction to the Criticism of the New Testament*, p. 382.

[59] Again, the old *Scofield Reference Bible* corrects this error (p. 1351).

Besides the seven previously mentioned manuscripts that Erasmus used in Basel for his Greek text, his *Annotationes* indicate that he had examined and collated a few other manuscripts in his various travels. One of these, which can be identified with certainty, is Codex 69, a 15th century manuscript of the entire NT with minor gaps. In a few places Erasmus selected distinctive readings from this manuscript.[60]

OTHER EDITIONS

A second edition of Erasmus' Latin-Greek NT was published in 1519 in which the title was changed from *Novum Instrumentum* to *Novum Testamentum*. In this edition his *Annotationes* almost doubled in size, and a new piece was added: *Capita argumentorum contra morosos quosdam ac indoctos,* "Summary arguments against certain contentious and boorish people." Erasmus also had access to other manuscripts, chiefly Codex 3[eap], a minuscule containing the entire NT except for Revelation, dated to the 12th century.[61] The Greek text differs from the first edition in hundreds of places, chiefly in the correction of misprints.[62] John Mill estimated these changes to number 400.[63] However, the real character of the text changed little, since the manuscripts that Erasmus consulted were primarily of the Byzantine family. As was noted earlier, his Latin translation for this edition was a more thoroughgoing revision of the Vulgate.

A third edition was published in 1522.[64] Erasmus had been criticized because his first and second editions did not contain the famous "heavenly witnesses" passage of 1 John 5:7b–8a *(Comma Johanneum),* which was in manuscripts of the Vulgate.

> [7]For there are three that bear record [*in heaven, the Father, the Word, and the Holy Ghost: and these three are one.* [8]*And there are three that bear witness in earth,*] the Spirit, and the water, and the blood; and these three agree in one.

One of Erasmus' critics was Diego López Zúñiga (better known by his Latin name, Stunica), who was one of the editors of the Complutensian NT.

---

[60] See Bentley, *Humanists and Holy Writ,* p. 126; Brown, "Date of Erasmus' Latin Translation," p. 368.

[61] Bentley, *Humanists and Holy Writ,* p. 133; Yamauchi, "Erasmus' Contributions," p. 12.

[62] Leon Vaganay, *An Introduction to New Testament Textual Criticism,* 2nd ed. rev. by Christian-Bernard Amphoux (Cambridge: Cambridge University Press, 1991), p.132.

[63] In his *Novum Testamentum Graecum* (Oxford, 1707), cited by Scrivener, *A Plain Introduction to the Criticism of the New Testament,* p. 385. From his own study, Scrivener believed that Mill's numbers were low.

[64] Mill estimated 118 changes were made.

The Complutensian NT had included 1 John 5:7, though they translated it from Latin into Greek. Stunica could never cite any Greek manuscript which included the text, but only argued that Latin manuscripts were more reliable than Greek.[65] Another critic was Edward Lee, who was later to become Archbishop of York. Lee accused Erasmus of encouraging Arianism. "Latin Christians since the early Middle Ages had considered this passage the clearest scriptural proof of the doctrine of the Trinity."[66] But Erasmus had excluded it from his first two editions because he found it in "no Greek manuscript, few Latin manuscripts of antique vintage, and only rarely in patristic works. He cited with approval the opinion of St. Jerome, that Latin copyists had introduced the passage on their own in order to refute the Arians and provide scriptural support for Trinitarian doctrine."[67]

In the many retellings of this famous episode, it has become the common tradition that Erasmus rashly made a promise to his critics that he would include the *Comma* if a single Greek manuscript could be brought forward as evidence.[68] However, Henk J. de Jonge has recently demonstrated that nothing in Erasmus' writings indicates he formally made such a promise.[69] De Jonge suggests that the notion of a promise came from a misinterpretation of a passage in a 1520 response to Edward Lee *(Responsio ad Annotationes Eduardi Lei)*. Erasmus wrote:

> If a single manuscript had come into my hands, in which stood what we read (sc. in the Latin Vulgate) then I would certainly have used it to fill in what was missing in the other manuscripts I had. Because that did not happen, I have taken the only course which was permissible, that is, I have indicated (sc. in the *Annotationes*) what was missing from the Greek manuscripts.[70]

De Jonge suggests that Erasmus included the *Comma Johanneum* because he did not want his reputation ruined over a minor detail in the Greek text that might prevent his Latin translation from receiving wide

[65] Bentley, *Humanists and Holy Writ,* pp. 95–96.

[66] Ibid., p. 95.

[67] Ibid., p. 152.

[68] E.g., Metzger, *Text of the New Testament,* p. 101; Jack Finegan, *Encountering New Testament Manuscripts* (Grand Rapids: Eerdmans, 1974), p. 57; Greenlee, *Textual Criticism,* p. 64; Bainton, *Erasmus,* p. 137.

[69] Henk J. de Jonge, "Erasmus and the *Comma Johanneum,*" *Ephemerides Theologicae Lovanienses* 56 (1980): 381–89.

[70] The translation is from de Jonge, "Erasmus and the *Comma Johanneum,*" p. 385.

distribution. When Erasmus was informed that the passage had been found in Codex 61, a 16th century manuscript then in England, he included it, though he notes in his *Annotationes* that he did not believe the *Comma* was genuine.[71]

Another part of this episode has also been incorrectly reported. Again, Metzger, among others, has said that Erasmus *believed* that Codex 61 "had been prepared expressly in order to confute him."[72] And Harris has shown that Codex 61 was, in fact, probably produced at the time of the controversy for the purpose of refuting Erasmus.[73] But Erasmus himself had a different theory as to why Codex 61 contained the *Comma*. He believed

> that the Codex, like many other manuscripts, contained a text which had been revised after, and adapted to, the Vulgate. This was one of Erasmus' stock theories, to which he repeatedly referred in evaluating Greek manuscripts of the New Testament. He regarded manuscripts which deviated from the Byzantine text known to him, and showed parallels with the Vulgate, as having been influenced by the Vulgate.[74]

Erasmus continued to include the *Comma* in his later editions.[75]

A fourth edition was published in 1527. Erasmus made use of the Complutensian Polyglot, especially in the book of Revelation. The text of the Vulgate was added in a third column. A fifth and final edition was published in 1535, one year before Erasmus' death. The Vulgate was no longer included.

---

[71] Erasmus was, of course, correct. That the *Comma* is a later addition to the text can be demonstrated from the fact that it is found in the text of only four manuscripts (61, 629, 918, 2318), the earliest of which is from the fourteenth century, and in the margin of four others (88, 221, 429, 636), the earliest of which is the tenth century. It was not cited in the 4th century Trinitarian controversies (Sabellian and Arian) by any Greek Father, an absolutely inexplicable omission had they been aware of the passage. The old *Scofield Reference Bible* says that it "has no real authority, and has been inserted" (p. 1325).

[72] *Text of the New Testament,* p. 101. In the Appendix to his 3rd edition, Metzger notes that these statements have now been demonstrated to be inaccurate by the research of de Jonge (p. 291, n 2).

[73] J. Rendel Harris, *The Origin of the Leicester Codex of the New Testament* (London, 1887), pp. 46–53.

[74] de Jonge, "Erasmus and the *Comma Johanneum,*" p. 387.

[75] Greenlee (*Textual Criticism,* p. 64) and Yamauchi ("Erasmus' Contributions," p. 12) incorrectly report that Erasmus dropped the *Comma* from his later editions. But see Bentley, *Humanists and Holy Writ,* p. 153.

REACTION TO THE *NOVUM INSTRUMENTUM*

The criticism that Erasmus received for his work was primarily directed toward his Latin translation and his *Annotationes,* not his Greek text directly, which few people could read.[76] The translation was criticized because the Vulgate, which Erasmus was correcting by examining Greek manuscripts, was considered to be inspired. Even before the *Novum Instrumentum* was published, Maarten van Dorp, a friend of Erasmus from the theology faculty at Louvain, wrote in a 1514 letter:

> Now I differ from you on this question of truth and integrity, and claim that these are qualities of the Vulgate edition that we have in common use. For it is not reasonable that the whole church, which has always used this edition and still both approves and uses it, should for all these centuries have been wrong.[77]

Dorp goes on to say if anything in the Vulgate "varies in point of truth from the Greek manuscript, at that point I bid the Greeks goodbye and cleave to the Latins."[78] Another critic of Erasmus, Petrus Sutor, a theologian at the University of Paris, said of the Vulgate:

> If in one point the Vulgate were in error the entire authority of Holy Scripture would collapse, love and faith would be extinguished, heresies and schisms would abound, blasphemy would be committed against the Holy Spirit, the authority of theologians would be shaken, and indeed the Catholic Church would collapse from the foundations.[79]

Besides failure to include the *Comma Johanneum* in his first two editions, Erasmus' Latin translation was the object of numerous attacks wherever it departed from the "inspired" Latin Vulgate. For instance, when the angel greets Mary in Luke 1:28, the Vulgate translates the Greek κεχαριτωμένη with *gratia plena* ("full of grace"). Erasmus, however, correctly believed the Greek is better translated by *gratiosa* ("favored").[80] This rendering

---

[76] For a discussion of some of the controversies surrounding Erasmus' work, see Rummel, *Erasmus' Annotations,* chapter 4 and "An Open Letter to Boorish Critics," pp. 438–59; Bentley, *Humanists and Holy Writ,* chapter 5 and "Erasmus' *Annotationes,*" pp. 33–53; Bruce E. Benson, "Erasmus and the Correspondence with Johann Eck: A Sixteenth-Century Debate over Scriptural Authority," *Trinity Journal* 6 (Autumn 1985): 157–65.

[77] Epistle 304, CWE 3:21.

[78] Ibid., p. 22.

[79] Cited by Bainton, *Erasmus,* p. 135.

[80] Rummel, *Erasmus' Annotations,* p. 167; Bentley, "Erasmus' *Annotationes,*" p. 41.

caused an uproar since the translation *gratia plena* had been understood by the church in the technical sense of "full of divine grace," and thus supporting the doctrine of Mary's sinlessness.

Erasmus was also attacked for some of his interpretative comments in the *Annotationes*. He was justly criticized because of his view of inspiration. He believed correctly that it extended only to the original authors, but incorrectly held that it protected them only in matters of faith. In a note on Acts 10 he stated that the apostles' Greek was in error. Divine inspiration extended only to their thoughts, not their words. "It was not necessary to ascribe everything in the apostles to a miracle. They were men, they were ignorant of some things, and they erred in a few places."[81] In the *Capita* he insisted that "there were in the apostle's speech some things that were not grammatically correct."[82] Because of this criticism Erasmus added a statement to the *Apologia* of his fourth edition (1527) in which he affirmed the authors of Scripture had made no mistakes but "that errors crept into Scripture only through inattentiveness of copyists and translators."[83]

THE GREEK TEXT AFTER ERASMUS

Erasmus' Greek text was reprinted with various changes by others. Robert Estienne (Latin, Stephanus) produced four editions (1546, 1549, 1550, 1551). His third edition of 1550 was the first to have a critical apparatus, with references to the Complutensian Polyglot and fifteen manuscripts.[84] It was republished many times and became the accepted form of the TR, especially in England.[85] It influenced all future editions of the TR. According to Mill, the first and second editions differ in 67 places, and the third in 284 places.[86] The fourth edition had the same text as the third but is noteworthy because the text is divided into numbered verses for the first time. It was the source for the NT of the Geneva Bible (1557).

Theodore Beza, the successor of John Calvin at Geneva, produced nine editions between 1565 and 1604. Only four are independent editions,

---

[81] Cited by Rummel, "An Open Letter to Boorish Critics," p. 454.

[82] Ibid.

[83] Bentley, *Humanists and Holy Writ,* p. 204.

[84] T. H. L. Parker, *Calvin's New Testament Commentaries* (London: SCM Press, 1971), p. 103.

[85] Philip Schaff, *A Companion to the Greek Testament and the English Version,* 4th ed. (New York: Harper and Brothers, 1896), p. 236.

[86] Cited by Scrivener, *A Plain Introduction to the Criticism of the New Testament,* pp. 387–88.

the others being smaller-sized reprints. His text was essentially a reprinting of Stephanus with minor changes.[87] A study of the KJV NT by F. H. A. Scrivener concluded that Beza's edition of 1598 was the main source for the translators.[88]

As was noted at the beginning of this article, Bonaventura and Abraham Elzevir produced seven editions between 1624 and 1678. And it was from their second and definitive edition of 1633 that the term Textus Receptus originated. In Europe the third edition of Stephanus (1550) became the standard form of the text in England and that of the Elzevirs (1633) on the continent. Scrivener suggests that they differ in 287 places.[89]

CONCLUSION

Upon receiving a copy of Erasmus' Latin Greek NT, John Colet responded: "The name of Erasmus shall never perish."[90] His "prophecy" has proved to be true for nearly 500 years. His "Textus Receptus" was the standard form of the Greek Text until challenged in the nineteenth century, but, as has been noted, still has many defenders in fundamental circles. Greenlee has wisely observed: "The TR is not a 'bad' or misleading text, either theologically or practically."[91] No one will be led into theological error from using the TR, either directly or in a translation based on it (e.g., KJV and NKJV). But is it, as Waite believes, "the exact words of the originals themselves"? Hardly! It is based on a few very late manuscripts, and in some cases has no Greek manuscript support whatsoever. Without question it is possible to produce a text that is closer to the autographs by comparing the more than 5,000 Greek manuscripts available today. Fundamentalists should reject the attempts by some in our movement to make the TR the only acceptable form of Greek text.

---

[87] Vaganay, *Introduction to New Testament Textual Criticism,* p. 134. Scrivener *(A Plain Introduction to the Criticism of the New Testament,* p. 391), citing Wetstein, says that Beza's text differs from that of Stephanus in about 50 places.

[88] *The New Testament in Greek: According to the Text Followed in the Authorised Version Together with the Variations Adopted in the Revised Version* (Cambridge: University Press, 1908), p. vii.

[89] *A Plain Introduction to the Criticism of the New Testament,* p. 392.

[90] Epistle 423, CWE 3:312.

[91] Greenlee, *Textual Criticism,* p. 63

THE PRESERVATION OF SCRIPTURE[1]

William W. Combs

One of the many issues in the current debate about Greek manuscript text-types and English versions is the question of the preservation of Scripture. In fact, as one analyzes the arguments for the King James-only, Textus Receptus (TR), and Majority Text (MT) positions, it soon becomes obvious that the doctrine of the preservation of Scripture is at the heart of many of these viewpoints.

It may be helpful, at the outset, to note the major differences among these three perspectives. The MT position differs from the TR position in that it argues that the text of the autographs is more perfectly preserved in the thousands of manuscripts that are part of the Byzantine text-type. Since, therefore, these manuscripts represent a majority of all extant Greek manuscripts, a Greek text derived from a consensus of these manuscripts can be called the Majority Text.[2] The TR viewpoint, on the other hand, suggests that the various printed editions of the Greek New Testament, beginning with Erasmus in 1516, more perfectly preserve the autographs. The name Textus Receptus was not formally attached to these printed editions until 1633.[3] Though the TR is Byzantine in character, yet, because it is based on only about seven out of the thousands of Byzantine-type manuscripts, it differs from the more broadly based MT. Daniel Wallace has counted 1,838 differences between the TR and the *Majority Text* of Hodges and Farstad.[4] There has been no English translation based on the MT. The KJV was, of course, translated from the TR, and the TR and King James-only positions are almost always inextricably tied to one another such that one can speak of the KJV/TR position. The King James-only view argues that the KJV is the only English Bible that may be called the Word of God.

Preservation is an underlying presupposition that often controls the text-critical arguments of the KJV/TR and MT positions.[5] For example,

---

[1] This article appeared in the 2000 issue of *DBSJ,* vol. 5, pp. 3–44.

[2] E.g., Zane C. Hodges and Arthur L. Farstad, eds. *The Greek New Testament According to the Majority Text* (Nashville: Thomas Nelson, 1982).

[3] See William W. Combs, "Erasmus and the Textus Receptus," *Detroit Baptist Seminary Journal* 1 (Spring 1996): 35; also available from http://www.dbts.edu/journal.html.

[4] "Some Second Thoughts on the Majority Text," *Bibliotheca Sacra* 146 (July–September 1989): 276.

[5] This assessment is also shared by other observers. See, e.g., Gordon D. Fee, "Modern Textual Criticism and the Revival of the *Textus Receptus,*" *Journal of the Evangelical*

Edward F. Hills argues that "the New Testament textual criticism of the man who believes the doctrines of the divine inspiration and providential preservation of the Scriptures to be true ought to differ from that of the man who does not so believe."[6] He goes on to add that the proper method of textual criticism, which he calls the *"consistently Christian"* method, "interprets the materials of New Testament textual criticism in accordance with the doctrines of the divine inspiration and providential preservation of the Scriptures."[7] The perspective of Hills is one that is universally shared by all those in the KJV/TR camp.[8]

The emphasis given to the preservation argument varies among members of the MT camp. The modern MT and KJV/TR movements owe their impetus to the writings of John Burgon (1813–1888). Though he is often identified with the KJV/TR camp, he himself held a position similar to the MT. This is commonly understood by most anyone who has studied Burgon's writings.[9] Burgon himself said: "Once for all, we request it may be clearly understood that we do not, by any means, claim *perfection* for the Received text. We entertain no extravagant notions on this subject. Again and again we shall have occasion to point out (*e.g.* at page 107) that the *Textus Receptus* needs correction."[10] Burgon's departure from the TR toward the MT is candidly admitted by TR supporters like Edward F. Hills and Theodore P. Letis.[11] However, Burgon is still claimed by most TR supporters as their

---

Theological Society 21 (March 1978): 21–24; Daniel B. Wallace, "The Majority-Text Theory: History, Methods and Critique," *Journal of the Evangelical Society* 37 (June 1994): 186–97; David D. Shields, "Recent Attempts to Defend the Byzantine Text of the Greek New Testament" (Ph.D. dissertation, Southwestern Baptist Theological Seminary, 1985).

[6] *The King James Version Defended,* 4th ed. (Des Moines, IA: Christian Research Press, 1984), p. 3.

[7] Ibid. Similarly, David W. Cloud has an article entitled "Preservation Is Missing in Standard Works on Textual Criticism" (Oak Harbor, WA: Way of Life Literature, 1999); available from http://wayoflife.org/~dcloud/fbns/preservationis.htm.

[8] The one exception may be the Trinitarian Bible Society, according to Shields ("Recent Attempts to Defend the Byzantine Text," pp. 104–6). But see an article on their official web site by G. W. Anderson, which is similar to the normal KJV/TR position on preservation: "What Today's Christian Needs to Know About the Greek New Testament"; available from http://biz.ukonline.co.uk/trinitarian.bible.society/articles/grktxt.htm.

[9] See, e.g., Wallace, "The Majority-Text Theory," pp. 187–89.

[10] *The Revision Revised* (reprint ed.; Paradise, PA: Conservative Classics, n.d.), p. 21, note 2.

[11] Hills, *The King James Version Defended,* p. 192; Theodore P. Letis, "Introduction," in *The Majority Text: Essays and Reviews in the Continuing Debate,* ed. Theodore P. Letis (Grand Rapids: Institute for Biblical Textual Studies, 1987), pp. 2–5.

champion, while at the same time they continue to denounce the modern MT movement. For example, Donald Waite inexplicably asserts: "I also maintain that [Burgon] would have defended the Textus Receptus over the so-called 'Majority' Greek text of Hodges and Farstad."[12]

For Burgon preservation was certainly an important factor in his text-critical views. He argued:

> There exists no reason for supposing that the Divine Agent, who in the first instance thus gave to mankind the Scriptures of Truth, straightway abdicated His office; took no further care of His work; abandoned those precious writings to their fate. That a perpetual miracle was wrought for their preservation—that copyists were protected against the risk of error, or evil men prevented from adulterating shamefully copies of the Deposit—no one, it is presumed, is so weak as to suppose. But it is quite a different thing to claim that all down the ages the sacred writings must needs have been God's peculiar care; that the Church under Him has watched over them with intelligence and skill; has recognized which copies exhibit a fabricated, which an honestly transcribed text; has generally sanctioned the one, and generally disallowed the other.[13]

Burgon's view of preservation was particularly tied to his High Church Anglicanism and apostolic succession, in that the correct text is to be found in what the Church through its bishops has preserved.[14] He observed: "The Church, remember, hath been from the beginning the 'Witness and Keeper of Holy Writ'...The Church, in her collective capacity, hath nevertheless—as a matter of fact—been perpetually purging herself of those shamefully depraved copies which once everywhere abounded within her pale..."[15] The "Witness and Keeper of Holy Writ" is a reference to the Thirty-Nine Articles of the Church of England, to which Burgon subscribed.[16] Thus, it may be, as Hills and Letis suggest, that Burgon's rejection of the TR was related to its origin with Erasmus, who was not a bishop.[17]

---

[12] *Fundamentalist Distortions on Bible Versions* (Collingswood, NJ: Bible for Today Press, 1999), p. 7.

[13] John W. Burgon, *The Traditional Text of the Gospels,* ed. Edward Miller (London: George Bell and Sons, 1896), pp. 11–12.

[14] See Hills, *The King James Version Defended,* pp. 140, 142 and idem, "A History of My Defense of the King James Version," *Burning Bush* 4 (July 1998): 102.

[15] *The Revision Revised,* pp. 334–35.

[16] See Edgar C. S. Gibson, *The Thirty-Nine Articles of the Church of England,* 5th ed. (London: Methuen & Co., 1906), p. 526.

[17] Hills, *The King James Version Defended,* p. 192; and Letis, "Introduction," p. 5.

Since preservation was an important ingredient in Burgon's text-critical views, it is not surprising that we should see the argument from preservation used by his followers in the MT camp. It is quite prominent in Wilbur Pickering's articulation,[18] though it receives less emphasis in Zane Hodges' writings.[19] However, Robinson and Pierpont deny that their text-critical methodology in defense of the MT is in any way tied to the doctrine of preservation.[20]

VIEWS ON PRESERVATION

The views of evangelical Christians who are currently engaged in the present debate about preservation can be classified a number of ways. At the most fundamental level, one can make a twofold division: (1) those who deny the Scriptures teach any doctrine of preservation and (2) those who affirm there is a doctrine of preservation taught by the Scriptures, either directly or indirectly. However, a threefold division is more helpful since those in group 2, who affirm a doctrine of preservation, are themselves sharply divided as to what that doctrine teaches. On one side are those who believe that the Scriptures have been preserved in the totality of the biblical manuscripts (Hebrew, Aramaic, and Greek), and, on the other side, are those who believe that the Scriptures have only been accurately preserved in the KJV/TR/MT tradition—that any other textual tradition is corrupt.

Right at the onset, we must distinguish between belief in a *doctrine* of preservation and, simply, belief in preservation. This is crucial in understanding exactly what those in group 1 are denying. To my knowledge, no one in that group denies *the preservation of Scripture,* that is, that the books of the Old and New Testaments have been

---

[18] "Contribution of John William Burgon to New Testament Criticism," in *True or False? The Westcott-Hort Textual Theory Examined,* ed. David O. Fuller (Grand Rapids: Grand Rapids International Publications, 1973), pp. 277–80; idem, *The Identity of the New Testament Text* (Nashville: Thomas Nelson, 1977), pp. 143–44. See especially the discussion by Daniel B. Wallace, "The Majority Text and the Original Text: Are They Identical?" *Bibliotheca Sacra* 148 (April–June 1991): 152–54.

[19] "Rationalism and Contemporary New Testament Textual Criticism," *Bibliotheca Sacra* 128 (January–March 1971): 29–30. In his later writings, however, Hodges holds the preservation argument in abeyance and argues the MT position on strict text-critical grounds. See, for example, "Modern Textual Criticism and the Majority Text: A Response," *Journal of the Evangelical Theological Society* 21 (June 1978): 145–46.

[20] Maurice A. Robinson and William G. Pierpont, *The New Testament in the Original Greek According to the Byzantine/Majority Textform* (Atlanta: Original Word Publishers, 1991), pp. xli–xliii.

substantially preserved to our day. But they do deny that Scripture anywhere promises, either directly or indirectly, its own preservation—a doctrine of preservation. That is, they can speak of the preservation of Scripture because it is a historical reality, but it is not a theological necessity. This then provides another way to distinguish between groups 1 and 2. Those in group 1, who deny a doctrine of preservation, believe Scripture has been preserved, but it is only a historical reality—a fact that is clear from the historical evidence. Those in group 2, who affirm a doctrine of preservaion, also believe that the historical evidence demonstrates the preservation of Scripture, but add that this preservation is a theological necessity— Scripture must be preserved because Scripture itself promises its own preservation. We will now turn to a more complete description of these views.

Denial of a Doctrine of Preservation

In an article entitled "Inspiration, Preservation, and New Testament Textual Criticism,"[21] by Daniel B. Wallace, we find what is apparently the first definitive, systematic denial of a doctrine of preservation of Scripture.[22] He has been joined in his view by W. Edward Glenny.[23] Though it is impossible to prove that most evangelical Christians have always affirmed a doctrine of preservation, the position of Wallace and Glenny appears to be a rather novel one. It is clearly the rise of the KJV/TR movement that has sparked the recent discussions by Wallace and Glenny, and it is principally the particular doctrine of preservation found in the KJV/TR position that they are seeking to refute—a preservation that hints at, and often openly declares, the perfect preservation of the text of Scripture. But in refuting that extreme view, they have eliminated any vestige of the preservation of Scripture as a doctrine.

It is important to remember that simple statements to the effect that "God has wonderfully preserved the Scriptures" or that "God has provi- dentially preserved the Scriptures" do not, in and of themselves, tell us

---

[21] *Grace Theological Journal* 12 (Spring 1991): 21–50. This article originally appeared in *New Testament Essays in Honor of Homer A. Kent, Jr.,* ed. Gary T. Meadors (Winona Lake, IN: BMH Books, 1991), pp. 69–102.

[22] Wallace's former teacher, Harry Sturz, did in fact precede him in the denial of any corollary between inspiration and preservation, but Sturz argued, contrary to Wallace, that preservation *is* promised in Scripture. See Harry A. Sturz, *The Byzantine Text-Type and New Testament Textual Criticism* (Nashville: Thomas Nelson, 1984), p. 38.

[23] "The Preservation of Scripture," in chapter 5 of *The Bible Version Debate: The Perspective of Central Baptist Theological Seminary,* ed. Michael A. Grisanti (Minneapolis: Central Baptist Theological Seminary, 1997). But, as I will demonstrate later, Glenny retreats from his denial in a footnote to his essay.

anything about one's belief, or lack thereof, in a doctrine of preservation. Whatever has been preserved, whether it is the Bible or, for instance, Julius Caesar's *Commentaries on the Gallic War,* has been preserved because God is in control of the universe. Any ancient document that is extant today owes its present existence to God's preservation. So we can say that all the works of ancient authors in existence today have been "providentially preserved." But again, this does not necessarily imply a doctrine of preservation—that God must preserve. God did not have to preserve Caesar's *Commentaries on the Gallic War,* and, as is well-known, many ancient documents that were once known to exist have long since perished (e.g., Origen's Hexapla[24]). A *doctrine* of preservation of the Scriptures says that they must be preserved—that they cannot have perished.

Both Wallace and Glenny put forth two major arguments against preservation. First, preservation is not a necessary corollary of inspiration; that is, while inspiration is a true doctrine, there is nothing in the doctrine itself that demands that what God inspired he was bound to preserve. Second, the biblical texts that are used to support a doctrine of preservation have been misinterpreted, and, in fact, do not teach such a doctrine. They take what might be called a minimalist approach to these texts. Both of these arguments will be examined in due course.

Preservation in the KJV/TR/MT Tradition

Though there are some differences among the King James-only and Textus Receptus positions, they both affirm a doctrine of preservation of Scripture, and it is this doctrine that is generally a controlling principle in their text-critical arguments. Although this doctrine receives greater emphasis and is more fundamental in the KJV/TR position, as we noted earlier, the preservation argument also shows up in most formulations of the MT position. The distinguishing factor in this expression of the doctrine of preservation is the notion that God has only accurately preserved the Scriptures in a particular translation (KJV) and printed Greek text (TR) or in a particular manuscript tradition (Byzantine). Other translations of the Bible and other Greek texts are corrupt to such a degree that they generally cannot be called the Word of God. Questions regarding the Old Testament text are usually not addressed in this debate.[25]

---

[24] Hexapla is Greek for "sixfold," and was so named because it was an edition of the Old Testament in six parallel columns. Unfortunately, only fragments of the Hexapla have survived since it was too massive to be copied in full, and the original was destroyed in A.D. 638 when Caesarea was overrun by the Arabs.

[25] See Roy E. Beacham, "The Old Testament Text and English Versions," in chapter 3 of *The Bible Version Debate: The Perspective of Central Baptist Theological Seminary,* ed. Michael A. Grisanti (Minneapolis: Central Baptist Theological Seminary, 1997).

This view of preservation is often described by its supporters as nothing more than *providential* preservation. When, for example, opponents charge that those who hold this view must actually believe in a continuing miracle of *inspiration*, advocates commonly protest that that is not their position, but that of Peter Ruckman, with which they do not wish to be identified.[26] They, we are told, believe in *providential* preservation. However, one gets the impression from their discussions that for the advocates of this viewpoint the word *providential* has taken on an unusual meaning, that *providential* preservation places the preservation of the Scriptures on a different level than other works.[27] However, this is a misunderstanding of *providential*. In reality, "providence is God's power in bringing the movement of the universe to its predetermined goal and design."[28] God brings about his will in the universe either directly (e.g., miracles) or indirectly, that is, through secondary causation. Concerning this latter means, Sproul explains: "We are creatures with a will of our own. We make things happen. Yet the causal power we exert is secondary. God's sovereign providence stands over and above our actions. He works out His will through the actions of human wills, without violating the freedom of those human wills."[29]

When most writers speak of the preservation of the Scripture as being providential, they mean Scripture has been preserved by secondary causation, through ordinary human means, rather than by God's direct, miraculous intervention. God has not chosen to preserve the Scriptures miraculously. Thus the preservation of Scripture is not different *in method* from any other ancient book God has determined to preserve, as, for example, Caesar's *Commentaries on the Gallic War*—both Scripture and Caesar's work have been preserved providentially, by secondary causation, by essentially ordinary human means. But we could also say that Origen's

---

[26] See, e.g., David W. Cloud, "What About Ruckman?" *O Timothy* 11 (November 1994); available from http://wayoflife.org/~dcloud/articles/ruckman.htm.

[27] For instance, Edward F. Hills says, "Dr. Warfield ignored the providential preservation of the Scriptures and treated the text of the New Testament as he would the text of any book or writing" ("A History of My Defense of the King James Version," p. 100). Of course, it is nonsense to suggest that Warfield "ignored the providential preservation of the Scriptures." See his "The Westminster Confession and the Original Autographs," in *Selected Shorter Writings of Benjamin B. Warfield,* vol. 2, ed. John E. Meeter (Nutley: NJ: Presbyterian and Reformed Publishing Company, 1973), pp. 588–94 (originally published in *The Presbyterian Messenger,* September 13, 1894). Hills's negative view of Warfield stems from Warfield's failure to subscribe to Hills's particular view of preservation.

[28] Rolland D. McCune, "Systematic Theology I" (class notes, Detroit Baptist Theological Seminary, 1997), p. 185.

[29] R. C. Sproul, *Essential Truths of the Christian Faith* (Wheaton, IL: Tyndale House Publishers, 1992), p. 62.

Hexapla has providentially *not* been preserved. A *doctrine* of preservation of the Scriptures would mean, however, that the preservation of Scripture was always assured even though God carried out his will to preserve the Scriptures primarily through the actions of human wills.

Advocates of the KJV/TR position, who themselves use the phrase *providential preservation,* often, in their further descriptions of what they mean by preservation, betray the fact that they do indeed believe in a preservation of the Scriptures that is beyond secondary causation. Ray, for example, on the one hand, says that "God has providentially preserved for us the Greek New Testament from which the Authorized King James Bible was translated in 1611";[30] on the other hand, he says that "the writing of the Word of God by inspiration is no greater miracle than the miracle of its preservation in the Textus Receptus."[31] David Cloud speaks of "the Scripture which has been providentially 'kept pure in all ages,'"[32] but then says: "The bottom line is that the same Bible that claims to be infallibly inspired also claims to be infallibly preserved."[33] And, amazingly, Richard Flanders, after arguing that the Bible "claims its God-given words will be providentially preserved,"[34] goes so far as to say that "the actual existence of the original text will continue eternally..."[35]

The first major plank of the KJV/TR viewpoint is that preservation is a corollary of inspiration. Hills argues:

> If the doctrine of the *divine inspiration* of the Old and New Testament Scriptures is a true doctrine, the doctrine of the *providential preservation* of the Scriptures must also be a true doctrine...If He gave the Scriptures to His Church by inspiration..., then it is obvious that He would not allow this revelation to disappear or undergo any alteration of its fundamental character.[36]

Second, we are told that the Bible actually teaches the doctrine of "infallible" preservation of the Scriptures. Many texts are commonly cited, including Psalm 12:6–7; 119:89; 119:152; 119:160; Isaiah 40:8; Matthew

---

[30] Jasper J. Ray, *God Wrote Only One Bible* (Junction City, OR: Eye Opener Publishers, 1955), p. 193.

[31] Ibid., p. 104.

[32] "Comments on James Price's *Textual Emendations in the Authorized Version*" (Oak Harbor, WA: Way of Life Literature, 1986); available from http://wayoflife.org/~dcloud/fbns/commentsonprice.htm.

[33] "Preservation Is Missing in Standard Works on Textual Criticism."

[34] "Does the Bible Promise Its Own Preservation?" p. 1. This is an unpublished paper by the pastor of the Juniata Baptist Church in Vassar, MI.

[35] Ibid., p. 6.

[36] *King James Version Defended*, p. 2.

5:17–18; John 10:35; Matthew 24:35, and 1 Peter 1:23–25. Finally, preservation means that the biblical text has always been publicly available throughout the history of the church. Hills says, "It must be that down through the centuries God has exercised a special, providential control over the copying of the Scriptures and the preservation and use of the copies, so that trustworthy representatives of the original text have been available to God's people in every age."[37] These last two points are quite important because they are used to rule out immediately any printed Greek text or version that is not based on the TR. Only the TR, we are told, displays the kind of "perfect" preservation that Scripture promises for itself, and the only Greek text available throughout all of church history, according this view, has been the TR. Any printed text or version not based on the TR must therefore be of necessity corrupt—not worthy of the title, "the Word of God."

Preservation in the Totality of Manuscripts

That God has preserved the Scriptures in the totality of the manuscript tradition has traditionally been the position of most evangelicals and fundamentalists on the subject of preservation. On the one hand, they have generally affirmed that a doctrine of preservation is taught in Scripture; on the other hand, they have rejected the view that preservation is restricted to just a single text-type (e.g., Byzantine text), printed text (e.g., TR), or version (e.g., KJV). For example, Detroit Baptist Theological Seminary has said:

> While the Bible clearly teaches the ultimate indestructibility of the verbal revelation of God (Matt 24:35; 1 Pet 1:25), it does not tell how and where the written manuscript lineage of that Word is preserved. We believe that God has providentially preserved His word in the many manuscripts, fragments, versions, translations, and copies of the Scriptures that are available, and that by diligent study, comparison, and correlation, the original text (words) can be ascertained.[38]

There is nothing new about this viewpoint. B. B. Warfield understood this to be the clear teaching of the Westminster Confession:

> We thus have brought before us by the Confession, in turn, the original autograph of Scripture, produced by the immediate inspiration of God; the preservation of this autographic text in a multitude of copies whose production is presided over by God's singular care and providence; and the ordinary Bibles

---

[37] Ibid.

[38] *Inspiration & Preservation of Scripture* (Allen Park, MI: Detroit Baptist Theological Seminary, 1996); available from http://www.dbts.edu/inspiration.html.

in the hands of the people, each of which conveys divine truth to the reader with competent adequacy for all the needs of the Christian life.[39]

Like the previous position, this view normally uses the argument based on a corollary between inspiration and preservation (though sometimes it is not formally stated as such). Wisdom, for example, says, "Verbal inspiration is useless without verbal preservation," and Houghton argues, "A view of inspiration without a corresponding view of preservation is of no value."[40] Though these statements could easily be made by someone in the KJV/TR camp, this view of preservation does not hold that the corollary between inspiration and preservation requires that preservation be restricted to the KJV, TR, or MT. The implications of this corollary will be explored later in this essay. In addition, this view of preservation appeals to some of the same biblical texts as the previous view, though they are interpreted quite differently. It obviously does *not* hold that the doctrine of preservation requires that the most accurate biblical text or, for that matter, any biblical text, be publicly available to God's people at all times.

EXAMINATION OF THE BIBLICAL DATA

Appeal has traditionally been made to a number of biblical texts in order to prove a doctrine of preservation. Those who deny that there is any doctrine of preservation discount all these texts, and even those who affirm a doctrine of preservation do not necessarily agree that every one of these texts is applicable. A number of the most commonly cited texts will now be examined. But before these texts are considered, it will be helpful to first look at a phrase whose meaning is central in a number of them—"the Word of God."

The Word of God

In order to prove a doctrine of preservation, a number of Scripture passages in which the phrase "the word(s) of God" (or Lord) is used are commonly appealed to. It is customarily assumed, usually with no supporting argumentation, that this expression universally refers to Scripture, God's written revelation. However, a study of this phrase suggests that, more often than not, God's written revelation is not in view.[41]

---

[39] "The Westminster Confession and the Original Autographs," p. 594.

[40] Thurman Wisdom, "Textus Receptus: Is It Fundamental to Our Faith?" *Faith for the Family,* October 1979, p. 3; Myron J. Houghton, "The Preservation of Scripture," *Faith Pulpit,* August 1999 (a publication of Faith Baptist Theological Seminary, Ankeny, IA).

[41] David W. Hay denies the expression "Word of God" is *ever* used in the Bible with reference to writings ("The Expression 'Word of God' in Scripture," *Canadian Journal of Theology* 2 [July 1956]: 139).

A glance at a concordance or lexicon will easily demonstrate that in the Old Testament the expression "the word of God" (or Lord) is used almost universally of oral communication.[42] Most of the time the phrase occurs in instances of God's communication to man, beginning in Genesis 15:1, "the word of the LORD came to Abraham in a vision, saying, 'Do not fear...,'"[43] and continuing throughout the OT. Also numerous are the occasions where the word of the prophet to his audience is designated as the "word of the LORD," beginning at Numbers 36:5, "Then Moses commanded the sons of Israel according to the word of the LORD, saying, 'The tribe of the sons...,'" and also continuing throughout the OT. Because what came orally to God's spokesmen was sometimes eventually written down, the phrase came to designate Scripture as well. For instance, when the copy of the Law was found in the temple during the reign of Josiah, the king says: "Go, inquire of the LORD for me and for those who are left in Israel and in Judah, concerning the words of the book which has been found; for great is the wrath of the LORD which is poured out on us because our fathers have not observed the word of the LORD, to do according to all that is written in this book" (2 Chr 34:21). But this usage is not common in the OT, with other terms being more frequently used to refer to the written word (e.g., law, testimonies, statutes, etc.). While the attributes of God's oral communication can often be easily transferred to God's written word, a one-to-one correspondence is not always possible; so texts that seem to promise preservation of "the word of God" need to be examined carefully to determine if such an application is valid.

At the beginning of the New Testament there is a continuation of the Old Testament usage when "the word of God came to John, the son of Zacharias, in the wilderness" (Luke 3:2). But once Jesus comes as "the Word" (John 1:1, 14), there is no further reference of the word of God coming to anyone. While "the word of God" does occasionally designate Scripture in the NT, most often "it is used to refer comprehensively to the

---

[42] Francis Brown, Samuel R. Driver, and Charles A. Briggs, eds., *A Hebrew and English Lexicon of the Old Testament* (Oxford: At the Clarendon Press), s.v. "דָּבָר ," pp. 182–83 and "אָמְרָה," p. 57 [hereafter cited as BDB]. See the discussions in *Theological Dictionary of the Old Testament,* s.v. "דָּבָר ," by W. H. Schmidt, 3:111–125; *Evangelical Dictionary of Theology,* s.v. "Word, Word of God, Word of the Lord," by H. D. McDonald, pp. 1185–88; *Evangelical Dictionary of Biblical Theology,* s.v. "Word," by H. Douglas Buckwalter, pp. 828–31; *Zondervan Pictorial Encyclopedia of the Bible,* s.v. "Word, Word of the Lord," by G. W. Bromiley, pp. 956–62. See also Wayne Grudem, *Systematic Theology* (Grand Rapids: Zondervan, 1994), pp. 47–50; idem, "Scripture's Self-Attestation and the Problem of Formulating a Doctrine of Scripture," in *Scripture and Truth,* ed. D. A. Carson and John D. Woodbridge (Grand Rapids: Zondervan, 1983), pp. 19–49.

[43] Unless otherwise noted, all Scripture quotations are from the *New American Standard Bible,* 1995 edition.

body of revealed truths which made up the apostolic gospel."[44] This is how it is used exclusively in Acts: for example, "they...*began* to speak the word of God with boldness" (4:31); "The word of God kept on spreading" (6:7); "the word of the Lord continued to grow and to be multiplied" (12:24); and "the word of the Lord was being spread through the whole region" (13:49). The phrases "the word of God" and "the word of the Lord" are used twenty-one times in Acts and in every case the referent is to the apostolic message of Christ, which was delivered orally. This is the normal usage in Paul's epistles as well. For instance, when Paul describes his enemies as those who "corrupt the word of God" (2 Cor 2:17, KJV), he is not making reference to the Scriptures, but the gospel message.[45] Those in the KJV/TR camp, because they incorrectly assume Paul's "word of God" is Scripture, commonly argue erroneously that here Paul is acknowledging the corrupting of "manuscripts and translations by false teachers."[46]

Psalm 12:6–7

[6]The words of the Lord *are* pure words: *as* silver tried in a furnace of earth, purified seven times. [7]Thou shalt keep them, O Lord, thou shalt preserve them from this generation for ever (KJV).

Several ideas are usually extracted from this verse in the KJV by those in the KJV/TR camp. The "words of the Lord" are understood to be the Bible, and these "pure words" are promised an eternal preservation. It is also understood that these "pure words" will be preserved in a pure form. There are several problems with this interpretation. Everyone would agree that the originally inspired words are "pure words" in the sense that they

---

[44] J. I. Packer, *"Fundamentalism" and the Word of God* (Grand Rapids: Eerdmans, 1958), p. 85. See also Walter Bauer, William F. Arndt, and F. Wilbur Gingrich, *A Greek-English Lexicon of the New Testament and Other Early Christian Literature,* 2nd ed., rev. and augmented by F. Wilbur Gingrich and Frederick W. Danker (Chicago: University of Chicago Press, 1979), s.v. "λόγος," p. 478 and "ῥῆμα," p. 735 [hereafter cited as BAGD]; *Theological Dictionary of the New Testament,* s.v. "λέγω, λόγος, et al.," by A. Debrunner, et al., 4:114; *New International Dictionary of New Testament Theology,* s.v. "Word, Tongue, Utterance," by B. Klappert, 3:1113.

[45] Paul Barnett, *The Second Epistle to the Corinthians,* New International Commentary on the New Testament (Grand Rapids: Eerdmans, 1997), p. 157; Ralph P. Martin, *2nd Corinthians,* Word Biblical Commentary (Waco, TX: Word Books, 1986), p. 50.

[46] David W. Cloud, "The Problems with Bible Preservation/Can You Answer All of the Questions?" (Oak Harbor, WA: Way of Life Literature, 1999 [available from http://wayoflife.org/~dcloud/fbns/problemswith.htm]); also Clinton Branine, *The History of Bible Families and the English Bible* (Greenwood, IN: Heritage Baptist University, n.d.), p. 1; Ray, *Only One Bible,* p. 4.

are "true and dependable, containing no hidden dross or deceit."[47] Truly, these "pure words" are inerrant words, but the passage does *not* say how *purely* they will be preserved, only that they will be preserved. Therefore, at most this verse might be a general promise of the preservation of God's Word. Even then it is somewhat problematic that God would promise only to preserve his Word from David forward ("from this generation"). What about the period between Moses and David?[48]

However, it is more probable that verse 7 ("Thou shall keep them… thou shalt preserve them") is not even referring to "the words of the LORD" in verse 6. That is, the antecedent of "them" in verse 7 is probably not the "words" of verse 6. The Hebrew term for "them" (twice in v. 7) is masculine, while the term for "words" is feminine. Therefore, most interpreters and versions understand the promise of preservation in verse 7 to apply to the "poor" and "needy" of verse 5. Note the NIV:

> [5]"Because of the oppression of the weak and the groaning of the needy, I will now arise," says the LORD. "I will protect them from those who malign them." [6]And the words of the LORD are flawless, like silver refined in a furnace of clay, purified seven times [7]LORD, you will keep us safe and protect us from such people forever.

David's subject in this Psalm is stated right in verse 1: "Help, LORD, for the godly man ceases to be, For the faithful disappear from among the sons of men." David is concerned about the righteous who are being oppressed by the wicked of "this generation." In the midst of this he declares his assurance that God will preserve the righteous forever. Taken in this sense, this passage has no bearing on the doctrine of preservation.

Psalm 119:89

Forever, O LORD, Your word is settled in heaven.

About this verse, D. A. Waite argues:

> God's Word is not in doubt. It is permanent. It is unconfused and plain. God has settled this. If it has been settled, that means it has been preserved, kept pure, Nothing has been lost…. Some people say, "Well, it is settled in Heaven but not on earth." But God doesn't need it in Heaven; He knows His Word.

---

[47] *New International Dictionary of Old Testament Theology and Exegesis,* s.v. "צרף," by Robin Wakely, 3:849.

[48] Glenny, "The Preservation of Scripture," p. 91.

We are the ones who need it. He is using this verse, Psalm 119:89, to show us
that God has given us Words that are settled.[49]

Thus we are to understand that there is a perfect copy of the Bible in
heaven, and this perfect Bible has been "given" to us here on earth.

There are a number of problems with this interpretation. For one, as
has been previously explained, it cannot be automatically assumed that
any reference to the word of God ("Your word") is to be identified with
God's written revelation. So the question in Psalm 119:89 becomes, Is
"Your word" a reference to Scripture or some other usage of the term
word? On the positive side, it is universally recognized that in Psalm 119
the term *word* (דָּבָר), used here, along with the expressions *law* (תּוֹרָה),
testimonies (עֵדוּת), *precepts* (פִּקּוּדִים), *statutes* (חֻקָּה), *commandments*
(מִצְוָה), *ordinances* or *judgments* (מִשְׁפָּטִים), and *promise* or *word* (אִמְרָה) are
commonly used as "synonyms for Scripture,"[50] particularly the Torah.[51]
And in this section of the Psalm (vv. 89–98), other verses do seem to make
reference to the Torah: "If Your law had not been my delight, Then I would
have perished in my affliction" (v. 92); "I will never forget Your precepts,
For by them You have revived me" (v. 93); "I am Yours, save me; For I
have sought Your precepts" (v. 94); "The wicked wait for me to destroy
me; I shall diligently consider Your testimonies" (v. 95); "I have seen a
limit to all perfection; Your commandment is exceedingly broad" (v. 96).
So the Psalmist could be referring to Scripture, and it must be admitted
that even some who do not share the KJV/TR viewpoint on preservation,
nevertheless, believe that verse 89 refers to "a copy of words that God in
heaven has permanently decided on and has subsequently caused to be
committed to writing by men."[52]

Granting for the moment that this verse is referring to God's written
revelation in heaven, it still says nothing about the preservation of that
revelation here on earth, not withstanding Waite's protestations to the
contrary. In fact, it says nothing about its initial inspiration here on earth.

---

[49] *Defending the King James Bible* (Collingswood, NJ: Bible for Today Press, 1992),
pp. 7–8.

[50] Derek Kidner, *Psalms 73–150* (Downers Grove, IL: InterVarsity Press, 1975), p.
417.

[51] Leslie C. Allen, *Psalms 101–150,* Word Biblical Commentary (Waco, TX: Word
Books, 1983), p. 139.

[52] Grudem, "Scripture's Self-Attestation and the Problem of Formulating a Doctrine of
Scripture," p. 33. See also John R. Rice, *Our God-Breathed Book— The Bible* (Murfreesboro,
TN: Sword of the Lord Publishers, 1969), p. 181. William D. Barrick understands Ps
119:89 to mean that the Word of God is preserved in heaven in the *mind* of God ("Ancient
Manuscripts and Exposition," *Master's Seminary Journal* 9 [Spring 1998]: 28).

In short, no direct promise of preservation here on earth can be gleaned from this verse.

Apart from this verse, there is nothing in the rest of Scripture to suggest the idea of an archetypal Bible in heaven, which, if true, might logically lead to a dictation view of inspiration.[53] While it might be accurate to describe some portions of the Bible as being dictated (e.g., The Ten Commandments), conservative explanations of the doctrine of inspiration have generally rejected a dictation methodology.[54] It seems more likely that "Your word" in verse 89 has no *direct* reference to God's written revelation. As Anderson notes, "thy word…is probably the expression of God's all-embracing purpose and will (cf. Isa 40:8)."[55] God's purpose, his will, is "firmly fixed" in heaven "beyond the reach of all disturbing causes."[56] This seems confirmed by the next two verses in Psalm 119:

> [90]Your faithfulness *continues* throughout all generations; You established the earth, and it stands. [91]They stand this day according to Your ordinances, For all things are Your servants.

What God says, his word, is determined and fixed; it can be counted on; thus, God is faithful. His word holds the universe in place.[57] Thus, it would appear that this verse has no direct application to the doctrine of preservation.

Psalm 119:152

Of old I have known from Your testimonies That You have founded them forever.

This verse would seem to offer stronger support for a doctrine of preservation. The context (vv. 145–52) makes clear reference to God's written revelation in the Torah. The Psalmist says he will observe the Lord's "statutes" (v. 145) and keep his "testimonies" (v. 146). He waits for his "words" (v. 147) and meditates in his "word" (v. 148) and asks to be revived according to the LORD's "ordinances" (v. 149). The Psalmist observes that the wicked do not obey his "law" (v. 150). Finally, he concludes in verses

---

[53] E.g., Rice, *Our God-Breathed Book—The Bible,* pp. 282–91.

[54] E.g., Millard J. Erickson, *Christian Theology,* 3 vols. (Grand Rapids: Baker, 1983–1985), 1:207.

[55] A. A. Anderson, *The Book of Psalms,* 2 vols., New Century Bible Commentary (Grand Rapids: Eerdmans, 1972), p. 831.

[56] J. A. Alexander, *The Psalms* (reprint of 1873 ed.; Grand Rapids: Baker, 1975), p. 495.

[57] Glenny, "The Preservation of Scripture," p. 88.

151–52, "You are near, O LORD, And all Your commandments are truth. Of old I have known from Your testimonies that You have founded them forever." These "testimonies," have been "founded forever," meaning, as the NIV puts its, "you established them to last forever."

Glenny seeks to deny any reference to preservation by suggesting the point of the verse is that "in contrast to the wicked, the Psalmist is trusting in God's Word (vv. 145–149). His confidence is that God's law is not fickle; it is trustworthy and based on God's unchanging moral character. That must be the meaning of verse 152 in its context."[58] All of this is true but it is doubtful if it goes far enough. If God has "established" the "testimonies" to "last forever," it is certainly true that "God's law is not fickle" and that "it is trustworthy and based on God's unchanging moral character." But since the Psalmist would have come to know these "testimonies" from the written Torah, probably through his own reading, it is difficult to imagine that he could divorce their being "founded," established, or caused to "last forever" apart from a *preserved* written form, the written form from which he was reading. The Torah could not likely be "established…to last forever" apart from a written form. Verse 152 appears to be a fairly direct promise of preservation.

Psalm 119:160

> The sum of Your word is truth, And every one of Your righteous ordinances is everlasting.

This verse is similar to Psalm 119:152 in that it is part of a section (vv. 153–60) in which the Psalmist makes numerous references to the Torah: "law" (v. 153), "word" (v. 154), "statutes" (v. 155), "ordinances" (v. 156), "testimonies" (v. 157), "word" (158), and "precepts" (159). Again, Glenny seeks to discount the preservation emphasis in verse 160 by interpreting it as he does verse 152. Concerning the last part of the verse, "And every one of Your righteous ordinances is everlasting," Glenny says: "[the Psalmist] must be expressing his confidence in the infallibility and absolute trustworthiness of God's Word. Every statement in God's Word is dependable."[59] Certainly that is true, but it seems to fall short of the meaning of the last part of the verse. God's special revelation is "truth"—it is "dependable," as Glenny notes; but it is also "everlasting." As in verse 152, the Psalmist is reflecting on God's Word in the written Torah, which he sees as both dependable and imperishable. This verse, then, like 152, would also seem to strongly imply a doctrine of preservation.

---

[58] Ibid.

[59] Ibid., p. 89.

Isaiah 40:8

The grass withers, the flower fades, But the word of our God stands forever.

In this verse we are again faced with the problem of identifying "the word of our God," as well as the meaning of "stands forever." The Hebrew word for "stands" (קוּם) when it is used figuratively can have the ideas of "fixed," "confirmed," "established," "endure," and according to BDB in this verse the particular sense is "be fulfilled."[60] BDB also suggests parallels with Isaiah 14:24, "The LORD of hosts has sworn saying, 'Surely, just as I have intended so it has happened, and just as I have planned so it will stand,'" and Isaiah 46:10, "Declaring the end from the beginning, And from ancient times things which have not been done, Saying, 'My purpose will be established, And I will accomplish all My good pleasure.'" Thus, the idea would be that "the word of our God stands forever" in the sense that it will "be fulfilled." However, commentators universally understand the emphasis to be more that of "permanence"—the permanence of God's word in contrast to "the grass" and "the flowers."[61] Motyer says that in verses 6–8 "the message is the contrast between human transience and divine permanence, designed to affirm that what the Lord promises he will most surely keep and perform."[62] Thus Isaiah says that the plans and purposes of the nations will fail, "but the word of our God stands forever"—his plans are fixed, established, permanent; they cannot be "annulled by the passage of time."[63] Alexander suggests that "there is a tacit antithesis between the word of God and man; what man says is uncertain and precarious, what God says cannot fail."[64] What God says, his word, cannot be changed; it is immutable.

[60] p. 878.

[61] So Edward J. Young, *The Book of Isaiah,* 3 vols. (Grand Rapids: Eerdmans, 1965, 1969, 1972), 3:35; John N. Oswalt, *The Book of Isaiah,* 2 vols., New International Commentary on the Old Testament (Grand Rapids: Eerdmans, 1986, 1998), 2:54; Claus Westermann, *Isaiah 40–66,* Old Testament Library (Philadelphia: Westminster Press, 1969), p. 42; Barry G. Webb, *The Message of Isaiah,* The Bible Speaks Today (Downers Grove, IL: InterVarsity Press, 1996), p. 163; George A. F. Knight, *Isaiah 40–55,* 2nd ed., International Theological Commentary (Grand Rapids: Eerdmans, 1984), pp. 14–15; R. N. Whybray, *Isaiah 40–66,* New Century Bible Commentary (Grand Rapids: Eerdmans, 1975), p. 51.

[62] J. Alec Motyer, *Isaiah,* Tyndale Old Testament Commentaries (Downers Grove, IL: InterVarsity Press, 1999), p. 245.

[63] *New International Dictionary of Old Testament Theology and Exegesis,* s.v. "עוֹלָם," by Anthony Tomasino, 3:349.

[64] J. A. Alexander, *The Prophecies of Isaiah,* 2 vols. (reprint of 1875 ed.; Grand Rapids: Zondervan, 1974), 2:98.

Glenny seeks to dismiss any implications this verse might have for the preservation of Scripture by arguing that "this OT context speaks of the infallibility of God's promises to deliver His people from their captivity in Babylon."[65] Earlier he says that "this promise from God 'stands forever'; it is infallible."[66] But this analysis seems to miss the clear emphasis of "permanence" in verse 8, an emphasis that would support the preservation of the word of God. However, it must still be determined if "the word of our God" refers to written revelation. Glenny argues that Isaiah is referring more generally to God's word, that is, "God's promise to deliver His people from the Babylonian Captivity and bring them back to Judah (vv. 9ff.)."[67] But most would not wish to restrict the phrase so narrowly. Grudem is probably more on target when he observes that "Isaiah 40:6–8…refers to the words of God spoken and/or written through the Old Testament prophets" and that verse 8 "is a statement about the character of God's words generally, without reference to any particular form in which they occur."[68]

Overall, then, it does not appear that verse 8 should be pressed to affirm a specific and direct promise of the preservation of God's written revelation. Instead, it may have a more indirect application to the doctrine.

Matthew 5:17–18

[17]Do not think that I came to abolish the Law or the Prophets; I did not come to abolish but to fulfill. [18]For truly I say to you, until heaven and earth pass away, not the smallest letter or stroke shall pass from the Law until all is accomplished.

This is one of the most commonly referenced passages used to support the preservation of Scripture. More familiar are the words of the KJV, which renders the last part of verse 18 thusly, "one jot or one tittle shall in no wise pass from the law, till all be fulfilled." It is universally agreed that the "jot" (ἰῶτα) refers to the Hebrew (or Aramaic) letter ʼ (*yôd*), the smallest letter in the Hebrew alphabet.[69] The "tittle" (κεραία) literally means "horn," that is, a "projection" or "hook."[70] This has often been understood to refer

---

[65] "The Preservation of Scripture," p. 89.

[66] Ibid.

[67] Ibid.

[68] Wayne Grudem, *1 Peter,* Tyndale New Testament Commentaries (Grand Rapids: Eerdmans, 1988), p. 90.

[69] E.g., BAGD, s.v. "ἰῶτα," p. 386; D. A. Carson, "Matthew," in vol. 8 of *The Expositor's Bible Commentary,* ed. Frank E. Gaebelein (Grand Rapids: Zondervan, 1984), p. 145; Robert H. Gundry, *Matthew* (Grand Rapids: Eerdmans, 1982), p. 80; R. T. France, *Matthew,* Tyndale New Testament Commentaries (Grand Rapids: Eerdmans, 1985), p. 115.

[70] BAGD, s.v. "κεραία," p. 428.

to small parts of letters, especially the small strokes distinguishing similar Hebrew letters (e.g., ר and ד).[71] The NASB's "smallest letter or stroke" very adequately conveys the sense.

Taken at face value, the phrase "not the smallest letter or stroke shall pass from the Law" could be understood to teach an absolutely perfect preservation of the "Law." And in fact Flanders says:

> Some say that this promise refers only to the *fulfillment* of scripture and not to its preservation. But notice that it says the text of the Bible (to the very letter) will not *"pass"* in the sense that *"heaven and earth"* shall one day *"pass."* The Greek word used here for *"pass"* is *parelthe,* and it refers to the physical extinction of the thing that shall pass. It can also be translated *"perish."* Just as God's creation *will* pass some day, God's Words will *never* pass! The actual existence of the original text of scripture will continue eternally, just as the physical existence of heaven and earth will not continue.[72]

Flanders's interpretation is just how Matthew 5:18 is commonly understood from the KJV/TR viewpoint. Cloud explains: "In summary, the Bible promises that God will preserve His Word in pure form, including the most minute details (the jots and titles [*sic*], the words), and that this would include the whole Scriptures, Old and New Testaments. The biblical doctrine of preservation is verbal, plenary preservation...."[73] Waite describes this as the "inerrant preservation of the Words of the Bible."[74] But, in fact, these advocates of KJV/TR position do not actually take Matthew 5:18 literally, even though they claim to do so. If not one "jot" or "tittle" is to be changed, then they should insist on using only the 1611 edition of the KJV since "jot" and "tittle" certainly involve spelling, and there have been thousands of spelling changes since 1611. In addition, if not one "jot" or "tittle" is to be changed, they should also insist upon the authority of the Apocrypha since it was also a part of the 1611 edition.

There are two things to be said about the KJV/TR interpretation of Matthew 5:18. First, it is an *incontrovertible* fact, obvious to anyone who has examined the manuscript evidence, that we do not now possess the

---

[71] E.g., Leon Morris, *The Gospel According to Matthew* (Grand Rapids: Eerdmans, 1992), pp. 109–110; Craig L. Blomberg, *Matthew,* New American Commentary (Nashville: Broadman Press, 1992), p. 104; John A. Broadus, *Commentary on the Gospel of Matthew* (Valley Forge, PA: Judson Press, 1886), p. 100; Other suggestions include the Hebrew letter ו (*wāw*), the hook at the top of the ancient י, or scribal ornamentation of certain letters (see Carson, "Matthew," p. 145; Gundry, *Matthew,* p. 80).

[72] "Does the Bible Promise Its Own Preservation?" p. 6.

[73] "Preservation Is Missing in Standard Works on Textual Criticism."

[74] *Fundamentalist Distortions on Bible Versions,* p. 23.

words of the autographs in an absolutely inerrant state. This assertion is most significant since it flatly contradicts the whole thesis of the KJV/TR position. I will demonstrate the truth of this assertion later in this essay. Second, Jesus is not teaching in this verse the "inerrant preservation of the Words of the Bible." We will now turn to the actual meaning of Jesus' words.

Matthew 5:18 is first of all an example of hyperbole,[75] "a conscious exaggeration or a type of overstatement in order to increase the effect of what is being said."[76] In a graphic way, then, this text makes a point similar to Isaiah 40:8—if "not the smallest letter or stroke shall pass from the Law until all is accomplished," the "Law" is immutable;[77] it "stands forever." "No part of the law, not the most insignificant letter, was to be set aside"[78]; "the law is unalterable."[79] But unlike Isaiah 40:8, this text is more directly tied to Scripture since "Law" in verse 18 is at least a reference to the Torah, more probably the entire OT.[80] But again, this is not to be taken literally, as though Jesus were promising that no Hebrew manuscript could be changed or that no copyist could make an error. This is simply a hyperbolic way of saying that God's written revelation cannot be changed.

If the Scripture cannot be changed, then it obviously remains valid, with full authority. Thus, the emphasis in Matthew 5:18 is more on the *authority* and *validity* of the OT, not primarily its preservation.[81] As Moo observes: "Probably, then, we should understand v. 18 to be an endorsement of the continuing 'usefulness' or authority of the law."[82] Thus, this verse makes no *direct* affirmation concerning preservation; however, the emphasis on the continuing authority of the Scriptures can *by implication* be used to argue for the preservation of those same Scriptures. This approach will be discussed later in this essay.

---

[75] So Craig S. Keener, *A Commentary of the Gospel of Matthew* (Grand Rapids: Eerdmans, 1999), p. 178; Robert H. Stein, *Difficult Sayings in the Gospels* (Grand Rapids: Baker, 1985), p. 36.

[76] Walter C. Kaiser, Jr. and Moisés Silva, *An Introduction to Biblical Hermeneutics* (Grand Rapids: Zondervan, 1994), p. 95.

[77] Keener, *Matthew,* p. 177; W. D. Davies and Dale C. Allison, Jr., *The Gospel According to Saint Matthew,* 3 vols., International Critical Commentary (Edinburgh: T. & T. Clark, 1988, 1991, 1997), 1:492.

[78] Broadus, *Matthew,* p. 100.

[79] France, *Matthew,* p. 115.

[80] Carson, "Matthew," p. 145.

[81] Douglas J. Moo, "The Law of Christ as the Fulfillment of the Law of Moses: A Modified Lutheran View," in *The Law, the Gospel, and the Modern Christian,* ed. Wayne G. Strickland (Grand Rapids: Zondervan, 1993), pp. 347, 353; Morris, *Matthew,* p. 110; Gundry, *Matthew,* p. 80; Blomberg, *Matthew,* p. 104; Carson, "Matthew," p. 145.

[82] "The Law of Christ as the Fulfillment of the Law of Moses," p. 353.

John 10:35

> If he called them gods, to whom the word of God came (and the Scripture cannot be broken),

This verse is also commonly used to prove a doctrine of preservation. Waite says: "The Lord Jesus Christ Himself is saying that the Words of God cannot be 'loosened, broken up, destroyed, dissolved, melted, or put off.' It is permanent and preserved by God."[83] Brake adds: "[John 10:35] maintains that the Scriptures cannot cease to exist, that they *will stand*. It is as direct and forceful as possible in maintaining the preservation of the Scriptures."[84] Contrary to Brake, Jesus' statement that "the Scripture cannot be broken" is probably not a "direct" assertion of the preservation of the Scriptures. The word "broken" (λύω) has the idea of "repeal, annul, abolish."[85] Büchsel suggests that here the best rendering is "to set aside," "to invalidate."[86] The Scripture cannot be emptied of its authority or, as Morris explains, "Scripture cannot be emptied of its force by being shown to be erroneous.[87] Thus, Jesus' statement that "the Scripture cannot be broken" is basically making the same point as Matthew 5:18. Murray argues that "in both passages it is the inviolability of Scripture that is asserted."[88] Thus, if Scripture cannot be emptied of its authority, it must have a continuing authority, and, therefore, John 10:35, like Matthew 5:18, has an important implication for the preservation of Scripture. Again, this will be addressed later in this essay.

Matthew 24:35

> Heaven and earth will pass away, but My words will not pass away.

Jesus' statement, "My words will not pass away," might at first seem to be a direct promise of preservation. Waite takes the promise quite broadly:

---

[83] *Defending the King James Bible,* p. 13.

[84] Donald L. Brake, "The Doctrine of the Preservation of the Scriptures" (Th.M. thesis, Dallas Theological Seminary, 1970), p. 14.

[85] BAGD, s.v. "λύω," p. 484. Cf. the NRSV, "and the scripture cannot be annulled."

[86] *Theological Dictionary of the New Testament,* s.v. "λύω et al.," by F. Büchsel, 4:336.

[87] Leon Morris, *The Gospel According to John,* 2nd ed., New International Commentary on the New Testament (Grand Rapids: Eerdmans, 1995), p. 468. See also D. A. Carson, *The Gospel According to John* (Grand Rapids: Eerdmans, 1991), p. 399; F. F. Bruce, *The Gospel of John* (Grand Rapids: Eerdmans, 1983), p. 235; J. Carl Laney, *John,* Moody Gospel Commentary (Chicago: Moody Press, 1992), p. 197.

[88] John Murray, "The Infallibility of Scripture," in *Collected Writings of John Murray,* 4 vols. (Carlisle, PA: Banner of Truth Trust, 1976–82), 1:15.

The Lord is talking of *His Words,* the New Testament. Not the Masoretic Hebrew Old Testament only, but His *Words* will not pass away. That means the promise extends to the New Testament. I believe, personally that the Lord Jesus was the Source and Author of every word of the Hebrew Old Testament text. He was the Revelator. He is the Word of God. In a very real sense, therefore, His *Words* include the entire Old Testament. He is also the Source and Author of all the New Testament books.[89]

However, this verse would seem to promise too much. It is simply not true that *all* of Jesus' words have been preserved. The apostle John reminds us that "there are also many other things which Jesus did, which if they were written in detail, I suppose that even the world itself would not contain the books that would be written" (John 21:25). Certainly, Jesus must have said some things that were not recorded in the NT, and some of those words *have* passed away. Though it is true that God (or Jesus) is the ultimate author of Scripture, this verse is not directly referring to any written revelation.

Matthew 24:35 uses the same hyperbolic language as Matthew 5:18. "Not the smallest letter or stroke shall pass [παρέλθῃ] from the Law" is saying much the same thing as "My words will not pass away [παρέλθωσιν]." Both the words of the Law and the words of Jesus are immutable; they cannot be set aside; they are unalterable. As the words of God, they "stand forever" (Isa 40:8). And just as "not the smallest letter or stroke shall pass from the Law" speaks of the *authority* and *validity* of the Law, so the fact that Jesus' "words will not pass away" gives them equal authority to the OT. Carson notes: "The authority and eternal validity of Jesus' words are nothing less than the authority and eternal validity of God's words (Ps 119:89–90; Isa 40:6–8)."[90] But unlike Matthew 5:18, which clearly refers to Scripture, 24:35 has reference to the authority of Jesus' oral words. And though it is true that some of Jesus' words were recorded in Scripture, written revelation is not the primary emphasis here. Any application to preservation would be indirect, much like Isaiah 40:8.

1 Peter 1:23–25

[23]for you have been born again not of seed which is perishable but imperishable, *that is,* through the living and enduring word of God. [24]For, "ALL FLESH IS LIKE GRASS, AND ALL ITS GLORY LIKE THE FLOWER OF GRASS. THE GRASS WITHERS, And this is the word which was preached to you.

[89] *Defending the King James Bible,* p. 11.

[90] Carson, "Matthew," p. 507.

Again, Waite says, commenting on this passage:

> That is a reference to *Bible preservation*, isn't it? The Word of God is *incor-ruptible*.... God's Words cannot be corrupted, corroded, or decayed like our bodies.... The words of God are incorruptible. They live and abide forever. That is a promise of God's preservation....The Words of God do not go away. They do not perish. They endure *for ever.*[91]

Waite's reference to the Word of God being "incorruptible" comes from the KJV translation: "Being born again, not of corruptible seed, but of incorruptible...." The Greek term (ἄφθαρτος) does not mean "incorruptible" in the modern sense of "without error," but "imperishable," as the NASB rightly translates.[92] Peter is not suggesting there can be no errors in the manuscript tradition.

But does this verse directly teach that God's written revelation is "imperishable"; in other words, does it directly affirm a doctrine of preservation? There are several problems with that interpretation. First, it is not certain that the phrase "living and enduring" in verse 23 modifies "word." A case can be made that it modifies God—"through the word of the living and enduring God."[93] The same two participles are applied to God in Daniel 6:27 (LXX). However, it must be admitted that this reading is rejected by most commentators. Second, Peter is quoting Isaiah 40:8 in verses 24 and 25, and we have already noted that this text is probably not a direct promise of the preservation of Scripture. Third, it is not clear that Peter's reference to the "word of God" in verse 23 and the "word which was preached" in verse 25 is a reference to Scripture. As was previously explained, in the New Testament the "word of God," more often than not, has reference to the gospel message, rather than God's special written revelation. Finally, the passage in Peter ends with the words: "And this is the word which was preached to you." This would seem to indicate that Peter's emphasis throughout has been on the gospel message as proclaimed to his readers, not on God's written revelation.[94] That gospel message may have included references to God's Word written, but it does not appear that this is

---

[91] *Defending the King James Bible,* p. 14.

[92] Also NIV. Cf. BAGD, s.v. "ἄφθαρτος," p. 125.

[93] E.g., J. Ramsey Michaels, *1 Peter,* Word Biblical Commentary (Waco, TX: Word, 1988), pp. 76–77. This is also the marginal reading of the NRSV and the NEB.

[94] Michaels, *1 Peter,* p. 79; J. N. D. Kelly, *A Commentary on the Epistles of Peter and Jude* (reprint of 1969 ed.; Grand Rapids: Baker, 1981), pp. 80–81; Edward G. Selwyn, *The First Epistle of St. Peter* (reprint of 1947 ed.; Grand Rapids: Baker, 1981), p. 151; D. Edmond Hiebert, *First Peter* (Chicago: Moody Press, 1984), p. 105. Though not a conclusive argument, Peter does use the term ῥῆμα, which is commonly used for oral communication (BAGD, s.v. "ῥῆμα," p. 735).

Peter's primary emphasis. Therefore, any reference to the preservation of Scripture in this passage is probably indirect at best.

Summary of Biblical Data

It has been demonstrated that many of the verses commonly claimed by those in the KJV/TR camp to directly prove a doctrine of preservation have been misinterpreted and misapplied. On the other hand, at least two verses, Psalm 119:152 and 160, would seem to suggest a more direct promise of preservation, with Isaiah 40:8 and Matthew 24:35 supplying more indirect support. In addition Matthew 5:18 and John 10:35 also strongly imply a doctrine of preservation with their emphasis on the continuing authority of Scripture—an argument that will be explored shortly. The attempt by Wallace and Glenny to discount the force of these passages for preservation is unconvincing.

Thus we conclude that some of the verses discussed above do teach a doctrine of preservation, some more directly and others more indirectly. However, they do not support the view of preservation that is put forth by the KJV/TR camp—that God has perfectly preserved the Bible to our day. Instead, they only suggest a general promise of preservation without specifying how (what method) or to what extent (how pure) God has chosen to preserve his Word.

IS PRESERVATION THE COROLLARY OF INSPIRATION?

Webster defines *corollary* as "(1) a proposition inferred immediately from a proved proposition with little or no additional proof, (2a) something that naturally follows: result, and (2b) something that incidentally or naturally accompanies or parallels."[95] Thus to say that preservation is the corollary of inspiration means that preservation is a doctrine that can be "inferred immediately" from the "proved proposition" of inspiration; preservation "naturally follows" or "parallels" inspiration. To say that there is a correlation or parallel between inspiration and preservation does not reveal anything about the exact nature of that preservation. It is perfectly reasonable to assert a corollary between inspiration and preservation without asserting that preservation be in every way equal to inspiration—for example, that inerrant inspiration demands inerrant preservation. This is

[95] *Merriam-Webster's Collegiate Dictionary,* 10th ed., s.v. "corollary," p. 259.

the fallacy of the KJV/TR position, which takes the corollary to demand a kind of preservation that is perfect, or almost perfect, and uses that argument to restrict preservation to a specific translation (KJV) or printed text (TR). It is this unreasonable, unbiblical, and unhistorical expression of the corollary that Sturz, Wallace, and Glenny have sought to refute.[96] Although the KJV/TR movement has misconstrued the corollary, the corollary is still valid.

A right understanding of the corollary suggests that there is no real purpose or value in inspiring a document that is not preserved. Skilton observes:

> But we must maintain that God who gave the Scriptures, who works all things after the counsel of his will, has exercised a remarkable care over his Word, has preserved it in all ages in a state of essential purity, and has enabled it to accomplish the purpose for which he gave it. It is inconceivable that the sovereign God who was pleased to give his Word as a vital and necessary instrument in the salvation of his people would permit his Word to become completely marred in its transmission and unable to accomplish its ordained end. Rather, as surely as that he is God, we would expect to find him exercising a singular care in the preservation of his written revelation.[97]

To illustrate, we might ask, What would be the purpose of producing an authoritative record (inspiration) and letting it perish? Why, for instance, let Paul write an inspired letter to the Romans and then have it perish on the way to Rome? Of course, that did not happen, but could it have happened? If one denies a corollary between inspiration and preservation, Paul's letter could have perished before it got to Rome.

The purpose of inspiration was to produce γραφή (2 Tim 3:16), a written record, a deposit of divine truth for the readers, not the writer. Without preservation the purpose of inspiration would be invalidated. Since it was clearly God's intention that Paul's inspired letter to the Romans be read by the Romans—it could not have perished—there must have been a divine work of preservation at work for at least a few weeks or months until the letter was received by the Romans. This suggests that there is some degree of correlation between inspiration and preservation. And the letter to the Romans was not meant just for the Romans. No Scripture was intended for just the original recipients—"For whatever was written in earlier times was written for our instruction, that through perseverance and

---

[96] Harry A. Sturz, *The Byzantine Text-Type,* pp. 37–39; Wallace, "Inspiration, Preservation, and New Testament Textual Criticism," pp. 31–33; Glenny, "The Preservation of Scripture," pp. 77–78.

[97] John H. Skilton, "The Transmission of the Scriptures," in *The Infallible Word* (reprint of 1946 ed.; Phillipsburg, NJ: Presbyterian and Reformed, 1980), p. 143.

the encouragement of the Scriptures we might have hope" (Rom 15:4). Similarly, Paul warns the Corinthians using the example of Israel's failure: "Now these things happened to them as an example, and they were written for our instruction, upon whom the ends of the ages have come" (1 Cor 10:11). If the Old Testament Scriptures ("these things") were "written," that is, inspired for the purpose of instructing future believers ("our instruction"), that purpose for the inspired writings demands their preservation.

The corollary between inspiration and preservation is so compelling that even Glenny, who denies this principle in the text of his chapter on preservation, is forced to recant his denial in a long footnote to that same chapter:

> An obvious truth is that a document that is to be included in the canon must be preserved. Therefore, since inspiration implies canonicity, in an indirect way inspiration is related to the preservation of the *documents* that are included in the canon. However, the preservation I have addressed and evaluated in this chapter is not the preservation of the *documents* that are in the canon, but rather the perfect preservation *of the words of the texts of all of those documents.*[98]

While it is true that Glenny's main concern in his chapter on preservation is to disprove "the perfect preservation *of the words of the texts of all those documents,*" in the process he absolutely denies any corollary between inspiration and preservation. But since this denial creates an untenable problem for his doctrine of the canon, Glenny permits the corollary to enter through the back door. Why is it that "a document that is to be included in the canon *must* be preserved"? (emphasis added)[99] Obviously, it is because God wanted the documents he *inspired* to be in the canon, and if he wanted his *inspired* documents to be in the canon, he "must" have preserved them. This line of reasoning ultimately is based on a corollary between inspiration and preservation. Glenny's *doctrine* of the "preservation of the documents"[100] is essentially the position I am arguing in this essay—preservation of the Scriptures in the totality of the manuscripts.

---

[98] "The Preservation of Scripture," pp. 104–05, note 36.

[99] In a letter to me, Glenny says: "It is inconsistent, and I think impossible, for a canonical document to be lost" (November 5, 1997).

[100] "I base my belief in the preservation of documents on theological reasoning from the doctrines of inspiration and canonicity. And, based on this theological reasoning, I believe we could call this belief in the *preservation of documents* a doctrine…" (Ibid.).

THE ARGUMENT FROM AUTHORITY

Closely tied to the argument for preservation based on a correlation between inspiration and preservation is another corollary between the *authority* of Scripture and preservation. Harold Stigers, in an article entitled "Preservation: The Corollary of Inspiration," never actually makes a *direct* case for a corollary between inspiration and preservation, in the sense argued above. Instead, he says: "The preservation of the Scriptures is bound up with their authority so that the two are really indissoluble. The former is a most necessary outgrowth of their inspiration."[101] The argument here is that since the Scriptures are authoritative, an authority that comes from their inspiration (2 Tim 3:16), the Scriptures can have no continuing authority unless they are preserved. Bahnsen correctly notes: "It is certainly legitimate for us to maintain that God in His sovereignty has preserved His Word in dependable form for all generations. To be a Christian *requires* the possession of God's words as a basis for faith and direction in life,... and men in all generations are *responsible* to be Christians."[102]

Concerning *authority,* Grudem says: "The authority of Scripture means that all the words in Scripture are God's words in such a way that to disbelieve or disobey any word of Scripture is to disbelieve or disobey God."[103] It is "the right to command belief and/or action."[104] This very principle is seen in the most fundamental text on inspiration itself, 2 Timothy 3:16–17: "All Scripture is inspired by God and profitable for teaching, for reproof, for correction, for training in righteousness; so that the man of God may be adequate, equipped for every good work." These purposes for Scripture, to teach, reprove, correct, and train, cannot be fulfilled unless Scripture is preserved. This is where Matthew 5:17–18 and John 10:35 also tie into the doctrine of preservation. Since both passages teach a continuing authority for Scripture, as we have demonstrated, they indirectly support a doctrine of preservation. But the same can be said for numerous texts that command the believer's obedience. If these texts are essential to the believer's sanctification, and they are, they must have been preserved.

THE METHOD AND EXTENT OF PRESERVATION

Though it has been demonstrated that a doctrine of preservation can be rightly affirmed both directly and indirectly from the overall biblical teaching, it is

---

[101] *Journal of the Evangelical Theological Society* 22 (September 1979): 217.

[102] Greg L. Bahnsen, "Autographs, Amanuenses and Restricted Inspiration," *Evangelical Quarterly* 45 (April–June 1973): 110.

[103] *Systematic Theology,* p. 73.

[104] Erickson, *Christian Theology,* 1:243.

important to make clear that none of these Scripture texts and arguments tell us *how* God would preserve his Word, only that he *would* preserve it. We are told neither the *method* nor the *extent* of this preservation.

The Method of Preservation

As far as the method of preservation is concerned, there are only two options. Scripture must be preserved either directly, by miraculous intervention in the transmission process, and/or indirectly, through secondary causation—"through the actions of human wills," as Sproul reminded us earlier. It is generally agreed that God's normal method of preservation has been indirect, through secondary causation. This method has usually been termed *providential,* though, as we previously noted, providence simply has to do with God carrying out his design for the universe, regardless of whether that is done directly or indirectly. But in discussions of preservation the term *providential* is used to signify that though God miraculously inspired his Word, he has normally chosen to preserve it via secondary causation, that is, through ordinary human means. And because preservation has been by ordinary human means, the transmission process has inevitably resulted in the introduction of errors.

As we have observed earlier, because advocates of the KJV/TR position commonly claim to believe in providential preservation through ordinary human means, they generally wish to distance themselves from the idea of a miraculous re-inspiration of manuscripts or versions. However, providential preservation via secondary causation cannot produce the kind of product this position claims to possess—an error-free TR and/or KJV. Speaking of the TR, Waite says:

> It is my own personal conviction and belief, after studying this subject since 1971, that the words of the Received Greek and Masoretic Hebrew texts that underlie the King James Bible are the very words which God has preserved down through the centuries, being the exact words of the originals themselves. As such, I believe they are inspired words.[105]

Of the KJV he adds that he has "not found any translation errors in the King James Bible."[106] In another place, Waite says that "the King James Bible is 'God's Word Kept Intact.'"[107] What does "intact" mean? Waite explains: "It means 'not harmed.' Nothing harms or defiles it.... The King James Bible—in my studied opinion—is the only translation that completely

---

[105] *Defending the King James Bible,* pp. 48–49.

[106] Ibid., p. 246.

[107] Ibid., p. 1.

and accurately reflects, in English, the original Hebrew/Aramaic and Greek."[108] Similarly, Cloud says: "I believe the King James Bible is an accurate and lovely translation of the preserved Greek and Hebrew text of Scripture. I do not believe the King James Bible contains any errors."[109] In like manner, Thomas Strouse writes: "The KJV is the Word of God in the English language. It has no errors in it because it carefully reflects the original language texts closest to the autographa."[110] Ian Paisley agrees: "I believe the Authorised Version preserves the Word of God for me in the English tongue and that it contains no errors."[111]

Although many of those in the KJV/TR camp refrain from using language associated with the original inspiration of the Scriptures, some are not so guarded. Paisley argues: "There is no such thing as verbal Revelation without verbal Inspiration and there is no such thing as verbal Inspiration without verbal Preservation. In all cases it is not partial but plenary i.e. full, complete, perfect."[112] Wallace Miller insists that the "Authorized 1611 Version is the preserved, inerrant, inspired, and perfect word of God in the English language."[113] And amazingly, Charles Perkins believes that "there are no mistakes in it [KJV] and not one word, comma, period, chapter heading, or verse number needs to be changed."[114]

No matter whether one uses the miraculous language of inspiration to describe preservation, or simply calls it providential, the Bible the KJV/TR position claims to possess—an infallible and inerrant Bible—requires a continuous chain of miracles throughout the transmission process. But in actuality the facts demonstrate nothing of the kind, as we will now prove.

The Extent of Preservation

How pure have the original words of the biblical writings been preserved? It is an indisputable fact, proven by the manuscript and versional evidence, that God has not perfectly (that is, without error) preserved the Scriptures throughout their long history of transmission. There is no single manuscript, printed text, or version that can be shown to be error free. This

[108] Ibid.

[109] David W. Cloud, *For Love of the Bible: The Battle for the King James Version and the Received Text from 1800 to Present* (Oak Harbor, WA: Way of Life Literature, 1995), p. 10.

[110] *The Lord God Hath Spoken: A Guide to Bibliology* (Virginia Beach, VA: Tabernacle Baptist Theological Press, 1992), p. 23.

[111] *My Plea for the Old Sword* (Belfast: Ambassador Productions, 1997), p. 9.

[112] Ibid., p. 102.

[113] *The Revelation of God to Man* (Cincinnati, Published by the author, 1992), p. 79.

[114] *Flaming Torch,* April–June 1998, p. 7.

is patently obvious to anyone who is at all familiar with the transmission history of the Scriptures. First, we should note that no two Greek manuscripts of the New Testament agree exactly; these thousands of manuscripts all differ from one another to some degree.[115] No one has ever suggested, even within the KJV/TR camp, that a particular one of these manuscripts is a perfect copy of the autographs—that it is error free. This conclusively demonstrates that God has permitted errors to enter the transmission process, which is the inevitable result of providential preservation. So clearly, at least for 1500 years, once the autographs had perished and before the age of printing, no one had access to an error-free Bible.

Even then, the coming of the printing press did not suddenly produce a perfect Bible. How could it? There were no inerrant Greek manuscripts available from which to produce an inerrant Greek New Testament. When Erasmus published the first Greek New Testament in 1516, he had access to only about seven of the several thousands of Greek manuscripts that are now extant, and even these seven were only partial copies of the New Testament.[116] For instance, for the book of Revelation Erasmus had only one manuscript available to him. Unless this copy of Revelation was an exact copy of the autograph, Erasmus' Greek New Testament was corrupted (i.e., contained errors) when it came off the press. And it is an indisputable fact that it did contain errors.[117] To be specific, the single manuscript of Revelation used by Erasmus was not really a separate manuscript of the text of Revelation but was actually imbedded in a commentary on Revelation by Andreas of Caesarea. As such it was difficult for the printer to read the text itself, so Erasmus had a fresh copy of the text made. The copyist himself misread the original at places, and thus a number of errors were introduced into Erasmus' printed text. One example is in Revelation 17:8, where the copyist mistakenly wrote καίπερ ἔστιν ("and yet is") instead of καὶ παρέσται ("and shall come"). This erroneous reading in Erasmus' Greek New Testament is not found in any manuscript of Revelation, yet it occurs

---

[115] Gordon D. Fee, "The Textual Criticism of the New Testament," in vol. 1 of *The Expositor's Bible Commentary,* ed. Frank E. Gaebelein (Grand Rapids: Zondervan, 1979), p. 420. Burgon himself said: "That by a perpetual miracle, Sacred Manuscripts would be protected all down the ages against depraving influences of whatever sort,—was not to have been expected; certainly, was never promised" (*The Revision Revised,* p. 335).

[116] Combs, "Erasmus and the Textus Receptus," p. 45.

[117] Cf. the oft-quoted appraisal of F. H. A. Scrivener: "Erasmus' first edition is in that respect the most faulty book I know" (*A Plain Introduction to the Criticism of the New Testament,* 2nd ed. [London: Deighton, Bell, and Co., 1874], p. 383).

in all editions of the TR that have followed Erasmus' first edition, including the widely used version published by the Trinitarian Bible Society.[118] Interestingly, Hills admitted that this *is* an error in the TR (and KJV).[119]

The subsequent history of the printed TR did not produce an error-free Bible. This can be seen from the fact that many indisputable errors introduced into Erasmus' first edition, such as the one just discussed, were never corrected, and also from the fact that there have been at least thirty editions of the TR, with hundreds of differences among them.[120] Even the Trinitarian Bible Society, which publishes the most commonly used edition of the TR, admits that no two of these thirty editions is exactly the same.[121] While it is common to speak of the TR as a single, fixed text, there is in fact no such thing.

Finally, when we come to the KJV, we still have not arrived at a perfect Bible. When some advocates of the KJV/TR position are pressed on this point, they may allow for some imperfections. Hills concedes: "Admittedly the King James Version is not *ideally* perfect. No translation ever can be. But it is the product of such God-guided scholarship that it is *practically* perfect. Its errors are few and very minor."[122] In a previous essay I have demonstrated that the current-day KJV clearly contains definite, unmistakable errors, so I will not

---

[118] Η ΚΑΙΝΗ ΔΙΑΘΗΚΗ. This version is subtitled *The New Testament: The Greek Text Underlying the English Authorised Version of 1611*. My copy is not dated, though it was apparently published in 1976. See Andrew J. Brown, *The Word of God Among All Nations: A Brief History of the Trinitarian Bible Society, 1831–1981* (London: Trinitarian Bible Society, 1981), p. 130.

[119] Edward F. Hills, *Believing Bible Study,* 3rd ed. (Des Moines, IA: Christian Research Press, 1991), p. 83.

[120] These include the Complutensian Polyglot of 1514 (though not published until 1520 or 1522), Erasmus' five editions between 1516 and 1535, the 1534 edition of Simon Colinaeus, the four editions of Robert Estienne (Latin, Stephanus) from 1546 to 1551, the nine editions of Theodore Beza from 1565 to 1604, the Antwerp Polyglot of 1571, the seven editions of Bonaventura and Abraham Elzevir from 1624 to 1678, the Paris Polyglot of 1630–1633, and the London Polyglot of 1657. For a listing of some of the differences, see Herman C. Hoskier, *A Full Account and Collation of the Greek Cursive Codex Evangelium 604* (London: David Nutt, 1890), appendix B.

[121] G. W. Anderson and D. E. Anderson, "The Received Text: A Brief Look at the Textus Receptus"; available from http://biz.ukonline.co.uk/trinitarian.bible.society/articles/tr-art.htm.

[122] *Believing Bible Study,* p. 83. In *The King James Version Defended,* he admitted: "As the marginal notes indicate, the King James translators did not regard their work as perfect or inspired, but they did consider it to be a trustworthy reproduction of God's holy Word…" (p. 216).

retrace all that ground here.[123] However, two points should be noted. First, the translators themselves argue in the preface to the 1611 edition that no translation can be expected to be free from error since translators are not superintended by the Holy Spirit in their work as were the apostles when they wrote inspired Scripture: "For has there been anything perfect under the sun in which Apostles or their colleagues, people endued with an extraordinary measure of God's Spirit and privileged with the privilege of infallibility, were not involved?"[124] Second, just as there is no single, fixed form of the TR, so also the KJV. There has never been one KJV, even in 1611. When the KJV was published, there were actually two printed editions in 1611, with 216 variations in the biblical text.[125] These are commonly called the "He" and "She" Bibles, from their respective readings in Ruth 3:15 ("he went into the city" and "she went into the city"). So if the 1611 KJV is without error, which one is it? And since 1611 the KJV has gone through many changes so that no modern-day Christian uses the 1611 KJV.[126] Even modern printings of the KJV differ among themselves. For instance, at Jeremiah 34:16, the Cambridge edition reads "whom ye had set at liberty," while the Oxford edition reads, "whom he had set at liberty."

In addition, those who would attempt to persuade us that the Bible has been perfectly preserved through the TR and KJV wish to give the impression that there are no differences between the Greek text and English version. Waite, for example, when confronted with the problem of how to defend his doctrine of perfect preservation in light of numerous editions of the TR, responds: "The one I am talking about is the exact Textus Receptus that underlies our King James Bible. It was printed by the Trinitarian Bible Society, London, England in the 1970's. It's Beza's 5th edition, 1598, with very few changes. It's the exact text that underlies our King James New Testament."[127] But this is simply false. There are places where the KJV differs from the Trinitarian Bible Society TR or any other

[123] See William W. Combs, "Errors in the King James Version?" *Detroit Baptist Seminary Journal* 4 (Fall 1999): 151–64.

[124] Erroll F. Rhodes and Liana Lupas, eds., *The Translators to the Reader: The Original Preface of the King James Version of 1611 Revisited* (New York: American Bible Society, 1997), p. 78.

[125] Ibid., p. 5.

[126] I have documented some of these changes in my "Errors in the King James Version?" pp. 160–61. For a much more comprehensive list, see F. H. A. Scrivener, *The Authorized Edition of the English Bible (1611), Its Subsequent Reprints and Modern Representatives* (Cambridge: At the University Press, 1884), pp. 148–202.

[127] *Fundamentalist Distortions on Bible Versions*, p. 16.

edition of the TR. A few examples will suffice.[128] In Hebrews 10:23 the KJV has "confession of faith," but the Trinitarian Bible Society TR has "confession of hope." Everyone concedes that the actual Greek word is *hope* (ἐλπίς), not *faith* (πίστις). *Hope* is found in all manuscripts and all editions of the TR. *Hope* and *faith* are two entirely different words, so one cannot sincerely argue that the translators simply decided on "faith" as the correct translation at this point. Besides, the Greek word for *hope* (ἐλπίς) is used 52 others times in the New Testament and in *every* case the translators of the KJV rendered it "hope," not "faith."

In Acts 19:20 the KJV reads "God" ("So mightily grew the word of God and prevailed"), whereas the Trinitarian Bible Society TR has "Lord." In Gal 4:15 the KJV has "Where" (ποῦ) ("Where is then the blessedness..."), while the Trinitarian Bible Society TR has "What" (τίς). "What" is not "Where," and, more particularly, "Lord" is not "God." One or the other must be in error. When pinned down on this point, Cloud, for example, concludes: "We are convinced that the KJV is accurate in all extual matters, and if there is a difference between a KJV reading and any certain edition of the Received Text, we follow the KJV."[129]

So we see that the evidence of manuscripts, texts, and versions means nothing to those in the KJV/TR camp. The KJV is the final authority upon which all manuscripts, texts, and versions are to be judged. How do we know this? It is, we are told, a matter of faith. Cloud informs us: "The doctrines of Biblical infallibility and preservation raise many questions that cannot be fully answered. On the final analysis, they must be accepted by faith."[130] Similarly, Moorman argues:

> Preservation must be approached in an attitude of faith. Like all other Bible truths, the Scripture's teaching on its own preservation is to be in the first instance accepted by faith. Edward F. Hills in his outstanding book, *The King James Version Defended,* calls it "the logic of faith." The facts and evidence of such preservation will then follow.[131]

---

[128] For others, see F. H. A. Scrivener, *The New Testament in Greek According to the Text Followed in the Authorised Version Together with the Variations Adopted in the Revised Version* (Cambridge: At the University Press, 1908), pp. 648–56.

[129] David W. Cloud, "Which Edition of the Received Text is the Preserved Word of God?" (Oak Harbor, WA: Way of Life Literature, 1996); available from http:// wayoflife. org/~dcloud/fbns/whichtr.htm.

[130] "The Problems with Bible Preservation/Can You Answer All of the Questions?"

[131] "Principles of Bible Preservation"; available from http://www.staggs.pair.com/ kjbp/kjb-docs/biblepre.txt.

In one sense Moorman is absolutely correct. What the Bible teaches about its own preservation is to be accepted by faith. But that can be said of everything the Bible teaches—everything the Bible teaches is to be accepted by faith. This argument from faith or "the logic of faith," as Hills likes to call it,[132] actually boils down to faith in the KJV as the perfectly preserved Word of God, in spite of all the evidence to the contrary. This is not faith, at least not in the biblical sense, but pure presumption.

The fundamental fallacy in KJV/TR position can be traced to the faulty premise that the Scriptures themselves teach a perfect and inerrant preservation of the actual words of the autographs. We saw this earlier in Flanders's statement that "the actual existence of the original text will continue eternally..."[133] It is not enough to hold a Bible in one's hand, even a King James Bible, and say this is the Word of God; the KJV/TR position insists that one must be able to say that these are the *Words* of God. Anything else, according to Waite, is "an apostate, heretical, modernistic, and liberal position."[134] Thus one cannot honestly, according to Waite, say that the NASB is the Word of God. He complains that if one holds "his King James in his hand and the New American Standard in his hand with 5,604 differences in their Greek texts in the New Testament alone, how can they both be the *'Word'* of God? *'Word'* of God' could not mean the *'Words'* of God' because of these differences in the Words."[135]

The true situation is this: God has preserved his Word to this day, but because of the means he has chosen to use to accomplish this preservation—providentially, through secondary causation—the words of the autographs have not been inerrantly preserved. Instead, God has chosen to allow for variations to occur—variants within the Hebrew, Aramaic, and Greek copies of the autographs. God has providentially provided all these copies in order to preserve the Scriptures. So it is proper to say that preservation has taken place in the totality of manuscripts. Because God chose this method of preservation, it was not possible to provide a perfectly pure text with no variations (errors). It was sufficient for God's purpose to preserve his Word in copies of the autographs whose exact wording contains some variation. This level of purity is sufficient for God's purposes.

---

[132] *Believing Bible Study,* pp. 36–37, 55–58.

[133] "Does the Bible Promise Its Own Preservation?" p. 6.

[134] *Fundamentalist Distortions on Bible Versions,* p. 45. See also pp. 1, 23, 42, 44, and 50.

[135] Ibid., p. 42.

THE QUESTION OF CERTAINTY

Advocates of the KJV/TR position are unwilling to accept this view of preservation, preservation within the totality of manuscripts. Several reasons are given for rejecting this position, but they all seem to funnel down to the problem of certainty. They believe that this position does not allow the average Christian to be certain that he has access to the Word of God. With so much variation, we are told, one cannot be sure what the Word of God is, and thus inspiration is practically invalidated. Hills argues:

> Has the special providence of God over the New Testament text done no more than to preserve the true readings somewhere, that is to say, in some one or other of the great variety of New Testament manuscripts now existing in the world? If Christ has done no more than this, how can it be said that He has fulfilled His promise always to preserve in His Church the True New Testament Text? How can His people ever be certain that they have the True New Testament Text?[136]

To accept the view that preservation is found in the totality of manuscripts leaves the Christian with what Hills calls "maximum uncertainty" about the text of Scripture, whereas the KJV/TR position results in "maximum certainty."[137] Echoing this same concern, Cloud says that "the average Christian (including the average preacher)" is thus put "at the mercy of textual scholars to tell them what parts of the King James Bible (or any other Bible) can be trusted and what parts are corruptions and mistakes."[138] But all this is simply a camouflage that seeks to give the impression that the words of the KJV or the TR are the words of the autographs and thus have no corruptions or mistakes in them. Cloud ignores the fact that all Christians are "at the mercy of textual scholars." Every English translation, including the KJV, has been based on a printed Greek text. That printed Greek text was the product of textual criticism. So, whether they acknowledge it or not, readers of the KJV are "at the mercy" of Erasmus, who did textual criticism on the manuscripts available to him in order to produce his printed Greek text; and they are at the mercy of the translators of the KJV, who, as we have shown, did not always follow the TR.

---

[136] *King James Version Defended*, p. 109.

[137] Ibid., p. 224.

[138] David W. Cloud, "Correspondence with a Fundamentalist Bible Teacher Who Denounces the King James Only & Received Text Only position" (Oak Harbor, WA: Way of Life Literature, 1999); available from http://wayoflife.org/~dcloud/fbns/correspondencewitha.htm.

When we examine the textual data, it may appear that the KJV/TR position does give greater certainty about the text of Scripture. If one takes into account all of the New Testament manuscripts, for example, there are more total variants among these manuscripts than the total number of variants found just within the Byzantine family, upon which the TR is based. Or if one looks only at various editions of the TR, the number of variants among them is small in comparison to the number of variants in all the New Testament manuscripts. Or if one examines the various editions of the KJV, the number of variants is also small. But this supposed certainty is simply an illusion. The admitted fewer variations in the Byzantine text-type do not necessarily mean that it is a purer text, one that is closer to the autographs. One could argue, and I *would* argue, that by excluding the other manuscript evidence, the KJV/TR position has left itself with a text that is not as pure as one obtained by giving consideration to the total manuscript evidence.[139] There is simply nothing in the biblical doctrine of preservation itself that says that the Byzantine text-type or TR is purer than any other text-type or printed Greek text. The Bible does not teach its own perfect preservation, and it is a serious error to claim otherwise.

As we have already noted, advocates of the KJV/TR position argue that only their view of preservation honestly permits the believer to hold in his hands a Bible (KJV) that can be called the Word of God. Cloud, for instance, says: "There is something wrong with a position on Bible preservation that leaves a man with no preserved Bible...."[140] Their premise is that they have a Bible (KJV) that has no errors; therefore, it, and only it, can be called the Word of God. It is interesting to note at the outset that the translators of the KJV held the exact *opposite* opinion. In their preface to the 1611 edition, they say:

> Now to answer our enemies: we do not deny, rather we affirm and insist that the very worst translation of the Bible in English issued by Protestants (for we have seen no Catholic version of the whole Bible as yet) contains the word of God, or rather, is the word of God. In the same way, when the King's speech delivered in Parliament is translated into French, German, Italian, and Latin, it is still the King's speech, even if it is not interpreted by every translator with the same skill, or perhaps with as appropriate phrasing or always with as great clarity. For as everyone knows, things are classified by their major characteristics. Anyone will admit that a person may be regarded as virtuous even though he has made many slips during his life, otherwise no

---

[139] For proof of this point, see Combs, "Erasmus and the Textus Receptus," pp. 35–53.

[140] David W. Cloud, "The Heresy of Believing the KJV-TR is the Preserved Word of God" (Oak Harbor, WA: Way of Life Literature, 1999); available from http://wayoflife. org/~dcloud/fbns/heresyofbelieving.htm.

one could be called virtuous, because "all of us make many mistakes" (James 3:2). A person may be called handsome and charming, even though he may have some warts on his hand, and not only some freckles on his face, but also scars. So there is no reason why the word when it is translated should be denied to be the word, or should be declared inauthentic, simply because there may be some imperfections and blemishes in the way it is published. For has there been anything perfect under the sun in which Apostles or their colleagues, people endued with an extraordinary measure of God's Spirit and privileged with the privilege of infallibility, were not involved?[141]

R. A. Torrey tackled this problem of identifying translations as the Word of God:

> I have said that the Scriptures of the Old and New Testaments *as originally given* were absolutely inerrant, and the question of course arises to what extent is the Authorized Version, or the Revised Version, the inerrant Word of God. The answer is simple; they are the inerrant Word of God just to that extent that they are an accurate rendering of the Scriptures of the Old and New Testaments as originally given, and to all practical intents and purposes they are a thoroughly accurate rendering of the Scriptures of the Old and New Testaments as originally given.[142]

Therefore, it is proper, and not any sort of deception, to speak of different printed Greek and Hebrew texts, and different translations, as the Word of God even though they have differences among them. God has preserved the Scriptures in a state of what might be called "essential purity."[143] Schnaiter reminds us, following the thought of B. B. Warfield, that we must be

> careful to distinguish between textual purity and the purity of the sense of any given message. There is a purity with regard to the wording of a text that is different from the purity of the message. This merely recognizes that the same thing can be said reliably in more than one way. For example, there is no effect on the meaning of a statement like "she denied her daughter permission to go," if the wording is altered to read "she refused to permit her daughter to go." For a textual researcher who is trying to determine which of those was the original wording of a particular author, it is a question of wording purity. He may thereby refer to one text as "corrupt" and the other as "pure" without reference to the substance of the passage.[144]

---

[141] Rhodes and Lupas, eds., *The Translators to the Reader,* p. 78.

[142] *The Fundamental Doctrines of the Christian Faith* (New York: George H. Doran, 1918), pp. 36–37.

[143] Skilton, "The Transmission of the Scriptures," p. 143.

[144] S. E. Schnaiter, "Review Article: *New Age Bible Versions,*" *Detroit Baptist Seminary Journal* 2 (Fall 1997): 113–14.

The essential message of Scripture has been preserved not only in the Byzantine text-type, but in the Alexandrian text-type as well; the KJV is the Word of God as well as the NASB. When we refer to either or both of these versions as the Word of God, we do so because we rightly assume they are tethered to the autographs and are thus sufficient representatives of them.

Supporters of the KJV/TR position like to point out differences between modern versions and the KJV, seeking to demonstrate that versions like the NASB and NIV are corrupt because they omit various passages and titles associated with the Lord Jesus Christ. However, they are committing the logical fallacy of begging the question, that is, assuming ahead of time what is to be proved. One cannot start with the KJV, point out differences between it and another version, and from that assume that the other version is incorrect. A difference may just as likely indicate that the KJV is incorrect.[145] In any case, these differences are overblown. In truth, doctrinal differences have no real basis in the different Greek texts or English versions. Silva reminds us:

> Christian assurance has little to do with certainty about details. Christ's promise that the Scriptures would be preserved is not affected in the least by modern text-critical methods. The Westminster Confession of Faith, for example, a very extensive summary of Christian doctrine, was produced on the basis of the Textus Receptus. Who would want to argue that the adoption of the UBS text requires a revision of that document?[146]

For a more concrete example, we might consider the doctrinal statement of Detroit Baptist Theological Seminary. It is a detailed declaration of about ten pages in length, consisting of fifteen different articles.[147] There are 920 different verses of Scripture cited in the statement, which are used to support the doctrinal affirmations; and, as one might expect in such a document, these verses represent the most important doctrinal passages in the Bible. Yet one can support these affirmations whether the verses are examined in the KJV, NASB, or NIV. No one is denying that different translations may sometimes disagree in the meaning of an individual verse, but these differences do not result in different formulations of fundamental doctrine. Burgon himself vehemently criticized the *Revised Version* of 1881, yet he admitted that

---

[145] For a full discussion of this issue, see James R. White, *The King James Only Controversy* (Minneapolis: Bethany House Publishers, 1995), chapters 6–9.

[146] Moisés Silva, review of *The Greek New Testament According to the Majority Text,* ed. Zane C. Hodges and Arthur L. Farstad, in *Westminster Theological Journal* 45 (Spring 1983): 185–86.

[147] See the current seminary catalog, 1999–2002, pp. 88–98; available from http://www.dbts.edu/faithstatem.html.

doctrinal differences are not at issue between versions: "Let it be also candidly admitted that, even where (in our judgment) the Revisionists have erred, they have never had the misfortune *seriously* to obscure a single feature of Divine Truth."[148] It cannot be denied that various Christians have some differences in their doctrinal formulations, such as between Presbyterians and Baptists, or between dispensationalists and covenant theologians; but these differences are not the result of using different Greek New Testaments or English versions. Instead, they are directly related to hermeneutical issues; the same words of Scripture are simply interpreted differently by various Christians.

IS PUBLIC AVAILABILITY A NECESSARY COMPONENT OF PRESERVATION?

Those in the KJV/TR camp commonly argue that the doctrine of preservation also includes the idea of public availability of the true text of Scripture. Hills, for example, argues: "It must be that down through the centuries God has exercised a special, providential control over the copying of the Scriptures and the preservation and use of the copies, so that trustworthy representatives of the original text have been available to God's people in every age."[149] And more specifically, he adds concerning the Scriptures: "He must have preserved them not secretly in holes and caves but in a public way in the usage of His Church."[150] The point of this argument is to rule out from consideration as the Word of God Greek texts other than the TR and translations not based on the TR. This argument can be traced back to Burgon and has been followed by most proponents of the MT.

> I am utterly unable to believe, in short, that God's promise has so entirely failed, that at the end of 1800 years much of the text of the Gospel had in point of fact to be picked by a German critic out of a waste-paper basket in the convent of St. Catherine; and that the entire text had to be remodelled after the pattern set by a couple of copies which had remained in neglect during fifteen centuries, and had probably owed their survival to that neglect; whilst hundreds of others had been thumbed to pieces, and had bequeathed their witness to copies made from them.[151]

Burgon was arguing that to set aside the MT (which he called the traditional text) and embrace the text of his adversaries Westcott and Hort would

---

[148] *The Revision Revised*, p. 232.

[149] *The King James Version Defended*, p. 2.

[150] Ibid., p. 86.

[151] Burgon, *The Traditional Text of the Gospels*, p. 12.

mean "that God kept hidden from the church the true text of the Word of
God from some time around the ninth century until the discoveries of the
Codex Sinaiticus and Vaticanus in the nineteenth century."[152]

There are two problems with this argument. First the use of "true text"
is loaded language that distorts the view of those who do not believe that
either the TR or MT is necessarily the closest text to the autographs. It is not
the case that with the publication of the Greek New Testament of Westcott
and Hort, we now have the "true text" that was unavailable before. Both
the TR and MT are the "true text" in the sense that both can be called the
Word of God, both accurately convey the message of the autographs. But
the text of Westcott and Hort as well as the more recent Nestle-Aland and
United Bible Societies' Greek texts can also be called the "true text" in that
they also accurately convey the message of the autographs. It has already
been argued that doctrinal differences among Christians do not stem from
differences in Greek texts or English versions. Many of us simply prefer
the more recent editions of the Greek New Testament because we honestly
believe they present a text that is somewhat more accurately representative
of the autographs.

Second, the belief that God must have made the Scriptures publicly
available at all times has no basis in Scripture itself or in the transmission history of the text. While there are, as I have argued, some texts that
promise the preservation of Scripture, both directly and indirectly, none of
these demands continuous public availability of the text. In fact, Scripture
itself records an instance where part of the Old Testament was not available for a period of probably more than fifty years. When the temple was
being repaired in the eighteenth year of the reign of Josiah (622 B.C.), we
read of the finding of "the book of the law" by Hilkiah the high priest (2
Kings 22:8–10; 2 Chr 34:14–18). Though it is not clear whether "the book
of the law" is a reference to the entire Pentateuch[153] or just the book of
Deuteronomy,[154] it is undeniable from the reaction of Josiah (vv. 11ff.) that
there had been general ignorance of the Law for some time (Josiah says
"our fathers have not obeyed the words of this book," v. 13). According to
Deuteronomy 31, Moses wrote down the Law and gave it to the Levites to
"place it beside the ark of the covenant" (v. 26). It is probable that normal
access to the Scriptures was through copies since the ark, and presumably
the Law, was placed in the most holy confines of the temple. But during

[152] Brake, "The Doctrine of the Preservation of the Scriptures," p. 4.

[153] E.g., Barrick, "Ancient Manuscripts and Exposition," p. 31.

[154] E.g., Raymond B. Dillard, *2 Chronicles,* Word Biblical Commentary (Waco, TX:
Word, 1987), p. 280.

the reign of Manasseh (697–642 B.C.) true Israelite religion was practically wiped out, and it may well be that all copies of the Law were destroyed, thus explaining the general ignorance of the Law until it was discovered during the reign of Josiah.[155]

CONCLUSION

In discussions of the doctrine of preservation by those in the KJV/TR camp, one is often presented with a long list of Scripture texts that purport to support that doctrine. However, as our analysis has shown, the Scriptures themselves have little to say about their own preservation. And, in fact, Wallace and Glenny have openly denied a doctrine of preservation. Yet two verses, Psalm 119:52 and 160, would seem to suggest a more direct promise of preservation, while Isaiah 40:8 and Matthew 24:35 may play a more indirect role. Beyond that, the seemingly undeniable existence of a corollary between inspiration and preservation demands a doctrine of preservation. Equally important are the implications from texts such as Matthew 5:18 and John 10:35, which teach a continuing authority for Scripture, an authority that demands their preservation.

While some have gone too far in their denial of the doctrine of preservation, those in the KJV/TR camp have moved to the other extreme by raising the providential preservation of Scripture to the level of inspiration. That is, the perfect Bible they claim to possess in the TR and LJV cannot have been produced by providential preservation, but only by the miraculous working of God. As Warfield reminded us long ago, inspiration was an immediate activity of God that "produced the plenarily inspired Bible, every word of which is the Word of God."[156] Preservation, on the other hand, was a mediate activity of God that "produced the safe transmission of that Word, but not without signs of human fallibility here and there in several copies."[157] The indisputable evidence from manuscripts, printed texts, and versions proves that the autographic text has not been preserved in any single one of them, but in their totality. Only by careful examination of the preserved documents can the most accurate form of the Scriptures be identified. While it is not possible to produce a text that is in all points identical to the autographs, nevertheless, carefully produced texts and versions are able to convey God's truth to the reader "with competent adequacy for all the needs of the Christian life."[158]

---

[155] John C. Whitcomb, Jr., *Solomon to the Exile* (Grand Rapids: Baker, 1971), p. 136; Leon Wood, *A Survey of Israel's History* (Grand Rapids: Zondervan, 1970), p. 367.

[156] The Westminster Confession and the Original Autographs," p. 593.

[157] Ibid., pp. 593–94.

[158] Ibid., p. 594.

Part 2:

Biblical & Theological Studies

A DEFENSE OF LITERAL DAYS
IN THE CREATION WEEK[1]

Robert V. McCabe

Over the past decade, there has been a proliferation of articles defending either a literal or a figurative[2] interpretation of the days in the creation week.[3] While some of the issues associated with the debate about a literal versus a figurative understanding of the creation days in Genesis 1 have been discussed since the early days of the church,[4] the figurative interpretation of the creation days representing each day as an extended period of time is of recent vintage.[5] Though a few significant interpreters prior

---

[1] This article appeared in the 2000 issue of *DBSJ*, vol. 5, pp. 97–123.

[2] In this paper, I am using the expression "literal" day to refer to a normal, 24-hour day and "figurative" day to refer to a period of time beyond a 24-hour day.

[3] For a recent collection of essays treating both the literal and figurative interpretation of the days in the creation week, see *Did God Create in Six Days?* ed. Joseph A. Pipa, Jr. and David W. Hall (Taylors, SC: Southern Presbyterian Press, 1999).

[4] For a historical survey of the interpretation of the creation days, see Jack Lewis, "The Days of Creation: An Historical Survey of Interpretation," *Journal of the Evangelical Theological Society* 32 (December 1989): 433–55.

[5] A recent article by Robert Letham attempts to demonstrate "that a non-literal view of Genesis 1 has a pedigree reaching back to the third century" ("'In the Space of Six Days': The Days of Creation from Origen to the Westminster Assembly," *Westminster Theological Journal* 61 [Fall 1999]: 151). Though it is true that there have been in the history of Christian doctrine dating back to the third century those interpreters of the creation days advocating a figurative understanding of these days, their non-literal interpretation was diametrically opposed to recent figurative understandings of the creation days. Under some influence from Greek philosophy, early figurative interpreters of the creation days, such as Origen and Augustine, taught that God instantaneously created the world (see Gerhard F. Hasel, "The 'Days' of Creation in Genesis 1: Literal 'Days' or Figurative 'Periods/Epochs' of Time?" *Origins* 21 [1994]: 6–7). While we understand that some early interpreters had theological and hermeneutical ambiguities, none of them argued for any of the days of the creation week to be millions of years old (see David W. Hall, "Evolution of Mythology," in *Did God Create in Six Days?* p. 275). Consequently, Letham's article is somewhat misleading and selective in his use of source material. For a more comprehensive and evenhanded treatment of the historical data, see David W. Hall, "The Westminster View of Creation Days," *Premise* 5 (July 1998), available at http://capo.org/premise/98/july/98/ p980710.html; David W. Hall, Mark A. Herzer, and Wesley A. Baker, "History Answering Present Objections," available at http://capo.org/1540–1740.html; and "The Patristics on Creation," available at http://capo.org/patristics.html. Although Hall's conclusions have been recently challenged by William S. Barker ("The Westminster Assembly on the Days of Creation," *Westminster Theological Journal* 62 [Spring 2000]: 113–20), Hall has effectively rebutted Barker's challenge by demonstrating that orthodox theologians prior to

to the Reformation did not consistently interpret the days of the creation week in a literal manner, they clearly did not support, nor could they have even envisioned, a figurative use for each of the creation days representing an extended period of time. However, since the days of the Reformation, with a renewed and more consistent emphasis on a grammatical-historical hermeneutic, a literal interpretation of the creation days has been the prevailing view of orthodox Christianity. This literal interpretation maintains that God created the heavens, the earth, and all things therein in six, successive 24-hour days.

The literal interpretation of the creation days has come under a more threatening and increasing assault within the last 150 to 200 years. With the rise of modern geology, it became apparent to some that if modern man were to be able to explain the earth's topography by the processes that he could observe, he would have to allow for an earth that has existed for millions of years.[6] Because the geological data for an old earth seemed so overwhelming, some who claimed loyalty to the teachings of Scripture felt compelled to reevaluate the literal understanding of the days of the creation week and to find novel ways to bring their exegetical and theological results into conformity with an old earth. Because of this, reevaluation has resulted in a polarization of thought concerning the earth's age. As in the time prior to the Reformation, two broad interpretative groups have again surfaced: those who interpret the days of creation figuratively and those who interpret the days literally. While those who interpret the creation days figuratively may have some level of hermeneutical continuity with a few pre-Reformation interpreters, their conclusions are radically different: an old earth model supported by modern scientific belief and by "scientifically correct" reinterpretations of key biblical texts. Those who currently interpret the creation days figuratively maintain either that each day corresponds to a long period of time,[7] perhaps millions of years or whatever amount of time is demanded by current geological study, or that

1800 clearly and uncompromisingly maintained that God created the world and all things therein in the space of six literal days ("Still the Only View Expressed by Westminster Divines on Creation Days," at http://capo.org/OpenLetter.html).

[6] See L. Berkhof, *Systematic Theology,* 4th ed. (Grand Rapids: Eerdmans, 1941), pp. 153–54.

[7] So Hugh Ross, *Creation and Time* (Colorado Springs, CO: NavPress, 1994), pp. 45–52; Derek Kidner, *Genesis: An Introduction and Commentary,* Tyndale Old Testament Commentaries (Downers Grove, IL: InterVarsity Press, 1967), pp. 56–57; James O. Buswell, *A Systematic Theology of the Christian Religion,* 4 vols. in 1 (Grand Rapids: Zondervan, 1962), 1:139–59; R. Laird Harris, "The Length of the Creative Days in Genesis 1," in *Did God Create in Six Days?* pp. 101–11.

the days of the creation week are literary forms picturing a topical account of creation that focuses on vegetation and humanity, rather than a chronological sequence,[8] and, concomitantly, providing tacit support for an old earth model.[9] Generally, the advocates of this figurative interpretation hold to some form of day-age theory, progressive creationism, framework hypothesis, analogical view, or theistic evolution.[10]

Against the figurative use of "day," the literal interpretation of the days of the creation week has been a clearly expressed orthodox interpretation since the Reformation. Martin Luther reflected this interpretation: "We assert that Moses spoke in the literal sense, not allegorically or figuratively, i.e., that the world, with all its creatures, was created within six days, as the words read."[11] John Calvin and Francis Turretin also clearly articulated a literal understanding of the days of the creation week.[12] Various

---

[8] Mark D. Futato, "Because It Had Rained: A Study of Gen 2:5–7 with Implications for Gen 2:4–25 and Gen 1:1–2:3," *Westminster Theological Journal* 60 (Spring 1998): 17; Futato's article is a complement to an article by Meredith G. Kline "Space and Time in the Genesis Cosmogony," *Perspectives on Science and Christian Faith* 48 (March 1996): 2–15; see also Kline's earlier article, "Because It Had Not Rained," *Westminster Theological Journal* 20 (May 1958): 145–57; so also Henri Blocher, *In the Beginning,* trans. David G. Preston (Downers Grove, IL: InterVarsity Press, 1984), pp. 49–59.

[9] While advocates of the framework hypothesis may not explicitly argue for an old earth, the reinterpretation of the creation week as a topical account, rather than a chronological account, is certainly coordinate with old earth creationism. If there is any doubt about what is, at the minimum, implied by the framework hypothesis, its implications are explicitly stated by Meredith Kline, when he maintains that his understanding of Scripture's teaching about biblical cosmogony "is open to the current scientific view of a very old universe and, in that respect, does not discountenance the theory of the evolutionary origin of man" ("Space and Time," p. 15, n. 47), though he also insists that he adheres to the historicity and federal headship of Adam. He further laments that young earth creationism "is a deplorable disservice to the cause of biblical truth" (ibid.).

[10] For a summary of these types of categories, as well as varying levels of interaction with each, see Thomas Allen McIver, "Creationism: Intellectual Origins, Cultural Context, and Theoretical Diversity" (Ph.D. dissertation, University of California, Los Angeles, 1989), pp. 403–530; C. John Collins, "Reading Genesis 1:1–2:3 as an Act of Communication," in *Did God Create in Six Days?* pp. 145–51. For a presentation and critique of progressive creationism and theistic evolution, as well as young earth creationism, see *Three Views on Creation and Evolution,* ed. J. P. Moreland and John Mark Reynolds (Grand Rapids: Zondervan, 1999).

[11] Martin Luther, *Luther's Works, Volume 1, Lectures on Genesis: Chapters 1–5,* ed. Jaroslav Pelikan (Saint Louis: Concordia, 1958), p. 5.

[12] John Calvin, *Commentaries on the First Book of Moses Called Genesis,* trans. John King, 2 vols. (reprint ed., Grand Rapids: Eerdmans, n.d.), 1:78; and Francis Turretin, *Institutes of Elenctic Theology,* trans. Francis Musgrave Giger, ed. James T. Dennison, Jr., 3 vols. (Phillipsburg, NJ: Presbyterian & Reformed, 1992), 1:444–45.

Protestant confessions of faith have also affirmed a literal understanding of the creation "days." From our own Baptist heritage, the literal interpretation of the creation days is clearly revealed in the Second London Baptist Confession of 1689: "In the beginning it pleased God the Father, Son, and Holy Spirit, for the manifestation of the glory of his eternal power, wisdom, and goodness, to create or make the world, and all things therein, whether visible or invisible, in the space of six days, and all very good" (chapter 4, paragraph 1).[13] Many evangelical and fundamentalist schools are still affirming this historic, literal understanding of the days of creation in our present day. In Article 6 on "Creation," Detroit Baptist Theological Seminary's statement of faith says, "We believe in the original direct creation of the universe, a voluntary act of God whereby for his own glory and according to his eternal counsel, in six successive days of twenty-four hours each, he gave existence to all things in distinction from himself."

A fair assessment of the historical data demonstrates that a literal interpretation of the days of the creation week has been the normal position of orthodox Christianity. If we consistently affirm the perspicuity of Scripture, the literal interpretation of the creation days provides the most internally consistent synthesis of Scripture's comprehensive message about the nature of the creation week. My objective in this article is to provide a biblical justification for a literal understanding of the six days of the creation week. To accomplish this objective, I will initially provide biblical evidence to support this literal interpretation and, subsequently, answer some of the reputed biblical problems encountered by this position.

EVIDENCE FOR LITERAL DAYS
IN THE CREATION WEEK

English versions of Genesis 1:1–31 consistently translate the Hebrew noun יוֹם as "day."[14] The semantic range of יוֹם includes uses such as "daytime," as opposed to nighttime, a calendrical "day" of 24 hours, a specific day, "lifespan," "time," "years." When יוֹם is part of a compound grammatical construction, it has an idiomatic nuance that allows for a non-literal sense,

---

[13] The Second London Baptist Confession's doctrinal affirmation about creation is derived from the earlier Westminster Confession of Faith (1646): "It pleased God the Father, Son, and Holy Ghost, for the manifestation of the glory of His eternal power, wisdom, and goodness, in the beginning, to create, or make of nothing, the world, and all things therein, whether visible or invisible, in the space of six days, and all very good" (chapter 4, paragraph 1).

[14] To cite a few examples, see the NASB, NASB '95, NIV, KJV, NKJV, RSV, NRSV, NLT, TEV, CEV, and NET BIBLE.

such as "when."[15] While the semantic range of יוֹם reflects that its various uses range from a literal day to a figurative use of "day" as an extended period of time, lexicographers consistently cite the enumerated days of Genesis 1:1–31 as examples of a literal day.[16]

In opposition to Hebrew lexicographers, many interpreters would contend that the figurative use of יוֹם warrants reinterpreting each of the enumerated days of the creation week as extended periods.[17] If this figurative use of יוֹם were consistent with Genesis 1, it would provide an acceptable harmonization of Scripture and many currents views of science. However, we are persuaded that a figurative use of יוֹם in Genesis 1 is incongruous with the semantics of the singular יוֹם,[18] its syntactical combinations, and its biblical parallels.

Do the semantical constraints of יוֹם permit a figurative use of it in Genesis 1:1–31, or do they suggest a literal use of יוֹם? Is the use of the singular number, as opposed to the plural, significant in this passage? How do the modifiers of יוֹם as well as surrounding phrases impact its literal or

---

[15] See David J. A. Clines, ed., *The Dictionary of Classical Hebrew*, 5 vols. to date (Sheffield: Sheffield Academic Press, 1994–), 2:166–85 [hereafter cited as *DCH*]); and William L. Holladay, *A Concise Hebrew and Aramaic Lexicon of the Old Testament* (Grand Rapids: Eerdmans, 1971), pp. 130–31 (hereafter cited as *CHAL*); see also the pertinent discussion by James Stambaugh, "The Days of Creation: A Semantic Approach," *Creation Ex Nihilo Technical Journal* 5 (1991): 70–78.

[16] For example, see *DCH*, 2:166; Francis Brown, Samuel R. Driver, and Charles A. Briggs, eds., *A Hebrew and English Lexicon of the Old Testament* (reprint ed., Oxford: At the Clarendon Press, 1972), p. 398 (hereafter cited as *BDB*); Ludwig Koehler and Walter Baumgartner, *The Hebrew and Aramaic Lexicon of the Old Testament*, 5 vols., rev. W. Baumgartner and J. J. Stamm (Leiden: Brill, 1994–2000), 2:399 (hereafter cited as *HALOT*). Not only do lexicons recognize the literal use, but it is also reflected in *Theological Dictionary of the Old Testament*, s.v. "יוֹם," by M. Saeboe, 6:23 (hereafter cited as *TDOT*); and *New International Dictionary of Old Testament Theology and Exegesis*, s.v. "יוֹם," by P. A. Verhoef, 2:420 (hereafter cited as *NIDOTTE*).

[17] Besides some of the previously cited sources in footnotes 7 and 8, see also Perry G. Phillips, "Are the Days of Genesis Longer than 24 Hours? The Bible Says, 'Yes!'" *IBRI Research Report* 40 (1990): 1–5; and Thomas Key, "How Long Were the Days of Genesis?" *Journal of the American Scientific Affiliation* 36 (September 1984): 159–61; Dick Fischer, "The Days of Creation: Hours or Eons?" *Perspectives on Science and Christian Faith* 42 (March 1990): 15–22; and R. Clyde McCone, "Were the Days of Creation Twenty-Four Hours Long? 'No,'" in *The Genesis Debate*, ed. Ronald F. Youngblood (Grand Rapids: Baker, 1990), pp. 12–35.

[18] While we do not endorse James Barr's denigration of biblical inerrancy (*The Bible in the Modern World* [London: SCM Press, 1973], pp. 13–34), we do concur with him when he maintains that biblical exegesis demands a literal interpretation of the creation days (*Fundamentalism* [Philadelphia: Westminster, 1978], pp. 40–43).

figurative use?[19] How do other Scriptural passages interpret the days of creation? In responding to these questions, we will set forth five reasons why the unambiguous meaning of Scripture affirms that the days of the creation week be interpreted as six, successive 24-hour days.

Semantic Constraints of the Singular Use of יוֹם

The noun יוֹם fits into the semantic domain of Hebrew words used for time. The emphases of the subdomains for time words may focus on the general nature and/or duration of time. This would include words like עֵת ("time"), עוֹלָם ("time," "long time," "eternity"), עַד ("always," "forever"), קֶדֶם ("ancient times," "antiquity"), זְמָן ("season"), and דּוֹר ("generation"). Another subdomain is more specific periods of time, such as שָׁנָה ("year"), חֹדֶשׁ ("month"), יֶרַח ("month"), שָׁבוּעַ ("week"), יוֹם ("day"), and בֹּקֶר ("morning"). While this listing of time words is not exhaustive,[20] it does suggest that the various biblical authors had at their disposal a more than adequate lexical stock to describe short or long periods of time, and, significantly for our purposes, יוֹם is a time word that may legitimately be used to describe a literal day. However, יוֹם, like our English word *day,* is polysemantic, involving literal and figurative uses. To determine if our specific time word, יוֹם, is used of a literal, 24-hour day or an extended period, we must more precisely consider its semantic constraints.

When יוֹם is used in the singular and is not part of a compound grammatical construction,[21] it is consistently used in reference to a literal day of 24 hours or to the daytime portion of a literal day. However, when יוֹם is used in the plural or is part of a compound grammatical construction, some of its uses in the plural may be extended to include the sense of "time," "year," or for any extended period of time. Hasel has stated the case in this manner:

---

[19] For a helpful study of the semantics of יוֹם, see Hasel, "Days," pp. 21–31.

[20] For other helpful treatments of Hebrew words for time, see Stambaugh, "The Days of Creation," pp. 73–74; Simon J. DeVries, *Yesterday, Today, and Tomorrow* (Grand Rapids: Eerdmans, 1975), pp. 39–47; *TDOT,* s.v. "יוֹם," 6:20–21; Russell Grigg, "How Long Were the Days of Genesis 1?" *Creation Ex Nihilo* 19 (December 1996–February 1997): 23–24; and *NIDOTTE,* s.v. "Time and Eternity," by P. A. Verhoef, 4:1252–55.

[21] By compound grammatical construction, I am referring to the following types of items: the noun יוֹם being a part of a complex prepositional construction, יוֹם being a part of a longer prepositional construction which has a verbal immediately following it, יוֹם being a part of the multi-word construction known as the construct-genitive relationship, יוֹם being reduplicated (יוֹם יוֹם). For a more complete development of this construction, see *TDOT,* s.v. "יוֹם," 6:14–20.

The extended, non-literal meanings of the term *yôm* are always found in connection with prepositions, prepositional phrases with a verb, compound constructions, formulas, technical expressions, genitive combinations, construct phrases, and the like. In other words, extended, non-literal meanings of this Hebrew term have special linguistic and contextual connections which indicate clearly that a non-literal meaning is intended. If such special linguistic connections are absent, the term *yôm* does not have an extended, non-literal meaning; it has its normal meaning of a literal day of 24-hours.[22]

The noun "day," יוֹם, is used in the Hebrew Old Testament 2,304 times. Of these uses, יוֹם appears in the singular 1,452 times. It is used in the Pentateuch 668 times. Of these, the singular form is used 425 times. It is used in Genesis 152 times, with 83 of these in the singular.[23] In Genesis 1, יוֹם is used 11 times, 10 times in the singular and once in the plural. This lone use of the plural noun יָמִים, "days," does not provide any support for the use of יוֹם as an extended period of time in the creation account. While the use of יָמִים, "days," is clearly not a reference to any of the creation days, its use in 1:14 specifically has reference to calendrical "days and years."

Of the 10 uses of the singular "day" in Genesis 1, 4 refer to "day" as opposed to "night," לַיְלָה (1:5, 14, 16, 17).[24] As such, each full day of the creation week is divided according to the natural phenomena of "daytime," יוֹם, and "nighttime," לַיְלָה. It is this day and night cycle that constitutes each full day of the creation week,[25] as Genesis 1:5 indicates: "God called the light day, and the darkness He called night. And there was evening and there was morning, the first day"[26] (see also in 1:16, where the greater light governs the daylight and the lesser light the nighttime).

---

[22] Hasel, "Days," pp. 23–24.

[23] These statistics are derived from *Theological Lexicon of the Old Testament,* s.v. "יוֹם," by E. Jenni, 2:526–27 (hereafter cited as *TLOT*).

[24] *HALOT,* 2:401.

[25] *TDOT,* s.v. "יוֹם," 6:22–23.

[26] All Scripture quotations, unless otherwise noted, are taken from the 1995 edition of NASB; however, in my quotation of Gen 1:5, I have changed NASB's translation of "one day" to "the first day." The difference between these two options for translation relates to how we render אֶחָד. While אֶחָד is often translated as a cardinal number, it may also be translated as an ordinal, "first"; see *HALOT,* 1:30. The very nature of the progression of "second" through "seventh" supports אֶחָד being taken as an ordinal. The grammatical significance of this has been stated: "The indefinite noun plus אֶחָד has a definite sense in the opening chapter of Genesis: יוֹם אֶחָד 'the first day' (Gen 1:5)" (Bruce K. Waltke and M. O'Connor, *An Introduction to Biblical Hebrew Syntax* [Winona Lake, IN: Eisenbrauns, 1990], p. 274); so Nahum M. Sarna, *Genesis,* JPS Torah Commentary (Philadelphia: Jewish Publication Society, 1989), p. 8, and see his discussion of this in his endnote 14, p. 353.

The remaining 6 uses of יוֹם make up the enumerated days of the creation week, the "first day," "second day," etc. (1:5, 8, 13, 19, 24, 31).

While we recognize that the semantic domain for the time word "day" is broad, the use of the singular in Genesis 1 suggests that a literal nuance is its intended meaning. In fact, the singular noun in the absolute state is consistently used in the Old Testament to refer to an ordinary day, and not to an extended period of time involving more than a 24-hour day.[27] In addition, this literal nuance may be corroborated by its patterns of collocation. When the singular "day" has a distinctive relationship with a numeral and the phrase "evening and morning," the unambiguous meaning "day" is a 24-hour day.[28]

Numeric Qualifiers and יוֹם

When each day of the creation week is summarized, the singular "day" is modified by a numerical qualifier, "first day" (v. 5), "second day" (v. 8), and sequentially continuing to the "sixth day" (vv. 13, 19, 23, 31). Immediately after the sixth day, God ceased from his work. This day of cessation from God's creative work is designated on three occasions as the "seventh day" (2:2 [twice], 3). The use of the numeric qualifier and sequential numbering suggest that this is a literal day.[29]

The singular and plural forms of "day" are used with a number in excess of 350 times in the Old Testament.[30] A number is used to qualify the singular use of יוֹם approximately 150 times.[31] When יוֹם is qualified by a number, it is almost invariably used in a literal sense.[32] An example

---

[27] Since Moses had at his disposal a number of time words that clearly describe an age, he could have chosen one of these words, such as עוֹלָם ("long time"); so Arthur C. Custance, *Hidden Things of God's Revelation,* The Doorway Papers, vol. 7 (Grand Rapids: Zondervan, 1977), p. 295.

[28] Hasel, "Days," p. 26.

[29] Terence E. Fretheim, "Were the Days of Creation Twenty-Four Hours Long? 'Yes,'" in *The Genesis Debate,* p. 18.

[30] See Stambaugh, "The Days of Creation," p. 3.

[31] *TLOT,* s.v. "יוֹם," 2:528.

[32] See Kenneth L. Gentry, Jr. "Reformed Theology and Six-Day Creation," *Chalcedon Report* 398 (September 1998): 28. There is a possible exception to this in Hos 6:2: "He will revive us after two days; He will raise us up on the third day, that we may live before him." Ross has attempted to use this passage to mitigate the force of this argument (*Creation and Time,* pp. 46–47). However, Hosea's use of numbers "two" and "third" as qualifiers is different than the pattern we see in Genesis 1. Hosea's use of these numbers is a common Semitic rhetorical feature known as a graded numerical device, or an x/x+1 pattern. As such, the emphasis is not on a literal numbering of days, but refers to a brief period of time

of this is found in Leviticus 12:3, "On the *eighth day* the flesh of his fore-skin shall be circumcised." The use of םוֹי with a numeric qualifier is also illustrated in Numbers 7. In this context, leaders from each tribe of Israel brought various gifts to the Lord on 12 sequential, literal days. A number qualifies each use of the word "day." Numbers 7:12 illustrates this point, "Now the one who presented his offering on the *first day* was Nahshon the son of Amminadab, of the tribe of Judah" (emphasis mine.) (For the remainder of the days along with their numerical qualifiers, see vv. 18, 24, 30, 36, 42, 48, 54, 60, 66, 72, 78). Thus, the use of day with a numerical qualifier is a clear reference to a literal day.[33]

Not only does the correlation of the singular "day" with a number support a literal understanding of each day, the use of consecutive ordinal numbers indicates a chronological arrangement of the creation days. The sequential use of the ordinal numbers "first" through "sixth" for each day of the creation week, followed by the "seventh day" (2:2 [twice], 3), indicates a chronological progression of days.[34] Hasel has concisely stated the issue:

> What seems of significance is the sequential emphasis of the numerals 1–7 without any break or temporal interruption. This seven-day schema, the schema of the week of six workdays followed by "the seventh day" as rest day, interlinks the creation "days" as normal days in a consecutive and non-interrupted sequence.[35]

(see David M. Fouts, "How Short an Evening and Morning?" *Creation Ex Nihilo Technical Journal* 11 [1997]: 307–8).

[33] This type of syntagmatic relationship with םוֹי and numbers is true for the numbers 1 through 1000 (so Hasel, "Days," p. 26). An exception to this literal understanding is found in Zech 14:7, where דָחֶא םוֹי is apparently used with a non-literal sense of a "unique day" or a "continuous day." In arguing against a chronological sequence in Genesis 1, David Sterchi suggests that there is a contextual correlation between Zech 14:7 and Gen 1:5 ("Does Genesis Provide a Chronological Sequence?" *Journal of the Evangelical Theological Society* 39 [December 1996]: 532). While Zech 14:7 may be an exception and presents some translation difficulties, as a comparison of various English versions reflects, it certainly cannot be used to undermine the clear usage in Genesis 1 (see Stambaugh, "The Days of Creation," p. 75).

[34] E. J. Young, *Studies in Genesis One* (Phillipsburg, NJ: Presbyterian & Reformed, 1964), p. 99; see also Joseph A. Pipa, Jr., "From Chaos to Cosmos: A Critique of the Non-Literal Interpretations of Genesis 1:1–2:3," in *Did God Create in Six Days?* p. 183.

[35] Hasel, "Days," p. 26.

"Evening" and "Morning" as Qualifiers of יוֹם

The singular יוֹם in Genesis 1 is qualified further with the words "evening" and "morning." The clauses in which these two nouns are found, "and there was evening and there was morning," stand in juxtaposition with each enumerated day of the creation week (1:5, 8, 13, 19, 23, 31). Whether "evening" and "morning" are used together in a context with יוֹם (19 times beyond the 6 uses in Genesis 1) or they are used without יוֹם (38 times), they are used consistently in reference to literal days.[36] Commonly, "evening" and "morning" have been taken as a reference to the entire 24-hour day.[37] With this understanding, "evening" is used to represent the entire night-time portion of a literal day, and "morning" to stand for the entire daytime segment of a day.[38] If the use of "evening" and "morning" were intended to recapitulate a whole day of creation, we would expect that the order of the two terms would be reversed: "morning" followed by "evening."[39] While it is true that "evening" and "morning" are always used as a reference to segments of literal days, I am persuaded that "evening" and "morning" in Genesis 1 refer exclusively to the beginning and conclusion of the nighttime period that concludes each of the creation days, after God had ceased from that day's creative activity.[40] There are two reasons for this understanding.

First, this understanding is consistent with other Old Testament uses of "evening" and "morning." The noun עֶרֶב, "evening," is related to a rarely used verb עָרַב, to "turn into evening."[41] In its Qal stem, this verb is used in Judges 19:9 to indicate "the arrival of evening, as indicated by its description as the ending of the day."[42] While it would be imprecise to define "evening" for the first three creation days as "sunset" since the sun is not actually created until the fourth day,[43] "evening" and "morning"

---

[36] These statistics are derived from Stambaugh, "The Days of Creation," p. 72; see also Abraham Even-Shoshan, *A New Concordance of the Bible* (Jerusalem: Kiryat Sefer, 1985), pp. 451–59.

[37] Fretheim, "Days," p. 19.

[38] Hasel, "Days," p. 28.

[39] Leon J. Wood, *Genesis,* Bible Study Commentary (Grand Rapids: Zondervan, 1975), p. 25.

[40] See Robert E. Grossmann's helpful article, "The Light He Called 'Day,'" *Mid-America Journal of Theology* 3 (1987): 7–34; and Sarna, *Genesis,* p. 8.

[41] *HALOT,* 2:877.

[42] *NIDOTTE,* s.v. "עָרַב" by A. H. Konkel, 1:715.

[43] Sarna, *Genesis,* p. 8. The sun is not created until the fourth day of creation; however, at God's command in v. 3, some form of cosmic light came into existence, with the earth possibly rotating on its axis (so Henry M. Morris, *The Genesis Record* [Grand Rapids:

basically refer to the same type of physical phenomenon. This is to say, it is a transitional period of light between the twilight of day and the darkness of night.[44] The noun בֹּקֶר, "morning,"[45] may refer to all the hours of daylight or from midnight until noon.[46] It may also indicate "the arrival of daylight."[47] This last use is the most consistent with the overall context of Genesis 1. The terms "evening" and "morning" "respectively signify the end of the period of light, when divine creativity was suspended, and the renewal of light, when the creative process was resumed."[48]

These two terms are used in a similar fashion in other passages in the Pentateuch and picture the "evening" and "morning" cycle as completing a day. In Exodus 27:21, Moses instructed Aaron and his sons to keep the lamps in the Tabernacle burning all night until they were extinguished in the morning: "In the tent of meeting, outside the veil which is before the testimony, Aaron and his sons shall keep it in order from *evening* to *morning* before the LORD; *it shall be* a perpetual statute throughout their generations for the sons of Israel." The command for Aaron and his sons to keep the lamp burning all night is reiterated in Leviticus 24:3: "Outside the veil of testimony in the tent of meeting, Aaron shall keep it in order from *evening* to *morning* before the LORD continually; *it shall be* a perpetual

---

Baker, 1976], p. 65), though this is not necessarily required. However, we must insist that the text of Genesis requires that the absolutely sovereign and omnipotent God created a cosmic light source that in some sense "waxed and waned in periods of 'evening' and 'morning'" (Frank Walker, Jr. "A Critique of the Framework Hypothesis," *Chalcedon Report* 398 [September 1998]: 32). This would suggest that the earth's relationship to the cosmic light source on the first three days of creation was the same as its relationship to the sun from the fourth day of creation and following; see Morton H. Smith, *Systematic Theology*, 2 vols. (Greenville, SC: Greenville Seminary Press, 1994), 1:187–88; and Robert C. Harbach, *Studies in the Book of Genesis* (n.p.: Grandville Protestant Reformed Church, 1986), p. 15. Because the sun is not created until the fourth day of creation, some have inferred that the first three days of creation were extended periods of time (so McCone, "Days," p. 24). Because each day of the creation week is successively numbered and qualified by the "evening" and "morning," the first three days and the last three days must be equivalent in duration. While John H. Stek is no friend of recent creationism, he also makes the same point about the duration of the six days, whether they be extended periods of time or, according to our interpretation, calendrical days ("What Says the Scripture?" in *Portraits of Creation*, ed. Howard J. Van Till, Robert E. Snow, John H. Stek, Davis A. Young [Grand Rapids: Eerdmans, 1990], pp. 237–38).

[44] See U. Cassuto, *A Commentary on the Book of Genesis: Part One—From Adam to Noah*, trans. Israel Abrahams (Jerusalem: Magnes, the Hebrew University, 1961), p. 28.

[45] *HALOT*, 1:151.

[46] *DCH*, 2:252.

[47] *NIDOTTE*, 1:711; see also *TDOT*, s.v. "בֹּקֶר," by Ch. Barth, 2:222.

[48] Sarna, *Genesis*, p. 8.

statute throughout your generations." In keeping records of Israel's wilderness wanderings, Moses describes in Numbers 9:15 how the theophanic
cloud would hover over the tabernacle all night when it had been set up:
"Now on the day that the tabernacle was erected the cloud covered the
tent of the testimony, and in the *evening* it was like the appearance of fire
over the tabernacle until *morning*" (emphasis added; see also v. 21). The
night cycle of evening to morning is also reflected in the description of the
Passover ritual in Deuteronomy 16:4: "For seven days no leaven shall be
seen with you in all your territory, and none of the flesh which you sacrifice
on the *evening* of the first day shall remain overnight until *morning*."[49]
These uses suggest that a literal use of "evening" and "morning" refer
to the nighttime. As such, the alternation of "evening" and "morning" in
Genesis 1 pictures the nighttime portion that concludes a literal day.[50]

Second, the general framework for each of the creation days also
reflects that "evening" and "morning" are used to describe the completion
of each day. The creative activity and its cessation are summarized by a
fivefold framework that is reflected in the days of creation: divine speech
("God said"), fiat ("let there be," or an equivalent, such as "let the waters
teem," v. 20),[51] fulfillment ("there was," "it was so," "God created," etc.),
evaluation ("God saw that it was good"),[52] and conclusion ("there was
evening and there was morning," the first day, etc.).[53] This framework

---

[49] The words *evening* and *morning* in the four verses cited in this paragraph, are
italicized for my own emphasis.

[50] Pipa, "From Chaos to Cosmos," p. 184.

[51] The verbs used in the fiat segment of this fivefold framework are usually jussives,
with the exception of v. 26 where a cohortative is found, "let us."

[52] The only exception to this evaluation ("God saw that it was good") is the second day.
In contrast to the Masoretic Text, the Septuagint contains an additional clause of evaluation
in v. 8. This addition was apparently to harmonize all the days of the creation week, but it
does not represent the reading of the original Hebrew text. The omission of this clause in
the Hebrew text may indicate that the author saw the creation of the expanse on this day
"as only a preliminary stage to the emergence of dry land in v. 10, and thus he reserved the
phrase until its most appropriate time" (Victor P. Hamilton, *The Book of Genesis: Chapters
1–17*, New International Commentary on the Old Testament [Grand Rapids: Eerdmans,
1990], p. 124). Whatever the reason for the omission of this by Moses, we understand that
this fivefold framework was intended only as a general framework.

[53] With some qualification, Young follows this fivefold pattern (*Studies in Genesis One*, p.
84); this framework is also recognized by critical scholar Claus Westermann, *Genesis 1–11: A
Commentary*, trans. John J. Scullion (Minneapolis: Augsburg, 1984), pp. 84–85. Others have
seen a sevenfold scheme; see Gordon F. Wenham, *Genesis 1–15*, Word Biblical Commentary
(Waco, TX: Word, 1987), pp. 17–19; see also the discussion in Harold G. Stigers, *A Commentary
on Genesis* (Grand Rapids: Zondervan, 1976), pp. 53–54. While either framework needs some
qualification, the fivefold framework is generally more consistent with the text of Gen 1.

reflects that the "evening-morning" conclusion is consistently used to conclude each creation day. This understanding of the "evening-morning" conclusion depicts "the period of darkness that completes a regular day."[54] This is to say, the "evening" and the "morning" mark "the beginning and end of the *night,* the period in which no creative activity is reported, the period which follows the day."[55]

Therefore, "evening" and "morning" are respectively used to represent the conclusion of the daylight portion of a literal day, when God suspended his creative activity, and the reemergence of daylight, when God resumed another day of his creative work. As such, each "evening-morning" cycle concludes a creation day and provides a transition to the next day of creative activity.[56]

Scriptural Parallels with יוֹם

Having examined the semantic and syntactic considerations associated with יוֹם, we must also consider the hermeneutical principle of "the analogy of faith," *analogia fidei.*[57] Because this hermeneutical guideline maintains that Scripture interprets Scripture, some feel a more appropriate designation is the *analogia scriptura.*[58] Since Scripture is a self-authenticating special revelation from the triune God, Scripture is a self-interpreting book.[59] As such, "what is obscure in one passage may be illuminated by another. No

---

[54] Pipa, "From Chaos to Cosmos," p. 184.

[55] Grossmann, "Day," p. 23.

[56] Pipa, "From Chaos to Cosmos," p. 184; so also C. F. Keil and F. Delitzsch, *The Pentateuch,* 3 vols. in 1, trans. James Martin, in *Biblical Commentary on the Old Testament* (reprint ed., Grand Rapids: Eerdmans, 1973), 1:50–51.

[57] For a concise treatment of this hermeneutical subject, see Milton S. Terry, *Biblical Hermeneutics* (reprint ed., Grand Rapids: Zondervan, 1974), pp. 579–81; and Gerhard Maier, *Biblical Hermeneutics,* trans. Robert W. Yarbrough (Wheaton, IL: Crossway, 1994), pp. 181–83.

[58] Grant Osborne observes that *analogia fidei* is at times understood as the interpreter's personal "faith" being the final interpreter of Scripture (*The Hermeneutical Spiral* [Downers Grove, IL: InterVarsity Press, 1991], p. 273). While this type of understanding misses the mark of the historical use of *analogia fidei* by the Reformers, it is perhaps better to describe this as the *analogia scriptura* (so also Robert Reymond, *A New Systematic Theology of the Christian Faith* [Nashville: Thomas Nelson, 1998], p. 394).

[59] This hermeneutical axiom is stated this way in the Second London Baptist Confession: "The infallible rule of interpretation of Scripture is the Scripture itself; and therefore when there is a question about the true and full sense of any Scripture (which is not manifold, but one), it must be searched by other places that speak more clearly" (chapter 1, paragraph 9). This axiom is predicated upon the earlier Westminster Confession of Faith (chapter 1, paragraph 9).

single statement or obscure passage of one book can be allowed to set aside a doctrine which is clearly established by many passages."[60] In essence, *analogia scriptura* maintains that the entirety of Scripture is the context and guide in interpreting the specific passages of Scripture. As applied to a literal interpretation of the days of the creation week, we should expect this to be confirmed by other Scriptural texts.[61] There are two passages, dealing with regulations for the observance of the sabbath that cogently reinforce a literal interpretation of the days in the creation week. These passages are Exodus 20:8–11 and 31:14–17.

The fourth commandment of the Decalogue in Exodus 20:8–11 is for Israel to set the sabbath day apart as a holy day to the LORD. This command is given in vv. 8–10:

> Remember the sabbath day, to keep it holy. Six days you shall labor and do all your work, but the seventh day is a sabbath of the LORD your God; *in it* you shall not do any work, you or your son or your daughter, your male or your female servant or your cattle or your sojourner who stays with you.

The motivation for this command is stated in v. 11: "For in six days the LORD made[62] the heavens and the earth, the sea and all that is in them, and rested on the seventh day; therefore the LORD blessed the sabbath day and made it holy."

While some have attempted to reduce the relationship between the fourth commandment and the creation week to one of "analogy," in that man's sabbath rest cannot be identical to God's rest, but only analogous to God's day of rest,[63] this understanding oversimplifies and misrepresents the correlation between these two texts. Exodus 20:11 has a number of connections with the creation week: a "six-plus-one" pattern, "the heavens and the earth," "the seventh day," "rested," "blessed," and "made it holy."[64] All of this suggests that, at the least, one of God's purposes in creating the world and all things therein in six successive literal days followed by a literal day of rest was to set up a pattern for his people to follow. According

---

[60] Terry, *Biblical Hermeneutics,* p. 579.

[61] See Noel Weeks, "The Hermeneutical Problem of Genesis 1–11," *Themelios* 4 (April 1978): 16–17.

[62] Collins's translation of the verb עָשָׂה as "worked on," rather than "made" is tenuous ("Reading Genesis 1:1–2:3," pp. 141–42); cf. *TLOT,* s.v. "עָשָׂה" by J. Vollmer, 2:949; Exod 20:11 is derived from Gen 2:2 where עָשָׂה is used in the sense of "done." The use of "done" focuses on the accomplishment of God's creative activities, as the use of "create," בָּרָא, in Gen 2:3 clearly indicates.

[63] So Collins, "Reading Genesis 1:1–2:3," p. 139.

[64] Hasel, "Days," p. 29.

to this text, Israel's workweek is patterned after God's creative activity.[65] If, for argument sake, we assume that each day was a geological age, we could interpret Exodus 20:11 in this fashion: "For in six geological ages of a million years or so, the LORD made heaven and earth, the sea, and all that in them is, and rested on the seventh geological age of a million years or so; therefore the LORD blessed the sabbath geological age of a million years or so and made it holy." Any interpretation other than literal days is problematic for Israel's proper observance of the sabbath, and seriously undermines a literal interpretation of the days of Genesis 1.[66]

This literal understanding of the creation week is reiterated in Exodus 31:14–17:

> Therefore you are to observe the sabbath, for it is holy to you. Everyone who profanes it shall surely be put to death; for whoever does any work on it, that person shall be cut off from among his people. For six days work may be done, but on the seventh day there is a sabbath of complete rest, holy to the LORD; whoever does any work on the sabbath day shall surely be put to death. So the sons of Israel shall observe the sabbath, to celebrate the sabbath throughout their generations as a perpetual covenant. It is a sign between Me and the sons of Israel forever; for in six days the LORD made heaven and earth, but on the seventh day He ceased *from labor,* and was refreshed.

In this context, Israel's observance of the sabbath is a sign of the Mosaic Covenant. God's commanding Israel to keep the sabbath is grounded in the creation week.[67] As in Exodus 20:11, 31:17 has a number of links with the creation week: a "six-plus-one" pattern, "heaven and earth," and "ceased" is the same Hebrew verb, שׁבת, translated as "rested" in Genesis 2:2. Obviously, Moses had six literal days in mind with the seventh day also being a 24-hour period.

Exodus 20:11 and 31:17 confirm that the days of the creation week are literal days.[68] According to these two texts, the references to the creation

---

[65] Noel Weeks, *The Sufficiency of Scripture* (Carlisle, PA: Banner of Truth, 1988), p. 112; see also Raymond F. Surburg, "In the Beginning God Created," in *Darwin, Evolution, and Creation,* ed. Paul A. Zimmerman (St. Louis: Concordia, 1959), p. 61.

[66] Robert L. Dabney, *Lectures in Systematic Theology* (reprint ed., Grand Rapids: Zondervan, 1972), p. 255; see also William Einwechter, "The Meaning of 'Day' in Genesis 1–2," *Chalcedon Report* 398 (September 1998): 13.

[67] J. Gerald Janzen, *Exodus,* Westminster Bible Companion (Louisville, KY: Westminster/John Knox, 1997), p. 222.

[68] While there are a number of New Testament passages that may have some bearing on this subject, our purpose is to treat those biblical texts that have direct impact

week are not analogous—man's rest is not simply like God's rest on the seventh day—instead, man is to imitate the divine Exemplar. Since God worked for six days and rested on the seventh, the nation of Israel must follow his example.[69]

Sequence of Events and יוֹם

The nature of certain aspects of the created order assumes a literal interpretation of the days of the creation week rather than a figurative understanding. On the third day of creation, God created vegetation with fruit trees and seed-bearing plants (Gen 1:11–12). Much vegetation needs insects for pollination. Insects were not created until the sixth day (vv. 24–25). If some plants were dependent upon insects for pollination, it would be impossible for them to survive if each creation day was an extended period of time.[70] This is to say, a symbiotic relationship between plants and animals is coordinate with literal and successive days in Genesis 1, but this would not be the case if the days refer to extended periods.

Furthermore, if the days are figurative and if there is any consistency in interpretation, then there must be extended periods of light corresponding to "morning" and of darkness corresponding to "evening." This would guarantee that both plant and animal life would be unable to survive.[71] Consequently, certain aspects of God's creation work are more readily harmonized with a literal understanding of the days in the creation week than with a figurative understanding.

In summarizing the evidence for a literal interpretation of the days of the creation week, we have provided five reasons supporting our argument that each day of the creation week was a 24-hour day and that these days immediately followed each other in the space of six days. If semantics, syntax, and overall Scriptural context mean anything in a literal hermeneutic, then יוֹם must refer to a literal day. Therefore, it is clear that the creation account unequivocally communicates that God created the universe and all things therein in six consecutive literal days.

---

on whether the days of Genesis 1 are to be interpreted as literal or figurative days. For more information on other texts used in the New Testament, see Douglas F. Kelly, *Creation and Change* (Fearn, Great Britain: Mentor, 1997), pp. 129–34; and Sid Dyer, "The New Testament Doctrine of Creation," in *Did God Create in Six Days?* pp. 221–42.

[69] Fretheim, "Days," p. 20.

[70] Morris, *The Genesis Record,* p. 64; see also Berkhof, *Systematic Theology,* p. 155.

[71] Hasel, "Days," p. 30.

ARGUMENTS AGAINST LITERAL DAYS IN THE CREATION WEEK

While we have attempted to argue positively for a literal interpretation of the days in the creation week, we have not fully interacted with some of the interpretative arguments used by those who deny this position. To demonstrate that a literal interpretation of the creation days is an internally consistent synthesis of Scripture's comprehensive message about the creation week, we will now show that the arguments against this position have no real merit and can be readily answered.

The Seventh Day

Opponents of literal creation days generally use the seventh day of the creation week as a justification for elongated days in Genesis 1. Since no "evening-morning" conclusion is explicitly stated in Genesis 2:1–3, it is argued that the seventh day of "God's rest was and is still going on."[72] According to Blocher, this is the "most simple and natural conclusion" that can be drawn from this deliberate omission.[73] Genesis 2:1–3 implies that the seventh day is unending. This implication supposedly becomes the basis for the use of Genesis 2:1–3 in other passages such as Psalm 95, John 5, and Hebrews 4.[74] According to this interpretation, Hebrews 4:3–11, while drawing from Psalm 95:7–11 and Genesis 2:2, suggests that God's "rest" began when God ceased from his creative activity and still continues until the present. The author of Hebrews uses God's sabbath rest to challenge his audience to enter into God's unending sabbath rest.[75] When the Jews were prepared to persecute Jesus for healing a man on the sabbath, Jesus responded in John 5:17 by claiming, "My Father is working until now, and I Myself am working." Blocher maintains that "Jesus' reasoning is sound only if the Father acts *during his* [Father's] *sabbath;* only on that condition has the Son the right to act similarly on the sabbath;... God's sabbath, which marks the end of creation but does not tie God's hands, is therefore co-extensive with history."[76] Based upon these passages and the deliberate omission of the "evening-morning" conclusion in Genesis 2:1–3, "the

---

[72] R. Laird Harris, "The Length of the Creative Days in Genesis 1," in *Did God Create in Six Days?* p. 109.

[73] Blocher, *In the Beginning,* p. 56.

[74] Ross, *Creation and Time,* p. 49.

[75] C. John Collins, "How Old Is the Earth? Anthropomorphic Days in Genesis 1:1–2:3," *Presbyterion* 20 (Fall 1994): 119.

[76] Blocher, *In the Beginning,* p. 57.

seventh day of Genesis 1 and 2 represents a minimum of several thousand years and a maximum that is open ended (but finite). It seems reasonable to conclude then, given the parallelism of the Genesis creation account, that the first six days may also have been long time periods."[77]

Is an open-ended seventh day the "most simple and natural conclusion" to draw from the omission of the "evening-morning" conclusion in Genesis 2:1–3? While it is true that this omission is significant, the textual data within Genesis 1:1–2:3 suggests a more natural interpretation. The omission of this "evening-morning" conclusion has a dual significance. We will initially look at the twofold significance of this omission and then interact with the texts used to support a figurative interpretation of the seventh day.

First, the "evening-morning" conclusion is one part of a fivefold framework that Moses uses in shaping the literary fabric for each of the creation days.[78] It should be noted that none of the other parts of this fivefold framework are mentioned on the seventh day.[79] Moses uses this fivefold literary framework to represent, in a concise yet accurate manner, God's work in creating the heavens, the earth, and all things therein for each of the six days of his six-phase program of creation. By excluding the fivefold framework, his theological emphasis is to demonstrate in literary form that the seventh day was a day of cessation from God's creative activity. This is to say the omission of the "evening-morning" conclusion is related to the omission of the other four parts of the fivefold framework. Since the other four parts of his framework are not needed in that God's creative activity is finished, his concluding formula is not needed either. The overall framework is not used for the obvious reason that God is no longer creating after the sixth day. Because the seventh day is a normal, 24-hour day, it is numbered like the previous six days.

---

[77] Ross, *Creation and Time,* p. 49; so also Mark Ross, "The Framework Hypothesis: An Interpretation of Genesis 1:1–2:3," in *Did God Create in Six Days?* p. 122.

[78] As Moses gave literary shape to represent in written form the events from the creation week, we should understand that the way he shaped his material was controlled by two necessary elements: the actual events that took place during the creation week and his divinely-given theological interpretation of the material (see John Sailhamer, "Genesis 1:1–2:4a," *Trinity Journal* 5 [Spring 1984]: 73). In the case of the creation week, God obviously had to give direct revelation concerning the details of the creation week to someone as early as Adam but no later than Moses, and Moses has accurately preserved this in written form. What actually happened during the creation week placed certain limitations on Moses' use of this material, and his actual message controls how he selects and arranges this material. Inerrancy allows for literary shaping but never at the expense of the historical accuracy of the actual events, and it requires that the historical account sets parameters on literary shaping.

[79] See earlier discussion about "'Evening' and 'Morning' as Qualifiers יוֹם."

Second, the "evening-morning" conclusion has another rhetorical effect in that it also functions as a transition to the following day.[80] If the first week is completed, there is no need to use the concluding formula for transitional purposes. Pipa has precisely summarized this argument.

> The phrase "evening and morning" links the day that is concluding with the next day. For example the morning that marks the end of day one also marks the beginning of day two. Thus, we do not find the formula at the end of the seventh day, since the week of creation is complete.[81]

Therefore, the more "natural conclusion" to draw from the omission of the "evening-morning" conclusion is that the seventh day was not a day of creation, but a day of rest. The focus of Genesis 2:1–3 is not on what occurred after a literal seventh day but what transpired on the seventh day. According to v. 3, "God blessed the seventh day and sanctified it, because in it He rested from all His work." In the first week of history, God set up a "six-plus-one" pattern of working six days and resting on the seventh.[82]

We now need to interact with those passages used to support a figurative interpretation of the seventh day. It is our contention that the biblical texts used to support an elongated seventh day do not provide explicit support for this interpretation. The "rest" used in Psalm 95:11 is a reference to the promised land of Canaan. Because of their disobedience, God prohibited the generation of Israelites who left Egypt from entering the Promised Land.[83] The use of John 5:17 to force a figurative interpretation upon the seventh day in Genesis 2:1–3 is also problematic. Blocher's logic is that Jesus' healing on the Sabbath is only valid if the Father works on *his Sabbath*. Therefore, the Father's Sabbath on which he works has continued from the seventh day up through the present.[84] Weeks correctly observes that Jesus' logic has "equal force if God was working on the regular weekly Sabbath. In context, the work in question would not be primarily a work of creation or providence but the work of redemption and mercy."[85]

---

[80] See earlier discussion about "'Evening' and 'Morning' as Qualifiers יוֹם."

[81] Pipa, "From Chaos to Cosmos," p. 168.

[82] Grossman, "Day," p. 21.

[83] Mark Van Bebber and Paul S. Taylor, *Creation and Time: A Report on the Progressive Creationist Book by Hugh Ross,* 2nd ed. (Mesa, AZ: Eden Communications, 1995), pp. 71–73.

[84] Blocher, *In the Beginning,* p. 57.

[85] Weeks, *The Sufficiency of Scripture,* p. 114; see also John Murray, *Principles of Conduct* (Grand Rapids: Eerdmans, 1957), p. 33.

The use of "rest" in Hebrews 4 does not provide unquestionable support for a figurative use of the seventh day. While the author of Hebrews, in 4:3–11, cites Genesis 2:2 and Psalm 95:7–11, his argument is to provide a warning against unbelief. If one does not persevere in the faith, he will not enter into God's eternal rest. The eternal rest described by the author of Hebrews is built off the model of God's sabbath rest in Genesis 2:1–3. The author of Hebrews apparently uses the Mosaic omission of the concluding formula as a type patterned after God's eternal rest. This is similar to what he does in 5:6–10 and 7:1–4 where he uses Melchizedek's lack of a genealogy in Genesis 14 as well as no mention of his death in Scripture to serve as a type of Christ. The silence of Scripture about Melchizedek's family background and death serve as a pattern for the eternal priest, Jesus Christ.[86] As it would be invalid to deny the historical reality of Melchizedek's family background and death based upon the omission of these two items in Hebrews, so it would also be invalid on this basis to deny the historical reality of a literal seventh day in Genesis 2:1–3.[87] As such, Hebrews 4:3–11 may be used to establish that God's eternal rest is patterned after God's rest on the literal seventh day of the creation week,[88] but it cannot be explicitly used to preclude the seventh day as a literal day.

Consequently, neither the omission of the "evening-morning" conclusion in Genesis 2:1–3 nor other biblical texts discussed provides indisputable evidence to sustain a figurative interpretation of the seventh day.[89] In reality, the omission of the concluding formula and the immediate context of Genesis 2:1–3, with the threefold repetition of the "seventh day" as well as the singular use of יוֹם along with a numeric qualifier, indicate that the "most simple and natural conclusion" to draw is that the seventh day was a literal day, just like the preceding six literal days of the creation week.

The Use of "Day" in Genesis 2:4

The use of "day" in Genesis 2:4 has been used by some as evidence that the singular form of יוֹם may be used to refer to the entire creation week, and it therefore substantiates interpreting each singular use of "day" in

---

[86] Homer A. Kent, Jr., *The Epistle to the Hebrews* (Grand Rapids: Baker, 1972), p. 82, n. 32.

[87] Pipa, "From Chaos to Cosmos," p. 169.

[88] See Murray, *Principles of Conduct,* p. 32.

[89] See Kelly, *Creation and Change,* p. 111.

Genesis 1 as referring to an extended period of time. This is the manner in which Wayne Grudem uses Genesis 2:4.

> In favor of viewing the six days as long periods of time is the fact that the Hebrew word *yôm*, "day," is sometimes used to refer not to a twenty-four-hour literal day, but to a longer period of time. We see this when the word is used in Genesis 2:4, for example: "In the *day* that the LORD God made the earth and the heavens," a phrase that refers to the entire creative work of the six days of creation.[90]

We would not deny that the singular noun יוֹם in Genesis 2:4b is used figuratively for more than a literal day in that it apparently summarizes the entire time covered during the first six days of creation. However, this type of comparison disregards the grammatical differences between the use of the singular, *absolute* noun "day" in Genesis 1 and the singular, *construct* noun "day" in Genesis 2:4. This construction in v. 4 requires further explanation.

In Genesis 2:4, "day" appears in a compound grammatical construction.[91] A literal translation of v. 4b will assist in explicating the significance of this construction: "in-the-day-of-making by the LORD God earth and heaven." The five hyphenated words in this translation are what constitute this compound grammatical relationship. These five words involve three closely related words in the Hebrew text: the inseparable preposition בְּ ("in"), immediately attached to the construct, singular noun יוֹם ("day"), and an infinitive construct עֲשׂוֹת ("making"). Thus, the "day" in 2:4 is not simply an example of a singular noun but is part of a compound grammatical construction.

When the preposition בְּ is prefixed to the construct noun יוֹם and these words are followed by an infinitive construct, this complex construction forms a temporal idiomatic construction.[92] The temporal nature of this

---

[90] Wayne Grudem, *Systematic Theology: An Introduction to Biblical Doctrine* (Grand Rapids: Zondervan, 1994), p. 293; this is the same argument used by Ross, *Creation and Time,* p. 52; Gleason L. Archer, Jr., *A Survey of Old Testament Introduction,* rev. ed. (Chicago: Moody, 1994), p. 20; and Otto J. Helweg, "How Long an Evening and Morning?" *Facts and Faith* 9 (1995): 8–9.

[91] For my earlier qualifications of a compound grammatical construction, see above, n. 21.

[92] E. Kautzsch, ed., *Gesenius' Hebrew Grammar,* rev. A. E. Cowley, 2nd English ed. (Oxford: Oxford University Press, 1910), pp. 347–48, sec. 114e; and Paul Jouön. *A Grammar of Biblical Hebrew,* 2 vols., trans. and rev. T. Muraoka (Rome: Pontifical Biblical Institute, 1993), 2:471, sec. 129p.

construction is reflected in its more than 60 uses in the Old Testament.[93]
When a particular day is in view in a specific context, it may be translated
as "on the day when." When the temporal reference is more general, this
construction is more generally translated as "when."[94] As a result, rather
than translating בְּיוֹם in Genesis 2:4b as "in the day of," a more concise
English equivalent would be to render it as "when."[95]

We should also note how the rendering of this construction as "when"
fits the immediate context of Genesis 2:4. This verse has a few overlapping concepts, and these are apparent in NASB's translation: "This is the
account of the heavens and the earth when they were created, in the day that
the Lᴏʀᴅ God made earth and heaven." The verbs "created" and "made"
are used synonymously. In addition, "heaven" and "earth" are used in both
clauses. The passive clause "when they were created" has a corresponding active clause where the agent is given "in the day that the Lᴏʀᴅ God
made earth and heaven." While we recognize that there are grammatical
differences between the two clauses, it appears that the passive clause is
balanced by the active clause. As a result, "in the day that" is best taken
as a temporal construction that functions in an equivalent manner to the
temporal conjunction "when." In contrast to NASB's translation, we
would prefer to translate v. 4 like this: "This is the account of the heavens
and the earth when they were created, when (בְּיוֹם) the Lᴏʀᴅ God made
earth and heaven."[96] Therefore, the use of Genesis 2:4 as a justification
for "day" being an extended period is grammatically invalid. Although he
supports an old earth model, Collins nevertheless recognizes the linguistic
deficiencies in justifying the figurative use of "day" with Genesis 2:4.

> Unfortunately, the linguistic case for this theory [day-age view] is weak. Gen
> 2:4 does not provide evidence of a broader semantic range for *yôm,* since
> the word appears in a bound expression. ...But when *běyôm* ("in the day")
> precedes an infinitive, as it does here (*'ăśôt*) it is properly translated "when"
> as in NIV. Thus the bound form *běyôm* in Gen 2:4, being part of an idiomatic
> expression, gives us no information on the range of meanings of *yôm* outside
> the bound form.[97]

---

[93] *TLOT,* s.v. "יוֹם," 2:529.

[94] *TDOT,* s.v. "יוֹם," 6:15; see also *NIDOTTE,* s.v. "יוֹם," 2:420; Cassuto, *Genesis,* p. 16; Westermann, *Genesis 1–11,* p. 183; and John C. Whitcomb and Donald B. DeYoung, *The Moon* (Grand Rapids: Baker, 1978), p. 77.

[95] See BDB, p. 400, and *HALOT,* 2:401.

[96] Waltke and O'Connor, *Biblical Hebrew Syntax,* p. 250.

[97] Collins, "How Old Is the Earth?" p. 110.

Texts Connecting "Day" with a Thousand Years

By equating a creation day with a thousand years, two other biblical texts have been used to support a figurative interpretation of "day" in Genesis 1: Psalm 90:4 and 2 Peter 3:8.[98] If these texts genuinely equate a creation day with a thousand years, the argument for a literal interpretation of the creation days is certainly weakened. However, a closer examination of these two texts reflects that they cannot legitimately be used to rule out a literal interpretation of the days in Genesis 1.

Psalm 90:4 is a passage that has often been used to suggest that "day" may refer to an extended period of time: "For a thousand years in Your sight are like yesterday when it passes by, or *as* a watch in the night." The argument is that Moses interprets his use of day in Genesis 1 in Psalm 90, the only psalm ascribed to him.[99] Psalm 90:4, as the argument goes, indicates that "God's days are not our days"; that is, God's days are not 24-hour days but long periods of time.[100]

Can this argument be sustained from Psalm 90:4? In comparing the use of "day" in this verse with its use in Genesis 1, three observations will be helpful. First, in Psalm 90:4 the comparison between "a thousand years" and "yesterday" involves a simile, "like" (כְּ). However, in Genesis 1 God describes his actual activities on each creation day. He is not making comparative statements, as is the case in Psalm 90:4. The simile in v. 4 compares "a thousand years" to two brief periods of time, "yesterday when it passes by" and "a watch in the night." This is to say, the author is not using "a thousand years" in comparison with a normal day, but with a short period of time. The point of this verse is that God does not evaluate time the way man does.[101]

Second, though "day," יוֹם, is used in Genesis 1 and Psalm 90:4, יוֹם is consistently used in Genesis 1 as a singular noun. However, in Psalm 90:4, יוֹם is part of a compound grammatical construction, "like-a-day-already-past" (i.e., "like yesterday," כְּיוֹם אֶתְמוֹל). As such, this comparison is grammatically deficient. Third, Psalm 90 is not a creation hymn, and the stanza in which v. 4 is located does not focus on any items from creation.[102] Therefore, if any attention is given to exegetical detail, Psalm 90:4 cannot be used to support a figurative interpretation of the days of Genesis 1.

---

[98] Phillips, "Days of Genesis," p. 4.

[99] Ibid.

[100] Ross, *Creation and Time,* p. 45.

[101] Hasel, "Days," p. 12.

[102] Ibid., p. 13.

The second text used to support a figurative interpretation of the creation days is 2 Peter 3:8: "But do not let this one fact escape your notice, beloved, that with the Lord one day is like a thousand years, and a thousand years like one day." It has been suggested that if we take this passage at face value along with Psalm 90:4, it explicitly rules out a literal interpretation of the days of Genesis 1.[103] In contrast to this type of naïve interpretation, we should notice that the immediate context of 2 Peter 3:8 is not a creation context. Furthermore, as in Psalm 90:4, a simile is used to make a comparison.[104] For those using this text to suggest that a "day" in Genesis 1 is a thousand years, or however many years, Whitcomb's response is apropos:

> The latter verse [2 Pet 3:8], for example, does not say that God's days last a thousand years, but that "one day is with the Lord *as* a thousand years." In other words, God is above the limitations of time in the sense that he can accomplish in *one literal day* what nature or man could not accomplish in a vast period of time, if ever. Note that one day is "*as* a thousand years," not "*is* a thousand years," with God. If "one day" in this verse means a long period of time, then we would end up with the following absurdity: "a long period of time is with the Lord as a thousand years." Instead of this, the verse reveals how much God can actually accomplish in a literal day of twenty-four hours.[105]

The Sixth Day

Another challenge to a literal interpretation of the creation days pertains to the many activities that took place on the sixth day. All the activities involving Adam's participation appear to be humanly impossible to accomplish in a portion of a literal day. Grudem provides a summary of this line of reasoning:

> An additional argument for a long period of time in these "days" is the fact that the sixth day includes so many events that it must have been longer than twenty-four hours. The sixth day of creation (Gen. 1:24–31) includes the creation of animals and the creation of man and woman both ("male and female he created them," Gen. 1:27). It was also on the sixth day that God blessed Adam and Eve and said to them, "Be fruitful and multiply, and fill the earth and subdue it; and have dominion over the fish of the sea and over the birds of the air and over every living thing that moves upon the earth" (Gen. 1:28). But that means that the sixth day included God's creation of Adam, God's putting Adam in the Garden of Eden to till it and keep it, and giving Adam directions regarding the tree of the knowledge of good and evil (Gen.

[103] Fischer, "The Days of Creation," p. 20.

[104] Hasel, "Days," p. 13.

[105] John C. Whitcomb, Jr., *The Early Earth,* rev. ed. (Grand Rapids: Baker, 1986), p. 28.

2:15–17), his bringing all the animals to man for them to be named (Gen. 2:18–20), finding no helper fit for Adam (Gen. 2:20), and then causing a deep sleep to fall upon Adam and creating Eve from his rib (Gen. 2:21–25). The finite nature of man and the incredibly large number of animals created by God would by itself seem to require that a much longer period of time than part of one day would be needed to include so many events.[106]

Against this type of reasoning, we should ask this question: Is *God* incapable of doing all these activities in one day, or a portion thereof? Of the many activities represented by old earth advocates, is not God the One performing most of them? One activity might superficially appear too involved for Adam to accomplish in a portion of a literal day—assigning names to the animals. However, Adam's giving names to the animals is not quite the mammoth task that old earth advocates would lead us to believe. There are three reasons for maintaining that Adam was capable of doing this in a portion of a literal day.

First, Genesis 2:19–20 specifically informs us that God "brought" the animals to Adam so that he could assign them names.

> Out of the ground the LORD God formed every beast of the field and every bird of the sky, and brought *them* to the man to see what he would call them; and whatever the man called a living creature, that was its name. The man gave names to all the cattle, and to the birds of the sky, and to every beast of the field, but for Adam there was not found a helper suitable for him.

If Adam had to round up the animals, this would have certainly increased the difficulty, but the text informs us that God "brought" them to Adam.

Second, Genesis 2:19–20 also inform us that Adam named only "all the cattle," "the birds of the sky," and "every beast of the field." To say that this was an "incredibly large number of animals" appears somewhat exaggerated. In considering the text of Genesis 1–2, Adam did not assign names to "creeping things" (Gen 1:24) and the sea creatures (1:20). Adam gave names only to those animals with which he would have primary contact as he exercised his rule over them (1:26–28). According to Henry Morris,

> At the most this would include only the birds and the higher mammals. Furthermore,…the created kinds undoubtedly represented broader categories than our modern species or genera, quite possibly approximating in most cases the taxonomic family. Just how many kinds were actually there to be named is unknown, of course, but it could hardly have been as many as a thousand.[107]

---

[106] Grudem, *Systematic Theology,* p. 294; so also Archer, *Old Testament Introduction,* p. 201; and Collins, "How Old Is the Earth?" pp. 118–19.

[107] Henry M. Morris, *The Biblical Basis for Modern Science* (Grand Rapids: Baker, 1984), pp. 128–29.

Just as God created the prototypes for the vegetation and for mankind, he also did the same in the animal kingdom. The DNA structure for Adam and Eve was undoubtedly designed to allow for their subsequent descendants. As Adam and Eve were the prototypes for humanity, so there would have been a male and female proto-dog. There would have also been a male and female proto-horse. Thus Adam's task as described in Genesis 2:19–20 is not nearly as large as many advocates of an old earth would suggest. This is to say that it would not require many days or years to do this. Adam was naming the prototypes of only a portion of the various created "kinds" (מִין): "all the cattle," "every beast of the field," and "the birds of the sky."[108]

Third, we should also keep in mind that Adam was created perfectly programmed. From an unfallen, human state, Adam's mind would have been programmed from the beginning to exercise his subordinate sovereign rights over the animal kingdom including the ability to name each "kind" (מִין). Even if Adam named a thousand animals, at the maximum, this would seem like a large task to us. However, this task must be balanced by the biblical fact that God directly and perfectly created Adam. As the perfection of humanity, he came equipped to function as God's vice-regent in exercising dominion on earth. Along this line Morris has said:

> It should be remembered that Adam was newly created, with mental activity and physical vigor corresponding to an unfallen state. He certainly could have done the job in a day and, at the very most, it would only have taken a few days even for a modern-day person, so there is nothing anywhere in the account to suggest that the sixth day was anything like a geological age.[109]

While I recognize that this explanation is not necessarily as explicit as the other exegetical data we have used, my intention is to demonstrate that recent creationism has a consistent biblical explanation to account for the many activities performed by God and man on the sixth day of the creation week. Because Adam was the quintessential man, was in an ideal environment where God brought the animals to him, and was naming the prototypes for "all the cattle," "every beast of the field" and "all the birds of the sky," I would understand that Scripture affirms that Adam gave names to these animals during a segment of the sixth day of the creation week. Not only is it feasible that Adam assigned names to these animals on the sixth day, but this explanation, given the nature of God's creating in six,

---

[108] The created "kinds" in Genesis 1–2 have also been referred to as *baramins* (*bara* [בָּרָא], "create," plus *min* [מִין], "kind"). For further information, see John C. Whitcomb, Jr., and Henry M. Morris, *The Genesis Flood* (Philadelphia: Presbyterian & Reformed, 1961), pp. 66–68.

[109] Ibid., p. 129.

successive 24-hour days, is highly probable, since it provides a consistent harmonization with the text.

SUMMARY AND CONCLUSIONS

The objective of this essay has been to provide a biblical justification for a literal understanding of the six creation days. To accomplish this, a dual approach was taken. First, five reasons were set forth to defend this literal interpretation. Because of the semantic constraints for "day," its syntactical constraints, and overall scriptural context, we concluded that Scripture univocally maintains that God created the universe in six consecutive normal days. Second, four arguments against literal days in the creation week were addressed: an open-ended seventh day, the appeal to Genesis 2:4 to support a figurative use of "day," the use of Psalm 90:4 and 2 Peter 3:8 to support figurative creation days, and a figurative understanding of the sixth day to account for the many activities of that day. These four objections do not provide clear-cut evidence to abandon what God has clearly communicated about a literal creation week.

In the final analysis, the figurative understanding of the creation days engenders more exegetical and theological problems than it solves, and is, therefore, indefensible when viewed from the perspective of Scripture's comprehensive message about the nature of the creation week. Consequently, the cumulative weight of the examined evidence demands that the literal interpretation of the days in Genesis 1 is the most internally consistent synthesis of this subject in Scripture.

While many Christians and Christian organizations relegate a literal creation week to a secondary or tertiary level of Christian doctrine, I would suggest that it is an essential part of the faith. To relegate literal creationism to a peripheral doctrinal level minimally suggests an inconsistent view of Scripture's perspicuity on this subject and pervasively promotes deterioration in other facets of orthodox doctrine.[110] Thus, this essay concludes that the sovereign triune God created, for his own glory and according to his eternal counsel, the heavens and the earth and all things therein.

---

[110] For a beneficial discussion of the theological ramifications of creationism, see Morton H. Smith, "The Theological Significance of the Doctrine of Creation," in *Did God Create in Six Days?* pp. 243–65.

THE PRE-MOSAIC TITHE:
ISSUES AND IMPLICATIONS[1]

Mark A. Snoeberger

In Leviticus 27 the Mosaic Law expressly commands the practice of tithing, codifying it for all Israel as a combined act of spiritual service and economic obligation for the advancement of the nation. This codification, however, was by no means the birth of the tithe, but a new expression of the ancient Near Eastern tithe infused with theological significance for the new political entity of Israel.[2]

The payment of tithes was no novel practice, having been performed for centuries by both biblical figures and pagans alike. It is well attested that the tithe[3] was present in the very earliest of cultures—Roman, Greek, Carthaginian, Cretan, Silician, Phoenician, Chinese, Babylonian, Akkadian, and Egyptian—stretching back to the earliest written records of the human race.[4] This extra-biblical practice of tithing must, of course, be considered when searching for the origin of the tithe. Was the tithe a divinely conceived custom, original with Yahweh and unique in its expression, or was tithing a divine adaptation of an originally pagan custom, bequeathed with theological significance by divine fiat? Further, was the tithe an act of worship alone, or a demonstration of political subservience: a primitive form of taxation? Or was it a combination of the two?

Many scholars (including most liberals) contend that the Levitical institution was borrowed strictly from early contemporary heathen practices.[5] On the other pole, some, generally more conservative, scholars

---

[1] This article appeared in the 2000 issue of *DBSJ*, vol. 5, pp. 71–95.

[2] Henry Landsell, *The Sacred Tenth or Studies of Tithe-Giving, Ancient and Modern*, 2 vols. (Grand Rapids: Baker, 1955), 1:56.

[3] The author intends the term in its technical sense—a tenth. As John E. Simpson notes of the nearly universal pagan practice of tithing, "the amount so given was almost invariably one-tenth" (*This World's Goods* [New York: Revell, 1939], p. 88). Cf., however, Joseph M. Baumgarten, "On the Non-literal Use of *ma'ăśēr/dekatē Journal of Biblical Literature 103* (June 1984): 245–51.

[4] Landsell, Sacred Tenth, 1:1–38; Arthur Babbs, *The Law of the Tithe As Set Forth in the Old Testament* (New York: Revell, 1912), pp. 13–24; E. B. Stewart, *The Tithe* (Chicago: Winona Publishing Co., 1903), pp. 7–13.

[5] H. Jagersma, "The Tithes in the Old Testament," in *Remembering All the Way*, Oudtestamentische Studiën XXI (Leiden: Brill, 1981), pp. 116–28; Marvin E. Tate, "Tithing: Legalism or Benchmark?" *Review and Expositor* 70 (Spring 1973): 153; *Encyclopedia Judaica*, s.v. "Tithe," by M. Weinfeld; *The Interpreter's Dictionary of the Bible*, s.v. "Tithe,"

contend that the universality of the tithe and the failure of attempts to
discover its origin within secular sources point to a much more ancient
practice—one instituted by God at the very dawn of human history.[6]

To make either claim, one must look to the early chapters of Genesis
for clues to the genesis of the tithe. If, indeed, concrete evidence for its
origin can be discovered here, one can be assured that the tithe originated
with God and that it was revealed by him from the very earliest times
to mankind. Failure to discover the origin here does not rule out the
possibility of divine origin, but it does render the origin of the tithe an
argument from silence for either position. It is, therefore, the purpose of
this essay to probe the OT material, beginning with the sacrificial practices
of Cain and Abel, continuing with the unprecedented payment of tithes by
Abram to the priest of the most high God, Melchizedek, and concluding
with Jacob's intention to tithe, for clues to the genesis of the pre-Mosaic
tithe. We will then decide whether sufficient evidence exists to confirm its
divine origin, then discuss briefly its relationship to the Levitical tithe and
its continuing applicability (or non-applicability) today.

THE GIVING PRACTICES OF CAIN
AND ABEL (GENESIS 4:3–7)

So it came about in the course of time that Cain brought an offering to
the LORD of the fruit of the ground. Abel, on his part also brought of
the firstlings of his flock and of their fat portions. And the LORD had
regard for Abel and for his offering; but for Cain and for his offering
He had no regard. So Cain became very angry and his countenance
fell. Then the LORD said to Cain, "Why are you angry? And why has
your countenance fallen? If you do well, will not *your countenance* be
lifted up? And if you do not do well, sin is crouching at the door; and
its desire is for you, but you must master it."[7]

In an attempt to establish the continuity of the tithe throughout human
history, several older conservative scholars adopted an alternative text and
translation to affirm that Cain's and Abel's sacrifices establish tithing as
early as Genesis 4. The LXX reading of verse 7 apparently reflects the
Hebrew לנתח (to dissect or divide) rather than the MT's לפתח (reflected in
NASB's "at the door"). The resulting English translation of verse 7 identifies

---

by H. H. Guthrie, Jr. Included in this group are all those who view Israel's "cultus" as
evolutionary and not revelational.

[6] Landsell, *Sacred Tenth*, 1:38; Babbs, *Law of the Tithe*, pp. 24–25.

[7] All Scripture quotations, unless otherwise noted, are taken from the 1995 edition of NASB.

Cain's sin as his failure to "*divide* rightly." Furthering this conclusion is an alternate reading of a NT text, Hebrews 11:4, namely, that "Abel offered unto God a *more abundant*[8] sacrifice than Cain." The conclusion drawn from these combined readings is that Cain's sin was specifically a failure to give an adequate percentage of his income to God. The percentage, it is deduced, must be none other than a tithe.[9] This understanding is not unreasonable, as it follows the reading of the LXX, the text (though not the interpretation) of the early church fathers.[10] However, the difficulty of this reading and the high degree of accuracy of the MT at this point have led most modern commentators to reject this reading out of hand,[11] and with it the implied reference to proportional tithing by Abel.

The Occasion

The preceding discussion does not render the Cain and Abel incident as having no value to the discussion of the tithe. On the contrary, herein is the first recorded instance of an offering presented to God in the OT—offerings that would later be expanded to include the tithe.[12]

---

[8] The term in question, πλείονα, includes in its range of meaning both the qualitative idea of excellence and the quantitative idea of abundance (BAGD, p. 689), though most NT commentators have understood the usage in Hebrews 11:4 to be qualitative, that is, "a better sacrifice."

[9] Landsell, *Sacred Tenth*, 1:40–41; Babbs, *Law of the Tithe*, p. 25.

[10] Clement, *The First Epistle of Clement 4,* in *The Ante-Nicene Fathers,* ed. Alexander Roberts and James Donaldson, 1st series, reprint ed., 10 vols. (Grand Rapids: Eerdmans, 1977), 1:6; Irenaeus, *Against Heresies* 4.18.3, in *The Ante-Nicene Fathers*, 1:485; *Tertullian, An Answer to the Jews 2*, in *The Ante-Nicene Fathers*, 2:153; See also the note on 1:40 of Landsell's *Sacred Tenth* for a survey of other patristic support.

[11] E. A. Speiser, *Genesis*, 2nd ed., AB (Garden City, NY: Doubleday, 1978), p. 32. Most commentators follow the MT without even entertaining the LXX reading in their discussions (e.g., S. R. Driver, *The Book of Genesis* [London: Methuen & Co., 1904], p. 65; Franz Delitzsch, *A New Commentary on Genesis*, 2 vols., trans. Sophia Taylor, reprint of 1888 ed. [Minneapolis: Klock & Klock, 1978], pp. 181–83; Victor P. Hamilton, *The Book of Genesis*, 2 vols., NICOT [Grand Rapids: Eerdmans, 1990, 1995], 1:225–26; and Gordon J. Wenham, *Genesis*, 2 vols., WBC [Waco, TX: Word, 1987, 1994], 1:96–106). Claus Westermann gives an otherwise complete list of philological options for the verse, but does not view the LXX reading as worthy of mention (*Genesis*, 3 vols., Continental Commentaries [Minneapolis: Augsburg, 1984–95], 1:299–301).

[12] The use of the word "expanded" is not intended to imply that the Israelite "cult" evolved on its own apart from the sovereign hand of God, as is asserted by many liberals (see below); instead, it simply recognizes the progress of divine revelation which expands man's knowledge and adjusts his responsibilities. We need not, indeed, must not see the shadow of the Mosaic code veiled in the Cain/Abel narrative; nonetheless, this first recorded sacrifice does give us insight into God's expectations and the means by which he communicated them to early believers.

The background of this incident is meager. We are no sooner told that Cain and Abel have been born when we suddenly find the boys as men, each with the respective occupations of agriculturalist and herdsman. After a period of time, both bring an offering to Yahweh. Cain brings some of the vegetables and fruits resulting from his labor as a farmer, Abel an offering of some of his livestock. For some reason not specified in this text, Yahweh rejects the former but receives the latter.

Several obvious questions arise from the narrative. How did Cain and Abel know to bring an offering to Yahweh? What was the nature of their offering? Why was Cain's offering rejected and Abel's accepted? And, ultimately, does their gift have any bearing on the Levitical tithe or on the NT believer? Naturally, a correct understanding of the term used for this offering (מִנְחָה) is essential to the understanding of the purpose of the sacrifices presented in Genesis 4. We begin here in our search for the tithe in the OT.

The Term Employed

Many have concluded that the offerings of Genesis 4 were intended as atoning, expiatory sacrifices, based on the assumption that God's displeasure with Cain's offering stemmed from his failure to give a blood sacrifice.[13] This theory fails on two counts. First, the term used to describe the offering, מִנְחָה, is elsewhere used of a bloodless sacrifice,[14] and is the standard term used in the Levitical code for the meal offering. Here in Genesis 4 Moses avoids using readily available, general terms that denote blood sacrifice (e.g., זֶבַח). While we may not extrapolate Levitical language anachronistically onto the Genesis 4 incident, Moses' usage of the same term he would later use for the meal offering strongly suggests that this

---

[13] Robert S. Candlish, *An Exposition of Genesis* (reprint ed., Wilmington, DE: Sovereign Grace Publishers, 1972), p. 65. Scofield sees the sin offering in the phrase "sin is crouching at the door." The term for sin (חַטָּאת) may refer to sin or to its sacrificial remedy, the "sin offering." Thus, Yahweh was informing Cain that he had not done well, and that his only solution was to offer a blood sacrifice (*The Scofield Reference Bible* [New York: Oxford, 1909], p. 11). The identification of this חַטָּאת as a crouching beast (רֹבֵץ), however, makes this option unlikely.

[14] J. H. Kurtz goes so far as to say that the מִנְחָה was "exclusively" bloodless (*Sacrificial Worship of the Old Testament*, reprint of 1863 edition [Minneapolis: Klock & Klock, 1980], pp. 158–59), as does Hamilton (Genesis, 1:223), though 1 Samuel 2:17 and 26:19 indicate otherwise. The term has a broader meaning than its technical sense as a meal offering (*New International Dictionary of Old Testament Theology and Exegesis*, s.v. מִנְחָה," by Richard E. Averbeck, 2:980–87). It is best to conclude that the מִנְחָה was usually bloodless, and in its prescriptive, Levitical sense (which is not the case here) was always bloodless.

sacrifice was not intended to be viewed as a sin or guilt offering.[15] Second, the event is predicated on the culmination ("in the course of time"—יָמִים מִקֵּץ [v. 3]) of a lengthy period of agricultural productivity ("Abel was a keeper of flocks, but Cain was a tiller of the ground" [v. 2]), indicating that this was a special offering of thanksgiving for God's abundant blessing. Thus it is roughly, though not exactly, equivalent to Israel's firstfruits or meal offerings, not to their regular sin offerings or tithes.

The term מִנְחָה, in its non-technical usage, is also frequently associated with payment of tribute or taxes (Gen 32:13 [14 MT]; Judg 3:15, 17–18; 1 Sam 10:27). For this reason, it may be suggested that Cain and Abel's gifts were mandatory. However, the term may simply be employed "as an expression of respect, thanksgiving, homage, friendship, dependence,"[16] which functions do not all imply obligation.

The Reason for Cain's and Abel's Offerings

Having deduced, then, that this was a thank offering, we move on to discover the specific basis for this gift. While biblical revelation gives us no precedent or mandate for this type of offering, God's displeasure with Cain's offering implies that Cain failed to meet some divinely revealed requirement. We have already rejected the possibilities of the inappropriate content or quantity of the sacrifice. Other options include inadequate quality in the offering,[17] deficient integrity in the

---

[15] Bruce K. Waltke, "Cain and His Offering," *Westminster Theological Journal* 48 (Fall 1986): 365–66.

[16] *HALOT* (in English), 2:601. Cf. also George B. Gray, *Sacrifice in the Old Testament: Its Theory and Practice* (New York: Ktav, 1971), pp. 16–17; *NIDOTTE*, s.v., "מִנְחָה," by Richard E. Averbeck, 2:986; and *TWOT*, s.v. "מִנְחָה," by G. Lloyd Carr, 1:514–15.

[17] Waltke suggests that the וְ opening v. 4 is adversative, highlighting the "fat" and "firstborn" elements of Abel's sacrifice in contrast to Cain's mere offer of "some" of his fruits and vegetables ("Cain and His Offering," p. 368; cf. also Delitzsch, *Genesis*, pp. 180–81; Hermann Gunkel, *Genesis* [Macon, GA: Mercer University Press, 1997], pp. 42–43; Allen P. Ross, *Creation & Blessing: A Guide to the Study and Exposition of Genesis* [Grand Rapids: Baker, 1988], pp. 157–58; Kenneth A. Mathews, *Genesis 1:1–11:26*, NAC (Nashville: Broadman & Holman, 1996), pp. 267–68. We note, however, that there is no equivalent of fat for Cain's offering, nor does Moses specify that Cain's offering was *not* of the firstfruits. John Sailhamer, in fact, suggests that Cain was also bringing his firstfruits ("Genesis," in vol. 2 of *The Expositor's Bible Commentary*, ed. Frank E. Gaebelein [Grand Rapids: Zondervan, 1990], p. 61).

offerer,[18] or even the simple possibility that Abel was the object of God's elective prerogative while Cain was not[19]—the text does not specify. The NT commentary is simply that Abel's offering was offered "in faith" while Cain's was not (Heb 11:4). This may imply that God had given explicit instructions regarding expiatory and other sacrifices;[20] however, this argument flows purely from silence. All that can be conclusively deduced is that Cain's sacrifice did not issue from faith, but from other, inferior, motivation.

Conclusion

The offerings of Cain and Abel give evidence that men professing to be God-fearers, from earliest times, brought offerings to Yahweh (v. 3) from their bounty. There was, however, no percentage specified, nor any purpose delineated other than direct worship and gratitude addressed to God. Thus, there is little to link these offerings with the basis of the ensuing Levitical tithe, nor to shed light on its continuing applicability. While it is possible that God may have established binding requirements for offerings in the OT apart from written revelation, we certainly cannot deduce from the Cain and Abel narrative that the tithe was among these requirements.

ABRAM'S TITHE TO MELCHIZEDEK
(GENESIS 14:17–24)

> Then after his return from the defeat of Chedorlaomer and the kings who were with him, the king of Sodom went out to meet him [Abram] at the valley of Shaveh (that is, the King's Valley). And Melchizedek king of Salem brought out bread and wine; now he was a priest of God Most High. He blessed him and said, "Blessed be Abram of God Most High, Possessor of heaven and earth; And blessed be God Most High, Who has delivered your enemies into your hand." He gave him a tenth of all. The king of Sodom said to Abram, "Give the people to me and take the goods for yourself." Abram said to the king of Sodom, "I have sworn to the LORD God Most High, possessor of heaven and earth, that I will not take a thread or a sandal thong or anything that is yours, for fear you would say, 'I have made Abram rich.' I will take nothing except what the young men have eaten, and the share of the men who went with me, Aner, Eshcol, and Mamre; let them take their share."

---

[18] John J. Davis, *Paradise to Prison: Studies in Genesis* (Grand Rapids: Baker, 1975), p. 99; John Calvin, *Commentaries on the First Book of Moses Called Genesis*, 2 vols., trans. John King (reprint ed., Grand Rapids: Eerdmans, 1948), 1:196; Hamilton, *Genesis*, 1:224; Driver, *Genesis*, p. 65.

[19] Gerhard Von Rad, *Genesis: A Commentary* (Philadelphia: Westminster, 1974), p. 104.

[20] Landsell, *Sacred Tenth*, 1:41.

We move onward from Cain and Abel in our quest for the genesis of the tithe in the OT to Abram's unprecedented tithe paid to Melchizedek, king of Salem and priest of the most high God. It is in this passage that the technical term "tithe" (מַעֲשֵׂר) is first used in Scripture, making it the first recorded instance of OT tithing. In this incident is found the most promising data for the current study, thus a large segment of the essay will be dedicated to it.

The Occasion

In Genesis 14, Abram is informed that a band of marauding monarchs led by Chedorlaomer had sacked the pentapolis that included Sodom, where his nephew Lot was living. Many of the goods of the city had been seized, and Lot had also been taken captive. Abram gathers a small band from his household, attacks and defeats the marauders in an unlikely nighttime foray, pursues them far to the north, and recovers what had been stolen. Emboldened by Abram's remarkable success, king Bera of Sodom travels northward to the "King's Valley" just south of Salem to meet Abram. He is joined by the local king, Melchizedek, in the valley. King Bera begrudges Abram the spoils but asks for the recaptured citizenry. Melchizedek, identified here as a priest of the most high God (אֵל עֶלְיוֹן), brings out bread and wine to refresh and reward Abram and his men, blesses Abram repeatedly, and blesses Abram's God for the victory. As a biblically unprecedented reciprocation, Abram gives to Melchizedek a tenth of all (presumably of all the spoils). The rest of the spoils are then meted out and the incident is closed.

The Term Employed

The Hebrew term for "tithe" (מַעֲשֵׂר) is simply the adjectival form of the number ten, עֶשֶׂר.[21] The term is used infrequently in Scripture apart from the Levitical and deuteronomic legislation concerning its contribution within the assembly. The term's employment is by no means complex, but it is precise. The tithe is an exact tenth, and is not used in a generic sense to refer to multiple types of offerings of varying amounts.[22]

In Ugaritic and Phoenician sources the tithe was generally paid as the standard unit of taxation owed to the throne. While priests sometimes collected this tithe, there was often no idea of worship involved—the

---

[21] BDB, p. 798.

[22] *NIDOTTE*, s.v. "מַעֲשֵׂר," by Richard E. Averbeck, 2:1035; cf. also H. Jagersma, "Tithes in the Old Testament," p. 117.

priests were viewed as any secular recipient of the tithe would be.[23] Further, it is apparent that, even when the priests collected the tithe, the state, and not the religious personnel, controlled its distribution.[24] This is contrary to the Mosaic legal practice, where, in all recorded situations save one (1 Sam 8:15–17), the tithe was paid to Yahweh through the hand of the priest, and presumably dispensed by the same.[25]

The ancient Near Eastern tithe was paid to the king on everything earned by the subjects of the throne, including produce, animals, and loot won in battle. For this reason it is not unusual that Abram paid a tithe. What is unusual is the abruptness of Melchizedek's appearance, the lack of explanatory details concerning his kingship and priesthood, and the mystery surrounding his relationship to Abram. These enigmas must be resolved along with other questions, such as whether Abram was paying tithes to Melchizedek as his king or as his priest (or both) and whether the tithe Abram paid was voluntary or mandatory. A brief look at Melchizedek is in order to answer these questions.

The Recipient of Abram's Tithe—Melchizedek

Because Abram's tithe, unlike that of the other pre-Mosaic offerings, involves a human as well as a divine recipient, and because that recipient's role seems even more prominent than Abram's in the context of the narrative, Melchizedek merits special study. Rising suddenly to prestige in verse 18 and vanishing just as suddenly a scant two verses later, Melchizedek's function raises many questions. This brief study cannot answer them all, but will endeavor to answer two: What did Melchizedek's offices entail, and what was Abram's relationship to these offices?

Melchizedek as King

Several questions must be answered concerning Melchizedek as king before conclusions may be drawn about the tithe paid him. First, what was the nature of his kingship and the extent of his realm? Second, and closely related to the first, what was Abram's political relationship to the king?

---

[23] *NIDOTTE*, s.v. "מַעֲשֵׂר," by Richard E. Averbeck, 2:1035–36; M. Heltzer, "On Tithe Paid in Grain at Ugarit," *Israel Exploration Journal* 25 (1975): 124–28. Cf., however, Averbeck's remarks on the Akkadian tithe (2:1036).

[24] Jagersma, "Tithes in the Old Testament," pp. 123–24.

[25] Ibid., p. 123. This is not to say that the Mosaic tithe had no secular function—the Mosaic tithe provided poverty relief (Deut 14:28). However, its primary function was to finance "the service of the tent of meeting" and to provide for the Levites "who have no inheritance" (Num 18:21–32).

Melchizedek's Realm

The term "king" (מֶלֶךְ) may be misleading for the reader accustomed to the pomp and prestige of present-day royalty. The fact that at least six kings occupied such a small area of southern Palestine suggests that the kingdoms were quite small and the kings little more than local chieftains[26] each of whom ruled a city and the small tract of surrounding land used by his constituency. This is further attested by the fact that little extrabiblical material survives to tell us about these "kingdoms." On the other hand the marauding eastern kings were apparently much more powerful, one each from the Elamite, Amorite, Hurrian, and Hittite empires.[27] This is not to say, however, that these kings represented the full force of these empires, nor that these empires were in the height of their glory when the invasion occurred.

Melchizedek's realm was the city of Salem. This inexplicable shortening of "Jerusalem" has led many scholars, even conservative ones, to at least entertain the possibility that this was not Jerusalem at all, but another town, perhaps Shiloh, Shechem, or Samaria.[28] Since, however, Psalms 76:2 (3 MT) and 110:2, 4 identify Melchizedek's realm with "Zion," and since the common identification of the valley of שָׁוֵה (v. 17) is confirmed by 2 Samuel 18:18 to be the junction of the nearby Kidron and Hinnom Valleys, there is no doubt that the city was Jerusalem. There is nothing to suggest, however, that Melchizedek's reign in Jerusalem had any special significance to the narrative.[29] Jerusalem was no "holy city" until David's establishment of the seat of his kingdom and the tabernacle (and later Solomon's temple) there.[30]

Melchizedek's Royal Relationship to Abram

Since it is widely held in liberal circles that the narrative concerning Melchizedek (vv. 18–20) is a fictional, secondary insertion, very little scholarship has been spent studying the historicity of Melchizedek or the

---

[26] Philip J. Nel indicates a wide range of meaning for the term, the minimum element being the exercise of rule over a realm, whether that be of a tribe, city-state, or larger territory such as a country or empire (*NIDOTTE*, s.v. "מלך," 2:956).

[27] Hamilton, *Genesis,* 1:399–400; Speiser, *Genesis,* 1:106–8.

[28] For an overview of the options posited, see J. A. Emerton's article, "The Site of Salem, the City of Melchizedek (Genesis xiv 18)," in *Studies in the Pentateuch*, ed. J. A. Emerton, *Supplements to Vetus Testamentum* XLI (Leiden: Brill, 1990): 45–71.

[29] Contra Driver, *Genesis*, p. 164.

[30] In fact, the Jebusite occupation of the city until David's conquest of the city in 998 B.C., recorded in 2 Sam 5:6–8, makes it one of the last Canaanite cities to be conquered by Israel.

correlation of the Melchizedek pericope with the local context.[31] This void of serious study makes Melchizedek's relationship to the surrounding kings and to Abram difficult to discern.

Some propose that Melchizedek's was the smallest of the kingdoms in the narrative, suggested by his lack of involvement in the defensive campaign.[32] Perhaps he could spare no men but could provide some provisions for the victors.

Others have suggested that Salem, since it is to be associated with Jerusalem (Ps 76:2 [3 MT]; 110:2, 4), the most prominent and advantageous geographical location for a city in the region, would have been the capital of a very important city-state in Palestine.[33] Its precedence over the "valley of kings," apparently a very famous and important place in the ancient Near East[34] also suggests that Melchizedek's kingship was a powerful, even a supervisory one. Wenham suggests that his dual role as king and priest would have made him a wealthy and hence a powerful king, as evidenced by his supply of "royal fare" for Abram.[35] He further suggests that his supply of bread and wine was his duty as the "dominant ally."[36] There is no explanation given, however, why Melchizedek, if he was so dominant, did not become involved in the military action. It is also inconclusive that bread and wine were "royal fare" or that Melchizedek's wealth exceeded that of the other local kings.

It seems, therefore, unlikely that Melchizedek exercised authority as an overlord over Abram and the five western kings. This factor is of considerable importance for discussing the tithe paid by Abram—it is unlikely that the tithe represented a tribute or tax paid as a matter of duty to Abram's ruler.

Melchizedek as Priest

Having established the unlikelihood that Melchizedek's regal authority extended over Abram, we now turn to Melchizedek's role as priest of the most high God (כֹהֵן לְאֵל עֶלְיוֹן). We face similar questions with Melchizedek's priesthood as we did with his kingship—What was the nature of his priesthood and the extent of his authority as priest? Second, and again related to the first, what was Abram's spiritual relationship to Melchizedek?

---

[31] Hamilton, *Genesis*, 1:408–9, n. 4.

[32] H. H. Rowley, *Worship in Ancient Israel* (Philadelphia: Fortress, 1967), pp. 17–18.

[33] J. A. Emerton, "The Riddle of Genesis XIV," *Vetus Testamentum* 21 (October 1971): 413.

[34] Gunkel, *Genesis*, p. 279.

[35] *Genesis*, 1:316.

[36] Ibid.

Melchizedek's Priesthood

Melchizedek is labeled by Moses as a כֹּהֵן—a priest. This is the first mention of a priest in the OT, though the concept was not new. A priest is someone who stands in the gap between God and man, representing man to God and God to man.[37] We note, then, that Abram, Noah, and presumably all godly familial heads and clan-leaders in the pre-Abrahamic era functioned as microcosmic priests in a limited capacity as primitive mediators of what would later become the theocratic kingdom.

The first consideration in the study of Melchizedek's priesthood is a very basic one—Whom was Melchizedek serving as priest? The text indicates that the deity served was called "the Most High God" (אֵל עֶלְיוֹן). What has been of considerable debate is whether this deity is to be identified with Yahweh, the God of Abram, or with some local deity.

Liberals have generally contended that אֵל עֶלְיוֹן was a local deity.[38] Based on their assumption that the Hebrew religion began with Abram and over time evolved into modern Judaism, they naturally contend that a reference to Abram's Yahweh in this pericope would be anachronistic. This contention is furthered by their conclusions that the shortened names for עֶלְיוֹן אֱלֹהִים and אֵל are very late developments,[39] heightening the anachronism of seeing Yahweh in Genesis 14:18–20. Further complicating the matter is the absence of the article on אֵל, suggesting that this is a local god, and not the Hebrew God. Instead, it is assumed that the use of אֵל is the widely used Semitic term for various and sundry gods, a term which Israel later borrowed as a designation for her evolving God.

This theory is fraught with bad exegesis and unbiblical assumptions. First, it must be noted that the absence of the article is common with compound names for God,[40] rendering its absence here ancillary to the discussion. Second, the Hebrew term עֶלְיוֹן has no secular parallels other than a rather recently developed Phoenician god, whom Philo labeled as 'Ελιοῦν, ὁ ὕψιστος, who even liberals admit emerged long after the Israelite usage had been established (Num 24:16, Deut 32:8, etc.). We conclude with Speiser and Gunkel that the term was not borrowed by Israel from her pagan neighbors; rather, Israel's neighbors borrowed the term from her.[41]

---

[37] *NIDOTTE*, s.v. "כהן," by Philip Jenson, 2:600.

[38] Speiser, *Genesis*, 1:104; Westermann, *Genesis*, 2:204; Driver, *Genesis*, p. 165; Gunkel, *Genesis*, pp. 279–80. Wenham also takes this view (*Genesis*, 1:316–17).

[39] Speiser, *Genesis*, 1:104.

[40] Delitzsch, *Genesis*, 1:409.

[41] Speiser, *Genesis*, 1:104; Gunkel, *Genesis*, p. 280.

Further, as Hamilton points out, the late Phoenician deity Ἐλιοῦν was the grandson of אֵל.[42] Thus, even if a correlation is attempted, it fails to give us a single god, but two separate ones. In only one other occasion in all known ancient Near Eastern literature are אֵל and עֶלְיוֹן found together—in Psalm 78:35 of the Hebrew canon, and that with reference to the God of Israel.[43] We conclude that there is simply no evidence for a god by the name of אֵל עֶלְיוֹן in the Canaanite or any other pantheon.

Furthering this conclusion is later revelation in Psalm 110, where Melchizedek's priesthood is discussed with reference only to יהוה—neither אֱלֹהִים nor its cognates are mentioned in the entire psalm. Sealing the matter is Hebrews 5:6, 10, where the Greek equivalents of both יהוה and אֵל (κύριος and θεός) are used interchangeably in the context of the priesthood of Melchizedek. There is no question that the אֵל עֶלְיוֹן whom Melchizedek served as priest was Abram's God, the God of Israel. Indeed, as Homer Kent points out, "it is inconceivable that [Abram] would have acknowledged the priesthood of anyone other than a representative of the true God."[44] We add to this that Abram would never have acknowledged anyone but the one true God as the "creator of heaven and earth" and the God who gave him victory in battle (vv. 19–20).

We move on now to discuss the extent of the authority of Melchizedek's priesthood. It apparently was a common practice in the ancient Near East for a king to function as a priest for his people.[45] In fact, it is apparent that Abram himself functioned in much the same capacity, building altars and offering sacrifices (functions of a priest) while functioning as the leader of his clan as a "mighty prince" (נְשִׂיא אֱלֹהִים), a term translated as "king" (βασιλεύς) in the LXX version of Genesis 23:6. This is in keeping with the dispensational setting of Melchizedek's day. As yet there had been no establishment of a single central altar. There had been no formal introduction of Abram as the priest for the world, though it had been privately revealed that his was to be the chosen line to bring blessing to all the nations. Thus it seems likely that, until this point, the dispensation of human government was in effect. God-fearers of this period approached God through their various God-fearing clan-leaders—such as Melchizedek.

This solution, however, only leads to another question. If Melchizedek had jurisdiction as priest only within his own clan (there being no biblical basis for regional high priests with hierarchical sovereignty over lesser priests) why did Abram recognize Melchizedek as his priest?

---

[42] *Genesis*, 1:410.

[43] Cf. also Psalm 7:17 (18 MT) for the use of עֶלְיוֹן, with יהוה.

[44] *The Epistle to the Hebrews* (Grand Rapids: Baker, 1972), p. 124.

[45] Gunkel, *Genesis*, p. 280; Westermann, *Genesis*, 2:204–5; Wenham, *Genesis*, 1:316.

Melchizedek's Spiritual Relationship to Abram

If Melchizedek's jurisdiction extended no further than his clan, the tithe paid by Abram to Melchizedek[46] seems a bit out of place. Hebrews 7:7, however, in discussing Abram and Melchizedek, insists that, "without any dispute, the lesser is blessed by the greater," thus implying that Melchizedek was in some sense greater than Abram when he blessed Abram, and, presumably, when he received tithes from Abram.

Alva J. McClain recognizes the complexity of this passage and acknowledges the possibility that "in the era before Abraham there were other kings who held a similar mediatorial authority between their subjects and the true God."[47] He goes on to theorize that it was "this precise point in Biblical history…[that] marks the end of an era and the beginning of a new order of things."[48] Melchizedek's blessing effectively heralded for the whole world that the mediatorial idea was being localized in "concrete form historically in miniature."[49] The theory makes Melchizedek roughly comparable to other transitional figures, such as Anna, Simeon, and John the Baptist, who, having announced the arrival of the Messiah, faded into oblivion. Representative of this view before McClain was none other than Robert S. Candlish, who, though no dispensationalist, on this one point sounds like one:

> Melchizedek, as the last preserver, as it were, of the primitive patriarchal hope, hands over his function to one more highly favored than himself, in the very spirit of the Baptist—"He must increase, but I must decrease" (John 3:30). His own occupation, as a witness and standing type of the Messiah, is over; one newly called out of heathenism is to succeed and to take his place.… He hails in Abram the promised seed, and blesses him accordingly.… Thus

---

[46] This essay assumes, with most commentators, that the tithe was paid by Abram to Melchizedek, although the text is perhaps less than absolutely explicit on this point. R. H. Smith contends that it was Melchizedek who paid the tithe as an attempt to bribe the warlike Abram to leave the area ("Abraham and Melchizedek," *Zeitschrift für die Alttestamentliche Wissenschaft* 77 [1965]: 134). This narrow view ignores, however, the broader context of Scripture (Hebrews 7) and the traditional understanding of the passage (LXX). J. A. Emerton objects to Smith's view, but asserts that leaving Abram as the tither contradicts verse 23, where Abram is said to have given all the spoil back to the king of Sodom ("Riddle," p. 408). But this is not what verse 23 says. It says, in fact, that Abram would not take anything that belonged to the king of Sodom. This statement does not preclude his tithing or giving the culturally accepted share owed to hired mercenaries (see below).

[47] *The Greatness of the Kingdom* (Grand Rapids: Zondervan, 1959), p. 50.

[48] Ibid., p. 51.

[49] Ibid., p. 50.

the Patriarchal, the Abrahamic, and the Levitical dispensations appear, all of them, in their true character, as subordinate and shadowy.[50]

Although the theory cannot be verified (McClain and Candlish argue from silence that Melchizedek relinquished his priestly functions after this incident), there is much to commend it. The timing is correct, since Abram's call was quite recent. The public announcement is appropriate, for without it no one would have been aware of the dispensational change. The prominence of Melchizedek's delivery of blessings (בָּרַךְ is employed three times in the two verses of Melchizedek's brief discourse) is also significant in light of the reciprocal blessings promised in the Abrahamic Covenant (Gen 12:1–3) to those who would bless Abram. Melchizedek's repeated blessings and his disclosure that God was blessing and being blessed[51] specifically through Abram announced to the listening world that Abram had been specially selected by God as his unique mediatorial representative.[52]

The question still remains, however, why Melchizedek was viewed as "greater" than Abram, able to give him a blessing, and worthy of receiving his tithe. The commentaries are generally silent on this issue, and the question is difficult to answer. It seems best to understand that Melchizedek was not permanently or personally superior to Abram, but that "at that moment Melchizedek stood between God and Abram and was the better."[53] Indeed, any time a person stands in the place of God his superiority is instantly, if temporarily, confirmed by virtue of the God he represents. McClain's comments (above) may also be informative: Melchizedek, representing the authority of the old dispensation, was ceding the reins of the incipient mediatorial kingdom to its new mediator, after which time Abram became superior to Melchizedek.

---

[50] *Genesis*, p. 143.

[51] The action of blessing implied in the term בָּרַךְ, as explained by Hebrews 7:7, always flows from the greater to the lesser. It is no contradiction, however, that Melchizedek "blessed" God. While active blessing (the impartation of something of value to someone) can never be offered by mortals to God, men can "bless" God in a "passive and stative sense" by speaking highly of him or attributing praise to him (*NIDOTTE*, s.v. "ברך," by Michael L. Brown, 1:764). Hebrews 7:7 is by no means at odds with Genesis 14:20.

[52] Victor Hamilton completely misses the point of the repeated use of בָּרַךְ; when he begrudges Abram his blessings while his 318 companions went unmentioned with the sarcastic comment, "As one would expect, it is the general, not the private, who gets the kudos" (*Genesis*, 1:409). It is not because Abram was the "general" that he got the "kudos"; it was because he was one with whom God had covenanted to make a great nation and to be a source of blessing to all the nations.

[53] Kent, *Hebrews*, p. 129.

We thus conclude that Abram's recognition of Melchizedek as a superior was not because Melchizedek was some type of regional high priest, hierarchically presiding over all other lesser priests in the area. Nonetheless, *for the moment*, Melchizedek stood in the place of God, and, as such, exercised temporary spiritual authority over Abram, an authority which Abram recognized by the giving of a tithe.

The Reason for Abram's Tithe

In the previous section we established that the basis for Abram's tithe was the (temporarily)[54] superior priesthood of Melchizedek. We now move to Abram's purpose for giving him a tithe. Was it a social (political) function or an act of pure worship? Was it mandatory or voluntary?

Some suggest that Abram's was a primitive payment to the deity for making him victorious in battle.[55] This is generally a liberal idea[56] and is held only by those who deny that Melchizedek was a priest of the one true God. Others, chiefly those who view Melchizedek as a theophany, view the gift as a direct act of worship to God.[57] Still others suggest that the tithe was rendered to Melchizedek as his share of the spoils of battle in compensation for his role in the conquest of the four invading kings, a "postbellum distribution of the booty, in which the spoils are distributed equally between those who personally fought...and for those who for one reason or another did not actively engage in the fighting."[58] This reminds us of similar incidents in Numbers 31:27 and 1 Samuel 30:21–25, where personnel left behind were afforded shares of the spoils despite their failure to actively participate in the battle.

---

[54] By using this qualifier the author is not intending to negate the arguments of Hebrews 5–7 or Psalm 110. For typological purposes, that moment of superiority was captured by the later authors and coupled with a few of the sudden and mysterious factors surrounding the appearance of Melchizedek in Scripture to provide vivid illustrations of the superiority of Christ. As with all types there is not a one-to-one correspondence between every detail, thus it is not necessary to elevate Melchizedek to some mysterious or supernatural plane to preserve the analogy between him and Christ (as some have done by suggesting that Melchizedek's appearance in Genesis 14 was a theophany). Melchizedek, it should be concluded, was simply a literal, historical human being whose life was directed by God to serve as a type of Christ (See Kent, *Hebrews*, pp. 124–27).

[55] Westermann, *Genesis*, 2:206; Speiser, *Genesis*, 1:109; Wenham, *Genesis*, 1:317.

[56] A more radically liberal idea, held by Gunkel (*Genesis*, p. 281) and Driver (*Genesis*, pp. 167–68), is that the character Melchizedek was pseudepigraphal, being invented, along with the legend of the Jebusite coalition, in David's time to lend legitimacy to the establishment of his new capital in Jerusalem.

[57] Candlish, *Genesis*, pp. 142–46.

[58] Hamilton, *Genesis*, 1:413.

While this last theory is attractive, it has a few flaws. First, the tithe to Melchizedek is set apart from the rest of the distribution of the spoils—the tithe occurs in verse 20, but the provisions for distribution of the spoils are not made until the very last verse of the chapter. Further, Abram's tithe is mentioned in close proximity to Melchizedek's priestly blessing of Abram, suggesting that his tithe-giving had a purely spiritual purpose, not a politico-cultural one. The king of Sodom clearly did not understand this exchange, and apparently thought that the division of spoils had begun in v. 20. He immediately jumped in and made his bid for the people of his city, abandoning all hope of regaining anything else. Abram's negative response is quite revealing: he wanted no blessings, material or spiritual, from the wicked king of Sodom to becloud or overshadow the priestly blessing he had just received from Melchizedek, nor create any sense of obligation of Abram to Sodom.[59] As a result, he renounced all claim to the spoils. Third, Abram's comments in verse 23, that he would not take anything that rightly belonged to the king of Sodom, seems to indicate that, after Melchizedek's tenth and a small mercenary stipend for the efforts of Abram's companions, the rest of the spoils went back to their previous owners. This is in contrast to the ancient Near Eastern custom. While the spoils belonged legally to Abram,[60] simple kindness required him to return the property to its rightful owners.

It seems most likely that the tithe was paid to Melchizedek as a voluntary reciprocation for the priestly functions performed by Melchizedek and a thank offering given to God for the success of the military excursion.[61] As such it represented a willing consecration of a portion of the goods to God through the hand of the priest, in acknowledgement that the whole belonged to God.[62] It also represented Abram's recognition that the dispensational baton, as it were, was being passed to him by its legitimate forebear.

Why Abram chose a tenth and not some other amount is not explained. As has been already demonstrated, payment of a tenth was a universal practice in the ancient known world. We may hypothesize that God, though unrecorded in the Hebrew Scriptures, established the tenth as a general figure to be spent on priestly administration, but it may be that this amount was simply selected by Abram as a reasonable amount to fulfill sacrificial

[59] Ibid., 1:413–14; Ross, *Creation and Blessing*, p. 300–302; Sailhamer, "Genesis," pp. 123–24.

[60] Wenham, *Genesis*, 1:317.

[61] Delitzsch, *Genesis*, 1:410.

[62] Candlish, *Genesis*, p. 142.

duty to God. Nor have we ruled out the idea that the custom was merely adopted from Abram's heathen neighbors. Genesis 26:5,[63] which informs us that Abraham obeyed God, along with all his commandments, statutes, and laws, could point to the first of these options, but there is no clear link of 26:5 with the specific statute of tithing.

We may only speculate about Melchizedek's subsequent usage of the tithes he received, but it seems likely that they went to finance the priestly services provided by Melchizedek as a mediator for God.[64]

Conclusion

While Abram's tithe apparently meets with God's approval, several factors lead us to conclude that it has little bearing on the Levitical tithe and on our current practice. First, the tithe mentioned here is unique to the transition between the dispensations of human government and promise and has no genuine parallels in the rest of Scripture. Second, the silence as to the origin of and the apparently voluntary nature of Abram's tithe render it unlike anything in the rest of biblical experience. Abram's tithe had a purpose, origin, and nature *distinct* from the Mosaic institution.

JACOB'S PROMISED TITHE (GENESIS 28:18–22)

[18]So Jacob rose early in the morning, and took the stone that he had put under his head and set it up as a pillar and poured oil on its top. [19]He called the name of that place Bethel; however, previously the name of the city had been Luz. [20]Then Jacob made a vow, saying, "If God will be with me and will keep me on this journey that I take, and will give me food to eat and garments to wear, [21]and I return to my father's house in safety, then the LORD will be my God. [22]This stone, which I have set up as a pillar, will be God's house, and of all that You give me I will surely give a tenth to You."

The second and only other OT mention of the tithe prior to the giving of the Mosaic Law comes in the form of a tithe promised to God by Jacob after his ladder vision at Bethel and God's reaffirmation of the Abrahamic Covenant to Jacob there (vv. 10–15). As in the Abram/Melchizedek narrative, the Hebrew term מַעֲשֵׂר is used, so we are sure that it is an actual tithe in question. Since this term has already been discussed, we move directly to a study of the occasion of this promised tithe to understand its

---

[63] See W. W. Barndollar's extensive discussion of this verse in his "The Scriptural Tithe" (Th.D. dissertation, Grace Theological Seminary, 1959), pp. 80–99.

[64] Ibid.

purpose and to glean insights into the validity and continuing applicability of Jacob's practice.

The Occasion

The event comes at a particularly turbulent period in Jacob's life, a fact which weighs heavily on our study. In chapter 27, Jacob, true to his name, had completed the two-fold deception of his father and brother, and had successfully stolen the birthright away from Esau. Esau's resultant rage and apparent intent to kill Jacob for the deception led Jacob, at his mother's bidding and with the blessing of his father, to flee to the house of his uncle, Laban, until his brother's anger abated.

En route to Laban's house Jacob is arrested by a dream in the city of Luz (which he later renamed "Bethel"). In the dream, Yahweh renewed the Abrahamic Covenant with Jacob. In so doing, Yahweh confirmed to Jacob that he was the chosen son through whom the covenant blessings would flow. Jacob awakens in fear and quickly erects an altar at the site of the dream and gives a sacrifice of oil on the altar to God. Upon making the sacrifice he offers up a vow to God that he would make Yahweh his God and give him a tenth, presumably of all his possessions, so long as Yahweh spared him, provided for his needs, and prospered him during his sojourn at his uncle's residence. God was true to his promise, but there is no indication whether or not Jacob fulfilled his vow.

Again, questions arise from the narrative that affect our understanding of the promised tithe. Was Jacob's promised tithe an act of faith or part of some sort of inappropriate "bargain" made with God? If the latter, can Jacob's tithe be considered normative or foundational to the study of the tithe in the rest of the OT, or have any bearing on its practice (or non-practice) today? Whether or not the vow was actually fulfilled, what was the reason and purpose for Jacob's tithe?

The Spiritual State of Jacob

While most evangelicals have maintained that this dream finds or at least leaves Jacob converted, there are three factors in the narrative and one in Genesis 32 which indicate that Jacob's vow to tithe to Yahweh was an illegitimate act of worship.

First, Jacob's reaction of fright upon the appearance of Yahweh indicates an improper relationship to God. Many commentators take the reaction by Jacob to be a healthy, reverential awe of God and his description of the site as "awesome," inducing genuine worship.[65] If this is the case, Jacob's succeeding actions denote consecration. This is a legitimate interpretation of the terms employed. In fact, the "fear of the Lord" seems to be the OT equivalent for faith (Prov 1:7). The Hebrew root ירא ("to fear"), represented in the Jacob narrative by the Qal imperfect and niphal participle respectively, however, has a wide range of meaning, extending from a meaning of "reverence" or "respect" at one pole to "terror" or "fright" at the other.[66] The present context favors the second pole.[67] First, whenever the term is used elsewhere of Jacob in subsequent contexts, it clearly denotes "fright," that is, fear that caused him to respond by running or conniving, rather than trusting (e.g., 31:31, 32:7, 11).[68] Second, Jacob's ignorance that God could be here in Luz (v. 16) may indicate that he was shocked to find God here.[69] Waltke and O'Connor concur, demonstrating from the emphatic adverb אָכֵן that the verse conveys "a sudden recognition in contrast to what was theretofore assumed."[70] If this is the case, then Jacob is betraying a woeful lack of knowledge and respect for the Almighty. Third, as Hamilton points out, this is the only instance in the patriarchal narratives (except possibly 15:12) that a theophany is ever met with astonishment or fright. The other patriarchs always "took theophanies in stride."[71]

Further developing the "fright" idea of the term ירא is Jacob's apparent lack of faith in the explicit promises of God. After hearing the promises, Jacob makes a conditional vow whose conditions were the very promises he had just received from Yahweh. In verse 15 Yahweh promises to be with Jacob, to keep him, and bring him back to the land. Jacob responds in verse 20 that if indeed God remains with him, keeps him safe, clothes and feeds him, and returns him to the land, *then* he would make Yahweh his God, pay tithes, etc.[72] By thus casting his conversion in the future,

---

[65] Candlish, *Genesis*, pp. 294–96; Delitzsch, *Genesis*, 2:165; Ross, *Creation and Blessing*, pp. 491–94; Wenham, *Genesis*, 2:223–25; John J. Davis, *Paradise to Prison*, pp. 243–44.

[66] BDB, s.v. "יָרֵא," p. 431.

[67] *NIDOTTE*, s.v. "ירא," by M. V. Van Pelt and W. C. Kaiser, Jr., 2:528–29.

[68] Hamilton, *Genesis*, 2:244.

[69] Ibid., 2:243–44.

[70] Bruce K. Waltke and M. O'Connor, *An Introduction to Biblical Hebrew Syntax* (Winona Lake, IN: Eisenbrauns, 1990), p. 670.

[71] *Genesis*, 2:245.

[72] Hamilton suggests that the latter half of verse 21 is actually part of the protasis, not part of the apodosis (*Genesis*, 2:248). As such the verses should read, "If God stays with

Jacob is apparently refusing to exercise faith at this time. Some suggest the conditional particle, אִם ("if") used here precludes a genuine contingency,[73] instead meaning "since," or "forasmuch as," much like the Greek first class condition. However, the grammar of this passage suggests otherwise. In his remarks about conditional clauses, Gesenius comments:

> With regard to the difference between אִם (אִם לֹא) and לוּ (לוּלֵא), the fundamental rule is that אִם is used if the condition be regarded either as already fulfilled, or if it, together with its consequence, be thought of as possibility (or probability) occurring in the present or future. In the former case, אִם is followed by the perfect, in the latter (corresponding to the Greek ἐάν with the present subjunctive) by the imperfect or its equivalent (frequently in the apodosis also).[74]

The immediately following lead verb (יִהְיֶה) is in the imperfect, and all the succeeding verbs of the protasis are cast in the perfect with the וְ consecutive (making their function equivalent to the imperfect), clearly demonstrating that the vow represents a genuine contingency.[75] Thus, his actions of building an altar and his promise to tithe on his livelihood are not deeds of faith; instead, they are wary, fearful acts of a trapped person to appease and "strike a bargain" with God.

To the grammatical argument we add an obvious theological one. The sheer brazenness of a mortal establishing a conditional covenant with the Almighty gives evidence to Jacob's unconverted state. To place God under obligation to act a certain way and to stipulate that God must fulfill certain obligations *before* one consecrates himself is not an act of faith but an audacious challenge to God's sovereignty, inspired by unbelief.

Finally, the events surrounding Jacob's dream at Peniel and his wrestling match there (32:24–32 [25–33 MT]) indicate that this latter event

---

me…protects me…gives me bread to eat and clothing to wear, and I return safely to my fathers house and *if Yahweh shall be my God*, then this stone…shall be God's abode… and a tenth will I tithe to you" (2:237–38). This interpretation does little to change the "bargaining" arrangement proposed by Jacob.

[73] Candlish, *Genesis*, pp. 294–95; also Barndollar, "Scriptural Tithe," p. 108.

[74] E. Kautzsch, ed., *Gesenius' Hebrew Grammar*, 2nd English ed., rev. A. E. Cowley (Oxford: Clarendon Press, 1910), pp. 494–95. On p. 496, the very passage in question is used as an example of genuine contingency. Cf. also Waltke and O'Connor, *Hebrew Syntax*, pp. 526–27.

[75] Barndollar makes a serious error in affirming that "all the verbs which follow אִם in verses 20 and 21 are perfect" ("Scriptural Tithe," p. 108), a faulty affirmation which he uses to support his theory that there was no actual contingency in Jacob's vow. The grammar, in fact, proves quite the opposite.

was the actual conversion of Jacob. The name change (v. 28 [29 MT]) from Jacob ("deceiver") to Israel (probably "let God rule"[76]) is not a mere change of name, but is representative of a change in character—from a depraved self-server to one who recognizes and submits to God's sovereignty. Likewise, Jacob's naming of the site "Peniel" ("the face of God") is not due to his struggling with God himself,[77] but because he has finally come to a point where he has recognized Yahweh as his God and, much to his relief, is enabled to exercise true faith in the promises made to him at Bethel so many years before.[78] The contention that Jacob's conversion experience took place at Peniel, then, naturally precludes its occurrence at Bethel or some prior occasion.

One notable objection to such a late conversion date for Jacob, and perhaps the reason why most commentators assume Jacob to be saved in Genesis 28, is the bequest of the Abrahamic promises to Jacob at Bethel. It is contended that God's reiteration of the Abrahamic promises to Jacob assumes his salvation. This, however, is a logical *non sequitur*. The OT teems with examples of beneficiaries of national election, even heads of the mediatorial kingdom, who were never converted (e.g., many of the judges and kings, most notably, Saul). The unconditional covenant promises given nationally to the patriarchs and their descendants had no direct bearing on their individual election to salvation (Rom 9:6). Thus it was not necessary for Jacob to have been a believer to receive the blessings of the Abrahamic Covenant.

This author, with a fair degree of confidence asserts, then, that Jacob's vow to tithe was made while he was yet unconverted. This fact, coupled with the silence as to the fulfillment of the vow render this reference to tithing a rather slender strand of evidence for affirming the foundation of the Levitical tithe or asserting an ongoing tithe in our present dispensation.

The Reason for Jacob's Promised Tithe

The fact that Jacob settled on a tithe as opposed to some other amount may indicate that he had some prior exposure to the tithe. Jacob may have been following the lead of his grandfather or other God-fearers with whom he

---

[76] Hamilton, *Genesis*, 2:334. There is a bit of debate regarding the exact meaning of this name. The scope of this essay, however, does not require interaction with the debate except to assert that the change of name signals a change of heart.

[77] Whether or not the "man" with whom Jacob struggled was a preincarnate form of Christ is a matter of considerable debate; however, since this is not, apparently, the source of the name "Peniel," the issue will be left unresolved.

[78] Hamilton, *Genesis*, 2:337.

was acquainted. In light of Jacob's faulty view of the extent of God's presence, authority, and faithfulness to his promises and of Jacob's willingness to demean God's sovereignty by "bargaining" with him, it is more likely that he was borrowing the tithing practice of the surrounding pagans. As with Abram, no clear conclusions may be drawn.

Nor is it certain what the purpose or method of payment was if, indeed, Jacob fulfilled his vow. While Abram still had a priest external to himself, it seems unlikely, if McClain's and Candlish's theory[79] is correct, that any legitimate priests of Yahweh remained to whom Jacob could pay his tithes.[80] Perhaps he would have consumed the tithe on an altar to Yahweh, or used it to finance priestly duties performed among his family. Again, the text gives us no sound answers.

Conclusion

Because Jacob's promised tithe resembles, even derives from, the heathen practices of his neighbors, it adds little to our study. The basis for the Levitical tithe certainly does not derive from Jacob's practice. This fact, coupled with Jacob's unconverted state and the silence of Scripture as to the fulfillment of Jacob's vow, should cause us to dismiss Genesis 28 from consideration in the quest for the genesis of the tithe.

IMPLICATIONS OF THE PRE-MOSAIC TITHE FOR PRESENT-DAY INSTITUTIONS

If tithing were confined to the Mosaic Law it would be easy to dismiss its validity today. In that the Mosaic Law has been set aside in the work of Christ (Rom 10:4, 2 Cor 3:7–11, etc.), tithing, as part of that unified legal corpus, would also be set aside.[81] The pre-Mosaic tithe complicates the issue, raising the possibility that the tithe might be a trans-dispensational practice, part of the moral code of God, and thus a continuing obligation for NT believers.

---

[79] Cf. above.

[80] Cf., however, Barndollar, "The Scriptural Tithe," p. 111.

[81] To be sure, many a covenant theologian would recoil at such a statement and assert that the law is still in effect and the command to tithe is still in vogue (e.g., Edward A. Powell and Rousas J. Rushdoony, *Tithing and Dominion* [Vallecito, CA: Ross House, 1979], pp. 11–14). The scope of this essay does not include this issue, so it will be left for others to debate. Instead this section will address the continuing validity of the tithe strictly on the basis of the pre-Mosaic practice.

There can be no denial of the fact of tithing before the Law; however, the assertion of a continuing principle necessitates more than a mere mention of the term "tithe" prior to the giving of the Law. As Pieter Verhoef, a non-dispensationalist, concedes, "a pre-Mosaic custom does not, as a matter of course, transcend the Old Testament dispensation, becoming an element of the universal and timeless moral code."[82] There must also be clear evidence that the tithe was divinely mandated before the Law or somehow sourced in God's nature. Further, there must be a parallelism between the practice of the tithe in the pre-Mosaic period and that in our present experience.

God's Nature and Mandate and the Pre-Mosaic Tithe

Many suggest that the universal practice of the tithe and the failure of attempts to identify its origin in the secular realm point to its divine origin and continuing practice from Adam onward.[83] Others do not trace the practice to Adam, but contend that God gave Abram direct revelation, and "started all over," establishing a new precedent with Abram that was continued by Israel,[84] and presumably today. There are many flaws with this theory.

First, it has already been established that neither Abel's nor Jacob's practices are legitimate paradigms for a biblical tithe. Thus, we are left with only Abram's practice to prove that the tithe was practiced by all God-fearers for the millennia prior to the giving of the Law. This hasty generalization from a single datum of evidence renders the argument very weak.

Second, universality of practice in the secular realm does not prove that God is the originator of the tithe. This is yet another logical *non sequitur*. It seems far more reasonable that Abram was not acting by divine mandate, but in accordance with the ancient Near Eastern customs of his day.[85]

---

[82] "Tithing: A Hermeneutical Consideration," in *The Law and the Prophets: Old Testament Studies Prepared in Honor of O. T. Allis,* ed. John H. Skilton (Phillipsburg, NJ: Presbyterian and Reformed, 1974), p. 122.

[83] Landsell, *Sacred Tenth,* 1:38; Babbs, *Law of the Tithe,* pp. 24–25. E. B. Stewart further maintains that "divine acceptance…is a demonstration of a divine institution" (*The Tithe,* p. 37). This is a classic example of a non sequitur.

[84] R. T. Kendall, *Tithing* (Grand Rapids: Zondervan, 1982), p. 45; Driver, *Genesis,* p. 166; John Skinner, *A Critical and Theological Commentary on Genesis,* ICC (Edinburgh: T. & T. Clark, 1910), p. 269.

[85] This possibility in no wise reduces Israel's religion to a conglomeration of pagan practices that evolved into a final form. God clearly created the OT Jewish legal system by divine fiat, and was by no means bound to pagan customs in his formation of the Law. On the other hand, neither was he obliged to avoid all pagan customs in the formation of

Third, there is no basis for claiming that Israel derived her practice of tithing from Abraham or Jacob. On the contrary, it is clear that "the normative significance of tithing must be considered within the context of the ceremonial law."[86] Indeed, both post-pentateuchal injunctions for Israel to pay tithes reference the Law as the impetus for the injunction, not the practice of the patriarchs (Neh 10:36–39; Mal 3:7–10).

Fourth, there is never an appeal to God's nature or to creation as a basis for tithing. How a mere percentage, apart from an explicit command, can take on moral value is impossible to establish.

Fifth and in summary, the hypotheses that the pre-Mosaic tithe had its basis in God's command, God's nature, or God's approval all argue from silence.

Parallels to the Pre-Mosaic Tithe

Another argument against the continuing applicability of the tithe is the simple lack of present-day parallels to the pre-Mosaic practice.

First, Abram's tithe was apparently a one-time act, not a regular giving pattern. There is no record of Abram's return to Melchizedek, and the references to his tithe in the singular in Hebrews 7:4, 6 point to a one-time gift.[87]

Second, Abram's tithe was made strictly on the spoils of war seized from the coalition of eastern kings. While the Hebrew and Greek texts simply state that Abram made a tithe of "all," this clearly cannot mean he gave Melchizedek a tenth of his entire possessions—Abram surely was not carrying such a percentage of his property on a swift military raid. It seems certain that it was only the spoils on which Abram tithed.

Third, there is no present-day recipient of a tithe that can parallel Melchizedek. The church bears little resemblance to a priest/clan-leader.

---

the Law. Timothy H. Fisher, for instance, notes that the pagan practice of circumcision predates God's institution of circumcision in Genesis 17 by hundreds of years ("A Study of the Old Testament Tithe," [Th.M. Thesis, Capital Bible Seminary, 1990] p. 11, n. 1). This issue is also addressed by David G. Barker ("The Old Testament Hebrew Tithe" [Th.M. Thesis, Grace Theological Seminary, 1979], p. 131).

[86] Verhoef, "Tithing," p. 122.

[87] Again, Barndollar shows extraordinary carelessness in his exegesis, maintaining in support of a regular tithe that "the writer of the Epistle to the Hebrews declares that Melchizedek 'received *tithes* of Abraham' (Heb. 7:6). The plural number of the word certainly suggests more than one visit by Abraham to Melchizedek for the purpose of the presentation of his tithes to the Lord's high priest" ("Scriptural Tithe," p. 60). While the King James Version does cast the tithe in verse 6 in the plural, and the Greek term for tithe, δεδεκάτωκεν (δεδεκάτωκε in the Majority Text and Textus Receptus), is inconclusive, a simple comparison with verse 4 results in a conclusion opposite Barndollar's.

Furthermore, the usage of the tithe by Melchizedek and the church (missions outreach, etc.) are dissimilar.

We conclude, then, that there is nothing in pre-Mosaic tithing practices to serve as a basis for viewing the tithe as a trans-dispensational and thus a continuing principle for the NT church. There is simply no evidence to support the claim.

CONCLUSION

In summary, this paper leaves the reader with the difficult and perhaps unsatisfying verdict that the pre-Mosaic title did not originate with divine revelation. In fact, the evidence suggests identifying the practice of the patriarch's pagan neighbors as the basis for patriarchal tithing practices. It is only as God placed theological significance on the tithe in Leviticus that the tithe became mandatory and meaningful.

One looks in vain for evidence of proportional giving in the Cain and Abel narrative, finding only a few short verses to fuel the possibility that any sacrifices at all were mandatory in the pre-Mosaic period. Certainly there is insufficient evidence to support a tithe.

The first OT mention of the tithe is in the context of an extraordinary event with no parallels in the Levitical system or today. Instead, it was a dispensational marker heralding the shift from the dispensation of human government to the dispensations of promise. The recipient of Abram's tithe and its purpose have no parallels in NT practice or in the Levitical system.

The second OT mention of the tithe is even less helpful, as the promised tithe of Jacob is never said to have been actually paid and the giver has been demonstrated to be unconverted at the time of the vow. The recipient and purpose of Jacob's tithe, if it ever materialized, are cloaked in such obscurity that the identification of any parallels in the present-day or in the Levitical system is impossible.

We conclude, therefore, that the pre-Mosaic tithe was merely a culture-bound, voluntary expression of worship reflective of the ancient Near Eastern practice of the time, and adapted by Abraham as a means of expressing gratitude and attributing glory to Yahweh.

THE MESSAGE OF ECCLESIASTES[1]

Robert V. McCabe

In the history of its interpretation, the book of Ecclesiastes has presented a plethora of difficulties. The book presents difficulties in interpreting its individual passages, unity of thought, textual criticism, language, and syntax. One of the major frustrations has been determining what is the basic message of this book. How do some of the negative elements such as Qohelet's[2] hating life (2:17) tie in with the more positive element of his commending the enjoyment of life (2:24)? Is the message of Ecclesiastes one of skepticism or hedonism? Many critical scholars have maintained that Qohelet was a skeptic. Crenshaw has stated that "Qohelet examines experience and discovers nothing that will survive death's arbitrary blow. He then proceeds to report this discovery of life's absurdity and to advise young men on the best option in the light of stark reality."[3]

However, this type of thinking is not confined to the critical scholar. A number of conservative scholars have interpreted the message of Ecclesiastes in a similar fashion. Stuart has stated that the perspective of Ecclesiastes "is the secular, fatalistic wisdom that a *practical* atheism produces. When one relegates God to a position way out there away from us, irrelevant to our daily lives, then Ecclesiastes is the result."[4] Another example of this is found in the introduction to Ecclesiastes in the *New Scofield Reference Bible.* "The philosophy it [Ecclesiastes] sets forth, which makes no claim to revelation but which inspiration records

---

[1] This article appeared in the Spring 1996 issue of *DBSJ*, vol. 1, pp. 85–112.

[2] Qohelet is a transliteration of the feminine participle קֹהֶלֶת. This feminine form has generally been understood as referring to one who holds an office. Since this Hebrew appellative is used to refer to the book's author, its transliterated form will be used in this article to refer to the author. The meaning of the term is uncertain. Following the Septuagint's translation of this with ἐκκλασιαστής, a number of translations have rendered קֹהֶלֶת as "preacher." The term קהל is used in reference to one who gathers an assembly and, consequently, may refer to the one who addresses the assembly, a teacher. In the Old Testament only קֹהֶלֶת is rendered as "preacher" in the KJV and NASB. Since the concept of preacher is more a New Tesament one, this translation appears to be historically inconsistent. It is better to see קֹהֶלֶת as an "assembler" or a "teacher."

[3] James L. Crenshaw, *Ecclesiastes*, OTL (Philadelphia: Westminster, 1987), p. 28.

[4] Gordon D. Fee and Douglas Stuart, *How to Read the Bible for All Its Worth*, 2nd ed. (Grand Rapids: Zondervan, 1993), p. 214. This is also the view advocated by Longman (Raymond B. Dillard and Tremper Longman III, *An Introduction to the Old Testament* [Grand Rapids: Zondervan, 1994], p. 254).

for our instruction, represents the worldview of one of the wisest of men, who knew that there is a holy God and that He will bring everything into judgment."[5] Perhaps we might think the editors of the *New Scofield Reference Bible* were inconsistent with their predecessor C. I. Scofield. But in his correspondence school course, Scofield reflects this same type of thought:

> It is not at all the *will of God* which is developed, but that of *man* "under the sun" forming his own code. It is, therefore, as idle to quote such passages as 2:24, 3:22, etc., as expressions of the divine will as it would be to apply Job 2:4, 5 or Genesis 3:4. The constant repetition of such expressions as "I perceived," "I said in my heart," "then I saw," etc., sufficiently indicate that here the Holy Spirit is showing us the workings of man's own wisdom and his reaction in weariness and disgust.[6]

Other interpreters have tended to interpret the message in a more positive manner. Gianto has advocated that the enjoyment motif plays a major emphasis in Ecclesiastes.[7] While recognizing that Qohelet is a realist, Whybray maintains that man should "enjoy to the full what *good* things

---

[5] *The New Scofield Reference Bible* (New York: Oxford University Press, 1967), p. 696. Though the editors of the Scofield Reference Bible surely did not intend it, their words could lead to an unwarranted dichotomy between inspiration and revelation. Paul affirms in 2 Tim 3:16 that "all Scripture is breathed by God." Since "Scripture" is a translation of the Greek word graphē, which denotes what is written, inspiration ("breathed by God") is what God originally produced in written form. In this context, special revelation relates to written truth (Scripture). Special revelation contains two forms of truth: descriptive and normative. Every word of the Bible as originally given is what we could label descriptive truth. This guarantees the accurate preservation of items such as Satan's lie in Gen 3 and his desire to get Job to curse God in Job 2:4–5. Whatever Scripture records, it has preserved with historical accuracy. The statement by the editors of the *Scofield Reference Bible* suggests that the whole book of Ecclesiastes is only descriptive truth with two theological exceptions: there is a holy God and he will bring everything into judgment. Thus the implication is that only these two statements are Qohelet's normative truth. If this is so, then Ecclesiastes is different from every other book in the Canon. Normative truth, on the other hand, pertains to those truths by which the people of God are to regulate their lives. I would understand that Ecclesiastes is affirming much more normative truth than the editors of the *Scofield Reference Bible* allow. For more on the subject of inerrancy, see Paul D. Feinberg, "The Meaning of Inerrancy," in Inerrancy, ed. Norman L. Geisler (Grand Rapids: Zondervan, 1980), pp. 267–304; and for information on how this relates to Ecclesiastes, see Weston W. Fields, "Ecclesiastes: Koheleth's Quest for Life's Meaning" (Th.M. thesis, Grace Theological Seminary, 1975), pp. 116–27.

[6] *Scofield Bible Correspondence Course*, 2 vols. (reprint ed., Chicago: Moody Bible Institute, 1959), 2:302.

[7] Agustinus Gianto, "The Theme of Enjoyment in Qohelet," *Biblica 73* (1992): 528–32; see also Norbert Lohfink, "Qoheleth 5:17–19—Revelation by Joy," *Catholic Biblical Quarterly* 52 (October 1990): 625–35.

God has given; and indeed this is what God *requires* of them."[8] In an earlier article, Whybray refers to Qohelet as a "Preacher of Joy."[9] Though we recognize that Qohelet's enjoyment motif is positive, the overall message of Ecclesiastes is not one of unbridled hedonism.

Each of these types of interpretations[10] suggests that Qohelet was either a skeptic or a hedonist. In either case, we are left with a book that either makes no contribution to biblical theology or at best a minimal contribution. What then would be the contribution of Qohelet to normative truth? By comparing the final two verses of Ecclesiastes as well as the normative theology of Scripture as a whole, Stuart states that it is in our canon to serve "as a foil, i.e., as a contrast to what the rest of the Bible teaches."[11] If this understanding of Ecclesiastes is correct, then this book is the antithesis of all other canonical books. However, we are persuaded that Qohelet[12] was a godly sage and that he made a significant contribution

---

[8] R. N. Whybray, *Ecclesiastes*, NCB (Grand Rapids: Eerdmans, 1989), p. 2.

[9] R. N. Whybray, "Qoheleth, Preacher of Joy," *Journal for the Study of the Old Testament* 23 (1982): 87–98.

[10] For an extensive summary of the history of interpretation of Ecclesiastes, see Christian D. Ginsburg, *The Song of Songs and Coheleth*, 2 vols. in 1 (reprint ed., New York: Ktav Publishing House, 1970), 2:27-243). For more concise summaries, see G. A. Barton (*The Book of Ecclesiastes*, ICC [Edinburgh: T. and T. Clark; 1908], pp. 18–31); Duane A. Garrett (*Proverbs, Ecclesiastes, Song of Songs*, New American Commentary [Nashville: Broadman, 1993], pp. 271–79); S. Holm-Nielsen ("On the Interpretation of Qoheleth in Early Christianity," *Vetus Testamentum* 24 [1974], pp. 168–87); R. E. Murphy (*Ecclesiastes*, Word Biblical Commentary [Dallas: Word, 1992], pp. xlviii–lvi); and Neal D. Williams ("A Biblical Theology of Ecclesiastes" [Th.D. dissertation, Dallas Theological Seminary, 1984], pp. 88–168).

[11] Fee and Stuart, *How to Read the Bible*, p. 214.

[12] Though I am using the appellative Qohelet to refer to the author of Ecclesiastes, I am using it in conformity with the book. However, I am persuaded that Qohelet is Solomon and that he is the author of this book. For a good defense of Solomonic authorship, see Gleason A. Archer (*A Survey of Old Testament Introduction*, rev. ed. [Chicago: Moody Press, 1994], pp. 528–37) and Garrett (*Ecclesiastes*, pp. 254–67). However, my persuasion is in contrast to the vast array of liberal and many conservative scholars. Childs notes that "there is almost universal consensus, shared by extremely conservative scholars, that Solomon was not the author of the book" (*Introduction to the Old Testament As Scripture* [Philadelphia: Fortress, 1979], p. 582). Some of these include Hengstenberg (*A Commentary on Ecclesiastes* [reprint ed., n.p.: Sovereign Grace Publishers, 1960], pp. 1–15), Delitzsch (*Proverbs, Ecclesiastes, Song of Solomon*, 3 vols. in 1, in *Commentary on the Old Testament*, vol. 6 [Grand Rapids: Eerdmans, 1973], 3:207–16), Young (*An Introduction to the Old Testament*, rev. ed. [Grand Rapids: Eerdmans, 1964], pp. 347–49), Harrison (*Introduction to the Old Testament* [Grand Rapids: Eerdmans, 1969], pp. 1072–78), and Longman (*Introduction*, pp. 248–50). Since the linguistic evidence against Solomon has been considered essentially irrefutable, how do conservatives explain passages such as 1:1

to biblical theology. How do we harmonize his apparently skeptical observations with his hedonistic advice? How do these tie in with the message
of Ecclesiastes? My purpose in this article is to delineate the message
of Ecclesiastes. This will be developed by initially examining Qohelet's
subject of inquiry, followed by his response to this inquiry.

QOHELET'S SUBJECT

In any attempt to discover a wisdom writer's subject, we should initially
consider his placement of it in prominent positions in his work. Our
understanding of the subject will be further enhanced by an examination
of the author's theological *a prioris*. The subject is further developed by
the book's dialectical nature.

Statement of the Subject

After a brief introduction in 1:1, Qohelet provides a sweeping generalization in
1:2, "Breath of breaths, says Qohelet, breath of breaths, all is breath."[13] Qohelet's
placement of this motif at the inception of the book is where we might expect
an author to place his subject. His catchword הֶבֶל, "breath," is used five times in
this verse. That this is the subject is further confirmed by the fact that Qohelet
concludes his work with three uses of הֶבֶל in 12:8. This forms an *inclusio*
marking the parameters of his work. Within this framework, הֶבֶל is used thirty
other times. Since this is undoubtedly a key term in this work, an understanding
of its semantics is necessary for interpreting Ecclesiastes. However, determining
its semantics in Ecclesiastes has been a problem of no small import.

---

and 1:12–2:26 that strongly imply Solomonic authorship? Following the lead of Young,
Bullock has referred to this as an "impersonation genre" (*An Introduction to the Old
Testament Poetic Books*, rev. ed. [Chicago: Moody Press, 1988], p. 185). By comparing
Ecclesiastes with Akkadian fictional autobiographical texts from the Cuthean Legend of
Naram-Sin and the Sin of Sargon, Longman has provided further support for this type
of genre; he has classified Ecclesiastes as a "framed autobiographical" genre (see his
Fictional Akkadian Autobiography [Winona Lake: Eisenbrauns, 1991]. For a simplified
form of Longman's position, see his "Comparative Methods in Old Testament Studies:
Ecclesiastes Reconsidered," *Theological Students' Fellowship Bulletin* 7 [March–April
1984]: 5–9). The significance of the linguistic evidence for a post-exilic date has recently
been challenged by Fredericks who has concluded that these earlier linguistic studies had
"neglected the genre and dialectical uniqueness of Qoh, and have resulted in a scholarly
consensus on a post-exilic date that is invalid" (*Qohelet's Language, Ancient Near Eastern
Texts and Studies*, vol. 3 [Lewiston, NY: Edwin Mellen Press, 1988], p. 266).

[13] This is a literal translation of 1:2; unless otherwise noted, all translations in this
paper are my own.

The noun הֶבֶל is used in the Hebrew Bible 73 times,[14] and 38 of these occurrences are found in Ecclesiastes.[15] The literal meaning of הֶבֶל is "vapor, breath." In Isaiah 57:13 a "breath" will carry away idols. In this context הֶבֶל, "breath," is parallel with רוּחַ, "wind," in the preceding colon. The metaphorical use of this term denotes that which is "evanescent, unsubstantial, worthless, vanity." Idols are הֶבֶל, "vain," in Deuteronomy 32:21, Psalm 31:6, and Jeremiah 8:19.[16] This metaphor is used of vain words in Job 35:16, for something that is "pointless" in Proverbs 21:6 or "fruitless" in Psalm 78:33.[17] Outside of Ecclesiastes the metaphorical use of הֶבֶל consistently denotes something that is vain or has no value. This understanding has been carried over into its use in Ecclesiastes.

We can trace this metaphorical rendering back to the Septuagint translation of Ecclesiastes which rendered הֶבֶל as ματαιότης, "emptiness, futility, purposelessness, transitoriness."[18] Since the Greek term includes the nuance of "transitoriness," it allows for a broader use than a strictly negative sense. However, the dominance of the pejorative sense of vanity owes its allegiance to Jerome, who translated הֶבֶל with *vanitas,* "unsubstantial or illusory quality, emptiness, falsity, untruthfulness."[19] Since that

---

[14] Abraham Even-Shoshan, *A New Concordance of the Bible* (Jerusalem: Kiryat Sefer, 1985), p. 279.

[15] My count is based on the MT. However, this count could be either 37 or 39 depending on how two text critical problems are treated. At 9:2 the Septuagint, Symmachus, and Vulgate have emended הַכֹּל to הֶבֶל. This would increase its uses to 39. Though it may be argued that this emendation provides an easier reading, there is no manuscript support for this. This is a case of *lectio difficilior.* In 9:9 הֶבֶל is found twice: כָּל־יְמֵי חַיֵּי הֶבְלֶךָ is found in the first line and is essentially repeated with כָּל יְמֵי הֶבְלֶךָ in the second line. The repetition of the phrase in the second line is not found in seven other manuscripts, nor the Septuagint, Vetus Latina, Targum, or the Vulgate. If this evidence is accepted, this is an example of homoteleuton and would reflect that our catchword is used only 37 times in Ecclesiastes. However, this phrase could have been repeated for emphasis (see Murphy, *Ecclesiastes,* p. 89, n. 9b).

[16] Francis Brown, Samuel R. Driver, and Charles A. Briggs, eds., *A Hebrew and English Lexicon of the Old Testament* (Oxford: At the Clarendon Press), p. 210 [hereafter cited as BDB].

[17] Ludwig Koehler and Walter Baumgartner, *The Hebrew and Aramaic Lexicon of the Old Testament,* 3 vols., rev. W. Baumgartner and J. J. Stamm (Leiden: Brill, 1994–), 1:237.

[18] Walter Bauer, William F. Arndt, and F. Wilbur Gingrich, *A Greek-English Lexicon of the New Testament and Other Early Christian Literature,* 2nd ed. revised and augmented by F. Wilbur Gingrich and Frederick W. Danker (Chicago: University of Chicago Press, 1979), p. 495.

[19] P. G. W. Glare, ed., *Oxford Latin Dictionary* (Oxford: At the Clarendon Press, 1982), p. 2010.

time most versions have rendered הֶבֶל as "vanity." This is the rendering found in the KJV, NKJV, RSV, and NRSV. The TEV deviates from this pattern by translating it as "useless" and the NIV does likewise with its rendering as "meaningless." The NASB translates הֶבֶל as "vanity" 22 times, "futility" 12 times, "fleeting" twice, and "emptiness" once.[20]

Besides translations, many individual scholars have also interpreted הֶבֶל as "vanity" or some equivalent reflecting the nuance of having no value. Some of these include C. D. Ginsburg, Hengstenberg, Bridges, Barton, H. L. Ginsberg, Whitley, Woudstra, and Scott.[21] Against this, a number of interpreters have recognized that this exclusively negative meaning of הֶבֶל does not harmonize with Qohelet's exhortations to enjoy the gifts of life and his commendation of wisdom. Furthermore, we should expect other synonymous words or phrases with הֶבֶל to be used by the author if his point was that life had no value.[22]

Gordis suggests that הֶבֶל was used in Ecclesiastes with two different senses: "unsubstantial" and "transitory."[23] In keeping with the first sense, he translates the vast majority of cases in the sense of "vanity" or "futile." However, he translates the second use of הֶבֶל in 9:9 as "brief" and in 11:10 as "fleeting breath."[24] Hamilton opts for three translation values of הֶבֶל: "vanity," "senseless," and "transitory."[25] Meek has suggested five different uses: "futile," "empty," "sorry," "senseless," and "transient."[26] Though the

---

[20] In 9:9 the translators of NASB have followed the emended form of the MT. As a result they have only 37 uses of הֶבֶל (see above, n. 15).

[21] Ginsburg (*Coheleth*, 2:259–60); Hengstenberg (*Ecclesiastes*, p. 46); Charles Bridges (*An Exposition of the Book of Ecclesiastes* [reprint ed., n.p.: The Banner of Truth Trust, 1960], p. 5); Barton (*Ecclesiastes*, pp. 46–50); H. L. Ginsberg ("The Structure and Contents of the Book of Koheleth," in *Wisdom in Israel and in the Ancient Near East,* ed. M. Noth and D. Winton Thomas, *VTSup* 3 [Leiden: E. J. Brill, 1955]: 138–40); Charles F. Whitley (*Koheleth* [Berlin: Walter de Gruyter, 1979], pp. 6–7); Sierd Woudstra ("Koheleth's Reflection upon Life" [Th.M. thesis, Westminster Theological Seminary, 1959], pp. 39–41); and R. B. Y. Scott (*Proverbs-Ecclesiastes*, AB [New York: Doubleday and Company, 1965], p. 209). Though using different words to translate הֶבֶל, the concept that ties these words together for Scott is that of having no value.

[22] For a listing of these, see Daniel C. Fredericks, *Coping with Transience* (Sheffield: JSOT Press, 1993), pp. 28–29.

[23] Robert Gordis, *Koheleth*, 3rd ed. (New York: Schocken Books, 1968), p. 205.

[24] Ibid., pp. 188, 196.

[25] *Theological Wordbook of the Old Testament*, s.v. "הֶבֶל," by Victor P. Hamilton, 1:205.

[26] Theophile J. Meek, "Translating the Hebrew Bible," *Journal of Biblical Literature* 79 (December 1960): 331.

translation of a Hebrew word used many times in a book may have two or more uses, this is a problem in Ecclesiastes. If Qohelet announces in 1:2 and 12:8 that "all is הֶבֶל" and then describes the specifics of the all and evaluates these as הֶבֶל, then it must have a common nuance in Ecclesiastes.[27] This has also been noted by Fredericks, who has perceptively observed that it is an error "to see distinct spheres of meaning for the word and to select the correct one for each context, ending in a multifarious description of reality that is contrary to a significant purpose for the unifying and generalizing agenda of Qoheleth—'everything is breath.'"[28]

If הֶבֶל does not contain distinct spheres of meaning, what is the common sphere of meaning? Fox has opted for "absurd"[29] and Fredericks for "transience."[30] The problem with Fox's rendering is that it is tied to the assumptions of existentialism, specifically those of Albert Camus. This understanding of Ecclesiastes represents an irrational and oppressive worldview.[31] Fredericks's understanding, on the other hand, does not do justice to texts such as 8:14 where Qohelet observes that righteous men get what the wicked deserve and the wicked receive what the righteous are expected to receive. The difficulty with this viewpoint is that if this kind of apparent injustice is only a "fleeting" problem, why then is Qohelet so troubled by it?[32]

Other options include "bubble,"[33] "ceaseless change,"[34] "contingency,"[35] and "incomprehensible."[36] The problem with "bubble" and "ceaseless change"

---

[27] Michael V. Fox, "The Meaning of Hebel for Qohelet," *Journal of Biblical Literature* 105 (September 1986): 411.

[28] Fredericks, *Coping with Transience*, pp. 23–24.

[29] Fox, "The Meaning of *Hebel*," pp. 414–27.

[30] Fredericks, *Coping with Transience*, pp. 18–32.

[31] Michael V. Fox, *Qohelet and His Contradictions*, JSOT Supplements, 71 (Sheffield: JSOT Press, 1989), pp. 33–34.

[32] Garrett, *Ecclesiastes*, pp. 282–83.

[33] F. C. Burkitt, "Is Ecclesiastes a Translation?," *Journal of Theological Studies* 22 (1921): 27–28.

[34] C. S. Knopf, "The Optimism of Koheleth," *Journal of Biblical Literature* 49 (1930): 196.

[35] John McKenna, "The Concept of *Hebel* in the Book of Ecclesiastes," *Scottish Journal of Theology* 45 (1992): 19–28.

[36] Graham S. Ogden, "'Vanity' It Certainly Is Not," *Bible Translator* 38 (July 1987): 301–7. In his commentary *Qoheleth* ([Sheffield: JSOT Press, 1987], p. 28), Ogden acknowledges that this concept had been suggested earlier by W. E. Staples ("The 'Vanity' of Ecclesiastes," *Journal of Near Eastern Studies* 2 [1943]: 95–104 and "Vanity of Vanities," *Canadian Journal of Theology* 1 [1955]: 141–56) and by Edwin M. Good

is that they are tied to a purely negative evaluation of life. If הֶבֶל represents a devaluation of life, can this legitimately be harmonized with his
motifs of enjoying life and praising wisdom? Qohelet's description of the
sovereignty of God in 3:1–15 is too absolute to allow for the ambiguity
associated with "contingency." Though it would appear that no English
term provides an equivalent to הֶבֶל, the closest of the options is probably "incomprehensible" or a synonym such as "enigma" or "mystery."[37]
However, a limitation of "incomprehensible" is that it does not necessarily
account for the emotive connotations of הֶבֶל. This is expressed in 2:17
where Qohelet states that he hates life because his work had been griev-
ous. We would grant that this is hard to comprehend, but it is more than
that. Life with its difficulties and vicissitudes as a result of the Fall is a
puzzle that finite man cannot figure out, and it frustrates Qohelet in his
search for meaning and purpose. In his attempt to master life, Qohelet
eventually realizes with defeated expectations that he cannot understand
God's scheme of things. Though in English we do not have a precise word
equivalent to the meaning associated with this Hebrew term, I would prefer
to translate it something like a "frustrating enigma" for three reasons.

First, the phrase רְעוּת רוּחַ, "chasing after wind," provides a qualifying
element to הֶבֶל. An example of this is found in 1:14 where רְעוּת רוּחַ is
used to complement הֶבֶל. This is also used in 2:11, 17, 26; 4:4, 6; 6:9. In
1:17 and 4:16 a closely related phrase is used, רַעְיוֹן רוּחַ, "chasing after
wind." Both רְעוּת רוּחַ and רַעְיוֹן רוּחַ are translated in the KJV as "vexation
of spirit." The translators of the NASB rendered these as "striving after
the wind," the NIV as "chasing after the wind," and NKJV as "grasping for
the wind." The reason for the different renderings of רְעוּת and רַעְיוֹן relates
to its different uses.[38] Whether this be a "vexation of spirit" or "striving
after the wind," the difference is of no consequence for our contention. If
the first is the case, this may reflect something that troubles one's thoughts.
The latter rendering reflects something that is beyond man's control. As
Shank has said, "A man may determine or make up his mind to accomplish
something eternally significant in a creation subjected to vanity, yet no
matter how hard he tries Qoheleth tells him it will be a fruitless endeavor.

---

with his translation "irony" (*Irony in the Old Testament*, 2nd ed., Bible and Literature
Series [Sheffield: Almond Press, 1981], pp. 176–83). Recently, Roland E. Murphy has ex-
pressed a preference for this nuance, see "On Translating Ecclesiastes," *Catholic Biblical
Quarterly* 53 (October 1991): 572–73.

[37] However, for some potential difficulties with this rendering, see *Theological
Dictionary of the Old Testament*, s.v. "הֶבֶל," by K. Seybold, 3:318–20.

[38] For a brief discussion of these, see Whitley, *Koheleth*, p. 13.

A man in his toil 'under the sun' grasps after the wind and attains precious little for all his labor."[39] Thus, the concept of "chasing after wind" supports our contention that the semantic range of הֶבֶל includes a cognitive sense.[40]

Second, if life has no value, how can we harmonize this with Qohelet's positive exhortations about life? At climactic points in this work, Qohelet gives us advice to enjoy God's gifts (2:24; 3:12, 22; 5:17 [in Eng. v. 18]; 8:15; 9:7–10). These gifts include food, drink, work, wealth, possessions, marital relationships, and youth. Though wisdom is not the panacea for all of life's adversities, Qohelet commended it as a solution to many of life's problems (2:13; 4:13; 7:11–12, 19; 9:13–18). These positive exhortations certainly suggest that life has some value.

Third, Qohelet recounts his quest for meaning and purpose in life. The very nature of this quest was to gain understanding into what gives life meaning. It was not a haphazard search but had been a thorough quest in that it took into account the range of activities occurring "under the sun." Rather than this prepositional phrase reflecting a limitation to "natural theology,"[41] it denotes the place where these activities occurred, "on the earth."[42] The epistemological nature of this search is emphasized in passages such as 1:13 where Qohelet sets his mind, לֵב, to seek and explore by his divinely given gift of wisdom all that had been done upon the earth.[43] This is further emphasized by Qohelet's observations. He saw, ראה, all of man's works in 1:14, wisdom and understanding in 1:16, madness and folly in 2:12, injustice in the halls of justice in 3:16, labor produced by rivalry in 4:4, riches hurting the one who possesses them in 5:13, one whom God has not enabled to enjoy his wealth in 6:1–2, retribution violating a strict cause and effect relationship in 7:15, unexpected victors in 9:11, inappropriate leadership in 10:7, and people dying in 12:3. The cognitive sense of הֶבֶל is also stressed in 6:1–11:6. Following Addison G. Wright's understanding of the structural unity of Ecclesiastes, this section

---

[39] H. Carl Shank, "Qoheleth's World and Life View As Seen in His Recurring Phrases," *Westminster Theological Journal* 37 (Fall 1974): 67.

[40] For other complementary phrases, see Ogden, *Qoheleth*, p. 21.

[41] H. C. Leupold, *Exposition of Ecclesiastes* (Grand Rapids: Baker, 1974), pp. 42–43.

[42] Shank, "Qoheleth's World and Life View," p. 67. The prepositional phrase תַּחַת הַשֶּׁמֶשׁ, "under the sun," is used 29 times in this book. An informative parallel is found in 8:14–15, Qohelet describes an event that occurs עַל־הָאָרֶץ, "on the earth," in v. 14; in the next verse, he replaces this with תַּחַת הַשֶּׁמֶשׁ, which also is found in 8:16–17.

[43] The Hebrew verb נתן followed by לֵב, denoting a serious deliberation, is used in 1:13, 17; 7:2; 8:9, 16; 9:1. The construction is used to show Qohelet's examining wisdom, folly, the house of death, injustice, everything done on earth that he could examine.

of material (6:1–11:6) revolves around finite man's inability to understand God's work. In 7:1–8:17, Qohelet punctuates this unit with "not discover" and "who can discover" in 7:14, 24, 28 (twice), and 8:17 (three times). In 9:1–11:6 Qohelet emphasizes "do not know" and "no knowledge" in 9:1, 5, 10, 12; 10:14, 15; 11:2, 5–6 (three times).[44] All of this suggests that the use of הֶבֶל in Ecclesiastes relates to the issue of man's frustrating inability to comprehend the activities in his earthly sphere of existence.

Therefore, הֶבֶל is an appropriate term to encapsulate Qohelet's frustrating and puzzling search for meaning and purpose in life. The use of this term in the sentence "all is הֶבֶל," as used in 1:2 and 12:8, sets the parameters for its use in Ecclesiastes. In every case where Qohelet evaluates life[45] with this catchword, we should translate it in a consistent manner with this understanding. We might translate 1:2 in this fashion: "Most frustratingly enigmatic, says Qohelet, most frustratingly enigmatic, all is frustratingly enigmatic."[46] Consequently, Qohelet's subject is the frustratingly enigmatic nature of all the facets of this life. However, did Qohelet draw upon this subject from his own rationalistic observations with a bare minimum of special revelation? Or were his observations influenced by a proper understanding of biblical theology? What were Qohelet's theological *a prioris?*

Theological Presuppositions

To gain a fuller understanding of Qohelet's subject, we need to consider the theological presuppositions that have influenced him. Qohelet did not simply know that there was a holy God and that He would bring everything into judgment.[47] We are persuaded that he reflects a solid theological grasp of the early chapters of Genesis. In wisdom literature such as Ecclesiastes, we should expect this type of influence. Zimmerli has stated that wisdom is found "within the framework of a theology of creation."[48] This is especially

---

[44] Addison G. Wright, "The Riddle of the Sphinx: The Structure of the Book of Qoheleth," *Catholic Biblical Quarterly* 30 (July 1968): 323.

[45] This would take into account 32 of its 38 uses in this work. Those sections where הֶבֶל is not used as a catchword are 6:4, 11, 12; 7:15; 9:9; and 11:10.

[46] See David A. Hubbard, *Ecclesiastes, Song of Solomon,* The Communicator's Commentary (Dallas: Word, 1991), p. 44; Hubbard has clarified his thoughts about הֶבֶל since his earlier work, *Beyond Futility* (Grand Rapids: Eerdmans, 1976), p. 15.

[47] *The New Scofield Reference Bible,* p. 696.

[48] Walter Zimmerli, "The Place and Limit of Wisdom in the Framework of Old Testament Theology," *Scottish Journal of Theology* 17 (March 1964): 148; see also William J. Dumbrell, *The Faith of Israel* (Grand Rapids: Baker, 1988), pp. 215–16.

true in Ecclesiastes where Qohelet's understanding of his frustrating and puzzling world is directly influenced by his understanding of Genesis.[49] We will briefly examine this influence.

The influence of Genesis is initially seen when Qohelet poses his thematic question in 1:3, "What is man's advantage from all his labor at which he toils under the sun?" Qohelet has not changed his emphasis from his generalized subject in 1:2 but has reduced his reflections on life's meaning and purpose to a specifically identifiable biblical idea of labor. He poses his question in terms of the dominion mandate originally given to Adam, who as God's vice-regent was to subdue the earth (Gen 1:28; 2:5, 15).[50] However, when Adam chose to disobey God, the Fall occurred. This included God cursing the land, making man's labor one of strenuous toil (Gen 3:17–19; cf. Eccl 2:22–23). It is this curse that brought death and destruction, causing the creation to groan under this bondage longing for God's redemption (Rom 8:19–21). It is this quest to find significance through toil that characterizes Qohelet's search.

The interrogative particle מַה, "what,"[51] introduces the rhetorical question in 1:3. The term translated as "advantage" is יִתְרוֹן.[52] Gordis indicates that this is a commercial term denoting "the surplus of the balance sheet."[53] In Ecclesiastes, it[54] is used in the sense of ultimate advantage.[55] For example, in 2:12–21 Qohelet shows how he as a sage evaluated wisdom. He found that there were some benefits to wisdom. In 2:13 he states that "wisdom is more advantageous [יִתְרוֹן] than folly as

---

[49] Charles C. Forman, "Koheleth's Use of Genesis," *Journal of Semitic Studies* 5 (1960): 256–63.

[50] Eugene H. Merrill, "A Theology of the Pentateuch," in *A Biblical Theology of the Old Testament*, ed. Roy B. Zuck, Eugene H. Merrill, and Darrel L. Bock (Chicago: Moody, 1991), pp. 13–16.

[51] מַה is used ten times in Ecclesiastes at significant junctures, 1:3; 2:2, 12, 22; 3:9; 5:11, 16; 6:8 (twice), 11.

[52] BDB, p. 452.

[53] Gordis, *Koheleth*, p. 205.

[54] יִתְרוֹן is used ten times in Ecclesiastes, 1:3; 2:11, 13 (twice); 3:9; 5:8 (Eng. v. 9), 15 (Eng. v. 16); 7:12; 10:10, 11. Other cognate terms are used such as מוֹתָר in 3:19 and יוֹתֵר is used in 6:8, 11; 7:11. יוֹתֵר is also used adverbially in 2:15; 7:16; 12:9, 12.

[55] We would agree with Ogden that יִתְרוֹן is used in reference to "ultimate advantage"; however, he correlates this advantage with the possibility of some advantage beyond death and suggests that this is significant for developing the concept of life after death which is more fully developed in the New Testament (*Qoheleth*, pp. 22–26). In the context of Ecclesiastes, this term is better interpreted as a reference to Qohelet's quest for meaning in this life; none of the facets of God's created order provide Qohelet with this ultimate advantage.

light is more advantageous [יִתְרוֹן] than darkness." However, in 2:14–16
Qohelet came to recognize that death happens to both the sage and the
fool. That death happens to both indicates that the benefits of wisdom are
relative and not absolute. Wisdom has an advantage in this life but it does
not provide the ultimate advantage in finding meaning in life. Therefore,
Qohelet's quest for meaning and purpose is exemplified with this struggle
to find significance by the sweat of his brow.

The Genesis account further informs the theology of Ecclesiastes
concerning life and death. Man was made from dust and to dust he shall
return (Gen 2:7; 3:19; cf. Eccl 3:20; 12:7). Furthermore, man's uncon-
firmed creature holiness in Genesis 1–2 and subsequent depravity in
Genesis 3 are also used as an informing motif in Ecclesiastes 7:29 (8:11;
9:3).[56] Drawing upon Genesis 3:16, Qohelet additionally notes the frac-
tured relations between husbands and wives in 7:26–28.[57] Another motif
drawn from the Mosaic account in Genesis is God's role as Creator. In
agreement with Genesis 1, God is the "Maker of all things" in 11:5 and
"Creator" in 12:1. In Genesis 1–3 God is also presented as the Sovereign.
In Ecclesiastes 3:1–15 Qohelet recognizes God's absolute sovereign
control over everything in life.[58]

In Genesis God created man in his image and likeness. As God's image
bearer, finite man has derivative wisdom. Not only did man's wisdom have
natural limitations as a created, finite being, but God also imposed other
limitations (e.g., "do not eat..." [Gen 2:17]). When Satan tempted Eve, he
challenged God's holy image bearers to gain more wisdom by eating from
the tree of knowledge of good and evil. What Satan did not tell Eve was
that while gaining increased wisdom, she and her husband would use this
increased wisdom in the context of their resulting depravity. The theology of Genesis has a profound effect on Ecclesiastes. As a sage, Qohelet
diligently studied and explored with wisdom every activity done on earth.
However, God's curse on man and creation made this a burdensome task
(Eccl 1:13). After his poem on God's coordination of earthly activities
with time, Qohelet observes that God has made everything beautiful in its
season (3:11, NASB footnote).

---

[56] Michael A. Eaton, *Ecclesiastes*, TOTC (Downers Grove, IL: InterVarsity, 1983),
pp. 116–17.

[57] Duane A. Garrett, "Ecclesiastes 7:25–29 and the Feminist Hermeneutic," *Criswell
Theological Review* 2 (Spring 1988): 309–21.

[58] Roy B. Zuck, "A Theology of the Wisdom Books and the Song of Songs," in *A
Biblical Theology of the Old Testament*, ed. Roy B. Zuck, Eugene H. Merrill, and Darrel L.
Bock (Chicago: Moody, 1991), pp. 246–47.

Though unable to comprehend God's work, our author is able to appreciate the beauty of God's providential work. Man's quest for the scheme of things is a God-given capacity within man that Qohelet calls הָעֹלָם. Because of its use in an equivalent manner in v. 14, this Hebrew term is best translated as "eternity." הָעֹלָם is apparently part of man's metaphysical constitution as God's image bearer.[59] Though man's longing to see God's scheme of things is divinely given, in v. 11 our writer also indicates that God has placed limitations on man's ability to understand the scheme of things. Because of man's finiteness and the Edenic curse, God's providence is veiled and burdensome to man. God has also limited man's ability to comprehend His moral governing of the cosmos (7:15–18; 8:14) and the future (8:7; 10:14). Qohelet has thoroughly grasped the message of Genesis that God did not want mankind to pursue all wisdom and, "therefore, thwarted their efforts in its pursuits. That his own views on the limitations of knowledge and frustration that comes in its quest were based on Genesis seems apparent."[60]

Qohelet's *Leitmotiv*[61] about celebrating life is also dependent upon Genesis. As Johnston has noted about this recurring theme: "Perhaps more importantly, Ecclesiastes and Genesis exhibit substantial agreement as to the central point of the creation motif—that life is to be celebrated as a 'good' creation of God."[62] Though we will look at this motif more fully in subsequent pages, we should notice at this point that this recurring theme reflects Qohelet's expectation that God will bring blessing to his creation. Nevertheless, Qohelet recognizes that the Fall can adversely affect man's ability to enjoy life. Because of the Fall, God imposed a curse on creation. Since God directly made Adam and Eve, he created them in a state of innocence. When temptation came, they succumbed to it, and rather than being confirmed in creature holiness, they became totally depraved. Because Adam was the representative of creation, his sin resulted in all his posterity and the rest of creation becoming subject to the curse. In Qohelet's attempt to understand and master life, he came to realize that this was an impossible task. To paraphrase Qohelet's words, all creation has become twisted and crooked because of the Fall (1:15; 7:13). The curse was directly imposed by God. Yet God began a process of bringing blessing to his creation (see

---

[59] Eaton, *Ecclesiastes*, p. 81.

[60] Forman, "Koheleth's Use of Genesis, " p. 261.

[61] This German term means "recurring theme." Because of its use in literature dealing with Ecclesiastes, I will be using this term frequently in the remainder of this paper.

[62] Robert K. Johnston, "'Confessions of a Workaholic': A Reappraisal of Qoheleth," *Catholic Biblical Quarterly* 38 (January 1976): 22.

Gen 1:28; 3:15; 9:1, 26–27; 12:2–3). He will deliver his creation from the bondage of the curse. Qohelet as a godly sage recognizes God's curse on his creation, yet he also understands that God is working to redeem his creation.[63] This is why Qohelet can strongly recommend the enjoyment of the blessings of God. Caneday has perceptively stated it:

> Qoheleth upholds the creational design to celebrate life as a divine gift which is to be enjoyed as good, something to be cherished reverently and something in which man delights continually. This, perhaps, is the greatest enigma in Qoheleth—his bold assertion of the meaninglessness of life "under the sun" and his resolute affirmation that life is to be celebrated joyfully…. He was a godly sage who could affirm both the aimlessness of life "under the sun" and the enjoyment of life precisely because he believed in the God who cursed his creation on account of man's rebellion, but who was in the process, throughout earth's history, of redeeming man and creation, liberating them from the bondage to decay to which they had been subjected.[64]

Consequently, Qohelet's subject has been directly affected by his theological grasp of Genesis. When Qohelet affirms in 1:2 that "everything is frustratingly enigmatic," this encompasses the negative features of life in a sin-cursed world and the positive dimensions of his expectation of God's restoration. Though he understands God's curse and blessing, he also lives in a world where God's providence is veiled. He desires to figure out God's scheme of things, but in his desire to understand and control life his expectations have been defeated. As such, Qohelet recognized that life has tensions. This reflects an antithetical character to life. Though living in a cursed world which frustrated his quest for meaning and purpose, our author was also a man of faith who recognizes that God is working to redeem his creation. It is this theological foundation that has also influenced our author to construct his work on what could be described as a dialectical model.

Dialectical Nature

As we read Ecclesiastes, we almost feel at first glance as if Qohelet has a "schizophrenic outlook on life."[65] Qohelet oscillates between a negative

---

[63] Two significant motifs in Genesis 1–11 are those of blessing and cursing; see Gary V. Smith, "Structure and Purpose in Genesis 1–11," *Journal of the Evangelical Theological Society* 20 (December 1977): 307–19.

[64] Ardel B. Caneday, "Qoheleth: Enigmatic Pessimist or Godly Sage?" *Grace Theological Journal* 7 (Spring 1986): 43–44.

[65] Grant R. Osborne, *The Hermeneutical Spiral* (Downers Grove, IL: InterVarsity, 1991), p. 200.

outlook on life and a positive perspective. These polarized perspectives reflect the dialectical nature of Ecclesiastes.[66] The antithetical nature of Qohelet's motifs has received various explanations. Some critical scholars have explained the opposed subjects as later additions.[67] Though this explanation may solve some problems, it leaves Ecclesiastes open to every new critic's innovation. If we are committed to a high view of bibliology, we must permit the biblical author to speak for himself, even when we cannot always harmonize the problems to every scholar's satisfaction. Another solution is that of Gordis who explains the opposed motifs as quotations. According to Gordis, Qohelet used quotations from orthodox teachings to refute them with his unorthodox teaching.[68] Gordis's quotation hypothesis is flawed because it tends to violate Qohelet's normal grammatical patterns.[69]

Another solution, proposed by Loader, is that Qohelet introduces a subject and then presents a counter thought. According to Loader, this presents a tension that the author leaves unresolved.[70] Qohelet begins his analysis with the divine control of time in 3:1–9, which is based on a genuine polar structure. Loader then superimposes this grid on the vast majority of Ecclesiastes.[71] Though his analysis is helpful in identifying a number of antithetical subjects, it is a creative oversimplification of the data. Fox has posed another solution to Qohelet's conflicting subjects. He has advocated that Qohelet intentionally used life's contradictions to demonstrate that life is absurd.[72] Though this sin-cursed world does have contradictory elements, his solution is that of an existential sage. If Qohelet is a godly sage, is it consistent with the general teaching of Scripture to have him affirming that life was absurd? If we see motifs in this work that are antithetical, does this necessarily demand the conclusion that life is absurd? While recognizing the contribution made by Loader and Fox, we are convinced that the contrasting material can be handled in a different manner.

There is a preferable solution in dealing with the antithetical motifs. Qohelet has crafted his work to reflect the realities of this world. The

---

[66] Leland Ryken, *Words of Delight* (Grand Rapids: Baker, 1987), pp. 320–28.

[67] For a summation of various ways of handling these contradictions, see Fox, *Qohelet and His Contradictions,* pp. 19–28.

[67] Gordis, *Koheleth*, p. 96

[69] See his discussion of 8:11–14 (Ibid., p. 105).

[70] J. A. Loader, *Ecclesiastes* (Grand Rapids: Eerdmans, 1986), pp. 33–34, passim.

[71] J. A. Loader, *Polar Structures in the Book of Qohelet* (Berlin: Walter de Gruyter, 1979).

[72] Fox, *Qohelet and His Contradictions*, pp. 11–14.

actual events behind the book of Ecclesiastes reflect Qohelet's search for meaning and purpose in life. He has examined perspectives and items of life such as wisdom, folly, building projects, pleasure, toil, and wealth. He leads us on a journey through his personal experiences in pursuit of his goal. He takes us down the path of wisdom but it comes to a dead end. He takes us down the path of pleasure but this also leads to a dead end. We are taken down various dead end trails until finally we come to the conclusion of the matter in 12:13, and he informs us that the answer to his quest is fearing God and keeping his commandments. None of the theories, thrills, or things of life could provide the answer to Qohelet's quest.[73]

Using various genres such as reflection stories, proverbs, comparative sayings, rhetorical questions, autobiographical material, Qohelet recounts his quest with a lyrical description. In recounting the details of his quest, Qohelet draws us into his world, where he takes us down a dead-end path. However, he abruptly changes paths to one reflecting the beauty of a theocentric worldview. Qohelet lives in a world where unresolved tensions are a part of the baffling puzzle of life. Rather than reflecting a sequential arrangement to his quest, he composes his work by using contrasting motifs to duplicate the tensions he faced in his fallen world. To legitimately interpret Ecclesiastes, we should follow an explanation that harmonizes passages asserting that life has many unresolved tensions with those advocating a celebration of God and his gifts. The overall plan of the book has negative passages being followed by positive passages. Ryken has tabulated that there are fifteen negative pericopes, thirteen positive passages, and three that combine the two perspectives.[74] Furthermore, in terms of space the negative passages exceed the positive ones by three or four to one.[75] As such, the negative passages receive major attention and the positive ones minor space. Qohelet's procedure initially is to treat a negative perspective and then follow up with the positive message. Why did he intermingle the two perspectives?

> His mingling of negative and positive is realistic and faithful to the mixed nature of human experience. The technique keeps the reader alert. It also creates the vigor of plot conflict for this collection of proverbs, as the writer lets the two viewpoints clash. The dialectical pattern of opposites is a strategy of highlighting: the glory of a God-centered life stands out all the more brightly for having been contrasted to its gloomy opposite.[76]

---

[73] Leland Ryken, "Ecclesiastes," in *A Complete Literary Guide to the Bible,* ed. Leland Ryken and Tremper Longman III (Grand Rapids: Zondervan, 1993), p. 271.

[74] Ryken, *Words of Delight,* p. 320.

[75] Ryken, "Ecclesiastes," p. 270.

[76] Ryken, *Words of Delight,* pp. 320–21.

To demonstrate its dialectical nature, we will look at some of these motifs in more detail. Qohelet initially sets up the contrasting nature of his work in 1:4–11. After stating his thematic question in v. 3, our author introduces his work with a poem contrasting temporal man with an enduring cosmos. Generations of people come and go, but the world continues in an uninterrupted manner (v. 4). However, the permanent terrestrial sphere is marked by changes such as the movement of the sun, the wind, and rivers flowing into the sea (vv. 5–7). By the nature of the enduring cosmos being cyclical, we might expect finite man to ultimately comprehend the underlying forces at work in the natural realm. However, man is always taking in what he perceives with his senses and is never able to adequately describe his world; it is an endless task for finite man (v. 8). Qohelet characterizes this search as wearisome (יְגֵעִים). Because man is endlessly taking in the facets of life, surely he will discover something new. What is constant for man is that there is no novelty in life, there is "nothing new under the sun" (v. 9); and if he thinks something is unique, it is because he has forgotten history (vv. 10–11). The enduring world is characterized by monotonous cycles and yet finite man will never be able to comprehend or describe his milieu. Consequently, Qohelet prepares us to view his work as a microcosmic representation of the realities of God's good creation subjected to the bondage of the Fall.

A wide range of polarized subjects is summarized in 3:1–8. Fourteen pairs of opposites are listed in vv. 2–7. These merisms range from birth and death, love and hate, war and peace, and many other contrasting features of life. These are part of the constant repetition in time that God directs according to his own good pleasure. Therefore, the activities of this life have a polarized nature.[77] Man's nature endeavors to understand how these polarized elements fit together, but God has not given this to him. Man can appreciate that this is part of God's plan and he can recognize that God's providential arrangement of all these activities is a symmetrical masterpiece (vv. 10–11), but God's ways are inscrutable for him. God has created us with a desire to comprehend what God is doing but our finiteness prevents this. By the nature of our depravity, our desire is marred by frustration and weariness.

In 2:11 Qohelet evaluates toil as being הֶבֶל. Furthermore he maintains that labor may not be satisfying because of envy (4:4–6) and selfish greed (4:7–12). This must be contrasted with his recommendation in 2:24 to find enjoyment in work (so also in 3:13, 22; 5:17 [Eng. v. 18]; 8:15).[78]

---

[77] Loader, *Polar Structures,* pp. 29–33.

[78] Donald R. Glenn, "Ecclesiastes," in *The Bible Knowledge Commentary: Old Testament*, ed. John F. Walvoord and Roy B. Zuck (Wheaton, IL: Victor Books, 1985), p. 976.

Another tension is between life and death. In 7:1 Qohelet states that the day of death is better than the day of birth; however, in 9:4–6 he states that anyone who is living has hope and that a living dog is better than a dead lion. On the one hand, he hates life (2:17); on the other hand, he commends its enjoyment (2:24–26). Furthermore, death is no respecter of animate beings. Man has no advantage over animal life in that both die (3:18–21). A person may strenuously work all his life accumulating wealth, yet he will die like the profligate. When death comes, he must leave behind the results of his work, "as he came, so he departs and what is his advantage since he labors after wind?" (5:15, Eng. 5:16). Like the rest of Adam's race, the sage has no control over the time of his death (8:2–8). Though one may live a godly life, death overtakes him just as it does the wicked (9:2–3). This reflects a life that is filled with tensions and distortions.[79]

Perhaps Qohelet's most vexing tension relates to the issue of justice. Our author teaches that there is divine justice, but he is plagued by the injustices that God permits in his providence. If there is any place on earth where we expect justice to occur, it is in the court. Contrary to this expectation, our author affirms in 3:16, "in the halls of justice, wickedness is there; and in the halls of righteousness, wickedness is there." However, in v. 17 he expresses confidence that God will bring to justice both the righteous and the wicked. In 5:7 (Eng. 5:8), he observes that the oppressed have their rights denied. In some sense, we might contend that the oppressed and the judicially victimized may not be truly righteous. However, in 7:15 Qohelet describes a situation where a genuinely righteous person receives what the wicked should get; and the wicked person receives what the righteous person should get. In the first colon of this verse Qohelet evaluates this scenario as a הֶבֶל situation. In 8:12–13 Qohelet maintains that God does take care of the righteous and the wicked. However, he once again describes the same two exceptions that he mentioned in 7:15 and again categorizes this as a הֶבֶל situation in 8:14. It is this incomprehensible situation that vexes our author.[80] While affirming that God is providentially controlling all aspects of life with their appointed times, he recognizes that divine providence is often veiled. Since the righteous and the wicked are under God's control and his providence is often veiled, no man knows

---

[79] Caneday, "Qoheleth," p. 40.

[80] Since Qohelet affirms God's justice, it is unwarranted to call this situation "vain." According to Fox, this involves a contradiction so he describes this situation as "absurd" (*Qohelet*, pp. 121–22). Since God does not bless or curse in an immediate fashion but always in accord with his timing, I feel it is unwarranted to call this "absurd." This is mysterious but not contradictory, hard to understand but not absurd.

whether his future holds "love or hate." Nevertheless, there is one event that everyone must experience, death (9:1–3). No one knows what his future will be or what is the way that will bring the most success in life (6:12; 7:14; 8:12; 10:14; 11:6).[81] To Qohelet these types of inequities make divine providence inscrutable.

> The almighty God who rules this world hides himself behind a frowning providence. It seldom appears that the benevolent God who created the universe has control of his own creation. It rarely seems that a rational and moral being gives motion to the world. Even the beauty of uniformity plagues man's thoughts about God. Uniformity becomes monotony in the present cursed world, for it is precisely upon the basis of the world's disjointed regularity that men scoff at God and his promises. The present world order becomes the occasion for wicked men to jeer God and for righteous men to vex their souls that divine justice is so long delayed.[82]

In his pervasive search for meaning and purpose, Qohelet makes a generalization that all the facets of life are frustratingly enigmatic. This search is not based solely on empirical observation. Rather his search is predicated upon his theological understanding of Genesis. He recognizes that the infinite God created a good world but with the Fall God in holy judgment subjected it to his curse. Qohelet observes that all the dimensions of this earthly sphere are influenced by this supernaturally imposed curse. As a result, Qohelet's attempt to fully fathom life has been marked by one exacerbating conflict after another. Qohelet came to recognize that he could not comprehend God's work. He has designed Ecclesiastes to reflect these conflicts by following a dialectical pattern. Because of the infinite nature of God's being and finite man's depravity, Qohelet's attempt to master life with wisdom was misdirected. If the only conclusion that we can draw from Ecclesiastes is that everything about life is frustratingly enigmatic, then Ecclesiastes only make a minimal contribution to normative theology. However, Qohelet as a godly sage realizes that God is actually working to restore his creation. Qohelet's biblical understanding of life thus has a profound influence on his response to the mysterious nature of life.

QOHELET'S RESPONSE

Since Qohelet's passion to master life was misdirected, we might expect him to respond with pessimism, existentialism, or secularism. Rather, he responds by exhorting us to use and enjoy our divinely bestowed gifts judiciously and reverentially in an attempt to make the most out of our

---

[81] Glenn, "Ecclesiastes," p. 977.

[82] Caneday, "Qoheleth," pp. 41–42.

God-given lives. In examining Qohelet's response, we will primarily focus on this *Leitmotiv* of celebrating life. Qohelet provides this alternative exhortation in order to assist us in navigating through the inscrutable maze of life. This exhortation to enjoy life repeatedly punctuates Ecclesiastes at key junctures. This refrain is found in 2:24–26; 3:12–13, 22; 5:17–19 (Eng. 5:18–20); 8:15;[83] 9:7–10;[84] and 11:9–12:1.[85] Based upon these, we can synthesize four responses in the face of life's baffling and incomprehensible nature. The first response relates to man's limitation in life. This limitation is highlighted by comparing this *Leitmotiv* with other portions of Ecclesiastes. Second, in each of the enjoyment motifs, Qohelet reflects a theocentric perspective of life. Third, each refrain challenges us to joyfully use God's good gifts. Finally, Qohelet views his advice as being normative truth for God's people.

Man's Limitations

Having presented a brief autobiographical sketch of his search for meaning in wisdom, pleasure, and the lack of permanence in life (1:12–2:23), our author introduces us to his first *Leitmotiv* about enjoying life in 2:24–26. In these verses, God enables those who belong to Him to enjoy their food, drink, and find satisfaction in their work. Furthermore, in v. 26 God gives those who are pleasing to him wisdom, understanding and joy, but to sinners God gives them the task of "gathering up" for his people. This is a way God has chosen to provide for his people by even using the labor of reprobates. What is indicated by this refrain's content is God's freedom in using people and their limitations to carry out God's plan. Man's limitations are further implied by the placement of 2:24–26 immediately after the description of Qohelet's search for meaning in his autobiographical

[83] Three of these refrains (2:24–26; 5:18–20; 8:15) have been used as dividing points for a fourfold outline of Ecclesiastes; see Walter C. Kaiser, *Ecclesiastes: Total Life* (Chicago: Moody, 1979), pp. 19–24. Kaiser's use of these refrains as dividing points is based on an anonymous article, "The Scope and Plan of the Book of Ecclesiastes," *Biblical Repertory and Princeton Review* 29 (July 1857): 419–40.

[84] Though discussed on a more popular level, the significance of these six refrains for interpreting Ecclesiastes has been observantly pointed out by J. Stafford Wright, "The Interpretation of Ecclesiastes," in *Classical Evangelical Essays*, ed. Walter C. Kaiser, Jr. (Grand Rapids: Baker, 1972), pp. 133–50. For a discussion of the rhetorical significance of אֵין טוֹב ("there is nothing better than") in 2:24; 3:12, 22; and 8:15, see Graham S. Ogden, "The 'Better'-Proverb (*tôb-spruch*), Rhetorical Criticism, and Qoheleth," *Journal of Biblical Literature* 96 (December 1977): 489–505.

[85] Often the first six passages are considered the refrains to enjoy life; I have included the last passage because it also includes this same motif. See Whybray, "Qoheleth," p. 87.

sketch. The longer negative perspective on life is contrasted by the shorter positive point of view. By placing these in juxtaposition, "the writer of Ecclesiastes has set for himself the task of making us feel the emptiness of life under the sun and the attractiveness of a God-filled life that leads to contentment with one's earthly lot."[86] One of Qohelet's key responses to his subject is his focus on our limitations.

The book of Ecclesiastes asserts that man is limited by his natural weaknesses and sin.[87] For example, in 1:12–18 Qohelet recognizes that increased wisdom results in increased grief. A further limitation is seen in his search for meaning in pleasure-seeking (2:1–11) and comparing wisdom and folly (2:12–23). In 4:1–3 oppression reflects another sinful limitation of man, as does laboring with wrong motives in 4:4–16. In 7:20 Qohelet affirms that everyone is a sinner and in v. 29 reflects that God had originally made man upright but he has gone in search of his own "sinful" schemes. Sin extends to the core of man's being. The issues of theodicy also vex our author in 3:16–21; 7:15–18; 8:12–14. Though our inability to understand God's moral governance of the world is part of our creaturely weakness, this inability has been exacerbated by our sinfulness. One of life's great frustrations is death. As indicated by its repetition, the frustration of death is also a major emphasis in Qohelet's thoughts (2:12–17; 3:18–21; 9:1–10; 12:1–7). The items mentioned here provide a sampling of man's limitations as a depraved, finite person.

Ecclesiastes also develops the limitations man has as a created being. The admonition in 12:1 exhorting youth to remember their Creator reflects a limitation in them as finite beings. As created beings, we have both a beginning and limited knowledge (3:11). Our limited knowledge is highlighted in 9:17–10:20, where wisdom, though having great value, cannot help the sage to know the future. Since we cannot know the future, we cannot know if a business investment will succeed. Qohelet, therefore, recommends that we diversify our business investments in 11:1–6. As a finite being man has natural limitations.

A specific application of man's limitations as a sinful, finite being relates to Qohelet's misdirected attempt at mastering life. He came to realize "that he is not the master of events."[88] As God's image bearer, man has a natural inquisitiveness about eternal things; however, God has not given

---

[86] Ryken, "Ecclesiastes," p. 271.

[87] There is a difference between our weaknesses as finite beings and our innate depravity. Prior to the Fall, Adam would still have needed to grow in wisdom since he was not created omniscient. He obviously had limitations in knowledge. Once he fell, his weaknesses would have been intensified because of sin.

[88] George R. Castellino, "Qohelet and His Wisdom," *Catholic Biblical Quarterly* 30 (January 1968): 27.

him the ability to understand these areas. In 3:10 Qohelet describes this as a "burden" and in 1:13 as a "heavy burden." God has designed life in this manner to demonstrate that we are finite (3:18). This inquisitiveness about eternal matters is undoubtedly part of Qohelet's motivation in attempting to master life. Our author makes an appeal to youth not to emulate his example. He recommends that they enjoy themselves during their "youth." After making a positive admonition in 11:9, he provides a negative exhortation in 11:10 to banish vexation from their heart and to cast off trouble from their body. The term for "vexation" (כַּעַס) is also used in 1:18 where it relates to the burden associated with the increase of wisdom. In light of 1:12–17 this vexation is associated with Qohelet's attempt to understand and master life. Because of Qohelet's burdensome search, the vexation and trouble of 11:10 may refer to the same type of anxiety that would be produced in a youth if he imitated Qohelet's search. Qohelet's point in 11:9–10 is that young men should not get caught up in attempting to master life with its vexation; rather, they should make the most of their youth. Since man is limited in his ability to master life, he should refrain from this quest. Qohelet's misdirected quest was an experiment in folly.

Theocentric Perspective of Life

Having searched for meaning and purpose in the gifts of life and, subsequently, realizing that this quest had been foolishly misdirected, Qohelet finds the answer in the incomprehensible God. Some interpreters have maintained that the only orthodox admonition about God is found in the conclusion of the book (12:13–14). However, this could not be further from the truth. Each of the exhortations commending the enjoyment of life not only places an emphasis on enjoying life but also on God's presence. We will briefly look at an example from the refrain in 3:12–14.

> [12]I know that there is nothing better for men than that they rejoice and do well in life; [13]and also that every man should eat and drink and find satisfaction in all his labor—this is the gift of God. [14]I know that everything God does will endure forever; nothing can be added to it and nothing taken from it. God does this so that men should fear Him.

This passage indicates that God enables men to be happy, prosper, enjoy their food and drink, and find satisfaction in their work. This refrain is in a context describing Qohelet's ability to see the beauty of God's ordered arrangement of life, yet he is grieved by his inability to comprehend how the details of God's plan are being accomplished (v. 11). In light of this frustration, he recommends that we enjoy the basic elements of life that

God has given us. With our limited capacity for knowledge, our author urges us to be content with what we do possess. In v. 14 he is convinced that nothing can change God's work and that the consequence of this is that men will fear God. From this, we should understand that Qohelet viewed life through a God-centered theology. In comparing 3:12–14 with the refrain in 2:24–26, this theocentric perspective is more strongly developed in 2:24–26. In the context of chapter two Qohelet despairs of life because he will have to leave the fruit of his labor to another who will not have labored over it and may not use it as wisely. The emphasis has been on what Qohelet had accomplished with God being excluded from his presentation; however, in vv. 24–26 the presence of God dominates every verse. In v. 25 Qohelet uses a rhetorical question, "Who can eat or find enjoyment without Him [God]?"[89] The point is no one can find enjoyment in life without God. Those enabled by God to find enjoyment are described in v. 26 as "those who please God." The emphasis is on a dynamic relationship with the Living God. Consequently, the refrain of 2:24–26 has a strong God-centered emphasis. Qohelet's theocentric perspective is seen in his other exhortations commending the enjoyment of life.

How extensive is Qohelet's theology? The editors of the *New Scofield Reference Bible* suggest that Qohelet used only two theological truths in the composition of his book, namely, that "there is a holy God and that He will bring everything into judgment."[90] If this is correct, then we would have to agree with Murphy that Qohelet did not have a "finished *Weltanschauung* ['worldview']."[91] However, the concept of fearing God in Ecclesiastes points us to a more satisfactory understanding of Qohelet's theology. Not only does Qohelet refer to this concept of fearing God in 3:14 but he also uses it in 5:6 (Eng. v. 7); 7:18; 8:12, 13; 12:13.[92] In 5:6 fearing God should correct insincerity in worship. Though God is external to creation in his transcendence (5:1 [Eng. v. 2]), in his immanence he is also involved with his people so that he knows their rash vows made in

---

[89] A comparison of this verse with the KJV and NKJV indicates that the prepositional phrase I translated as "without Him" has been rendered as "more than I." My translation is consistent with the translation found in both the NASB and NIV. There are a number of textual difficulties in this verse. See Whitley, *Koheleth*, p. 29; and J. De Waard, "The Translator and Textual Criticism," *Biblica* 60 (1979): 509–29.

[90] *The New Scofield Reference Bible*, p. 696.

[91] Roland E. Murphy, "The Pensées of Coheleth," *Catholic Biblical Quarterly* 17 (1955): 306; see also Robert H. Pfeiffer, "The Peculiar Skepticism of Ecclesiastes," *Journal of Biblical Literature* 53 (March–December 1934): 108.

[92] For an excellent discussion of the fear of God, see John Murray, *Principles of Conduct* (Grand Rapids: Eerdmans, 1957), pp. 229–42.

worship. In 8:12 God in his providence takes care of those who fear him, but in v. 13 he punishes those who do not fear him by not prolonging their lives. In 12:13, fearing God is coordinate with keeping his commandments, with the attached motivation in v. 14 that God will bring all things into judgment, even those things done in secret. God in his omniscience and omnipresence knows all things and will consequently prosecute his holy judgment (see also 3:17).

In 11:9–10 Qohelet commends the enjoyment of youth. In v. 9 Qohelet gives this exhortation: "Rejoice, young man, during your youth, and let your heart be glad in the days of young manhood. Follow the ways of your heart and the desires of your eyes." This might be misunderstood as support for an uncontrolled hedonistic lifestyle; however, this is not the case, for the last part of this verse reads: "But know that for all these things God will bring you to judgment." The point is to enjoy life, but keep it within the God-given boundaries. Qohelet's enjoyment motif is coordinate with God's commandments. He follows up his exhortation in 11:9–10 with another exhortation in 12:1 to remember our Creator during the time of youth.

Furthermore, as we have already seen, Qohelet recognizes the Fall and curse in Genesis 3. He also recognizes that God is working to restore his creational design (see Gen 1:28; 3:15; 9:1, 26–27; 12:2–3). Qohelet is so bold to proclaim in 7:14 that God sovereignly disposes all the events of life, "in the days of prosperity, be glad; but in the days of trouble, consider: God has made the one as well as the other." How God does this is beyond Qohelet's comprehension, according to 3:11. Because of his creaturely ignorance, he concludes in the last colon of 7:14, "Therefore, no man can discover anything about the future." Qohelet's system of belief stresses the supremacy of God's knowledge and our limited knowledge.[93] This belief emphasizes the Creator-creature distinction, God's incomprehensibility.[94] Qohelet's God is the Sovereign Lord who in His infinite wisdom created the earth and all living things, who is governing the world in his providence and will bring it to its appointed end, and who judged the world at the Fall and who will also judge all people at his eschatological judgment. Does this sound as if Qohelet was theologically deprived? As a biblical theologian, Qohelet's view of life is God-centered; this is to say his observations

---

[93] Derek Kidner, *The Message of Ecclesiastes* (Downers Grove, IL: InterVarsity, 1976), p. 16.

[94] This does not mean that God cannot be known, but that our knowledge is not equivalent to God's knowledge. We can know what he has revealed in his word about himself, but we can never know God in the same sense that he knows himself.

about life were conditioned by his understanding of special revelation. As Shank has stated,

> Qoheleth's perception…refers to a knowledge which is a 'reflex-action' of his fear of God and which penetrates to the essence of the *meaning* of what this world of vanity is all about. Surely, Qoheleth does perceive the vanity 'under the sun' which does not *exclude* the intellectual element of knowledge of these things. Yet that perception also *includes* a deep, spiritual insight into the effects of the curse of God upon life and labor 'under the sun.'[95]

In light of Qohelet's God-centered emphasis, we should conclude that Qohelet, rather than having a theocentric deficiency, has a theocentric perspective of life.

Enjoyment of Life

The enjoyment-of-life motif has been one of the most misunderstood portions of Ecclesiastes. An example of this misunderstanding is reflected by Scott. He has suggested that the mood of Ecclesiastes reflects disillusionment and that Qohelet's ethic is not based on divine commands. Consequently, Scott sees Qohelet's enjoyment of life as the only resignation open to man. For Scott, Qohelet "is a rationalist, an agnostic, a skeptic, a pessimist, and a fatalist."[96] Rather than following this conclusion about this *Leitmotiv,* we are convinced that in their contexts these passages do not lead to the skeptical conclusions of Scott.

When considered in light of death, Qohelet found no satisfaction in wisdom, pleasure, and toil (1:12–2:23). Everything that he labored to accumulate will be left to someone after him. In light of this he recommends in 2:24–26 that as God enables us, we should enjoy our food, drink, and work. He further affirms that God also gives wisdom, understanding, and joy to those who please him. The second refrain is found in the context dealing with God's sovereign appointment of life's events with their divine timing. The God-given desire to understand God's sovereign appointments haunts Qohelet because he recognizes that it is a symmetrical masterpiece, but he is unable to comprehend it. His second refrain advocates that we should be happy and accomplish good in life. He further recommends again the enjoyment of our food, drink, and the fruits of our labor. His third refrain is found in 3:22. The context of this relates to injustice being permitted to take place in this world.[97] Qohelet affirms that God will judge the righteous

---

[95] Shank, "Qoheleth's World and Life View," p. 68.

[96] Scott, *Ecclesiastes*, pp. 191–92.

[97] Whybray, "Qoheleth," p. 90.

and the wicked. He further notes that we are finite beings. Recognizing the infinite God's judgment and our finite limitations in this temporal sphere, he again recommends that we find satisfaction in our work.

The fourth refrain in 5:17–19 (Eng. 5:18–20) is situated in a chapter dealing with the liabilities associated with an excessive desire for wealth. In this context, he recommends that the value of riches is relative and that we should enjoy our wealth and possessions as God enables us. He again commends making the most of our food, drink, and work. The fifth refrain is in 8:15. While confident that God will judge, Qohelet is perplexed by how God morally governs his universe (8:1–14). In this refrain, Qohelet again commends the enjoyment of life, food, drink, and work. One of his more elaborate exhortations celebrating life is his sixth refrain in 9:7–10. In this context, Qohelet affirms that both the righteous and wicked are in the hands of God and neither know whether love or hate will occur in their future. All men share the same destiny of death. This being the case, he commends joy while we are alive, for the activities of this life will not take place in Sheol.[98] In vv. 7–10 he commends eating and drinking with a joyful heart, the enjoyment of fine clothes, perfume, and our wives.[99] He further commends that we labor diligently and astutely. The final exhortation is in 11:9–12:1. In a context dealing with the uncertain timing of death, Qohelet recommends that young people enjoy their youth commensurate with God's moral laws and that they have a faithful remembrance of their Creator. This examination of these passages reveals that Qohelet challenges us to be actively engaged in and to enjoy our food, drink, work, results from our work, spouse, clothes, perfume, and youth. Since this enjoyment is correlated in some contexts with God's judgment and the fear of God motif, this certainly does not seem to be the remarks of a skeptic advocating unbridled hedonism. Qohelet sounds like an orthodox biblical theologian who had a solid understanding of antecedent revelation.

Normative Theology

Some have claimed that enjoyment-of-life refrains do not reflect normative truth for God's people. Illustrative of this is C. I. Scofield, who correlated

---

[98] This text of Ecclesiastes has been used by cultic groups such as the Jehovah's Witnesses to deny conscious life after death; however, the emphasis in this context is not to teach what life is like beyond the grave. It tells us what will not be there, but the point of the passage is not to affirm what is there. The point of this passage is to make the most of our earthly joys in life. To deal with the doctrine of life after death we need to go to passages dealing with this subject. For a helpful treatment of this subject in Ecclesiastes, see Ginsburg, *Coheleth*, 2:999.

[99] Hubbard, *Ecclesiastes*, p. 93.

the refrain of 2:24 with Satan's lie in Genesis 3:4.[100] Since Qohelet has coordinated these refrains with man's accountability to God, these cannot mean "Do what you will."[101] Instead, we should notice that in the last part of 2:24, he said "this also I saw, that it was from the hand of God." This is to say, that the items enumerated in vv. 24–26 are from God. He makes a similar statement in 3:13 where the blessings enumerated are referred to as "the gift from God." In 3:22 the gifts given to man are referred as "his portion" (חֵלֶק). This term denotes what has been apportioned or divided.[102] It indicates what portion God has assigned to man. Man receives a portion but not all of God's blessings. Qohelet uses חֵלֶק twice in 5:17–18 (Eng. vv. 18–19). This same expression is used again in 9:9. In 8:15 "God gives" these blessings. I would conclude from this that Qohelet has designed his advice to be normative theology.

SUMMARY AND CONCLUSION

Having made a thorough study of life to discover meaning and purpose, our author has presented the results of his study in Ecclesiastes. He has presented the subject of his work in 1:2 and 12:8, "Everything is frustratingly enigmatic." This is to say, everything about life is a burdensome mystery. This subject was not based simply on empirical observations, but his observations were sifted through his theological grid. Qohelet understood that God created an originally perfect cosmos, but he subsequently imposed a curse on his cosmos and its inhabitants. However, he also recognized that God is working to restore his creational design. Because of his theological understanding of the early chapters of the Torah, his subject in Ecclesiastes has been shaped by his theologi-cal *a prioris.* In his search, Qohelet had attempted to master life but was faced with one frustration after another. He came to realize that he could not accomplish his objective and that the object of his search was not the creation but the Creator. As a result, he has used a dialectical structure to reflect the conflicts he encountered and to commend the enjoyment of life from a theocentric perspective.

In responding to his subject, Qohelet in summary form has exhorted us to use and enjoy our divinely bestowed gifts judiciously and rever-entially. The primary thrust of his response focused on his *Leitmotiv* of

---

[100] Scofield, *Scofield Bible Correspondence Course,* 2:302.

[101] J. Stafford Wright, "Ecclesiastes," in *The Expositor's Bible Commentary,* 12 vols., ed. Frank E. Gaebelein (Grand Rapids: Zondervan, 1991), 5:1146.

[102] BDB, p. 324.

enjoying life. From the placement and content of this *Leitmotiv,* four responses were synthesized. First, the placement of this motif highlighted our limitations as depraved, finite beings. Because of our limitations, we should not attempt to master life but to make the most of and enjoy what God has given us. Second, each of the refrains exhorting the celebration of life reflected a theocentric perspective on life. Third, the enjoyment-of-life motif has emphasized that we be actively engaged in and enjoy our food, drink, work, fruits of our labor, spouse, clothes, perfume, and youth. Because of this theme's coordination with God's judgment and the fear-of-God motif, this is a judicious and reverential use of God's gifts. Fourth, Qohelet regarded his exhortation to enjoy life as normative truth. In the midst of a sin-cursed world and a veiled providence, Qohelet has counseled us to have a submissive faith in our sovereign God, to be diligently involved in our responsibilities of life, and to enjoy God's blessings.

Qohelet ties everything together in his conclusion (12:8–14). In v. 8 he restates his subject, "Everything is frustratingly enigmatic." In vv. 9–10, he reminds us that he was a wise man and studied out the issues of life. In v. 9 he has carefully arranged his words. In v. 10 he wrote "acceptable words." The "acceptable words" are a reference to those which are delightful or profitable. This is to say, these words are compelling words designed to skillfully impact his audience. He further wrote "upright and true words." This is to say, these words are profitable for faith and practice. In v. 11 he states that the sayings of sages are like "goads." Goads were prods used to drive cattle.[103] Ecclesiastes was designed by our author to serve as a guide. What he has advised is special inscripturated revelation because ultimately it was given to him by the One Shepherd, God. Qohelet is claiming divine authority and inerrancy for his book. He reminds us then, in vv. 13–14, that we are to fear God and be obedient, something that only a believer can hope to do, and that we are accountable for our actions to God. Qohelet's intent is not to solve life's vexing mysteries but to recommend "an acceptance of life as given by God with both its joys and sorrows, and he argues for an active participation and engagement with life, despite its uncertainties."[104]

---

[103] Gordis, *Koheleth,* p. 353.

[104] Johnston, "Confessions of a Workaholic," p. 21.

THE MEANING OF "BORN OF WATER AND THE SPIRIT" IN JOHN 3:5[1]

Robert V. McCabe

The Holy Spirit's role in regeneration or the new birth has been the subject of many theological discussions. A text that has received considerable attention is John 3:5, "Truly, truly, I say to you, unless one is born of water and the Spirit, he cannot enter into the kingdom of God."[2] A major interpretative problem with this verse is the meaning of "born of water and the Spirit" (γεννηθῇ ἐξ ὕδατος καὶ πνεύματος). Is "water" (ὕδατος) to be equated with baptism? Should water be correlated with procreation? Or, is water used as a symbol for the Word of God or cleansing? Furthermore, what is the relationship between "water" (ὕδατος), and "spirit" (πνεύματος)? Is water set in contrast to the spirit, or do water and spirit reflect a conceptual unity?

This article will attempt to determine the meaning of "born of water and the Spirit" by examining the immediate context of John 3 and other pertinent theological data. After this, we will survey some of the more dominant and popular interpretations of "water and the Spirit."

AN EXAMINATION OF JOHN 3:5

In the history of Christian interpretation, John 3:5 has often been associated with Christian baptism.[3] Undoubtedly, the sacramentalism associated with a broad spectrum of Christianity has influenced some to interpret this verse in light of a sacramental grid. However, we must determine what this verse means in its immediate and overall canonical context. To determine the meaning of John 3:5, we will initially examine the key concepts within this text, followed by an examination of its literary features.

An Examination of Key Concepts

Nicodemus is identified in 3:1 as a Pharisee, a "ruler of the Jews" (ἄρχων τῶν Ἰουδαίων). This identification would suggest that he was not simply

---

[1] This article appeared in the 1999 issue of *DBSJ*, vol. 4, pp. 85–107.

[2] All Scripture quotations, unless otherwise noted, are taken from the 1977 edition of NASB.

[3] Raymond E. Brown, *The Gospel According to John*, 2 vols., AB (Garden City, NY: Doubleday, 1966–70), 1:141.

a community leader, but a Jewish leader and perhaps a member of the Sanhedrin.[4] After presenting his discussion of the supernatural origination of the new birth, Jesus chides Nicodemus in v. 10 for being "the teacher of Israel" (ὁ διδάσκαλος τοῦ Ἰσραήλ), yet unable to comprehend the subject of Jesus' discourse, "Are you the teacher of Israel, and do not understand these things?" Two items are significant in v. 10. First, "the teacher of Israel" is a title reflecting that Nicodemus was a recognized teacher of Scripture. Second, as a well-known teacher, Nicodemus should have grasped the connection between Jesus' doctrine of regeneration and its Old Testament foundation. The nature of Jesus' berating Nicodemus would clearly suggest that Jesus' discourse on the new birth is rooted in the Old Testament. Carson has correctly observed that "nothing could make clearer the fact that Jesus' teaching on the new birth was built on the teaching of the Old Testament."[5] We will survey four key concepts in 3:5, along with a correlation of each with its appropriate Old Testament background.

Born of

In a similar manner to the use of "Amen" in 3:3 and 1:51, Jesus stresses the importance of his teaching by introducing his remarks with a double "Amen."[6] He next sets forth a condition for entering the kingdom of God, viz., being "born of water and the Spirit." The verbal phrase is comprised of an aorist subjunctive passive verb followed by a preposition, γεννηθῇ ἐξ, "is born of." We should initially observe that Jesus' use of the passive voice unequivocally stresses that the human participant in the new birth is completely passive.[7] In addition, we should observe that this specific metaphor of God's giving "birth" to an individual is not used in the Old Testament. It is possible that Jesus draws upon a common experience of childbearing to illustrate the new birth.[8] However, it is equally plausible that the seed form of this specific metaphor may be seen in those passages where God's covenant relationship with Israel is portrayed in a familial relationship. Yahweh is presented as Israel's "Father" (Deut 32:6), and the covenant nation as his "sons" (Deut 8:5; 14:1; Jer 3:19; Hos 11:1) or

---

[4] C. K. Barrett, *The Gospel According to St. John*, 2nd ed. (Philadelphia: Westminster, 1978), p. 204.

[5] D. A. Carson, *The Gospel According to John* (Grand Rapids: Eerdmans, 1991), p. 198.

[6] F. F. Bruce, *The Gospel of John* (Grand Rapids: Eerdmans, 1983), pp. 172, 173.

[7] Anthony A. Hoekema, *Saved by Grace* (Grand Rapids: Eerdmans, 1989), p. 97.

[8] Linda L. Belleville, "'Born of Water and Spirit': John 3:5," *Trinity Journal* 1 (Fall 1980): 137.

"first-born" (Exod 4:22; Jer 31:9).[9] The relationship between Yahweh and the promised Davidic king is also portrayed in familial terms, "Father" and "son" (2 Sam 7:14; 1 Chr 17:13; 22:10; 28:6). David is specifically referred to as Yahweh's "firstborn" (Ps 89:27).[10] It is not until the postexilic period that we find pious individual Jews designated as "sons of God" (Jub 1:23–25; Sir 4:10; 23:1, 4; Wis 2:13, 16, 18).[11] While familial terms are used of Israel and the Davidic ruler, the concept of God's giving "birth" to individuals is not specifically used in Old Testament thought. However, the familial terms may provide a potential informing background for Jesus' use of γεννάω. According to Brown, the familial terms should have provided an informative, though limited, background for Nicodemus.[12]

Though the Old Testament context does not provide a complete picture about the new birth, John presents a more complete picture, for he uses γεννάω more often to refer to God's sovereign role in regeneration[13] than any other writer in the New Testament.[14] In Johannine literature, γεννάω is used 28 times;[15] 16 of these refer to the new birth, with 6 in John's gospel and 10 in 1 John.[16] In John's gospel, those who receive Christ in 1:12–13 are "born" (ἐγεννήθησαν), "from God" (ἐκ θεοῦ). In 3:3–8, an aorist passive form of γεννάω, followed by ἐκ or an equivalent, is used 5 times (vv. 3, 4 [twice], 5, 7) to express the concept of a spiritual birth produced by God. In particular, Jesus says in v. 3 if one is to see the kingdom of God, he must "be born from above" (or "born again," γεννηθῇ ἄνωθεν). Verse 5 closely parallels v. 3. Jesus' replacement of ἄνωθεν with ἐξ ὕδατος καὶ

---

[9] *New International Dictionary of Old Testament Theology and Exegesis*, s.v. "Adoption," by Victor P. Hamilton, 4:363 (hereafter cited as *NIDOTTE*).

[10] Ibid.

[11] Brown, *John*, 1:139.

[12] Ibid.

[13] It is beyond the scope of this paper to develop the theological ramifications of the doctrine of regeneration; for fuller treatments of this doctrine, see Robert L. Reymond, *A New Systematic Theology of the Christian Faith* (Nashville: Nelson, 1998), pp. 718–21; Wayne Grudem, *Systematic Theology* (Grand Rapids: Zondervan, 1994), pp. 699–707; and Hoekema, Saved by Grace, pp. 93–112.

[14] In 1 Cor 4:15 Paul uses the aorist active indicative, ἐγέννησα, to speak of his own role as a proclaimer of the gospel which resulted in the Corinthians experiencing the new birth. Outside of the Johannine material, other synonyms for γεννάω are used, such as ἀναγεννήσας in 1 Pet 1:3, 23, παλιγγενεσίας in Tit 3:5, and ἀπεκύησεν in Jas 1:18.

[15] *New International Dictionary of New Testament Theology*, s.v. "γεννάω," by A. Ringwald, 1:178 (hereafter cited as NIDNTT).

[16] Excluding 2 uses in 3:6b, 8, the other 10 examples are used in a physical sense (3:6; 8:41; 9:2, 19, 20, 32, 34; 16:21 [twice], and 18:37).

πνεύματος in v. 5 strongly suggests that he is describing the same type of birth in both verses. 1 John further supports the divine origination of the new birth. Excluding an aorist active participle in 5:1, γεννάω is used in a passive form 9 times in 1 John, all of which refer to a birth produced by God, γεγεννημένος ἐκ τοῦ θεοῦ or an equivalent (2:29; 3:9 [twice]; 4:7; 5:1 [twice], 4, and 18 [twice]). This would suggest that "born of God" in 1 John expresses the same concept as "born of the Spirit" and its equivalent expressions in John 3. By his consistent use of γεννάω, as well as his use of this verb in the passive voice, John stresses that this spiritual birth, regeneration, is a sovereign work of God alone. Hoekema summarizes the significance of this use of γεννάω with the following:

> The passive voice of the verb tells us that this is an occurrence in which human beings are wholly passive. In fact, the very verb used, even apart from the passive, tells us the same thing. We did not choose to be born; we had nothing to do with our being born. We were completely passive in our natural birth. So it is also with our spiritual birth.[17]

Although Hoekema may place too much emphasis on the passive voice alone, it is nevertheless true that to be "born of the Spirit," in John 3, connotes the Spirit producing new spiritual life.

Water

The Old Testament presentation of water provides an informing background for Jesus' reference to ὕδωρ. Water was used in the Old Testament to symbolize cleansing and renewal. Water was used in priestly ablutions to denote ceremonial cleansing. Before the Aaronic priests entered their vocation, they were consecrated by ablutions (Exod 29:4). Water was also used by priests for ritual cleansing of their hands and feet (Exod 30:17–21; 40:30–32). Cleansing with water was also required after sexual emissions (Lev 15).[18] Not only may water be associated with cleansing, but it is also used figuratively for renewal. On the one hand, to forsake Yahweh is to forsake "the fountain of living water" (Jer 2:13; 17:13).[19] On the other hand, to come to God for the satisfaction of one's thirst is to experience life (Isa 55:1–3). Therefore, water may be used as a metaphor for spiritual

---

[17] Hoekema, *Saved by Grace*, p. 97.

[18] *NIDNTT*, s.v. "ὕδωρ," by O. Bocher, 3:989; and *NIDOTTE*, s.v. "מַיִם," by Michael A. Grisanti, 2:930.

[19] See *Theological Wordbook of the Old Testament*, s.v. "מַיִם," by Walter C. Kaiser, 1:502–3.

life. Water as a symbol for renewal is also connected with God's fulfilling his promises of a physical restoration (Ezek 47:9; Zech 14:8). In addition, when it is used as a metaphor for cleansing and renewal, God is the source of this cleansing water (Isa 4:4).

In John's gospel, ὕδωρ is used 21 times. Excluding John 3:5, it is used of literal water 13 times,[20] and is used as a metaphor 7 times.[21] As a metaphor, "living water" represents life that is produced by the Spirit.[22] In 4:14, the water given by Jesus becomes "a well of water [ὕδατος] springing up to eternal life [εἰς ζὼν αἰώνιον]." In 6:63, "it is the Spirit [πνεῦμα] who gives life [ζῳοποιοῦν]." In 7:38–39, "from his innermost being shall flow rivers of living water [ὕδατος ζῶντος]. But this He spoke of the Spirit [πνεύματος]."[23] Consequently, if the metaphorical examples of ὕδωρ are consistently used in John for spiritual vivification, this would suggest that ὕδωρ is used in 3:5 in a similar manner.

Spirit

In John 3:3–12, πνεῦμα is used five times and reflects Jesus' theological emphasis in this passage. In the Old Testament "spirit"[24] may denote God's animating principle of life (Gen 2:7; 6:3). While "spirit" may be used in this sense on a general level to describe God's animating force in all living creatures, it is more specifically used to denote the Spirit who will quicken his people and produce God's eschatological blessings. The Old Testament predicts that a time will come when God pours out his Spirit on all mankind (Joel 2:28). This pouring out of his Spirit involves a transformation that includes a cleansing from sin and a spiritual renewal

---

[20] For example, water is used of John's baptism (1:26, 31, 33; 3:23), for satisfying one's thirst (4:7, 13), at the pool of Bethesda (5:7), for washing feet (13:5), being turned into wine (2:7, 9 [twice]; 4:46), and as flowing from Jesus' side (19:34).

[21] The metaphorical use of ὕδωρ is found in 4:10, 11, 14 (three times), 15; 7:38.

[22] Leon Morris, *The Gospel According to John*, New International Commentary on the New Testament (Grand Rapids: Eerdmans, 1971), p. 260.

[23] Support for this position is more fully developed by James D. G. Dunn, *Baptism in the Holy Spirit* (London: SCM Press, 1970), p. 187; see also Kylne R. Snodgrass, "That Which Is Born from *Pneuma Is Pneuma*: Rebirth and Spirit in John 3:5–6," *Covenant Quarterly* 49 (February 1991): 19.

[24] The Hebrew term רוח, "spirit," is found in the Masoretic Text 377 or 378 (the count of 377 uses is taken from *NIDNTT*, s.v. "Spirit, Holy Spirit," by E. Kamlah, 3:690; the count in Even-Shoshan, based upon the edition of the Koren Publishers in Jerusalem, is 378 in Hebrew and 11 in Aramaic [*A New Concordance of the Bible* (Jerusalem: Kiryath Sepher, 1985), pp. 1063–66]). Of the 377 or 378 times the Hebrew term רוח is found in the MT, 264 of these are translated in the LXX with πνεῦμα.

of God's covenant people (Ezek 11:18–20; 36:25–27). This time will also include a restoration of God's blessings and righteousness (Isa 32:15–20; 44:3; Ezek 39:29).[25] The use of πνεῦμα in John is consistent with the Old Testament predictions of the Spirit's quickening work in salvation. John uses πνεῦμα 24 times,[26] and he generally uses it as reference to the Holy Spirit producing spiritual life.[27]

Water and the Spirit

There is a coordination of water and spirit in a few key Old Testament texts, literature from the intertestamental period, and John's gospel. Water and spirit are correlated in Isaiah 44:3–5 and Ezekiel 36:25–27. The setting of these two passages provides significant Old Testament material for our understanding of John 3:5. Both Old Testament books provide a number of references to the new covenant promises[28] and place an emphasis on Israel's eschatological future.[29] In keeping with this twofold theological emphasis, both Isaiah and Ezekiel use the Old Testament term רוּחַ ("breath, spirit, wind") over 50 times. Of the 377 or 378[30] uses of רוּחַ in the Masoretic Text, רוּחַ is found in Isaiah 51 times and Ezekiel 52 times.[31] Because of the major emphases of Isaiah and Ezekiel, these are texts with which a Jewish teacher such as Nicodemus should have been acquainted.

In Isaiah 44:3–5 water is associated with restoration of the land and God's Spirit with the transformation of his people.

> [3]For I will pour water on the thirsty land and streams on the dry ground; I will pour out My Spirit on your offspring and My blessing on your descendants; [4]And they will spring up among the grass, like poplars by streams of water. [5]This one will say, "I am the Lord's"; and that one will call on the name of Jacob; And another will write on his hand, "Belonging to the Lord," and will name Israel's name with honor.

---

[25] *NIDNTT*, s.v. "Spirit, Holy Spirit," 3:692.

[26] The noun πνεῦμα is used in 1:32, 33 (twice); 3:5, 6 (twice), 8 (twice), 34; 4:23, 24 (twice); 6:63 (twice); 7:39 (twice); 11:33; 13:21; 14:17, 26; 15:26; 16:13; 19:30; 20:22.

[27] Dunn, *Baptism*, p. 189.

[28] See R. Bruce Compton, "An Examination of the New Covenant in the Old and New Testaments" (Th.D. dissertation, Grace Theological Seminary, 1986), pp. 32–33, 66–129.

[29] On Israel's eschatological future in Isaiah and Ezekiel, see Robert B. Chisholm, Jr., "A Theology of Isaiah," in *A Biblical Theology of the Old Testament*, ed. Roy B. Zuck (Chicago: Moody Press, 1991), pp. 325–26; 335–38; and in the same book, see Eugene H. Merrill, "A Theology of Ezekiel and Daniel," pp. 376–83.

[30] See above, n. 24.

[31] See chart in *Theological Lexicon of the Old Testament*, s.v. "רוּחַ," by R. Albertz and C. Westermann, 3:1202–3.

This passage reflects a close association of water and spirit. "I will pour water" (אֶצָּק־מַיִם) is parallel with "I will pour out My Spirit" (אֶצֹּק רוּחִי). The significance of the parallelism is that one could legitimately correlate being "born of water" with being "born from above," as Hodges has clearly indicated:

> Accordingly, the Holy Spirit's activity is here presented as an effusion of water *from above,* the effect of which in those on whom it falls is that they spring up like freshly watered plants (v. 4). But this, in turn, is connected with the realization that the individuals thus blessed are now truly "the Lord's" (v. 5). Hence it would be difficult to discover a passage more apposite to the experience of new birth than this, and one might reasonably describe the recipients of such an experience as "born of water" *and* "born from above."[32]

The context of Ezekiel 36:1–37:28 focuses on Israel's future restoration. To develop how this restoration will be accomplished, Ezekiel places an emphasis on the Spirit's life-giving operation. Two facets of the Spirit's quickening work are stressed in 36:25–27, cleansing and transformation. Ezekiel further develops the transforming work of the Spirit in 37:1–14. In this context, Ezekiel uses the Hebrew term רוּחַ to develop his message about the life-giving operation of the Spirit. In v. 1 the Spirit (רוּחַ) of Yahweh transports Ezekiel to the valley of dry bones. The key question for this chapter is found in v. 3, "Son of man, can these bones live?" After Ezekiel's ambiguous response ("O Lord God, Thou knowest"), Yahweh answers His own question by affirming that He would make "breath" (רוּחַ) to enter the dry bones and bring them back to life (vv. 5–6). However, the issue in this context is not simply about bringing bones back to life, but about the Spirit's life-giving operation, as vv. 11–14 explain.

> [11]Then He said to me, "Son of man, these bones are the whole house of Israel; behold, they say, 'Our bones are dried up, and our hope has perished. We are completely cut off.' [12]Therefore prophesy, and say to them, 'Thus says the Lord GOD, "Behold, I will open your graves and cause you to come up out of your graves, My people; and I will bring you into the land of Israel. [13]Then you will know that I am the LORD, when I have opened your graves and caused you to come up out of your graves, My people.[14]And I will put My Spirit [רוּחַ] within you, and you will come to life, and I will place you on your own land. Then you will know that I, the LORD, have spoken and done it," declares the LORD.'"

---

[32] Zane C. Hodges, "Water and Spirit — John 3:5," *Bibliotheca Sacra* 135 (July–September 1978): 217.

According to these verses, not only does God's future work involve Israel's restoration to the land, but it also emphasizes a placing of God's Spirit within his people to bring them to life. Thus a focus of Ezekiel 37:1–14 is on God's future vivification of his people.[33] As such, this assists in establishing the overall context for Ezekiel 36–37. However, a key informing text for John 3:5 is Ezekiel 36:25–27.

Ezekiel 36:25–27 is set in a new covenant context.[34] This eschatological setting conjoins water and spirit in the context of cleansing from sin and a spiritual transformation.

> [25]Then I will sprinkle clean water on you, and you will be clean; I will cleanse you from all your filthiness and from all your idols. [26]Moreover, I will give you a new heart and put a new spirit [רוּחַ] within you; and I will remove the heart of stone from your flesh and give you a heart of flesh. [27]And I will put My Spirit [רוּחִי] within you and cause you to walk in My statutes, and you will be careful to observe My ordinances.

In v. 25 water cleanses from sin, and in vv. 26–27 God's Spirit (רוּחַ) produces a new heart and new spirit (רוּחַ) that enable obedience to God's law. Though this transformation of heart is for the corporate nation, this would suggest that individuals also undergo a spiritual transformation (cf. Jer 31:31–34).[35] Therefore, Ezekiel 36:25–27 provides a significant informing text for our interpretation of John 3:5.[36]

From the intertestamental period, Judaism reflects the concepts of divine sonship, cleansing and renewal. In the pseudepigraphical book of Jubilees 1:23–25, it is stated by God: "I shall create for them a holy spirit, and I shall purify them so that they will not turn away from following me from that day and forever.... And I shall be a father to them, and they will be sons to me. And they will all be called 'sons of the living God.'"[37]

---

[33] For a development of the details of the connection between Ezekiel 36:26–27 and 37:1–14, see Daniel I. Block, "The Prophet of the Spirit: The Use of *rwh* in the Book of Ezekiel," *Journal of the Evangelical Theological Society* 32 (March 1989): 37–39.

[34] Though בְּרִית ("covenant") is not used in Ezekiel 36:25–27, the placement of God's Spirit within man suggests that this is a new covenant context; see Compton, "An Examination of the New Covenant," pp. 32–33.

[35] Block develops the similarities between Jer 31:31 and Ezek 36:27–28 ("The Prophet of the Spirit," pp. 39–40).

[36] For other connections between Ezekiel and John, see *NIDOTTE*, s.v. "Ezekiel, Theology of," by J. B. Job, 4:633.

[37] For additional texts, see Rudolf Schnackenburg, *The Gospel According to John*, 3 vols., trans. Kevin Smyth, 2nd ed. (New York: Crossroad, 1982), 1:370.

The Qumran community also reflects the motifs of cleansing and renewal. According to the *Rule of the Community,*

> God will refine, with his truth, all man's deeds, and will purify for himself the configuration of man, ripping out all spirit of deceit from the innermost part of his flesh, and cleansing him with the spirit of holiness from every irreverent deed. He will sprinkle over him the spirit of truth like lustral water (in order to cleanse) from all the abhorrences of deceit and from the defilement of the unclean spirit (1QS 4:20–22).[38]

Thus the connection of water and spirit denoting a spiritual transformation finds a parallel in the context of Palestinian Judaism.[39]

In John's gospel, the noun ὕδωρ is found only three times on the lips of Jesus (3:5; 4:7–15; and 7:38–39). In 4:10, 11, 14, Jesus correlates living water with eternal life, and in 7:38–39 he correlates water with the Spirit. This suggests that Jesus uses water as a metaphor for the Spirit in his function of imparting life. If we attribute any significance to the fact that Jesus refers to water in only three contexts and that in two he connects "water" to the Spirit or life, this would suggest that his use of water in the one other context, "3:5 likewise symbolizes the life-giving operation of the Spirit."[40]

An Examination of the Literary Context

To determine the intended meaning of a given passage, we must discover that meaning which is consistent with the sense of its literary context. We will attempt to examine the literary context in two ways. First, we will consider the theological emphasis of John 3. The theological emphasis in this passage is greatly assisted by a number of parallel expressions to γεννηθῇ ἐξ ὕδατος καὶ πνεύματος. Second, we will examine those syntactical features in v. 5 that have an impact on our study of γεννηθῇ ἐξ ὕδατος καὶ πνεύματος.

Parallel Expressions

When John repeats a statement, whether it be Jesus' words or someone else's, part of the Johannine style is to include minor variations in the

---

[38] This translation is taken from Florentino García Martínez, *The Dead Sea Scrolls Translated*, trans. Wilfred G. E. Watson, 2nd ed. (Grand Rapids: Eerdmans, 1996), p. 7.

[39] Schnackenburg, *John*, 1:370.

[40] Dunn, *Baptism*, p. 189.

repeated statements. For example in John 6:35 and 48 Jesus says, "I am the bread of life" (ὁ ἄρτος τῆς ζωῆς); however, he varies this in v. 51, "I am the living bread" (ὁ ἄρτος τῆς ζῶν).[41] In the immediate context of John 3, Jesus informs Nicodemus in v. 3 that unless one experiences the new birth, he cannot "see (ἰδεῖν) the kingdom of God." In v. 5 Jesus replaces ἰδεῖν with εἰσελθεῖν ("enter"). Though entering the kingdom of God may be a slightly stronger statement than seeing the kingdom, the meaning of both is essentially the same.[42] Therefore, "variation of expression is not intended to convey different ideas, but is typical of the style of the Fourth Gospel."[43] Jesus describes the new birth five different times in this passage, yet each statement has a variation as the following reflects:

> γεννηθῇ ἄνωθεν, "born from above" (v. 3) γεννηθῇ ἐξ ὕδατος καὶ πνεύματος, "born of water and the Spirit"(v. 5) τὸ γεγεννημένον ἐκ τοῦ πνεύματος πνεῦμά ἐστιν, "that which is born of the Spirit is spirit" (v. 6) γεννηθῆναι ἄνωθεν, "be born from above" (v. 7) ὁ γεγεννημένος ἐκ τοῦ πνεύματος, "born of the Spirit" (v. 8).

We should initially note that τὸ γεγεννημένον ἐκ τοῦ πνεύματος πνεῦμά ἐστιν ("that which is born of the Spirit is spirit," v. 6), and ὁ γεγεννημένος ἐκ τοῦ πνεύματος ("born of the Spirit," 3:8), are restatements of v. 5, with the exception that ὕδατος καὶ has been eliminated. This suggests that Jesus is emphasizing a birth produced by the Spirit. Though ἄνωθεν in 3:3, 7 is generally translated as "again,"[44] it may also be translated as "from above." Either translation is lexically[45] possible, and there is also a possibility that ἄνωθεν is a double entendre.[46] As such, ἄνωθεν can be taken in three ways. First, some have taken ἄνωθεν as having a double meaning.[47] Support for this has been drawn

---

[41] For a full development of John's use of variation as a stylistic feature, see Leon Morris, *Studies in the Fourth Gospel* (Grand Rapids: Eerdmans, 1969), pp. 293–319; see also Wayne A. Meeks, "The Man from Heaven in Johannine Sectarianism," *Journal of Biblical Literature* 91 (March 1972): 49–55.

[42] Carson, *John*, p. 191.

[43] Snodgrass, "Rebirth and Spirit," pp. 16–17.

[44] The adverb ἄνωθεν is translated as "again" in the KJV, NASB, NIV, and NKJV.

[45] Walter Bauer, William F. Arndt, and F. Wilbur Gingrich, *A Greek-English Lexicon of the New Testament and Other Early Christian Literature*, 2nd ed. revised and augmented by F. Wilbur Gingrich and Frederick W. Danker (Chicago: University of Chicago Press, 1979), p. 77 (hereafter cited as BAGD).

[46] Each translation has its list of supporters; see Morris, *Gospel*, p. 213, n. 13; and Belleville, "Born of Water and Spirit," p. 138, n. 75.

[47] This is the suggestion made by the editors of BAGD, p. 77.

from Johannine style.[48] Though this understanding is perhaps possible, it misses the force of Jesus' argument in vv. 5–8. Second, others have taken ἄνωθεν in a temporal sense as "again." If this is the case, we should understand that Jesus informs Nicodemus that he must reenter his mother's womb and be born a second time.[49] A common support for this interpretation is drawn from Nicodemus's interpretation of Jesus' words in v. 4, "How can a man be born when he is old? He cannot enter a second time into his mother's womb and be born, can he?" The problem with this understanding is that Nicodemus misconstrues Jesus' statement in v. 3. The point of vv. 5–8 is that one needs an impartation of life by the Spirit. Third, other commentators have argued for taking ἄνωθεν in a spatial sense, "from above."[50] With this understanding Jesus informs Nicodemus that he must have a heavenly birth.[51] This understanding is supported from the only three other uses of ἄνωθεν in John, 3:31; 19:11, 23. In each case, ἄνωθεν means "from above."[52]

If we take ἄνωθεν in the third sense, this is another way of clearly indicating that one must be born of God.[53] As such, γεννηθῇ ἄνωθεν is equivalent to John's emphasis in 1 John of being born from God. In our immediate context of John 3, this forms a tight parallel with Jesus' other uses of γεννάω, for in each case Jesus is saying that if one is to enter the kingdom of God, he must be born of the Spirit. Thus, it is this third use of ἄνωθεν that Nicodemus must grasp. Therefore, this tight parallel thought of Jesus provides assistance in understanding what it means to be born of "water and the Spirit." In keeping with this, Hodges appropriately says: "The expression ἐξ ὕδατος καὶ πνεύματος, therefore, which replaces ἄνωθεν in the statement of verse 5, will fit

---

[48] So Grant R. Osborne, *The Hermeneutical Spiral* (Downers Grove, IL: InterVarsity Press, 1991), pp. 88–89; and Barrett, John, pp. 205–6.

[49] From either end of the theological spectrum, this is followed by Rudolf Bultmann, *The Gospel of John*, trans. G. R. Beasle-Murray (Philadelphia: Westminster, 1964) pp. 135–38; and Frederic Louis Godet, *Commentary on John's Gospel* (reprint ed., Grand Rapids: Kregel, 1978), pp. 376–77.

[50] For support of this understanding of ἄνωθεν, see Matthew Vellanickal, *The Divine Sonship of Christians in the Johannine Writings* (Rome: Biblical Institute Press, 1977), pp. 172–74.

[51] Gary M. Burge, *Interpreting the Gospel of John*, Guides to New Testament Exegesis (Grand Rapids: Baker, 1992), pp. 143–44.

[52] NASB's idiomatic translation of the last part of John 19:23 obscures my point. NASB's marginal reading better reflects the use of ἄνωθεν: "woven from the upper part (ἄνωθεν) through the whole." "The upper part" reflects what is above.

[53] Hoekema, *Saved by Grace*, p. 97.

the narrative most naturally if it is seen as an effort to communicate what it really means to be born *from above.*"[54]

Syntactical Features

Two pertinent syntactical items of John 3:5 need to be addressed. First, in v. 5 the preposition ἐκ governs two nouns, ὕδατος and πνευματος, that are coordinated by καί. This indicates that Jesus regards ὕδατος καὶ πνεύματος as a conceptual unity. If ὕδατος καὶ πνεύματος is a conceptual unity, this phrase may be taken either as a "water-spirit" source[55] or a "water-and-Spirit" source of birth.[56] A good case can be presented for either view in the context of John 3:1–8. With either view, there is one birth that is characterized either as "water-spirit," or "water-and-Spirit." Neither of these understandings suggests that there are two births, physical and spiritual. Furthermore, there is no suggestion of a contrast "between an external element of 'water' and an inward renewal achieved by the Spirit."[57] The origin of regeneration is a ὕδωρ and πνεῦμα source.[58]

Second, the anarthrous use of πνεῦμα may suggest that this is not a reference to the Spirit per se, but to "the impartation of God's nature as πνεῦμα."[59] As such, πνεῦμα, like the anarthrous ὕδωρ, would emphasize the quality of the new birth. This is to say, the emphasis of πνεῦμα in v. 5 is on the nature and work of the Spirit, and not on the Spirit as a person.[60] In addition, this use of πνεῦμα could be suggested by the nature of the prepositional phrase in v. 5. The preposition ἐκ governing the two nouns, ὕδωρ and πνεῦμα, coordinated by καί naturally suggests that this phrase is a conceptual unity: a "water-spirit" birth.[61] Furthermore, this use of πνεῦμα as "spirit" is strengthened by a syntactical parallel in John 4:23, "the true worshipers shall worship the Father in spirit and truth (ἐν

---

[54] Hodges, "Water and Spirit," p. 213.

[55] Belleville, "Born of Water and Spirit," p. 135; so also Carson, *John*, p. 195.

[56] Dunn, *Baptism*, p. 192.

[57] *NIDNTT*, s.v. "Prepositions and Theology in the Greek New Testament," by Murray J. Harris, 3:1178.

[58] Carson, *John*, p. 194. This is not the same position as Morris, who takes "water" and "spirit" as having the same referent and, consequently, meaning to be "born of 'spiritual water'" (*Gospel*, p. 218). Instead, "water" and "spirit" have different referents, but they are a part of one birth (Carson, *John*, p. 194, n. 3).

[59] Carson, *John*, p. 194.

[60] Belleville, "Born of Water and Spirit," p. 135, n. 66.

[61] Carson, *John*, p. 194.

πνεύματι καὶ ἀληθείᾳ)." As in 3:5, a preposition (ἐν) governs two nouns, πνεῦμα and ἀλήθεια, coordinated by καί. Thus, in John 4:23 a case can be made that πνεῦμα is not a reference to the person of πνεῦμα, but to the nature of πνεῦμα. As a result, this position argues that ὕδωρ is that which internally purifies and "πνεῦμα that which partakes of the essential nature of God himself."[62]

Though this understanding of πνεῦμα is exegetically compatible with John 3, a legitimate argument can be made for interpreting Jesus' reference to πνεῦμα in 3:5 as a reference to the Holy Spirit. There are three reasons for this. First, an anarthrous noun may be definite;[63] and, if this is so, then the anarthrous use of πνεῦμα in 3:5 may be treated as a definite noun referring to the Holy Spirit. In 7:39 πνεῦμα is used twice. The first use of πνεῦμα is with the article and the second is without it. Both are clearly references to the Holy Spirit. Furthermore, "when the noun is the object of a preposition, it does not *require* the article to be definite: if it has the article, it *must* be definite; if it *lacks* the article, it *may* be definite."[64] Thus, the anarthrous πνεῦμα may be a reference to the Holy Spirit.

Second, as we have argued, the prepositional phrase in John 3:5 (ἐξ ὕδατος καὶ πνεύματος) cogently argues for a conceptual unity. Does this conceptual unity suggest that both ὕδωρ and πνεῦμα focus strictly on a twofold source defining the nature of this spiritual birth, a "water-spirit" birth,[65] as opposed to a "water-and-Spirit" birth? While I recognize that John 4:23 provides support for a "water-spirit" birth, Matthew 3:11, in contrast, provides support for taking this as a "water-and-Spirit" birth. In this text John the Baptist proclaims that Jesus would "baptize with the Holy Spirit and fire (βαπτίσει ἐν πνεύματι ἁγίῳ καὶ πυρί)." As in John 3:5, we have a preposition ἐν governing two anarthrous nouns, πνεῦμα and πυρός. The baptism that would be performed by Jesus is accomplished by two means: the Holy Spirit[66] and fire, with the preposition ἐν embracing

---

[62] Belleville, "Born of Water and Spirit," p. 140.

[63] See Daniel B. Wallace, *Greek Grammar Beyond the Basics* (Grand Rapids: Zondervan, 1996), p. 247; Maximilian Zerwick, *Biblical Greek Illustrated by Examples* (Rome: Pontificii Instituti Biblici, 1963), pp. 58–59; and A. T. Robertson, *A Grammar of the Greek New Testament in the Light of Historical Research* (Nashville: Broadman, 1934), p. 791.

[64] Wallace, *Greek Grammar*, p. 247.

[65] Belleville, "Born of Water and Spirit," p. 140.

[66] In describing the Holy Spirit as a means, I am following Wallace's use of "means" (*Greek Grammar*, p. 374). Christ is the personal agent who baptizes by the instrument of the Holy Spirit. Though the Holy Spirit is a person, He is being used by Christ as His baptizing instrument.

both of these elements. Therefore, we have a "Spirit-and-fire" baptism.[67] Though πνεῦμα, in John 3:5, is not qualified by the adjective ἅγιος, we are suggesting that the prepositional phrase in this verse is analogous to the prepositional phrase in Matthew 3:11. Since "born of water and the Spirit" is parallel with "born from above" in vv. 3, 7 and "born of the Spirit" in vv. 6, 8, this would also provide some support for identifying Jesus' use of πνεῦμα as a reference to the person of the Holy Spirit.[68] While recognizing that a "water-spirit" birth is certainly a conceptual unity, we conclude that a "water-and-Spirit" birth can also be regarded as a valid conceptual unity.[69]

Third, Johannine literature uses a passive form of γεννάω with the preposition ἐκ ("born of") to describe a believer's spiritual birth as originating with God.[70] The construction "born of" is used 14 times in Johannine literature. Excluding John 3:5 for the moment, in every use the object of the preposition denotes the source from which the birth is produced. God is the object of the preposition 10 times,[71] the Spirit 2 times,[72] and the flesh once.[73] In 12 of the 13 examples, God or the Holy Spirit produces spiritual birth. Since John 3:5 contains the same type of construction with πνεῦμα as the object of the preposition, this suggests that Jesus uses πνεῦμα to refer to the Holy Spirit.

Consequently, though it is possible that the anarthrous use of πνεῦμα in 3:5 may be a reference to the nature and work of πνεῦμα, I am convinced from these three reasons that Jesus uses πνεῦμα as a reference to the person of πνεῦμα. However, my point is not to set up an absolute dichotomy between the person of πνεῦμα and the nature imparted as πνεῦμα. In some theological discussions, it is necessary to distinguish between the principle of new spiritual life implanted, regeneration, and the person of the Spirit; however, in contexts focusing on regeneration, as in John 3, regeneration and the Spirit are inseparable. Our contention is

---

[67] *NIDNTT*, s.v. "Prepositions and Theology," 3:1178; see also Dunn, *Baptism*, pp. 8–14; and D. A. Carson, "Matthew," in *The Expositor's Bible Commentary*, 12 vols., ed. Frank E. Gaebelein (Grand Rapids: Zondervan, 1991), 8:105.

[68] Snodgrass, "Rebirth and Spirit," p. 17.

[69] This is also recognized by Harris (NIDNTT, s.v. "Prepositions and Theology," 3:1178), Dunn (*Baptism*, p. 190), and Ladd (*A Theology of the New Testament* [Grand Rapids: Eerdmans, 1974], p. 284).

[70] *NIDNTT*, s.v. "γεννάω," 1:179.

[71] John 1:13; 1 John 2:29; 3:9 (twice); 4:7; 5:1 (twice), 4, 18 (twice).

[72] John 3:6, 8.

[73] John 3:6; this use of σάρξ as the object of ἐκ does not violate our point, for that which comes from human procreation is human in nature (see Hoekema, *Saved by Grace*, p. 98).

that the use of πνεῦμα in v. 5 is the Spirit himself who regenerates. There are two reasons for this contention. First, Jesus maintains in v. 6 that the Spirit produces spiritual life, "that which is born of the Spirit is spirit." It is the Holy Spirit who imparts new spiritual life. Second, an important new covenant context from the Old Testament, Ezekiel 36:26–27, correlates the Spirit with spiritual life. "I [Yahweh] will give you a new heart [לֵב חָדָשׁ] and put [אֶתֵּן] a new spirit [רוּחַ חֲדָשָׁה] within you [בְּקִרְבְּכֶם]" is tantamount to "I will put [אֶתֵּן] My Spirit [רוּחִי] within you [בְּקִרְבְּכֶם]." The parallelism in these two verses suggests an inseparable connection between "new heart," "new spirit," and Yahweh's "Spirit." Therefore, to be born of πνεύματος is to experience new spiritual life produced by the Holy Spirit.

In summation, Jesus has told Nicodemus in 3:5 that, if one is to enter the kingdom of God, he must be the recipient of the life-giving and purifying work produced by the Spirit. This interpretation was supported by comparing γεννάω, ὕδωρ, and πνεῦμα with other uses in Johannine literature and the Old Testament. Comparing v. 5 with other parallel expressions in the immediate context and two syntactical items in this verse further supported it. As Jesus substantiated his case with Nicodemus, he highlighted theological truth about regeneration from key Old Testament texts. As a recognized Jewish teacher, Nicodemus should have been familiar with eschatological contexts such as Isaiah 44 and Ezekiel 36–37, affirming the cleansing and transformation produced by the Spirit. Jesus clarified for Nicodemus how this applied to him. Consequently, being "born of water and the Spirit" is the Spirit's work of cleansing from sin and imparting new spiritual life.[74]

SURVEY OF INTERPRETATIONS

Having examined some of the exegetical and theological aspects of John 3:5, it must now be asked how this verse has been understood by other interpreters. Historically, there have been numerous interpretations of John 3:5.[75] We will summarize and evaluate six leading proposals. The first two views have been dominant interpretations in church history and the last four are interpretations found more currently among interpreters having a high view of bibliology.

---

[74] *Evangelical Dictionary of Biblical Theology*, s.v. "New Birth," by Carl B. Hoch, Jr., pp. 558–59.

[75] For a good examination of various interpretations, see Belleville, "Born of Water and Spirit," pp. 125–34.

Christian Baptism and the Spirit

Many Christian interpreters have interpreted ὕδατος καὶ πνεύματος as a reference to the sacrament of Christian baptism and the Holy Spirit. It is argued that Jesus' use of ὕδωρ in John 3:5 would have readily been identified by a first century audience as the waters of baptism. C. H. Dodd reflects this interpretation when he asserts that "the instructed Christian reader would immediately recognize a reference to Baptism, as the sacrament through which the Spirit was given to believers, and by which they were initiated into that new order of life described as the Kingdom of God, which was historically embodied in the Church."[76]

Though some who take "water" as Christian baptism see Jesus' use of ὕδατος as a reference either to His own baptizing ministry (so Dodd)[77] or to John's (so Lenski),[78] they are united by maintaining that both Jesus' baptizing ministry and John's are part of the one sacrament of Christian baptism.[79] Others of a Christian baptism persuasion do not view ὕδατος καί as coming from the lips of Jesus, but as a later editorial addition to the text. Those maintaining that this is a subsequent addition to Jesus' words fall into two groups. On the one hand, Bultmann maintains that a subsequent ecclesiastical redactor added ὕδατος καί.[80] On the other hand, Bernard maintains that John himself added this to Jesus' words as an interpretation for the following generation.[81] Whether ὕδατος καί is genuine to Jesus or a subsequent interpretative addition to Jesus' words, they are united in their position that ὕδατος is a reference to Christian baptism.

Support for taking ὕδωρ as Christian baptism is drawn from John's other references to the ordinances. In 1:26–34 the Evangelist highlights the baptizing ministry of John the Baptist. In v. 33 "water" and "Spirit"

---

[76] C. H. Dodd, *The Interpretation of the Fourth Gospel* (Cambridge: Cambridge University Press, 1953), p. 309.

[77] Ibid., pp. 310–11.

[78] R. C. H. Lenski, *The Interpretation of St. John's Gospel* (Minneapolis: Augsburg Publishing House, 1943), pp. 237–38.

[79] Dodd, Interpretation, pp. 310–11, and Lenski, *John's Gospel*, p. 23; a secondary reference to baptism is seen by some, such as Brown, *John*, 1:141–42, and Dunn, *Baptism*, pp. 193–94.

[80] Bultmann, *The Gospel of John*, p. 139; this has also recently been followed by Ernst Haenchen, *A Commentary on the Gospel of John*, 2 vols., trans. Robert W. Funk, Hermenia, ed. Robert W. Funk with Ulrich Busse (Philadelphia: Fortress, 1984), 1:206.

[81] J. H. Bernard, *A Critical and Exegetical Commentary on the Gospel According to St. John*, 2 vols., ICC (Edinburgh: T. and T. Clark, 1928), 1:104–5. This is also followed by J. N. Sanders and B. A. Mastin, *A Commentary on the Gospel According to St. John* (London: Adam and Charles Black, 1968), p. 124.

are closely associated. In 3:22 and 4:1 the baptizing ministry of Jesus and his disciples is also emphasized. Further support for a sacramental understanding is drawn from supposed references to the Lord's Supper in John 6. For example, Beasley-Murray says: "As in 6:51ff the exposition on eating the flesh of the Son of Man and drinking His blood cannot fail to bring to mind the Lord's Supper, so the reference to new birth by water and Spirit inevitably directs attention to Christian baptism."[82]

Many advocates of Christian baptism maintain that there is a close connection between Christian baptism and πνεῦμα as a reference to the Holy Spirit. Some would maintain that the new birth takes place at the time of baptism, while others would see a less rigid association between the new birth and baptism. In the former case, Dodd interprets πνεύματος as a reference to the gift of the Spirit that accompanies Christian baptism.[83] Sanders and Mastin state that John believed that baptism conveyed "the gift of the spirit, as the occasion of the new birth."[84] In the latter case, Lenski maintains that "strictly speaking, this repentance (contrition and faith) itself constitutes the rebirth in all adults yet not apart from Baptism which as its seal must follow."[85]

In evaluating this position, we should notice that baptism does not fit with the parallelism of this passage. Because "born of water and the Spirit" is parallel with "born from above" in vv. 3, 7 and "born of the Spirit" in vv. 6, 8, this indicates that the emphasis of this passage is on a birth produced by the Spirit. If the emphasis of John 3 is coordinate with the ten uses of "born of God" in 1 John, this further corroborates our interpretation that "born of water and the Spirit" refers to a birth produced by a divine source. This understanding is further supported in v. 8 where Jesus compares the Spirit's regenerating work with the wind in two ways. First, the Spirit's work is sovereign, "the wind blows where it wishes." In regeneration, the Spirit works monergistically, and not synergistically. Second, the Spirit's life-giving work is mysterious and invisible: "you hear the sound of it, but do not know where it comes from and where it is going." Since water baptism is a visible and comprehensible act, it certainly cannot fit Jesus' analogy in v. 8. The Spirit's work in regeneration "is not bound to any external rite such as baptism."[86]

---

[82] G. R. Beasley-Murray, *Baptism in the New Testament* (Grand Rapids: Eerdmans, 1973), pp. 228–29.

[83] Dodd, *Interpretation*, p. 311.

[84] Sanders and Mastin, *St. John*, p. 124.

[85] Lenski, *John's Gospel*, p. 238.

[86] Gordon R. Lewis and Bruce A. Demarest, *Integrative Theology*, 3 vols. (Grand Rapids: Zondervan, 1994), 3:96.

John's Baptism and the New Birth

A variation of the Christian baptism position is one that takes ὕδωρ as a reference to John's baptism and πνεῦμα to the new birth. According to this view, when Nicodemus heard Jesus refer to a birth ἐξ ὕδατος, he would have naturally thought of John's baptism, for John's baptism was currently creating an immense reaction in Israel.[87] Support for this is further drawn from John 1:33 and 3:23. In 1:33 baptism with water and the Spirit are specifically mentioned, and in 3:23 reference is made to John's baptizing ministry. John's baptism was a baptism of repentance (Matt 3:11). With this view ὕδατος is an outward symbol of an inward repentance.[88]

Those maintaining this view of ὕδατος interpret the connection between ὕδωρ and πνεῦμα in two different ways. First, some see ὕδωρ, a baptism of repentance, and πνεῦμα, the new birth, as coordinate requirements to enter into the kingdom of God.[89] With this understanding, ὕδωρ and πνεῦμα are coordinate. Second, others see John's baptism, though important, as not being sufficient to enter the kingdom of God — there must also be a birth of the Spirit.[90] This understanding sees a contrast between John's baptism and birth of the Spirit.

While this proposal suffers from the same deficiencies as the Christian baptism proposal, it does provide more immediate contextual support, as the references to John's baptism in 1:33 and 3:23 reflect. However, this contextual support is tangential rather than substantive.[91] The point of the references to John's baptism is not to emphasize its importance, but rather to stress its comparative insignificance, as clearly presented in 1:23, 26, and 3:30.[92]

The Word of God and the Spirit

This view maintains that there are two necessary elements in the new birth: the Word of God and the Holy Spirit. Boice summarizes his understanding

---

[87] Frederick Louis Godet, *Commentary on the Gospel of John* (reprint ed., Grand Rapids: Kregel, 1978), p. 379.

[88] B. F. Westcott, *The Gospel According to St. John* (reprint ed., Grand Rapids: Eerdmans, 1971), pp. 49–50; see also Gary M. Burge, *The Anointed Community* (Grand Rapids: Eerdmans, 1987), pp. 162–63.

[89] Westcott, *John*, pp. 49–50.

[90] William Hendriksen, *Exposition of the Gospel According to John*, 2 vols. (Grand Rapids: Baker, 1953), 1:134.

[91] Larry P. Jones, *The Symbol of Water in the Gospel of John* (Sheffield: Sheffield Academic Press, 1997), p. 71.

[92] Belleville, "Born of Water and Spirit," p. 127.

of this passage in this way: "When we see Christ's words in this light, we see that God is here pictured as the Divine Begetter, the Father of His spiritual children, and we learn that the written Word of God together with the working of His Holy Spirit is the means by which the new birth is accomplished."[93] This metaphorical significance of ὕδωρ is seen in Ephesians 5:26 where Paul writes that Christ gave himself for the church "that He might sanctify her, having cleansed her by the washing of water [τοῦ ὕδατος] with the word." The new birth is further connected with the Word of God in passages such as 1 Peter 1:23, "for you have been born again not of seed which is perishable but imperishable, that is, through the living and abiding word of God." Further support is drawn from James 1:18, "In the exercise of His will He brought us forth by the word of truth, so that we might be, as it were, the first fruits among His creatures."[94]

Though we agree that the Holy Spirit uses the Word of God in regenerating the totally depraved sinner, this verse does not emphasize the Spirit's use of the Word of God in the same manner as 1 Peter 1:23. Since seven of the eight uses of ὕδωρ in John picture spiritual vivification, it follows that the eighth use in 3:5 would also be taken in a similar manner. Though Ephesians 5:26 provides support for taking "water" as the Word [ῥῆμα] of God, it seems more likely that Jesus would have used ῥῆμα, as He does in John 6:63, instead of ὕδωρ.[95]

Natural Birth and the New Birth

This view argues that ὕδατος καὶ πνεύματος refer to both a natural birth and a spiritual birth. In order to enter the kingdom of God, it is necessary for one to be physically born and, subsequently, to experience a spiritual birth. This view is supported by connecting ὕδωρ with the amniotic fluid that surrounds an unborn child in its mother's womb and ruptures at

---

[93] James M. Boice, *The Gospel of John* (Grand Rapids: Zondervan, 1985), p. 175.

[94] Homer A. Kent, Jr., *Light in the Darkness* (Grand Rapids; Baker, 1974), p. 60. This view is also supported by Herman A. Hoyt, *The New Birth* (Findlay, OH: Dunham Publishing, 1961), pp. 47–51; and Arthur W. Pink, *Exposition of the Gospel of John*, 3 vols. (Grand Rapids: Zondervan, 1945), 1:110–11. For a variation of this view, where ὕδωρ is taken to be a reference to the Torah, see the citations in Belleville, "Born of Water and Spirit," p. 130.

[95] Hodges, "Water and Spirit," pp. 214–15.

delivery,[96] or by taking it as a metaphor for semen.[97] Witherington draws upon Proverbs 5:15–18 and Canticles 4:12–15 to demonstrate that water is a metaphor for fecundity and reproduction.[98] Contextual support in John 3 is drawn from Nicodemus's reference to a mother's womb in v. 4 and Jesus' apparent interpretation of ὕδατος in v. 6, "That which is born of the flesh is flesh." In support of this understanding, Laney has stated:

> In Jesus' analogy, then, the fleshly, or natural, birth corresponds to being "born of water." During pregnancy the unborn child floats in the amniotic fluid within the mother's womb. During delivery, this water is expelled. The child is literally born "out of water" (*ek hudatos*). The expression "of water" is used here as a figure for physical birth.[99]

However, this view presents some syntactical problems. The syntactical linkage using one preposition to govern two coordinated nouns affirms that one birth associated with "water" and "Spirit" is in view. This syntactical linkage poses a problem if two births, natural and spiritual, are in view. Advocates of this view circumvent this syntactical problem and point to v. 6 to support their view, "That which is born of the flesh is flesh, and that which is born of the Spirit is spirit." The problem with this is that there is a conjunctive relationship between "water" and "Spirit" in v. 5, and a contrastive relationship between "flesh" and "Spirit" in v. 6. Consequently, "water" in v. 5 cannot be equated with "flesh" in v. 6.[100]

Double Metaphor for the New Birth

Another recent interpretation of John 3:5 understands that the new birth is pictured by two metaphors of "water" and "wind" (πνεῦμα). This is the position of Zane Hodges, who argues that ὕδατος καὶ πνεύματος should be consistently translated in their "most natural semantic association....

---

[96] Russell Fowler, "Born of Water and the Spirit (John 3⁵)," *Expository Times* 82 (February 1971): 159, and D. G. Spriggs, "Meaning of 'Water' in John 3⁵," *Expository Times* 85 (February 1974): 149–50.

[97] This is mentioned as a possibility by Ben Witherington III, "The Waters of Birth: John 3.5 and 1 John 5.6–8," *New Testament Studies* 35 (1989): 156. A variation of this view is that "water" represents spiritual semen or seed, see Hugo Odeberg, *The Fourth Gospel* (Amsterdam: B. R. Grüner, 1968), pp. 48–71.

[98] Witherington, "The Waters of Birth," pp. 155–60; see also Margaret Pamment, "Short Notes," *Novum Testamentum* 25 (April 1983): 189–90.

[99] J. Carl Laney, *John* (Chicago: Moody Press, 1992), p. 78.

[100] Gerald L. Borchert, *John 1–11*, New American Commentary (Nashville: Broadman, 1996), p. 170.

The association of 'water and wind' as elements in the physical world is one that is both readily and frequently made."[101] Water and wind are used in the Old Testament as metaphors to picture the quickening work of the Holy Spirit, "water" in Isaiah 44:3–5 and "wind" in Ezekiel 37:9–10.[102] Support for interpreting πνεῦμα as "wind" is found in 3:8 where πνεῦμα is used twice, translated respectively as "wind" and "spirit."[103]

Though there are some commendable elements in Hodges' proposal, his discussion of πνεῦμα is unconvincing. The Johannine use of πνεῦμα is based upon Old Testament material focusing on the Spirit's life-giving work. In John πνεῦμα is consistently used in the sense of "spirit." The only exception to this pattern is where contextual evidence would clearly demand otherwise. Such a case is found in 3:8. Since πνεῦμα is the subject of the verb πνεῖ ("blows"), πνεῦμα must be taken as a reference to "wind." However, πνεῦμα in v. 6 could not make sense if it were not used in its normal sense of "spirit." In fact, the use of πνεῦμα in v. 6 with its consistent sense of "spirit" is what prepares for Jesus' analogical argument where "wind" pictures "spirit."[104] Consequently, Hodges interpretation of πνεύματος in 3:5 as "wind" is improbable.

Purification and the New Birth

This position interprets ὕδατος καὶ πνεύματος as a reference to the purifying and life-giving work of the Holy Spirit. According to this position, Jesus tightly connects ὕδωρ and πνεῦμα to remind Nicodemus of key aspects of Old Testament eschatological promises that focus on God's purifying and transforming activity on behalf of his people.[105] The terms "water" and "spirit" are used in Ezekiel 36:25–27 to stress the Spirit's future purification of His nation.[106] Though the Old Testament promises are primarily related to the nation, advocates of this view maintain that this certainly presupposes that the Spirit would regenerate individuals.[107] Jesus' dropping of the concept of water and, consequently, emphasizing only the Spirit's work in vv. 6–15 further supports this view.[108]

---

[101] Hodges, "Water and Spirit," p. 216.

[102] Ibid., pp. 217–18.

[103] Ibid., p. 216.

[104] Carson, *John*, pp. 193–94.

[105] John Murray, *Redemption—Accomplished and Applied* (Grand Rapids: Eerdmans, 1955), p. 96; Hoekema, Saved by Grace, p. 96; Belleville, "Born of Water and Spirit," p. 134.

[106] Bruce, *John*, p. 84.

[107] Carson, *John*, p. 195.

[108] Belleville, "Born of Water and Spirit," p. 134.

While advocates of this position agree that ὕδωρ is used figuratively for the Spirit's work in cleansing and renewal, the interpretation of πνεῦμα can be taken either as a reference to the implanting of God's nature as spirit,[109] or to the Spirit.[110] Though these are two viable interpretations of πνεῦμα, the evidence suggests that it is preferable to interpret πνεῦμα as a reference to the Holy Spirit. In the final analysis, this view appears to harmonize best with the exegetical and theological details associated with John 3:5.

CONCLUSION

The purpose of this article has been to determine the meaning of "born of water and the Spirit" in John 3:5. Initially, we examined the key concepts and literary context. We next surveyed and evaluated six interpretations of this phrase. From our examination, we understand that Jesus' description of the new birth has two aspects: purification and transformation. Three reasons support this interpretation. First, it harmonizes with the literary context of John 3. Second, this interpretation is consistent with the Johannine use of γεννάω, ὕδωρ, and πνεῦμα. Finally, Jesus' berating Nicodemus in John 3:10 for his failure to comprehend the Old Testament indicates that the new birth is predicated upon the Old Testament. John 3:5 has an informing foundation in Ezekiel 36:25–27 where "water" and "Spirit" are used in parallel. The coordinate relationship between John 3:5 and Ezekiel 36:25–27 demonstrates that "water" is a cleansing from sin, and that God's "Spirit" transforms the heart. In commenting on John 3:5, Murray has appropriately summarized Ezekiel's influence:

> These elements, the purificatory and the renovatory, must not be regarded as separable events. They are simply the aspects which are constitutive of this total change by which the called of God are translated from death to life and from the kingdom of Satan into God's kingdom, a change which provides for all the exigencies of our past condition and the demands of the new life in Christ, a change which removes the contradiction of sin and fits for the fellowship of God's son.[111]

Therefore, we conclude that "born of water and the Spirit" refers to the life-giving and purifying activity of the Spirit.

---

[109] So Belleville, "Born of Water and Spirit," p. 140; and Carson, *John*, p. 195.

[110] A few supporters are Murray (*Redemption*, pp. 96–104), Hoekema (*Saved by Grace*, pp. 96–98), and Ladd (Theology, p. 284).

[111] Murray, *Redemption*, p. 100.

WATER BAPTISM AND THE
FORGIVENESS OF SINS IN ACTS 2:38[1]

R. Bruce Compton

Then Peter *said* to them, "Repent, and let each of you be baptized in the name of Jesus Christ for the forgiveness of your sins, and you shall receive the gift of the Holy Spirit" (Acts 2:38).[2]

Peter's exhortation delivered at Pentecost has been the source of ongoing debate. Virtually all engaged in the debate take the command "be baptized" as referring to water baptism rather than Spirit baptism,[3] and most understand the phrase "the forgiveness of sins" as a synonym for salvation.[4] The question that has stirred the debate is, What is the relationship between the commands "repent" and "be baptized" and the phrase "for the forgiveness of sins"? Or, more specifically, how are we to understand "be baptized…for the forgiveness of sins"? Is Peter identifying water baptism as a condition for salvation, or should Peter's statement be interpreted in some other way?

---

[1] This article appeared in the 1999 issue of *DBSJ*, vol. 4, pp. 3–32.

[2] Πέτρος δὲ πρὸς αὐτούς, μετανοήσατε, [φησίν], καὶ βαπτισθήτω ἕκαστος ὑμῶν ἐπὶ τῷ ὀνόματι Ἰησοῦ Χριστοῦ εἰς ἄφεσιν τῶν ἁμαρτιῶν ὑμῶν καὶ λήμψεσθε τὴν δωρεὰν τοῦ ἁγίου πνεύματος. All translations are the author's own, unless otherwise noted. There are a few minor textual questions with this verse, none of which impacts significantly the debate on its interpretation. See Bruce M. Metzger, *A Textual Commentary on the Greek New Testament*, 2nd ed. (New York: The United Bible Societies, 1994), pp. 261–62. The textual issues are addressed as necessary in the ensuing discussion of the verse.

[3] This identification is supported by the fact that v. 38 distinguishes the command, "be baptized," from the gift of the Spirit, "and you shall receive the gift of the Holy Spirit" (cf. Acts 8:15–17; 10:45–47, where a similar distinction between water baptism and the gift/activity of the Spirit is found). Furthermore, this "gift of the Spirit" is specifically identified in Acts 11:16–17 as Spirit baptism. For other uses of βαπτίζω in Acts referring to water baptism, see 2:41; 8:12–13, 16, 36, 38; 9:18; 10:47–48; 16:15, 33; 18:8; 19:3–5; 22:16. Also see the discussion in *NIDNTT*, s.v. "Baptism, Wash," by G. R. Beasley-Murray, 1:145–46.

[4] By "salvation" it is meant the initial aspects of spiritual redemption and renewal, including regeneration, justification, forgiveness, adoption, etc. Following his exhortation in v. 38 involving the forgiveness of sins, Peter urges his audience in v. 40 to "be saved," thereby associating the concepts of forgiveness and salvation (cf. vv. 21 and 47). See *TDNT*, s.v. "σῴζω," by W. Foerster, 7:996–97. Foerster states, "Again and again in Ac. the content of σωτηρία is the forgiveness of sins, 3:19, 26; 5:31; 10:43; 13:38; 22:16; 26:18."

The purpose of this article is to interact with recent discussions of this verse and to arrive at an interpretation that is consistent with the immediate and larger contexts of Peter's exhortation.[5] The major views on the meaning of the verse are presented first. These are then examined to identify those views that are both syntactically and theologically viable. Finally, a conclusion to the interpretation of the verse is offered.

MAJOR INTERPRETATIONS

Five interpretations are commonly found in the literature on this verse:[6] (1) Baptism as a condition for salvation, normative for the Church; (2) Baptism as a condition for salvation, not normative for the Church; (3) Baptism as a parenthetical remark, not directly related to salvation; (4) Baptism as a sign of conversion-initiation, the evidence of genuine repentance; (5) Baptism as a consequence of salvation, not a condition for salvation.

Baptism as a Condition for Salvation, Normative for the Church

Proponents of this interpretation include both sacramentalists (those who see baptism as the effective means whereby God imparts the grace of salvation)[7] and baptismal regenerationists (those who see baptism simply

---

[5] Recent articles on Acts 2:38, championing diverse understandings of Peter's exhortation, testify to the continuing interest in the verse and to the vitality of the debate over its interpretation. See, for example, Luther B. McIntyre, Jr., "Baptism and Forgiveness in Acts 2:38," *BSac* 153 (January–March, 1996): 53–62 and a response by Ashley L. Camp, "Reexamining the Rule of Concord in Acts 2:38," *ResQ* 39 (1997): 37–42. The use of this verse as a linchpin in support of baptismal regeneration— the belief that water baptism is a prerequisite for salvation— heightens the importance of further examination.

[6] See Lanny Thomas Tanton, "The Gospel and Water Baptism: A Study of Acts 2:38," *Journal of the Grace Evangelical Society* 3 (Spring 1990): 27–52. Tanton lists six views, two of which have been combined under a single designation in this article. Tanton's is a well-researched and reasoned article that provides a helpful survey of the major interpretations of the verse.

[7] Principally in view here are Roman Catholic and Greek or Eastern Orthodox Churches. According to the Council of Trent, session 7, canon 6, "If any one saith, that the sacraments of the New Law do not contain the grace which they signify; or, that they do not confer that grace on those who do not place an obstacle thereunto; as though they were merely outward signs of grace or justice received through faith,…let him be anathema." Canon 8 is even clearer, "If any one saith, that by the said sacraments of the New Law grace is not conferred through the act performed [*ex opere operato*], but that faith alone in the divine promise suffices for the obtaining of grace, let him be anathema" (Philip Schaff, *The Creeds of Christendom, with a History and Critical Notes*, rev. David Schaff [reprint ed., Grand Rapids: Baker, 1985] 2:121–22). In a similar way, the Longer Catechism of

as a step of obedience which, together with faith, is necessary for salvation).[8] The distinction between the two is somewhat artificial in that sacramentalists generally hold to baptismal regeneration.[9] However, not all who hold to baptismal regeneration define baptism as a sacrament. The distinction may be a matter of semantics, but the designation "baptismal regenerationists" is used in this paper for those who would make this distinction.

The two groups take the phrase "for the forgiveness of sins" in Acts 2:38 as modifying both the commands "repent" and "be baptized," and understand the preposition "for" (εἰς) associated with forgiveness as signifying purpose or goal. The resulting translation would be "repent and...be baptized in order to *receive* the forgiveness of your sins." Thus, water baptism, along with repentance, represents a necessary condition for salvation, apart from which one cannot be saved. For example, H. Mueller, a Roman Catholic, writes concerning water baptism, "Described in the NT as the sacramental entrance into the people of God...Baptism into Christ, when received in faith, effects forgiveness of sin, bestows the Holy Spirit, and unites the believer to Christ's Mystical Body."[10] Similarly, Alexander

---

the Eastern Church, article 10, question 284, states, "What is a Mystery or Sacrament? A Mystery or Sacrament is a holy act, through which grace, or, in other words, the saving power of God, works mysteriously upon man" (Schaff, *Creeds*, 2:490). See also *ISBE*, rev. ed., s.v. "Sacraments," by R. Wallace and G. Bromiley, 4:256–58 and *NCE*, 3rd ed., s.v. "Sacraments, Theology of," by J. Quinn, 12:806–13.

[8] The term "baptismal regeneration" comes from an interpretation of passages such as Titus 3:5, "...He saved us by the washing of regeneration and the renewing of the Holy Spirit." Those who fall under this heading view regeneration here as the result of this "washing" and interpret the washing as a reference to water baptism, hence, a regeneration accomplished through water baptism (cf. also John 3:5 and Eph 5:26). Included in this category are the various denominations within the Restoration Movement, including the Christian Church, the Disciples of Christ, and the Churches of Christ. While many of these disavow the term "baptismal regeneration," the concept is applicable nevertheless. See the *Dictionary of Christianity in America*, s.v. "Baptism," by S. Grenz, pp. 105–8; s.v. "Restoration Movement," by J. North, pp. 1005–8; and the *Encyclopedia of Religion in the South*, s.v. "Disciples of Christ," by S. Pearson, pp. 201–5.

[9] For example, the Council of Trent, Catechism, part 2, chapter 2, question 5 states, "... it hence follows that baptism may be accurately and appositely defined to be the sacrament of regeneration by water in the word; for by nature we are born from Adam children of wrath, but by baptism we are regenerated in Christ children of mercy" (J. Donovan, ed. *Catechism of the Council of Trent* [Dublin: James Duffey and Company, 1908], p. 144).

[10] *NCE*, 3rd ed., s.v. "Baptism (in the Bible)," by H. Mueller, 2:54. Note along with this the Council of Trent, session 7, canon 5 (On Baptism), "If any one saith, that baptism is free, that is, not necessary unto salvation: let him be anathema" (Schaff, *Creeds*, 2:123). Mueller's statement is similar to what is found in the Longer Catechism of the Eastern Church, article 10, question 288, "What is Baptism? Baptism is a Sacrament, in which a man who believes, having his body thrice plunged in water...is born again of the Holy Ghost

Campbell, a representative of the baptismal regenerationist group, argues, "To every believer…[water] baptism is a formal and personal remission, or purgation of sins. The believer never has his sins formally washed away or remitted until he is baptized."[11]

It is difficult to know where to place mainline Protestant denominations within this discussion.[12] According to the pertinent confessions, certain of these denominations appear to view water baptism as a sacrament which, when combined with faith, is instrumental in the reception of salvation and, therefore, necessary for salvation.[13] The Augsburg Confession, for example, states, "it [water baptism] is necessary to salvation, and that by Baptism the grace of God is offered."[14] In his Shorter Catechism, Martin Luther remarks on the efficacy of water baptism, "It worketh forgiveness of sins, delivers from death and the devil, and gives everlasting salvation to all who believe, as the Word and promise of God declare."[15]

Others of these denominations, however, demur, preferring to describe baptism as the "ordinary means" that God works in salvation, but allowing that salvation can be received apart from the rite.[16] For example, the Westminster

---

to a life spiritual and holy (Schaff, *Creeds*, 2:491). See also *NCE*, 3rd ed., s.v. "Baptism (Theology of)," by T. De Ferrari, 2:62–68; and the *Oxford Dictionary of the Christian Church*, s.v. "Orthodox Church," pp. 1197–99.

[11] Alexander Campbell and W. L. Maccalla, *A Public Debate on Christian Baptism* (Kansas City: Old Paths Book Club, n.d.), p. 116, quoted in John Mark Hicks, "'God's Sensible Pledge:' The Witness of the Spirit in the Early Baptismal Theology of Alexander Campbell," *Stone-Campbell Journal* 1 (Spring 1998): 14.

[12] In view here are the Lutheran, Anglican, and Reformed Churches, together with those traditions closely associated with these.

[13] See *The Oxford Dictionary of the Christian Church*, s.v. "Baptism," pp. 151–52.

[14] Part 1, article 9 (Schaff, *Creeds*, 3:13). The Lutheran position differs from the Roman Catholic position in at least two respects. The Lutheran Church holds to only two sacraments, Baptism and the Lord's Supper, rather than to the seven of the Catholic Church. In addition, the Lutheran confessions reject the traditional Catholic concept that the sacraments confer saving grace merely by the operation of the sacrament itself (*ex opere operato*).

[15] Small Catechism, part 4, question 2 (Schaff, *Creeds*, 3:85). In his subsequent discussion, Luther is clear to note that faith must be present for the rite to be efficacious (see question 3, *Creeds*, 3:86). A similar view is expressed by the Anglican Church in their Thirty-nine Articles. The twenty-seventh article defines baptism as "…a sign of regeneration or new birth, whereby, as by an instrument, they that receive Baptism rightly are grafted into the Church; the promises of forgiveness of sin, and of our adoption to be the sons of God by the Holy Ghost, are visibly signed and sealed; Faith is confirmed and Grace increased by virtue of prayer unto God" (Schaff, *Creeds*, 3:504–5).

[16] L. Berkhof, *Systematic Theology* (Grand Rapids: Eerdmans, 1941), p. 608. According to the Westminster Confession of Faith, 1647, chapter 27, paragraph 6, "The efficacy of baptism is not tied to that moment of time wherein it is administered; yet,

Confession (1647) adds a note of caution against linking too closely the rite with the spiritual transaction with which it is associated, "Although it is a great sin to contemn or neglect this ordinance, yet grace and salvation are not so inseparably annexed unto it, as that no person can be regenerated or saved without it, or that all that are baptized are undoubtedly regenerated."[17] Perhaps the best approach is to place these denominations generally within this category, while recognizing that not all involved would hold to this interpretation of Acts 2:38 or hold to it with the same degree of dogmatism.

Baptism as a Condition for Salvation, Not Normative for the Church

Defenders of this interpretation fall into one of two groups. The first group, often referred to as ultra-dispensationalists, takes the verse in the same way as the previous view in the sense that repentance and baptism are the necessary conditions for salvation. They limit the application of the verse, however, to first century Jews living in the period between the ministry of Jesus and the start of the Church. Once the Church began (at some point after Acts 2), salvation was conditioned by faith alone.[18] Charles Baker, a well-known proponent of this position, describes the role of water baptism in the period before the Church.

> No religious ordinance ever had the power in itself to impart grace or forgiveness, but it appears very evident that in God's dealings with Israel He

---

notwithstanding, by the right use of this ordinance the grace promised is not only offered, but really exhibited and conferred by the Holy Ghost..." (Schaff, *Creeds,* p. 663).

[17] The Westminster Confession, chapter 27, paragraph 5 (Schaff, *Creeds,* 3:663). Calvin, in his *Institutes* (book 4, chapter 16, section 26), remarks, "The passage [John 5:24] only serves to show that we must not deem baptism so necessary as to suppose that every one who has lost the opportunity of obtaining it has forthwith perished" (John Calvin, *Institutes of the Christian Religion,* trans. Henry Beveridge, 2 vols. [Grand Rapids: Eerdmans, 1966], 2:547).

[18] There is no unanimity among ultra-dispensationalists as to when the Church actually began. The common denominator within this group is that the Church began at some point in Paul's ministry. Baker lists three options championed by ultra-dispensationalists: (1) The Church began with Paul's conversion in Acts 9; (2) the Church began with Paul's call to the ministry in Acts 13; (3) the Church began at the end of Acts with the final rejection of the Kingdom by the Jews (Acts 28:28). Baker himself argues for the second option. See Charles F. Baker, *A Dispensational Theology* (Grand Rapids: Grace Bible College Publications, 1971), pp. 496–505. In any case, ultra-dispensationalists generally hold that water baptism, along with faith, was a condition for salvation during the period of transition. But, with the start of the Church, salvation is conditioned by faith alone. (Baker, *Dispensational Theology,* pp. 407–8; see also pp. 543–54).

channeled His blessings through the instrumentality of ordinances, but not apart from faith. Therefore it would appear that baptism was an ordinance which was an instrumental means of grace....[19]

However, with the dispensation of the Church, Baker avers, "Whereas in other dispensations faith required the exercise of various ordinances and sacrifices, in this present dispensation…it is faith alone apart from such ordinances."[20]

The second group, represented by some traditional dispensationalists,[21] offers an interpretation that is considerably more complex. This group limits the application of the verse to first century Jews who were familiar with the baptizing ministries of both John the Baptist and Jesus. As Zane Hodges writes,

> The situation in Acts 2 is apparently exceptional. It is not repeated in the experience of Gentile converts (Acts 10:43–48).… Neither are such terms presented anywhere in the epistles of the New Testament. They evidently belong to the historic record of God's dealings with that generation of Palestinians who had been exposed to, but had rejected, the ministries of both John the Baptist and Jesus Himself.[22]

Although these Jews were able to obtain justification and eternal life on the basis of faith alone, they had to repent and undergo Christian baptism in order to receive the forgiveness of sins and the gift of the Holy Spirit. "Those who heard Peter's message in Acts 2 and believed it were regenerated at the moment of their faith, whether that occurred before or after their repentance. However, in order to receive the forgiveness of sin and the gift of the Holy Spirit, Peter's audience had to repent and be baptized."[23]

The requirements of Acts 2:38 were placed on these Jews, proponents argue, because of the heinous nature of their sin. They had rejected the message of both John and Jesus and had crucified the Lord. Thus, for these Jews, forgiveness and the gift of the Spirit were conditioned by repentance and water baptism.[24] All other Jews and all Gentiles, in contrast, receive these and the other benefits of salvation on the single condition of faith alone. As Hodges comments, "Normative Christian experience takes the

---

[19] Baker, *Dispensational Theology,* pp. 407–8.

[20] Ibid., p. 408.

[21] The principal advocates of this position are those associated with the Grace Evangelical Society, their most prominent representative being Zane Hodges. See Zane C. Hodges, *The Gospel Under Siege: A Study of Faith and Works* (Dallas, TX: Redención Viva, 1981), pp. 99–107; Tanton, "The Gospel and Water Baptism," pp. 47–52.

[22] Hodges, The Gospel Under Siege, pp. 102–3.

[23] Tanton, "The Gospel and Water Baptism," p. 47.

[24] Hodges, *The Gospel Under Siege,* pp. 102–3.

form set forth in the crucial story of the conversion of Cornelius in Acts 10. There forgiveness and the reception of the Sprit take place at the moment of faith (10:43, 44). Water baptism *follows* and in no way conditions these blessings."[25]

Baptism as a Parenthetical Remark, Not Directly Related to Salvation

Advocates of this position come from both Reformed and dispensational traditions.[26] As with the preceding interpretations, these too argue that the preposition "for" in the prepositional phrase, "for the forgiveness of sins," signifies purpose. However, the phrase itself, along with the reference to the reception of the Spirit that follows, is to be taken exclusively with the command to repent. The second command, "and let each one of you be baptized," is a parenthetical remark and, therefore, does not factor into the equation between repentance and forgiveness.[27] The resultant translation is, "Repent (and let every one of you be baptized in the name of Jesus Christ) in order to *receive* the forgiveness of your sins."

Supporters argue that the command to repent is plural whereas the command to be baptized is singular. The phrase "for the forgiveness of your sins" includes the plural pronoun "your," making the reference plural and linking it with the plural "repent" rather than the singular "be baptized." For example, Stanley Toussaint writes,

> The verb [verse?] makes a distinction between singular and plural verbs and nouns. The verb 'repent' is plural and so is the pronoun 'your' in the clause *so that your sins may be forgiven....* Therefore the verb 'repent' must go with the purpose of forgiveness of sins. On the other hand the imperative 'be baptized' is singular, setting it off from the rest of the sentence.[28]

Proponents further argue that tying forgiveness to repentance alone is consistent with what Peter and Luke say elsewhere about how forgiveness

---

[25] Ibid., p. 104.

[26] The Reformed tradition is represented, for example, by N. B. Stonehouse ("Repentance, Baptism and the Gift of the Holy Spirit," *WTJ* 13 [1949–51]: 13–15), while the dispensational by Stanley D. Toussaint ("Acts," *The Bible Knowledge Commentary*, 2 vols., ed. J. Walvoord and R. Zuck [Wheaton, IL: Victor, 1983], 2:359). Stonehouse does not use the term "parenthesis." He does link both forgiveness and the gift of the Spirit to repentance, speaking of baptism as "subordinated to repentance" (p. 15).

[27] Toussaint describes the preferred view in this way, "A third view takes the clause *and be baptized, every one of you, in the name of Jesus Christ* as parenthetical" ("Acts," *BKC*, 2:359).

[28] Ibid.

is obtained.[29] For instance, the Lord's commission to His disciples recorded by Luke simply states, "and *that* repentance for the forgiveness of sins be proclaimed in His name to all the nations."[30] Here repentance is the sole condition for forgiveness; nothing is said about baptism.[31] Consequently, supporters conclude that Peter's statement in Acts 2:38 should be interpreted in the same way.

Baptism as a Sign of Conversion-Initiation, the Evidence of Genuine Repentance

A variety of interpreters hold to this understanding of the verse.[32] Proponents assert that Christian conversion-initiation involves the three things mentioned in Acts 2:38: repentance, water baptism, and the gift of the Spirit.[33] Of these three items, repentance functions as the efficacious element and the reception of the Spirit as the culminating or concluding element. The significance of water baptism as a factor in conversion-initiation is that, among its other roles, it is the vehicle by which true repentance is expressed. Commenting on forgiveness in Acts 2:38, James Dunn states,

> We have already seen...that in Luke where repentance is joined to water-baptism it is the former alone which is really decisive for forgiveness. So in 2.38, Peter's basic and primary demand is for repentance; the forgiveness of sins can be promised to the baptisand [*sic*] only because his baptism is his act and expression of repentance.[34]

---

[29] Ibid.

[30] Luke 24:47 (καὶ κηρυχθῆναι ἐπὶ τῷ ὀνόματι αὐτοῦ μετάνοιαν εἰς ἄφεσιν ἁμαρτιῶν εἰς πάντα τὰ ἔθνη).

[31] See also Acts 5:31; 10:43.

[32] See especially G. R. Beasley-Murray, *Baptism in the New Testament* (Grand Rapids: Eerdmans, 1962), pp. 31, 35, 43, 90, 100–4, 107–8, 120–22, 263–66, 271–79, 303–5, 393–95, and *Baptism Today and Tomorrow* (New York: St. Martin's Press, 1966), pp. 13–32; James D. G. Dunn, *Baptism in the Holy Spirit* (London: SCM Press, 1970), pp. 4–7, 90–93, 96–102, 227–29; Richard N. Longenecker, "Acts," in *The Expositor's Bible Commentary*, 12 vols., ed. F. E. Gaebelein (Grand Rapids: Zondervan, 1981), 9:283–85, 287; Richard E. Averbeck, "The Focus of Baptism in the New Testament," *GTJ* 2 (Fall 1981): 265–301.

[33] According to this view, repentance and the gift of the Spirit address the inward subjective aspects of conversion, while water baptism designates the external objective rite of initiation. Supporters aver that becoming a Christian embraces both conversion and initiation, hence the designation conversion-initiation. Cf. Dunn, *Baptism in the Holy Spirit*, pp. 6–7.

Furthermore, advocates recognize that the sequence between water baptism and the gift of the Spirit varies in the conversion accounts in Acts. Sometimes, for example, water baptism is mentioned before the gift of the Spirit as in Acts 8:14–17 with the Samaritan converts and in Acts 19:1–6 with John's disciples in Ephesus. At other times, water baptism is mentioned after the gift of the Spirit as in Acts 10:44–48 with the conversion of Cornelius.[35] Because Acts 2:38 is in a position of prominence— it is placed early in the conversion accounts in Acts and is associated with the events surrounding Pentecost— supporters argue that the sequence in Acts 2:38 is normative for the Church. The other conversion accounts in Acts are simply *ad hoc* variations of this intended pattern.[36] According to Richard Longenecker, "We should understand Peter's preaching at Pentecost as being theologically normative for the relation in Acts between conversion, water baptism, and the…Holy Spirit, with the situations having to do with the Samaritan converts, Cornelius, and the twelve whom Paul met at Ephesus…to be more historically conditioned and circumstantially understood."[37]

Applying all of this to the verse itself, adherents argue that the preposition "for" shows purpose and that the prepositional phrase "for the forgiveness of sins" modifies both commands.[38] The focus with the second command, "be baptized," is not on the ordinance itself, however, but on what the ordinance signifies. In other words, water baptism is viewed as an initiatory rite where the believer not only publicly identifies with Christ, but also publicly gives allegiance to Christ.[39] Peter's first command was

---

[34] Dunn, *Baptism in the Holy Spirit,* pp. 97–98. Averbeck adds, "The point is that baptism was not the means of obtaining regeneration. Rather, it was an *instrument* adopted by the apostles and the apostolic church…for the purpose of *implementing* the *expression* of the repentance necessarily associated with regeneration as well as the discipleship commitment that was inherent within that repentance [emphasis original]" ("The Focus of Baptism in the New Testament," p. 292, n. 66. See also Beasley-Murray, *Baptism in the New Testament,* p. 35, 100–2, 120–21, 271–72.

[35] See Dunn, *Baptism in the Holy Spirit,* p. 90; Longenecker, "Acts," 9:284.

[36] Dunn, *Baptism in the Holy Spirit,* pp. 90–91. He states, "Luke probably intends Acts 2.38 to establish the pattern and norm for Christian conversion-initiation in his presentation of Christianity's beginnings. At the close of the first Christian sermon the leading apostle sets the precedent for the instruction of enquirers" (p. 90).

[37] Longenecker, "Acts," 9:285. See also Dunn, *Baptism in the Holy Spirit,* pp. 90–91.

[38] E.g., Averbeck, "The Focus of Baptism in the New Testament," p. 292.

[39] Averbeck states, "As part of the new believer's incorporation into the Christian community he or she must be baptized…. In effect, the initiate by his submission to baptism, declared himself a disciple of Christ and committed himself to the kind of lifestyle pertinent to that declaration" ("The Focus of Baptism in the New Testament," p. 288).

for the hearers to repent of their sins. Those whose repentance was sincere would obey Peter's second command and be baptized, thus identifying with Christ and proclaiming publicly their allegiance to Him. Hence, it is these, the ones who were baptized as an expression of their true repentance, who had their sins forgiven and who received the gift of the Holy Spirit. Technically, then, water baptism is understood here not so much as a condition for forgiveness and the Spirit as it is the mark of those whose repentance is genuine. As F. F. Bruce comments,

> It would indeed be a mistake to link the words "for the forgiveness of sins" with the command "be baptized" to the exclusion of the prior command to repent. It is against the whole genius of biblical religion to suppose that the outward rite could have any value except insofar as it was accompanied by the work of grace within.... So here the reception of the Spirit is conditional not on baptism in itself but on baptism in Jesus' name as the expression of repentance.[40]

Baptism as a Consequence of Salvation, Not a Condition for Salvation

This view too has a variety of supporters.[41] These take the phrase "for the forgiveness of sins" as modifying only the second command, the command to be baptized. Unlike the previous interpretations, however, forgiveness is viewed here, not as the goal or outcome of baptism, but rather as the basis or motivation for it. In other words, Peter is saying, "repent, and [having done that] let everyone of you be baptized in response to the forgiveness of sins." The critical difference here is the interpretation of the preposition "for" (εἰς). As with the previous views, it can point to the purpose or goal of that which precedes it. However, proponents argue that it can also

---

[40] F. F. Bruce, *The Book of Acts,* rev. ed., NICNT (Grand Rapids: Eerdmans, 1988), p. 70. Averbeck concurs, "The Qumran emphasis upon repentance as the key to real efficacy in water informs us concerning the intent of this type of statement. As mentioned previously, even John, in his preaching, made it clear that his baptism was only valid if accompanied by genuine repentance (Matt 3:5–8; Luke 3:7–8). This association of baptism with repentance was carried directly into the church. The rite, as far as the NT canon is concerned, found its formative and ideological base in John the Baptist. Neither John the Baptist nor the apostolic church would have conceived of the rite as being efficacious in the absence of genuine repentance" ("The Focus of Baptism in the New Testament," p. 292). See also Dunn, *Baptism in the Holy Spirit,* p. 100.

[41] Included are A. T. Robertson, *A Grammar of the Greek New Testament in Light of Historical Research* (Nashville: Broadman, 1934), p. 592 and, especially, *Word Pictures in the New Testament,* 6 vols. (Nashville: Broadman, 1930), 3:35–36; H. E. Dana and Julius R. Mantey, *A Manual Grammar of the Greek New Testament* (New York: Macmillan, 1927), pp. 103–5; James A. Brooks and Carlton L. Winbery, *Syntax of New Testament Greek* (Lanham, MD: University Press of America, 1979), p. 60.

identify the cause or basis for what precedes it. In the latter case, it would be translated "because of," "in response to," or "on the basis of." Thus, Peter is saying that those who responded to his message and repented are to be baptized because, having repented, their sins are [already] forgiven.

Although the causal use of this preposition is not common in the New Testament, advocates note, neither is it unprecedented. As A. T. Robertson comments,

> In themselves the words can express aim or purpose for that use of *eis* does exist as in 1 Cor. 2:7 *eis doxan hēmōn* (for our glory). But then another usage exists which is just as good Greek as the use of *eis* for aim or purpose. It is seen in Matt. 10:41 in three examples *eis onoma prophētou, dikaiou, mathētou* where it cannot be purpose or aim, but rather the basis or ground, on the basis of the name of prophet, righteous man, disciple, because one is, etc. It is seen again in Matt. 12:41 about the preaching of Jonah (*eis to kērugma Iōnā*). They repented because of (or at) the preaching of Jonah. The illustrations of both usages are numerous in the N.T. and the *Koine* generally.[42]

Furthermore, elsewhere in Luke-Acts, the forgiveness of sins is normally associated with repentance and/or faith and not with baptism at all.[43] In fact, defenders argue, with the possible exception of Acts 22:16, there is no other passage in Acts where baptism is "presented as bringing about the forgiveness of sins."[44]

ANALYSIS AND EVALUATION

Although the meaning of the verse is highly contested, several points can be established that will help in arriving at a proper interpretation. The above views will be critiqued in connection with the discussion of these points. The critique itself focuses on the salient problem(s) identified with each view.

---

[42] Robertson, *Word Pictures in the New Testament,* 3:35. For others who allow for a limited use of the preposition in this sense, in addition to those already mentioned, see Maximilian Zerwick, *Biblical Greek,* trans. J. Smith (Rome: Pontifical Biblical Institute, 1963), p. 32; Nigel Turner, *A Grammar of New Testament Greek* (Edinburgh: T. & T. Clark), 3:255 (but note 3:266–67); *TDNT,* s.v. "εἰς," by A. Oepke, 2:427–28. On the issue of extra-biblical examples, see the debate between J. R. Mantey ("The Causal Use of *Εἰς* in the New Testament," *JBL* 70 [1951]: 45–48; "On Causal *Εἰς* Again," *JBL* 71 [1952]: 309–11) and Ralph Marcus ("On Causal *Εἰς,*" *JBL* 70 [1951]: 129–30; "The Elusive Causal *Εἰς,*" *JBL* 71 [1952]: 43–44).

[43] E.g., Luke 24:47; Acts 3:19; 5:31; 10:43; 13:38–39; 26:18.

[44] See John B. Pohill, *Acts,* New American Commentary (Nashville: Broadman, 1992), p. 117.

Baptism as a Condition for Salvation,
Normative for the Church

Supporters argue that the prepositional phrase "for the forgiveness of sins" modifies both commands "repent" and "be baptized." The preposition itself signifies purpose or goal and makes water baptism, as well as repentance (and faith), a condition for salvation. The chief problem with this interpretation is that by making water baptism a condition for salvation it appears to violate the gracious nature of the gospel. In other words, salvation is no longer by faith alone, but by faith plus water baptism.

The tension here is that Peter's statement needs to be interpreted in harmony with what Scripture teaches elsewhere regarding salvation. This point expresses a standard principle of interpretation. Namely, we are to interpret the difficult passages in the Bible in light of those passages whose teachings are clear.[45] Taken in their entirety, the Scriptures describe salvation as an unmerited gift, received by faith and not by works.[46] Paul states in Romans 3:24, 28, "being justified as a gift by His grace through the redemption that is in Christ Jesus,…we maintain that a man is justified by faith apart from works of the law."[47] The same is found in Ephesians 2:8–9, "for by grace you have been saved through faith; and this not of yourselves, it is the gift of God; not of works, so that no one can boast."[48]

Those defending water baptism as a condition for salvation argue that the works in view in these passages should be limited either to those associated with the Mosaic regulations or to those done in a legalistic spirit. In other words, passages such as these do not rule out all works as a basis for salvation, only those improperly motivated or those based on the Old Testament Law. However, these interpretations are problematic.[49] Paul's exclusion in Romans 3:28 and elsewhere is not limited to works of the Law or to works with wrong motivations. His exclusion is open-ended.

---

[45] See Bernard Ramm, *Protestant Biblical Interpretation,* 3rd ed. (Grand Rapids: Baker, 1970), pp. 104–7. Ramm identifies two overlapping principles germane to this discussion. The first is that "obscure passages in Scripture must give way to clear passages" (p. 104). The second is the "analogy of faith" by which he means "that the interpretations of specific passages must not contradict the total teaching of Scripture on a point" (p. 107).

[46] See Gen 15:6; Hab 2:4; John 20:31; Rom 3:21–28; 4:1–5; Gal 2:16; 3:8–14; etc.

[47] δικαιούμενοι δωρεὰν τῇ αὐτοῦ χάριτι διὰ τῆς ἀπολυτρώσεως τῆς ἐν Χριστῷ Ἰησοῦ·…λογιζόμεθα γὰρ δικαιοῦσθαι πίστει ἄνθρωπον χωρὶς ἔργων νόμου.

[48] τῇ γὰρ χάριτί ἐστε σεσῳσμένοι διὰ πίστεως· καὶ τοῦτο οὐκ ἐξ ὑμῶν, θεοῦ τὸ δῶρον· οὐκ ἐξ ἔργων, ἵνα μή τις καυχήσηται.

[49] See R. Bruce Compton, "James 2:21–24 and the Justification of Abraham," *DBSJ* 2 (Fall 1997): 24–26.

Paul is using "works of law"[50] in the sense of anything done in obedience to God's Word and, by extension, anything that a person does. As others have argued,

> (1) The closest Paul comes to a definition of "works" is in Romans 9:10–11, where "works" refers to anything that a person does, whether "good or bad." (2) In Romans 4:1ff., the "works" of Abraham, in which he could not boast, clearly refer to good works— hence the potential for Abraham's boasting (cf. Rom 3:27). At the same time, the Abraham illustration in Romans 4 is closely tied to Paul's argument in Romans 3:20–28 where "works of law" is used. (3) What appears to be the case is that Paul uses "works of law" in 3:20–28 to refer to a specific kind of works, those done in obedience to the Mosaic Law, in order to show that even these are excluded. (4) At the same time, from Romans 4 and elsewhere, it may be seen that Paul's purpose in Romans 3:28 "is to exclude *all* works—not just certain works or works done in a certain spirit—as a basis for justification."[51]

Although faith is described in Scripture as an act of obedience and, specifically, as an act of obedience in response to the gospel, yet this does not make faith a work.[52] Faith is not some task that a person performs. Rather, it is the response of the will that trusts in what God has accomplished in providing salvation through the person and work of Christ.[53] In that sense, faith and works are antithetical.[54] Salvation, as Paul and others declare, is

---

[50] ἔργων νόμου. The phrase also occurs in Rom 3:20; 9:32; Gal 2:16; 3:2, 5, 10. The genitive is variously identified as objective, subjective, possessive, etc. Regardless, the meaning appears clear. The expression refers to works required by the Law or done in response to the Law. See Douglas J. Moo, *The Epistle to the Romans,* NICNT (Grand Rapids: Eerdmans, 1996), p. 209, n. 61; Joseph A. Fitzmyer, *Romans,* AB (Garden City, NY: Doubleday, 1993), pp. 337–38.

[51] This represents a synopsis of Douglas J. Moo's arguments (*The Letter of James,* TNTC [Grand Rapids: Eerdmans, 1985], pp. 101–2), which was developed in Compton, "James 2:21–24 and the Justification of Abraham," p. 25, n. 24. See also D. J. Moo, "'Law,' 'Works of the Law' and Legalism in Paul," *WTJ* 45 (Spring 1983): 73–100, esp. pp. 90–100; *The Epistle to the Romans,* pp. 209–10.

[52] Cf. Rom 10:16; 2 Thess 1:8. For a discussion of the pertinent constructions, see Moo, *The Epistle to the Romans,* pp. 51–53.

[53] See *ISBE,* s.v. "Faith," by G. W. Bromiley, 2:271–72; Leon Morris, *The Epistle to the Romans* (Grand Rapids: Eerdmans, 1988), pp. 196–99. Morris states, "This is not to regard it [faith] as a meritorious work; it is the very absence of all work…. Paul is speaking of a system that requires him to produce nothing. All he does is to reach out in faith for God's good gift" (p. 99). For a definition of faith, see the discussion below under the subheading "The Command to Repent."

[54] As Jas 2:14–26 and other passages indicate, faith and works are not ultimately antithetical. They are antithetical only insofar as they are viewed as the basis for salvation. The importance of works in connection with faith may be seen in that works serve as the

based on the principle of faith and not on the principle of works, whether good or otherwise. In fact, in Romans 4 and elsewhere, Paul argues that faith and works are mutually exclusive principles as a basis for salvation (See Rom 3:27; 4:4–5, 13–14; Gal 3:18).[55]

This being the case, the view that identifies water baptism as a condition for salvation violates this principle. There is every indication that water baptism falls within the definition of a work and therefore cannot be a condition for salvation. A comparison between circumcision in the Old Testament and water baptism in the New Testament supports this conclusion: Both are religious ceremonies. Both were commanded by God. Both involve an act of obedience. Both are one-time acts. Both are somewhat passive in the sense that the participant is acted upon by another. Paul's argument in Romans 4 regarding the salvation of Abraham requires circumcision to be understood as a work, albeit a good work (See Rom 3:27–4:25).[56] By definition, then, circumcision could not have been a condition for Abraham's salvation, a point Paul establishes in Romans 4:9–11. The same must be said of water baptism. By definition, it too is a work. Therefore, Acts 2:38 cannot be requiring water baptism as a condition for salvation.

Baptism as a Condition for Salvation, Not Normative for the Church

As with the preceding interpretation, advocates take the prepositional phrase "for the forgiveness of sins" as modifying both commands "repent" and "be baptized." The preposition indicates purpose and identifies both

---

necessary evidence of genuine faith. As such, though, works are the fruit of salvation, not its condition. See Compton, "James 2:21–24 and the Justification of Abraham," pp. 19–45.

[55] See, especially, John Murray, *The Epistle to the Romans,* NICNT (Grand Rapids: Eerdmans, 1977), pp. 122–23; 132–33; 140–43. Similarly, C. K. Barrett, *A Commentary on the Epistle to the Romans,* HNTC (New York: Harper & Row, 1957), pp. 82, 88, 94–95; Morris, *The Epistle to the Romans,* pp. 185–86; 197–99; 205–6; Moo, *The Epistle to the Romans,* pp. 246–50; 263–65; 273–75; Thomas Schreiner, *Romans,* Baker Exegetical Commentary on the New Testament (Grand Rapids: Baker, 1998), pp. 213–15. Schreiner comments on Paul's argument in Rom 4, "Verses 4–5 restate the substance of verses 2–3, so that the polarity between faith and works will be grasped. Paul specifically and emphatically contrasts 'working' and 'believing' in verses 4–5" (pp. 214–15).

[56] See Morris, *The Epistle to the Romans,* pp. 193, 201–2, 205; Moo, *The Epistle to the Romans,* pp. 267, 273; Schreiner, *Romans,* pp. 228–29. Commenting on Paul's argument involving Abraham's circumcision in Rom 4:9–12, Morris notes, "Paul insisted that it is faith (and by implication not any outward ceremony) that brings salvation" (p. 201). A similar argument is put forward by Paul in Gal 5:2–12. See, for example, Ronald Y. K. Fung, *The Epistle to the Galatians,* NICNT (Grand Rapids: Eerdmans, 1988), p. 221.

repentance and water baptism as conditions for salvation. However, supporters limit the application of the verse in one of two ways. Ultra-dispensationalists limit its application by placing it before the start of the church. They argue that for the church salvation is by faith alone. For those saved before the church, salvation was by both faith and water baptism. Certain other dispensationalists limit the application of the verse by restricting it to those Jews who rejected the ministry of the Lord and who were guilty of crucifying Him. These Jews could receive some of the benefits of salvation by faith alone. But, in order to receive forgiveness and the gift of the Spirit, these Jews must repent and be baptized.

The problems with this interpretation are two-fold. For the ultra-dispensationalists, the problem is over the starting point of the church. For the other dispensationalists holding to this interpretation, the problem is over the relationship of faith and repentance.

The Command to Repent

As mentioned above, the issue here is not so much the meaning of the command as it is the relationship between repentance and faith. For the sake of discussion, the New Testament word group representing repentance[57] is defined in its theological use as a fundamental change of mind,[58] and, in particular, a change of mind about God, sin, and the need of salvation.[59] In his message to the Athenians at the Areopagus, Paul declares, "since we are God's offspring, we should not think that the divine being is like gold or silver or stone, an image formed by man's skill and thought. God has overlooked these times of ignorance *but* now commands all men everywhere to repent, in that He has set a day wherein He will judge the world in righteousness."[60] Here, Paul calls for repentance involving

---

[57] The principal Greek words associated with repentance in the New Testament are ἐπιστρέφω, μεταμέλομαι, μετανοέω, and μετάνοια.

[58] *NIDNTT,* s.v. "Conversion et al.," by F. Laubach, 1:355; *ISBE,* s.v. "Repent," by B. H. DeMent and E. W. Smith, 4:136; *ABD,* s.v. "Repentance," by A. Boyd Luter, Jr., 5:672. For example, DeMent and Smith state, "...the exhortations of the ancient prophets, of Jesus, and of the apostles show that the change of mind is the dominant idea of the words employed...." Luter concurs, "The generally recognized core idea of these words is a 'change of mind.'"

[59] "Intellectually, human beings must apprehend sin as unutterably heinous, the divine law as perfect and binding, and themselves as falling short of the requirements of a holy God" (*ISBE,* s.v. "Repent," by B. H. DeMent and E. W. Smith, 4:136).

[60] Acts 17:29–31a (γένος οὖν ὑπάρχοντες τοῦ θεοῦ οὐκ ὀφείλομεν νομίζειν χρυσῷ ἢ ἀργύρῳ ἢ λίθῳ, χαράγματι τέχνης καὶ ἐνθυμήσεως ἀνθρώπου, τὸ θεῖον εἶναι ὅμοιον. τοὺς μὲν οὖν χρόνους τῆς ἀγνοίας ὑπεριδὼν ὁ θεός, τὰ νῦν παραγγέλλει

a change of mind because of the Athenians' misconceptions about God, misconceptions which will certainly bring divine judgment if they are not corrected.[61] This fundamental change of mind in New Testament repentance includes an emotional dimension involving sorrow over sin.[62] In terms of the emotional aspect, Paul speaks of a "godly [produced] sorrow" bringing about a "repentance *that leads* to salvation."[63] True repentance entails a volitional element as well, an element that expresses itself in a decisive turning from sin.[64] Paul describes repentance in Acts 26:18–20 as a turning "from darkness to light and from the power of Satan to God."

The word group representing the concept of faith in the New Testament[65] is defined in its active or subjective sense[66] as the unreserved and undivided trust[67] in God and, specifically, in His provision for salvation through the person and work of Christ.[68] For example, in John 3:16, John records that God sent His Son into the world so that humanity might not perish but, by believing

---

τοῖς ἀνθρώποις πάντας πανταχοῦ μετανοεῖν, καθότι ἔστησεν ἡμέραν ἐν ᾗ μέλλει κρίνειν τὴν οἰκουμένην ἐν δικαιοσύνῃ). See also 2 Tim 2:25.

[61] See, for example, Bruce, *The Book of Acts,* p. 340, "If ignorance of the divine nature was culpable before, it is inexcusable now. Let all people everywhere (the Athenian hearers included) repent therefore of their false conception of God...and embrace the true knowledge of his being now made available in the gospel."

[62] "A change in emotional attitude is necessarily involved in genuine repentance.... Before there can be a hearty turning away from unrighteousness, there must be a consciousness of sin's effect on humanity and its offensiveness to God.... But the type of grief that issues in repentance must be distinguished from that which simply plunges into remorse. There is a godly sorrow and a worldly sorrow: the former brings life, the latter death (cf. Mt. 27:3–5; Lk. 18:23; 2 Cor. 7:9f.)" (*ISBE,* s.v. "Repent," 4:136).

[63] 2 Cor 7:10 (ἡ γὰρ κατὰ θεὸν λύπη μετάνοιαν εἰς σωτηρίαν ἀμεταμέλητον ἐργάζεται·).

[64] "Repentance is that change of a sinner's mind that leads him or her to turn from evil ways and live" (*ISBE,* s.v. "Repent," 4:136). As may be seen from the definition, genuine repentance involves "the entire personality, including the intellect, the emotions, and the will" (Ibid.).

[65] The principal Greek words associated with faith in the New Testament are πιστεύω, πίστις, and πιστός.

[66] This would be in contrast to the passive or objective sense of faith involving a body of truths which together comprise the content of what is to be believed. For example, Jude states in v. 3 "exhorting [you] to contend for the faith that has been once for all delivered to the saints." See *ISBE,* s.v. "Faith," 2:270

[67] *TDNT,* s.v. "πιστεύω κτλ.," by R. Bultmann and A. Weiser, 6:203; *ISBE,* s.v. "Faith," 2:270; *NBD2,* s.v. "Faith," by L. Morris, pp. 366–67. For example, Bromiley states, "The main sense of the word 'faith' in the NT is that of trust or reliance" (*ISBE*).

[68] See *NBD2,* s.v. "Faith," pp. 366–67. Morris writes, "The stress on faith is to be seen against the background of the saving work of God in Christ. Central to the NT is the thought that God sent his Son to be the Saviour of the world.... It is the attitude of complete trust in Christ, of reliance on him alone for all that salvation means."

on His Son, have eternal life. Similar to repentance, genuine faith has both an intellectual and a volitional dimension.[69] In terms of the intellectual, faith entails a knowledge of the facts contained in the gospel, a comprehension of the truths communicated about God and His provision of salvation in Christ.[70] As Paul declares in Romans 10:14, 17, "How then shall they call upon Him in whom they have not believed? And how shall they believe in Him whom they have not heard? And how shall they hear without a preacher?... So then, faith *comes* from hearing and hearing by the word of Christ."[71] Accordingly, a person believes based on the message heard, and the message heard specifically includes the revelation about Christ.

The volitional aspect of faith, on the other hand, involves the idea of reliance or trust. As such, faith represents a confidence in the truths of the gospel and a surrender or commitment to them and to their author for salvation.[72] Thus, the writer of Hebrews describes the message of salvation as "the elementary teachings about Christ." In connection with these teachings, the writer contrasts a confidence or trust in works, which must be abandoned ("repentance from dead works"), with a confidence or trust in God, which must be embraced

---

[69] *ISBE,* s.v. "Faith," pp. 270–71; L. Berkhof, *Systematic Theology* (Grand Rapids: Eerdmans, 1941), pp. 503–6. Berkhof at the outset identifies faith as composed of three elements — knowledge (intellect), assent (emotion), trust (will); he concludes by combining knowledge and assent as constituents within the intellectual element (p. 505). See also Anthony A. Hoekema, *Saved by Grace* (Grand Rapids: Eerdmans, 1989), pp. 140–43.

[70] *ISBE,* s.v. "Faith," p. 271. Again, Bromiley states, "To have faith in a person is to believe certain things about this person, his nature, word, and work.... One cannot really trust in Jesus Christ without believing that He is the Messiah, the incarnate Son, the crucified and risen Savior. The words and works, the essential being of Jesus, are all part of His person.... True faith is confident attachment to the Jesus of the NT."

[71] Πῶς οὖν ἐπικαλέσωνται εἰς ὃν οὐκ ἐπίστευσαν; πῶς δὲ πιστεύσωσιν οὗ οὐκ ἤκουσαν; πως δὲ ἀκούσωσιν χωρὶς κηρύσσοντος;...ἄρα ἡ πίστις ἐξ ἀκοῆς, ἡ δὲ ἀκοὴ διὰ ῥήματος Χριστοῦ. See *ISBE,* s.v. "Faith," p. 271. Bromiley concludes, "The content of faith is given in and by the Word of God. The Word of God is, of course, Jesus Himself. But it is also the word written and the word preached.... It is by receiving and believing the words and works recorded in Holy Scripture and proclaimed by ministers of the gospel that Jesus Himself is received and believed."

[72] *TDNT,* s.v. "πιστεύω κτλ.," 6:210–12. Bultmann notes, "Faith accepts the existence of Christ and its significance for the believer. It rests on the message, but as faith in the message it is faith in the person whom the message mediates" (*TDNT,* one vol. ed., s.v. "πιστεύω κτλ.," p. 854).

("faith in God").[73] Scripture speaks of both repentance and faith as gifts from God.[74]

On the level of their respective definitions, repentance and faith are complementary activities. Repentance is the turning from sin, while faith is the corresponding turning to God. As mentioned earlier, Paul describes the purpose or goal of the Lord's sending him to the Gentiles in Acts 26:18 as "to open their eyes so that they may turn from darkness to light and from the power of Satan to God, in order that they may receive forgiveness of sins and an inheritance among those who have been sanctified by faith in Me."[75] This "turning to God" Paul defines in the last part of the verse as faith, and the "turning from darkness" he defines in v. 20 as repentance ("...that they should repent and turn to God").[76]

An examination of how these terms are used in salvation contexts substantiates the inter-relationship between the two concepts. Scripture identifies repentance and faith not only individually, but also collectively as the sole prerequisites for salvation. Thus, in Acts, for example, forgiveness of sins is linked with repentance in 3:19 and 5:31, with faith in 10:43, and with both repentance and faith in 26:18, 20. What must be concluded from this is that repentance and faith are fundamental corollaries; they are essentially two sides of the same coin.[77] Both must be exercised in

---

[73] Heb 6:1 (Διὸ ἀφέντες τὸν τῆς ἀρχῆς τοῦ Χριστοῦ λόγον ἐπὶ τὴν τελειότητα φερώμεθα, μὴ πάλιν θεμέλιον καταβαλλόμενοι μετανοίας ἀπὸ νεκρῶν ἔργων καὶ πίστεως ἐπὶ θεόν,). A number of interpreters define the dead works here in terms of vices or sinful behavior, based on the use of the expression in 9:14 (see F. F. Bruce, *The Epistle to the Hebrews,* rev. ed., NICNT [Grand Rapids: Eerdmans, 1990], pp. 139–40). However, the Jewish background and orientation of Hebrews would argue that dead works refers to cultic observances, works of the Law. What is in view with the expression "repentance from dead works" is a turning away from confidence in such observances for salvation. See Homer A. Kent, *The Epistle to the Hebrews: A Commentary* (Grand Rapids: Baker, 1972), p. 106; William L. Lane, *Hebrews,* 2 vols., WBC (Dallas: Word, 1991), 1:140; and the discussion in Philip Edgcumbe Hughes, *A Commentary on the Epistle to the Hebrews* (Grand Rapids: Eerdmans, 1977), pp. 197–98.

[74] For repentance as a gift, see Acts 5:31 ("This one God exalted...to grant repentance to Israel, and the forgiveness of sins.") and Acts 11:18 ("Therefore to the Gentiles also God has granted the repentance *that leads* to life."). For faith, see Phil 1:29 ("For it has been granted to you on behalf of Christ not only to believe on him...").

[75] ἀνοῖξαι ὀφθαλμοὺς αὐτῶν, τοῦ ἐπιστρέψαι ἀπὸ σκότους εἰς φῶς καὶ τῆς ἐξουσίας τοῦ Σατανᾶ ἐπὶ τὸν θεόν, τοῦ λαβεῖν αὐτοὺς ἄφεσιν ἁμαρτιῶν καὶ κλῆρον ἐν τοῖς ἡγιασμένοις πίστει τῇ εἰς ἐμέ.

[76] μετανοεῖν καὶ ἐπιστρέφειν ἐπὶ τὸν θεόν.

[77] *IDB,* s.v. "Repentance," by W. A. Quanbeck, 4:34; *TDNT,* s.v. "μετανοέω κτλ.," by J. Behm, 4:1004; *NIDNTT,* s.v. "Conversion et al.," by F. Laubach and J. Goetzmann, 1:355, 358; *ABD,* s.v. "Repentance," 5:673.

order for someone to be saved.[78] When one appears without the other in a passage such as Acts 2:38, the other is to be understood as well.[79] Hence, Peter's command to repent in Acts 2:38 necessarily implies the command to believe the gospel, that is, to exercise saving faith in the person and work of Jesus Christ. The implications of all of this for the present discussion will be brought out in connection with the following point.

The Church and Acts 2

Taken at face value, the evidence from the New Testament points to Acts 2 as the beginning of the church.[80] The principal arguments in support of this are threefold. *First,* the church is defined in the New Testament as the body of Christ.[81] For example, Paul states in Ephesians 1:22–23[a], "And He [God] has placed all things under his [Christ's] feet and appointed him *to be* head over all things for the church, which is his body."[82] The same thought is found in Colossians 1:18[a], "And he [Christ] is the head of the body, the church."[83] Both the larger and the more immediate contexts of these passages indicate that the term "body" is used metaphorically[84] and

---

[78] *Baker Encyclopedia of the Bible,* s.v. "Repentance," by P. Helm, 2:1837; *ABD,* s.v. "Repentance," 5:673. Luter states, "Any conception of repenting not wedded to faith in the gospel falls short of the full biblical message."

[79] *ABD,* s.v. "Repentance," 5:673. Luter describes the relationship in this way: "Parallel to the phenomena in the gospels, repentance in Acts may be complementary to faith (20:21) or include faith (17:30) and leads to forgiveness of sins (2:38; 5:31) and eternal life (11:18)."

[80] See, for example, Dunn, *Baptism in the Holy Spirit,* pp. 38–54; Earl D. Radmacher, *The Nature of the Church* (Portland, OR: Western Baptist Press, 1972), pp. 193–220; Robert L. Saucy, *The Church in God's Program* (Chicago: Moody, 1972), pp. 57–68; Charles C. Ryrie, *Basic Theology* (Wheaton, IL: Victor Books, 1986), pp. 397–402; *Dispensationalism,* rev. ed. (Chicago: Moody, 1995), pp. 123–44. On the various uses of ἐκκλησία in the NT, see, in addition to the above, *TDNT,* s.v. ἐκκλησία, by K. L. Schmidt, 3:502–13; *NIDNTT,* s.v. "Church, Synagogue," by L. Coenen, 1:296–305.

[81] See *TDNT,* s.v. "σῶμα κτλ.," by E. Schweizer, 7:1068–81; *NIDNTT,* s.v. "Body," by S. Wibbing, 1:236–38; Radmacher, *The Nature of the Church,* pp. 222–40; Saucy, *The Church in God's Program,* pp. 24–32; Donald Guthrie, *New Testament Theology* (Downers Grove, IL: Inter-Varsity Press, 1981), pp. 744–46. The body imagery is one of several employed in the NT to describe the church. In addition to the above, see Paul S. Minear, *Images of the Church in the New Testament* (Philadelphia: Westminster, 1960).

[82] καὶ πάντα ὑπέταξεν ὑπὸ τοὺς πόδας αὐτοῦ καὶ αὐτὸν ἔδωκεν κεφαλὴν ὑπὲρ πάντα τῇ ἐκκλησίᾳ, ἥτις ἐστὶν τὸ σῶμα αὐτοῦ.

[83] καὶ αὐτός ἐστιν ἡ κεφαλὴ τοῦ σώματος τῆς ἐκκλησίας·

[84] See Edmund P. Clowney, "Interpreting the Biblical Models of the Church: A Hermeneutical Deepening of Ecclesiology," in *Biblical Interpretation and the Church:*

refers to believers in a collective or corporate sense as those who have responded to the gospel and have experienced salvation.[85] Thus, Paul says of the Corinthian believers, "Now you are Christ's body, and individually members *of it.*"[86]

Second, this body is formed or brought into existence in connection with the baptism of the Holy Spirit.[87] Again, the apostle Paul writes, "For just as the body is one and has many members, and all the members of the body, though they are many, are one body, so also is Christ. For by one Spirit we were all baptized into one body..." (1 Cor 12:12–13ᵃ).[88] Paul draws an analogy in verse 12 between the human body and the body of Christ to underscore the twin themes of unity and diversity within the body of Christ.[89] He then supports the idea of unity in verse 13 by stating how

---

Text and Context, ed. D. A. Carson (Grand Rapids: Baker, 1984), pp. 64–109; Robert H. Gundry, *Sôma in Biblical Theology* (Grand Rapids: Zondervan, 1987), pp. 223–44;

[85] As with the use of "church" in the NT, interpreters generally recognize that the expression "body of Christ" when referring to believers can be used in both a local sense of a specific congregation (e.g., 1 Cor 12:27) as well as in a universal sense of the sum total of believers in the present era (e.g., Eph 1:22–23). In addition to the resources previously cited above in n. 81, see Millard J. Erickson, *Christian Theology,* 2nd ed. (Grand Rapids: Baker, 1998), pp. 1047–49.

[86] 1 Cor 12:27 (' Ὑμεῖς δέ ἐστε σῶμα Χριστοῦ καὶ μέλη ἐκ μέρους). The term "body" (σῶμα) in this verse is anarthrous and there have been various attempts at capturing the precise nuance of the construction. See Robert L. Thomas, *Understanding Spiritual Gifts: A Verse by Verse Study of 1 Corinthians 12–14,* rev. ed. (Grand Rapids: Kregel, 1999), pp. 232–33. The issue does not affect the present argument.

[87] See Dunn, *Baptism in the Holy Spirit,* pp. 49–52; 127–31; Radmacher, *The Nature of the Church,* pp. 210–11; Saucy, *The Church in God's Program,* pp. 64–66. On the meaning of Spirit baptism as a metaphor and its comparison and contrast to the literal sense when used of water baptism, see the discussion in Dunn, *Baptism,* pp. 127–31. Dunn defines the metaphor as "the spiritual transformation which puts the believer 'in Christ,' and which is the effect of receiving the gift of the Spirit..." (p. 130).

[88] Καθάπερ γὰρ τὸ σῶμα ἕν ἐστιν καὶ μέλη πολλὰ ἔχει, πάντα δὲ τὰ μέλη τοῦ σώματος πολλὰ ὄντα ἕν ἐστιν σῶμα, οὕτως καὶ ὁ Χριστός· καὶ γὰρ ἐν ἑνὶ πνεύματι ἡμεῖς πάντες εἰς ἓν σῶμα ἐβαπτίσθημεν. For a discussion of the interpretive issues in these two verses, see D. A. Carson, *Showing the Spirit: A Theological Exposition of 1 Corinthians 12–14* (Grand Rapids: Baker, 1987), pp. 42–48; Gordon D. Fee, *The First Epistle to the Corinthians,* NICNT (Grand Rapids: Eerdmans, 1987), pp. 600–6; Thomas, *Understanding Spiritual Gifts,* pp. 40–46; 224–30. The interpretation of v. 13 is particularly debated. As Carson notes, "Almost every word and syntactical unit in this verse is disputed" (p. 43).

[89] Technically, the verse draws the analogy between the human body and Christ. However, Christ is used in the verse as a metonymy for the body of Christ, as the following verses make clear. See Simon J. Kistemaker, *Exposition of the First Epistle to the Corinthians,* New Testament Commentary (Grand Rapids: Baker, 1993), p. 429; Fee, *The First Epistle to the Corinthians,* p. 603. For a discussion of the views, see Thomas, *Understanding Spiritual Gifts,* pp. 224–25.

the Corinthian believers had all been placed into one body through the baptism of the one Spirit.[90] Regardless of the precise nuance of the phrase "by one Spirit,"[91] Spirit baptism is clearly in view.[92] Paul declares that it was through this baptism that the Corinthian believers had been made or formed into one body,[93] a body Paul specifically identifies as the body of Christ.[94] Thus, it is through Spirit baptism that the church as the body of Christ is formed.

Third, the baptism of the Holy Spirit had its inception in the events recorded in Acts 2.[95] Although the expression "baptism of the Spirit" is not found in Acts 2, the evidence nevertheless supports this conclusion.

---

[90] On the development of Paul's argument in these verses, see Fee, *The First Epistle to the Corinthians,* pp. 600–1. Paul uses the first person plural in verse 13, which could suggest he has the experience of all believers in view. In this case, the reference to Christ's body would carry its universal sense. See Kistemaker, *Exposition of the First Epistle to the Corinthians,* p. 430. However, Paul's statement in v. 27 describing specifically the Corinthians as the body of Christ suggests that Paul may have had the local sense in mind. See Fee, *The First Epistle to the Corinthians,* p. 617, n. 5.

[91] The preposition (ἐν) in this phrase has been translated as instrumental ("with"), agency ("by"), and locative ("in"). For a survey of the syntax, see *TDNT,* s.v. "βαπτίζω κτλ.," by A. Oepke, 1:539–40; and for a discussion of the various approaches, see Thomas, *Understanding Spiritual Gifts,* pp. 43–44; 227–28. The argument here does not rest on the precise sense of the preposition.

[92] Several interpreters see both Spirit and water baptism in this verse, based on the use of the word *baptize* and the association of water and Spirit baptism elsewhere. See, for example, Beasley-Murray, *Baptism in the New Testament,* pp. 167–71. For a convincing rebuttal in defense of a singular reference to Spirit baptism, see Dunn, *Baptism in the Holy Spirit,* pp. 129–31.

[93] The prepositional phrase "into/unto (εἰς) one body" could be given a local sense, in which case it would describe the Corinthian believers being placed into something that already existed. This would fit well with the universal sense of the body of Christ. However, the phrase could also identify the goal, in which case it would indicate that through this baptism something was brought into existence. If this were the sense, the local body of Christ would be in view. See the discussion in Fee, *The First Epistle to the Corinthians,* p. 606. Fee concludes, "In the present case the idea of 'goal' seems more prominent. That is, the purpose of our common experience of the Spirit is that we be formed into one body. Hence, 'we all were immersed in the one Spirit, so as to become one body.'"

[94] See 1 Cor 12:27. A number of interpreters have attempted to divorce Spirit baptism in this verse from conversion, Spirit baptism being a later experience of some, but not all, believers. However, that position has now been generally abandoned. As Carson notes, "the main point is now largely conceded: that the Spirit baptism in v. 13a is to be linked with conversion" (*Showing the Spirit,* p. 45, n. 88).

[95] See Dunn, *Baptism in the Holy Spirit,* pp. 38–54; Radmacher, *The Nature of the Church,* pp. 210–12; Saucy, *The Church in God's Program,* pp. 64–66; Ryrie, *Basic Theology,* pp. 399–402; *Dispensationalism,* pp. 125–27; and the discussions in *TDNT,* s.v. "πνεῦμα κτλ.," by E. Schweizer, 6:409–13; *NIDNTT,* s.v. "Spirit, Holy Spirit," by J. D. G. Dunn, 3:698–701.

References to the baptism of the Holy Spirit occur on several occasions in the gospels. On each occasion, Spirit baptism is described as a future event. Mark, for example, records the words of John the Baptist, "I baptize you with water, but he will baptize you with the Holy Spirit" (Mark 1:8).[96] In Acts 1:4–5, the Lord reaffirms John's promise when He tells his disciples on the eve of his ascension "not to leave Jerusalem but to wait for the promise of the Father which you have heard about from me, for John baptized with water, but you will be baptized with the Holy Spirit not many days from now."[97] From the Lord's statement it is evident that the baptism of the Spirit was still future, and, at the same time, something that was soon to take place.[98]

The next reference in Acts to this baptism is found in Acts 11:15–16. Reporting on the conversion of Cornelius, Peter states, "And as I began to speak, the Holy Spirit fell on them just as *He had* upon us at the beginning. And I remembered the words of the Lord, how He used to say, 'John baptized with water, but you will be baptized with the Holy Spirit.'"[99] Peter's words indicate that the baptism of the Spirit had taken place with the outpouring of the Spirit on Cornelius, and that Peter and the other disciples had experienced this same baptism "at the beginning."[100] This expression, "at the beginning," must be a reference to Acts 2 and the dramatic outpouring of the Spirit recorded there,[101] especially in light of the Lord's statement in Acts 1:5 about the nearness of Spirit baptism.[102]

---

[96] ἐγὼ ἐβάπτισα ὑμᾶς ὕδατι, αὐτὸς δὲ βαπτίσει ὑμᾶς ἐν πνεύματι ἁγίῳ. The other references in the gospels are Matt 3:11, Luke 3:16, and John 1:33. Although John's reference does not include the future tense, it parallels the other accounts where the future tense is employed and, therefore, it may be assumed the sense is the same. Carson, for example, translates the present participial clause, "The man on whom you see the Spirit come down and remain is he who will baptize with the Holy Spirit" (*The Gospel According to John* [Grand Rapids: Eerdmans, 1991], p. 151).

[97] ἀπὸ Ἰεροσολύμων μὴ χωρίζεσθαι ἀλλὰ περιμένειν τὴν ἐπαγγελίαν τοῦ πατρὸς ἣν ἠκούσατέ μου, ὅτι Ἰωάννης μὲν ἐβάπτισεν ὕδατι, ὑμεῖς δὲ ἐν πνεύματι βαπτισθήσεσθε ἁγίῳ οὐ μετὰ πολλὰς ταύτας ἡμέρας.

[98] See, for example, Bruce, *The Book of Acts,* p. 35, "The time was now drawing very near, said Jesus, when these words of John would be fulfilled: 'you will be baptized with the Holy Spirit in a few days' time.'"

[99] ἐν δὲ τῷ ἄρξασθαί με λαλεῖν ἐπέπεσεν τὸ πνεῦμα τὸ ἅγιον ἐπ' αὐτοὺς ὥσπερ καὶ ἐφ' ἡμᾶς ἐν ἀρχῇ. ἐμνήσθην δὲ τοῦ ῥήματος τοῦ κυρίου ὡς ἔλεγεν, Ἰωάννης μὲν ἐβάπτισεν ὕδατι, ὑμεῖς δὲ βαπτισθήσεσθε ἐν πνεύματι ἁγίῳ.

[100] ἐν ἀρχῇ. See Bruce, *The Book of Acts,* pp. 222–23.

[101] See Acts 2:33.

[102] See I. Howard Marshall, *The Acts of the Apostles,* TNTC (Grand Rapids: Eerdmans, 1980), pp. 197–98.

The conclusion from the above arguments is that the church, as the body of Christ, formed by the baptism of the Holy Spirit, began in Acts 2.[103]

The evidence from this and from the previous discussion on the relationship between repentance and faith seriously undermines the second interpretation. Ultra-dispensationalists limit the application of the verse to those living in the period prior to the start of the church. Prior to the start of the church, these argue, both faith and water baptism were required for salvation. Once the church began, salvation was by faith alone. The evidence above has shown that the church did in fact begin in Acts 2. Whatever Acts 2:38 is saying, it is speaking to those who were placed in the body of Christ. That being the case, salvation for those in Acts 2 cannot be conditioned by faith alone and, at the same time, by faith plus water baptism.

Those dispensationalists holding to the second interpretation limit the application of Acts 2:38 to Jews guilty of the crucifixion of the Lord. Advocates argue that these Jews were saved, that is, were justified on the basis of faith alone. Forgiveness of sins and the gift of the Spirit, on the other hand, were conditioned for these Jews by repentance and water baptism. All others, they purport, receive the collective benefits of salvation on the sole condition of faith. However, the discussion above on repentance and faith has shown that these are integrally connected and that both must be exercised for salvation. Any interpretation of Acts 2:38 that endeavors to divide repentance and faith or to make salvation conditioned by something other than repentance and faith is in conflict with the biblical evidence.

Baptism as a Parenthetical Remark, Not Directly Related to Salvation

The third interpretation takes the command "be baptized" as a parenthesis and links the phrase "for the forgiveness of sins" with the first command "repent." Support for this, proponents aver, is that the command to repent is plural whereas the command to be baptized is singular. The phrase "for the forgiveness of your sins" contains the plural pronoun "your,"[104] thus associating the phrase with the plural "repent" and not with the

---

[103] Dunn states, "We can therefore say that Pentecost is the beginning of the Church and the coming into existence of the Church as the Body of Christ. And this is the work of the Spirit" (*Baptism in the Holy Spirit,* p. 51).

[104] A few witnesses omit the pronoun ὑμῶν after ἁμαρτιῶν, apparently to harmonize the phrase with the shorter form found elsewhere in the NT (Matt 26:28; Mark 1:4; Luke 3:3; 24:47). The evidence decidedly favors the longer reading. See James H. Ropes, *The Beginnings of Christianity,* Part 1: *The Acts of the Apostles,* 5 vols. (London: Macmillan, 1926), 3:22; Metzger, *A Textual Commentary on the Greek New Testament,* pp. 261–62.

singular "be baptized." The resultant translation is, "Repent (and be baptized everyone of you in the name of Jesus Christ) for the forgiveness of your sins." In this case, forgiveness is understood as the goal or outcome of the command "repent." The chief obstacle with this view is its understanding of the syntax between the command to be baptized and the prepositional phrase "for the forgiveness of sins."

Without question, the command "repent" is plural, the command "be baptized" is singular, and the personal pronoun in the prepositional phrase "for the forgiveness of your sins" is plural. However, to argue from this that the prepositional phrase itself cannot modify the second command fails to consider the pronoun modifying the subject of the second command. Following the command to repent, Peter says, "and let each one of you be baptized." Peter switches from the plural "repent" to the singular "let each be baptized" to stress individual participation in the second command.[105] At the same time, Peter modifies the subject of the second command "each" with the plural pronoun "of you."[106] In other words, although the expressed subject of the second command is singular, Peter still has the plural subjects in view with the second command, as shown by his use of the plural pronominal modifier.[107]

In addition, the closest antecedent to the plural pronoun in the prepositional phrase is not the plural subject implied in the first command, but the plural pronoun modifying the subject of the second command. It is "let each *of you* be baptized...for the forgiveness of *your* sins."[108] None of this necessarily rules out having the prepositional phrase modify both commands. It does appear to rule out excluding the second command as being modified by the prepositional phrase. Having said that, the close connection between the pronouns "each *of you*" and "for the forgiveness of *your* sins" weighs in favor of taking the prepositional phrase specifically with the second command, rather than with both commands.

---

[105] See Longenecker, "Acts," p. 283; Carroll D. Osburn, "The Third Person Imperative in Acts 2:38," *ResQ* 26 (1983): 83–84.

[106] καὶ βαπτισθήτω ἕκαστος ὑμῶν.

[107] See C. K. Barrett, *The Acts of the Apostle,* 2 vols., ICC (Edinburgh: T & T Clark, 1994), 1:153–54; and the discussion in Ashby L. Camp, "Reexamining the Rule of Concord in Acts 2:38," *ResQ* 39 (1997): 37-42.

[108] It is surprising that proponents who take the second command as a parenthesis, based in large part on the force of the plural pronoun (ὑμῶν) modifying "sins," fail to note the identical plural pronoun (ὑμῶν) modifying the subject of the second command. See, for example, McIntyre, "Baptism and Forgiveness in Acts 2:38," pp. 54–59.

Baptism as a Sign of Conversion-Initiation, The Evidence of Genuine Repentance

The fourth interpretation, referred to as conversion-initiation, takes the prepositional phrase "for the forgiveness of sins" as indicating purpose and as modifying both commands "repent" and "be baptized." The focus with the second command, "be baptized," is not on the rite itself, but on the rite as an expression of genuine repentance. Repentance is the efficacious element, proponents argue; the rite is simply the vehicle wherein true repentance is expressed. By making repentance the effective element in the forgiveness of sins, advocates endeavor to harmonize their interpretation of Acts 2:38 with other passages where forgiveness is addressed and the rite is not mentioned. Dunn, for example, states,

> Luke never mentions water-baptism by itself as the condition of or means to receiving forgiveness; he mentions it only in connection with some other attitude (repentance— Luke 3:3; Acts 2:38) or act (calling on his name— Acts 22:16). But whereas water-baptism is never spoken of as the sole prerequisite to receiving forgiveness, Luke on a number of occasions speaks of repentance or faith as the sole prerequisite (Luke 5:20; 24:47; Acts 3:19; 5:31; 10:43; 13:38; 26:18; cf. 4:4; 9:35, 42; 11:21; 13:48; 14:1; 16:31; 17:12, 34).[109]

The challenge with this approach is in its understanding of the second command and its relationship to the phrase "for the forgiveness of sins."

While there is much to commend this interpretation of Acts 2:38, adherents are confronted with a dilemma. To begin with, the interpretation appears to link too closely water baptism and the forgiveness of sins. If the prepositional phrase, "for the forgiveness of sins," indicates the purpose or goal of both commands, and if the second command involves the rite of water baptism, there is a sense in which forgiveness is conditioned by the rite. Again, Dunn argues,

> In Acts faith and baptism are normally closely linked (2:38, 41; 8:12f.; 8:37 (D); 16:14f., 31–33; 18:8). In the case of the Ephesians the sequence of Paul's questions indicates the πιστεῦσαι and βαπτισθῆναι are interchangeable ways of describing the act of faith: baptism was the *necessary* expression of commitment, without which they could not be said to have truly 'believed.'[110]

---

[109] Dunn, *Baptism in the Holy Spirit,* p. 97.

[110] Dunn, *Baptism in the Holy Spirit,* p. 96 (emphasis added). Dunn is using faith here as the corollary to repentance.

The problem with linking repentance and water baptism too closely and, in effect, with making the rite necessary for forgiveness is that this interpretation faces the same liabilities as the first interpretation. Salvation involving the forgiveness of sins is now conditioned by both faith (repentance and faith) and water baptism and is no longer by faith alone.[111]

Proponents have sensed something of the tension with their understanding of Acts 2:38 and have taken pains to qualify their interpretation to avoid the problem. Dunn is quick to add,

> It is false to say that water-baptism conveys, confers or effects forgiveness of sins. It may symbolize cleansing, but it is the faith and repentance which receives the forgiveness, and the Holy Spirit who conveys, confers and effects it.... In other words, water-baptism is neither the sole preliminary nor in itself an essential preliminary to receiving forgiveness.[112]

By stating that water baptism is not "in itself an essential preliminary to receiving forgiveness," Dunn appears to have driven a wedge between the two, between water baptism and forgiveness.[113] In other words, Dunn is saying that forgiveness can be and, in fact, has been received by faith apart from the rite. Earlier in this same discussion, Dunn acknowledges, "But whereas water-baptism is never spoken of as the sole prerequisite to receiving forgiveness, Luke on a number of occasions speaks of repentance or faith as the sole prerequisite."[114]

But once Dunn makes that concession, then in what sense can he say that Peter's two commands are conditions for the forgiveness of sins? Either water baptism is the necessary expression of saving faith, apart from which forgiveness is not received, or water baptism is not necessary. But if it is not essential, as Dunn's quote above indicates, then how does the expression "for the forgiveness of sins" represent the purpose or goal of both "repent" *and* "be baptized?" Although Acts 2:38 is reportedly

---

[111] Tanton, for example, states "Dunn appears to say that C (the reception of the Holy Spirit) comes because of A (faith), but A is not truly A unless it is accompanied by B (baptism). This raises the question: how does this argument avoid the logical deduction that B is as necessary as A in order to receive C?" (Tanton, "The Gospel and Water Baptism," pp. 44–45).

[112] Dunn, *Baptism in the Holy Spirit,* p. 97.

[113] By the expression "in itself," Dunn means "apart from faith." However, the point still stands. To say that water-baptism "in itself" is not an essential preliminary to forgiveness implies that forgiveness could be gained apart from the rite, a point Dunn has already acknowledged in his discussion of conversion-initiation in Acts (*Baptism in the Holy Spirit,* p. 97).

[114] Dunn, *Baptism in the Holy Spirit,* p. 97.

the norm for conversion-initiation in Acts, supporters like Dunn have recognized the numerous exceptions to the norm.[115] Once exceptions are allowed, then this interpretation of Peter's exhortation appears to be countermanded.

Baptism as a Consequence of Salvation, Not a Condition for Salvation

The fifth and final interpretation restricts the prepositional phrase "for the forgiveness of sins" to the second command "be baptized" and interprets the prepositional phrase as identifying the cause or basis for the second command. The resultant translation is "repent, and [following that] let each one of you be baptized...on the basis of the forgiveness of your sins." In other words, Peter says that those who have responded to his message and have repented are to be baptized because, having repented, their sins are [already] forgiven. Basically two objections have been levied against this interpretation. The first is that there is limited support for the causal use of this preposition, and the support that has been offered has been strongly contested.[116] The second is that in the other four uses of the prepositional phrase "for the forgiveness of sins" in the New Testament, the preposition appears to have a telic force.[117] Undoubtedly, the critical issue with this interpretation is the use of the preposition.

While recognizing that a number of interpreters discount the causal use of the preposition altogether, there are at least two passages in the New Testament that appear to support it. The first is Matthew 12:41. In this verse, Matthew writes, "The men of Nineveh will stand up in the judgment with this generation and condemn it, for they repented at (εἰς) the preaching of Jonah, and behold, one greater than Jonah is here."[118] The

---

[115] It seems somewhat strange that Dunn and others holding to this interpretation identify Acts 2:38 as the norm for conversion-initiation when, as Dunn notes, "it is the only verse in Acts which directly relates to one another the three most important elements in conversion-initiation: repentance, water-baptism, and the gift of the Spirit— repentance and faith being the opposite sides of the same coin" (*Baptism in the Holy Spirit*, p. 91). The fact that this is the only verse that relates these three items and that there are a number of passages where one of the items— water baptism— is not a factor in the equation seems to raise questions as to the normative nature of this verse.

[116] See, for example, J. W. Roberts, "Baptism for Remission of Sins— A Critique," *ResQ* 1(1957): 226–34; and J. C. Davis, "Another Look at the Relationship Between Baptism and Forgiveness," *ResQ* 24 (1984): 80–88.

[117] See Davis, "Another Look at the Relationship Between Baptism and Forgiveness," pp. 80–81. The other four uses are Matt 26:28; Mark 1:4; Luke 3:3; 24:47.

[118] ἄνδρες Νινευῖται ἀναστήσονται ἐν τῇ κρίσει μετὰ τῆς γενεᾶς ταύτης καὶ κατακρινοῦσιν αὐτήν, ὅτι μετενόησαν εἰς τὸ κήρυγμα Ιωνᾶ, καὶ ἰδοὺ πλεῖον

key to the interpretation of the preposition in this verse is to identify the precise relationship between the two expressions the preposition connects, that is, between repentance and the preaching of Jonah. In order to make this identification, two questions need to be asked and answered.

The first question is, Is there a temporal sequence between the preaching of Jonah and the repentance of the Ninevites? The answer to the first question is clearly yes. According to the historical record, Jonah preached, and, following this, the Ninevites repented.[119] The second question is, Is there, in addition, a logical relationship between these two activities? Again, the answer to this question is also clearly yes. The repentance of the Ninevites was in response to or based on Jonah's preaching. According to Jonah 3:9, the king's call for national repentance was in the hope that God would relent of the impending judgment that Jonah had proclaimed. Thus, the nation's repentance was in direct response to Jonah's message.

The issue ultimately is not whether there are other ways this prepositional phrase in Matthew 12:41 could be rendered. Undoubtedly there are. The issue centers on what is the most probable relationship suggested by the immediate and larger contexts of the phrase. If the meaning of a word is based on its use in a given context, the evidence strongly supports that the relationship between Jonah's preaching and the Ninevites' repentance is that they repented "in response to" the preaching of Jonah.[120] By any other name, this is what is meant by the causal use of the preposition.

The second verse in the New Testament supporting the causal use of the preposition is Matthew 3:11. In this verse, Matthew records a statement by John the Baptist where John contrasts his baptism with that of the Lord's. Describing his own baptism, John declares, "I indeed baptize you with water for (εἰς) repentance...."[121] John's declaration is significant for the present discussion in that both here and in Acts 2:38 the verb "baptize" is used and, in both, the verb is modified by the same preposition (εἰς). As with Matthew 12:41, the question that needs to be considered is, What is the relationship between the two activities connected by the preposition, between John's baptism and repentance? From Matthew 3:7–8, it is apparent that John demanded repentance as a prerequisite for his baptism.

Ἰωνᾶ ὧδε. Translating the prepositional phrase as "at the preaching of Noah" follows the rendering of several modern translations. Cf. AMPLIFIED, NASB, NAS95, NEB, REB, NIV, NKJV, NLB, RSV, NRSV.

[119] Note the sequence of *waw consecutives* in Jonah 3:4–5: "And Jonah cried out and proclaimed...and the men of Nineveh believed...."

[120] See, for example, D. A. Carson, "Matthew," in *The Expositor's Bible Commentary*, 12 vols., ed. F. E. Gaebelein (Grand Rapids: Zondervan, 1984), 8:297.

[121] ἐγὼ μὲν ὑμᾶς βαπτίζω ἐν ὕδατι εἰς μετάνοιαν.

When the Pharisees and Sadducees came to John to be baptized by him, he rebuked their hypocrisy and demanded that they "bring forth fruit in keeping with repentance."[122] It may be concluded from this that one could not undergo John's baptism without first showing evidence of repentance. Thus, a baptism "for repentance" meant a baptism that was based on repentance.[123] Again, by any other name, this is what is meant by the causal use of the preposition.

Having addressed the first objection to this interpretation, the second objection needs to be discussed. The second objection is that in the four other New Testament uses of the prepositional phrase "for the forgiveness of sins," the preposition appears to have a telic force, indicating purpose or goal. In response, it should be noted that in two of the uses, Matthew 28:26 and Luke 24:47, water baptism is not mentioned. While a telic force of the preposition may be granted in these two verses, the lack of correspondence with the construction in Acts 2:38 lessens the significance of these verses for the interpretation of Acts 2:38. Of the remaining two uses, Mark 1:4 and Luke 3:3, water baptism is mentioned. In these, the text reads "a baptism of repentance for the forgiveness of sins."[124] As such, there is correspondence between these verses and the construction in Acts 2:38.

Having said that, the interpreter is faced with the same options for the prepositional phrase in these verses as in Acts 2:38. Is the preposition in these two verses telic or causal? From the discussion above on Matthew 3:11, it could be argued that the preposition in these two passages has a causal force, not a telic force. In fact, the construction in Mark 1:4 and Luke 3:3 is somewhat parallel with the construction in Matthew 3:11. All three are describing John's baptism. In Mark 1:4 and Luke 3:3, it is called a baptism "for the forgiveness of sins."[125] In Matthew 3:11, it is referred to as a baptism "for repentance." The conclusion drawn above with Matthew

---

[122] ποιήσατε οὖν καρπὸν ἄξιον τῆς μετανοίας.

[123] See, for example, Leon Morris, *The Gospel According to Matthew* (Grand Rapids: Eerdmans, 1992), p. 326. Interestingly enough, there is extra-biblical corroboration for this interpretation of Matt 3:11. Josephus writes concerning those coming to John for baptism, "They must not employ it [baptism] to gain pardon for whatever sins they committed, but as a consecration of the body implying that the soul was already thoroughly cleansed by right behaviour" (*Antiquities*, XVIII, 117). See Louis H. Feldman, trans., *Josephus*, 10 vols., in The Loeb Classical Library (Cambridge, MA: Harvard University Press, 1965), 9:80–83.

[124] βάπτισμα μετανοίας εἰς ἄφεσιν ἁμαρτιῶν. The construction is identical in both passages.

[125] The prepositional phrase "for the forgiveness of sins" modifies "baptism" and not the intervening genitive "of repentance." See, for example, the discussion in Robert A. Guelich, *Mark*, 2 vols. (in progress), WBC (Dallas: Word Books, 1989–), 1:18–20.

3:11 was that a baptism "for repentance" meant a baptism based on repentance. The same could be argued for these other two passages. In other words, a baptism "for the forgiveness of sins" could mean a baptism based on the forgiveness of sins.

CONCLUSION

Scripture unequivocally presents salvation as an unmerited gift, received by faith alone, apart from works. This being true, any of the last three views on the interpretation of Acts 2:38 are viable candidates. Viewing the command for baptism as a parenthesis, taking the verse as describing Christian conversion-initiation, or interpreting the preposition as causal all roughly support the gracious nature of salvation. Having said that, the last view is preferred. The causal use of the preposition, although certainly not common in the New Testament, is supported from Matthew 12:41 and Matthew 3:11. The latter of these two verses places the causal use of the preposition within the context of water baptism, the same construction as found in Acts 2:38. In addition, the same plural pronoun found with both the command to be baptized and the prepositional phrase "for the forgiveness of sins" in Acts 2:38 closely links this command with the prepositional phrase. In fact, with the repetition of the identical pronoun, the prepositional phrase is best taken specifically with the second command. The last interpretation, involving the causal use of the preposition, alone holds to this relationship of the prepositional phrase.

While none of the interpretations is free of questions, the last poses the least number of problems and is deemed the superior alternative. Peter's first command is to repent; implied in the command is the exercise of faith. His second command, the command to be baptized, is best taken as the response of those whose sins are forgiven rather than as a condition for forgiveness. While water baptism is important as a step of obedience and as a public affirmation of saving faith, faith alone saves. Peter's words, when properly interpreted, do not argue to the contrary.

IS *APOSTASIA* IN 2 THESSALONIANS 2:3 A REFERENCE TO THE RAPTURE?[1]

William W. Combs

In 2 Thessalonians 2:3, Paul says: "Let no one in any way deceive you, for *it will not come* unless the apostasy comes first...."[2] The word translated "apostasy" is ἀποστασία.[3] Instead of understanding ἀποστασία as apostasy, some sort of religious departure, a number of modern interpreters (pretribulational, premillennial) have suggested that ἀποστασία refers to a spatial departure—specifically, the Rapture of the church. It is generally recognized that this view can be traced to a series of articles by E. Schuyler English, entitled "Re-Thinking the Rapture," which first appeared in *Our Hope* magazine from October 1949 to March 1950. It is the purpose of this paper to reexamine this view, especially in light of its recent championing in an extensive treatment by H. Wayne House.[4]

CONTEXT OF 2 THESSALONIANS 2:3

Before examining the arguments for and against the Rapture view, we would do well to look briefly at the surrounding context, specifically, 2 Thessalonians 2:1–3.

The Appeal for Calmness Concerning the Day of the Lord, 2:1–2

Subject of the Appeal, v. 1

Now we request you, brethren, with regard to the coming of our Lord Jesus Christ, and our gathering together to Him,

Paul begins chapter two with an appeal for the Thessalonians to remain calm. It is in the nature of a "request" (ἐρωτῶμεν[5]) and is directed toward

---

[1] This article appeared in the 1998 issue of the *DBSJ*, vol. 3, pp. 63-87.

[2] All Scripture references are taken from the NASB unless otherwise noted.

[3] Barbara and Kurt Aland, *Novum Testamentum Graece,* 27th ed. (Stuttgart: Deutsche Bibelgesellschaft, 1993), p. 539. This Greek text is used throughout this paper.

[4] "Apostasia in 2 Thessalonians 2:3: Apostasy or Rapture?" in *When the Trumpet Sounds,* ed. Thomas Ice and Timothy Demy (Eugene, OR: Harvest House, 1995), pp. 261–96.

[5] Some believe that ἐρωτάω is used here as practically an equivalent to παρακαλέω (cf. 1 Thess 4:1; 5:12, 14). See F. F. Bruce, *1 and 2 Thessalonians,* Word Biblical Commentary (Waco, TX: Word Books, 1982), p. 163; D. Michael Martin, *1, 2 Thessalonians,* New

Paul's Christian "brethren" at Thessalonica. Paul's request concerns ("with regard to," ὑπέρ[6]) "the coming of our Lord Jesus Christ, and our gathering together to Him." Both posttribulationists[7] and pretribulationists[8] agree that "our gathering together (ἐπισυναγωγῆς) to him" clearly speaks of the Rapture described in 1 Thessalonians 4:13–17. The word translated "coming" (παρουσία) is used numerous times in the NT to refer to the return of Christ. It can be used of the Rapture (1 Thess 4:15) as well as the return of Christ to the earth at the end of the Tribulation (2 Thess 2:8). Pretribulationists separate these events by the seven-year Tribulation period, while posttribulationists do not. Because Paul clearly identifies the Rapture with the phrase "our gathering together to Him," pretribulationists have sensed some difficulty in accounting for the addition of παρουσία.

The phrase "the coming of our Lord Jesus Christ, and our gathering together to Him" involves two nouns joined by καί with the article preceding only the first noun (τῆς παρουσίας...καὶ...ἐπισυναγωγῆς). This single article joining both παρουσία and ἐπισυναγωγή has usually been interpreted to mean that there is some close connection between the two. Ward says that "the *coming* and the *assembling* are united by one Greek article. Paul was thinking of one event, not two."[9] Williams goes even further: "The two nouns, coming (*parousia*...) and being gathered (*episynagogē*) are governed by the one article and are thus depicted as the one (complex) event.... Therefore, those who use this verse to make a distinction between the time of the so-called Rapture of the saints and

---

American Commentary (Nashville: Broadman and Holman, 1995), p. 223; Paul Ellingworth and Eugene A. Nida, *A Translator's Handbook on Paul's Letters to the Thessalonians* (London: United Bible Societies, 1976), p. 156; and cf. the NRSV, "beg."

[6] The preposition ὑπέρ is here equivalent to περί. See Walter Bauer, William F. Arndt, and F. Wilbur Gingrich, *A Greek-English Lexicon of the New Testament and Other Early Christian Literature,* 2nd ed., revised and augmented by F. Wilbur Gingrich and Frederick W. Danker (Chicago: University of Chicago Press, 1979), s.v. "περί," p. 839 [hereafter, BAGD]; A. T. Robertson, *A Grammar of the Greek New Testament in the Light of Historical Research* (Nashville: Broadman, 1934), p. 632; C. F. D. Moule, *An Idiom-Book of New Testament Greek,* 2nd ed. (Cambridge: Cambridge University Press, 1959), p. 65. It is often suggested that the "by" of the KJV (as if it were a formula of adjuration) was erroneously adopted from the Latin *per adventum.* See, e.g., George Milligan, *St. Paul's Epistles to the Thessalonians* (reprint ed.; Old Tappan, NJ: Fleming H. Revell, n.d.), p. 96.

[7] E.g., Robert H. Gundry, *The Church and the Tribulation* (Grand Rapids: Zondervan, 1973), pp. 113–114.

[8] E.g., Paul D. Feinberg, "2 Thessalonians 2 and the Rapture," in *When the Trumpet Sounds,* ed. Thomas Ice and Timothy Demy (Eugene, OR: Harvest House, 1995), p. 301.

[9] Ronald A. Ward, *Commentary on 1 & 2 Thessalonians* (Waco, TX: Word Books, 1973), p. 153.

the Parousia, do so in defiance of the syntax...."[10] This argument seeks to invalidate pretribulationism by arguing that both terms must refer to the post-tribulational return of Christ.[11] Pretribulationists, like Hiebert, have countered by arguing that "the aspect of the coming in view here is made clear by the added expression 'and our gathering together unto him.'"[12] In other words, the aspect of παρουσία in view is defined by the additional phrase, "our gathering together to Him," so that just one event is in view, the pretribulational event.

This assumption that παρουσία and ἐπισυναγωγή must have the same referent is probably tied to a misunderstanding of the so-called Granville Sharp rule.[13] Sharp's rule is often understood to mean that when two nouns are joined by καί with the article preceding only the first, both nouns refer to the same person or thing. Various studies, in recent years, by several scholars, especially Daniel B. Wallace, have now clarified Sharp's rule and shed light on the semantics of similar constructions.[14] Sharp's rule states that if two or more nouns (or participles or adjectives, used as nouns) are joined by καί and the article precedes only the first noun, then the other noun(s) refers to the same person. As Sharp himself phrased it: "the second noun...denotes a farther description of the first-named person."[15] In order for the rule to be

---

[10] David J. Williams, *1 and 2 Thessalonians,* New International Biblical Commentary (Peabody, MA: Hendrickson, 1992), p. 122.

[11] This is precisely what F. F. Bruce argues (*1 and 2 Thessalonians,* p. 163).

[12] D. Edmond Hiebert, *The Thessalonian Epistles* (Chicago: Moody Press, 1971), p. 300. See also Robert L. Thomas, "2 Thessalonians," in *The Expositor's Bible Commentary,* 12 vols., ed. Frank E. Gaebelein (Grand Rapids: Zondervan), 11:318; Thomas L. Constable, "2 Thessalonians," in *The Bible Knowledge Commentary: New Testament Edition,* ed. John F. Walvoord and Roy B. Zuck (Wheaton, IL: Victor, 1983), p. 717.

[13] Granville Sharp, *Remarks on the Uses of the Definite Article in the Greek Text of the New Testament Containing Many New Proofs of the Divinity of Christ, From Passages Which Are Wrongly Translated in the Common English Version* (reprint of 1803 ed.; Atlanta: Original Word, 1995). Sharp presents six rules related to the use of the article in Greek; it is the first that has become known as the Granville Sharp rule.

[14] Daniel B. Wallace, "The Semantic Range of the Article-Noun-Καί-Noun Plural Construction in the New Testament," *Grace Theological Seminary* 4 (Spring 1983): 59–84. For an exhaustive study of these issues, see his "The Article with Multiple Substantives Connected by Καί in the New Testament: Semantics and Significance," (Ph.D. dissertation, Dallas Theological Seminary, 1995). A more concise treatment is found in his *Greek Grammar Beyond the Basics: An Exegetical Syntax of the New Testament* (Grand Rapids: Zondervan, 1996), pp. 270–90. For a list of studies predating Wallace, see his "The Article with Multiple Substantives," pp. 75–76.

[15] *Remarks on the Uses of the Definite Article,* p. 8.

valid, the nouns cannot be plural, cannot be impersonal nouns (e.g., love, righteousness), and cannot be proper names (e.g., Jesus).[16]

In 2 Thessalonians 2:1 the two nouns παρουσία and ἐπισυναγωγή do, in fact, fit the Granville Sharp construction, but the rule is not valid because the nouns are impersonal. Wallace has demonstrated that in the case of impersonal nouns, five semantic categories are theoretically possible: (1) distinct entities, though united (e.g., "truth and love"); (2) overlapping entities (e.g., "wisdom and knowledge"); (3) first entity subset of second (e.g., "the hour and day of his coming") (4) second group subset of first (e.g., "the day and hour of his coming"); and (5) both entities identical (e.g., the city of the great king, that is, Jerusalem).[17] There is no example of category (2) in the NT and only one of category (5), none involving concrete impersonals, like παρουσία and ἐπισυναγωγή. Category (3) would seem to be easily ruled out since it is doubtful Paul viewed the παρουσία as a subset of the ἐπισυναγωγή — no eschatological system posits such a view. This leaves either (1) or (4), that is, the παρουσία and the ἐπισυναγωγή are distinct, though united, or the ἐπισυναγωγή is a subset of the παρουσία. Actually, either of these could fit both pretribulationism and posttribulationism. The παρουσία and the ἐπισυναγωγή could be viewed as distinct events though united in time (posttribulationism) or distinct events though united thematically (pretribulationism), that is, two elements of one complex event.[18] If the ἐπισυναγωγή is taken as a subset of the παρουσία, the latter would be viewed in a general way, something of a complex event; but, again, neither eschatological system is favored. In summary, the attempt by some to rule out pretribulationism based on this text is founded on a misunderstanding of the grammatical structure and its semantic implications.

Content of the Appeal, v. 2a

> that you may not be quickly shaken from your composure or be disturbed either by a spirit or a message or a letter as if from us,

---

[16] See the discussion by Wallace, "The Semantic Range of the Article-Noun-Καί-Noun Plural Construction," p. 62; "The Article with Multiple Substantives Connected by Καί in the New Testament," pp. 47–48; *Greek Grammar*, pp. 271–72.

[17] "The Article with Multiple Substantives Connected by Καί in the New Testament," pp. 167–84; *Greek Grammar*, pp. 286–290.

[18] Cf., e.g., Paul D. Feinberg, "The Case for the Pretribulational Rapture Position," in *The Rapture: Pre-, Mid-, or Post-Tribulational?* ed. Richard R. Reiter, et al. (Grand Rapids: Zondervan, 1984), pp. 84–85.

There is some question about the relationship between verse 1 and the clause in verse 2 made up of εἰς τό plus the two infinitives (σαλευθῆναι and θροεῖσθαι). Though this clause may give Paul's purpose,[19] here it would seem to indicate the content of Paul's "request" from verse 1.[20] The request is two-fold: first, that they would not be "quickly shaken from [their] composure." The adverb "quickly" (ταχέως) does not primarily refer to "haste." Rather, it is used here in the unfavorable sense of "too easily."[21] The second request is for the Thessalonians not to "be disturbed." Thus we can conclude that the Thessalonians had rashly lost their composure about end-time events.

This loss of composure was the result of some false teaching that came to the Thessalonians by one of three possible avenues: "a spirit or a message or a letter." Paul is thus saying that although he knows the Thessalonians have received a false report, he does not know the means (διά) through which it has come to them. Most commentators understand "spirit" (πνεύματος) to be some sort of prophetic utterance; "message" (λόγου), an oral report or teaching; and "letter" (ἐπιστολῆς), a written message.[22] But there is some question as to how the next phrase, "as if from us" (ὡς δι' ἡμῶν), relates to these three items. Is it to be taken only

---

[19] Charles A. Wanamaker, *The Epistles to the Thessalonians,* New International Greek Text Commentary (Grand Rapids: Eerdmans, 1990), p. 238.

[20] James E. Frame, *A Critical and Exegetical Commentary on the Epistles of St. Paul to the Thessalonians,* International Critical Commentary (Edinburgh: T. & T. Clark, 1912), p. 245; Ernest Best, *A Commentary on the First and Second Epistles to the Thessalonians* (London: Adams and Clark, 1972), p. 275. Some commentators suggest that εἰς τό with the infinitives expresses both "the content and the purpose of the plea" (Williams, *Thessalonians,* p. 122). See also Hiebert, *Thessalonian Epistles,* p. 301. More likely, σαλευθῆναι and θροεῖσθαι are infinitives of indirect discourse after ἐρωτῶμεν in v. 1, giving the content of Paul's request (Daniel B. Wallace, "2 Thessalonians 2:1–2" [Class Notes, Grace Theological Seminary, May 1982], p. 3). For other examples of this construction, cf. Acts 13:42; Rom 4:18?; 1 Thess 2:12; 3:10. See also Richard A. Young, *Intermediate New Testament Greek* (Nashville: Broadman and Holman, 1994), p. 168. Burton and Robertson, though using different terminology, come to the same conclusion. See Ernest D. Burton, *Syntax of Mood and Tenses in New Testament Greek* (reprint of 1900 ed.; Grand Rapids: Kregel, 1976), p. 162 and Robertson, *Grammar,* p. 1072.

[21] BAGD, s.v. "ταχέως," p. 806. See also Gordon D. Fee, "Pneuma and Eschatology in 2 Thessalonians 2:1–2: A Proposal About 'Testing Prophets' and the Purpose of 2 Thessalonians," in *To Tell the Mystery: Essays on New Testament Eschatology in Honor or Robert H. Gundry,* ed. Thomas E. Schmidt and Moisés Silva, Journal for the Study of the New Testament— Supplement Series 100 (Sheffield: Sheffield Academic Press, 1994), p. 198.

[22] E.g., Bruce, *Thessalonians,* pp. 163–64.

with the last term ("letter"[23]), the last two ("message" and "letter"[24]), or, as it is more commonly understood, with all three?[25] Since the language of the last two items (διὰ λόγου, δι᾿ ἐπιστολῆς) is repeated in v. 15 with reference to Paul's own teaching ("stand firm and hold to the traditions which you were taught, whether by word *of mouth* or by letter from us"), it may be that the false teaching was a misrepresentation of what Paul had taught orally, when he was at Thessalonica, or what he had written in a previous letter (1 Thessalonians).

It is more important, however, to determine what "as if from us" means. It is normally seen as expressing Paul's uncertainty over the *means* by which the false teaching was communicated. However, as Gordon Fee has recently argued, the way in which this false teaching came to the Thessalonians is really of minor importance to Paul. It may have come through some supposed prophetic utterance at Thessalonica, or through a (deliberate?) misunderstanding of Paul's oral teaching or his first letter (1 Thess 5:1–11). What really concerns Paul is that the false teaching is being attributed to him, "as though through us" (ὡς δι᾿ ἡμῶν), that is, from Paul and his associates.[26] Thus the phrase "as though through us" is better understood as anticipating what follows ("that the day of the Lord has come"), denying that what the Thessalonians are presently believing can be attributed to him.

Erroneous Teaching that Prompted the Appeal, v. 2b

to the effect that the day of the Lord has come.

The false teaching that was somehow being attributed to Paul was "to the effect that the day of the Lord has come." "Has come" is the perfect tense of ἐνίστημι. There is almost universal agreement that in the perfect tense it

---

[23] Ibid., p. 164.

[24] Hendricksen thinks this is the "most natural" (William Hendricksen, *Exposition of 1 & 2 Thessalonians* [Grand Rapids: Baker, 1955], p. 168, n. 119).

[25] E.g., Hiebert, *Thessalonian Epistles,* p. 302; Leon Morris, *The First and Second Epistles to the Thessalonians,* 2nd ed. New International Commentary on the New Testament (Grand Rapids: Eerdmans, 1991), p. 215, n. 11; Frame, *Thessalonians,* p. 246; Best, *Thessalonians,* p. 278; J. B. Lightfoot, *Notes on the Epistles of St. Paul* (reprint of 1895 ed.; Winona Lake, IN: Alpha Publications, 1979), p. 109. As Fee has noted, it seems difficult connecting "as if from us" with "spirit" since Paul had not recently been in Thessalonica to make such an utterance (Fee, "Pneuma and Eschatology," p. 205). For a contrary view, see Lightfoot, *Notes on the Epistles,* p. 109.

[26] Fee, "Pneuma and Eschatology," p. 199.

has the sense of "be present," "have come" rather than the KJV's "at hand."[27] Hiebert observes that

> the rendering "at hand" is not due to the acknowledged meaning of the word; it is due rather to a doctrinal difficulty felt by the translators. They could not conceive how anyone could really think that the "the day of the Lord" had actually arrived. The supposed doctrinal difficulty lies in the failure to distinguish between the *parousia* and the day of the Lord.[28]

Pretribulationists argue that the Thessalonians could not distinguish their present troubles from those of the Day of the Lord, and thus they concluded it must already be present.

Numerous problems surround the interpretation of the Day of the Lord. Most pretribulational writers have held that all references to the Day of the Lord in both the Old and New Testaments refer strictly to an eschatological period beginning with the Tribulation, extending through the Millennium.[29] However, not all pretribulationists believe the Millennium is included in the Day of the Lord,[30] but, fortunately, the *terminus ad quem* is not a determining factor in the pretribulational/posttribulational debate nor the Rapture view of ἀποστασία. However, the *terminus a quo* of the Day of the Lord is of major importance in both of these issues. Posttribulationists begin the Day of the Lord with the end of the Tribulation. Pretribulationists have generally viewed it as commencing at the beginning, but this has not been, nor is it now, the universal opinion of all pretribulationists. Some older dispensationalists were in agreement with the posttribulational viewpoint. The old *Scofield Reference Bible* noted that "the day of Jehovah (called, also, 'that day,' and 'the great day') is that lengthened period of time beginning with the return of the Lord in

---

[27] BAGD, s.v. "ἐνίστημι," p. 266. See especially the discussion by Frame, *Thessalonians*, pp. 248–49 and cf. Rom 8:38 and 1 Cor 3:22 where it is contrasted with μέλλω.

[28] *Thessalonian Epistles*, p. 304.

[29] E.g., Charles C. Ryrie, *What You Should Know About the Rapture* (Chicago: Moody Press, 1981), p. 94. This is not universally true, of course. Mayhue, for instance, says that the Day of the Lord "is a multiple fulfillment term which is limited in occurrences only by its mention in Biblical revelation" (Richard L. Mayhue, "The Prophet's Watchword: Day of the Lord" [Th.D. dissertation, Grace Theological Seminary, 1981], p. 31. See also his "The Prophet's Watchword: Day of the Lord," *Grace Theological Journal* 6 [Fall 1985]: 245). Thus he holds that some of the OT references have already been fulfilled.

[30] Mayhue, "The Prophet's Watchword," Th.D. dissertation, pp. 67, 109; "The Prophet's Watchword," *GTJ*, p. 246; John A. Sproule, *In Defense of Pretribulationism* (Winona Lake, IN: BMH Books, 1980), p. 35.

glory, and ending with the purgation of the heavens and the earth...."[31] Some modern pretribulationists have returned to this view.[32] Another pretribulationist, Paul Feinberg, believes the Day of the Lord begins about the middle of the Tribulation period.[33] The Rapture view of ἀποστασία as an argument for pretribulationism has no validity unless the Day of the Lord begins with the opening of the Tribulation, that is, the fact that the ἀποστασία (i.e., Rapture) precedes the Day of the Lord does not prove a pretribulational Rapture unless the commencement of Day of the Lord also marks the opening of the Tribulation. Therefore, those who hold the Rapture view of ἀποστασία always assume as much. This article will not try to settle this issue but will assume, at least for argument's sake, that the Day of the Lord does begin with the Tribulation.

The Majority text and the second corrector of D (9th century[34]) read "Day of Christ" instead of "Day of the Lord" against all earlier evidence in all forms (Greek, versions, fathers).[35] The "Day of Christ" (or "Lord Jesus," "Lord Jesus Christ," or "Christ Jesus") occurs six times in the NT (1 Cor 1:8; 5:5; 2 Cor 1:14; Phil 1:6, 10; 2:16).[36] "Day of Christ" and "Day of the Lord" are usually seen as being roughly synonymous.[37] However, some pretribulationists see a distinction in the terms, with Day of Christ more closely associated with the Rapture events and Day of the Lord with those of the Second Advent. Pentecost, for instance, says that "each case in which Day of Christ is used it is used specifically in reference to the expectation of the Church, her translation, glorification, and examination for reward."[38] Some pretribulationists hold to only a difference in

---

[31] C. I. Scofield, ed., *The Scofield Reference Bible* (New York: Oxford University Press, 1945), p. 1349, n. 1. Note also Lewis S. Chafer, *Systematic Theology,* 8 vols. (Dallas: Dallas Seminary Press, 1948), 4:398.

[32] Mayhue, "The Prophet's Watchword," Th.D. dissertation, 109; "The Prophet's Watchword," *GTJ,* p. 246; Sproule, *Defense of Pretribulationism,* p. 35.

[33] "Case for the Pretribulational Rapture Position," p. 61.

[34] Aland, *Novum Testamentum Graece,* p. 48.

[35] Ibid. p. 539.

[36] There are textual variations involved with each of these occurrences except for Phil 2:16.

[37] E.g., Gordon D. Fee, *The First Epistle to the Corinthians,* New International Commentary on the New Testament (Grand Rapids: Eerdmans, 1987), p. 43 and Peter T. O'Brien, *Commentary on Philippians,* New International Greek Testament Commentary (Grand Rapids: Eerdmans, 1991), p. 65.

[38] J. Dwight Pentecost, *Things to Come* (reprint of 1958 ed.; Grand Rapids: Zondervan, 1970), p. 232.

emphasis between the terms but no chronological distinction.[39] Thus the textual variant is viewed as not being significant to the interpretation of this verse.[40] Other pretribulationists do, apparently, make a chronological distinction between Day of Christ and Day of the Lord.[41] And because they limit the Day of Christ to events surrounding the Rapture, the reading "Day of Christ" in 2 Thessalonians 2:2 would seem to rule out pretribulationism since, according to 2 Thessalonians 2:3 the Day of Christ (and thus the Rapture) does not take place until after the revelation of "the man of lawlessness," an undisputed tribulational event. As might be expected, those who hold to a chronological distinction between Day of Christ and Day of the Lord opt for the latter reading in 2 Thessalonians 2:2.[42] Thus it appears that either reading can be harmonized with the Rapture view of ἀποστασία, though, apparently, those who take the Rapture view generally point to "Day of the Lord" as the correct reading.[43] This paper will assume that "Day of the Lord" is the correct reading.[44]

Events that Must Precede the Day of the Lord, 2:3

> Let no one in any way deceive you, for *it will not come* unless the apostasy comes first, and the man of lawlessness is revealed, the son of destruction.

In order to correct the error that had been propagated among the Thessalonians, Paul seeks to prove that the Day of the Lord was not, after all, present. He does this by naming two events, in verse 3, which must precede the Day of the Lord. But before naming these two events, Paul

---

[39] Ibid. Cf. also Mason: "While generally *day of Christ* and its variants are used concerning the church's translation to heaven, and *the day of the Lord* comes into the New Testament with heavy overtones from the Old Testament concerning God's dealings with Israel and the nation [*sic*] (Zech. 14:1–4, 9), the difference is not primarily one of time or of words but rather of emphasis (Clarence E. Mason, Jr., "The Day of Our Lord Jesus Christ," *Bibliotheca Sacra* 125 (October–December 1968): 356).

[40] Ibid., p. 358.

[41] E. Schuyler English, *Re-Thinking the Rapture* (Travelers Rest, SC: Southern Bible Book House, 1954), p. 66; Kenneth S. Wuest, "The Rapture— Precisely When?" *Bibliotheca Sacra* 114 (January–March 1957): 63–64.

[42] Ibid.

[43] Gordon R. Lewis does seem to speak of the "day of Christ" in his discussion ("Biblical Evidence for Pretribulationism," *Bibliotheca Sacra* 125 [July–September 1968]: 217).

[44] Fee suggests the reading Χριστοῦ "seems to be a later attempt to make sure that 'Lord' equals 'Christ' in this passage, which in fact it undoubtedly does" ("Pneuma and Eschatology," p. 198).

issues a warning: "Let no one in any way deceive you." This exhortation sums up what has been said in verses 1 and 2.

"The Apostasy"

The first event that must take place before the Day of the Lord is "the apostasy." That the apostasy comes before the Day of the Lord is made clear by the direct statement of the verse 3: "*it will not come* unless the apostasy comes first." However, as the italics in the NASB indicate, the words "*it will not come*" have been added. Paul has written the protasis of a third class condition[45] (ἐὰν μὴ ἔλθῃ ἡ ἀποστασία πρῶτον καὶ ἀποκαλυφθῇ ὁ ἄνθρωπος τῆς ἀνομίας,...) without an apodosis. Although the apodosis is not stated, it is almost universally agreed that it must come from verse two: "the day of the Lord has come" or "is present."[46] The adverb πρῶτον is generally understood to modify the entire protasis; thus Paul is understood to mean that the Day of the Lord is not present unless *first* both the apostasy comes and the man of lawlessness is revealed.[47]

The ἀποστασία has been understood in primarily four different ways.[48] Many church fathers took ἡ ἀποστασία as equal to ὁ ἀποστάτης ("the apostate") and thus in apposition to "the man of lawlessness."[49] The majority view today understands ἀποστασία as religious apostasy. This option is further divided according to whether the participants in this apostasy are professing believers,[50] Jews,[51] or non-Christians.[52] Then

---

[45] Following the classification of Wallace, *Greek Grammar,* p. 696.

[46] Apparently, the lone exception is Charles H. Giblin, who argues that it is to be found in what follows (*The Threat to Faith: An Exegetical and Theological Re-examination of 2 Thessalonians 2* (Rome: Pontifical Biblical Institute, 1967), pp. 122–39.

[47] The exception is Thomas ("2 Thessalonians," pp. 320, 323). He understands πρῶτον to be modifying only ἔλθῃ so that Paul would mean that the Day of the Lord is not present unless the apostasy comes *first* and, then, following the apostasy, the man of lawlessness is revealed. He also understands these events to take place *within* the Day of the Lord, one after the other. The position of πρῶτον is probably of little help in solving this question (cf. Luke 9:59 with 9:61; also, Giblin, *Threat to Faith,* p. 83). But it is generally thought that if Paul intended πρῶτον to be indicating a temporal order between the apostasy and the revelation of the man of lawlessness, he would have written καί ἔπειτα before ἀποκαλυφθῇ (Giblin, *Threat to Faith,* p. 83, n. 3; Wanamaker, *Thessalonians,* p. 243).

[48] See the survey by House, "Apostasia in 2 Thessalonians 2:3," pp. 262–69.

[49] E.g., Cyril of Jerusalem, *Catechetical Lectures* 15.9 and Chrysostom, *Homilies on 2 Thessalonians* 3.3.

[50] E.g., Hiebert, *Thessalonians,* p. 306; Constable, "2 Thessalonians," p. 718.

[51] E.g., Wanamaker, *Thessalonians,* p. 244; Marvin Rosenthal, *The Pre-Wrath Rapture of the Church* (Nashville: Thomas Nelson, 1990), p. 198.

[52] Frame, *Thessalonians,* p. 251; I. Howard Marshall, *1 and 2 Thessalonians,* New Century Bible Commentary (Grand Rapids: Eerdmans, 1983), p. 189. Actually, in my copy

there are those who take ἀποστασία to be an actual revolt or rebellion against God. It is a rebellion against God in the sense of a revolt against the governing authorities, who have been instituted by God.[53] Finally, there are those who understand ἀποστασία as a reference to the Rapture.[54] It is this last view with which this paper is concerned.

The Revealing of "The Man of Lawlessness"

The second event that must precede the Day of the Lord is the revelation of the "man of lawlessness." The manuscripts are divided on whether he is the "man of lawlessness" (ἀνομίας) or "man of sin" (ἁμαρτίας).[55] Since sin is essentially lawlessness with regard to God (1 John 3:4), perhaps the difference is not that great. This "man of lawlessness" is further described as the "son of destruction." This phrase is usually regarded as a Hebraism "indicating the one who belongs to the class destined to destruction."[56] The same expression is used of Judas Iscariot in John 17:12. Attempts to identify this one with someone in the past or present are futile. Paul is talking about a future "man of lawlessness" connected with events surrounding the Second Coming. He will not be revealed until that time. Most premillennialists identify him as the Antichrist.

HISTORY OF THE RAPTURE VIEW

As was noted earlier, the Rapture view of ἀποστασία is thought to have originated with work of E. Schuyler English. His series of articles, "Re-Thinking the Rapture," was later assembled in a book by the same name.[57] English cites no prior sources for his view, and so we are led to believe that it originated with him. However, this is not the case. English

---

of the text, Marshall says "the thought is of a general increase in godliness with the world at large"; but the context indicates "godliness" should read "godlessness."

[53] E.g., Bruce, *Thessalonians,* p. 167.

[54] E.g., House, "Apostasia in 2 Thessalonians 2:3, pp. 267–69

[55] Ἀνομίας is usually preferred since it is considered the harder reading, in that it is a word rarely used by Paul, which copyists would have altered to the more frequently used ἁμαρτίας. "Furthermore, γάρ...ἀνομίας in ver. 7 seems to presuppose ἀνομίας here" (Bruce M. Metzger, *A Textual Commentary on the Greek New Testament,* 2nd ed. [Deutsche Bibelgesellschaft: United Bible Societies, 1994], p. 567). However, ἀνομίας has only Alexandrian support, while ἁμαρτίας is supported by each of the three text types.

[56] Frame, *Thessalonians,* p. 254. Under Wallace's system τῆς ἀπωλείας would be a genitive of destination (*Greek Grammar,* pp. 100–01). Cf. the NIV's "the man doomed to destruction."

[57] *Re-Thinking the Rapture* (Travelers Rest, SC: Southern Bible Book House, 1954).

may have come to this view independently, but he was not the first to suggest it. Reiter has pointed out that, as early as 1895, J. S. Mabie argued for the Rapture view.[58] Apparently, this view was not unknown among pretribulationists before English. This would also explain why John R. Rice could suggest his support for the view in 1945, five years before English's work appeared.[59] However old the Rapture view is, it is clearly English who has popularized the view in recent times. English has been followed by Wuest, Walvoord, Lewis, Tan, Ellisen, Wood, Davey, and House.[60] Although Walvoord initially supported the view, he was later persuaded to the contrary by the arguments of Gundry[61] and has now abandoned the view.[62] The Rapture view of ἀποστασία has received little attention in recent years until House's article. He has produced the most thorough and well-reasoned defense of the Rapture view.

ARGUMENTS FOR THE RAPTURE VIEW

Appeal to Earlier Versions

Proponents of the Rapture view have generally followed English in his appeal to early English Bibles, noting that they translated ἀποστασία in 2 Thessalonians 2:3 as "departing." English says: "William Tyndale's version

---

[58] Richard R. Reiter, "A History of the Development of the Rapture Positions," in The *Rapture: Pre-, Mid-, or Post-Tribulational?* ed. Richard R. Reiter, et al. (Grand Rapids: Zondervan, 1984), p. 32. Mabie suggested this interpretation during an address at the Annual Conference on the Lord's Coming, Los Angeles, in November 1895. His address was later published. See J. S. Mabie, "Will the Church Be in the Tribulation—The Great One?" *Morning Star* 5 (November 1898): 123–24.

[59] John R. Rice, *The Coming Kingdom of Christ* (Murfreesboro, TN: Sword of the Lord Publishers, 1945), p. 152. Rice gives no argumentation; he simply says about the "falling way" in 2 Thess 2:3: "I believe that this refers to the rapture of the saints, when the invisible ties of gravity will be broken and we will suddenly fall away into the air to meet Jesus."

[60] Wuest, "The Rapture," pp. 64–67; John F. Walvoord, *The Rapture Question* (Grand Rapids: Zondervan, 1957), pp. 71–72; Lewis, "Biblical Evidence for Pretribulationism," pp. 216–18; Paul L. Tan, *The Interpretation of Prophecy* (Winona Lake, IN: BMH Books, 1974), p. 341; Stanley A. Ellisen, *Biography of a Great Planet* (Wheaton, IL: Tyndale House, 1975), pp. 121–23; Leon J. Wood, *The Bible and Future Events* (Grand Rapids: Zondervan, 1977), pp. 87–88; Daniel K. Davey, "The Apostasia of 2 Thessalonians 2:3" (Th.M. Thesis, Detroit Baptist Theological Seminary, 1982); House, "Apostasia in 2 Thessalonians 2:3," pp. 261–96.

[61] Gundry, *Church and the Tribulation,* pp. 114–18.

[62] John F. Walvoord, "Posttribulationism Today, Part X: Is the Tribulation Before the Rapture in 2 Thessalonians?" *Bibliotheca Sacra* 134 (April–June 1977): 110; idem, *The Rapture Question,* 2nd ed. (Grand Rapids: Zondervan, 1979), pp. 239–40.

of the N.T., translated and published at Worms, c. 1526, renders *hee* [*sic*] *apostasia,* 'a departynge.' Coverdale (A.D. 1535), Cranmer (1539), and the Geneva Bible (1537) render it the same way. Beza (1565) translates *apostasia* departing.'"[63] The implication of these appeals to the translation "departing" in earlier versions is that they give support or credence to the Rapture view since they can be understood to be referring to a spatial departure. House adds to the list of early translators, suggesting that the Wycliffe Bible of 1384 has the rendering "departynge" and that Jerome, in his Vulgate, used the "Latin word *discessio,* meaning 'departure.'"[64] In fact, House goes so far as to say that Jerome used *discessio* because he specifically understood ἀποστασία to mean a spatial departure.[65]

In arguing against the appeal by English to early versions, Gundry suggested that

> the appeal to early English translations unwittingly reveals weakness, because in the era of those versions lexical studies in NT Greek were almost nonexistent and continued to be so for many years. The papyri had not yet been discovered, and the study of the LXX had hardly begun. That subsequent versions uniformly departed from the earlier renderings points to a correction based on sound and scholarly reasons.[66]

House criticizes Gundry's argument at this point:

> I fail to follow Gundry's logic here. He argues that these early translations err in translating *apostasia*...as "departure" because they did not have the advantage of lexical studies in the New Testament and the LXX. He then indicates that subsequent versions deviated from this translation because they are based on sounder and more scholarly sources. How can this be? The 1611 King James Version, without any better access to more New Testament or Septuagintal studies than its predecessors, not to mention papyriological and other extra-biblical sources, changed from "departure" to "fall away." With the King James Version winning the day as the translation of the English-speaking world, translators characteristically, if not slavishly, followed its lead on *apostasia.*[67]

House has a point about the KJV. Its translation of ἀποστασία as "falling away" would not normally be understood as a spatial departure; and, if

---

[63] *Re-Thinking the Rapture,* p. 69, footnote *. See also Wuest, "The Rapture," p. 65.

[64] House, "Apostasia in 2 Thessalonians 2:3," p. 270.

[65] Ibid., p. 273.

[66] *Church and the Tribulation,* p. 116.

[67] House, "Apostasia in 2 Thessalonians 2:3," pp. 281–82.

future translators followed the KJV, they would render ἀποστασία accordingly. However, his observation probably works against him since, as we shall shortly demonstrate, it is not clear that the change from "departing" to "falling away" proves that the translators of the KJV understood ἀποστασία in 2 Thessalonians 2:3 in a different sense than previous translators—that they were, in effect, changing the meaning of ἀποστασία.[68]

Actually, the appeal to early English versions is of practically no importance in settling the issue at hand. For one thing, the translation "departing" does not give any more credence to the Rapture view since the English word *departing* can be used in both a spatial and nonspatial sense. In Hebrews 3:12 the KJV says: "Take heed, brethren, lest there be in any of you an evil heart of unbelief, in departing from the living God." Obviously, this "departing" is not a spatial one. Numerous examples could be cited from the KJV.[69] Interestingly, other early versions also translate Hebrews 3:12 as "depart."[70] The use of this English word to translate ἀποστασία in 2 Thessalonians 2:2 does not mean that these versions were less disposed to the idea of "religious departure" as the correct understanding of the term. As was noted previously, House says that the first English Bible by Wycliffe rendered ἀποστασία as "departynge." However, this is probably the reading of the second Wycliffe edition. The original edition apparently rendered ἀποστασία with "discencioun,"[71] which is an older spelling of the word *dissension.*[72] *Dissension* does not refer to a spatial departing.[73] Also, House's appeal to Jerome's rendering of ἀποστασία as *discessio* does not prove that Jerome had a spatial meaning in view since the meaning of *discessio* is not limited to only spatial "departing."[74] In fact, Jerome also used *discessio* to translate ἀποστασία in Acts 21:21, which unquestionably refers to religious apostasy.

---

[68] House suggests that the view of ἀποστασία as "apostasy" originated with the KJV (p. 273).

[69] E.g., Dan 9:5; 9:11; Hos 1:2; 1 Tim 4:1; 2 Tim 2:19.

[70] *The English Hexapla* (London: Samuel Bagster and Sons, n.d. The versions are Wyclif, Tyndale, Cranmer [Coverdale], Geneva, and Rheims.

[71] Ibid. This edition claims to represent the first Wycliffe edition of 1380 (p. 57). It is generally agreed that there were two Wycliffe versions—the first in 1380, and a second edition completed after Wycliffe's death in 1384 (see David Ewert, *A General Introduction to the Bible* [Grand Rapids: Zondervan, 1983], pp. 184–85).

[72] *The Oxford English Dictionary,* 12 vols. (Oxford: At the Clarendon Press, 1933), s.v. "dissension," 3:506.

[73] Ibid.

[74] *Oxford Latin Dictionary,* ed. P. G. W. Glare (Oxford: At the Clarendon Press, 1982), s.v. *"discessio,"* p. 550.

By translating ἀποστασία with words that can refer to a spatial departing as well as a figurative one (i.e., religious apostasy), early English translators do not provide us with any clear evidence of their understanding of the term in 2 Thessalonians 2:3. Additionally, there is no other positive evidence that they would have understood the "departing" in any sense other than a figurative one. No evidence is forthcoming that anyone in the church ever understood ἀποστασία to refer to a spatial departure until rather recent times. The translation of the KJV, "falling away," probably reflects how the passage was generally understood.

Meaning of *Apostasia*

Obviously, the crucial issue in evaluating the Rapture view of ἀποστασία is deciding how likely it is the word refers to a spatial departure in 2 Thessalonians 2:3. English built his case around the extra-biblical usage of ἀποστασία and, particularly, the usage of its cognate verb ἀφίστημι. Most interpreters, including most pretribulationists, have found the evidence wanting, especially after Gundry's critique of English.[75] House has recently sought to mitigate Gundry's arguments and to reestablish the cogency of spatial departure as the most probable meaning of ἀποστασία in 2 Thessalonians 2:3.[76] A complete review of the lexical data thus becomes essential.

The Lexical Evidence

Outside of our text, ἀποστασία is found only one other time in the NT—Acts 21:21: "and they have been told about you, that you are teaching all the Jews who are among the Gentiles to forsake Moses [ἀποστασίαν...ἀπὸ Μωϋσέως]...." Here it is agreed that ἀποστασία refers to religious apostasy. In the LXX ἀποστασία is found five times: Joshua 22:22; 2 Chronicles 29:19; 33:19; Jeremiah 2:19; 1 Maccabees 2:15.[77] It also occurs seven times in Aquila (Deut 15:9; Judg 19:22; 1 Kgdms 2:12; 10:27; 25:17; Prov 16:27; Nah 1:11), once in Theodotion (3 Kgdms

---

[75] *Church and the Tribulation,* p. 115–16.

[76] "Apostasia in 2 Thessalonians 2:3," pp. 277–86.

[77] J. Lust et al., eds. *A Greek-English Lexicon of the Septuagint: Part I* (Stuttgart: Deutsche Bibelgesellschaft, 1992), p. 56; Edwin Hatch and Henry A. Redpath, *A Concordance to the Septuagint and Other Greek Versions of the Old Testament,* 3 vols. (Oxford: At the Clarendon Press, 1895), 1:141 [hereafter, Hatch and Redpath]. Hatch and Redpath also list 3 Kgdms 20:13, but this is apparently an error. In three out of the five (Josh 22:22; 2 Chr 33:19; 1 Macc 2:15) there is some variation among the manuscripts between ἀποστασία and a cognate noun ἀποστάσις, which means "defection" or "revolt."

21:13), and twice in Symmachus (1 Kgdms 1:16; 2:12).[78] In every one of these instances from the OT and Apocrypha, the meaning is religious or political defection.

In other koine literature, as illustrated by Moulton and Milligan, only the idea of religious or political defection is found.[79] No example of spatial departure is given.

Both English and House, who argue that ἀποστασία means "spatial departure" in 2 Thessalonians 2:3, and Gundry, who does not, all agree that outside the koine period the idea of spatial departure is only a "secondary meaning" of the word.[80] This conclusion is drawn from the Liddell and Scott lexicon, which lists the primary meaning of ἀποστασία as "defection, revolt" and gives "departure, disappearance" as a secondary meaning.[81] However, the only example given for this secondary meaning comes from the 6th century A.D. Apparently, it is assumed that ἀποστασία can be understood to have the meaning of "spatial departure" in the earlier classical period because it is said that ἀποστασία is a later construction for ἀπόστασις, which *was* used of spatial departure in classical Greek.[82] However, one wonders if this has been proven. 'Αποστασία and ἀπόστασις are not simply spelling variations of the same word. Schlier also says that ἀποστασία is "a later construction for ἀπόστασις," but then seems to distinguish the two when he notes that ἀποστασία "presupposes the concept ἀποστάτης 'to be an apostate,' and thus signifies the state of apostasy, whereas ἀπόστασις denotes the act."[83] 'Αποστασία itself, apparently, first occurs in Greek literature outside the Bible in the first century B.C.[84]

Lampe's lexicon of the patristic period also lists "revolt, defection" as the primary meaning of ἀποστασία; however, there is one example

---

[78] Hatch and Redpath, 1:141; 3:200.

[79] James H. Moulton and George Milligan, *The Vocabulary of the Greek Testament Illustrated from the Papyri and Other Non-Literary Sources* (reprint of 1930 ed.; Grand Rapids: Eerdmans, 1976), pp. 68–69.

[80] English, *Re-Thinking the Rapture,* p. 68; House, "Apostasia in 2 Thessalonians 2:3," p. 273; Gundry, *Church and the Tribulation,* p. 115.

[81] Henry G. Liddell and Robert Scott, comp., *A Greek-English Lexicon,* 9th ed. (Oxford: Clarendon Press, 1996), p. 218 [hereafter, LSJ].

[82] Ibid.

[83] Gerhard Kittel et al., eds., *Theological Dictionary of the New Testament,* 10 vols. (Grand Rapids: Eerdmans, 1964–76), s.v. "ἀφίστημι, ἀποστασία, διχοστασία," by Heinrich Schlier, 1:513 [hereafter, *TDNT*].

[84] BAGD, s.v. "ἀποστασία," p. 98.

given of spatial departure.[85] This interesting reference does not seem to
have been discussed by supporters of the Rapture view.[86] This reference
to a spatial departure is found in a NT apocryphal work entitled *The
Assumption of the Virgin.* In sections 31–32 we read:

> But the Holy Ghost said to the apostles and the mother of the Lord, "Behold,
> the governor has sent a captain of a thousand against you, because the Jews
> have made a tumult. Go out therefore from Bethlehem, and fear not; for
> behold, I will bring you by a cloud to Jerusalem…." The apostles therefore
> rose up straightaway and went out of the house, bearing the bed of their lady
> the mother of God, and went forward towards Jerusalem: and immediately,
> just as the Holy Ghost said, they were lifted up by a cloud and were found at
> Jerusalem in the house of their lady.[87]

Here we clearly have the description of a "rapture" of the apostles and
mother of the Lord. The story continues in section 33:

> But when the captain came to Bethlehem and did not find there the mother
> of the Lord, nor the apostles, he laid hold upon the Bethlehemites,… For the
> captain did not know of the departure of the apostles and the mother of the
> Lord to Jerusalem.[88]

This "rapture" is now described as a "departure," the Greek word being
ἀποστασία.[89] Here is clear evidence that ἀποστασία can refer to a
"rapture"; however, *The Assumption of the Virgin* can be dated no earlier
than the fifth century A.D.[90]

The cognate verb of ἀποστασία, ἀφίστημι, is found fourteen times
in the NT. It is used in both a spatial and nonspatial sense. Only three times
is it used of religious apostasy (Luke 8:13; 1 Tim 4:1; Heb 3:12). No one

---

[85] G. W. H. Lampe, ed., *A Patristic Greek Lexicon* (Oxford: At the Clarendon Press, 1961), p. 208.

[86] It was brought to my attention by David G. Winfrey, *An Examination of the Pretribulational Rapture Interpretation of 2 Thess. 2:7* (Hollywood, FL: Lighthouse Ministries, 1980), p. 8.

[87] J. K. Elliott, *The Apocryphal New Testament* (Oxford: Clarendon Press, 1993), p. 705.

[88] Ibid.

[89] The Greek text is found in Constantin von Tischendorf, *Apocalypses Apocryphae* (reprint of 1866 ed.; Hildesheim: Georg Olms Verlagsbuchhandlung, 1966), p. 105.

[90] Edgar Hennecke, *New Testament Apocrypha,* 2 vols., ed. Wilhelm Schneemelcher, trans. R. McL. Wilson (Philadelphia: Westminster Press, 1963), 1:429.

questions the fact that the word most often designates a spatial departure. It is found with that meaning throughout all periods of Greek literature[91]

Evaluation

As was noted earlier, a major part of the case for understanding ἀποστα-σία as a spatial departure is its relationship to its cognate verb ἀφίστημι. The argument suggests that the meaning of the verb can also be applied to the noun. English says:

> It is evident, then that the verb *aphisteemi* [*sic*] does have the meaning *to depart* in the New Testament, in a very general sense which is not specialized as being related to rebellion against God or forsaking the faith. And, since a noun takes it meaning from the verb, the noun, too, may have such a broad connotation.[92]

Gundry argues that English is mistaken — one cannot say the cognate verb determines the meaning of the noun.[93] It may be that nouns often have a similar semantic range as their cognate verbs, but that must be demonstrated in each case — it cannot be assumed. Gundry points to the noun ἀποστάσιον, which is also cognate to ἀφίστημι, yet it relates only to "*divorce* or some other legal act of separation."[94] The cognate noun ἀποστατήρ means "one who has power to dissolve an assembly" or "to decide a question."[95] These derivative nouns do not carry the meaning of "spatial departure" found in ἀφίστημι. Though the cognate verb may be a guide and help to establishing the meaning of derivative nouns, the meaning of a noun must be established by its own usage.

When the usage of ἀποστασία itself is examined, the case is not entirely clear. If ἀποστασία is understood to be the same word as ἀπόστασις, then the

---

[91] LSJ, p. 291.

[92] English, *Re-Thinking the Rapture,* p. 69. Essentially the same argument is made by Wuest ("The Rapture," pp. 64–65), Lewis ("Biblical Evidence for Pretribulationism," p. 218), Ellisen (*Biography of a Great Planet,* p. 122), Wood (*The Bible and Future Events,* p. 87), Davey ("The Apostasia of 2 Thessalonians 2:3," pp. 7–10), and House ("Apostasia in 2 Thessalonians 2:3," pp. 282–83).

[93] *Church and the Tribulation,* p. 116. Davey carries the root idea even further: "Since the root verb has this meaning of 'departure' from a person or place in a geographical sense, would not its derivatives have the same foundational word meaning. If, not, then word meanings may be divorced from root meanings which is contrary to the linguistic rules governing semantics" (p. 9). On the contrary, it is Davey's understanding which is contrary to the regular use of language. This is the well-known root fallacy. See, for example, D. A. Carson, *Exegetical Fallacies,* 2nd ed. (Grand Rapids: Baker, 1996), pp. 28–35 and Grant R. Osborne, *The Hermeneutical Spiral* (Downers Grove, IL: InterVarsity Press, 1991), pp. 66–69.

[94] Gundry, *Church and the Tribulation,* p. 116.

[95] LSJ, p. 219..

meaning of "spatial departure" can be found in classical Greek. In the koine period no example of "spatial departure" is to be found, unless, of course, 2 Thessalonians 2:3 is the exception.[96] But even if the classical support is found wanting, clearly, ἀποστασία did come to have the meaning of "spatial departure," but the earliest example is from the 5th century A.D. At this point one must decide how to evaluate the data for ἀποστασία.

Gundry has argued that the "meaning and connotation of a NT word are determined from four sources: (1) other appearances in the NT; (2) the LXX; (3) the *koinē* (of which NT Greek is a species); and (4) classical Greek."[97] He goes on to note that the least important of these is classical Greek and observes that it is from this source that English draws his argument.[98] It is difficult to see why anyone would disagree with Gundry's procedure for evaluating lexical data. Even House, who quotes Gundry at this point, does not actually question the appropriateness of his procedure.[99] Since words change in meaning over time and since classical Greek is furthest from the NT, it is only proper that it be weighted least important. About the LXX, Gundry rightly observes:

> In matters of vocabulary and style the LXX strongly influenced the NT writers, whose Bible for the most part was the LXX. The high number of occurrences of ἀποστασία in the LXX and their broad distribution evince a well-established usage. And we ought to bear in mind that Paul was thoroughly familiar with and greatly influenced by the language of the LXX, for in quoting the OT he follows the LXX most of the time.[100]

Thus, the evidence from the most important sources gives no support for the meaning of "spatial departure" for ἀποστασία. This is probably why this meaning is not found in the standard NT lexicon by Bauer, nor by its predecessor Thayer.[101] The same is true for the *Theological Dictionary of the New Testament, The New International Dictionary of*

---

[96] In a search of the *Thesaurus Linguae Graecae* database from the second century B.C. through the first century A.D., Feinberg did not find a single instance where ἀποστασία means "spatial departure" ("2 Thessalonians 2 and the Rapture," p. 310).

[97] *Church and the Tribulation*, p. 115.

[98] Ibid.

[99] After quoting Gundry, House does say: "I find it extremely interesting that Gundry limits the determination of word meanings to four and omits (possibly by accident) the most important factor in determining the specific meaning of any given word; namely, context" ("Apostasia in 2 Thessalonians 2:3," p. 279). This is an unfair criticism since it is clear that Gundry is speaking of "sources" for determining the semantic range of a word, which can then can be evaluated by the context.

[100] *Church and the Tribulation*, p. 115.

[101] BAGD, s.v. "Ἀποστασία," p. 98; John H. Thayer, *Greek-English Lexicon of the New Testament* (reprint of 1889 ed.; Grand Rapids, Zondervan, 1975), s.v. "Ἀποστασία," p. 667.

New Testament Theology, and the more recent *Exegetical Dictionary of the New Testament.*[102] Considering all the lexical evidence, it seems unlikely that ἀποστασία means "spatial departure" in 2 Thessalonians 2:3. Yet, because of the evidence for such a meaning possibly before the koine period but clearly after it, it cannot be entirely ruled out. While not an impossibility, it seems improbable.

Contextual Arguments

Although the Rapture view is based mainly on the lexical argument surrounding ἀποστασία, it is also supported by several contextual arguments that are somewhat related. First, it is said that ἀποστασία "does not inherently carry the meaning of [religious] defection or revolt. It does so only because of the contexts."[103] It is, we are told, the presence of certain qualifying phrases (e.g., "from the faith," from the living God"[104]) that give the word this meaning.

It is true that qualifying phrases, as in the case of Acts 21:21 (lit. "apostasy...from Moses"), do clearly establish the meaning of the word. However, not every use of ἀποστασία in the LXX, for instance, includes a qualifying phrase, though in every case religious apostasy is in view. For example, in 1 Maccabees 2:15 we read: "The king's officers who were enforcing the apostasy came to the town of Modein to make them offer sacrifice" (Καὶ ἦλθον οἱ παρὰ τοῦ βασιλέως οἱ καταναγκάζοντες τὴν ἀποστασίαν εἰς Μωδεῖν τὴν πόλιν, ἵνα θυσιάσωσιν).[105] House admits this, but argues that in the case of 1 Maccabees 2:15, it is the immediate

---

[102] *TDNT,* s.v. "ἀφίστημι, ἀποστασία, διχοστασία," 1:513–14; Colin Brown, ed., *The New International Dictionary of New Testament Theology,* 3 vols. (Grand Rapids: Zondervan, 1975–78), s.v. "Fall, Fall Away," by W. Bauder, 1:606–08; Hortst Balz and Gerhard Schneider, eds., *Exegetical Dictionary of the New Testament,* 3 vols. (Grand Rapids: Eerdmans, 1990–93), s.v. "ἀποστασία," 1:141. House does not accurately represent the evidence in Kittel. He says: "Moreover, Kittel recognizes that *apostasia* and its cognates can carry the spatial sense" ("Apostasia in 2 Thessalonians 2:3," p. 281). Then he cites the first paragraph of the discussion of ἀφίστημι to prove his statement. The article in Kittel in no way "recognizes that *apostasia* and its cognates can carry the spatial sense." There is not the slightest hint of such an idea. Ἀποστασία is discussed in a separate section which does not even hint at a connection with ἀφίστημι.

[103] House, "Apostasia in 2 Thessalonians 2:3," p. 273. Similarly, Wuest, "The Rapture," p. 65.

[104] English, *Re-Thinking the Rapture,* pp. 68–69;

[105] NRSV. The Greek text is from Alfred Rahlfs, ed. *Septuaginta,* 2 vols. (Stuggart: Deutsche Bibelstiftung, 1935), 1:1043. Of the four other uses of ἀποστασία in the LXX, it appears that only 2 Chron 28:19 has a qualifying phrase (ἀπὸ κυρίου), excepting for personal pronouns (contra House, "Apostasia in 2 Thessalonians 2:3," p. 273).

context which gives ἀποστασία its meaning, while in 2 Thessalonians 2:3 the context does not support the idea of religious departure.[106] There is some truth to House's argument about a lack of context for religious departure, at least as far as most pretribulationists understand the apostasy. They believe the ἀποστασία in 2 Thessalonians 2:3 is a religious apostasy by professing believers which precedes the revelation of the man of lawlessness. Thus, there is, in their understanding, no mention of this apostasy in the immediate context following verse 3.[107] Perhaps the force of House's argument is blunted by Gundry's suggestion that by the time of the koine, ἀποστασία had acquired the limited meaning of "religious apostasy or political defection," and so no qualifying phrases were necessary.[108] There may be some cogency to this suggestion since, as we have before noted, every known instance of ἀποστασία in the koine has this limited meaning; and again, as we have shown, all lexical authorities support only this meaning. Our next discussion will also have a bearing on this issue.[109]

The second contextual argument supporting the Rapture view is based on the observation that ἀποστασία is articular, "ἡ ἀποστασία." It is argued that the article with ἀποστασία points to something well-known to the Thessalonians and explained in the previous context.[110] That previous context would be references to the Rapture in verse 1 ("our gathering together to Him") and 1 Thessalonians 4:13–17. That the article points to an ἀποστασία previously known to the Thessalonians is probably the most likely explanation of the article.[111] Gundry seeks to mitigate this difficulty by suggesting that the article points forward to what follows, the

---

[106] House, "Apostasia in 2 Thessalonians 2:3," pp. 273–74.

[107] E.g., Thomas, "2 Thessalonians," pp. 321–22; Hiebert, *Thessalonians,* p. 306; Constable, "2 Thessalonians," p. 718.

[108] Gundry, *Church and the Tribulation,* p. 116.

[109] This lack of reference to apostasy in the immediate context is not a problem for Gundry (*Church and the Tribulation,* pp. 117–18) and for at least one pretribulationist (See Charles E. Powell, "The Identity of the 'Restrainer' in 2 Thessalonians 2:6–7," *Bibliotheca Sacra* 154 [July–September 1997: 327]). They do find a description of the apostasy in 2 Thess 2. For them it comes about as a result of the activity of the man of lawlessness (2 Thess 2:4, 10–11).

[110] English, *Re-Thinking the Rapture,* pp. 69–70; Wuest, "The Rapture," p. 66; Ellisen, *Biography of a Great Planet,* p. 122; House, "Apostasia in 2 Thessalonians 2:3," pp. 284–86.

[111] Following Wallace's categories, the article, as understood in the Rapture view, would probably fall more into his "anaphoric" category rather than "well-known" (*Greek Grammar,* pp. 217–220, 225). Understanding ἀποστασία as religious apostasy places the article in the "well-known" category.

apostasy brought on by the man of lawlessness (vv. 4, 10–11).[112] However, this use of the article, while possible, is quite rare.[113]

But ἡ ἀποστασία would not have to be a reference to the Rapture in order to point to something well-known to the Thessalonians. If ἀποστασία is a reference to religious apostasy, Paul could have easily made reference to it during his previous visit. In fact, later in verse 15, Paul makes explicit reference to his previous oral (διὰ λόγου) teaching: "So then, brethren, stand firm and hold to the traditions which you were taught, whether by word *of mouth* or by letter from us." And, even more striking, in verse 5 he asks: "Do you not remember that while I was still with you, I was telling you these things?" "These things" could easily include the ἀποστασία of verse 3. While it might seem unlikely that Paul would, almost out of the blue, make reference to a religious apostasy not mentioned previously in the Thessalonian correspondence, yet, in fact, he does something quite similar in verse 6 with reference to the "restrainer": "And you know what restrains him now, so that in his time he may be revealed." This reference to τὸ κατέχον also seems to come from nowhere, yet Paul says the Thessalonians "know" (οἴδατε) it. How do they know it since this is a topic not previously mentioned in the Thessalonian correspondence? — obviously, because of Paul's previous oral teaching.

In one way the Rapture view does fit well with the overall context of how pretribulationists understand 2 Thessalonians 2. Since the Thessalonians were apparently connecting their present troubles with the Day of the Lord, thinking that it was present, and if Paul had previously taught them pretribulationism, posttribulationists ask why did he not simply tell them that they were not in the Day of the Lord because the Rapture had not taken place?[114] Of course, the Rapture view argues that is exactly what Paul did do with his reference to the ἀποστασία.[115] Thus Paul says, according to the Rapture view, that the Thessalonians need not be fearful that they are in the Day of the Lord, for that Day must be preceded by the Rapture, followed by the revelation of the man of lawlessness. Those who hold the Rapture view also point out that this interpretation corresponds, *in sequence,* with the common pretribulational understanding of verses 6–7:

---

[112] See footnote 108 above.

[113] Wallace calls this usage "kataphoric" (*Greek Grammar,* p. 220).

[114] E.g., Douglas, J. Moo, "The Case for the Posttribulation Rapture Position," in *The Rapture: Pre-, Mid-, or Post-Tribulational?* ed. Richard R. Reiter, et al. (Grand Rapids: Zondervan, 1984), p. 189.

[115] English, *Re-Thinking the Rapture,* p. 70. House, "Apostasia in 2 Thessalonians 2:3," p. 275.

the Holy Spirit indwelling the church is now restraining the revelation of the man of lawlessness until "he is taken out of the way" at the Rapture.[116]

This would seem to be a strong argument except for one problem. As has been previously noted, pretribulationists assume Paul had taught the Thessalonians a pretribulational Rapture, and now because of their present troubles, they thought they were in the Day of the Lord and thus had missed the Rapture. If Paul responds by saying that they are not in the Day of the Lord because the Rapture (ἀποστασία) must take place before the Day of the Lord, he would seem to be offering no real proof to allay their fears. That is, he would simply be telling them what he had taught them before, not really responding to their fear of having missed the Rapture. But, however, if he offers proof that the Day of the Lord cannot have commenced by pointing out that they have obviously not seen the apostasy and the revelation of the man of lawlessness, events he had previously taught them about, then their fears should be allayed.

CONCLUSION

The case for understanding ἀποστασία as the Rapture in 2 Thessalonians 2:3 has not been proven. The appeal to the translation of the word in versions prior to the King James has no merit whatsoever. While the English translation "departure" can refer to spatial departure, there is no evidence that this is the intended meaning of the word in these early versions in 2 Thessalonians 2:3. The lexical argument that ἀποστασία itself could have that meaning in this verse seems unlikely. The strongest argument for the Rapture view is the contextual considerations. These certainly have merit, but in my opinion do not rise to the level of probability. 'Αποστασία most likely refers to a religious apostasy, and therefore its occurrence in 2 Thessalonians 2:3 should not be used as evidence for the pretribulational Rapture.

---

[116] English, *Re-Thinking the Rapture,* pp. 70–71. House, "Apostasia in 2 Thessalonians 2:3," pp. 276–77.

PERSEVERING AND FALLING AWAY: A REEXAMINATION OF HEBREWS 6:4–6[1]

R. Bruce Compton

[4]For in the case of those who have once been enlightened and have tasted the heavenly gift and have been made partakers of the Holy Spirit, [5]and have tasted the good word of God and the powers of the age to come, [6]and *then* have fallen away, it is impossible to renew them again to repentance, since they again crucify to themselves the Son of God and put Him to open shame (Heb. 6:4–6).[2]

The warning passage in Hebrews 6:4–6 continues to be a notorious crux in New Testament interpretation. The difficulty comes in harmonizing the description in vv. 4–5 of those who have tasted the heavenly gift and have become partakers of the Holy Spirit with the statement in v. 6 about their falling away and not being able to be brought back to repentance. The juxtaposition of these verses has raised a number of questions. Are the experiences predicated in vv. 4–5 tantamount to salvation, or are they describing something that approximates salvation but falls short of it? If vv. 4–5 are describing salvation, is v. 6 describing the loss of salvation? Furthermore, why does v. 6 say that it is impossible to restore those who fall away, or is restoration possible? And, lastly, what precisely is the danger being warned about in these verses? Are those in view being threatened with the loss of reward or with eternal condemnation and judgment, with hell itself?

The purpose of this article is to survey the views found in the commentaries and related literature on this passage[3] and to update the

---

[1] This article first appeared in the Spring 1996 issue of *DBSJ,* vol. 1, pp. 135–167.

[2] Unless otherwise noted, all Scripture references are from the *New American Standard Bible*, 1995 edition. Verses in brackets represent the Hebrew text, when the Hebrew text differs from the verses of the English translation or the Septuagint (LXX).

[3] The verses under discussion fall within the context of what is generally referred to as the third warning passage, or 5:11–6:8. While scholarly opinion varies somewhat as to the number of these warnings and the verses involved, five warning passages are commonly identified in Hebrews: 2:1–4; 3:7–4:13; 5:11–6:8; 10:26–39; and 12:14–29. Furthermore, the warnings themselves are interrelated since they appear to have the same audience in view, the same underlying problem as the occasion for the warnings, and the same consequences if the warnings are not heeded. Consequently, they should not be treated in isolation, but synthetically, in order to arrive at a proper interpretation of each. On both the form and content of all five warning passages in Hebrews, see Scot McKnight, "The Warning Passages of Hebrews: A Formal Analysis and Theological Conclusions," *Trinity Journal* 13 (Spring 1992): 22–23.

arguments for the view that supports both the eternal security of the believer and the need for believers to persevere in the faith.

MAJOR VIEWS

The various interpretations of this passage in contemporary literature may be conveniently catalogued under four views.[4] The views themselves are generally distinguished according to their understanding of the spiritual status of those addressed and the nature of the warning being issued. The four views are (1) *true believer: apostasy/loss of salvation;*[5] (2) *true believer: apostasy/loss of reward;* (3) *true believer: hypothetical apostasy/loss of salvation;* and (4) *false believer: apostasy/eternal judgment.* These views are briefly discussed in this section to identify their salient strengths and weaknesses and to establish a basis for a more detailed examination of the passage in the following section.

True Believer: Apostasy/Loss of Salvation

Advocates of this view interpret vv. 4–5 as describing salvation and v. 6 as describing apostasy and the loss of salvation.[6] This view has

---

[4] E.g., Homer A. Kent, *The Epistle to the Hebrews* (Grand Rapids: Baker, 1972), pp. 111–14. Not all of the views currently championed on Heb 6 fit precisely into one of these four views. For somewhat different listings, see McKnight, "Warning Passages," pp. 23–25, and Herbert W. Bateman IV, ed., *Four Views on the Warning Passages in Hebrews* (Grand Rapids: Kregel, 2007). Other interpretations are addressed where appropriate in connection with the four views identified above. A history of the interpretation of this passage is provided by James K. Solari, "The Problem of *Metanoia* in the Epistle to the Hebrews" (Ph.D. dissertation, Catholic University of America, 1970).

[5] *Apostasy* means the renunciation of the gospel by those who had previously embraced it (*New Dictionary of Theology,* s.v. "Apostasy," by I. Marshall, pp. 39–40). For further treatment, see the discussion under v. 6. *Salvation* refers to the initial aspects of individual redemption, including regeneration, justification, forgiveness, adoption, etc. Conversely, *loss of salvation* refers to the forfeiture of these items. The end for those who are saved is heaven or glorification; the end for those who are not saved is hell or eternal condemnation and punishment. See Wayne Grudem, "Perseverance of the Saints: A Case Study from Hebrews 6:4–6 and the Other Warning Passages," in *The Grace of God, The Bondage of the Will, Volume One: Biblical and Practical Perspectives on Calvinism,* ed. Thomas R. Schreiner and Bruce A. Ware (Grand Rapids: Baker, 1995), pp. 134–37. Grudem's article appeared during the writing of the present article. He holds to the same position on Heb 6:4–6 as this author and uses a number of the same arguments.

[6] Brooke Foss Westcott, *The Epistle to the Hebrews* (reprint ed., Grand Rapids: Eerdmans, 1974), pp. 150, 166–67; James Moffatt, *A Critical and Exegetical Commentary on the Epistle to the Hebrews,* International Critical Commentary (Edinburgh: T. and T. Clark, 1924), pp. 76–82; R. C. H. Lenski, *The Interpretation of the Epistle to the Hebrews*

several strengths. First, it interprets the statements in vv. 4–5 as they are commonly understood. "Enlightened" in v. 4 is generally interpreted in a figurative sense of instruction or illumination.[7] "Tasted of the heavenly gift" is frequently understood as a metaphor for experiencing salvation.[8] Similarly, "partakers of the Holy Spirit" is often viewed as meaning "to share in the person and work of God's Spirit."[9] Second, this view interprets v. 6 as it is also commonly understood. "Fallen away" is defined as apostasy, a conscious and willful rejection of Christ and the gospel. The consequence of this act is the loss of salvation, resulting in eternal condemnation and judgment.[10] And the construction "it is impossible to renew them again to repentance" means that the subsequent condition of those who fall away is irreversible.[11]

At the same time, there are several liabilities with this interpretation. The overriding problem is that it contradicts a number of passages in Scripture, which argue that salvation once received cannot be lost.[12] In

---

and The Epistle of James (reprint of 1937 ed., Minneapolis: Augsburg, 1966), pp. 180–81; I. Howard Marshall, *Kept by the Power of God: A Study of Perseverance and Falling Away* (Minneapolis: Bethany Fellowship, 1969), pp. 148–53; Harold W. Attridge, *The Epistle to the Hebrews,* Hermenia (Philadelphia, Fortress, 1989), pp. 166–73; William L. Lane, *Hebrews,* 2 vols., Word Biblical Commentary (Dallas: Word, 1991), 1:141–43; Scot McKnight, "Warning Passages," pp. 24–25, 43–48; Grant R. Osborne, "A Classical Arminian View," in *Four Views on the Warning Passages in Hebrews,* ed. Herbert W. Bateman IV (Grand Rapids: Kregel, 2007), pp. 86–128.

Similarly, from a sacramental perspective where salvation is described in terms of membership in the Christian or new covenant community and the loss of salvation as exclusion from this community, see Hugh Montefiore, *A Commentary on the Epistle to the Hebrews,* Black's New Testament Commentaries (London: Adam and Charles Black, 1964), pp. 107–10; George Wesley Buchanan, *To the Hebrews,* Anchor Bible (Garden City, NJ: Doubleday, 1972), pp. 105–10.

[7] *Theological Dictionary of the New Testament,* s.v. "φῶς," by H. Conzelmann, 9:355 [hereafter cited as *TDNT*].

[8] *TDNT,* s.v. "γεύομαι," by J. Behm, 1:676–77; *The New International Dictionary of New Testament Theology,* s.v. "Hunger, Taste," by E. Tiedtke, 2:270 [hereafter cited as *NIDNTT*].

[9] *TDNT,* s.v. "μέτοχος," by H. Hanse, 2:832.

[10] *NIDNTT,* s.v. "Fall, Fall Away," by W. Bauder, 1:610–11; s.v. "Sin," by W. Gunther and W. Bauder, 3:586.

[11] *NIDNTT,* s.v. "Might," by O. Betz, 2:606; *TDNT,* s.v. "ἀνακαινίζω," by J. Behm, 3:451.

[12] Included among these passages are John 5:24; 6:37; 10:28–30; Rom 8:1, 28–30; Eph 4:30; Phil 1:6; and, by implication, Heb 8:12. For a recent defense of eternal security in the writings of Paul, see Judith M. Gundry-Volf, *Paul and Perseverance: Staying in and Falling Away* (Louisville: Westminster/John Knox Press, 1990). Her conclusion on the

addition, proponents of this view do not offer a consistent explanation on why it is impossible to restore those who fall away.[13]

True Believer: Apostasy/Loss of Reward

Proponents of this position interpret vv. 4–5 as referring to salvation and v. 6 as referring to a falling away from commitment to Christ and the gospel. What is in jeopardy for those who fall away is not the loss of salvation or eternal judgment, but rather the loss of blessing and reward.[14] The extent of this falling away varies among the proponents from a simple waning in devotion to Christ to a complete rejection of the faith, to apostasy itself. In addition, the tendency among the advocates is to interpret the expression "it is impossible" in v. 6 in a relative or restricted sense. The impossibility is from the human perspective alone. In other words, it is impossible for man, but not for God, to restore those who have fallen.[15]

Like the preceding view, this approach has certain strengths. It takes vv. 4–5 in their frequently understood sense as describing salvation. Furthermore, since there is no concept of a loss of salvation with this view, it avoids the liability of the previous view. There is no conflict here with those passages in Scripture that teach eternal security.

Yet this view faces serious problems. First and foremost, the threat in the warning passages appears to be much more extensive than simply

security of the believer in Paul's writings accurately reflects the position of all of Scripture on this subject.

Paul gives clear and ample evidence of his view that Christians' salvation is certain to reach completion. This thought is integral to his understanding of individual salvation. Though threats to the consummation of Christians' salvation may and will appear, they cannot successfully challenge it. God's faithfulness and love make divine triumph the unquestionable outcome. For Paul, certainty of final salvation rests on God's continued intervention to that end (p. 82).

[13] The explanation most often given is that apostasy, like the blasphemy against the Holy Spirit (cf. Matt 12:31–32; Mark 3:28–30; Luke 12:10), is an unforgivable sin. E.g., Lenski, *Hebrews,* pp. 180–81. Others demur, saying that those having fallen *can* be renewed, if they will turn from their rebellion and seek God's pardon. See the discussions in Moffatt, *Hebrews,* p. 79; and Attridge, *Hebrews,* pp. 166–72.

[14] Zane C. Hodges, "Hebrews," in *The Bible Knowledge Commentary,* 2 vols., ed. John F. Walvoord and Roy B. Zuck (Wheaton, IL: Victor Books, 1983), 2:794–96; Thomas Kem Oberholtzer, "An Analysis and Exposition of the Eschatology of the Warning Passages in the Book of Hebrews" (Th.D. dissertation, Dallas Theological Seminary, 1970) and, more recently, "The Thorn-Infested Ground in Hebrews 6:4–12," *Bibliotheca Sacra* 145 (July–September 1988): 319–28; Rodney J. Decker, "The Warning of Hebrews Six," *The Journal of Ministry & Theology* 5 (Fall 2001): 26–48; Randall C. Gleason, "A Moderate Reformed View," in *Four Views on the Warning Passages in Hebrews* (Grand Rapids: Kregel, 2007), pp. 336–77.

[15] Hodges, "Hebrews," p. 796; Oberholtzer, "Thorn-Infested Ground," p. 323.

the loss of blessing and/or reward. In 4:11, the defection warned against involves a falling into judgment and a missing out on God's Sabbath rest (4:9).[16] The Sabbath rest that those in view are in jeopardy of missing is nothing less than heaven itself.[17] In 10:27, the threat is presented as a terrifying expectation of judgment involving a raging fire that will consume the enemies of God.[18] This consuming of the enemies of God with a raging fire can hardly be a description of God's treatment of the redeemed.[19] The same may be said in 10:39, where those who persevere in the faith to the saving of the soul are contrasted with those who shrink back unto destruction.[20] The contrast between saving the soul and destroying the soul is found elsewhere in the NT of the contrast between salvation and eternal judgment.[21]

---

[16] Walter Bauer et al., *A Greek-English Lexicon of the New Testament and Other Early Christian Literature,* 3rd ed., rev. and ed. by Frederick W. Danker (Chicago: University of Chicago Press, 2000), s.v. "πίπτω," p. 815 [hereafter cited as BDAG]; *NIDNTT,* s.v. "Fall, Fall Away," by W. Bauder, 1:611.

[17] Kent, *Hebrews,* pp. 84–88. This conclusion is based on three lines of evidence. First, the "Sabbath rest" is future. According to 4:9, 11, it is something that the readers have not yet entered. Second, it is called a "Sabbath" rest because it is associated with God and His "rest" in heaven (comparing 4:4 with 4:9). Third, it is the same rest that Christ entered (4:10, "For the one [Christ] who has entered His rest has himself also rested from his works..."). This identification of the "Sabbath rest" in 4:9 still stands, even if 4:10 is referring to the believer rather than to Christ. For further support, see *TDNT,* s.v. "σαββατισμός," by E. Lohse, 7:34–35. The point is not that saved individuals may miss out on heaven, but that those who miss out on heaven do so because they are not saved.

[18] φοβερὰ δέ τις ἐκδοχὴ κρίσεως καὶ πυρὸς ζῆλος ἐσθίειν μέλλοντος τοὺς ὑπεναντίους.

[19] This verse includes an allusion to the LXX of Isa 26:11 where the enemies whom God destroys are distinguished from the righteous whom God blesses. This same distinction is maintained in Heb 10:27. The parallel reference in Heb 10:30 to the Lord judging His people does not militate against this conclusion. The statement in 10:30 is from the LXX of Deut 32:36 (cf. Ps 134:14 [135:14]). In Deut 32, Moses recounts the history of the nation and its failures and gives a forecast of the nation's anticipated rebellion as a warning to the generation about to enter Canaan (32:44–47). The "people" in view are not the righteous but the entire nation of Israel. Both the context of Deut 32 and the critique of the nation in Heb 3:7–19 suggest that the majority of the nation at that time were unbelievers. These are the people whom God judges (cf. Deut 32:43). For further discussion, see *NIDNTT,* s.v. "Judgment," by W. Schneider, 2:365–66.

[20] ἡμεῖς δὲ οὐκ ἐσμὲν ὑποστολῆς εἰς ἀπώλειαν ἀλλὰ πίστεως εἰς περιποίησιν ψυχῆς. Translating πίστεως as "persevere in the faith" is based on the antecedent exhortation in 10:35–36 calling the readers to perseverance. For taking περιποίησιν as "saving," see BDAG, p. 804; *NIDNTT,* s.v. "περιποιέομαι," by E. Beyreuther, 2:839.

[21] E.g., Matt 10:28, 39; 16:25–26. The noun "destruction" (ἀπώλειαν) is frequently used in the NT of eternal judgment. See BDAG, p. 127; *TDNT,* s.v. "ἀπώλειαν," by A. Oepke, 1:396–97.

Finally, in 12:15, the danger warned about involves being excluded from[22] the grace of God.

The unmistakable impression from these combined threats is that nothing short of eternal condemnation and punishment is in view for those guilty of not heeding these warnings.[23] Added to this is the *a fortiori* argument employed in several of the warning passages in Hebrews comparing and contrasting the judgment of those in the OT who rejected the Law with the judgment of those in the present era who spurn the gospel (2:1–4; 10:26–31; 12:25–27).[24] The argument is that the judgment of those who reject the gospel is not only more certain but also more severe. The force of the logic appears compelling. Those in the OT who rejected the Law forfeited their lives and were excluded from the rest associated with entering the land of promise (3:7–19; 10:28). The more certain and severe corollary must be that those who spurn the gospel face nothing less than eternal punishment and exclusion from heaven.[25]

A second liability with this view concerns the problem that has elicited the warnings. If the problem is simply a lack of spiritual maturity or commitment, as some have suggested, then why is it impossible, to bring those who are guilty to repentance?[26] On the other hand, if the problem is that of apostasy, as others have argued, how can apostasy be describing the action of a saved individual?[27] This is particularly problematic in that the author of Hebrews has specifically identified persevering in the faith as the mark of a partaker of Christ, that is, as the mark of a genuine believer, one who is truly saved (3:14).[28]

---

[22] BAGD, s.v. "ὑστερέω," p. 849; *TDNT,* s.v. "ὕστερος," by U. Wilckens, 8:596.

[23] McKnight, "Warning Passages," pp. 33–36; Grudem, "Perseverance of the Saints," pp. 151–52. For further support, see the discussion in connection with v. 6.

[24] Attridge, *Hebrews,* pp. 292 passim.

[25] McKnight, "Warning Passages," pp. 33–36.

[26] Oberholtzer, "Thorn-Infested Ground," pp. 323–24. Oberholtzer says what is impossible is others bringing the lapsed to repentance. He elsewhere states, "Since God is sovereign,… [He] is able to do as He pleases in human affairs," implying that God could overrule and bring to repentance those who fall away (p. 323).

[27] Hodges states, "The assertion that such a failure is not possible for a regenerate person is a theological proposition which is not supported by the New Testament" ("Hebrews," p. 795). His only defense of his own assertion is to cite 2 Tim 2:17–18 about Hymenaeus and Philetus destroying the faith of some. Oberholtzer adds 1 Tim 1:20; 5:15 to this list with the statement that these verses give examples of believers who "abandon their faith" and become subject to divine discipline ("Thorn-Infested Ground," p. 323). It is unclear how 1 Tim 5:15 fits into this discussion. 1 Tim 1:20 mentions Hymenaeus and Alexander as those who have made shipwreck of their faith. Neither in 1 Tim 1:20 nor in 2 Tim 2:17–18 is it demonstrated that the individuals mentioned were saved to begin with.

[28] The perfect tense of γεγόναμεν in the apodosis in 3:14 indicates that the following conditional statement in the protasis about persevering in the faith, "if indeed we hold our

True Believer: Hypothetical Apostasy/Loss of Salvation

Supporters of this view interpret vv. 4–5 as pointing to salvation and v. 6 as pointing to apostasy and the loss of salvation. The warning in v. 6, however, is both hypothetical and impossible. True believers could neither apostatize nor lose their salvation.[29] The purpose of the warning is not to suggest that such could actually happen, but rather to jar the readers from their spiritual lethargy and to spur them on to maturity.[30]

This view shares some of the strengths of the previous views. It takes vv. 4–5 in their commonly understood sense as describing salvation. It views the warning in v. 6 as referring to apostasy and the loss of salvation. Lastly, by understanding the warning as hypothetical *and* impossible, it avoids conflict with other verses in Scripture which teach the eternal security of the saved.

However, this interpretation encounters several difficulties. In order to take the warning as hypothetical, v. 6 is generally viewed as a conditional statement, "If they fall away."[31] Such an interpretation may be legitimately questioned. The expression "fall away" is the fifth in a series of five parallel participles which begin in v. 4. These five participles are joined by simple conjunctions and are preceded by a single article.[32] While an adverbial participle can introduce the protasis of a conditional clause, such does not appear to be the case here. The first four of these five participles are invariably taken with the article as adjectival and, specifically, as substantives in a series of relative clauses ("those who have once been enlightened and have

---

original confidence firm to the end (ESV)," is not a condition for becoming a partaker of Christ; rather, it is the mark of those who are already partakers. See, for example, D. A. Carson, *Exegetical Fallacies* (Grand Rapids: Baker, 1984), p. 88.

[29] Charles C. Ryrie, *Biblical Theology of the New Testament* (Chicago: Moody, 1959), pp. 256–58, and *Basic Theology* (Wheaton, IL: Victor Books, 1986), pp. 333–34; Thomas Hewitt, *The Epistle to the Hebrews,* Tyndale New Testament Commentaries (Grand Rapids: Eerdmans, 1960), pp. 106, 108, 111; Kent, *Hebrews*, pp. 113–14; Donald Guthrie, *The Letter to the Hebrews,* Tyndale New Testament Commentaries (Grand Rapids: Eerdmans, 1983), pp. 144–47; Thomas R. Schreiner & Ardel B. Caneday, *The Race Set Before Us: A Biblical Theology of Perseverance & Assurance* (Downers Grove, IL: InterVarsity Press, 2001), pp. 193–213.

[30] McKnight, "Warning Passages," p. 23.

[31] This interpretation treats the participle παραπεσόντας as conditional (RSV, NIV). Among others, see Hewitt, *Hebrews,* pp. 108, 111; Guthrie, *Hebrews,* p. 143; and Lane, *Hebrews,* 1:133.

[32] "τοὺς...φωτισθέντας...γευσαμένους τε...καὶ...γενηθέντας... καὶ...γευσαμένους... καὶ παραπεσόντας." All five of the participles are in the same tense (aorist), and all agree with the definite article that precedes them in gender, case, and number (masculine, accusative, plural).

tasted…"). Because all five appear to be parallel, there is every indication that the fifth should also be taken with the article as an adjectival substantive, continuing the series of relative clauses ("and have fallen away").[33] As such, it would not be adverbial and, hence, not conditional.[34]

Furthermore, advocates of this position understand "hypothetical" to mean that none of the readers had actually committed this sin.[35] But this explanation poses a problem as well. In the fourth warning passage, 10:26–39, the author of Hebrews warns the readers about not forsaking their assembling together (10:25).[36] In the following verses, he refers to the prohibited activity as sinning willfully (10:26),[37] and identifies the consequence as the wrath of God, which is meted out against God's enemies (10:27).[38] Since the two passages are parallel, it is assumed that the warning about falling away in 6:6 is parallel to the warnings about forsaking in 10:25 and sinning willfully in 10:26. Yet, according to 10:25, this forsaking is described as the habit of some.[39] In other words, the warning in these verses is in direct response to certain ones who had forsaken or abandoned the Christian community as it gathered for public worship. The point of the expression in v. 25 is that some had actually done this and were guilty of this sin.[40]

False Believer: Apostasy/Eternal Judgment

Supporters of this interpretation take the statements in vv. 4–5 as depicting the experience of those who had been exposed to the gospel, had made a

---

[33] NRSV.

[34] John A. Sproule, "Παραπεσόντας in Hebrews 6:6," *Grace Theological Journal* 2 (Fall 1981): 327–32. See also, A. T. Robertson, *A Grammar of the Greek New Testament in the Light of Historical Research* (Nashville: Broadman, 1934): 1103–41. Robertson places the conditional participle (p. 1129) under the broader category of circumstantial participles (p. 1124). This category is separate and distinct from his category of attributive participles (p. 1105) under which he places all articular participles (p. 1106).

[35] Guthrie, *Hebrews*, p. 145.

[36] μὴ ἐγκαταλείποντες τὴν ἐπισυναγωγὴν ἑαυτῶν.

[37] ἑκουσίως γὰρ ἁμαρτανόντων ἡμῶν. The γὰρ in v. 26 is explanatory and indicates the close connection between the prohibition in 10:25 and the activity described in 10:26. In 10:26–27, the author of Hebrews gives the reason why the readers should not forsake the Christian community as it gathers for worship. Such an act involves sinning willfully and brings God's judgment. See, for example, Lane, *Hebrews*, 2:290–91.

[38] τοὺς ὑπεντίους.

[39] καθὼς ἔθος τισίν.

[40] Kent, a proponent of the hypothetical-impossible position, acknowledges both the reality and seriousness of what is being described in 10:25 and the connection between the activity in v. 25 and the warning in vv. 26–39. However, he fails to see the implications of this for his position (*Hebrews*, pp. 202–5). For further treatment of this passage, see the discussion under v. 6.

profession of faith, had been associated with the community of believers, but who were not actually saved. Verse 6 is understood to say that these, under pressure of persecution, reject the faith and become hardened by this act of apostasy so that there is no possibility of bringing them again to repentance. The only prospect for these is the certainty of eternal judgment.[41]

Like the preceding views, this approach has several strengths. Chief among them is that it interprets v. 6 in its commonly understood sense as referring to apostasy with the consequence that the guilty face eternal condemnation and judgment. Furthermore, because it interprets vv. 4–5 as pointing to something close to but not identical with salvation, it avoids

---

[41] Philip E. Hughes, "Hebrews 6:4–6 and the Peril of Apostasy," *Westminster Theological Journal* 35 (Winter 1973): 137–55, and *A Commentary on the Epistle to the Hebrews* (Grand Rapids: Eerdmans, 1977), pp. 206–22; Roger Nicole, "Some Comments, on Hebrews 6:4–6 and the Doctrine of the Perseverance of God with the Saints" in *Current Issues in Biblical and Patristic Interpretaton,* ed. Gerald F. Hawthorne (Grand Rapids: Eerdmans, 1975), pp. 355–64; Leon Morris, "Hebrews," in *The Expositor's Bible Commentary,* ed. Frank E. Gaebelein (Grand Rapids: Zondervan, 1981), pp. 54–57; Stanley D. Toussaint, "The Eschatology of the Warning Passages in the Book of Hebrews," *Grace Theological Journal* 3 (Fall 1982): 67–80; Simon J. Kistemaker, *Exposition of the Epistle to the Hebrews* (Grand Rapids: Baker, 1984), pp. 157–64; F. F. Bruce, *The Epistle to the Hebrews,* rev. ed., New International Commentary on the New Testament (Grand Rapids: Eerdmans, 1990), pp. 144–45; Grudem, "Perseverance of the Saints," pp. 171–73; Buist M. Fanning, "A Classical Reformed View," in *Four Views on the Warning Passages in Hebrews,* ed. Herbert W. Bateman IV (Grand Rapids: Kregel, 2007), pp. 172–219.

A similar conclusion, though from a somewhat different perspective, is that offered by Verlyn D. Verbrugge, "Towards a New Interpretation of Hebrews 6:4–6," *Calvin Theological Journal* 15 (April 1980): 61–73. Verbrugge argues that the warning is not speaking of individuals who are in danger of falling away, but of a local Christian community. He bases his interpretation on the relationship between the illustration in Heb 6:7–8 and its alleged antecedent in Isa 5:1–7. Both, he argues, address a covenant community, which fails to bring forth fruit commensurate with true repentance and is consequently judged of God. He guards against the charge that he is allowing for true believers to apostatize and to lose their salvation by saying that what is said of a community is not necessarily true of every individual in that community. The community may fall into apostasy, but the true believer would and, in fact, could not. "In other words, God's rejection of his covenant community does not jeopardize the doctrine of election and the preservation or perseverance of the saints as it applies to the individual believer" (p. 62).

As intriguing as it is, Verbrugge's view has gained few supporters and has been justly criticized. See, for example, McKnight, "Warning Passages," pp. 53–54; Grudem, "Perseverance of the Saints," pp. 150–51. Both the warnings themselves and the exhortations for the readers to persevere in Hebrews are addressing individuals (e.g., 3:12, "See to it, brethren, that *none of you* has an evil, unbelieving heart that falls away from the living God."). Furthermore, the link between Heb 6:7–8 and Isa 5:1–7 is less than obvious. As McKnight notes, "the agricultural illustration of Heb 6:7–8 is very common in the ancient Mediterranean world, and the parallels to Isa 5:1–7, though possible, are at best inexact and incomplete" (p. 54).

conflict with other verses that argue for the eternal security of the saved. Those who fall and are condemned, it is argued, were never truly saved. On the other hand, the chief liability with this view, as may be anticipated, is that it gives a reading of vv. 4–5 that does not follow the frequently understood interpretation. It interprets these verses, not as referring to the saved, but to the unsaved.

PROPOSED SOLUTION

As has been seen in this brief survey, none of the above approaches is free from difficulty. Advocates of each interpret this and the other warning passages based on the larger context of Scripture and their own theological presuppositions and arrive at an interpretation that creates, for them, the least amount of tension. The same may be said of what follows. At the same time, the fourth view offers the most consistent interpretation of the verses within their own and related contexts and leaves the least number of questions unanswered.

According to the fourth view, the passage refers to those who have heard the gospel, have made a profession of faith, and yet are not saved. Under the pressure of persecution, these abandon the faith and are faced with eternal condemnation and judgment.[42] The argumentation given below is in support of the fourth view. The procedure is to examine first the interpretation of vv. 4–5, then to treat the interpretation of v. 6, the illustration in vv. 7–8, and the statements in v. 9. Elements within the other warning passages in Hebrews are discussed as appropriate in conjunction with the above verses.

Verses 4–5

Taken by themselves, the individual phrases in vv. 4–5 appear to identify experiences consistent with salvation, as a consensus of interpreters have

---

[42] While all interpreters agree that the readers were experiencing persecution, not all agree with the specific circumstances involved. Fortunately, the identification of the readers and the nature of the persecution do not materially affect the debate on the interpretation of Heb 6:4–6. The position embraced here is that the readers were Jewish Christians who were being pressured because of persecution to return to the OT system of worship. For a recent discussion on these and other introductory matters, see Donald Guthrie, *New Testament Introduction,* 4th ed. (Downers Grove, IL: InterVarsity, 1990), pp. 668–721; Lane, *Hebrews,* 1:xlvii–clvii; Paul Ellingworth, *The Epistle to the Hebrews,* The New International Greek Testament Commentary (Grand Rapids: Eerdmans, 1993), pp. 3–85; D. A. Carson & Douglas J. Moo, *An Introduction to the New Testament,* 2nd ed. (Grand Rapids: Zondervan, 2005), pp. 596–618.

endeavored to show.[43] If that is true of the phrases individually, then their collective force simply heightens this impression.[44] Added to this is the statement in v. 6 about the impossibility of renewing the lapsed again to repentance. The initial impression from this statement is that the repentance in view is genuine repentance. To renew these "again" would mean that the individuals addressed had previously expressed this repentance and were thus saved.[45]

This is all to say that the burden of proof rests on those who argue that the phrases in vv. 4–5 are describing ones who are not saved. Yet the nature of this burden must be clarified. All that really needs to be demonstrated with vv. 4–5 is that the phrases themselves are ambiguous or undetermined concerning the spiritual status of those in view.[46] In other words, while these phrases describe what may be *consistent* with saved individuals, the phrases themselves are not *inconsistent* with those who have made a profession of faith but who are not saved.[47]

Those who have once been enlightened (v. 4).[48] The term enlightened is used figuratively in the NT in the sense of "to reveal," "to instruct," "to illumine." In the passive voice as here, it has the force of "to be instructed" or "to be illumined," principally by God and/or His word.[49] It is often

---

[43] The interpretation of the individual phrases in vv. 4–5 as referring to saved individuals has been discussed under the first view.

[44] Osborne emphatically states, "In conclusion, we must say there is no more powerful or detailed description of the true Christian in the New Testament" ("Soteriology in the Epistle to the Hebrews," in *Grace Unlimited*, ed. Clark H. Pinnock (Minneapolis: Bethany Fellowship, 1975), p. 149). Even Grudem acknowledges this point, "What more could the author say to indicate a genuine experience of salvation?" ("Perseverance of the Saints," p. 139).

[45] The issue raised here is discussed in connection with the interpretation of v. 6.

[46] The terms "ambiguous" and "undetermined" simply mean that the spiritual status of those in view cannot be identified on the basis of these expressions alone. The question must be decided from the larger context.

[47] Nicole, "Some Comments on Hebrews 6:4–6," pp. 359–62; Grudem, "Perseverance of the Saints," pp. 139–50. Grudem gives an extensive treatment of these phrases, building on the discussion of John Owen, *An Exposition of Hebrews,* 4 vols. (reprint of 1855 ed., Marshallton, DE: National Foundation for Christian Education, 1969), 3:68–91, as well as the treatments of Nicole ("Some Comments on Hebrews 6:4–6," pp. 355–64) and Hughes (*Hebrews,* pp. 206–22). His conclusion is that "verses 4–6 by themselves are inconclusive, for they speak of events that are experienced both by genuine Christians and by some people who participate in the fellowship of a church but are never really saved (p. 139)."

[48] τοὺς ἅπαξ φωτισθέντας.

[49] John 1:9; 1 Cor 4:5; Eph 1:18; 2 Tim 1:10; and Heb 10:32. See BDAG, p. 1074. Lane provides a concise definition, "In the NT the term is used metaphorically to refer to spiritual or intellectual illumination that removes ignorance through the action of God or

assumed that the expression carries a connotation that is either equivalent to or associated with conversion or salvation.[50] This assumption is based on three reasons. First, the term and its cognates are commonly found in the NT with this sense, and there is an *a priori* likelihood that it carries this same meaning here.[51] Second, the adverb "once" which modifies enlightened suggests a decisive, once-for-all act consistent with the initial hearing and responding to the gospel.[52] Third, the only other use of enlightened by the author is in 10:32. There it identifies the readers as saved individuals and that argues for a similar understanding in this passage.[53]

The cumulative weight of these arguments is impressive, yet the evidence is capable of a different analysis and conclusion. While the cognate forms of the verb enlighten are used where the meaning is associated with salvation, it is questionable whether the verb itself is ever used in this sense.[54] Furthermore, there are clear examples in the NT where this word cannot refer to salvation. For example, John 1:9 refers to Christ as the true light who "enlightens every man."[55] Assuming "every man" means all humanity, enlightens cannot mean saves.

Second, the modifier "once" can suggest something of a decisive, once-for-all event consistent with conversion or salvation. However, it can also be used where the idea is "initially" or "at the first" in sequence with

---

the preaching of the gospel" (*Hebrews*, 1:141). Beginning in the second century, the term was used to refer to Christian baptism and became popularized in that sense in the centuries following. There is no clear evidence, however, that it was used in this sense prior to the second century (ibid.).

[50] E.g., Osborne, "Soteriology in Hebrews," p. 149; Attridge, *Hebrews*, p. 169; Lane, *Hebrews*, 1:141; McKnight, "Warning Passages," p. 46.

[51] McKnight, "Warning Passages," pp. 45–46.

[52] Lane, *Hebrews*, 1:132; similarly Bruce, *Hebrews*, pp. 145–46.

[53] Hodges, "Hebrews," p. 794; Oberholtzer, "Thorn-Infested Ground," p. 321.

[54] Grudem, "Perseverance of the Saints," pp. 141–43. Grudem concedes that the cognate noun φωτισμός is used in the sense of conversion (e.g., 2 Cor 4:4–6). He rejects the idea, however, that the verb itself is ever employed with this meaning in the NT. The verb is used eleven times in the NT, primarily as a metaphor for imparting or receiving knowledge/instruction. Only in Eph 1:18 can a case be made for the meaning of conversion. However, even here its meaning is debated. Lincoln, for example, argues that it refers to the conversion of the readers (*Ephesians*, Word Biblical Commentary [Dallas: Word Books, 1990], p. 58). Bruce, on the other hand, sees a reference here to the instruction of those who are already saved (*The Epistles to the Colossians, to Philemon, and to the Ephesians*, New International Commentary on the New Testament [Grand Rapids: Eerdmans, 1984], p. 270).

[55] See also 1 Cor 4:5.

a subsequent activity, and not carry the idea of once for all.[56] The use of the adverb "again" in v. 6 argues for the meaning of "at the first" in v. 4.[57] The thought would be that it is impossible for those who *initially* or *at the first* were enlightened and who subsequently fell away to be brought back *again* to repentance.

Lastly, what is often used as the critical text, 10:32, is not as decisive as some have suggested. The expression in 10:32, "after having been enlightened," is parallel with the expression in 10:26, "after having received the knowledge of the truth." There is no indication in the latter that receiving the knowledge of the truth suggests the idea of conversion or salvation. It simply means that the readers had been taught or instructed in the truth of God's Word. The same may be said of the expression in 10:32.[58]

The point of all of this is that the evidence for taking enlightened to mean either saved or simply instructed is inconclusive. In terms of probability, the evidence favors the concept of instructed rather than that of saved.

And have tasted the heavenly gift (v. 4).[59] Similar to the previous construction, this clause and its counterpart in v. 5 ("and have tasted the good word of God and the powers of the age to come") are commonly interpreted as synonyms for salvation.[60] Thus, to taste the heavenly gift means to participate in the gospel and its attendant blessings.[61] Support for this interpretation is based on two arguments. The first is that the word taste, used metaphorically, does not mean simply to sample something but to experience something and to experience it fully.[62] Its only other use in

---

[56] BDAG, p. 97. In 10:2, the adverb ἅπαξ carries the idea of once for all, but in 9:7; 12:26, 27 it does not.

[57] ἅπαξ...πάλιν. See Attridge, *Hebrews,* pp. 169–70; Ellingworth, *Hebrews,* p. 319.

[58] Hughes, *Hebrews,* p. 207; Grudem, "Perseverance of the Saints," pp. 141, 176–77.

[59] γευσαμένους τε τῆς δωρεᾶς τῆς ἐπουρανίου. The use of τε...καί...καί...καί and the precise relationship among the participial clauses in vv. 4–6 has been variously understood. As discussed earlier, the sequence of conjunctions and the construction of the participles argue that the clauses are coordinate. See BDAG, p. 993; Westcott, *Hebrews,* pp. 147–148; Attridge, *Hebrews,* p. 167.

[60] See, for example, Osborne, "Soteriology in Hebrews," p. 149. The expressions in v. 5 are discussed later.

[61] Lane, *Hebrews,* 1:141.

[62] Moffatt, *Hebrews,* p. 78; Ellingworth, *Hebrews,* p. 320. Some see eucharistic overtones with the use of the verb here, especially those who identify "enlightened" in the previous clause with baptism (e.g., Bruce, *Hebrews,* p. 146). The majority, however, rightly reject such overtones. Hughes, for example, notes that if the eucharist were in view, a literal meaning for the verb would be required, whereas the context clearly argues for a metaphorical sense (*Hebrews,* pp. 208–9).

Hebrews is in 2:9, where it describes Christ tasting death for every man. Clearly, the meaning there is "to experience fully," and that is its meaning here as well.[63] The second argument is that the heavenly gift is a reference to the gospel and/or its related blessings.[64] The word gift is used in the NT of Christ (John 4:10), the Holy Spirit (Acts 2:38; 8:20; 10:45; 11:17), and justification/salvation (Rom 5:15, 17). Thus, to taste any of these could only be said of one who is saved.

The evidence, however, is capable of a different interpretation that does not support the above conclusions. It must be granted that the figurative use of taste carries with it the idea of "to experience."[65] As mentioned with reference to Hebrews 2:9, Christ is said to taste death for every man. Without question, for Christ to taste death meant that he experienced death. In addition, every such tasting, as in 2:9, involves a real or genuine experience. Consequently, tasting the heavenly gift in v. 4 must mean that these genuinely experienced this gift.

Granting the above, the term taste involves an experience that could be momentary, temporary, or continuing. This is true whether it is used literally as in Matthew 27:34 of Christ tasting wine while on the cross or figuratively as in Hebrews 2:9. Christ's tasting death for every man was an experience that did not continue indefinitely. It took place within a specific period of time. Furthermore, while every figurative use of taste in the NT involves a genuine experience, not every use involves a saving experience.[66] In other words, there is a sense in which everyone experiences the grace and goodness of God. At the same time, many who taste God's goodness do not continue in that experience nor does that experience constitute salvation.[67] Therefore, the questions in v. 4 are not whether

---

[63] Marshall, *Kept by the Power of God,* p. 137; McKnight, "Warning Passages," pp. 46–47. Based on the use of γεύομαι with the genitive here in v. 4 and with the accusative in v. 5, some have suggested that the tasting in v. 4 is partial (e.g., Westcott, *Hebrews,* p. 149; Montefiore, *Hebrews,* p. 109; Attridge, *Hebrews,* p. 170). However, most reject this distinction and see the change between the genitive and accusative in these verses as primarily stylistic (e.g., Moffatt, *Hebrews,* p. 78; Ellingworth, *Hebrews,* p. 320).

[64] Attridge, *Hebrews,* p. 170.

[65] *TDNT,* s.v. "γεύομαι," by J. Behm, 1:676–77. BDAG, p. 195, lists "to come to know something; to partake of; to experience" for the figurative uses.

[66] Grudem, "Perseverance of the Saints," pp. 145–46. His argument is based primarily on the uses of γεύομαι in extra-biblical literature of this same period. The figurative uses of γεύομαι in the NT where the object involves some divine provision are limited to this passage and 1 Pet 2:3. In 1 Pet 2:3 the object of γεύομαι is "that the Lord is good" (ὅτι χρηστὸς ὁ κύριος). While χρηστὸς in 1 Pet 2:3 does appear to refer to the *saving* goodness of God, such does not prove that γεύομαι itself carries this sense. This meaning of 1 Pet 2:3 is based on the use of χρηστός, not γεύομαι.

[67] E.g., Matt 5:45; Acts 17:25; Titus 2:11.

taste means experience or whether the experience was real. Rather, the questions concern the extent of the experience and its efficacy for salvation. Since this same word may involve one or the other of these nuances, the word itself cannot determine whether those in view are saved or not.

Furthermore, the object "heavenly gift" is not determinative in deciding these issues either. It is true that the term gift is used of God's saving grace in salvation, but the term has a number of other uses in the NT. A good case could be made that it refers to the Holy Spirit.[68] The Holy Spirit is described as a gift (Acts 2:38) and as one that comes from heaven (1 Pet 1:12). Assuming for the moment this identification in v. 4 is correct, tasting the Holy Spirit does not equate with experiencing salvation. According to John 16:8, the Holy Spirit convicts the world of sin, yet the whole world is not saved as a result of this activity, this "tasting" of the Spirit's work. The problem is that this tasting of the heavenly gift is subject to more than one meaning. Because the options do not equal a saving experience in every case, the phrase cannot prove the spiritual status of those in view.

And have become partakers of the Holy Spirit.[69] As with the previous constructions, many argue that this clause refers to the saving ministry of the Holy Spirit.[70] This interpretation is based on similar uses in Hebrews of constructions with "partake." The most frequently mentioned example is in 3:14. There the expression "partakers of Christ" is found where the construction clearly refers to those who are saved, those who partake of Christ's saving activity. Thus, the corresponding phrase "partakers of God's Spirit" in v. 4 must have a similar sense.[71] To partake of the Holy Spirit means to participate in the saving ministry of God's Spirit.

This is perhaps the most difficult statement in vv. 4–5 to counter. There are several cross references in Hebrews where "partakers" is used of the saved. As was just mentioned, in 3:14 the author of Hebrews states that

---

[68] Ellingworth, *Hebrews,* p. 320; Grudem, "Perseverance of the Saints," p. 146. The Holy Spirit is identified as the antecedent simply for the sake of the argument. Since the Holy Spirit is specifically mentioned in the following verse, some other aspect of divine provision may be in view. See Marshall, *Kept by the Power of God,* p. 137. Assuming that the clauses in these two verses are synthetic rather than synonymous, the broader concepts of God's *grace* or God's *provisions* could be intended.

[69] καὶ μετόχους γενηθέντας πνεύματος ἁγίου.

[70] Marshall, *Kept by the Power of God,* p. 138; Osborne, "Soteriology in Hebrews," p. 149; Attridge, *Hebrews,* p. 170; Lane, *Hebrews,* 1:141. Those who interpret the preceding two clauses as conceptually linked to baptism and the eucharist suggest a similar link between this clause and the reference to the laying on of hands mentioned in 6:2. See the discussion in Hughes, *Hebrews,* pp. 208–10.

[71] McKnight, "Warning Passages," p. 47.

those who have become partakers of Christ are those who persevere in the faith.[72] It is difficult to see from this verse how partakers of Christ could be describing anyone other than those who are saved.[73] The same may be said of 3:1 and 12:8. It could be argued in 3:1 that the heavenly calling of which the readers are partakers is the call of God unto salvation.[74] This reference to the readers' calling in 3:1 is preceded by the parallel description of the readers as holy brethren, a common designation in the NT for the saved.[75] In 12:8 the discipline of which all are partakers is the discipline that God administers to his children, to the saved.[76] According to this same verse, not to partake of this discipline means that one is not God's child. Conversely, to be a partaker of this discipline is an indication that one is a true child, that one is saved.

Despite all this, the expression "partakers" does not prove that those in view are saved. In each case, the context, and not the word itself, must argue for such an understanding.[77] The term partake means "to share in something," often with others, hence, "to be a partner, a companion."[78] Furthermore, the degree of involvement in this sharing may vary from a loose association to a more direct and personal participation.[79] Only the context can indicate the nature of the sharing and the spiritual condition of those involved.[80]

For example, many argue that "partakers of a heavenly calling" in 3:1 refers to the saved. This understanding is based on the preceding expression "holy brethren," a common designation in the NT for the saved. However, a case could be made that "partakers of a heavenly calling" does not equal salvation. Assuming that the calling in 3:1 is the calling of God through

---

[72] Literally, "if we hold firm the beginning of our confidence to the end" (ἐάνπερ τὴν ἀρχὴν τῆς ὑποστάσεως μέχρι τέλους βεβαίαν κατάσχωμεν).

[73] This is based on the larger context of the NT where similar concepts are used to describe the saved. E.g., 1 John 5:11–12.

[74] κλήσεως ἐπουρανίου μέτοχοι.

[75] ἀδελφοὶ ἅγιοι. See. *TDNT*, s.v. "ἀδελφός," by H. von Soden, 1:145–46.

[76] ἧς μέτοχοι γεγόνασιν πάντες.

[77] Carson provides a helpful reminder of this principle in *Exegetical Fallacies,* pp. 25–66.

[78] BDAG, p. 643; *TDNT*, s.v. "μέτοχος," by H. Hanse, 2:830–32.

[79] Nicole, "Some Comments on Hebrews 6:4–6," p. 360; Ellingworth, *Hebrews,* p. 321; Grudem, "Perseverance of the Saints," p. 147.

[80] It is used in Luke 5:7, for example, of those who were companions with Peter and the disciples in the task of fishing. Here, the idea is probably fellow fishermen. In the LXX, it is used of those who are companions with God-fearers (Ps 118:63 [119:63]), as well as of those who are companions with idolaters (Hos 4:17).

the gospel,[81] not all who hear this call respond, and not all who respond, respond with saving faith.[82] Thus, "partakers of a heavenly calling" could refer to those who have heard the gospel, but who have not responded in saving faith.

The same may be said of the expression in Hebrews 6:4. To be partakers of the Holy Spirit could mean to share in his saving activity.[83] But, it could also refer to participating in some non-salvific activity. This may include a sharing in the general convicting ministry of God's Spirit, as was argued earlier, or being the beneficiary of the Spirit's miraculous gifts, or simply observing these gifts as exercised by others.[84] Again, the expression is open to several interpretations, some of which do not require that those so described are saved. All that can be said with certainty is that those in view share in some way in the Spirit's ministry.

And have tasted the good word of God and the powers of the age to come (v. 5).[85] The expression "tasted" is the same word previously

---

[81] BDAG, p. 549; *TDNT*, s.v. "κλῆσις," by K. Schmidt, 3:491–93; *NIDNTT*, s.v. "Call," by L. Coenen, 1:273–76. Theologians frequently distinguish between the general call of God and the effectual call of God. Both are accomplished in conjunction with the gospel, but the former does not invariably lead to salvation whereas the latter does (*New Dictionary of Theology*, s.v. "Calling," by R. Letham, pp. 119–20). It is the general calling of God that is argued for in Heb 3:1.

[82] See, for example, 2 Pet 1:10 where Peter exhorts his readers to "make sure of your calling and election." The exhortation directs his readers to demonstrate by the acquisition of the spiritual characteristics previously enumerated (vv. 5–7) that they had responded properly to the divine call and were indeed numbered among the chosen of God (vv. 8–9). See also the cognate expression in Matt 22:14, "many are called, but few are chosen." The same may be said of Heb 12:8. Experiencing divine chastisement is not the sole domain of the redeemed. On occasion, unbelievers are subject to divine chastisement as well. This was certainly true of the nation of Israel during its sojourn in the wilderness, where the majority were unbelievers (Heb 3:16–19). The point in 12:8 is that believers *invariably* experience God's hand of discipline. To be without divine chastisement is to be without the necessary mark of divine sonship. Conversely, to experience divine chastisement is not an invariable proof of sonship.

[83] Similarly, Rom 8:9.

[84] Grudem, "Perseverance of the Saints," pp. 147–48. A number of commentaries interpret the expression as referring to spiritual gifts, whether this included the actual exercising of such or simply observing and/or benefiting from these gifts as exercised by others. E.g., Hughes, *Hebrews*, p. 210; Kistemaker, *Hebrews*, p. 159; Bruce, *Hebrews*, pp. 146–47. Bruce suggests a possible parallel with Simon Magus (Acts 8:9–24), whom he describes as one who heard the gospel, responded to it, was baptized, witnessed the exercising of spiritual gifts, but who was later shown not to be saved.

[85] καὶ καλὸν γευσαμένους θεοῦ ῥῆμα δυνάμεις τε μέλλοντος αἰῶνος. An alternate rendering, suggested by C. F. D. Moule and others and followed by the NIV, is to take καλόν as substantival and translate it "tasted the goodness of the Word of God."

discussed in v. 4 ("tasted the heavenly gift"). What must be determined in this verse is the identification of the "word of God" and the "powers of the age to come" and whether those tasting these are saved or not. The word of God is generally understood to refer to divine revelation, whether spoken or written, and specifically to the gospel.[86] Likewise, the powers of the age to come is taken either as a reference to salvation[87] or, much more frequently, to the miracles that accompanied and validated the apostolic proclamation of the gospel in the early church.[88] In fact, the majority of commentaries see a parallel with 2:1–4, where a similar sequence is found of hearing the gospel and of witnessing the miracles that accompanied its proclamation.[89]

The evidence weighs in favor of the majority in seeing the same sequence in v. 5 as in 2:1–4. First, the author of Hebrews uses the phrase "word of God" in connection with God's activity in creating the universe (11:3), in giving revelation at Sinai (12:19), and in communicating the gospel through the Son (cf. 1:1–2, "God...has spoken to us in His Son," and 2:3, "so great a salvation...spoken through the Lord").[90] Of these possibilities, the parallel expressions in Hebrews argue for taking the word of God in v. 5 as referring specifically to the gospel. In 4:12, "the word of God" has in view the "good news" proclaimed by Christ and the apostles (4:2). In 13:7, "the word of God" refers to the preaching ministry of church leaders. In 6:1, the expression "word of Christ" is used of the gospel. The predominant meaning of this and related phrases in Hebrews is the gospel, and that appears to be its meaning here. It is the gospel that

---

C. F. D. Moule, *An Idiom-Book of New Testament Greek,* 2nd ed. (Cambridge: Cambridge University Press, 1959), p. 36; Lane, *Hebrews,* 1:133. Bruce prefers calling it a predicate use of the adjective, though arriving at the same translation (*Hebrews,* p. 147). The translation above takes καλόν as attributive, modifying the neuter noun ῥῆμα. The differences are minimal for the present discussion. The adjective signifies that which is excellent or blameless (BDAG, p. 505).

[86] *TDNT,* s.v. "λέγω," by G. Kittel, 4:113–19; *NIDNTT,* s.v. "Word," by O. Betz, 3:1121–23.

[87] Lenski, *Hebrews,* p. 184; Marshall, *Kept by the Power of God,* p. 138. Marshall states that these powers "are unlikely to be miracles," but does not offer any evidence to support his statement or explain why this is so.

[88] *TDNT,* s.v. "δύναμαι," by W. Grundmann, 2:310–15; Bruce, *Hebrews,* p. 147.

[89] E.g., Hughes, *Hebrews,* p. 211; Bruce, *Hebrews,* p. 147; Attridge, *Hebrews,* p. 170; Lane, *Hebrews,* 1:141; Ellingworth, *Hebrews,* p. 321.

[90] While some make a distinction between λόγος in 2:2 and ῥῆμα in 6:5 (e.g., Westcott, *Hebrews,* p. 149), the majority of commentaries argue for synonymy (e.g., Ellingworth, *Hebrews,* p. 321).

was first proclaimed by Christ (2:3) and then by the apostles and others (2:3; 13:7).[91]

Second, the plural term *powers* is regularly used of miracles in the NT.[92] This is the unanimous translation of the word in 2:4,[93] the only other use of the plural in Hebrews, and this is the likely meaning for the plural in v. 5. In addition, to describe these powers as belonging to the age to come means that the miracles that will characterize the eschaton were being experienced in connection with the apostolic preaching of the gospel.[94] According to 2:3–4, these miracles served as a witness and confirmation to the truth of the gospel.[95] All of this leads to the conclusion that the "word of God and the powers of the age to come" in v. 5 refer to the proclamation of the gospel and the miracles accompanying that proclamation.

The question still remains whether those who have tasted the word of God and the miracles accompanying it can be other than saved. To say that someone has tasted or experienced the gospel could be another way of saying that they were saved.[96] Yet, as was mentioned earlier, not everyone who has experienced or been exposed to the gospel has responded positively to it. Neither has everyone who has responded positively to it responded in saving faith and experienced salvation.

A number of examples in the NT support this. Simon Magus, for example, heard the gospel, assented to it, received baptism, and observed many miracles.[97] However, when he sought to purchase the ability to impart the Spirit through the laying on of hands, Peter denounced him in terms that show he was unsaved.[98] Furthermore, many others who

---

[91] In these passages, λόγος is used rather than ῥῆμα.

[92] BDAG, s.v. "δύναμις," pp. 262–63.

[93] KJV, RSV, NASB, NIV, et al.

[94] The expression "age to come" (μέλλοντος αἰῶνος) refers to the age following Christ's return and, specifically, to His millennial reign or kingdom. The construction μέλλων αἰών has this meaning in Matt 12:32 and Eph 1:21. The parallel construction αἰῶνι ἐρχόμενῳ has this meaning in Mark 10:30 and Luke 18:30. In Heb 2:5, the similar construction τὴν οἰκουμένην τὴν μέλλουσαν is found with the same sense. Furthermore, the author of Hebrews refers to the future return of Christ (1:6; 9:28; 12:14) as well as to a future kingdom (12:28; 13:14 ["*the city* which is to come"]). It is to these that the expression "age to come" points. For the association between miracles in the NT and their relationship to the future age, see Matt 12:28.

[95] See Mark 16:20 for a similar statement.

[96] Again, this appears to be the sense of 1 Pet 2:3. See also Titus 3:3–6.

[97] Acts 8:9–24.

[98] Note particularly v. 21, "You have no part nor portion in this matter, for your heart is not right before God." The same may be said of those passages in the Gospels which

witnessed miracles in the NT, both in the Gospels and in Acts, were not saved. In addition, not everyone who performed miracles was saved. For example, Jesus said of those who perform miracles in His name without submitting to the Father's will, "I never knew you, depart from me you evildoers." [99] The expression in v. 5, therefore, is equivocal. It can refer to both the saved as well as the unsaved.

As was mentioned earlier, the burden of proof for the fourth view rests on showing that the statements in vv. 4–5 can describe other than the saved. The discussion above has demonstrated the viability of such an interpretation. The statements could refer to those who are saved. But they can also depict those who have heard and understood the gospel and have even consented to it, have experienced the grace of God and the convicting ministry of the Holy Spirit, have witnessed miracles, but who have never responded in saving faith and are therefore not saved. Thus, it may be concluded that the phrases themselves are inconclusive. They cannot identify the spiritual status of those in view apart from the larger context.[100] Furthermore, what is true of the phrases individually is also true of their collective force. If the individual statements are ambiguous in this sense, then they are collectively ambiguous as well. The decision about the spiritual status of those in view must be based on evidence from the wider context, particularly from the verses that follow.[101]

---

describe individuals who hear the gospel, respond to it, follow Jesus, but later turn away from Him (e.g. John 6:60–66, note, especially, v. 64). This also is supported by the parable of the sower in Matt 13:3–9 (cf. Mark 4:3–20; Luke 8:4–15). Of the four groups depicted in this parable, at least three of the four respond to the gospel but only the last gives evidence of salvation (vv. 18–23). See D. A. Carson, *Matthew*, in vol. 8 of *The Expositor's Bible Commentary*, ed. Frank E. Gaebelein (Grand Rapids: Zondervan, 1984), pp. 312–15.

[99] Matt 7:22–23.

[100] There is one statement from the other warning passages that needs to be included in this discussion. In 10:29, the warning describes those in view as "sanctified" by the blood of the covenant (ἐν ᾧ ἡγιάσθη). The majority of interpreters understand "sanctified" in this verse to mean "cleansed, forgiven" and as equivalent to "saved." See, for example, McKnight, "Warning Passages," p. 43. It must be acknowledged that the verb is frequently used in Hebrews to describe those who are saved. This is true of its other two uses in the same chapter (10:10, 14). However, the term can also mean "to treat as holy" or "to associate with what is holy" where salvation is not in view (BDAG, s.v. "ἁγιάζω," pp. 9–10). The former may be the meaning in Heb 13:12, where the purpose of Christ's death is to sanctify the "people," the entire nation (note also 9:13). The latter is certainly its use in 1 Cor 7:14, where it refers to unbelieving children as "sanctified" by a believing parent. Either of these options could be applied to 10:29 without requiring those in view to be saved. See the discussion in Grudem, "Perseverance of the Saints," pp. 177–78.

[101] "Words derive their specific sense (within a possible range) from the context, and, among the possible meanings (those that have been attested elsewhere), there is no such

Verse 6

According to the fourth view, v. 6 depicts the apostasy of those who professed faith, but who were not saved. Furthermore, this apostasy is an irremediable act which exposes the guilty to the certainty of eternal judgment. Several questions with this verse need to be addressed in defense of the fourth view. The first is whether "fall away" means apostasy.[102] The second is whether the expression "bring again to repentance" means that these had previously exercised repentance and were saved. The third is whether the term "impossible" (v. 4) describes an irremediable act, and, if so, why is it irremediable?[103]

And then have fallen away.[104] The term "fallen away," found only here in the NT, is by itself somewhat ambiguous.[105] However, its use in the LXX, the parallel expressions in the other warning passages, and the descriptive phrases accompanying it here and elsewhere in Hebrews lead

---

thing as a 'more likely' meaning for a term apart from its context. In this case, the most relevant context includes the author's continuation of this discussion in verses 7–12" (Grudem, "Perseverance of the Saints," p. 152).

[102] The debate on this passage is not over the definition of apostasy. The debate is whether apostasy is in view and, if so, who can commit such. For a definition, see note 5 above.

[103] This expression is treated here rather than at v. 4 because of its conceptual and grammatical links with the clauses in v. 6. There is general consensus on the syntax of this passage. The conjunction "for" (postpositive γάρ) in v. 4 is connected either with vv. 1–3a, giving the reason why the readers must go on to maturity (because failure to do so would open them to further regression and perhaps even apostasy) or with v. 3b, clarifying what God does not permit (renewing those who fall away). The verbal adjective "impossible" (ἀδύνατον) is a predicate adjective, with an impersonal subject added by ellipsis, and governs the infinitive "to renew" (ἀνακαινίζειν). The infinitive, used transitively and without a specific subject, has the five aorist participles in vv. 4–6a as its objects. The two present participles in v. 6 are causal, modifying the predicate and answering the question why is it "impossible." See the discussion in Attridge, *Hebrews,* p. 167 and McKnight, "Warning Passages," p. 40.

For alternatives, see P. Proulx and L. Alonso Schokel, "Heb 6, 4–6: εἰς μετάνοιαν ἀνασταυροῦντας," *Biblica* 56 (1975): 193–203 and L. Sabourin, "'Crucifying Afresh for One's Repentance' (Heb 6:4–6)," *Biblical Theology Bulletin* 6 (October 1976): 264–71. Hagner's critique of the alternatives is apropos, "attempts to avoid the difficulty of the verse by assuming a transposition of words and different punctuation…is a drastic and unconvincing expedient." (Donald A. Hagner, *Hebrews,* New International Biblical Commentary [Peabody, MA: Hendrickson, 1900], p. 95).

[104] καὶ παραπεσόντας.

[105] It is ambiguous in the sense that the expression is not a technical term for apostasy, as seen by its use outside the Bible and in the LXX (BDAG, p. 770).

inevitably to the conclusion that the sin of apostasy is meant.[106] In the LXX, this term is used to translate several Hebrew expressions for sin, often in contexts involving gross unfaithfulness or spiritual adultery.[107] The same is true of the parallel expression in 3:12, translated "falls away."[108] It too is employed both in the OT and in the NT in the sense of "to come to reject," "to commit apostasy."[109]

This definition for the expression in v. 6 is further supported by the use of "sinning willfully" in the parallel warning in 10:26. The sin in 10:26 is "willful" because it involves a deliberate act.[110] Furthermore, according to the same verse, it is committed by one who has received "the knowledge of the truth." Moreover, its OT use suggests that this sin is equivalent to sinning "defiantly," not just a conscious violation of God's Law but a thorough and deliberate repudiation of divine revelation.[111]

In addition, the accompanying phrases both here and elsewhere in Hebrews are best understood in light of this definition. Those falling away in 3:12 are described as having an "evil, unbelieving heart."[112] In 6:6, they are said to "crucify to themselves the Son of God and put Him to open shame."[113] These last two statements seem particularly apt for those who

---

[106] This is clearly the consensus among the commentaries. See the listings in Bruce, *Hebrews*, pp. 147–48.

[107] Frequently with an intensifying cognate accusative. See Ezek 14:13; 15:8; 18:24; 20:27; 22:4; Wis 6:9; 12:2. *TDNT*, s.v. "παραπίπτω," by W. Michaelis, pp. 170–71.

[108] ἐν τῷ ἀποστῆναι.

[109] BDAG, pp. 157–58; *TDNT*, s.v. "ἀφίστημι," by H. Schlier, 1:513; *NIDNTT*, s.v. "Fall, Fall Away," by W. Bauder, 1:607–8.

[110] *TDNT*, s.v. "ἑκούσιος," by F. Hauck, 2:470.

[111] Most commentaries connect the sin here with Num 15:22–31 where the distinction is made between the so-called "unintentional" sin (LXX ἀκουσίως) and the "defiant" sin (LXX ἐν χειρὶ ὑπερηφανίας ["with a proud or arrogant hand"]). See, for example, Lane, *Hebrews*, 2:291–93. It is best to interpret the defiant sin in Num 15 as apostasy. This sin is not simply intentional, but defiant (LXX ὑπερηφανίας; MT רָמָה[from רום]). It involves blasphemy against God (v. 30) and hatred of God's word (v. 31). Furthermore, the one guilty is cut off from the nation (v. 30–31), with no hope of forgiveness (v. 31; cf. Heb 10:26, "no sacrifice for sins").

[112] Note also 3:17–19. The warning in 3:12 is based on the actions of apostate Israel who rejected God's promises and were prevented from entering God's rest.

[113] The debate over whether to translate ἀνασταυροῦντας as "crucify" (NASB) or "crucify again" (NIV) is not germane to the discussion. See Bruce, *Hebrews*, p. 138. The reflexive pronoun "to themselves" (ἑαυτοῖς) may be taken either as an ethical dative (Attridge, *Hebrews*, p. 171) or as a dative of disadvantage (Lane, *Hebrews*, 1:133; Ellingworth, *Hebrews*, pp. 324–25). The expression "put Him to open shame" (παραδειγματίζοντας) is used of public executions which expose the victim to humiliation and serve as a warning to others (e.g., Num 25:4 [LXX]). *TDNT*, s.v. "παραδειγματίζω," by H. Schlier; Bruce, *Hebrews*, p. 149.

have been enlightened by the gospel but who come to disdain its message. By such an act, they have placed themselves in the same company as those who rejected the claims of Christ and nailed Him to the cross. The same may be said of the expressions in 10:29, "trampled under foot the Son of God," "regarded as unclean the blood of the covenant," and "insulted the Spirit of Grace."[114] The author of Hebrews intentionally employs highly emotive phrases to communicate the magnitude involved in knowingly and deliberately spurning the grace of God in the gospel of Christ. The combined weight of all of this leads inexorably to the conclusion that the sin in these verses is apostasy.[115] It is the premeditated act of one who has been exposed to the gospel, has understood it and even agreed with it for a period of time, but who ultimately has come to reject it.

To renew again unto repentance.[116] The question raised with this clause is whether "repentance" means true repentance and whether those in view were thus saved.[117] The tension with the fourth view which says these were not saved is, why would it be desirable to restore these to repentance, if it were not true repentance? Without question, Scripture speaks of a repentance that leads to salvation.[118] Furthermore, true repentance and saving faith are corollaries. They are identified individually and collectively as the sole conditions for salvation.[119] At the same time, Scripture also speaks of a repentance that does not lead to salvation.[120] In other

---

[114] The expression "trampled under foot" (καταπατήσας), used here in a figurative sense, means to treat something with contempt (BDAG, p. 523). The same may be said of the expression "insulted" (ἐνυβρίσας, BDAG, p. 342). The "blood of the covenant" refers to Christ's sacrificial death in connection with the new covenant (Heb 9:11–22). By treating the blood of Christ as "common" (κοινόν), these were saying that Christ's death was ordinary in the sense that it had no real soteriological efficacy (Lane, *Hebrews,* 2:294–95).

[115] McKnight, "Warning Passages," pp. 36–43.

[116] πάλιν ἀνακαινίζειν εἰς μετάνοιαν.

[117] The infinitive ἀνακαινίζειν means "to renew" or "to restore" (BDAG, p. 64). The entire construction with the adverb πάλιν and the prepositional phrase εἰς μετάνοιαν means to bring (someone) back to repentance. The implication from this is that those in vv. 4–6 had previously been brought to repentance; they had previously repented.

[118] E.g., Acts 11:18; 2 Cor 7:10. Repentance is defined as a change of mind concerning personal sin and guilt, which may be accompanied by remorse and/or sorrow. Several argue that repentance is often used in the NT as a synonym for conversion. See, for example, *TDNT,* s.v. "μετανοέω, μετάνοια," by J. Behm, 4:999–1006; *Evangelical Dictionary of Theology,* s.v. "Repentance," by C. Kromminga, p. 396.

[119] E.g., Luke 5:20; 24:47; Acts 3:19; 5:31; 10:43; 13:38–39; 16:31; 20:21; 26:18.

[120] The implication from Acts 11:18 and 2 Cor 7:10 is that there is a repentance that does not lead to salvation.

words, just as there is a faith that does not save, so there is a repentance that does not save.[121] This is certainly the case with the repentance exercised by Esau in Hebrews 12:17 and Judas in Matthew 27:3.[122]

The question in v. 6 is, which kind of repentance is in view? Since either is a possibility, the answer must be based on the larger context. As previously argued, the sin in these verses is apostasy. It is the sin of those who made a profession of faith in Christ but who later repudiated Christ. In addition, the threat in the warning passages is the threat of eternal condemnation and punishment. It points to God's judgment of the lost, not of the saved. Lastly, the Scriptures teach the eternal security of those who are saved. Salvation once gained cannot be lost. In light of this, the repentance which those in Hebrews 6:6 had previously exercised was a repentance that did not lead to salvation.[123] The question remains, why, if that is the case, is it desirable to bring the lapsed back to this repentance, assuming that were possible. The answer is that the repentance in Hebrews 6:6 would involve conviction of sin and could serve as the foundation upon which the Spirit of God would work true repentance.

For it is impossible (v. 4).[124] Opinion is divided whether "impossible" is to be taken in a relative sense (impossible for man but not for God) or in an absolute sense (impossible for God or for anyone).[125] Several lines of

---

[121] For a reference in the NT to a faith that does not save, see Jas 2:14–20. In v. 14, James asks a rhetorical question, "can that faith save him" (μὴ δύναται ἡ πίστις σῶσαι αὐτόν)? The faith in view, from this verse, is a faith without works. The construction James uses in asking his question indicates that the answer intended is "no." James's point is that a faith without works is not a saving faith.

[122] Matt 27:3 uses the semantic cognate μεταμέλομαι (see BDAG, p. 639). The construction in Heb 12:17 is variously interpreted. Some argue that Esau sorrowed over the loss of his birthright, but did not repent (e.g., Attridge, *Hebrews,* pp. 369–70). Others argue that he repented, but that his repentance was ineffective (e.g., Kent, *Hebrews,* pp. 267–68). In either case, there is agreement that Esau had changed his mind about his birthright and was filled with remorse that he had sold it.

[123] McKnight, "Perseverance of the Saints," p. 150.

[124] ἀδύνατον γάρ.

[125] For the former, see Bruce, *Hebrews,* p. 144. He states, "We know, of course, that nothing of this sort is ultimately impossible for the grace of God, but as a matter of human experience the reclamation of such people is, practically speaking, impossible." For the latter view, see Moffatt, *Hebrews,* p. 179; Hughes, *Hebrews,* pp. 212–13; Attridge, *Hebrews,* pp. 167–69. Attempts by some to take the present participles in v. 6 as temporal, "it is impossible...*while* they crucify the Son of God," suggesting that were they to stop doing this then it would be possible to restore them, have generally been rejected. The oft quoted dictum by Bruce is frequently cited as an effective rebuttal, "To say that they cannot be brought to repentance so long as they persist in their renunciation of Christ would be a truism hardly worth putting into words" (*Hebrews,* p. 149).

evidence point to the second of these two as being the proper understanding. The word impossible is used four times in Hebrews. In the other three instances, the force of the term is clearly absolute. In 6:18, the author of Hebrews writes, "in which it is impossible for God to lie." In 10:4, he asserts that, "it is impossible for the blood of bulls and goats to take away sins." In 11:6, he states, "without faith it is impossible to please *Him.*" The context in each of these instances rules out the possibility of exceptions. "Impossible" in all three cases means absolutely, without exceptions.

Furthermore, the parallel expressions in the other warning passages add support to this interpretation. The force of the rhetorical question in the warning in 2:2–3, "how will we escape," is that there is no escaping the consequences of this sin.[126] The same may be said of the similar statement in 12:25, "much less *will we escape.*"[127] Similarly, in 10:26, those guilty of this act face the harsh reality that "there no longer remains a sacrifice for sins." No sacrifice means no forgiveness.[128] Moreover, the corollary to no forgiveness, according to 10:27, is "a terrifying expectation of judgment."[129] In other words, for those who commit this sin, there is no forgiveness; there is only the terrifying certainty of divine judgment.[130] The distinct impression is that the statement in 6:4 is absolute. It is impossible for God, or for anyone else, to restore those who have fallen away. Their sin is irremediable.

This conclusion raises a second question, why this sin is irremediable. Two explanations have been offered. The first is that it is irremediable because the sin of apostasy rejects the sole means of salvation. Salvation is an act of divine grace, conditioned by faith alone in the gospel alone. These, by rejecting the gospel, are rejecting the only means for their deliverance.[131] The second interpretation is that such sin, similar to the unpardonable sin in the Gospels, brings with it the invariable response of divine hardening.[132] Of the two explanations, the second is preferred as

---

[126] πῶς ἡμεῖς ἐκφευξόμεθα.

[127] εἰ γὰρ ἐκεῖνοι οὐκ ἐξέφυγον...πολὺ μᾶλλον ἡμεῖς.

[128] Hughes, *Hebrews,* 2:419.

[129] φοβερὰ δέ τις ἐκδοχὴ κρίσεως. The term ἐκδοχή ("expectation") carries with it the thought of certainty, that which is inevitable (Ellingworth, *Hebrews,* p. 534).

[130] Lane, *Hebrews,* 2:291–93.

[131] Attridge, *Hebrews,* p. 169; Lane, *Hebrews,* 1:142. Lane states, "The ἀδύνατον, which is used absolutely and without qualification in v 4, expresses an impossibility because the apostate repudiates the only basis upon which repentance can be extended."

[132] McKnight, "Warning Passages," p. 33, concludes, "...'impossible' is to be understood as 'God will not work in them any longer so it is impossible for them to be restored.'" On parallels outside of Hebrews, see Hughes, *Hebrews,* pp. 215–18.

more consistent with the meaning of impossible in the context of Hebrews. The first explanation allows for the possibility of restoration, if the apostate were to turn from rebellion. To summarize, the author of Hebrews is saying that it is impossible to restore those who heard and understood the gospel but who reject it. This irreversible act has as its only prospect the judgment of God.

Verses 7–8

> [7]For ground that drinks the rain which often falls on it and brings forth vegetation useful to those for whose sake it is also tilled, receives a blessing from God; [8] but if it yields thorns and thistles, it is worthless and close to being cursed, and it ends up being burned (Heb. 6:7–8).

In vv. 7–8, the author of Hebrews uses an illustration from agriculture to reinforce and clarify his warning in vv. 4–6.[133] The illustration describes land that receives rain and produces a diverse yield, and the contrasting outcomes that result from this. The outcomes in each case illustrate the consequences of those who persevere in the faith and those who fall away.[134] As such, the illustration functions as an extension of the warning and must be taken into consideration in the interpretation.[135]

The focus of the debate over this passage is with v. 8 and the interpretation of the consequences mentioned there.[136] The question raised is whether v. 8, in illustrating the consequences of falling away, refers to the chastisement of the saved or the punishment of the unsaved.[137] In other words, taking "land" in v. 8 as corresponding to the one falling away, are

---

[133] Postpositive γάρ is taken either as causal or as explanatory. In either case, it would be supporting and clarifying the warning in vv. 4–6. See the discussion in Verbrugge, "Towards a New Interpretation," pp. 62–63. On the background of the illustration, see Attridge, *Hebrews,* p. 172, and on the structure, see Ellingworth, *Hebrews,* pp. 325–27.

[134] Virtually all agree that v. 7 illustrates the consequences of those who persevere and v. 8 the consequences of those who fall away (e.g., Bruce, *Hebrews,* pp. 149–50). Debate over whether it is the same parcel of land in vv. 7–8 or two different parcels is not a critical issue and may be pressing the illustration too far. For discussion, see Grudem, "Perseverance of the Saints," p. 155. The focus of the illustration, in any case, is on the contrasting yields and the contrasting consequences that result from those yields (Lane, *Hebrews,* 1:143).

[135] McKnight, "Warning Passages," p. 35.

[136] ἐκφέρουσα δὲ ἀκάνθας καὶ τριβόλους, ἀδόκιμος καὶ κατάρας ἐγγύς, ἧς τὸ τέλος εἰς καῦσιν.

[137] Those who champion the second of the four views hold to the former; those who champion the first, third, and fourth views hold to the latter.

the expressions "worthless," "close to being cursed," and "ends up being burned" best understood as referring to the saved or the lost? The evidence favors the latter.

The expression "worthless" is used in the NT of that which has failed some test and is viewed as disqualified, disapproved, or rejected.[138] Based on 1 Corinthians 9:27 and the statement about Paul's guarding himself while ministering to others lest he himself should be disapproved, some argue that the term can refer to the saved.[139] However, it is questionable whether it has this sense in 1 Corinthians 9:27 or elsewhere in the NT. The expression is employed of the unbeliever, and, together with its antonym "approved," contrasts the lost with the saved.[140] It is used in Romans 1:28, for example, to describe the mind of the unbeliever, that is, the mind of the lost. In 2 Corinthians 13:5, it is used of false believers, those not in the faith. In 2 Timothy 3:8, it is used of Jannes and Jambres, who opposed Moses and were disapproved, shown to be false with regard to the faith. In all likelihood, that is its sense in 1 Corinthians 9:27. Paul is saying that he must exercise self-control lest he himself should fail the test and be rejected as one who is false and not true. Probability rests on the side that sees the same meaning for the expression here. Those who fall away do, by that act, fail the test of a genuine believer and are rejected by God.

The same may be said of the phrase "close to being cursed." The adverb "close" does not suggest that this curse is close by but may be avoided. Identical to its use in 8:13 of the demise of the old covenant, it carries the idea of what is imminent and inevitable.[141] In 8:13, the author of Hebrews describes the old covenant as growing old and obsolete, whose disappearance was close at hand. The thought is that with the promise of a new covenant in Jeremiah 31:31–34 (Heb 8:8–12) there is the anticipation that the old covenant would be replaced and set aside. According to 8:6, this new covenant has now been enacted with the death of Christ.

---

[138] BAGD, p. 18

[139] Oberholtzer, "Thorn-Infested Ground," p. 325.

[140] *TDNT,* s.v. "δόκιμος," by W. Grundmann, 2:255–60; *NIDNTT,* s.v. "δόκιμος," by H. Haarbeck, 3:808–10. Haarbeck's comments (p. 808) are noteworthy, "*dokimos* is used…in the sense of recognized, approved, accepted (Rom 14:18; 16:10; 1 Cor 11:19; 2 Cor 10:18); correspondingly *adokimos* means worthless, rejected, not in the sense of that which is seen from the first to be unsuitable (not even in Heb 6:8), but meaning that which has not stood the test, that which has been shown to be a sham, and has therefore been rejected (Rom 1:28; 1 Cor 9:27; 2 Cor 13:5; 2 Tim 3:8; Titus 1:16)."

[141] *TDNT,* s.v. "ἐγγύς," by H. Preisker, 2:330–32; Moffatt, *Hebrews,* p. 82; Hughes, *Hebrews,* pp. 223–24; Attridge, *Hebrews,* p. 173.

Without question, what is close at hand in 8:13 is what is both imminent and certain. The context argues for the same sense for "close" in v. 8.

In addition, the concept of a curse is difficult to understand, if it refers to the saved, but easily understood, if the reference is to the unsaved. The term is used elsewhere in the NT to describe God's condemnation and judgment of the lost, and that is its likely sense in this passage.[142] Not only are those who fall away rejected by God, they also face the imminent and certain threat of divine judgment.

Finally, it has been argued that the burning in v. 8 is the same as that mentioned in 1 Corinthians 3:13, 15. In both passages, works are burned, and in both, the saved are judged.[143] This is consistent, it is further argued, with the common practice in the ancient Near East of burning a field to rid it of weeds and to clear it for productive growth.[144] The thought is that the judgment in v. 8 is for the restoring of the saved, not the punishing of the lost.

While such an interpretation of the burning is possible, the concept of judgment and the reference to fire in the other warning passages weighs against seeing a judgment of the saved in v. 8. Elsewhere in the warning passages, as has been shown, the judgment is against the unbeliever, the one who is not saved. For example, the description of this judgment in 10:27 as a raging fire that will consume the "enemies" of God hardly sounds like God's judging the saved. The same may be said of the reference in 12:29 to God as a consuming fire. The context of 12:29 is God's future shaking or judging the created order prior to the establishing of His kingdom. The judgment there is the outpouring of divine wrath (12:26–28).[145] The

---

[142] *TDNT,* s.v. "ἀρά," by F. Buchsel, 1:448–51.

[143] Oberholtzer, "Thorn-Infested Ground," pp. 325–26.

[144] Oberholtzer, "Thorn-Infested Ground," p. 326. Oberholtzer differentiates between the present, temporal judgment of believers and the eschatological judgment of believers at the judgment seat of Christ. Heb 6:8 refers to the former whereas 1 Cor 3 refers to the latter, though the two are interrelated. His efforts to distinguish the thorns and thistles from the land as that which is burned in order to strengthen his interpretation of v. 8 is not supported by the syntax. The relative pronoun (ἧς) identifying that which is to be burned is feminine singular, agreeing with "land" (γῆ) in the preceding verse and not with the feminine plural "thorns" (ἀκάνθας) or the masculine plural "thistles" (τριβόλους) in v. 8. See Attridge, *Hebrews,* p. 173; Ellingworth, *Hebrews,* p. 328.

[145] Heb 12:26 incorporates a citation from the LXX of Hag 2:6 where Haggai reminds the post-exilic community of God's future, eschatological judgment of the nations (2:7) and of the entire created order (2:6). Heb 12:29 adapts the thought in Deut 4:24 where Moses is warning the nation to honor the covenant and shun idolatry (4:15–23). Both contexts address God's retributive judgment against those who rebel against Him and reject His revelation. For discussion on the background and interpretation of Heb 12:25–29 in support of the above, see Attridge, *Hebrews,* pp. 378–83.

evidence from all of this decisively favors taking the judgment in v. 8 as
the judgment of God upon the lost. The fire represents the eschatological
wrath of God that will be poured out against all who have rebelled against
Him and have rejected His word (12:25).

Taken together, the evidence from the illustration in vv. 7–8 further
confirms the fourth view and its interpretation of vv. 4–6. The application
of the illustration to vv. 4–6 is straightforward. Those who receive the
good things of God enumerated in vv. 4–5 and demonstrate the genuineness of their faith by the fruit they bear obtain God's blessing. On the
other hand, those who experience these same good things but fail the test
of genuineness by falling away from the faith are rejected by God and are
under His curse.

Verse 9

> But, beloved, we are convinced of better things concerning you, and things
> that accompany salvation, though we are speaking in this way (Heb 6:9).

In vv. 9–12, the author of Hebrews transitions from words of warning
to words of encouragement. He addresses the readers as "beloved" and
expresses his confidence in their salvation. Two questions in particular are
raised with these words of encouragement that are pertinent to the discussion of the warning passage. The first involves again the identification
of those in view in the warning. Some argue that the author frequently
uses the expression "we" when giving the warnings, indicating that he
includes himself in the warnings. Furthermore, he calls those who have
been warned "beloved" and says that he is confident of their salvation. All
of this suggests that the warnings are addressed to saved individuals.[146]
The second question, related to the first, concerns the interpretation of
the expression "better things concerning you, and things that accompany
salvation" and the force of the construction "though we are speaking in
this way." Specifically, what is the antecedent of the expression "better
things," and how do this and the following statements assist in the interpretation of v. 4–6?

Without question, the warnings are addressed to the readers of the
epistle, as seen by the frequent use of the second person plural in the
warnings themselves.[147] In addition to the second person plural, the author

---

[146] E.g., McKnight, "Warning Passages," p. 43.

[147] 3:12; 4:1; 5:11–12; 6:9–12; 10:35–36; 12:18, 22, 25.

of Hebrews also uses the first person plural in the same warnings.[148] However, this does not prove that everything said in the warnings applies equally to the readers, nor that each statement is describing those who are saved. The author's use of "we" is not employed consistently throughout the warnings and may be the "we" of accommodation. In other words, he may mean "we believers" or "we who have made a profession of faith," without intending to include himself. This is suggested in the second warning passage in 4:1 where the author of Hebrews begins with the first person plural. When addressing the actual warning, however, he switches to the second person ("let *us* fear if...*any one of you*...").[149] In any case, the use of the first person plural does not prove that every statement in the warning passages describes those who are saved. That must be determined by the nature of the statement and the form of address (viz., first, second, third person) used in each instance.

In terms of the form of address, the evidence suggests that the author of Hebrews intentionally distances his readers from the statements in the warnings describing the action of an apostate. For example, in the third warning passage, the author of Hebrews begins by admonishing his readers in the second person: "*you* have become dull of hearing," 5:11; "*you* ought to be teachers,"[150] "*you* have need again for someone to teach *you*," "*you* have come to need milk," 5:12. Following this, he exhorts his readers to maturity, using the first person plural: "let *us* press on," 6:1; "this *we* will do," 6:3. However, when addressing the actual warning where he gives a description of the apostates, he uses third person constructions: "*those* who have," 6:4–6; "*they* again crucify to *themselves*," 6:6.[151] Then, when returning to his exhortation in 6:9–12, he once again uses second person plurals: "better things concerning *you*," 6:9; "we desire that each of *you*," 6:11; "that *you* will not be sluggish," 6:12). The distinct impression from what appears to be a conscious variation in the form of address is that the author of Hebrews intentionally distances his readers from the description of the apostates in vv. 4–6.[152]

---

[148] E.g., 2:1–4.

[149] See also 12:25.

[150] The second person translation is based on taking the participial construction ὀφείλοντες εἶναι διδάσκαλοι as referring to the readers.

[151] The third person translation is based on taking the articular participles as substantival ("those who...") and the reflexive pronoun ἑαυτοῖς as third person ("themselves"). See BDAG, s.v. "ἑαυτοῦ," p. 268.

[152] Grudem, "Perseverance of the Saints," p. 157. A similar variation is found in 10:26–39. The author of Hebrews begins the warning in v. 26 by making a conditional

The other statements in v. 9 further support this conclusion. The author of Hebrews describes the readers as "beloved," a common expression in the NT for addressing believers.[153] Furthermore, he expresses his confidence that "better things"[154] could be said of them and, specifically, the "things that accompany salvation."[155] The basis for his confidence is the evidence of their salvation shown in the good works they had performed and were continuing to perform (v. 10).[156] The contrast between his confidence expressed here and the description of the apostates in the preceding verses is brought out in the statement "though we are speaking in this way."[157] This construction forms the protasis of a concessive clause that has as its apodosis the statement "[nevertheless] we are convinced..."[158] The thrust of the concession is to contrast what the author of Hebrews has been saying previously with his present expression of confidence in the salvation of the readers. The verse could be paraphrased in this way, "Although we were warning about God's eternal condemnation and judgment of the lost, nevertheless, we are confident that you are saved."

---

statement using the first person plural. But, when describing the actual actions of the apostate in vv. 28–29, he transitions to third person constructions. Then, when returning to exhortation in vv. 32–39, he switches back to first and second person plural forms.

[153] ἀγαπητοί. The term may denote one who is loved of God or simply be used as a term of endearment (BDAG, p. 7). Contrary to Oberholtzer, the expression "beloved" can be used of unbelievers (Rom 11:28) but that is not its force in v. 9 ("Thorn-Infested Ground," p. 327).

[154] τὰ κρείσσονα. There is debate both on the use of the article and the force of the comparative. A number of commentaries take the article as anaphoric and understand the comparative as making a positive statement, the entire construction referring to the "good" things in v. 7 in contrast to the "bad" things in v. 8. See Attridge, *Hebrews*, p. 174; Lane, *Hebrews*, 1:144; Ellingworth, *Hebrews*, p. 329. Grudem, on the other hand, takes the article as making the adjective substantival and argues that the construction "better" is used comparatively elsewhere in Hebrews (1:4; 7:7, 22; 8:6; 9:23; 10:34; 11:16, 35, 40; 12:24) and should have that meaning in this verse as well ("Perseverance of the Saints," p. 158). The comparison in this case is between the good things mentioned in vv. 4–5, which are the evidence of divine blessing, and the better things in vv. 10–12, which are the evidence of salvation. Although either interpretation is consistent with the position argued here, the use of the adjective elsewhere in Hebrews supports Grudem's interpretation.

[155] καὶ ἐχόμενα σωτηρίας. The construction represents a common Greek idiom for what is connected with or pertaining to something, here of salvation. See, for example, Moffatt, *Hebrews*, p. 83; Attridge, *Hebrews*, p. 174.

[156] The γάρ in v. 10 indicates that v. 10 identifies the basis for the author's confidence in his readers' salvation expressed in v. 9. Attridge, *Hebrews*, p. 174; Lane, *Hebrews*, 1:144.

[157] εἰ καὶ οὕτως λαλοῦμεν.

[158] RSV, NASB, NIV. Note the use of εἰ καί. On the form and function of concessive clauses, see Ernest De Witt Burton, *Syntax of the Moods and Tenses in New Testament Greek*, 3rd ed. (reprint of 1898 ed., Edinburgh: T. & T. Clark, 1973), pp. 112–16.

From this it can be seen that vv. 9–12 further validate the fourth view and its interpretation of vv. 4–6. Had the author of Hebrews intended vv. 4–6 to describe those who were saved, it is difficult to understand why he would say in v. 9 that he was persuaded of better things of the readers, and particularly, of the things that belong to salvation.[159]

With this in mind, the question that remains is how such warnings apply to the readers whom the author of Hebrews assumes are saved. The answer to that question involves the outworking of God's decrees. There is a sense in which God preserves for final salvation or glorification only those who persevere in the faith.[160] Yet, it is equally true that God insures that those who are truly saved persevere in the faith.[161] Thus, these warning passages may be viewed as the divinely appointed means, provoking true believers to persevere in the faith, to accomplish God's divinely appointed ends, the preservation of true believers for final salvation. At the same time, the warnings inform those who have made a profession of faith but who are not saved of the fatal consequences for rejecting the gospel. As such, the warnings could be used by God's Spirit to bring these to true repentance and saving faith.[162]

CONCLUSION

The chief strength with the fourth view is its interpretation of v. 6. Specifically, it defines the sin in the warning passages as the sin of apostasy, a conscious and deliberate rejection of the gospel. Furthermore, this sin is an irremediable act whose ultimate consequence is eternal condemnation and judgment. The preceding discussion has substantiated this interpretation. This rules out the second view, which argues that the judgment in these verses is that of the saved. The judgment in the warning passages is not that of the saved. It is the final and eternal judgment of God against the lost.

In addition, it has been demonstrated from v. 6 that this sin is neither hypothetical nor impossible. In fact, it was argued from the parallel warning in 10:25–26 that some who had been associated with the readers had actually committed this sin. This negates the third view, which argues that this sin was both hypothetical and impossible. Lastly, it was argued that

---

[159] Grudem, "Perseverance of the Saints," p. 159.

[160] E.g., Mark 13:13; Col 1:23.

[161] E.g., Rom 16:25; 1 Cor 1:8; Phil 1:6; Jude 24.

[162] Grudem, "Perseverance of the Saints," p. 183; Schreiner and Caneday, *The Race Set Before Us*," pp. 204–13.

Scripture teaches the eternal security of those who are saved. Salvation, once received, can never be lost. This rules out the first view, which argues that the warning involved the loss of salvation. Neither this nor the other warning passages, in describing the action of an apostate, are describing those who are saved. That leaves the fourth view as the only alternative.

The author of Hebrews had confidence in the salvation of his readers, as was seen in vv. 9–11. Yet, in 10:26, he indicates that some had forsaken the services of the local congregation and had repudiated the faith they had at one time professed. Moreover, in 5:11–14, the author of Hebrews chastises the readers for growing inattentive to God's word and to their responsibilities for spiritual growth. This combination compels him to exhort his readers to perseverance and to warn any who might fall away of the dire consequences of such an act. They were to persevere in the faith, because only those who persevere show themselves to be partakers of Christ and truly saved. This does not mean that perseverance in the faith is a condition for salvation. Rather, perseverance in the faith is understood as the mark of those who are saved. Were any to fall away, they would show they had not been partakers of Christ and were never saved. Furthermore, by falling away they would be committing an irremediable act, which would inevitably bring God's condemnation and judgment.

DOES THE BELIEVER HAVE
ONE NATURE OR TWO?[1]

William W. Combs

In recent times the popular radio preacher and author, John MacArthur, has attacked the idea of two natures in the believer. He says at one point: "If you are a Christian, it's a serious misunderstanding to think of yourself as having both an old and new nature. We do not have a dual personality!"[2] Similar attacks have come from a number of others. J. I. Packer says: "A widespread but misleading line of teaching tells us that Christians have two natures: an old one and a new one."[3] John Gerstner labels the two-nature viewpoint "Antinomianism."[4] Are these attacks justified? Is it unbiblical to speak of two natures within the believer? This essay purposes to tackle the issue.

I should begin by stating that I *do* think there is a sense in which the believer can properly be said to have two natures, and yet there is also a sense in which the believer can properly be said to have one nature. Whether the believer can more correctly be described as having one nature or two is *partly* a matter of semantics—a difference in the *usage* of the term *nature.* Those who insist that a believer has only one nature are using the term *nature* differently from the two-nature proponents. But, as I will demonstrate, more important than the issue of the semantics of one- or two-nature terminology, there lies below the surface of this debate a serious disagreement regarding the character of regeneration and sanctification within the believer. Those who argue against two natures in the believer usually do so because they view most of the two-nature proponents as having a defective understanding of these two doctrines, which is merely reflected in their two-nature terminology. Thus, it is important to note at the outset that the debate between one or two natures has both semantic and substantive elements of disagreement. Both of these areas will now be explored.

---

[1] This article appeared in the 1997 issue of *DBSJ,* vol. 2, pp. 81–103.

[2] "The Good-Natured Believer," *Masterpiece* (March–April 1990): 18.

[3] *Rediscovering Holiness* (Ann Arbor, MI: Servant Publications, 1992), p. 83.

[4] John H. Gerstner, *Wrongly Dividing the Word of Truth: A Critique of Dispensationalism* (Brentwood, TN: Wolgemuth & Hyatt, Publishers, 1991), p. 143.

MEANING OF *NATURE*

We might begin our discussion by looking at the word *nature*. It is important
to note that the meaning of the term *nature* as it is used in the debate over
one or two natures in the believer is primarily a theological issue, not one
of scriptural usage. Thus we observe that neither the KJV nor the NASB, for
instance, ever uses the terms *old nature, sinful nature,* or *new nature*. This
does not necessarily invalidate the legitimacy of these terms since, as we are
well aware, it sometimes behooves us to use a term to describe a theological
teaching of Scripture even though the term itself is not found therein—the
well-known example being, of course, the term *Trinity*.

Scriptural Data

It is not exactly true that Scripture *never* uses *nature* in the sense we are
discussing. Here I have reference to the Greek term φύσις, commonly
translated "nature," which is used fourteen times in the NT. On two of
those occasions, it may, in fact, be used in a sense similar to the way *nature*
is used in the debate at hand. In Ephesians 2:3 Paul says: "Among them
we too all formerly lived in the lusts of our flesh, indulging the desires
of the flesh and of the mind, and were by nature children of wrath, even
as the rest."[5] Though the meaning of the phrase "by nature children of
wrath" is debated, at least some commentators understand "nature" to
mean "sinful human nature."[6] Also, in 2 Peter 1:4 we are told that God
"has granted to us His precious and magnificent promises, in order that
by them [we] might become partakers of the divine nature." "Partakers
of the divine nature" could be understood to refer to the Christian's "new
nature."[7] However, neither of these verses can ultimately settle the debate
at hand, for, as we will later observe, some who argue for one nature would
admit that an individual can be said to have an old nature or a new nature,
but they do not allow that the Bible ever refers to both these natures in the
saved person.[8]

---

[5] Unless otherwise noted, all Scripture quotations are taken from the NASB, 1988.

[6] E.g., Homer A. Kent, Jr., *Ephesians: The Glory of the Church,* Everyman's Bible
Commentary (Chicago: Moody Press, 1971), p. 35; Andrew T. Lincoln, *Ephesians,* Word
Biblical Commentary (Dallas: Word, 1990), p. 99.

[7] D. Edmond Hiebert, *Second Peter and Jude* (Greenville, SC: Unusual Publications,
1989), p. 48; Renald E. Showers, "The New Nature" (Th.D. dissertation, Grace Theological
Seminary, 1975), pp. 86–88.

[8] E.g., B. B. Warfield, review of *He That Is Spiritual,* by Lewis S. Chafer, in *Princeton
Theological Review* 17 (April 1919), reprinted in Michael Horton, ed., *Christ the Lord: The
Reformation and Lordship Salvation* (Grand Rapids: Baker, 1992), p. 215.

It should also be noted that the term *nature* is used in both the RSV and NRSV in 2 Corinthians 4:16, "So we do not lose heart. Even though our outer nature is wasting away our inner nature is being renewed day by day" (NRSV). Here it might seem the Bible does refer to two natures in the believer. However, "outer nature" and "inner nature" are literally "outer man" (ὁ ἔξω ἄνθρωπος) and "inner man" (ὁ ἔσω). These terms may be contrasting Paul's outward physical life ("outer man") with his inward spiritual life ("inner man"),[9] though this is debated. What is certain is that no one is claiming they are to be equated with the old or new natures and thus have no bearing on the present debate. *Nature* is also found in the RSV's translation of Colossians 3:9–10, "Do not lie to one another, seeing that you have put off the old nature with its practices and have put on the new nature, which is being renewed in knowledge after the image of its creator." Here, however, "old nature" and "new nature" are literally "old man" (τὸν παλαιὸν ἄνθρωπον) and "new man" (τὸν νέον).[10] However, in this case the terms "old man," "new man" in Colossians 3:9–10 (as well as Rom 6:6 and Eph 4:22, 24) have often been identified with old and new natures, respectively. Therefore, we must necessarily discuss these three passages more carefully later in this paper. Finally, we should note that the phrase "sinful nature" is found numerous times in the NIV; however, this is not φύσις, but σάρξ (flesh). We will later examine the appropriateness of this translation and its relevance to the question of one or two natures.

Theological Usage

As was previously noted, the use of the term *nature* as it relates to the question of one or two natures does not stem primarily from a particular text. Instead, it can more correctly be viewed as a theological term, essential to the discussion at hand, but whose meaning is generally derived from its common, ordinary usage. Webster, for example, defines *nature* as "the inherent character or basic constitution of a person or thing: essence, disposition, temperament."[11] Smith helpfully observes that "except when it is used for the material world or universe, the term 'nature' does not designate a substance or an entity. Instead, it is a word which refers to the inherent or essential qualities of any substance or entity."[12] We might

---

[9] Homer A. Kent, Jr., *A Heart Opened Wide: Studies in 2 Corinthians* (Winona Lake, IN: BMH Books, 1982), p. 76.

[10] The NRSV has replaced "old nature," "new nature" with "old self," "new self."

[11] *Merriam-Webster's Collegiate Dictionary*, 10th ed., s.v. "nature," p. 774.

[12] Charles R. Smith, "Two Natures—Or One? An Attempt at Theological Clarification," *Voice* 62 (July–August 1983): 20.

simplify by saying that *nature* can be defined as "the characteristics which make a thing what it is," or as Smith says, "a set of characteristics."[13] The important thing to remember is that *nature* and *person* must be carefully distinguished. Here we have been helped by the discussion of Buswell, who argues that "a nature is by definition a complex of attributes." His more complete statement reads: "A person is a non-material substantive entity, and is not to be confused with a nature. A nature is not a *part* of a person in the substantive sense. A nature is a complex of attributes, and is not to be confused with a substantive entity."[14] Thus a nature cannot act and the Bible never speaks of a nature as acting.

By defining *nature* as a "complex of attributes" we can, for instance, correctly speak of Christ as having both a human and divine nature. By a human nature we mean he possessed all those attributes or characteristics essential for true humanity and, in like manner, by a divine nature we mean he possessed all those attributes or characteristics essential for true deity. Natures are not persons and natures do not act; thus Christ was one person with two natures. Therefore, it is perfectly acceptable to use two-nature terminology to describe Jesus Christ. Orthodox theology has traditionally used such terminology even though it is not found in the Bible. But, as Smith has wisely observed, "it is perfectly proper to speak of *the* (single) nature of Jesus as the God-Man. In so doing one would cite all those characteristics which are true of Him as the unique God-Man."[15] In describing Christ as having one nature or two natures, a different *meaning* is not being given to the term *nature*—"a complex of attributes"; rather, we are simply grouping various attributes of the one person into either one or two groups emphasizing different aspects of the one person. Though, admittedly, not our normal perspective, if, hypothetically, we were to describe the God-man as having one nature, we would include all those attributes that are essential to both natures—human and divine. If, as is our normal practice, we describe the God-man as having two natures, we are separating and grouping those attributes according to their distinctive qualities, whether they are human or divine. We are not suggesting by this two-nature terminology that these two natures are separate entities or persons. But we may conclude that, theologically, two-nature terminology seems quite helpful, if not essential, for understanding the one God-man.

---

[13] Ibid.

[14] J. Oliver Buswell, *A Systematic Theology of the Christian Religion,* 2 vols. in 1 (Grand Rapids: Zondervan, 1962, 1963), 2:52.

[15] Smith, "Two Natures—Or One?" p. 21.

By understanding *nature* as a complex of attributes, one is perfectly justified in using the term to describe the believer as having either one or two natures. In two-nature terminology the believer is usually said to have an old or sinful nature as well as a new nature. This old nature can be defined as "a continuing tendency to sin or rebel against God,"[16] or "as that capacity to serve Satan, sin, and self acquired through Adam."[17] When the believer is viewed from the perspective of his old nature, the focus is on those attributes or characteristics that dispose him to sin. The old nature is in effect a disposition to sin which remains in the regenerate person. In similar fashion the new nature can be defined as "the capacity to serve God and righteousness acquired through regeneration."[18] It is a disposition toward holiness. Two-nature terminology provides us with what Smith calls a "useful abstraction," enabling us to "speak of our 'old nature' when referring to the set of characteristics which is intrinsically ours by virtue of being born into this world as sinful persons—in contrast with those characteristics which are ours as a result of regeneration."[19]

In similar fashion, our understanding of *nature* as a complex of attributes permits us to view the believer as having one nature. By this we would be referring to all those attributes, whatever they are, necessary to describe the individual as a fallen human creature who has also been regenerated. In actuality, however, it is difficult to find a critic of the two-nature view who, in rejecting that view, argues instead that the believer has only one nature. Critics of the two-nature view mostly avoid using the term *nature* at all. Packer rejects its use since he believes the two-nature view employs the term contrary to its use "both in life and in Scripture." He adds "that 'nature' means the whole of what we are, and the whole of what we are is expressed in various actions and reactions that make up our life."[20] I have previously suggested, contrary to Packer, that Scripture may in fact use *nature* in the same way the two-nature view does (Eph 2:3; 2 Pet 1:4); but, even if Packer were correct on that point, he certainly falters when he insists that *nature* must mean "the whole of what we are." Clearly, he would not want us to believe that when he speaks of Christ's human nature, he intends "the whole" of what the God-man is. In truth *nature* can refer to "the whole of what we are," but it does not have to. As Smith explains:

---

[16] Anthony A. Hoekema, *Saved by Grace* (Grand Rapids: Eerdmans, 1989), p. 214.

[17] Gordon R. Lewis and Bruce A. Demarest, *Integrative Theology,* 3 vols. (Grand Rapids: Zondervan, 1994), 3:196.

[18] Ibid.

[19] Smith, "Two Natures—Or One?" p. 21.

[20] *Rediscovering Holiness,* p. 83.

It is proper to speak of a believer as having only one nature if the term is used to mean a "complex of attributes" which characterize an individual, and if this "complex" includes *all* the characteristics, good and bad, which describe the individual. But this does not disallow the use of the term as an abstraction to label various complexes of attributes such as that complex due to my Adamic inheritance.[21]

So, it may be concluded, contrary to Packer, there is nothing illegitimate about using *nature,* especially as a theological term, to refer to those characteristics, both good and bad within the believer— the new and old natures. Neither is it illegitimate to speak of the believer as having one nature, one complex of attributes, as long as those attributes describe the whole individual— including both good and bad characteristics. Thus, the difference between one-nature and two-nature terminology is not over the *meaning* of the term *nature* but rather the *usage* of *nature* to describe different complexes of attributes. The value and attraction of two-nature terminology is that it provides convenient terminology to describe the struggle with sin within every believer. Those who decry the idea of two-natures in the believer would still strongly affirm that struggle, but they simply believe that it is not theologically accurate to describe it as a struggle between the old and new natures. Such terminology, they feel, can be misleading.

But, in reality, those who object to two natures in the believer have a difficult time ridding themselves of two-nature terminology. One could hardly find a more strident opponent of the two-nature view than John Gerstner, yet his own position is that "the Christian is one person *with two struggling principles* [emphasis added]."[22] Another opponent of the two-nature view, J. I. Packer, explains that "believers find within themselves contrary urgings," which he identifies as their "regenerate desires and purposes" and their "fallen, Adamic instincts."[23] Thus it seems that it is difficult to accurately describe the struggle which takes place within the believer without talking about two opposing somethings— principles, desires, urgings, etc. While it is true that two-nature terminology can be misleading and has sometimes been tied to inadequate views of sanctification, this is not necessarily so. The problem is not with two-nature terminology per se, but with a defective theology that happens to use two-nature terminology. But before we deal with this issue, it behooves us to

---

[21] Charles R. Smith, review of *Birthright: Christian, Do You Know Who You Are?* by David Needham, in *Grace Theological Journal* 3 (Fall 1982): 288.

[22] *Wrongly Dividing the Word of Truth,* p. 232.

[23] J. I. Packer, *Concise Theology* (Wheaton, IL: Tyndale House, 1993), p. 171.

look more carefully at the scriptural descriptions of the believer's struggle with sin.

THE OLD MAN/NEW MAN

In Romans 6, Ephesians 4, and Colossians 3, Paul contrasts the old man with the new man, though, actually, Romans 6 speaks only of the old man. Whereas the KJV has "man" (ἄνθρωπος) in these passages, the NASB uses "self."

Romans 6:6

knowing this, that our old self was crucified with Him, that our body of sin might be done away with, that we should no longer be slaves to sin;

Ephesians 4:20–24

[20]But you did not learn Christ in this way, [21]if indeed you have heard Him and have been taught in Him, just as truth is in Jesus, [22]that, in reference to your former manner of life, you lay aside the old self, which is being corrupted in accordance with the lusts of deceit, [23]and that you be renewed in the spirit of your mind, [24]and put on the new self, which in the likeness of God has been created in righteousness and holiness of the truth.

Colossians 3:9–10

[9]Do not lie to one another, since you laid aside the old self with its evil practices, [10]and have put on the new self who is being renewed to a true knowledge according to the image of the One who created him

Advocates of the two-nature view have found support for their position in Paul's description of this old man/new man contrast. The old man is equated with the old nature, and the new man with the new nature. Numerous interpreters, especially in earlier years, have understood the old-man/new-man contrast as a struggle between the believer's two natures.[24] Bavinck explains:

The spiritual struggle which the believers must conduct inside their souls has a very different character. It is not a struggle between reason and passion, but between the flesh and the spirit, between the old and the new man, between the sin which continues to dwell in the believers and the spiritual principle of life which has been planted in their hearts.[25]

---

[24] E.g., Charles Hodge, *A Commentary on the Epistle to the Ephesians* (New York: Robert Carter and Brothers, 1857), p. 259; idem, *Systematic Theology,* 3 vols. (reprint ed.; Grand Rapids: Eerdmans, 1982), 3:221–224; Lewis S. Chafer, *Systematic Theology,* 8 vols. (Dallas: Dallas Seminary Press, 1947), 2:348.

[25] Herman Bavinck, *Our Reasonable Faith,* trans. Henry Zylstra (Grand Rapids: Baker, 1956), p. 493.

However, there has always been a problem with this interpretation. On the one hand, the Ephesians passage would seem to support the equation of old man/new man equals old nature/new nature since there Paul does appear to speak of a present situation within the believer: he must "put off the old man" and "put on the new man." This interpretation is probably more clearly seen in the NIV's translation: "You were taught, with regard to your former way of life, to put off your old self,…and to put on the new self."[26] In other words, the Ephesians passage would seem to argue for the two-nature view of the believer— he has both an old man and a new man.

On the other hand, the Romans and Colossians passages make it difficult to identify the old man with the old nature since the old man is said to have been "crucified" (Rom 6:6) and to have been "laid aside" (Col 3:9), both past circumstances for the believer. If the old nature has been "crucified" and "laid aside," how can one say the believer still has an old nature? Godet comes to the rescue by suggesting that Paul does not say our old nature was killed, only crucified— "He may exist still, but like one crucified, whose activity is paralyzed."[27] However, this is probably not Paul's thought. As Moo wisely reminds us:

> The image of crucifixion is chosen not because Paul wants to suggest that our "dying with Christ" is a preliminary action that the believer must complete by daily "dying to sin," but because Christ's death took the form of crucifixion. The believer who is "crucified with Christ" is as definitely and finally "dead" as a result of this action as was Christ himself after his crucifixion (as Paul stresses in v. 10: the death Christ died he died "once for all"). Of course, we must remember what this death means. This is no more a physical, or ontological, death, than is our burial with Christ (v. 4) or our "dying to sin" (v. 2). Paul's language throughout is forensic, or positional; by God's act, we have been placed in a new position. This position is real, for what exists in God's sight is surely (ultimately) real, and it carries definite consequences for day-to-day living. But it is status, or power-structure, that Paul is talking about here.[28]

[26] This same interpretation would seem to be found in the NASB and KJV.

[27] Frederic L. Godet, *Commentary on Romans* (reprint of 1883 ed.; Grand Rapids: Kregel, 1984), p. 244. Also, C. E. B. Cranfield, *A Critical and Exegetical Commentary of the Epistle to the Romans,* 2 vols., International Critical Commentary (Edinburgh: T. & T. Clark, 1975, 1979), 1:309.

[28] Douglas J. Moo, *The Epistle to the Romans,* New International Commentary on the New Testament (Grand Rapids: Eerdmans, 1996), p. 373.

As Moo stresses, Paul's old-man/new-man language is not ontological, but relational or positional in orientation. Paul is not describing aspects of the individual, but the person as a whole. The contrast between the old and new man does not refer to a change in nature but a change in relationship. Our old man is "what we were 'in Adam'— the 'man' of the old age, who lives under the tyranny of sin and death."[29] The old man is my old unregenerate self. The new man is my new regenerate self. Thus, the believer is properly described as only a new man. While one can, as I have argued, correctly speak of a believer as having both an old and new nature; "it is," as Murray reminds us, "no more feasible to call the believer a new man and an old man, than it is to call him a regenerate man and an unregenerate.... The believer is a new man, a new creation, but he is a new man not yet made perfect. Sin dwells in him still, and he still commits sin. He is necessarily the subject of progressive renewal."[30] Paul's point, then, in the old-man/new-man contrast is that there has been a radical change in the believer's relationship to sin. While the believer still sins, he is no longer a slave to sin, sin no longer reigns (Rom 6:14, 17, 18, 20)— that is the condition of the old man, the unregenerate person.

However, if this is true, and the believer is no longer an old man, but a new man, we still face a problem with the Ephesians passage, where, as we have seen, Paul seems to be commanding Christians to "put off the old man" and to "put on the new man." How can Paul command the putting off of the old man if the old man is the old unregenerate self? The answer is that Paul is probably not giving commands in Ephesians 4:22-24; instead, he is describing a past event for the Ephesian believers, the same situation we saw in Romans and Colossians. To understand Ephesians in this way, one might look to Murray's solution, which takes the infinitives in v. 22 ("put off," ἀποθέσθαι) and v. 24 ("put on," ἐνδύσασθαι) as indicating result. Thus he translates: "But ye have not so learned Christ, if so be ye have heard him and have been taught by him as the truth is in Jesus, so that ye have put off, according to the former manner of life, the old man who is corrupted according to the lusts of deceit, and are being renewed in the spirit of your mind, and have put on the new man who after God has been created in righteousness and holiness of the truth."[31] Though Murray presents a well-reasoned grammatical case for his translation, it is probably not the best way to understand Paul's syntax; result infinitives

---

[29] Ibid.

[30] John Murray, *Principles of Conduct* (Grand Rapids: Eerdmans, 1957), pp. 218–19.

[31] Ibid., pp. 215–16.

are not likely here. Wallace suggests they are more likely infinitives used in indirect discourse, following the verb "taught" (ἐδιδάχθητε), which could represent an indicative in the direct discourse.[32] Thus we should translate: "you have been taught in him...that you have put off...the old man...and that you have put on the new man...." This is supported by the "therefore" (διό) in 4:25, which usually follows a statement of fact in order to make an application; that is, because the Ephesians have already put off the old man and have put on the new man, they should "therefore... speak truth," etc.[33]

The conclusion to be drawn is that, although it has been common to equate old nature/new nature with old man/new man, this is not a correct understanding of how Paul uses the terms old man/new man. This lack of correlation does not in and of itself deny the legitimacy of the two-nature, only that the old-man/new-man contrast has a different point to make. We will now turn to two passages that do directly describe the believer's struggle with sin.

GALATIANS 5:16–17

[16]But I say, walk by the Spirit, and you will not carry out the desire of the flesh. [17]For the flesh sets its desire against the Spirit, and the Spirit against the flesh; for these are in opposition to one another, so that you may not do the things that you please.

It is universally recognized that this passage describes the believer's battle with sin—the flesh against the Spirit. Though Paul sometimes uses flesh (σάρξ) for the physical aspect of man, it is widely conceded that in this passage we find Paul's well-known "ethical" use of the term—fallen human nature. Longenecker explains:

It has often been noted that σάρξ used ethically has to do with humanity's fallen, corrupt, or sinful nature, as distinguished from the human nature as originally created by God.... Translating σάρξ as "flesh" in ethical contexts (as KJV, ASV, RSV) has often encouraged ideas of anthropological dualism, with the physical body taken to be evil per se and the mortification of the body viewed in some manner as necessary for achieving a true Christian experience. In reaction to such ideas, various translators have tried to give to the expression a more interpretive and descriptive rendering....

---

[32] Daniel B. Wallace, *Greek Grammar Beyond the Basics: An Exegetical Syntax of the New Testament* (Grand Rapids: Zondervan, 1996), p. 605.

[33] For a different view of how to harmonize the Ephesians passage, see Moo, *Romans,* pp. 374–75.

Probably the best of the interpretive translations are those that add the adjective "corrupt" or "sinful" to the noun "nature" (i.e., KNOX, NIV), thereby suggesting an essential aspect of mankind's present human condition that is in opposition to "the Spirit" and yet avoiding the idea that the human body is evil per se.[34]

Paul's use of "flesh," or "sinful nature" as the NIV renders the term, in Galatians 5:16–17 is viewed by two-nature advocates as a direct reference to the believer's old nature— his continuing tendency to sin or rebel against God. Those who argue against the two-nature view would not refer to the flesh as a nature, yet they still define flesh similarly. Packer, for instance, says:

> Believers find within themselves contrary urgings. The Spirit sustains their regenerate desires and purposes; their fallen Adamic instincts (the "flesh") which, though dethroned, are not yet destroyed, constantly distract them from doing God's will and allure them along paths that lead to death (Gal 5:16–17; James 1:14–15).[35]

Galatians 5:16–17 does not say that there is, in the believer, a struggle between the old nature (flesh) and new nature, but between flesh (old nature) and Spirit. However, Lenski, following Luther, among others, has understood "Spirit" as "spirit" and interpreted it as a direct reference to the new nature.[36] But this view has found few supporters, and, as Fung observes, "is highly unlikely in view of the Spirit-flesh contrast Paul develops elsewhere (cf. Rom 8:4–6, 9, 13), particularly in Gal 3:3, and in view of the clear reference to the divine Spirit in both the preceding and the following verses (5:16, 18, 22, 25)."[37]

Because Paul's language speaks specifically of a struggle between the flesh (old nature) and the Spirit, does that mean it is invalid to characterize that struggle as also one between the old and new natures? It is interesting to read Calvin's discussion of Galatians 5:17, where, in the same paragraph he speaks of the "Spirit" as both the "Spirit of God" and "the

---

[34] Richard N. Longenecker, *Galatians,* Word Biblical Commentary (Dallas: Word, 1990), pp. 239–40.

[35] *Concise Theology,* p. 171.

[36] R. C. H. Lenski, *The Interpretation of St. Paul's Epistles to the Galatians, to the Ephesians, and to the Philippians* (Columbus, OH: Wartburg Press, 1946), p. 281; Martin Luther, *A Commentary on St. Paul's Epistle to the Galatians*, ed. Philip S. Watson (Westwood, NJ: Fleming H. Revell, n.d.), p. 501. Also, J. C. Ryle, *Holiness* (reprint ed.; Westwood, NJ: Fleming H. Revell, n.d.), p. 21.

[37] Ronald Y. K. Fung, *The Epistle to the Galatians,* New International Commentary on the New Testament (Grand Rapids: Eerdmans, 1988), p. 249.

renewed nature, or the grace of regeneration."[38] While, as Pink observes, "we must distinguish between the Holy Spirit and the principle of which he imparts at regeneration,"[39] and while it is almost certainly true that Paul's contrast in Galatians 5:16–17 is between the flesh and the Holy Spirit, we should not attempt to drive a wedge between the Spirit himself and the new disposition (new nature) he imparts at regeneration. Stott concludes: "By 'the Spirit' he seems to mean the Holy Spirit Himself who renews and regenerates us, first giving us a new nature and then remaining to dwell in us."[40]

Even those who oppose the two-nature viewpoint strongly affirm that the Holy Spirit works in conjunction with the believer's new disposition. Warfield, perhaps the greatest foe of the two-nature view, says that in the process of sanctification the work of the Spirit includes "the development of the implanted principle of spiritual life and infused habits of grace,"[41] and, in addition, "holy dispositions are implanted, nourished and perfected."[42] As was previously observed, Packer says that while "believers find within themselves contrary urgings, the Spirit sustains their regenerate desires and purposes," and Packer ends this sentence with a reference to Galatians 5:16–17 (see p. 267).

So, it may be concluded that the struggle which Paul describes in Galatians 5:16–17 as being that of the flesh against the Spirit is no less a struggle between the believer's old and new natures.

---

[38] John Calvin, *Calvin's Commentaries: Romans–Galatians* (reprint ed.; Wilmington, DE: Associated Publishers and Authors, n.d.), p. 1921.

[39] Arthur W. Pink, *The Doctrine of Sanctification* (Grand Rapids: Baker, 1955), p. 245.

[40] John R. W. Stott, *The Message of Galatians,* The Bible Speaks Today (London: Inter-Varsity Press, 1968), p. 146. Cf. Homer A. Kent, Jr., "It is preferable, therefore, to regard the contrast as between the old nature of man ('flesh') and the new nature controlled by the Holy Spirit" (*The Freedom of God's Sons: Studies in Galatians* [Grand Rapids: Baker, 1976], p. 156) and William Hendriksen, "Verse 16 clearly implies that there is a conflict between the Spirit and the flesh, therefore also between the believer's new, Spirit-indwelt, nature and his old, sinful, self" (*Exposition of Galatians* [Grand Rapids: Baker, 1968], p. 214).

[41] John E. Meeter, ed., *Selected Shorter Writings of Benjamin B. Warfield,* 2 vols. (Nutley, NJ: Presbyterian and Reformed, 1973), 2:327.

[42] B. B. Warfield, "On the Biblical Notion of Renewal," in *Biblical and Theological Studies,* ed. Samuel G. Craig (Philadelphia: Presbyterian and Reformed, 1968), p. 372.

ROMANS 7:14–25

Paul's description of the struggle between the old and new natures is not confined to the flesh/Spirit contrast of Galatians 5:16–17. Paul can, as Romans 7:14–25 illustrates, use somewhat different terminology to describe the same conflict. Though there is considerable debate about this section of Romans, there would appear to be more than sufficient reasons for understanding this passage as describing Paul as a regenerate person. Some of the more important ones would include: (1) The shift from the past tenses of verses 7–13 to the present tenses beginning in verse 14 is inexplicable unless Paul has now shifted to his present regenerate status. (2) In verse 22 Paul says: "For I joyfully concur with the law of God in the inner man," and in verse 25b: "I myself with my mind am serving the law of God." Murray argues that "this is service which means subjection of heart and will, something impossible for the unregenerate man."[43] (3) In answer to the longing of verse 24, "Wretched man that I am! Who will set me free from the body of this death?" Paul gives a triumphant answer in the first part of verse 25, "Thanks be to God through Jesus Christ our Lord!" This is the confession of Paul, the regenerate man, which is immediately followed by a concluding summary concerning his continuing struggle with sin as a believer: "So then, on the one hand I myself with my mind am serving the law of God, but on the other, with my flesh the law of sin." This is the same struggle that has been recounted beginning in verse 14.

Numerous verses in 7:14–25 describe Paul's struggle with sin. There is, in general, a conflict between "willing" (θέλω, used 7 times) and "doing" (various words used 11 times). Paul says: "I am not practicing what I would like to do, but I am doing the very thing I hate" (v. 15). "For the good that I wish, I do not do; but I practice the very evil that I do not wish" (v. 19). Sometimes Paul's description sounds like he is split into two persons: "So now, no longer am I the one doing it, but sin which indwells me" (v. 17). "But if I am doing the very thing I do not wish, I am no longer the one doing it, but sin which dwells in me" (v. 20). The key here is to understand that Paul uses "I" in a more comprehensive sense in verses 15 and 19 than in verses 17 and 20.[44] The "I" in the former verses is the comprehensive Paul, the "I" who wishes to do good but finds himself doing evil. The "I" in the latter verses is viewed more narrowly. Thus, when Paul says, "if I [#1] am doing the very thing I do not wish, I [#2]

---

[43] John Murray, *The Epistle to the Romans,* New International Commentary on the New Testament, 2 vols. in one (Grand Rapids: Eerdmans, 1959, 1965), 1:258.

[44] Anthony A. Hoekema, "The Struggle Between Old and New Natures in the Converted Man," *Bulletin of the Evangelical Theological Society* 5 (May 1962): 47.

am no longer the one doing it," it may sound like there are two different personalities inside him. But, in fact, Paul is attempting to describe, within the limits of language, the experience of every Christian. He is viewing himself from the conflicting dispositions (natures) resident within himself. "I" [#1] is Paul viewed from the aspect of his old nature; "I" [#2] is Paul viewed from the aspect of the new nature: "If I [viewed from the perspective of my old nature] am doing the very thing I do not wish, I [viewed from the perspective of my new nature] am no longer the one doing it" (v. 20). We should not necessarily be surprised at Paul's language since he makes similar, seemingly contradictory statements in other places. "It is no longer I who live, but Christ lives in me" (Gal 2:20). "I labored even more than all of them, yet not I, but the grace of God with me" (1 Cor 15:10). As Hodge notes: "No one supposes that the labours and life here spoken of were not the labours and life of the apostle."[45]

Obviously, Paul is not trying to evade responsibility for his sin when he says "I am no longer the one doing it, but sin which dwells in me" (v. 20). Moo explains:

> His point is that his failure to put into action what he wills to do shows that there is something besides himself involved in the situation. If we had only to do with him, in the sense of that part of him which agrees with God's law and wills to do it, we would not be able to explain why he consistently does what he does not want to do. No, Paul reasons, there must be another "actor" in the drama, another factor that interferes with his performance of what he wants to do. This other factor is indwelling sin.[46]

When Paul says "I am no longer the one doing it, but sin which dwells in me," the conflict is specifically between the "I" of the new nature and sin. But "sin," as Moo continues, "is not a power that operates 'outside' the person."[47] Neither is it some abstract concept or some alien force in the believer, but the corruption of the old nature itself. Just as the conflict between the old and new natures can be described in Galatians 5:16–17 as a conflict between flesh (old nature) and Spirit, so here in Romans it can be described as a conflict between sin and the new nature. But it is still the same struggle. "Sin" is not an alien force distinct from the believer, but the corruption of the old nature itself. Hodge observes: "Sin, in this, as in

---

[45] Charles Hodge, *Commentary on the Epistle to the Romans* (reprint of 1886 ed.; Grand Rapids: Eerdmans, 1972), p. 232.

[46] *Romans,* pp. 457–58.

[47] Ibid. p. 458.

so many other places in Scripture, is presented as an abiding state of the mind, a disposition or principle, manifesting itself in acts."[48]

As was noted previously, Paul describes this same struggle in verse 25: "So then, on the one hand I myself with my mind am serving the law of God, but on the other, with my flesh the law of sin." Here the struggle is described as between the "mind" and the "flesh." "Mind" is used here, as Hodge reminds us, to refer not to "the reason, nor the affections, but the higher or renewed nature."[49] So we conclude that although Paul expresses his struggle with sin in Romans 7:14–25 using a variety of terminology, in reality he is describing one and the same conflict, the same conflict found in Galatians 5:16–17. While it is true that Paul never mentions the Spirit in Roman 7:14–25, this is only a factor of Paul's emphasis at this point in Romans. As Calvin notes, commenting on 7:15: "This conflict, of which the Apostle speaks, does not exist in man before he is renewed by the Spirit of God."[50] It is only, as Ferguson observes, "the presence of the Spirit that produces these conflicts."[51]

CRITICISMS OF THE TWO-NATURE VIEW

Though I have argued that the two-nature view is a theologically accurate way to describe the believer's struggle with sin and that Scripture itself supports such a view; nevertheless, the two-nature view has been subjected to severe criticism. That criticism has come mainly from within the Reformed camp. One of the most outspoken critics was B. B. Warfield. His views are found in an article entitled, "The Victorious Life," which was originally written for the *Princeton Theological Review* in 1918 and later reprinted as part of his two-volume work, *Perfectionism,* in 1931.[52] Equally important is Warfield's review of Lewis Sperry Chafer's book, *He That Is Spiritual,* which appeared in the *Princeton Theological Review* in 1919.[53] The significant point to note about Warfield's opposition to the two-nature view is that his criticism was based on a particular formulation of the two-nature view. Warfield criticized Chafer's presentation

---

[48] *Romans,* p. 232.

[49] Ibid., p. 237.

[50] *Romans,* p. 1419.

[51] Sinclair B. Ferguson, "The Reformed View," in *Christian Spirituality: Five Views of Sanctification,* ed. Donald L. Alexander (Downers Grove, IL: InterVarsity Press, 1988), p. 63.

[52] The most important essays from the two-volume set have been reprinted in one volume by Presbyterian and Reformed (1958).

[53] See note 8 above.

of two natures in the believer, not so much because of his two-nature terminology, but because Warfield believed Chafer's particular two-nature viewpoint was defective as it related both to regeneration and sanctification. Warfield's chief objection to Chafer was theological, not semantic. That this is the case can be demonstrated from the fact that Warfield's own teacher in theology at Princeton Theological Seminary, Charles Hodge, used two-nature terminology,[54] and, as we would expect, Warfield's views on regeneration and sanctification are in full agreement with those of Hodge.[55] A more recent Reformed theologian, Anthony Hoekema, whose views are substantially the same as Warfield's, also firmly supports the concept of two natures in the believer.[56]

The two-nature view, as it was understood by Chafer and those who have followed him, is open to a number of criticisms. The Chaferian view[57] of the two natures is defective, not because it is a two-nature view, but because of how the two natures are defined. Let us begin with Chafer's explanation: "Having received the divine nature (2 Pet 1:4) while still retaining the old nature, every child of God possesses two natures; one is incapable of sinning, and the other is incapable of holiness."[58] This defini-

---

[54] Hodge, *Systematic Theology,* 3:221–224. Cf. John F. Walvoord, "The Augustinian-Dispensational Perspective," in *Five Views on Sanctification* (Grand Rapids: Zondervan, 1987), p. 200.

[55] Warfield's textbook in his theology classes was Hodge's *Systematic Theology* (David B. Calhoun, *Princeton Seminary,* 2 vols. [Carlisle, PA: Banner of Truth Trust, 1994, 1996], 2:204). Warfield's immediate predecessor in the chair of theology at Princeton, A. A. Hodge, also used two-nature terminology (A. A. Hodge, *Evangelical Theology* [London: T. Nelson and Sons, 1890], p. 296).

[56] "The Struggle Between Old and New Natures in the Converted Man," pp. 42–50 and *Saved by Grace,* p. 214.

[57] This label has been suggested by Charles C. Ryrie ("Contrasting Views on Sanctification," in *Walvoord: A Tribute,* ed. Donald K. Campbell [Chicago: Moody Press, 1982], p.191). As Randall Gleason has pointed out ("B. B. Warfield and Lewis S. Chafer on Sanctification," *Journal of the Evangelical Theological Society* 40 [June 1997]: 245), Chafer's view on sanctification and the two natures is exactly the same as his mentor, C. I. Scofield (cf. Scofield's view in his *Rightly Dividing the Word of Truth* [Chicago: Bible Institute Colportage Association, n.d.], pp. 66–74). It is also, according to Charles Ryrie, the view of himself and John F. Walvoord ("Contrasting Views on Sanctification," p. 199). In his own article on sanctification, Walvoord calls his view "The Augustinian-Dispensational Perspective" (in *Five Views on Sanctification,* pp. 199–226). Whatever the title, Walvoord's view is essentially that of Chafer. Gleason observes that "Walvoord's expression 'the Augustinian-Dispensational perspective'…appears to be a misnomer, since there is little theological relationship between Chafer's unique perspective on sanctification and his dispensational distinctives" ("Warfield and Chafer on Sanctification," p. 241, n. 2).

[58] Lewis S. Chafer, *Major Bible Themes* (Chicago: Bible Institute Colportage Association, 1927), p. 161.

tion of the two natures is immediately problematic because it moves away from the truth that a nature is a complex of attributes, a set of characteristics, a disposition that characterizes the individual. To say that the new nature cannot sin suggests that it is an autonomous, separate entity, since only an entity can sin. This opens up the Chaferian view to the charge of an additional personality within the believer. Though Chafer naturally denies any suggestion of two personalities;[59] nevertheless, it is still a problem, as Warfield illustrates:

> At any rate it belongs ineradicably to "the Christian" to turn on the old carnal nature, or the new Spiritual nature, as he may choose, and let it act for him. Who this "Christian" is who possesses this power it is a little puzzling to make out. He cannot be the old carnal nature, for that old carnal nature cannot do anything good—and presumably, therefore, would never turn on the Spirit in control. He cannot be the new Spiritual nature, for this new Spiritual nature cannot do anything evil—and the "Christian" "may choose to walk after the flesh." Is he possibly some third nature: We hope not, because two absolutely antagonistic and noncommunicating natures seem enough to be in one man.[60]

The Chaferian view of the natures is also defective because it denies that they are subject to change. The new nature is, according to Chafer, "incapable of sinning" and the old nature is "incapable of holiness." The new nature "is a regeneration or creation of something wholly new which is possessed in conjunction with the old nature so long as the child of God is in this body."[61] Thus the believer has two equally powerful natures that remain in him as long as he lives and that remain unchanged during that time. This, of course, leads to a continual conflict within the believer and results in a view of sanctification that Ryrie calls the "counteraction of the new nature of the believer against the old."[62] The believer makes progress in sanctification as he yields to the Holy Spirit who is able to counteract the old nature and empower the new. Lawrence explains it well:

> The flesh will never change.... This means that the flesh will always and only do what sin, under the control of Satan, directs it to do. All efforts to change

---

[59] *Systematic Theology,* 2:347.

[60] *Perfectionism* (Philadelphia: Presbyterian and Reformed, 1958), p. 374.

[61] Chafer, *Systematic Theology,* 2:347.

[62] "Contrasting Views on Sanctification," p. 191

the flesh are futile; the only thing that can be done with the flesh is to bring it under the control of a greater power.[63]

That "greater power" is the Holy Spirit who counteracts the old nature as believers are filled with the Spirit. "The filling of the Spirit," as Walvoord says, "is the secret to sanctification."[64]

The problem with the Chaferian view is that it seems to leave a part of the individual— the old nature— untouched by either regeneration or sanctification. Again, this sounds like the old nature is some sort of autonomous entity. But if the old nature is a part of the individual, which, of course, it must be; then some aspect of the believer would appear to be unaffected by regeneration and resulting sanctification. The same could be said for the new nature. If, as Chafer says, it is incapable of sinning, we are left with another part of man that needs no saving.

The more correct and more "biblical teaching is rather that the Christian's total self is progressively renewed and restored throughout the sanctifying process."[65] At regeneration a new disposition (new nature) is created within the soul. Sanctification affects both this new disposition as well as the old (old nature). Hoekema defines sanctification "as that gracious operation of the Holy Spirit, involving our responsible participation, by which he delivers us from the pollution of sin, renews our entire nature according to the image of God, and enables us to live lives that are pleasing to him."[66] By "pollution" Hoekema means the "corruption of our nature which is the result of sin and which, in turn, produces further sin." He adds: "In *sanctification* the pollution of sin is in the process of being removed (though it will not be totally removed until the life to come)."[67] This was Warfield's point when he argued that in sanctification God

> cures our sinning precisely by curing our sinful nature; He makes the tree good that the fruit may be good. It is, in other words, precisely by eradicating our sinfulness — "the corruption of our hearts" — that He delivers us from sinning...

---

[63] William D. Lawrence, "The Traitor in the Gates: The Christian's Conflict with the Flesh," in *Essays in Honor of J. Dwight Pentecost,* ed. Stanley D. Toussaint and Charles H. Dyer (Chicago: Moody Press, 1986), pp. 128–29.

[64] *Five Views on Sanctification,* p. 101.

[65] Packer, *Rediscovering Holiness,* p. 111.

[66] *Saved by Grace,* p. 192

[67] Ibid., pp. 192–93.

> To imagine that we can be saved from the power of sin without the eradication of the corruption in which the power of sin has its seat, is to imagine that an evil tree can be compelled to bring forth good fruit.[68]

Warfield's use of the term *eradication* may seem somewhat strange to those of us who have been used to using the term in a pejorative sense as it is applied to those types of Christian experience which tend toward perfectionism— the complete eradication of the sinful nature as a present experience for the believer— but, of course, Warfield was violently opposed to any such idea of sanctification. By eradication, Warfield means a progressive and gradual process, not an instantaneous one. Neither does Warfield diminish the role of the Holy Spirit in the believer's sanctification. But he argues

> that the Spirit dwells within us in order to affect us, not merely our acts; in order to eradicate our sinfulness and not merely to counteract its effects. The Scriptures' way of cleansing the stream is to cleanse the fountain; they are not content to attack the stream of our activities, they attack directly the heart out of which the issues of life flow. But they give us no promise that the fountain will be completely cleansed all at once, and therefore no promise that the stream will flow perfectly purely from the beginning. We are not denying that the Spirit leads us in all our acts, as well as purifies our hearts. But we are denying that His whole work in us, or His whole immediate work in us, or His fundamental work in us, terminates on our activities and can be summed up in the word "counteraction." Counteraction there is; and suppression there is; but most fundamentally of all there is eradication; and all these work one and the self-same Spirit.[69]

At regeneration the believer is changed, but it is not a change of substance. Instead, it is a change in direction, a change in disposition. Whereas the unbeliever has only one direction, one disposition— toward sin and away from God— the believer is now a "new creature" (2 Cor 5:17) with a new direction, a new disposition—toward God and holiness. He now has characteristics or attributes which incline him toward holiness— a new nature—what Warfield calls the implantation of holy dispositions.[70] Though *genuinely* new, the believer is not *totally* new.[71] Therefore, he still retains those old characteristics or attributes that incline him toward

---

[68] *Perfectionism,* p. 368.

[69] Ibid., p. 371.

[70] "On the Biblical Notion of Renewal," p. 372.

[71] Hoekema, *Five Views on Sanctification* (Grand Rapids: Zondervan), p. 231.

sin— his old nature— what Warfield calls the "native tendencies to evil."[72] In sanctification the old nature is progressively being eradicated and the new nature is being "nourished"[73] so that it will ultimately supplant the old. However, ultimate perfection, final and complete sanctification— the total eradication of the old nature and the complete implantation of the new nature— is not, as Scripture makes clear, the believer's portion as long as he dwells in this mortal body; but it is the ultimate destiny of every believer, for one day "we shall be like Him, because we shall see Him just as He is" (1 John 3:2).

PROBLEMS WITH THE ONE-NATURE VIEW

Properly delineated, the two-nature view can accurately and correctly represent the Bible's teaching on regeneration and sanctification, but so can the one-nature view, *if* it is properly delineated. An advantage for the two-nature view— and thus a minor difficulty for the one-nature view— is that the two-nature view more easily describes the believer's struggle with sin. As we have previously observed, one-nature advocates usually end up using two-nature terminology even though they disavow the term *nature.* A potential and much more serious problem for the one-nature view can arise if that one nature is not carefully defined. For instance, Warfield says: "For the new nature which God gives us is not an absolutely new somewhat, alien to our personality, inserted into us, but our old nature itself remade."[74] Thus Warfield can call the believer's one nature, the new nature. But, of course, Warfield is careful to explain that something old remains in that new nature.

Unfortunately, sometimes, those who argue for the one-nature position have been unable to correctly express it. A well-known example of someone who has misunderstood one-nature terminology is John MacArthur, Jr. By mixing elements of the Chaferian view of the two natures while at the same time denying the two-nature view, MacArthur has sketched out a picture of the believer's struggle with sin that is theologically problematic. As was previously noted, MacArthur denies that the believer has two natures: "No matter how radical our outer transformation at the time of salvation may have been for the better, it is difficult to comprehend that we no longer have the fallen sin nature and that our new nature is actually divine."[75]

---

[72] "On the Biblical Notion of Renewal," p. 372.

[73] Ibid.

[74] Review of *He That Is Spiritual,* p. 215.

[75] John F. MacArthur, Jr., *Romans,* 2 vols. (Chicago: Moody Press, 1991, 1994), 1:334.

Thus, right away MacArthur has presented us and himself with a dilemma. If the believer has only one nature, and that nature is "divine," then how do we account for the believer's sinning? We get a glimpse of MacArthur's solution when he says: "Although sin is not the product of our new self, we're still bound to some degree by the body we dwell in."[76] Apparently, we are to understand that since we no longer have a fallen nature but only one new divine-nature, which cannot sin, the believer's sinning must be due to his physical body. This becomes clearer:

> As every mature Christian learns, the more he grows in Christ, the more he becomes aware of sin in his life. In many places, Paul uses the terms *body* and *flesh* to refer to sinful propensities that are intertwined with physical weaknesses and pleasures…. New birth in Christ brings death to the sinful self, but it does not bring death to the temporal flesh and its corrupted inclinations until the future glorification. Obviously, a Christian's body is potentially good and is intended to do only good things, else Paul would not have commanded believers to present their bodies to God as "a living and holy sacrifice, acceptable to God" (Rom 12:1). It can respond to the new holy disposition, but does not always do so.[77]

We can only assume that the body's failure to "respond to the new holy disposition" is due to some failure (sin) in the body.

But if we had any doubts that the believer's sinfulness is to be located in the body we only have to read a little further:

> Because a believer is a new creature in Christ, his immortal soul is forever beyond sin's reach. The only remaining beachhead where sin can attack a Christian is in his mortal body. One day that body will be glorified and forever be out of sin's reach, but in the meanwhile it is still mortal, that is, subject to corruption and death. It still has lusts — because the brain and the thinking processes are part of the mortal body…. [God] does not warn about sin reigning in our souls or our spirits, but only about its reigning in our bodies, because that is the only place in a Christian where sin can operate.[78]

MacArthur's argument is perfectly logical, if we accept his premise. Since the believer's "immortal soul is forever beyond sin's reach" — after all "sin is not the product of our new self" and "our new nature is actually divine" — there remains only one location left for sin to dwell — the body with its "brain" and "thinking processes." Sin is not to be located in the believer's immaterial being, his soul or spirit, but only in the physical body.

---

[76] "The Good-Natured Believer," p. 20.

[77] *Romans,* 1:325–26.

[78] Ibid., 1:337.

But all this assumes MacArthur's premise, that the believer's immaterial part, his soul and spirit, is sinless. This is far afield from traditional theology, but it is in perfect agreement with the radical dualism of the Greek philosophical tradition, which viewed the body as inherently evil. To be fair, MacArthur disavows any connection with that tradition,[79] but, unfortunately, his denials cannot overturn his clear statements to the contrary.

We might ask ourselves how MacArthur could have wandered so far from the way of traditional theology. Here one can only speculate, but if we read enough of MacArthur on this subject, it soon becomes clear how indebted he is to the teaching of John Murray on the old-man/new-man contrast, to which we have previously referred.[80] Murray correctly demonstrates, as we have previously explained, that the old-man/new-man contrast is not the same as the old-nature/new-nature contrast, but that the old man is the unregenerate person as a whole, while the new man is the regenerate person as a whole. It is this understanding of the old man/new man that appears to be behind MacArthur's thinking:

> The old man, the old self, is the unregenerate person. He is not part righteous and part sinful, but totally sinful and without the slightest potential *within himself* for becoming righteous and pleasing to God. The new man, on the other hand, is the regenerate person. He is made pleasing to God through Jesus Christ and his new nature is *entirely godly and righteous.*[81]

What MacArthur has apparently failed to grasp from Murray is that although Murray said "the believer is a new man, a new creation," he went on to add that "he is a new man not yet made perfect. Sin dwells in him, and he still commits sin."[82] And, more importantly, when Murray said "sin dwells in him," he meant the believer's immaterial being, not his body.[83] The believer is a new man in whom sin dwells, not in his body but in every aspect of his immaterial being.

But perhaps there is another source for MacArthur's view of the sinful body. After all, does not Paul himself speak of "our body of sin" (Rom 6:6) and "putting to death the deeds of the body?" (Rom 8:13). Traditional theology has always rejected any interpretation of these statements that would suggest that sin resides in the corporeal. There are two ways in

---

[79] Ibid., 1:386.

[80] Murray's discussion of the old-man/new-man contrast in *Principles of Conduct* is cited by MacArthur in *Romans,* 1:324 and "The Good-Natured Believer," p. 20.

[81] *Romans,* 1:318.

[82] *Principles of Conduct,* p. 219.

[83] Cf. his *Romans,* 1:221, n. 11.

which Paul's language might be explained. If, on the one hand, Paul does in fact mean the physical body in these verses, then the genitive modifier ("of sin") would not mean that the body is inherently sinful but "that the body is particularly susceptible to, and easily dominated by, sin."[84] This would seem to be Ladd's explanation:

> The body is not only weak and mortal but also an instrument of the flesh. Sin and death do not, however, reside in corporeality itself or in the natural body but in the flesh. Since sin can reign in the mortal body (Rom 6:12), the body viewed as the instrumentality of sin can be called a sinful body (Rom 6:6); and therefore the person indwelt by the Spirit must put to death the deeds of the body (Rom 8:13). This, however, is not mortification of the body, itself, but of its sinful acts.[85]

Another possibility, not unrelated to the first, is that Paul is using the word *body* (σῶμα) metaphorically to refer to the whole person, a figure of speech called synecdoche—"a part for a whole." This clearly seems to be the case in Romans 6:12–13, where Paul tells his readers, "do not let sin reign in your mortal body" and "do not go on presenting the members of your body to sin," but, on the contrary, "present yourselves to God." In these verses "yourselves" is equated with "body" (cf. also Rom 12:1–2). Thus it is the person who indwells the body who is sinful, not the body itself. Whichever way we may view Paul's language, it is clear that the Bible does not teach that the body is inherently evil but that sin resides in man's immaterial being, not his physical; yet the body is where we commonly see the outworkings of sin.

However MacArthur arrived at his view, the "good-natured believer" as he calls it in one place, it is out of step with traditional theology and a proper understanding of the one-nature view.

CONCLUSION

I have sought to demonstrate that it is perfectly valid to speak of the believer as having two natures—old and new—as long as the term *nature* is understood to refer to a complex of attributes, a set of characteristics, or disposition. These natures are not substantive entities and do not act. But the believer himself can be viewed as acting from the perspective of his old or new nature—his disposition may be toward sin or holiness. While some two-nature advocates have used two-nature terminology to present a

---

[84] Moo, *Romans,* p. 375.

[85] George E. Ladd, *A Theology of the New Testament,* rev. and ed. Donald A Hagner (Grand Rapids: Eerdmans, 1993), p. 508.

view of sanctification that is inherently defective, the fault lies with their deficient theology, not with two-nature terminology itself. Two-nature terminology combined with a proper understanding of regeneration and sanctification accurately represents the believer's struggle with sin as presented in Scripture.

Part 3:

Historical Studies

THE SELF-IDENTITY OF FUNDAMENTALISM[1]

Rolland D. McCune

Dr. William R. Rice, the founder of Baptist Theological Seminary, was trained for the ministry in the 1930s and 40s at Bob Jones University, a clearly militant fundamentalist institution, and at Grace Theological Seminary, then also an outspoken fundamentalist school. He began his pastoral ministry in the post-World War II era when fundamentalism's identity was not only self-assured but recognized outside its own confines as well. Over the years he witnessed many of his friends and former classmates leave the ranks of fundamentalism for the more congenial and inclusive camp of new evangelicalism. But his identity as a fundamentalist and that of his ministry of well over forty years were never in doubt nor questioned.

Today, fundamentalism is said to be in an identity crisis. It is allegedly trying to discover what it is. New self-definitions are being heard which say that a fundamentalist is one who is faithful to expository preaching, practices church discipline, repudiates easy believism, and is aggressive in evangelism. Or some imply that a fundamentalist is one who believes in inerrancy and does not cooperate with Roman Catholics, or is one who believes the "fundamentals" but is less militant and separatistic than formerly thought. The truth is that these are things that new evangelicals and self-proclaimed non-fundamentalists also believe and practice, leaving a distinctly *fundamentalist* self-identity completely vacuous. This all points up the fact that many are simply confused, and this includes would-be leaders as well as followers and well-wishers. Judging by some of the prevalent ambiguity, one is sometimes tempted to ask, Will the real fundamentalist please stand up?

The purpose here is to address some reasons for the present confusion, define fundamentalism as a bona fide religious movement, delineate a complex of doctrine around which the movement has rallied, and demonstrate that there are some other distinctives that make it what it is. In other words, I propose to set forth what I consider to be the real, historic identity markers of fundamentalism and thus to bring some sense of order out of the developing chaos on this question in certain sectors of the fundamentalist ranks.

---

[1] This article appeared in the Spring 1996 issue of *DBSJ*, vol. 1, pp. 9–34.

MODERN FUNDAMENTALIST CONFUSION
OVER SELF-IDENTITY

From one perspective fundamentalism may be difficult to define and identify. One has said, "The term fundamentalism has become the most elusive term on the American (and world) religious scene."[2] If referring to the theologically and historically unaware, this may be true since the term has been used to refer to a spectrum that goes all the way from Pentecostalism to the most extreme forms of Islam. Also, professing fundamentalist leaders have sometimes introduced confusion and ambiguity into the term.[3] From another standpoint, however, the term should not be ambiguous.

Dubious Justification

The grounds for the present fundamentalist confusion are tenuous at best. There is a seeming needlessness for it. For one reason, up until the 1970s fundamentalism was self-assured about its identity and direction. Historic fundamentalists rarely, if ever, quibbled over the boundary markers of their cause. As will be discussed, the most clearly observable distinctives of the movement are militancy and separatism. Separatism did become a point of controversy, and thus to some degree a question of fundamentalism's self-identity, in the 1970s when John R. Rice dogmatically rejected "second degree" separation.[4] Rice took fundamentalist separatism on a different tack, but it was Jerry Falwell who seriously challenged fundamentalism from within when he became very critical of old-line fundamentalism. Going beyond John R. Rice, with whom he identified himself, Falwell caustically attacked the separatist mentality of fundamentalism and essentially put his non-separatist, or at least his greatly modified separatist, views on notice.[5] In a similar vein, Jack Van Impe, a fundamentalist evangelist, tried to carve a new channel for fundamentalism,[6] though

---

[2] John Fea, "Understanding the Changing Facade of Twentieth-Century American Protestant Fundamentalism: Toward A Historical Definition," *Trinity Journal* 15 (Fall 1994), p. 181.

[3] For example, Jerry Falwell, Jack Van Impe, and Jack Hyles have each defined fundamentalism in terms of their own agendas, historical perceptions, and peculiar emphases.

[4] See his numerous articles in *The Sword of the Lord* (such as in the following issues: Sept 3, 1971; Oct 3, 1971; Mar 2, 1973; Aug 20, 1976; Sept 3, 1976; Dec 17, 1976).

[5] This was in an address to the Southwide Baptist Fellowship, Charlotte, NC, Oct 5, 1977.

[6] Jack Van Impe, *Heart Disease in Christ's Body* (Royal Oak, MI: Jack Van Impe Ministries, 1984). He had expressed major disagreement with historic fundamentalism in an address to the Sword of the Lord Convention in Detroit, Aug, 1977.

less successfully than Falwell. More recently Jack Hyles has sought to define fundamentalism in terms of the Landmarkian independent Baptist movement that came out of the Southern Baptist Convention over the last several decades.[7] The Falwell, Van Impe, and Hyles innovations brought a certain amount of confusion in some minds about the meaning and direction of the movement.

While the main fundamentalist distinctives (militancy and separatism) were challenged from within during the 1970s and 80s, there appears to be no lack of assurance among fundamentalists about their identity prior to the 1970s. The controversy and subsequent division caused by the rise of the new evangelicalism in the 1940s and 50s seemed to galvanize fundamentalist self-identity if anything. The innovations of the 1970s and 80s notwithstanding, it is still difficult to exculpate the present questioners since many of them lived through that period and thus should have sufficient historical and theological self-awareness to understand those proposals for what they were.

Another reason why it is not easy to justify the present confusion is the long history of fundamentalism's beliefs, practices, and heritage. This history has been well chronicled. There has been a veritable landslide of books, doctoral dissertations, and journal articles on fundamentalism in the last ten to fifteen years, many by non-fundamentalist but historically self-critical scholars. The traditional view, somewhat of a caricature of fundamentalism as an obscurantist and bellicose cultural reaction to modernity, has been largely disproven.[8] A "revisionist" historiography has arisen[9] that has brought the accounts of the roots and ongoings of the movement more in line with historical reality. Fundamentalists themselves have produced scholarly and well-researched material on the history of their

[7] Hyles's sermon, "Let Baptists Be Baptists," in which he delineated these views, was preached numerous times. See the critique by Pastor John K. Hutcheson, "The Arrogance and Heresy of Jack Hyles," *The Biblical Evangelist* (May 1, 1991), p. 1. Hyles also wrote an article entitled "True Fundamentalism" in *The Reclaimer* (n.d.), and this was reviewed by Andrew Sandlin in his paper, *The Biblical Editor* (Fall 1991), p. 11.

[8] Representatives of this discredited approach would be Stewart Cole, *The History of Fundamentalism* (New York: Richard R. Smith, 1931) and Norman Furniss, *The Fundamentalist Controversy, 1918–1931* (New Haven, CT: Yale, 1954).

[9] Representatives of the revisionist approach are George Marsden, William Vance Trollinger, Mark Noll, Grant Wacker, and others. See Mark Sidwell, "The Revisionist View of Fundamentalist History," *Biblical Viewpoint* 26 (Nov 1992), and John Fea, "American Fundamentalism and Neo-Evangelicalism: A Bibliographic Survey," *Evangelical Journal* 11 (Spring 1993).

cause.[10] Some liberals early on in the fundamentalist-modernist controversy also wrote with a good measure of historical integrity.[11] This historical material is readily available for investigation and information today.

Yet another reason for the tenuous nature of some of the current confusion is the fundamentalist self-identity of the early new evangelicals. In a very insightful article, Douglas Sweeney amply demonstrates the "largely fundamentalist demeanor of those who agreed to neo-evangelical unity."[12] He shows how the early new evangelicals considered themselves fundamentalists, using the term with reference to themselves until the mid to late 1950s. Events of the 1960s changed the course of the new evangelical movement so radically that some of the early founders eventually questioned the movement's evangelical credentials; nearly all of the early leaders lamented its liberalization.[13] But Harold John Ockenga said in a sermon in December 1957, "I wish to be always classified as a Fundamentalist." In 1947 he said that "fundamentalism most nearly approximates theological truth" despite all that he felt was wrong with it.[14] In the now-famous *Christian Life* article in 1956, the conclusion was that "fundamentalism has become evangelicalism,"[15] a tacit admission that up until then the new evangelicals considered themselves fundamentalists. Vernon Grounds wrote in 1956 that "undeniably evangelicalism

[10] The best from the fundamentalist perspective is David O. Beale, *In Pursuit of Purity: American Fundamentalism Since 1850* (Greenville, SC: Unusual Publications, 1986).

[11] Kirsopp Lake, a liberal, wrote with historical honesty in 1925 when he said, "It is a mistake, often made by educated persons who happen to have but little knowledge of historical theology, to suppose that Fundamentalism is a new and strange form of thought. It is nothing of the kind: it is the...survival of a theology which was once universally held by all Christians.... The Fundamentalist may be wrong: I think that he is. But it is we who have departed from the tradition, not he, and I am sorry for the fate of anyone who tries to argue with a Fundamentalist on the basis of authority. The Bible and the *corpus theologicum* of the Church is on the Fundamentalist side" (*The Religion of Yesterday and Tomorrow* [Boston: Houghton Miflin, 1925], pp. 61–62).

[12] Douglas A. Sweeney, "Fundamentalism and the Neo-Evangelicals," *Fides et Historia* 24 (Winter/Spring 1992), p. 81.

[13] See Harold Lindsell, *The Battle For the Bible* (Grand Rapids: Zondervan, 1976), pp. 139, 210, 211; and its sequel, *The Bible in the Balance* (Grand Rapids: Zondervan, 1979), pp. 319–320. Later he wrote, "Evangelicalism today is in a sad state of disarray. In many quarters it has ceased to be what its founding fathers intended" (*Moody* [Dec 1985], p. 113). See also Carl F. H. Henry, *Confessions of A Theologian* (Waco, TX: Word, 1986), chap. 19, and David F. Wells, *No Place For Truth* (Grand Rapids: Eerdmans, 1993), especially chap. three.

[14] Harold John Ockenga, "Can Fundamentalism Win America?" *Christian Life* (June 1947), p. 13.

[15] "Is Evangelical Theology Changing?" *Christian Life* (Mar 1956), p. 17.

is fundamentalism, if by fundamentalism is meant a tenacious insistence upon the essential and central dogmas of historic Christianity."[16] Edward John Carnell, in his 1948 book on apologetics, spoke of it as "a defense of Fundamentalism" and as "drawing out implications for Fundamentalism."[17] Fuller Theological Seminary was founded, according to George Marsden, to "reform" fundamentalism.[18] While it is true that most of the early new evangelicals were not as separatistic as their forebears, they still had a fundamentalist self-awareness.

This is all to say that one would expect that present day fundamentalists should know who they are and should not be in too much indecision about self-identification and authenticity. If the older fundamentalists had an assured self-identity, and if the new evangelicals who were in the process of reforming fundamentalism used the title with reference to themselves for a decade and a half, there should be minimal confusion on the matter in the fundamentalist camp at the closing of the twentieth century.

Evidence of the Present Confusion

Documentable, written evidence of this matter is a little difficult to ascertain. Much of the present confusion is heard in sermons, talks, or private conversations. But one fundamentalist pastor wrote, for example, "Fundamentalism, like happiness, is different things to different people." He calls himself a "centrist" fundamentalist, which he acknowledges somewhat tongue-in-cheek is a self-fulfilling and self-validating term lacking any objective content or verification. He does conclude by saying, "I guess all of us need to determine where we stand and to determine to stand there regardless of the criticism."[19] This seems to suggest that fundamentalism is in the eye of the beholder or in the person of the bearer. Such a subjective definition of fundamentalism, if consistently held, naturally would not

---

[16] Vernon Grounds, "The Nature of Evangelicalism," *Eternity* (Feb 1956), p. 13.

[17] Edward John Carnell, *An Introduction to Christian Apologetics* (Grand Rapids: Eerdmans, 1948), pp. 7–8. It would be more than ten years before he would caustically say that fundamentalism had gone "cultic" and thus constituted a "peril" to orthodoxy (*The Case For Orthodox Theology* [Philadelphia: Westminster Press, 1959], p. 113), or that he would talk about "Post-Fundamentalist Faith" (*The Christian Century* [Aug 26, 1959], p. 971).

[18] George M. Marsden, *Reforming Fundamentalism* (Grand Rapids: Eerdmans, 1987). The book claims to be "a narrative built around the theme of Fuller Seminary's leading role in the original new evangelical (or neo-evangelical) attempt to reform fundamentalism" (p. x).

[19] Charles R. Wood, *A Pastoral Epistle* (Dec 1994) [published by the author, pastor of the Grace Baptist Church, South Bend, IN], p. 2.

foster much of a valid consensus within the fundamentalist movement. In addition, there are instances where fundamentalism is discussed without any definition at all. This is not to say that the authors have no idea of what it is, but a definition is simply not given a formal place in the treatment.[20] One may read an article or a book on fundamentalism and not know very clearly what is being handled, again yielding a definition or an idea of fundamentalism based on one's preunderstanding or prior formulation.

In March, 1995, there was held a National Leadership Conference among fundamentalists which was called specifically to address the question, "What's at the heart of fundamentalism?"[21] This query seemed to signal some kind of identity search. Given the current milieu, calls for such meetings are probably necessary if not inevitable, but they are somewhat of a window into the fundamentalist soul and sound like concerns that were settled seventy or eighty years ago.

Some Causes and Remedies

No doubt there are several factors leading to the present period of questioning. In light of the previous point, these are not actually valid, excusable reasons, but they are none-the-less observable causes that can be identified and remedied.

In some cases there was a failure to communicate adequately the fundamentalist principles and heritage. This has at least two sides. For one, many churches, schools, and other institutions have not sufficiently informed their constituencies about the history of fundamentalism. Thus many may have grown up in the fundamentalist environment ignorant of their roots. However, this would seem to be easily corrected. Fundamentalist people can be apprised of who they are by hearing illustrations of incidents in fundamentalist history, or by hearing or reading of someone's personal experiences of involvement in the cause. Many have entered fundamentalist self-awareness by being in a church where the pastor was personally

---

[20] An example of this is Douglas R. McLachlan, *Reclaiming Authentic Fundamentalism* (Independence, MO: American Ass'n of Christian Schools, 1993). See the reviews of the book by Robert Delnay in *The Review* (Oct 1994) [published by the Independent Baptist Fellowship of North America], p. 6, and Rolland D. McCune in *The Sentinel* (Spring 1995) [published by the Detroit Baptist Theological Seminary]. Also James Singleton implied this criticism in *The Tri-City Builder* (Jan–Feb 1995) [published by the Tri-City Baptist Church, Tempe, AZ], p. 3.

[21] Promotional letter dated December 1994.

at the front lines of the battle.[22] Special meetings or services devoted to an issue, personality, or movement as it encroaches on a fundamentalist ministry are very educational. Inclusivist, ecumenical endeavors easily attract fundamentalist attention, and their unbiblical elements can be cause for exposure and teaching. Ecumenical evangelism is a perennial problem. Public rallies of quasi-evangelical but non-fundamentalist groups such as Promise Keepers, or even more remote stirrings such as Evangelicals and Catholics Together, have a certain effect on the fundamentalist community. These can be turned into pedagogical opportunities for conveying the history, principles, and practices of biblical fundamentalism and thereby facilitate a correct self-identity.

Sunday school or Bible Institute courses on fundamentalism, biblical separation, and related themes can be offered. Fundamentalist colleges and seminaries can develop in-depth, scholarly courses on fundamentalism, new evangelicalism, or contemporary issues, making them required subjects if necessary. At the very least a chapel series can be given on these matters, question and answer time set aside, and other such means. I have found that people in fundamentalist circles like to hear about their heritage. They are interested in names and events, and quite often want to know more about their own church's or institution's history and its involvement in the fundamentalist cause.

Obviously these educational efforts rise and fall on leadership. A benign, non-militant, pietistic pastor, for example, can hardly be expected to develop a knowledgeable fundamentalist church. Nor can one who is overly sensitive to emotions and feelings, his own and others', be very effective in this regard.

Another side to the lack of communication is the failure to provide adequate and biblical reasons why fundamentalism is correct or why a strong stand is needed on crucial issues. Some of the previous leaders may have taken too much for granted and did not spell out clearly enough the issues of the battles and why they were going in a certain direction. As a result, some of the younger heirs of the cause saw only the firm but necessary insistence of farsighted leadership and did not see the intermediate

---

[22] It was my good fortune for fourteen years to be associated with and participate in the ministry of Dr. Richard V. Clearwaters, pastor of the Fourth Baptist Church of Minneapolis from 1940 to 1982. In a meaningful sense an heir to the legacy and labors of W. B. Riley of the First Baptist Church of Minneapolis with whom he was closely associated in many endeavors, Clearwaters was an acknowledged national militant fundamentalist leader. He often sprinkled his preaching with anecdotes from fundamentalist history and consistently regaled the daily coffee break time with incidents from his long experience in standing for the Cause. Unfortunately, most of this valuable information went unrecorded.

factors that went into the decision-making process. Too many who grew up in fundamentalism now regard their forebears as power-seeking ladder-climbers, empire builders, or mean-spirited old saints who have led the movement into a hopeless maze of carnality and ineffectiveness. The remedy here would seem to be the same as for the previous point—instruction and education by any number of creative means.

A second contributing factor to the identity crisis is the notion that fundamentalism is constantly changing, that it is a dynamic and not a static movement.[23] Obviously if the defining rubrics of a movement are always on the move and its parameters in a continuous state of flux, to whatever degree, self-identification will become very perplexing. Now in one sense fundamentalism does change, as all things do that go from one day to the next. Time itself is measured by change, and all time-space-mass phenomena partake of the transitoriness of a finite universe. Change in that sense is inevitable. But that is not the point under discussion. What appears to be meant by the dynamic or constant change in fundamentalism includes its identity markers, almost change for its own sake. This must be seriously challenged because if consistently thought out, the "fundamentals" will not be what they were in the early twentieth century, the principles and practices based on the Word of God will be relative, and fundamentalism itself will be left in a continual state of "becoming." Confusion is bound to follow. This is the logic of the case; but, while most are spared the logical results of their inconsistencies, from a biblical standpoint fundamentalism is not given to substantive change any more than biblical Christianity itself. All biblical propositions and principles are part of the "once-having-been-delivered-unto-the-saints-faith" (Jude 3, lit.). There is no progress there or much room for dynamic and creative change.

These things seem to have been forgotten by many in the present fundamentalist quest for identity. True, the religious scene is never static; Satan is very creative and innovative with his strategies. Methods of implementing the fundamentalist agenda do involve adaptation to be sure. Emphases may change as well. But the defining genius of fundamentalism should not be subject to change. It is the same as it has always been, and that ultimately goes back to the first century. There is a certain core of crucial doctrine, mainly concerning Christ and the Scriptures, along with certain identifying characteristics, chiefly having to do with militant separatism, that make fundamentalism what it is. These need to

---

[23] This is the motif of John Fea, "Understanding the Changing Facade." See also David Burggraff, "Fundamentalism At the End of the Twentieth Century," *Calvary Baptist Theological Journal* 11 (Spring 1995), p. 29.

be stated and not necessarily debated. Fundamentalism's identity markers may need rediscovery on the part of some or fuller understanding on the part of others, and certainly more explication on the part of all. But their redefinition would alter the direction of the movement and compromise its genius.

Before the distinguishing characteristics of fundamentalism are explored, there is need for a brief statement that fundamentalism is a distinct, identifiable movement.

FUNDAMENTALISM IS A DISTINCT MOVEMENT.

David F. Wells, a new evangelical writing about the doctrinal collapse of the new evangelicalism, said that a movement must have certain ingredients: (1) A commonly held direction; (2) A common basis on which that direction is held; (3) An *esprit* that informs and motivates those who are joined in the common cause.[24] His (debatable) point is that evangelicalism has been incorrectly identified as a movement because it lacks those ingredients. On the other hand, fundamentalism does fulfill those requirements and can be seen as an identifiable historic religious movement. It has moved in a certain direction, i.e., in a biblically conservative direction whose distinctive path has by now been well documented. Its common basis is a set of biblical doctrines and beliefs, and its motivating *esprit* is essentially its militant separatism. Perhaps other characteristics of its *esprit* such as evangelism, revival, prayer, missions, or holiness could be mentioned, but these are not really the private property of fundamentalism's defining motivation.

Fundamentalism is a movement and not an attitude of belligerence, a spirit of ugliness, or a negative mentality of some sort as is sometimes depicted even by those agitating for change from within. Nor does it consist of a posture of self-aggrandizement or other self-serving attributes. While it is clearly arguable that certain fundamentalists may have exhibited those characteristics on occasion, it is also demonstrable that these do not constitute fundamentalism. Fundamentalism is intrinsically a movement and not a mood.[25]

---

[24] David F. Wells, *No Place For Truth*, p. 8.

[25] Joel A. Carpenter said it crisply, "Fundamentalism was a popular movement, not merely a mentality; it had leaders, institutions and a particular identity. Fundamentalists recognized each other as party members as it were, and distinguished themselves from the other evangelicals" ("Fundamentalist Institutions and the Rise of Evangelical Protestantism: 1929–1942," *Church History* 49 [Mar 1980], p. 64). He also said, "Fundamentalism bears all the marks of a popular religious movement which drew only part of its identity from opposition to liberal trends in the denominations" (p. 74).

As a distinct movement, the roots of fundamentalism go back to nineteenth century America. David Beale puts the antecedents of fundamentalism in the great urban revivals in the USA in the mid-nineteenth century.[26] Others put them in the Bible Conference movement of the last quarter of the nineteenth century.[27] Some would put the roots of fundamentalism in a cluster of persons, institutions, and events in the latter nineteenth century such as the Bible Conference movement, the Bible Institute movement, influential pastors and evangelists, and a stream of literature that arose.[28] Fea pinpointed 1893 as the start of the first phase of fundamentalism, for various reasons.[29]

Some of the early names connected with the fundamentalist movement were R. A. Torrey, John Roach Straton, Billy Sunday, A. C. Gaebelein, W. B. Riley, T. T. Shields, J. Frank Norris, and Bob Jones, Sr., to name a few. Some of the Bible Conferences of the early days were Niagara (ONT, 1876), Northfield (MA, 1880), Winona Lake (IN, 1895), Sea Cliff (NY, 1901), and Montrose (PA, 1908). Some of the Bible Institutes and Training Schools in the early part of the movement were Moody (1886), Gordon (1889), Practical Bible Training (1900), Northwestern (1902), Bible Institute of Los Angeles (1907), Northern Baptist Seminary (1913), Philadelphia School of the Bible (1916), and Bob Jones (1927). The stream of literature included *The Scofield Bible*, *The Fundamentals*, *Our Hope*, *The Watchman Examiner*, *The King's Business*, *The Sunday School Times*, and publications put out by individual fundamentalists such as *The Baptist Beacon* and *The Pilot* (W. B. Riley), *The Searchlight* (J. Frank Norris), and *The Gospel Witness* (T. T. Shields).

These tributaries all converged ultimately to give the fundamentalist movement a common direction, articulated the common biblical basis, and provided a large measure of its *esprit*. Other organizations and institutions eventually spun out of these tributaries such as the World's Christian Fundamentals Association (1919), the Baptist Bible Union (1923), and the Evangelical Theological College (1924; now Dallas Seminary), among others.

---

[26] David O. Beale, *In Pursuit of Purity*, chap. 2.

[27] George W. Dollar, *A History of Fundamentalism in America* (Greenville, SC: Bob Jones University Press, 1973), p. 27ff.

[28] Larry D. Pettegrew, "The Niagara Bible Conference and American Fundamentalism," *Central Bible Quarterly* 19 (Winter 1976), p. 8ff. Although dealing with a later period of fundamentalist history, Joel Carpenter reflects this cluster ("Fundamentalist Institutions and the Rise of Evangelical Protestantism: 1929–1942").

[29] John Fea, "Understanding the Changing Facade," p. 184.

Fundamentalism is a distinct movement and as such has an honorable history and is a noble heritage. It is not just a mood or a series of passing religious fads. The doctrinal aspect or theological content of its self-identity now needs to be identified.

CRUCIAL DOCTRINE

Fundamentalism has always been defined in the main by biblical doctrine. The parameters of that doctrinal complex are the subject of some debate, especially among non-fundamentalists. Charles Colson equated fundamentalism with orthodox Christianity. "Everyone who believes in the orthodox truths about Jesus Christ—in short, every Christian—is a fundamentalist."[30] John MacArthur's parameters are a little broader but run in similar lines as Colson's. He includes doctrines that are clear in Scripture, doctrines that are forbidden to be denied, and doctrines that are essential to saving faith. These are "all summed up in the person and work of Jesus Christ."[31] While MacArthur does not explicitly call this set of doctrines "fundamentalism," the context and implications of his treatment point to that.

Neither Colson nor MacArthur wishes to be identified with the fundamentalist *movement* but what they describe may well be "orthodoxy" or "evangelicalism" and would be a part of fundamentalist doctrine. The so-called fundamentals are in reality the core beliefs of orthodoxy/evangelicalism but should not be equated with fundamentalism as such. There have always been a few voices who would equate fundamentalism simply with the fundamentals.[32] But this is too broad an approach. However, the point here is that there is a certain complex of orthodox doctrine to which other distinctives must be appended to account for the phenomenon of fundamentalism.

Historically, fundamentalists have held to a certain core of biblical teaching, mainly concerning Christ and the Scriptures, with the added doctrinal distinctive of ecclesiastical separation. These, coupled with the practical distinctive of militancy, have formed the essence of fundamentalism as a movement. The purpose here is to determine this core of doctrine.

---

[30] Charles Colson, *The Body* (Waco, TX: Word, 1992), p. 186.

[31] John MacArthur, *Reckless Faith* (Westchester, IL: Crossway, 1994), p. 113.

[32] For example, Jerry Falwell, ed., *The Fundamentalist Phenomenon* (Garden City, NY: Doubleday, 1981), pp. 1–11.

Christianity Itself Is a Doctrinal Movement.

New Testament Christianity is a belief-system of divinely revealed propositions. It is a series of absolute truth claims that must be mentally appropriated, emotionally accepted, and volitionally trusted. There are popular misconceptions often heard concerning what Christianity really is. Some would say that Christianity is Jesus Christ. Others would say it is the new birth. While there is a measure of truth in each, these are actually reductionist in scope. True Christianity consists of *what the Bible says* about each of these and many more. There is "another Jesus" (2 Cor 11:4), but the way to God and eternal life is through the Christ of Scripture, the one whose coming was written "in the roll of the book" (Heb 10:7). There is also "another spirit" and "another gospel" (2 Cor 11:4) circulating under the guise of Christianity that yield all manner of subjective experiences, some even termed a new birth. But these are invalid because they do not conform to the real genius of the Christian religion which consists of the revealed truths of the New Testament.

Christianity's Fundamental Predication Is the Self-Witness of Scripture.

The Christian religion is an authoritarian one. It rests on the absolute authority of the revelation of God. As with everything about God, the Bible's witness to its divine authority is self-referential; it is a self-attesting revelation in human language. One cannot delegate authority to Scripture, he can only assent to it. The Bible bears its own marks of inspiration and authority; the human options it leaves are faith or unbelief. While some have attempted to come up with external "proofs" of inspiration, the biblical pattern consistently presents only one underlying proof or evidence of divine inspiration—its own claim to have come from God via the miracle of inspiration (1 Cor 2:13; 2 Tim 3:16). This claim can be appropriated and realized as true only by an act of supernaturally endowed faith. No one has natural ability to do so; in fact, everyone is born with a native hostility to God and His revelation (1 Cor 2:14).[33]

---

[33] One of the finest treatments of this subject is still the essay by John Murray, "The Self-Attestation of Scripture," in *The Infallible Word*, ed. Ned Stonehouse and Paul Wooley (Philadelphia: Presbyterian and Reformed, 1946), chap. 1.

Saving Faith Must Appropriate an Irreducible Number of Biblical Truth Claims.

There is a *sine qua non* of truth that must be appropriated by faith or one will perish in hell forever. This irreducible corpus of truth or gospel tenets is sometimes known as the *kerugma*, the proclamation or preachment of the good news. While there is a tendency, even within a certain element of fundamentalism, to proclaim a somewhat reduced gospel or a "simple gospel" that is much simpler than the New Testament allows, the biblical pattern of the *kerugma* generally consists of at least four elements. They are the Bible's witness to God, sin, Christ, and faith and repentance.[34] But again, these are articles of *faith*, i.e., propositional revelation that must be processed correctly by the cognitive/volitional faculties of human beings, because the good news of Christianity is a belief-system.

Fundamentalism Embraces Certain Crucial Doctrines.

There are certain tenets out of the broader doctrinal base of Christianity that form the hard core of historic fundamentalism. These doctrines are not the private property or sole possession of fundamentalism, but fundamentalists have held, guarded, defended, and propagated them with a tenacious militancy and separatism not found in other circles.

The founders and early leaders of fundamentalism were cognizant of the centrality of truth and because of that they gave first place to doctrine. They correctly gave priority to matters of *faith*. Doctrine determined who belonged within the ranks and doctrine was the criterion for ecclesiastical cooperation and separation. What one believed was of prime importance in these areas.

Since fundamentalism has as perhaps its main historical tributary the Bible Conference movement, it is instructive to observe the articles of faith of the Niagara Bible Conference, the first on the American continent. The 1878 Confession of Faith listed fourteen articles.[35] They were:

---

[34] See J. I. Packer, *Evangelism and the Sovereignty of God* (Downers Grove, IL: InterVarsity Press, 1961), pp. 57–73.

[35] See David O. Beale, *In Pursuit of Purity*, appendix A, pp. 375–79. For a comprehensive work on the origins, beliefs, history, and contributions of the Niagara Bible Conference, see Larry D. Pettegrew, "The Historical and Theological Contributions of the Niagara Bible Conference to American Fundamentalism" (Th.D. dissertation, Dallas Theological Seminary, 1976).

1. The verbal, plenary inspiration of the Scriptures in the original manuscripts.
2. The trinity.
3. The creation of man, the fall into sin, and total depravity.
4. The universal transmission of spiritual death from Adam.
5. The necessity of the new birth.
6. Redemption by the blood of Christ.
7. Salvation by faith alone in Jesus Christ.
8. The assurance of salvation.
9. The centrality of Jesus Christ in the Scriptures.
10. The true church made up of genuine believers.
11. The personality of the Holy Spirit.
12. The believer's call to a holy life.
13. The souls of believers go immediately to be with Christ at death.
14. The premillennial second coming of Christ.

The 1910 General Assembly of the Presbyterian Church drew up a five-point doctrinal statement of truths that were considered crucial and essential.[36] These became the historic "five fundamentals" of Presbyterian fundamentalism.

1. The inerrancy of the original manuscripts of Scripture.
2. The virgin birth of Christ.
3. The vicarious atonement of Christ.
4. The bodily resurrection of Christ.
5. The reality of biblical miracles.

The Confession of Faith of the Baptist Bible Union, drawn up on May 15, 1923, in conference in Kansas City, MO, had eighteen articles along the same lines as above.[37] Its main difference with other statements was the inclusion of articles on Satan, justification, repentance and faith, the eternal difference between the righteous and the wicked, and civil government.

Fundamentalism's historic doctrinal core concerned principally the Scriptures, Jesus Christ, and the way of salvation. Other doctrines were sometimes included for specific endeavors or institutions. There were certain essential doctrines that were simply understood but not stated, such as the genuine humanity of Christ, the indwelling of the Holy Spirit, or the imputation of Adamic guilt. Thus an exact number of "official" fundamentalist doctrines would be impossible to ascertain, for there was none. The consensus was general; the parameters were generally understood. Fundamentalism thus has a nucleus of crucial doctrines or biblical teachings that are clear and unambiguous. These do not of themselves comprise

---

[36] David O. Beale, *In Pursuit of Purity*, p. 149.

[37] Published by the Baptist Bible Union, n.d.

the full doctrinal identity of the movement, but a denial of any of them calls into serious question any claim to be a fundamentalist.

FUNDAMENTALISM HAS THE DISTINCTIVE OF MILITANCY.

Militancy has been a defining characteristic of fundamentalism from the beginning. On that there is near unanimity of opinion. George Dollar made militancy an aspect of the definition of fundamentalism, saying that fundamentalism consists in part of "the militant exposure of all non-biblical expositions and affirmations and attitudes."[38] Larry Pettegrew similarly said that "fundamentalism is a militant attitude that exposes the non-biblical exposition of the basic doctrines."[39] David Beale likewise consistently stressed militancy as one of the trademarks of fundamentalism.[40]

Non-fundamentalists also have been able to recognize this distinctive of the fundamentalist movement. John Fea, no fundamentalist himself, calls the "second phase" of fundamentalism (1919– 1940) "militant fundamentalism." (He called the first phase "irenic fundamentalism" [1893– 1919]).[41] George Marsden used the term "fundamentalist" (that of the 1920s to the 1940s) to mean one who was "theologically traditional, a believer in the fundamentals of evangelical Christianity, and willing to take a militant stand against modernism."[42] Elsewhere he noted the same militant anti-modernism as a characteristic of the 1920s fundamentalism.[43] Mark Noll, a thoroughgoing new evangelical, observed that a "militant defense of the faith" was one characteristic among others that could be found in the somewhat amorphous fundamentalism prior to World War I.[44]

Both self-confessed fundamentalists and non-fundamentalists alike recognize militancy as a mark of fundamentalism's identity. Evidently, militancy is not all that difficult to define and see.

---

[38] George W. Dollar, *A History of Fundamentalism in America*, p. xv.

[39] Larry D. Pettegrew, "Will the Real Fundamentalist Please Stand Up?" *Central Testimony* (Fall 1982) [published by the Central Baptist Theological Seminary of Minneapolis].

[40] David O. Beale, *In Pursuit of Purity*, pp. 10, 18, 268.

[41] John Fea, "Understanding the Changing Facade," p. 184.

[42] George M. Marsden, *Reforming Fundamentalism*, p. 10.

[43] George M. Marsden, *Fundamentalism and American Culture* (New York: Oxford University Press, 1980), p. 4.

[44] Mark A. Noll, *Between Faith and Criticism* (Grand Rapids: Baker, 1986), p. 38.

The Nature of Fundamentalist Militancy

George Houghton writes concerning militancy:

> What exactly is militancy, anyway? One dictionary says it is to be "engaged
> in warfare or combat…aggressively active (as in a cause)." It springs from
> one's values, is expressed as an attitude, and results in certain behavior. One's
> values are those things in which one strongly believes. They are what one
> believes to be fundamentally important and true. From this comes an attitude
> which is unwilling to tolerate any divergence from these fundamentally
> important truths and which seeks to defend them. It results in behavior which
> speaks up when these truths are attacked or diluted and which refuses to
> cooperate with any activity which would minimize their importance. The
> term is a military one and carries the idea of defending what one believes to
> be true.[45]

Fundamentalist militancy originally had a very anti-modernist expression
because modernism was the focal point of the battle.[46] This spirit has
continued to the present although the deviancies of the 1920s and 30s
are not currently the principal focus of fundamentalism's aggressive
defense. In the 1940s, 50s, and 60s, it was new evangelicalism against
which fundamentalism's militancy was especially deployed. By somewhat
common consent, new evangelicalism peaked and began to decline in the
1970s[47] and thus as a movement has been less aggressively attacked and
exposed than before by fundamentalists. In the 1970s and 80s the so-called
pseudo-fundamentalism of the Jerry Falwell making was of pressing
concern. Recent objects of fundamentalist militancy have been resurgent
new evangelical spin-offs such as Promise Keepers, the psychological
self-movement and its undermining of a sufficient Bible, Evangelicals and
Catholics Together, the teachings of Charles Swindoll on "free grace," the
inclusivism of John MacArthur, Tim Lee, and others, and, in some cases,
the non-militant, soft underbelly of professing fundamentalism itself.

Fundamentalist militancy has as its base and starting point the doctrines
of the Bible, especially the doctrine of ecclesiastical separation. Militancy
and separatism are in tandem. A practice of one necessitates the other; a

---

[45] George Houghton, "The Matter of Militancy," *Faith Pulpit* (May 1994).

[46] The early new evangelicals were also anti-modernist at least in an intellectual
sense. See Douglas A. Sweeney, "Fundamentalism and Neo-Evangelicalism," p. 89.

[47] Harold Lindsell, "Evangelicalism's Golden Age," *Moody* (Dec 1985), pp. 113–114.
Harold O. J. Brown, "Evangelicalism in America," *Dialog* (vol. 24, no. 3), pp. 188–92.
David F. Wells, *No Place For Truth.*, p. 127ff. Millard J. Erickson, *The Evangelical Heart
and Mind* (Grand Rapids: Baker, 1993), p. 191ff.

decline in one reflects a decline in the other. Militancy is simply being aggressive and combative about the faith, especially the nucleus of crucial doctrine, including the doctrine of ecclesiastical separation in its two-fold structure of separation from the apostasy and from disobedient brethren.

Militancy is not to be confused with having a domineering personality nor with mere belligerence for its own sake. It has to do with aggressive adherence to principle rather than the possession of a certain type of personality. Non-militancy cannot be excused on the basis of having a reticent personality. Everyone is militant about certain things. Those who decry fundamentalist militancy are saying more about what they consider worth defending than about their personalities. Forceful personalities rise to the fore and are entrusted with leadership somewhat naturally. A retiring type of personality may not have the fortitude to lead the battles for the faith, but he can at least stand with and support those who do. It is observable that those who deprecate or minimize militancy are usually quite militant about non-militancy, as oxymoronic as that may seem. Their writings and comments against militant fundamentalists are often classic demonstrations of the militancy they otherwise profess to disdain.

The Decline In Fundamentalist Militancy

In the last decade or so there has been a noticeable decline in fundamentalist militancy. Questions are being raised as to what constitutes militancy anyway. Some propose the need to explore and define militancy very precisely. This all seems highly anachronistic given the role of militancy in fundamentalism from the start. There are several reasons one could give to explain this general loss of militancy and aggressiveness in the movement.

The Influence of the General Culture. There is a disdain for militancy on almost any subject today. The 1960s brought a revolt against absolutes in nearly every realm. Personal preferences and value-options are all considered *equal* in today's mentality, creating a contempt for the aggressive prosecution of any idea or agenda, at least that of a conservative stripe. Evangelical scholarship loathes dogmatism no matter what the evidence for a position. This attitude eventually trickles down into the fundamentalist environment. A helpful corrective can be found in the example of Paul and Barnabas and their difference of opinion over John Mark (Acts 15:36–41). This was anything but an affirming, irenic, non-confrontational form of meekness often argued for today. Also in a militant vein, Paul opposed Peter "to his face" for his duplicity before the Gentiles, and he did it "before them all" (Gal 2:11–14). There was no smorgasbord of equal opinion in either of these incidents.

Dissatisfaction With Past Leadership. Certain fundamentalists have felt insulted by some of the unwise statements and misguided zeal of some other fundamentalists in the heat of battle. Thus they feel that to be militant is to be pugnacious, ugly, or careless with the truth. In turn they may propose a "militant meekness" or a "militancy for the meekness of Christ."[48] Sermons on "gentleness," for example, carry an overload of innuendo if not plain statement against fundamentalist militancy which for some conjures up a resurrection of the "J. Frank Norris syndrome." In point of fact, however, militancy and gentleness are compatible. There is no real dichotomy between them. True, "the servant of the Lord must...be gentle" (2 Tim 2:24; cf. 1 Thess 2:7; Titus 3:2), and "the wisdom from above is gentle" (Jas 3:17). But one need not be harsh or strident to be militant.

Pietism. Pietism is "a recurring tendency within Christian history to emphasize more the practicalities of Christian life and less the formal structures of theology or church order."[49] Its practical legacy in evangelical and fundamentalist circles includes the promotion of an emotional approach to controversial issues, a failure to observe long range effects and wider implications in the interests of immediate sensitivity to feelings and friendships, a tendency to opt for a warm-hearted "blessing" rather than face the cold reality of an issue, and a counsel of "let's pray about it" or an attempt to "put out a fleece" when decisive obedience is mandated. Pietistic people feel that militancy and aggressiveness in defending the faith and combating an issue are simply unspiritual.

There has always been a stratum of pietism in fundamentalism inherited principally from the Keswick and higher/deeper life movements that influenced its early formation. But the tension between militancy and spirituality is a false one as Jesus demonstrated when He cleansed the temple (John 2:14–16) and when He denounced the Pharisees in some of the most blistering language ever uttered (Matt 23). It must not be forgotten that Jesus of Nazareth was holy and harmless (Heb 7:26), the very incarnation of gentleness and love. Yet He was militant. "Servant leadership" does not necessitate a piously benign attitude toward error or toward individuals who hold and propagate error or who are tolerant of those who do.

Ambiguity Over the Meaning of Fundamentalism. The current search for self-identity among certain fundamentalists betrays a general lack of clarity about the genius of the movement itself. One cannot be militant about a cause that lacks specific content.[50] There may be some discernible

---

[48] Douglas R. McLachlan, *Reclaiming Authentic Fundamentalism*, p. 140.

[49] *Evangelical Dictionary of Theology*, s.v. "Pietism," by Mark A. Noll, p. 855.

[50] David M. Doran, "In Defense of Militancy," *Sentinel* (Spring 1995). The same article appeared with some modification in *Frontline Magazine* (vol. 5, no. 5, 1995), pp. 24–25.

reasons for this lack of clarity, as indicated earlier, but part of the aftermath of such a lack is a loss of aggressiveness or an inability to press the battle.

Lack of Strong Convictions. There has been a decline within fundamentalism of feelings of strong conviction about the content and direction of the movement. Perhaps the disdain for dogmatism in the general culture is partly to blame. It is also to be acknowledged that some influential fundamentalists have taken strong stands on the wrong issues, or have taken the right position in the wrong spirit. Furthermore, the biblical bases and rationale for some of these occasions may have been poorly thought out or simply not even there.[51] As a result there was a loss of confidence in some cases or at least a disappointment that significantly eroded enthusiasm for the fundamentalist cause. Militancy for any cause must be backed by strong convictions and wholehearted dedication in order to be effective. The younger heirs of fundamentalism are especially sensitive to the doctrinal and exegetical foundations for the positions and directions taken by their leaders and forebears. This is healthy and good, but it rightfully imposes a heavy responsibility on leadership. It does not take a whole lot of discernment to distinguish between preaching the Word of God with conviction and preaching a conviction about the Word of God. The two are not always synonymous. At any rate, militancy for the cause of fundamentalism diminishes as the certainty about the cause recedes.

Ignorance and Naiveté. There is a feeling among some professing fundamentalists that the religious environment today is short on issues, personalities, and movements against which a fundamentalist must be militant. The idea is that we live in a less hostile environment and therefore the concept of militancy must be rethought.[52] This appears to be a naive understanding of the present milieu, or worse, an ignorance of what is really pressing in on the fundamentalist community. This attitude naturally leads to a less militant approach.

The remedies for these causes would seem to be self-evident. The relativism of the general culture must be rejected in favor of the dogmatic absolutism of the teaching of Scripture and the examples of Jesus Christ, the apostle Paul, and others. Past leadership must be judged by the same criteria, noting that the sins of some do not invalidate the need for militancy nor do they characterize the Cause itself. The pietistic dichotomy between spirituality and militancy must be exposed as false and unwarranted. Ambiguity over the meaning of fundamentalism can easily be offset by presenting the clear case for historic fundamentalism. Lack of convictions

---

[51] Ibid.

[52] See Doran's account of one such claim made in his hearing. Ibid.

can only be replaced by feelings of strong dedication as one understands the Cause and gets involved in the fight. Ignorance and naiveté about the present religious scene are remedied by looking at the current scenario through biblical and historical eyes.

FUNDAMENTALISM HAS THE DISTINCTIVE OF ECCLESIASTICAL SEPARATION.

Another vital facet of the self-identity of fundamentalism is the doctrine and practice of ecclesiastical separation. It is at once both the most maligned and/or misunderstood distinctive of fundamentalism and probably the most defining one. Fundamentalism and separatism walk in lock step. James Singleton said correctly, "Without an authentic separation there can be no authentic fundamentalism."[53]

Various Types of Religious Separation

Civil. One of the Baptist distinctives is the separation of church and state, the separation of organized religion from the organized civil state. One may envision a scenario of the state over the church as in some totalitarian and/ or authoritarian governments. In some cases the church is over the state as in the old Holy Roman Empire or in certain present day Islamic countries. There may be a configuration of the church alongside the state in some kind of ecclesiastical and civil parity as in certain European countries. Or one may have a free church in a free state as in our own republic. The latter is the ideal separation of church and state and a rendering to Caesar those things that are his and a rendering to God that which is his (Matt 22:21).

Personal. This has to do with the individual believer and his personal relationship to the "world." The world in the biblical sense is that organized system that is in opposition to God. It is the transient though ever present arrangement of things—the "now," the cosmos. Its god is the devil (2 Cor 4:4), and it is structured by autonomous man and his "I'm worth it" philosophy. A biblical Christian will separate from the world (1 John 2:15; Rom 12:2).

Ecclesiastical. Ecclesiastical separation takes place on the organizational level where religious groups and leaders interact. Broadly speaking, it is the refusal to collaborate with, or a withdrawal of cooperation from, an ecclesiastical organization or religious leader that deviates from the Word of God in doctrine and practice. This is the distinctive form of fundamentalist separatists.

---

[53] James E. Singleton, *The Tri-City Baptist Builder* (Jan–Feb 1995), p. 2.

The Separatistic Nature of Fundamentalism

Fundamentalism has always been "separatistic" at heart and in principle. One may rightfully distinguish between non-conformist fundamentalism (pre-1930) and separatist fundamentalism (post-1930).[54] Beale notes that "the separatist position did not solidify as a distinct, militant movement until the 1930s."[55] This is true but it seems that even the non-conformists were at heart separatistic. They attempted to purge their denominations and institutions of unbelief, i.e., they tried to separate the liberals from their midst. When that did not prove successful, they separated themselves from the liberals in a more formal practice of ecclesiastical separation.

The Doctrine of Ecclesiastical Separation

The Basis. Ecclesiastical separation is more than a stance of anti-modernism. The new evangelicals also were against modernism. The National Association of Evangelicals, for example, began (in 1942) with an anti-liberal spirit, and continued it for some time. But those evangelicals were not separatists as such.[56] At best they had only a very low degree or thin veneer of separation that within a decade or less had been compromised in the interests of scholarly dialogue and ecumenical evangelism. The new evangelicals had a fundamentalist doctrinal core but repudiated the fundamentalist distinctive of ecclesiastical separation in favor of denominational infiltration.[57] Fundamentalists were both aggressive anti-modernists and ecclesiastical separatists.

---

[54] David O. Beale, *In Pursuit of Purity*, p. 5.

[55] Ibid.

[56] John Fea, "Understanding the Changing Facade," p. 189.

[57] Harold John Ockenga's news release of Dec 8, 1957, said clearly, "The new evangelicalism has changed its strategy from one of separation to one of infiltration." One of the points in the ground-breaking *Christian Life* article (March 1956) was "a growing willingness of evangelical theologians to converse with liberal theologians" (p. 19). In the same article Vernon Grounds said idealistically, "An evangelical can be organizationally separated from all Christ-denying fellowship and yet profitably engage in an exchange of ideas with men who are not evangelicals" (p. 19). While this may be formally true on a theoretical level, in practice the dialogue technique was disastrous for evangelicalism. And the infiltration principle was a total failure. Carl Henry said that the mainline denominations are now "irrelevant" ("Know Your Roots: Evangelicalism Yesterday, Today, and Tomorrow" [Videocassette by the Trinity Evangelical Divinity School, 1991]).

The biblical doctrine of ecclesiastical separation is grounded firmly in the character of God Himself; it is an expression of His eternal holiness. Holiness in Scripture means an apartness or separation from that which is common or profane. God's holiness is His apartness from all that is morally unclean, a holiness of moral purity. In some sense holiness qualifies or regulates His other moral attributes. It characterizes His "name" (Matt 6:5). Thus God has a constitutional reaction against anything that contradicts His holiness. Therefore He demands that His people be like Him in character and conduct (Matt 5:48; Rom 12:1; 1 John 2:1). Separatism arises out of God's intrinsic being.[58]

The Components. There are two components to ecclesiastical separation. The first is organizational separation from the apostasy. Early fundamentalists were sometimes slow to implement ecclesiastical separation in a more formal sense, hence Beale's distinction between non-conformist and separatist fundamentalism. Ecclesiastical separatism in the sense of withdrawal of all organizational cooperation with the apostasy began in about 1930. Prior to that there were numerous efforts of "separation from within," which were efforts to eliminate the apostate or unorthodox elements from a denomination, institution, or agency. Often those attempts took on a "loyal opposition" stance.[59] Sometimes friendships and retirement funds deterred a more forthright separation from a liberal institution.[60] W. B. Riley thought that God would use the fundamentalists to clean up the Northern Baptist Convention and give them triumph over the forces of darkness at last.[61] He also felt that to leave

---

[58] Fred Moritz, *"Be Ye Holy": The Call To Christian Separation* (Greenville, SC: Bob Jones University Press, 1994), chap. 1. See also Rolland D. McCune, "An Inside Look At Ecclesiastical Separation" (Detroit Baptist Theological Seminary, pamphlet, n.d.), pp. 6–7.

[59] Many within the Fundamentalist Fellowship of the Northern Baptist Convention had this motivating principle, including its first president, J. C. Massee. See William Vance Trollinger, *God's Empire* (Madison, WI: University of Wisconsin Press, 1990), p. 59. See also Beale, *In Pursuit of Purity*, pp. 180, 216.

[60] Dr. R. V. Clearwaters often made this point in my hearing either from the pulpit, in the classroom, or in the hallway. He spoke from personal knowledge, having been a fundamentalist leader against modernism in the Northern Baptist Convention, having served in Convention local churches and in leadership in the Iowa Baptist Convention and the Minnesota Baptist Convention, having been graduated from the Northern Baptist Theological Seminary, having served on the school's board of trustees, and having been given an honorary doctorate by the Seminary. He used to say wryly that he "made a heave offering" of his M and M Fund (a Convention-held retirement account for ministers and missionaries) when he separated from the Convention.

[61] Trollinger says this of Riley who stayed in the Northern Baptist Convention virtually until his deathbed when he withdrew on a personal basis (ibid., pp. 44, 60–61).

the denomination was to abandon the many orthodox missionaries and evangelists still in the Convention.[62] While a few struggled with the issue, the biblical and logical fundamentalist doctrine of ecclesiastical separation was being practiced by many others who were withdrawing from their liberal surroundings and were forming around strong leaders new schools, associations, mission agencies, and other institutions.

Some of the biblical considerations or grounds demanding this aspect of ecclesiastical separation are:

> False doctrine (1 Tim 6:3–5; 2 Tim 2:16–21; Rev 2:14–16)
> Divisiveness caused by false teaching (Rom 16:17–18)
> Error concerning the person of Christ (1 John 4:1–3; 2 John 10–11)
> Unequal alliances (2 Cor 6:14–18)
> A "gospel" different from the grace of God (Gal 1:8–10; 2 Cor 11:4)
> Organized apostasy (Rev 18:4. While this refers to the tribulation period, the principle is clear.)

The second component of ecclesiastical separation is organizational separation from disobedient brethren. This form of separatism came to the fore when the non-separatist new evangelicals broke away from fundamentalism in the 1940s and 50s. However, separation from disobedient brethren was being practiced in the early 1930s already. When the Baptist Bible Union was succeeded by the General Association of Regular Baptist Churches in 1932, one of the requirements for membership in the new group was a severance of all fellowship from liberalism and from those who were tolerant of it. This set the GARBC apart from the Fundamentalist Fellowship within the Northern Baptist Convention and the mentality that later formed the Conservative Baptist movement.

Ecumenical evangelism as practiced especially by Billy Graham eventually forced the separation issue, and by the time of the 1957 New York Crusade, the fundamentalist and new evangelical camps were irreconcilable.[63] As it was in the fundamentalist-modernist controversy, fundamentalists were again presented with conflict, only this time from fellow believers and churchmen, those from within the ranks of professing fundamentalism itself. And again they maintained the distinctive of ecclesiastical separation, in this case from new evangelical brethren.

Some, such as John R. Rice, took an ambivalent stance by separating from modernists but decrying "secondary separation" and refusing

---

[62] Ibid., p. 61.

[63] Farley P. Butler, Jr., "Billy Graham and the End of Evangelical Unity" (Ph.D. dissertation, University of Florida, 1976), pp. 191–94.

to separate from fellow brethren who loved the Lord and won souls to Christ.[64] Many of this persuasion more or less went off to themselves and dropped out of the mainstream of fundamentalism. Remnants of that mentality, however, continue to renew the controversy, especially among the younger heirs of fundamentalism, some of whom openly disavow "secondary separation." Andrew Sandlin contends that "it is not legitimate to extrapolate from Paul's express statements [in 2 Thess 3:7–12] to some sort of amorphous principle to justify an academic practice of separation."[65] By this he means that the only subject here is lazy Christians and not Christians in general who disobey apostolic teaching and principles in the Word of God. This effectively relieves almost everyone today from looking too closely at a brother's doctrine and practice, especially since "laziness" easily can become an ambiguous, amorphous rubric in itself. This kind of hermeneutic (used by the same author on other separation passages) specifically exempts new evangelicals as objects of ecclesiastical separation.[66] Exactly to whom Paul's strictures may apply today is not altogether clear.

"Secondary separation" may not be the best of expressions but it is one that has been used for quite some time. A newer term, "familial separation," has arisen lately to designate separation from disobedient brethren. However, while more innocuous as a term than secondary separation, it appears at times to lack specific organizational or ecclesiastical content. It could be taken to mean little more than local church discipline without any broader application to ecclesiastical or organizational levels.[67]

Ecclesiastical separation from erring brethren is based principally on 2 Thessalonians 3:6–15. Note several things about the passage. (1) The *problem* was the brother's disobedience to divine revelation in apostolic preaching and teaching (vv. 6, 14). Its *manifestation* was idleness or laziness (v. 6). Many confuse the problem with its local, first century manifestation.[68] The brother in view here had the example of Paul's work ethic (vv. 7–9), specific apostolic instruction (v. 10; cf. 2:15), and divine

---

[64] See his articles in *The Sword of the Lord* noted in footnote 4.

[65] Andrew Sandlin, "Some Thoughts on Secondary Separation," *Target* (Aug 1994), p. 9.

[66] Ibid., p. 13.

[67] Douglas R. McLachlan, *Reclaiming Authentic Fundamentalism*, pp. 125–37. He treats familial separation as something different from ecclesiastical separation, leaving some doubt that familial separation can actually be organizational in application. "Functional severance" is the explanation given for the term familial separation (p. 132), but the whole point seems to be set in distinction from ecclesiastical separation.

[68] As does Sandlin, "Some Thoughts on Secondary Separation," p. 13.

revelation in Paul's previous letter (1 Thess 4:11–12; 5:14). (2) The directive was to separate from this person (v. 6, "withdraw;" v. 14, "have no company with him"). It was authoritative (v. 6, "we command you") and affectionate (v. 6, "brethren"). (3) Separation was to be based on a pattern of disobedience (v. 6, "leads an unruly life;" v. 14, "does not obey our instruction." Both verbs are in the present tense.). (4) Local church discipline is a minimum understanding. But such apostolic directives and examples were warnings to other assemblies and leaders as well so that they would not collaborate with the disobedient brethren (e.g., 1 Tim 1:18–20). That is, the command to separate took on an organizational and ecclesiastical function that transcended the local church being addressed. Ecclesiastical separation from disobedient Christians is in principle the same as local church discipline of disobedient Christians. There is no real dichotomy.

Putting this in a more modern flesh and blood context, the category of erring brethren includes leaders or institutions who compromise some aspect of the core doctrines, or who cooperate with ecumenism/inclusivism in its various forms, or who are tolerant of those who tolerate compromise, or who are immoral or otherwise disqualified for religious leadership.

CONCLUSION

It would appear that fundamentalism still retains its original biblical and historic identity markers. These have not changed. Only the religious and cultural milieu has changed. The impact of the relativism of the 1960s has had a trickle-down effect on certain aspects of the fundamentalist movement, causing some now to begin a new search for self-identity and to come to a somewhat revisionist and reductionist idea of fundamentalism's content and history. This in turn has dictated certain proposals of change and course corrections for the movement and thus for the prospects of its future as well.

There will always be a remnant of historic fundamentalists despite the changes and calls for "relevancy" that seem to be increasing. And it seems outwardly, at least, that that remnant decreases in size and influence in proportion to the calls from within and without to tone down on militancy and separatism in favor of a fundamentalism more palatable to current tastes. The present cultural setting wants a non-confrontational, affirming, need-meeting, and positive message from the church, if it wants to hear the church at all; what one calls "hot tub religion."[69] Fundamentalists

---

[69] J. I. Packer, *Hot Tub Religion* (Wheaton: Tyndale House, 1988), chap. 4. While Packer is anything but a fundamentalist, he has diagnosed correctly much of the present religious scene.

are not immune from the temptation to be drawn in that direction and to tone down, or at least pronounce less clearly, their historic distinctives in the interests of gaining a larger hearing. There are calls from within the general new evangelical community for "reforging" a biblical identity[70] or "revisioning" evangelical theology.[71] Some of these are cogent remedies for the evangelical malaise; some are not. Other observers are apparently pessimistically uncertain about the whole future of evangelicalism.[72] Similar assessments were made of fundamentalism in the 1940s and 50s and again in the 1970s. These came from within its own ranks. We now can see that this attitude of "reforming" fundamentalism was actually alien and detrimental to the real genius of the movement. Thus one wonders if the present uncertainty about the self-identity of fundamentalism and the proposals for its restructuring are signs of a deterioration that has already taken place in some influential minds.

Fundamentalism may be defined as a religious movement committed to a certain core of biblical, orthodox, and historic doctrine, mainly concerning the Bible and Jesus Christ, a movement that is particularly distinguished by the doctrine and practice of ecclesiastical separation along with an aggressive affirmation and defense of those doctrines and a militant exposure of non-biblical expressions and practices.

[70] John Seel, *The Evangelical Forfeit* (Grand Rapids: Baker, 1993), chap. 5.

[71] Stanley J. Grenz, *Revisioning Evangelical Theology* (Downers Grove, IL: InterVarsity Press, 1993).

[72] David F. Wells, *No Place For Truth*, and its sequel, *God In the Wasteland* (Grand Rapids: Eerdmans, 1994), chaps. 8, 9.

DOCTRINAL NON-ISSUES IN
HISTORIC FUNDAMENTALISM[1]

Rolland D. McCune

Historic fundamentalism has always been characterized by a core of biblical, historic, orthodox doctrines.[2] Those concerned mainly the Scriptures and Jesus Christ. Coupled with the doctrine of ecclesiastical separation and the practice of a militant propagation and defense of those beliefs, they have given fundamentalism its identity. The precise number of explicit doctrines or an "official" list of fundamentalist beliefs would be difficult if not impossible to ascertain since the agreement among fundamentalists has been somewhat general. Most fundamentalists would be content with terms like "major doctrines" or "cardinal doctrines" to describe their consensus.

Periodically, other doctrinal issues, usually on matters peripheral to the basic orthodox core, have arisen and have caused concern and controversy. In some cases efforts were made to make a particular insight an article of fundamentalist faith. Historically, these attempts have not been successful and the movement has not been characterized as a whole by these kinds of views. They remain non-issues in that regard. Fundamentalist individuals and groups have almost always gone beyond the general doctrinal consensus so as to positionalize more definitively their own local church, association, or cause but have not insisted on those same distinctives for fundamentalism as a movement.

BIBLE VERSIONS, TEXTS, AND TEXT TYPES

Historically, fundamentalists have held that the inspiration and inerrancy of the Bible pertained to the autographs only and that copies, translations, and reproductions of the Scriptures derived inspiration from the original manuscripts insofar as they faithfully reproduced those originals. Historic fundamentalists did not accord any special, much less miraculous, protection to any particular reproduction of the biblical text. They held that God preserved His Word providentially in the various manuscripts, copies, and reproductions of the original biblical text, and by diligent study and comparison, the original words of the Scriptures are available for translation into the English language.

---

[1] This article appeared in the Fall 1996 issue of *DBSJ,* vol. 1, pp. 171–85.

[2] See Rolland D. McCune, "The Self-Identity of Fundamentalism" elsewhere in this anthology.

The biblical evidence indicates that inspiration proper is confined to the autographs. Paul categorically affirmed that the things which "I write" are the Lord's commandment (1 Cor 14:37). In Acts 1:16 Peter said that the Holy Spirit spoke the Scripture "by the mouth of David" (cf. Acts 4:25). In Acts 28:25 Paul said that the Holy Spirit spoke "through Isaiah" unto the fathers. In other words, inspiration and inerrancy took place miraculously when the Spirit breathed out the Scriptures through a David or an Isaiah. Inspiration proper did not take place when the scribe or copyist made the manuscript that Peter or Paul was using. Edward J. Young captured this point when he wrote that if holy men spoke when they were borne along by the Spirit (2 Pet 1:21), "then only what they spoke under the Spirit's bearing is inspired. It would certainly be unwarrantable to maintain that copies of what they spoke were also inspired, since those copies were not made as men were borne of the Spirit."[3]

Writing in *The Fundamentals,* a series of articles written in 1910–1915, James M. Gray said,

> *The record for whose inspiration we contend is the original record*—the autographs or parchments of Moses, David, Daniel, Matthew, Paul or Peter, as the case may be, and not any particular translation or translations of them whatever. There is no translation absolutely without error, nor could there be, considering the infirmities of human copyists, unless God were pleased to perform a perpetual miracle to secure it."[4]

Another wrote, "We take the ground that on *the original parchment*—the membrane—every sentence, word, line, mark, point, pen-stroke jot, tittle was put there by God. On *the original parchment.* There is no question of other, anterior parchments."[5] L. W. Munhall wrote in *The Fundamentals,* "The original writings, *ipsissima verba,* came through the penmen direct from God."[6] Also R. A. Torrey, an undisputed scholar in early fundamentalism, said concerning the extent of inspiration, "Because of this inspiration of Prophets and Apostles, the writers of the Bible, the whole Bible *as originally given* becomes the absolutely inerrant word of God"[7]

---

[3] Edward J. Young, *Thy Word is Truth* (Grand Rapids: Eerdmans, 1959), p. 55.

[4] James M. Gray, "The Inspiration of the Bible," in *The Fundamentals: A Testimony to the Truth,* 4 vols., ed. by R. A. Torrey, A. C. Dixon, et al. (Grand Rapids: Baker reprint, 1980), 2:12.

[5] George S. Bishop, "The Testimony of the Scriptures to Themselves," *The Fundamentals,* 2:92.

[6] L. W. Munhall, "Inspiration," in *The Fundamentals,* 2:44.

[7] R. A. Torrey, *The Fundamental Doctrines of the Christian Faith* (New York: George H. Doran, 1918), p. 34.

(italics added). And again, "'The Word of God' which we have in the Old and New Testaments, *as originally given,* is absolutely inerrant down to the smallest word and smallest letter or part of a letter"[8] (italics added).

Going back to the 1878 Confession of Faith of the Niagara Bible Conference,[9] we read in Article I that inspiration is to be understood

> in the sense that the Holy Ghost gave the very words of the sacred writings to holy men of old; and that His Divine inspiration is not in different degrees, but extends equally and fully to all parts of these writings, historical, poetical, doctrinal and prophetical, and to the smallest word, and inflection of a word, *provided such word is found in the original manuscripts* (italics added).

The Confession of Faith of the Baptist Bible Union,[10] drawn up in 1923, states concerning the Scriptures (Article I): "By 'THE HOLY BIBLE' we mean that collection of sixty-six books from Genesis to Revelation, which, *as originally written,*…IS the very Word of God" (italics added). One of the famous "five fundamentals" of the 1910 General Assembly of the Presbyterian Church was "the inerrancy of the *original manuscripts* of Scripture"[11] (italics added).

In a recent (1995) annual meeting of the Fundamental Baptist Fellowship (the continuation of the original Fundamentalist Fellowship of the old Northern Baptist Convention, begun in 1920), this clear resolution was passed:

> The FBF, while recognizing that God has used the King James Version of the Bible in a special way in the English speaking world, reaffirms its belief that the original manuscripts of Scripture are the documents which are inspired by God and that Bible translations may be considered trustworthy only if they accurately reflect the original manuscripts (2 Timothy 3:16).

The historic fundamentalist position was given classic expression by the General Assembly of the Presbyterian Church in America in 1893 and was quoted by more than one contributor to *The Fundamentals.*[12]

> The Bible as we now have it, in its various translations and revisions, when freed from all errors and mistakes of translators, copyists and printers, is the very Word of God, and consequently without error.

---

[8] Ibid., p. 35.

[9] See David O. Beale, *In Pursuit of Purity* (Greenville, SC: Unusual Publications, 1986), appendix A, pp. 375–79.

[10] Distributed by the Baptist Bible Union of America (no publishing data), p. 3.

[11] See Beale, *In Pursuit of Purity,* p. 149.

[12] For examples, see *The Fundamentals,* 2:43, 45.

A. Torrey also framed the issues very clearly regarding inspiration and translations when he wrote:

> I have said that the Scriptures of the Old and New Testaments as originally given
> were absolutely inerrant, and the question of course arises to what extent is the
> Authorized Version, or the Revised Version, the inerrant Word of God. The an-
> swer is simple; they are the inerrant Word of God just to that extent that they are
> an accurate rendering of the Scriptures of the Old and New Testaments as origi-
> nally given, and to all practical intents and purposes they are a thoroughly accurate
> rendering of the Scriptures of the Old and New Testaments as originally given.[13]

Early fundamentalists did not champion a particular version of the Bible
as their official version or elevate a particular codex, text type, or translation to the special status of being inspired or of being the very Word of
God to the exclusion of all others. While the King James Version was used
overwhelmingly in public, the American Standard Version (1901), for example, was widely assigned and used as a study Bible in fundamentalist
schools and was used by many teachers in the classroom. Pastors, evangelists, and Bible teachers had no hesitation in recommending it for clarity of
reading and understanding. Even the Revised Standard Version New Testament, in use from 1946 to 1952, before the Old Testament came out, was
used, recommended, and even advertised for sale by some fundmentalists.[14]
Bible versions, text types, and manuscript preferences were non-issues.

---

[13] A. Torrey, *The Fundamental Doctrines of the Christian Faith*, pp. 36–37.

[14] There was very little, if any, fundamentalist opposition to the RSV New Testament
when it came out in 1946. It was not until the Old Testament was published in Sept 1952
that there was a general fundamentalist outcry concerning some of the translations (notably
Isa 7:14), the lack of orthodox credentials on the translation committee, and the sponsorship
of the National Council of Churches. One early fundamentalist review of the RSV New
Testament appeared somewhat tepid (J. Oliver Buswell, Jr., *The Sunday School Times*,
Mar 16 and 23, 1946). Writing in 1952 of his earlier (1946) review, Buswell said that it
recognized "the general merits of the work yet pointed out a number of instances of bad
judgment and even doctrinal bias in the translation of particular passages" (The Sunday
School Times, Nov 1, 1952, p. 319). Buswell went on to state that in the six years the
New Testament had been out, he had recommended it for English-speaking nationals on
the foreign mission field. Nothing was ever said at the time against the RSV regarding its
textual background. Even more interesting is the fact that John R. Rice as late as Oct 17,
1952 ran an ad in *The Sword of the Lord* (p. 8) for the RSV New Testament, with an order
form to purchase it from his establishment. The following issue (Oct 24, 1952, p. 2) carried
an answer by Rice to a letter regarding the RSV. In it he acknowledged the modernistic
leadership of the National Council of Churches but also said that "this modernism did
not have much chance to come out since the translation made by many scholars would be
checked so that one man's opinion would be corrected somewhat by another." His main
reply was that the RSV was not as good as the ASV or the KJV for accuracy of translation.
In the Oct 31, 1952 issue (p. 2), Rice printed a statement by Carl McIntire about the RSV.
The thrust of this statement was that the RSV should not displace the KJV for a number

In the early 1970s an element in fundamentalism developed a "King James-only" type of thinking, breaking with fundamentalist scholarship and history. The spectrum of this group is fairly wide. Some feel that the KJV in English is inspired and inerrant, although which KJV is meant is debatable among them, ranging from the original 1611 version (which contained the Apocrypha) to the KJV in standard use today (which is actually the 1769 edition, one of many revisions of the 1611 edition[15]). Others claim superiority for the Textus Receptus, a Greek text put out in the 16th century that became the received or standard text in Europe. Still others hold to the Majority or Byzantine text as the special, God-protected text type from which the KJV came. Granted, some of these may only be textual preferences and not intended declarations that the King James Version is the only Word of God today. But often these nuances are too subtle to detect easily.

The truth is that the KJV is principally a revision of the Bishops' Bible, and in the preface the translators expressly disclaimed that their version or any other version was inerrant. This has been the fundamentalist consensus historically and continues to be the mainstream position. The King James-only proposal met strong opposition from some fundamentalist standard-bearers of the time. Bob Jones University faculty member, Edward Panosian, argued that "no *version* is inspired, except to the degree that it conforms to the original meaning of the words of the original manuscripts.

---

of reasons such as the translation of Isa 7:14, the copyright of the National Council of Churches, the liberal scholarship on the committee, and the omission of italics to show words added by the translators. The Nov 7, 1952 issue of the *Sword* (p. 1) carried a short review of the RSV by McIntire which pointed out three key Old Testament passages in which the deity of Christ was "consistently removed or toned down." On Nov 14, 1952 (p. 2) Rice put in an "Important Correction" in which he asked his readers for forgiveness for carrying the ad for the RSV on Oct 17, citing some of the criticisms made by McIntire previously printed in the *Sword*. Rice still maintained that the RSV was not as accurate as the KJV although he personally continued to use it for "reference and comparison." In the Nov 28, 1952 issue (p. 12) he advertised a pamphlet by McIntire, "The New Revised Standard Version—Why Christians Should Not Accept It." Later on the *Sword* published numerous articles "denouncing and showing the perversion of the RSV" (as so stated in the *Sword*, June 4, 1965, p. 7).

However in all of this comment, text types and matters pertaining to textual criticism and theories of translation were never an issue. In fact the Oct 17, 1952 ad in *The Sword of the Lord* expressly said that "inaccuracies and errors of older versions have been corrected in the light of ancient manuscripts." This statement brought no notice whatever, much less objection.

[15] Geddes MacGregor, *The Bible in the Making* (Philadelphia: J. B. Lippincott, 1959), p. 183.

Fundamentalists have always contended this."[16] Another, Stewart Custer, wrote a booklet setting forth the errors of attributing inspiration and inerrancy to the Authorized Version.[17] Paul Tassel, then the National Representative for the General Association of Regular Baptist Churches, issued a call to resist the "new fundamentalists" who were making the KJV issue a test of fellowship. He called also for a rallying around the doctrine of the verbal inerrancy of the Scriptures in the original manuscripts.[18]

The 75th annual meeting (1995) of the Fundamental Baptist Fellowship passed a resolution on the issue that reflects and reiterates the historic fundamentalist position. It says in part:

> In light of the considerable discussion among fundamentalists about the issue of manuscripts and textual theories, no particular belief about the best textual theory should be elevated to the place of becoming a core fundamentalist belief. Fundamentalists may hold the doctrine of inspiration with equal strength without embracing the same belief about textual criticism. Additionally, proper evaluation of the doctrinal integrity of any particular English translation can only be done by examining its faithfulness to the original languages, not by comparing it to another English translation. While the process of comparing it with other translations may be profitable for matters of clarity and readability, this process cannot pass as the test of doctrinal accuracy since it is illegitimate to check one copy by another; one must compare the copy to the original. In a day when translations abound, fundamentalists must exercise careful discernment in both the selection and rejection of translations. Some professing fundamentalists have wrongfully declared one translation to be the only inspired copy of God's Word in the English language and have sought to make this a test of fundamentalism. Since no translation can genuinely claim what only may be said of the original, inspired writings, any attempt to make a particular English translation the only acceptable translation of fundamentalism must be rejected.

The danger facing certain fundamentalists who wish to elevate a particular version or text type to a special, miraculous, God-protected status is that of confusing inspiration with preservation and thereby compromising verbal inspiration and inerrancy. Inspiration is a miracle of God by which He caused His propositional revelation to be written and recorded without error in the original human languages. Inspiration was a direct work of the Holy Spirit on the biblical authors (2 Pet 1:21). Biblical inspiration was a confluence of God and the human writer in a unitary authorship that resulted in a miraculous, inerrant product with a divine and a human aspect.

---

[16] Edward M. Panosian, "What Is the Inspired Word of God?" *Faith For the Family* (Feb 1979), p. 3. See also other articles that were negative toward the King James-only position (July–Aug 1979; Oct 1979; July–Aug 1982).

[17] Stewart Custer, *The Truth About the King James Version Controversy* (Greenville, SC: Bob Jones University Press, 1981).

[18] Paul Tassel, "Information Bulletin" (Sept 1981). He issued a similar plea in *The Baptist Bulletin* (Oct 1981, p. 10).

Copyists, translators, and revisers had no such ministry of the Spirit nor was any promise made by God for it. As a result, mistranslation, miscopying, or misprinting has crept into every version and reproduction of the biblical text, however minor.[19] Thus to attribute either direct inspiration or miraculous preservation to any translation or reproduction would appear to deny verbal inerrancy, given the inevitability of these mistakes. This seems to create the anomaly of affirming both a miracle (inspiration or preservation) and a non-miraculous result (erroneous versions). The biblical and historic fundamentalist approach is that copies and reproductions of the text *providentially* derive inspiration and authority in linear fashion from previous copies and reproductions to the extent that they accurately convey the autographs which were directly, *miraculously* given by God.

Controversy over text, text types, and translations of the Bible is one of fundamentalism's greatest present distractions. Historically, this has been a non-issue and, in the interests of the integrity of the Bible and the future of the fundamentalist movement, should remain so.

CALVINISM AND ARMINIANISM

Fundamentalism has never had a united voice on Calvinism-Arminianism issues although by and large it has been moderately Calvinistic, probably three or four-point Calvinism. But some have been five-point Calvinists and others outright Arminians. While there have been provincial skirmishes on the subject,[20] fundamentalism has never spoken with anything like unanimity on it. Occasionally someone may assert that fundamentalism is too Calvinistic or excessively Arminian,[21] but these complaints often reflect a local brush fire or a fundamentalist turf war of some kind. Robert

---

[19] Some were not so minor, such as the omission of the word "not" in the Seventh Commandment (Exod 20:14) of the 1631 edition of the King James Version, earning that translation the dubious label of "The Wicked Bible." See David Ewert, *From Ancient Tablets To Modern Translations* (Grand Rapids: Zondervan, 1983), p. 202.

[20] The General Association of Regular Baptist Churches went through some stress on this subject in the 1970s. See Kenneth H. Good, *Are Baptists Calvinists?* (Oberlin, OH: Regular Baptist Heritage Fellowship, 1975) (a pro-Calvinist stance), and the definitive but favorable review by Gregg J. Farrier in *The Baptist Reformation Review* 4 (Winter 1975). For the Arminian response to the controversy, see Robert L. Sumner's anti-Calvinist review of Good in *The Biblical Evangelist* (Jan 1976, p. 4). His *An Examination of Tulip* (Brownsburg, IN: Biblical Evangelist Press, 1972) is a general attack on five-point Calvinism. The issue subsided after the Association in 1975 voted down a proposed article of faith supporting unconditional election.

[21] For example, Douglas McLachlan, *Reclaiming Authentic Fundamentalism* (Independence, MO: American Ass'n of Christian Schools, 1993), lists "excessive Calvinism" as one of the "stifling factors" to authentic evangelism along with pervasive materialism, oppressive fundamentalism, and traditionalism (pp. 57–69).

Delnay put the matter in proper perspective when he wrote, "And wherever we [fundamentalists] find ourselves along the line between strong Arminianism and strong Calvinism, we have tried to treat each other with Christian grace; and even though somebody must be in error, we have refused to divide over that matter."[22] While individual fundamentalists and specific groups or institutions may rightfully take a definitive position on certain Calvinism-Arminianism issues, these have not achieved the status of fundamentalist articles of faith. In terms of the movement, they are non-issues.

DENOMINATIONAL DISTINCTIVES AND POLITY

Fundamentalism has been non-denominational/interdenominational as a movement. Humanly speaking, this was probably unavoidable given the transdenominational character of liberalism and the need to combat it on different denominational fronts.

The speakers and leaders of the Bible Conference era out of which fundamentalism formally emerged were mainly Baptists and Presbyterians, but representatives of the Congregationalists, Methodists, Lutherans, Dutch Reformed, and Anglicans, among others, could also be found.[23] The fundamentalist-modernist controversy largely took place among the northern Baptists and the northern Presbyterians. This does not mean that all fundamentalists could and did cooperate organizationally with each other in every endeavor. Nor does it suggest that they must and do hold hands in every common cause today. Most separatist Baptists today would explain that "fundamentalist" does not go far enough in positionalizing them and would hastily say they are "fundamental Baptists." But that is not to deprecate the term and connotations of fundamentalism. The majority of fundamentalists today are probably Baptists. Baptists and baptistic fellowships have been the predominant stratum for quite some time. But it would be a mistake to make denominational distinctives and polity part of the *sine qua non* of fundamentalism.

PREMILLENNIALISM AND DISPENSATIONALISM

The nearly unanimous consensus on eschatology in fundamentalism has been premillennial, and the major portion of that consensus has been dispensational. This viewpoint has dominated the Bible Conference era and the Bible Institute/Training School/College movement even to this

---

[22] Robert G. Delnay, "Ecclesiastical Separation," *Faith Pulpit* (July–Aug 1987) [published by the Faith Baptist Theological Seminary].

[23] Beale, *In Pursuit of Purity,* pp. 47–67.

day. There have been exceptions. T. T. Shields was amillennial as was J. Gresham Machen, although the latter somewhat disdained the title fundamentalist.[24] The Free Presbyterians of today have amillennialism in their ranks along with premillennialism, but their fundamentalist credentials are not questioned because of it.

One could say that fundamentalism has been characterized by premillennialism, especially through its legacy from the Bible Conference movement. But the premillennialism of the Bible conferences was not always solidly dispensational. The Niagara Bible Conference, for example, broke up in 1900 over the tribulation issue, with A. C. Gaebelein taking the pretribulational aspects to Sea Cliff, New York, and beginning the Sea Cliff Bible Conference in 1901.[25] There were also pretribulational premillennial fundamentalists who were not dispensational. John R. Rice is one such example.[26] The current revisionism going on in certain dispensational circles known as "progressive dispensationalism" raises serious doubts in some minds, including my own, if it is actually dispensationalism anymore.[27] It seems to make far-reaching concessions to covenant theology. But neither the tenets of dispensationalism nor covenant theology are part of the defining doctrine of the fundamentalist movement.

It would appear to be unwise to cast fundamentalism into an exclusive mold of dispensational premillennialism.[28] Distinctions and convictions on eschatology can and must be maintained individually and institutionally, but they have not been definitive rubrics for fundamentalism as a movement.

---

[24] Daryl G. Hart put it interestingly: "Machen himself did not like the term *fundamentalism* because it suggested 'some strange new sect.' Yet when forced to choose between fundamentalism and modernism, he admitted he was a fundamentalist 'of the most pronounced type'" (*Defending the Faith: J. Gresham Machen and the Crisis of Conservative Protestantism in Modern America* [Grand Rapids: Baker, 1994], p. 63).

[25] David O. Beale, *In Pursuit of Purity*, pp. 29, 35.

[26] John R. Rice, "Not Landmark Nor Dispensational," *The Sword of the Lord* (Mar 15, 1975). He said clearly, "I do not regard myself as a dispensationalist" (p. 11).

[27] Charles C. Ryrie, *Dispensationalism* (Chicago: Moody Press, 1995), p. 162. See also Bruce A. Waltke, "A Response," in *Dispensationalism, Israel and the Church* (Grand Rapids: Zondervan, 1992), p. 348.

[28] William R. Sandeen's thesis is that fundamentalism grew out of the British and American millenarianism of 1800–1930 as coalesced in the Bible Institute movement. See his *The Roots of Fundamentalism* (Grand Rapids: Baker reprint, 1978). John Fea regards Sandeen's proposal as reductionist ("Understanding the Changing Facade of Twentieth-Century American Protestant Fundamentalism: Toward A Historical Definition," *Trinity Journal* 15 [Fall 1994], p. 188).

THE MORAL EFFICACY OF THE PHYSICAL
BLOOD OF CHRIST

In the 1980s the issue concerning the physical blood of Christ arose in fundamentalism. It had to do with the preservation of His literal blood and the efficacy of its material components to make payment for sin and grant a genuine remission of ethical guilt.

It appears that fundamentalists have always generally held that the physical blood of Christ was literally shed on the cross and that the phrase "blood of Christ" stood principally for His sacrificial death for sin.[29] One of the earliest notices of Christ offering His own physical blood in the heavenly courts was by J. Vernon McGee in 1937.[30] The moral efficacy of Christ's literal blood was also addressed by M. R. DeHaan.[31] R. B. Thieme, Jr., in the early 1970s, openly deprecated the physical blood of Christ, but this had little influence, if any, on fundamentalism as a whole although there was some reaction from certain fundamentalists.[32] In the mid 1970s John MacArthur drew a theological distinction between Christ's physical bleeding and His atoning death as far as eternal saving

---

[29] The shedding of Christ's blood in sacrificial atonement is that of a sinless, infinitely meritorious life yielded up in death in the place of the guilty sinner. For an early source on the meaning of the blood of Christ, see Dyson Hague, "At-One-Ment By Propitiation," in *The Fundamentals,* 3:78–97. The expression he most often used is "death of Christ" and is obviously in synonymy with "blood of Christ." Hague says, "This atonement consisted in the shedding of blood. The blood-shedding was the effusion of life; for the life of the flesh is in the blood." Later on the same page he noted: "Shed blood represented the substitution of an innocent for a guilty life" (p. 79).

[30] J. Vernon McGee, "Theology of the Tabernacle," *Bibliotheca Sacra* 94 (April–June 1937), pp. 169–74.

[31] M. R. DeHaan, *The Chemistry of the Blood* (Grand Rapids: Zondervan, 1943), pp. 9–44. DeHaan taught that sin resided in the literal physical blood of human beings (pp. 13–14). He also held that this blood is contributed by the father to the child (p. 31ff.) so that all people except Christ have Adam's sinful blood coursing in their veins (p. 13). Jesus, not having a human father, did not have human blood and therefore was sinless because "the Holy Spirit contributed the blood of Jesus" (p. 36); His blood was "directly from God" (p. 41). He "escaped having one single drop of Adam's human blood within Him" (p. 26); He was "without one drop of human blood in His veins" (p. 25). Christ's blood, being non-human, was materially and ethically sinless and thus could make atonement for sinners. DeHaan's views were never widely accepted because they contradicted both theology and genuine biological science. In the early 1950s, when I was in Bible college, the president of the school took a chapel to address the basic problems of DeHaan's views.

[32] John R. Rice, "Colonel Thieme Again," *The Sword of the Lord* (Oct 20, 1972), p. 5; Robert G. Walter, "The False Themes of Pastor Thieme!" *The Baptist Bulletin* (Oct 1972); and Stewart Custer, *What's Wrong With the Teaching of R. B. Thieme, Jr.?"* (Greenville, SC: Bob Jones University Press, 1972).

efficacy was concerned.[33] But it was not until the mid to late 1980s that his views were made a point of controversy within fundamentalism.

There are fundamentalists today who do not believe that the physical/chemical components of Christ's blood in and of themselves give it its power to forgive sin.[34] The blood of Christ is efficacious because of His infinitely meritorious life which was yielded up in a sacrificial, atoning death in the place of the guilty sinner. The reason that animal blood could not finally expiate sin (Heb 10:4) is that it had no such moral worth (Heb 9:25–26; 10:10, 12). The efficacy of the death of Christ on the cross is in His perfect *obedience* to the moral law of God (Rom 5:19; Phil 2:8) so that infinite merit was earned (Rom 8:4; 1 Cor 1:30; 2 Cor 5:21) and payment for the guilt of God's broken law was made (Rom 8:1–3; 1 Pet 3:18). Both forgiveness and merit are necessary to go to heaven; both remission and righteousness are required to stand before God. Jesus kept all the positive demands of God's moral law (Matt 3:15; John 8:46) and paid the last farthing of its penal sanctions in an infinite substitutionary death (1 Pet 1:19; Rom 6:23). Because of this there is "power in the blood."

On the other hand, there are fundamentalists who do believe that the material/chemical elements of the physical blood of Christ have eternal moral saving efficacy.[35] These would generally hold that Christ's literal blood is divine and not human blood, totally unlike the physical blood of the rest of the human race, and as such has the ability in and of itself to bring about remission of sin.

The field on this subject is full of theological land mines having to do with the full and complete humanity of Christ. Fundamentalists have always insisted on the full and complete deity of Jesus of Nazareth, but some are apparently oblivious of the problems with not affirming His genuine and total humanity. Some of these problems concern the integrity of His person as the God-man, that is, One with a fully human nature and a

---

[33] John MacArthur, "Letter To A Learning Member," *Today* (May 1976). See also, among others, *The MacArthur New Testament Commentary: Hebrews* (Chicago: Moody Press, 1983), p. 237, and his article, "I Believe In the Precious Blood," *Grace To You* (Summer 1988). His point was that the physical blood of Christ did not have magical or mystical saving power, that it was not materially preserved in heaven, and that the expression "shedding of blood" was not simply a reference to bleeding but to violent death in sacrificial atonement.

[34] Daniel T. Borkert and Ken R. Pulliam, "The Blood of Christ," *Calvary Baptist Theological Journal* 3 (Fall 1987). See also Samuel Fisk, "The Blood of Christ," *Biblical Evangelist* (April 1, 1990), p. 3.

[35] Curtis Hutson, "Editor Answers Dr. John MacArthur," *The Sword of the Lord* (March 4, 1988), p. 1.

fully divine nature united inseparably in an indivisible person. Any denial or diminishing of His full humanity is to that extent a denigration of the hypostatic union and thus His person as the God-man. Furthermore, the integrity of His person as the God-man is necessary to enable His death to provide an ethical basis of atonement for human sin. If He is less than fully human, He could not atone for human sin. And that calls into question the moral justice of His forgiveness of human sin.[36]

The doctrinal implications of denying the genuine and complete humanity of the physical blood of Jesus Christ are far-reaching indeed. Most who attribute deity to His material blood do not seem to be aware of the depth of the problem they are causing themselves. In a theological sense this whole matter, as in other doctrinal matters, can become a profoundly serious issue because of the factors outlined above, factors dealing with the person of Christ, atonement, and forgiveness of sin. But it should not become such an issue or a load-bearing point in the fundamentalist structure.

LORDSHIP SALVATION

This is a phrase that has become attached to an issue that really has to do with the essence or genius of saving faith. The real question is, does saving faith involve a commitment of oneself, a trust in and an obedience to the sovereign Savior, or are these to be reserved for an experience subsequent to salvation? Is the title "Lord" an expression of the deity of Christ only or is it also of the claims He makes on a would-be follower? Is discipleship synonymous with believing or is it something a Christian enters into at a crisis experience of consecration after the initial salvation experience? Fundamentalists are divided on the issue,[37] but the greater question here is, is a particular position on this matter a necessary part of fundamentalism's self-identity? The answer historically has been no.

---

[36] For a good handling of the meaning of "the blood of Christ," see Leon Morris, *The Apostolic Preaching of the Cross* (Grand Rapids: Eerdmans, 1955), pp. 108–24. For the necessity of His full humanity, see Wayne Grudem, *Systematic Theology* (Grand Rapids: Zondervan, 1994), pp. 540–43. Loraine Boettner framed the necessity of both His full humanity and deity in almost classic fashion: "It was necessary that the Redeemer of mankind should be both human and Divine. It was necessary that He be human if He was actually to take man's place and suffer and die, for Deity as such was not capable of that. And it was necessary that He should be Divine if His suffering and death were to have infinite value" (*Studies in Theology* [Philadelphia: Presbyterian & Reformed, 1964], pp. 198–99; see also p. 203).

[37] John G. Balyo, "Lord of All," *The Baptist Bulletin* (Mar 1989), p. 23 (favorable). Manfred E. Kober, "Lordship Salvation: A Forgotten Truth or a False Doctrine?" *Faith Pulpit* (Mar 1989; Apr–May 1989) (unfavorable).

There is evidently a certain amount of semantic confusion among fundamentalists on the issue. The real heart of the controversy seems to be whether or not saving faith has a genuinely significant volitional element, leaving aside for the moment the meaning of Jesus Christ as "Lord" (Rom 10:9, 12; 1 Cor 12:3) and what constitutes "discipleship" (Matt 28:19). The common testimony of theologians, at least since the Reformation, is that faith must converge on biblical content as well as have a personal assent and a volitional reliance or commitment. Even non-lordship proponents recognize this.[38] If it is agreed that trust is ultimately the defining ingredient of saving faith, and it seems difficult to avoid the conclusion that this faith commitment in principle cannot be less than total, there appears to be more consensus on the issue than is usually recognized.

Saving faith is a complete reliance on the finished work of Christ as revealed in the Scriptures that precludes all vestiges of self-help. Put another way, how much *doubt* can one entertain about the truth claims and saving work of Christ and still exercise genuine faith, since any degree of doubt is not simply a lesser amount of faith but a frontal assault on true faith? This is especially poignant since saving faith is termed "obedience" in numerous contexts (Acts 5:32; 6:7; Rom 1:5; 15:18; Heb 5:9) and, conversely, unbelief is called "disobedience" (John 3:36; Heb 3:18–19). Fundamentalists probably have more unanimity on this issue than they realize, but in the last analysis it is not a defining element.

CONCLUSION

The founders and early leaders of fundamentalism were very solicitous about Bible doctrine. For that reason they gave first place to matters of faith. Failure to do so can result only in decline and eventual malaise. This has already happened before our eyes to the new evangelicalism. It has experienced a doctrinal collapse in recent years, mostly at the hands of the psychological self movement and the market-oriented philosophy of church growth.[39] It is difficult to find evangelical publishers whose name you can really trust.[40] And one wonders how much longer Clark Pinnock,

---

[38] Zane C. Hodges, *Absolutely Free* (Grand Rapids: Zondervan, 1989), pp. 31, 38–39. Charles C. Ryrie, *Basic Theology* (Wheaton, IL: Victor, 1987), pp. 326–27.

[39] David F. Wells, *No Place For Truth* (Grand Rapids: Eerdmans, 1993). This is a withering analysis of evangelicalism's doctrinal woes.

[40] InterVarsity Press seems to be making a name for the avant-garde in evangelical theological novelties. Books such as *Revisioning Evangelical Theology* by Stanley J. Grenz (1993) and *The Openness of God* by Clark Pinnock, et al. (1994) make doctrinal proposals not heard of before in historic evangelical circles. Eerdmans departed from its publishing philosophy decades ago.

for example, will go on claiming to be, and be recognized as, an evangelical, given his leftward pilgrimage of the last twenty-five years or so.

Lest fundamentalists be tempted to infer that the doctrinal non-issues in
the movement can become an excuse for a general doctrinal complacency,
consider the example of one fundamentalist institution that crossed over to
the less restrictive and more inclusive (developing) new evangelicalism in
the late 1940s and 50s. This happened during a relatively few years after
the passing of its leader. W. B. Riley, founder of the Northwestern Bible
Training School in Minneapolis in 1902, was a great fundamentalist leader
and a militant defender of the faith against modernism. The foundation of
his ministry was always doctrinal. While interdenominational in much of
his practice, he based it on doctrine when most others were purely pragmatic. That is, he fellowshipped with those who held to the same biblical
core of fundamental truth that he did. It was his intent and burden that
his successor at Northwestern Schools be a doctrinally oriented fundamentalist. This proved not to be the case. Following his death in 1947,
his immediate successor (Billy Graham) and those thereafter did not have
strong doctrinal moorings. As a result Northwestern went in a different
direction from its founder, and today it is most unlikely that it will return
to the fundamentalist convictions and practices of its early years.[41]

Fundamentalism's doctrinal saga suggests at least two lessons applicable to this study. One, doctrine is extremely important. It is very easy
for doctrinal matters to give way to the "practical" when the concerns of
lost and hurting people are all around. This relaxation of doctrine soon
shows up not only in how ministry is done but also in how it is prepared
for. Christian college and seminary curricula are constantly pressured to
reduce content courses in favor of methods courses. But the track record
of such proposals is not very good. The practical usually comes at the
expense of slow but sure doctrinal disintegration. "How-to-do-it" and relational courses tend to suffocate a curriculum by the sheer momentum and
weight of their appeal. Two, fundamentalists must be doctrinally grounded
so that what should be non-issues do not rise to be become divisive turf
wars. Some would-be fundamentalist leaders and spokesmen are actually
skating near the thin ice of heresy and seem totally unaware of where
they are going. Biblical and theological ignorance can rapidly lead to a

---

[41] For an excellent chronicle of the turn-about of Northwestern Schools and related
incidents, see Dell G. Johnson, "Fundamentalist Responses in Minnesota to the Developing
New Evangelicalism" (Th.D. dissertation, Central Baptist Theological Seminary of
Minneapolis, 1982).

situation where a non-issue suddenly becomes the big issue and division results.

Fundamentalism has a core of crucial orthodox doctrines or biblical teachings that are clear and unambiguous, centered principally on the Scriptures and Jesus Christ. These do not of themselves comprise the full identity of the movement, but a denial of any of them calls into serious question any claim to be a fundamentalist. At the same time there are other doctrinal distinctives that some may claim for themselves as fundamentalists. But to make these beliefs articles of fundamentalist faith would cut the movement's channel more narrowly than history will allow.

WILLIAM JENNINGS BRYAN AND THE SCOPES TRIAL: A FUNDAMENTALIST PERSPECTIVE[1]

Gerald L. Priest

During the last few years of the life of William Jennings Bryan (1860–1925), when the Fundamentalist–Modernist controversy was at its height, few men linked science with creationism (or Adamism as some evolutionists called it).[2] Very little scientific formulae and geological evidence for creationism were available in Bryan's day.[3] His critics suggest that, even if the facts were available, he would not have used them. His final and sufficient defense for divine creation was Genesis; God's answer was enough. Evolutionists were critical of fundamentalists for their "unscientific" approach to the biological origin and development of species, while the latter, under the leadership of Bryan, adamantly maintained that any system which contradicts the biblical account of creation cannot be true. Although the Bible, they said, is not a textbook on science, it nevertheless speaks authoritatively on any subject it addresses because it is divinely inspired and can be clearly understood.[4] Whenever it makes

---

[1] This article appeared in the 1999 issue of *DBSJ*, vol. 4, pp. 51–83.

[2] L. Sprage DeCamp, *The Great Monkey Trial* (Garden City, NY: Doubleday, 1968), p. 493.

[3] During the trial, Bryan did cite self-taught geologist and Seventh Day Adventist George McCready Price (1870–1963) as an opponent of evolution. The most systematic and comprehensive of Price's two dozen anti-evolution books was *The New Geology* (1923), written shortly before the trial. Price made many valid assertions that have now been accepted by creation scientists, but evolutionary geologists refused to take him seriously because of his lack of scientific credentials (Ronald L. Numbers, "Creationism in 20th–Century America," *Science* 218 [November 1982]: 539–40).

[4] Bryan believed in the Protestant hermeneutic of the perspicuity of Scripture, that most biblical statements are plain, self-interpreting, and self-authenticating. The Bible was clear about divine creation. This truth is not only perspicuous but it is immutable, and any so-called scientific view that attempted to circumvent or distort it was condemned by fundamentalists. Bryan's anti-evolution arguments rested on what he considered the popular belief in America that a literally interpreted Bible was the final authority and "court of appeal" on any issue (Nathan O. Hatch and Mark A. Noll, "Introduction," and George M. Marsden, "Everyone One's Own Interpreter? The Bible, Science, and Authority in Mid-Nineteenth-Century America," in *The Bible in America: Essays in Cultural History,* ed. Nathan O. Hatch and Mark A. Noll [New York: Oxford University Press, 1982], pp. 4–5, 9, 80–81). Marsden argues that science and biblical authority were compatible until the assumption of the "Baconian ideal" that made the sciences "neutral and freed from religious review at their starting points. Faith in the Bible was not in principle antagonistic to scientific

statements bearing on scientific questions (such as the origin of man), it is absolutely trustworthy. To contradict it is to impugn the character of God and undermine Christian doctrine. Bryan, therefore, refused to call evolution a science or even a theory but only a hypothesis.[5] This refusal, rooted deeply in a firm commitment to a literal interpretation of Scripture and a personal faith in Jesus Christ, led the Great Commoner into confrontation with evolution proponents, culminating in the famous Scopes trial of July 10–21, 1925.[6]

Much of what has been written about Bryan's fundamentalism and his involvement in the trial is superficial, tainted by invective and ridicule of the man's character and intelligence. The sensational atmosphere connected with the trial coupled with adverse press coverage has tended to give a distorted rather than an accurate view of Bryan,[7] the classic misrepresentation being the play and movie, *Inherit the Wind.*[8] Paul

---

inquiry. If, however, it was made to rest so heavily on the latest scientific findings it was always liable to disruption.... For nineteenth-century Americans this vulnerability became startlingly apparent with the coming of Darwinism—science without the tacit Christian premises of design and purpose." The result was that the preeminent place of biblical authority in academia lost out to autonomous intellectual inquiry apart from revelation (see ibid., p. 94). Bryan believed there was yet, in early twentieth century America, a popular consensus of reliance on biblical authority sufficient to counter scientific speculation.

[5] W. J. Bryan, *Seven Questions in Dispute* (New York: Fleming H. Revell, 1924), pp. 153–54. Bryan states this in his opening speech at the Scopes trial as well. Fundamentalists saw no contradiction between true verifiable science and the Bible. "Religion and science are not in conflict with each other," Curtis Lee Laws wrote ("Science and Religion," *Watchman–Examiner* 13 [July 23, 1925]: 941). Since evolution was not factual, but conjecture, it could not be science. See A. C. Dixon, "The Whole Christ and the Whole Bible for the Whole World" and L. W. Munhall, "The Bible and Science," in *Scriptural Inspiration Versus Scientific Imagination: Messages Delivered at the Great Christian Fundamentals Conference at Los Angeles, California* (Los Angeles: Biola Book Room, 1922), pp. 103–07, 121–29. Both Dixon and Munhall believed that the Bible was scientific since the works of God as stated in Scripture are observable and verifiable. Munhall said what most fundamentalists avowed: "The Bible is not a text-book for the schools, upon the physical sciences; but, it has not a little to say about the works of God, and what it does say, is said accurately and well, and can always be relied upon" (p. 122).

[6] See C. Allyn Russell, "William Jennings Bryan: Statesman–Fundamentalist," in *Modern American Protestantism and Its World: Fundamentalism and Evangelicalism,* ed. Martin E. Marty (Munich: K. G. Saur, 1993), pp. 78–79.

[7] For a detailed description of the phenomenal publicity associated with Dayton and the trial, see Edward J. Larson, *Summer of the Gods: The Scopes Trial and America's Continuing Debate Over Science and Religion* (Cambridge, MA: Harvard University Press, 1997), pp. 87–110.

[8] Jerome Lawrence and Robert E. Lee, *Inherit the Wind* (New York: Random House, 1955). The movie came out in 1960.

Waggoner points out that cynical analyses of the trial and Bryan by liberal commentators are guilty of caricaturing not only Bryan, but of fundamentalism as a whole. That is, they defined the movement by what they considered the "Dayton debacle" instead of interpreting the trial by a fair assessment of fundamentalism.[9] Beginning in the 1960s, however, historians began a more realistic appraisal of Bryan and the trial. The first significant revisionist study was made by Lawrence Levine, who challenged nearly every stereotype, every liberal carica- ture, and found them wanting.[10] Other biographers, following Levine's lead, have handled Bryan and the trial responsibly by placing the Great Commoner and his views in the larger contexts of (1) his humanitarian contributions as a Christian statesman[11] and (2) his place in fundamen- talism's crusade against evolution as malevolent to American society. Not many fundamentalists have written on Bryan and the trial.[12] The few who have addressed these subjects have perpetuated the consensus view

---

[9] Paul M. Waggoner, "The Historiography of the Scopes Trial: A Critical Re- Evaluation," *Trinity Journal* 5 (Autumn 1984): 164, esp. n. 3, and 166. Ernest Sandeen wrote, "No stereotype of the Fundamentalist dies harder than the picture provided by the Scopes trial" (*The Roots of American Fundamentalism: British and American Millenarianism, 1800–1930* [reprint of 1970 ed., Grand Rapids: Baker, 1978]), p. xv.

[10] Lawrence Levine, *Defender of the Faith, William Jennings Bryan: The Last Decade, 1915–1925* (New York: Oxford, 1965). Cf. Waggoner, "Historiography of the Scopes Trial," pp. 168–69. Waggoner describes Levine's treatment as "simply suggestive, other times overly cautious, but often simply brilliant." Other writers disarming the old stereotypes are Ferenc Szasz in several essays and his monograph, *The Divided Mind of Protestant America 1880–1930* (Tuscaloosa: University of Alabama Press, 1982), pp. 92–125; Paola E. Coletta in his comprehensive three volume work *William Jennings Bryan,* especially volume 3: *Political Puritan, 1915–1925* (Lincoln: University of Nebraska Press, 1969); and Willard H. Smith, who gives probably the most sympathetic treatment, in his *Social and Religious Thought of William Jennings Bryan* (Lawrence, KS: Coronado Press, 1975).

[11] According to Coletta, it was Bryan's evangelical Christianity that drove his social progressivism: "His [Bryan's] uniqueness lay in his double dedication, first to his God, second to the ideal of imbuing America's domestic and foreign relations with Christian ethics and morality. In each case he was a humanitarian" (cited in Robert D. Linder, "Fifty Years After Scopes: Lessons to Learn, A Heritage to Reclaim," *Christianity Today* 19 [July 18, 1975]: 9). It was in his role as humanitarian that Bryan defended personal property rights and promoted world peace. As secretary of state (1913–1915) under Wilson, he negotiated arbitration treaties with thirty nations. As a moral reformer, he stood against alcohol and promoted women's suffrage. Bryan believed that "the humblest citizen in all the land, when clad in the armor of a righteous cause, is stronger than all the hosts of error" (cited in ibid., p. 10).

[12] George Dollar does not treat the Scopes trial at all and mentions Bryan only briefly (*A History of Fundamentalism in America* [Greenville, SC: Bob Jones University Press, 1973], p. 309).

that "the fundamentalist movement was brought to an abrupt halt in 1925 at the Scopes Trial,"[13] due in large part to Bryan's supposed incompetent testimony which ostensibly humiliated the fundamentalists. However, I believe that this estimate is inaccurate. Fundamentalism did not wane; on the contrary, it experienced unprecedented growth partly *because* of Bryan's part in the trial, not in spite of it. Moreover, Bryan is worthy of vindication (1) when we measure his involvement in the trial by his consistent orthodoxy and his insistence upon the preservation of historic biblical Christianity as a moral force in America against a conspiracy of modernism he believed threatened it, and (2) when we consider that many of his warnings against evolution as detrimental to the moral fabric of society have been corroborated.[14]

Interpretation of important issues is subject to prejudice. The participation of Bryan in the Scopes trial is no exception. And because the trial involved such opposing views of far-reaching consequence, retaining an unbiased opinion is virtually impossible. One has only to sample the myriad accounts of the event and its principals to understand this. The trial was a battle between two great conflicting ideologies: the one conceiving an epistemology derived from unchanging absolutes and faith in a supernatural creator God as revealed in the Bible; the other, envisioning a universe of naturalistic origin and development and characterized by religious agnosticism.[15] The parties representing these beliefs were the fundamentalists on the one hand, centering hope in their champion Bryan, and the modernists, on the other, looking to Clarence Darrow who, in the name of academic freedom, would marshal the attack against fundamental Christianity. Each hated intensely what the other stood for. The Scopes trial, therefore, was a contest between two opposing world views.[16]

---

[13] Jerry Falwell, ed. with Ed Dobson and Ed Hindson, *The Fundamentalist Phenomenon* (New York: Doubleday Galilee, 1981), pp. 75–76. David Beale commends Bryan for his defense of Christianity, but writes that the Scopes trial was only a Pyrrhic victory for fundamentalism, and Bryan's death shortly after was a bad omen for the movement (*In Pursuit of Purity: American Fundamentalism Since 1850* [Greenville, SC: Unusual Publications, 1986], pp. 220–22).

[14] See Allen Birchler, "The Anti-Evolutionary Beliefs of William Jennings Bryan," *Nebraska History* 54 (April 1973): 545–59. The "conspiracy view," held by most fundamentalist leaders of the 1920s, including Bryan, proposed that modernists were plotting the overthrow of conservative Christianity in favor of materialistic and agnostic philosophies. For further comments on this phenomenon, see Smith, *Social and Religious Thought,* p. 188; Levine, *Defender of the Faith,* pp. 268, 347; and Stewart Cole, *The History of Fundamentalism* (Westport, CT: Greenwood Press, 1931), p. 308.

[15] DeCamp, *Monkey Trial,* p. 490.

[16] Warren Allem, "Backgrounds of the Scopes Trial at Dayton, Tennessee" (M.A. thesis, University of Tennessee, 1959), p. 40. This author does a commendable job of placing the issues of the trial in the broader context of the Fundamentalist–Modernist controversy. See also, Walter D. Buchanan, "The Significance of the Scopes Trial: From the Standpoint of Fundamentalism," *Current History* 23 (September 1925): 883–89.

After examining the facts connected to the trial, I believe that neither Bryan nor the fundamentalist movement proved to be a failure as a result of it. Nor was Bryan an embarrassment to the movement; on the contrary, there is every reason to believe that he added new vitality to it even after his death.

BRYAN, FUNDAMENTALIST CRUSADER

While adherents claim that fundamentalism is generally a reaffirmation of historical New Testament Christianity, it actually surfaced as a movement in the latter part of the nineteenth century, via Bible and prophetic conferences, as a protest against German rationalism (reflected in the higher critical theories of the Bible) and evolution.[17] Representatives of these schools of thought believed that Christianity should be reinterpreted according to recent "scientific" findings. This reinterpretation required that "out-dated" orthodox affirmations would have to be abandoned, followed by a relaxation of creedal requirements in denominational institutions and churches. This was the "modern" approach to Christianity; it meant the accommodation of orthodox doctrine to cultural and scientific change. A new generation of stalwart opponents rose up to contest this modernistic view, men who believed, like President James M. Gray of Moody Bible Institute, that modernism is really "a revolt against the God of Christianity."[18] In a similar vein, fundamentalist leader William B. Riley called modernism the greatest menace of the twentieth century because it is a flagrant denial of divine revelation.[19] The reason for fundamentalists' heated rhetoric against evolution was its twofold threat to both the biblical account of creation and to a civilized society. To fundamentalists, evolution was essentially and consequentially evil. It was diametrically opposed to the scriptural record of direct creation and thus its acceptance meant contradicting God's Word. Additionally, it produced a plethora of social and moral evils. Applied to society, the evolutionary dictum of "survival of the fittest" was militaristic and sinister. Most early fundamentalists

---

[17] C. Allyn Russell, *Voices of American Fundamentalism* (Philadelphia: Westminster Press, 1976), pp. 15–17; George M. Marsden, *Fundamentalism and American Culture: The Shaping of Twentieth–Century Evangelicalism 1870–1925* (Oxford: Oxford University Press, 1980), pp. 3, 5, 17–21.

[18] James M. Gray, "Modernism a Foe of Good Government," *Moody Monthly* 24 (July 1924): 545.

[19] William B. Riley, *The Menace of Modernism* (New York: Alliance Publishing, 1917), p. 2. Baptist leader A. C. Dixon made a nearly identical comment: "The modernism which is based upon evolution is the greatest menace in the world today" ("Dixon's Comments on Dr. Love's Letter," *Western Recorder* 99 [January 3, 1924]: 8).

believed it was Germany's application of this philosophy via Nietzsche that produced World War I.[20] Other implications of evolution were equally detrimental. The Bible teaches that man is immediately created by God in *his image.* If man was a descendant of an ape, he could not be a creature made in the image of God, but of a beast; at the heart of evolution, then, is an anthropological and theological perversion. If man fell because of sin, then sin is an intrusion into the human race and must be expelled by divine redemption. To the evolutionist, however, sin against a holy God is only a myth, an illusion, and therefore an atonement for it is unnecessary. Such teaching, fundamentalists preached, will undermine the Bible as the church's authority and destroy the moral foundations of civilized society.[21] Even more seriously, fundamentalists, taking their cue from Princeton theologian Charles Hodge, identified Darwinism as atheism. Hodge argued that Darwinism was atheistic not only because it is utterly inconsistent with the Scriptures, but Darwin's teaching of natural selection and corresponding denial of design in nature is virtually the denial of God.[22] Such denial is not only blasphemous, Bryan claimed, but is

---

[20] "Nietzsche carried Darwinism to its logical conclusion and denied the existence of God, denounced Christianity as the doctrine of the degenerate, and democracy as the refuge of the weakling; he overthrew all standards of morality and eulogized war as necessary to man's development" (Bryan, *Seven Questions,* p. 146). Confirming the link between Darwin and WWI were two influential works: Vernon Kellogg's *Headquarters Nights* (1917) and Benjamin Kidd's *Science of Power* (1918). For a description of how these related to the anti-evolution crusade, see Numbers, "Creationism in 20th–Century America," pp. 538–39. Interestingly, Darrow, in another "trial of the century"—the Leopold–Loeb case (1924)—pleaded mercy for the defendants whose murderous actions, he said, were due to misguided social Darwinist thinking. Ironically, since that trial, "Bryan had used Darrow's arguments about the psychological impact of the defendants' study of Nietzsche as a prime example of the need to stop teaching evolution" (Larson, *Summer of the Gods,* p. 100; cf. Mary Shiela McMahon, "King Tut and the Scopes Trial," in *Transforming Faith: The Sacred and Secular in Modern American History,* ed. M. L. Bradbury and James B. Gilbert [New York: Greenwood Press, 1989], pp. 89–90). For an incisive description of how Nietzsche's nihilism has invaded evangelicalism, see R. Albert Mohler, "Contending for Truth in an Age of Anti-Truth" in *Here We Stand: A Call from Confessing Evangelicals,* ed. James Montgomery Boice and Benjamin E. Sasse (Grand Rapids: Baker Books, 1996), pp. 59–76.

[21] Louis Gasper's definition of fundamentalism logically suggests this antipathy toward evolution: fundamentalism is "that movement which arose in opposition to liberalism, reemphasizing the inerrancy of the Scriptures, separation [from ungodliness] and Biblical miracles, especially the Virgin Birth, the physical Resurrection of Christ and the Substitutionary atonement (*The Fundamentalist Movement* [The Hague: Mouton, 1963], p. 13).

[22] Charles Hodge, *What Is Darwinism? And Other Writings on Science and Religion,* ed. Mark A. Noll and David N. Livingstone (Grand Rapids: Baker, 1994), pp. 138, 155–57.

tantamount to a practical removal of God from society, and this would inevitably result in barbarism and brutality.

In order to organize for combat and initiate strategies for defeating evolution, fundamentalists formed the World's Christian Fundamentals Association (WCFA) in 1919. Its agenda included a definite plan to purge schools, seminaries, and pulpits of liberals and heretics. The "heresy" of evolution was at the top of the list. In 1924, William Jennings Bryan made an appearance at the WCFA convention in Minneapolis. Gasper states, "This event raised the enthusiasm of the Fundamentalists to a new high. They now had a nationally known and popular figure to lead them in their crusade."[23] It was this Christian statesman who, two years before the meeting, brought fundamentalism to national attention through his relentless attacks on evolution.[24]

But why did Bryan, the silver-tongued politician, enter the ranks for the fundamentalist crusade, and in his twilight years at that? His wife, Mary Baird Bryan, tells us why in her husband's memoirs: "His soul arose in righteous indignation when he found from the many letters he received from parents all over the country that state schools were being used to undermine the religious faith of their children." Later she added that, "whenever Mr. Bryan took a stand upon any subject, the matter at once became an issue. People began to fall in line. The vigor and force of the man seemed to compel attention."[25] To the accusations of Bryan's enemies

---

Refusing to accept Darwin's random natural selection process, but admitting to what they considered compelling geological and paleontological evidence in favor of evolution, some conservatives suggested that evolution was God's method of creation, without necessarily discounting divine intervention. They believed that a Christian could therefore believe in the Bible and also believe in evolution. Some noteworthy examples are Benjamin B. Warfield, A. H. Strong, and James Orr. Bryan, however, refused to make such a concession, believing that any type of evolution is inimical to faith. "He saw the issue as a clear choice between godless materialistic Darwinian evolution or belief in a literal Bible and special creation. No other alternative existed" (L. Gordon Tait, "Evolution: Wishart, Wooster, and William Jennings Bryan," *Journal of Presbyterian History* 62 [Winter 1984]: 311).

[23] Gasper, *Fundamentalist Movement,* p. 14.

[24] Russell, *Voices,* p. 162; Ferenc Szasz, "The Scopes Trial in Perspective," *Tennessee Historical Quarterly* 30 (March 1971): 291.

[25] William Jennings Bryan and Mary Baird Bryan, *Memoirs of W. J. Bryan* (Philadelphia: John C. Winston, 1925), pp. 459, 480. Supporting this view is Norman F. Furniss's citation of James Leuba's landmark study of college students' loss of faith as the chief cause of the Great Commoner's entrance into the controversy (*The Fundamentalist Controversy, 1918–1931* [New Haven: Yale University Press, 1954], p. 17). Levine states the similar purpose of strengthening the values and faith of the common people (*Defender of the Faith,* p. 272). Russell gives a less complimentary view that Bryan was governed by the selfish motive of fulfilling a psychological need after bitter political defeats (*Voices,* p. 182).

that he was motivated to enter the anti-evolution fray because of personal ambition, demagoguery, and even senility(!), Levine responds that positing some kind of selfish compensation for his political frustrations cannot account for the activities of his final years.

> Bryan's entry into the fundamentalist crusade was neither sudden nor surprising. Bryan was raised with the common fundamentalist belief that all religious verities rested upon an infallible Bible, and if this were shaken nothing else could stand. He had objected to the theory of evolution as early as 1904, and while his later objections were more developed and specific, they were substantially the same as his earlier statements. What had changed was not Bryan's conception of evolution but his toleration of it. By 1921 he had become convinced that the evolutionary thesis was no longer a potential but an immediate threat.[26]

In his lectures and writings we find Bryan opposing evolution for several reasons. His two most famous speeches, "The Menace of Darwinism" (1921) and "The Origin of Man" (1922), and the book, *In His Image* (1922), listed them, including ones he would draw upon during the Scopes trial. In addition to standard fundamentalist arguments against evolution already mentioned, he added that evolution is only a guess at best and, more importantly, it was eliminating man's accountability to God. He declared,

> The hypothesis that links man to the lower forms of life and makes him a lineal descendent of the brute—is obscuring and weakening all the virtues that rest upon the religious tie between God and man.... [There] is no mention of religion, the only basis for morality; not a suggestion of a sense of responsibility to God—nothing but cold, clammy materialism! Darwinism transforms the Bible into a story book and reduces Christ to man's level. It gives him an ape for an ancestor.[27]

Because Bryan believed that the philosophy of evolution was contributing to the dissolution of morals in the nation's youth, he directed his offensive

---

[26] Levine, *Defender of the Faith,* p. 266. The year 1904 marked the publication of Bryan's famous "Prince of Peace" lecture wherein he objected to Darwinism "until more conclusive proof is produced." At a celebration of the Nebraska Centennial in Lincoln (March 19, 1960), William Jennings Bryan, Jr., stated that political expediency never controlled his father. "He loved his friends and gave consideration to their views, but he was adamant against any suggestion that for personal or political advantage, he soft pedal here or be silent there. He never counted the odds against him for he would cheerfully accept defeat rather than surrender a principle" (cited in Franklin Modisett, ed., *The Credo of the Commoner, William Jennings Bryan* [Los Angeles: Occidental College, 1968], p. 127).

[27] W. J. Bryan, *In His Image* (New York: Fleming H. Revell, 1922), p. 112.

against the teaching of evolution in the public schools.[28] As a populist Democrat, he advocated the right of free speech: it is "guaranteed in this country and should never be weakened." But this freedom entails personal responsibility. "The moment one takes on a representative character, he becomes obligated to represent faithfully...those who have commissioned him." The majority rules—in this case, the taxpayers—and no minority opinion that contradicts or undermines their wishes should be tolerated. He never tired of repeating, "The hand that writes the pay check rules the school."[29]

In various settings prior to the Scopes trial, Bryan was only partly successful in combating evolution. During the Presbyterian General Assembly at Indianapolis in 1923, he introduced a resolution demanding "that his church refuse to support schools that permitted the teaching of evolution 'as a proven fact.'" He cried amidst the opposition's uproar, "I am trying to save the Christian Church from those who are trying to destroy her faith."[30] Although the resolution did not pass, Bryan was effective in persuading the Assembly to reaffirm the five fundamental articles of faith which had been made a test of denominational orthodoxy in 1910. Fundamentalists assured themselves that, indirectly, points one and five supported divine creation as described in the Bible.[31] Through Bryan's influence, the Oklahoma legislature passed an anti-evolutionary textbook bill in March, 1923, and two months later his own adopted state of Florida approved a resolution he wrote forbidding the teaching of evolution as fact. Since government schools cannot teach religion, he argued, neither should they be permitted to allow religion to be attacked in the class room.[32] After addressing the North Carolina legislature, Bryan was hopeful that a similar bill would pass this body; it failed by one vote. These partial victories were one reason why Bryan welcomed the publicity of the Scopes trial. He was sure that a decision to uphold an anti-evolutionary bill in Tennessee would provide the catalyst necessary to prompt other states to enact similar legislation.

---

[28] Ibid., pp. 123–35.

[29] Bryan, *Seven Questions,* pp. 152, 154. The reference is to tax-paying parents who should have the final say about what their children are being taught in the public school.

[30] Coletta, *William Jennings Bryan. Vol. 3: Political Puritan, 1915–1925,* p. 223; Tait, "Evolution: Wishart, Wooster, and William Jennings Bryan," pp. 314–17.

[31] The first doctrine in the five-point declaration was the inerrancy of the original manuscripts of Scripture and the fifth was the reality of miracles as recorded in the Scriptures.

[32] Bryan, *Memoirs,* p. 460.

The Bryan papers between 1923 and 1925 deal extensively with the subject of evolution, especially in the correspondence with other fundamentalists. These, along with other evidence, point to the fact that the Commoner was recognized by them as a national leader of their movement. He was continually being asked to speak at fundamentalist gatherings and to take an active part in their organizations. Curtis Lee Laws, editor of the Baptist periodical *Watchman–Examiner,* wrote that "the newspapers, because of his prominence, made him the leader of interdenominational fundamentalism."[33] W. B. Riley commented after Bryan's death that he "was, while he lived, the great outstanding man of our movement, and that was particularly true of the last three years of his life."[34] Presbyterian fundamentalists Mark Matthews and Clarence E. Macartney strongly supported him; in addition to Riley, the Baptists John Roach Straton and J. Frank Norris recognized his leadership role. Straton, pastor of Calvary Baptist Church in New York City, took up the same battle and preached the same things against evolution as Bryan.[35] Norris extolled Bryan frequently in his paper *The Searchlight.* The Fort Worth pastor's invitation to Bryan to speak in his church drew a crowd of over six thousand. In a letter to Norris dated December 20, 1923, Bryan accepted the request and stated, "I am sure we will have a great meeting at Forth Worth. I am going to take as my subject, 'Is the Bible True?' and will discuss evolution under this heading because the objection to evolution is that it is undermining faith in God, the Bible, and Christ."[36] Norris responded in his usual hyperbolic flare that what Martin Luther was to the Reformation, William Jennings Bryan was to fundamentalism.[37] Bryan was frequently on the platform of the WCFA and was offered the presidency of the organization at its Memphis meeting only two months before the trial.[38]

But was Bryan really a fundamentalist? Most of his biographers agree that his brand of fundamentalism was unique: he was more conciliatory with those opposing him, he was not a premillennialist, and he advo-

---

[33] Editorial, "William Jennings Bryan," *Watchman–Examiner* 13 (August 6, 1925): 1005.

[34] Riley, "Bryan, The Great Commoner and Christian," *Christian Fundamentals in School and Church* 7 (October–December 1925): 5.

[35] John Roach Straton, *The Famous New York Fundamentalist Modernist Debates* (New York: George H. Doran, 1924–25).

[36] J. Frank Norris, editorial in *The Searchlight* 8 (January 11, 1924): 1.

[37] Ibid.

[38] W. B. Riley Sermon, Bryan papers, Library of Congress, Washington, D.C.

cated a form of the social gospel which he called "applied Christianity."[39] Nevertheless, he did not hesitate to identify with the movement, particularly in the advocacy of its essential doctrines. And he was more than willing to take up the fundamentalist attack against the common enemy of evolution. It appears that most fundamentalists were eager to have him do so.[40] Since Bryan was not a theologian, nor a pastor, and certainly not a scientist, one may legitimately ask if he was the logical choice to represent fundamentalism's cause before, not only a Tennessee jury, but an American public. Probably so. He had legal training (although he had not practiced court room law for thirty years); he was well-known nationally as the acknowledged interdenominational spokesman for fundamentalism; and he was immensely popular with most Tennesseans.[41] Finally, he had distinguished himself as a knowledgeable critic of evolution. It is true that his polemics were not scientifically informed, but he was well-acquainted with the hypotheses of Darwinism and he knew them to be antithetical to the Bible. This was his primary reference and authority for any subject, including origins: "If we accept the Bible as true we have no difficulty in determining the origin of man."[42] Yet Bryan did not rely solely on scriptural "proof texts." Theologian William Hordern, far from sympathetic with fundamentalism, nonetheless states that its leaders "have never rested their case against evolution upon blind acceptance of biblical questions. In William Jennings Bryan's *In His Image,* one finds a rational criticism of

---

[39] No doubt it was the agrarian populist mentality that influenced Bryan's view of religion. For example, he seemed to have an unbounded confidence in the civil righteousness of the American people. To him, most folks were basically good, God-fearing, and hardworking. He wrote to creationists, "Forget, if need be, the high-brows both in the political and college world, and carry this cause to the people. They are the final and efficiently corrective power" (editorial in the *Christian Fundamentalist* 2 [1929]: 13). This idealism would not have conformed to his denomination's creed regarding man's total depravity, however. But such a theological incongruity evidently did not pose a problem for him. This is very important to realize in the context of the Scopes trial. Bryan sincerely believed that he represented the "moral majority" of Americana when he spoke for the State of Tennessee as prosecuting attorney. "How could the taxpayers be morally wrong?" was a question that probably never entered his mind. He represented the "people;" Darrow represented a minority "special interest group" trying to undermine American morality.

[40] Cf. Smith, *Social and Religious Thought,* p. 181; Russell, *Voices,* p. 171; and Levine, *Defender of the Faith,* p. 251.

[41] Although Dayton itself was predominantly Republican, Bryan carried the State of Tennessee in each of his three presidential bids. See Ferenc M. Szasz, "Three Fundamentalist Leaders: The Roles of William Bell Riley, John Roach Straton, and William Jennings Bryan in the Fundamentalist–Modernist Controversy" (Ph.D. dissertation, University of Rochester, 1969), p. 242; and Furniss, *Fundamentalist Controversy,* p. 6.

[42] Bryan, *In His Image,* p. 88.

evolution.... In fact, science has come to accept some of the points made by Bryan."[43]

A few Bryan supporters thought it best that he not get involved in the trial. Methodists, some of whom were on the fringe of fundamentalism, such as southern bishop Warren A. Candler, thought Bryan better off to stay away.

> The issues were far too grave to rely upon such a spectacle.... It was clearly foolish to stake everything on a trial court which lacked the authority and ability to rule on the veracity of the theory of evolution, yet, when reported in the press, might convey to readers the impression that it could reach such a determination.[44]

So Candler turned down Bryan's request for assistance; nevertheless, Bryan believed the cause worthy of national attention in such a forum—a practice perfectly consistent with his manner of bringing all issues before the public. He wrote a friend on the eve of the trial, "[It] will be a success in proportion as it enables the public to understand the two sides and the reasons on both sides. Every question has to be settled at last by the public and the sooner it is understood the sooner it can be settled."[45] He was quoted in the *New York Times* as saying, "From this time forth the Christians will understand the character of the struggle also. In an open fight the truth will triumph."[46] It is clear that Bryan saw in the Scopes trial not merely the adjudication of a Tennessee law, but the opportunity to defend a righteous cause before a populace he believed would rally behind him once the issues were made clear.

BRYAN, TRIAL PROSECUTOR AND WITNESS

When Dayton city attorney Sue K. Hicks wrote Bryan on May 14, 1925, "We will consider it a great honor to have you with us in this prosecution," Bryan readily accepted.[47] Upon hearing this, famous Chicago lawyer and agnostic Clarence Darrow agreed to become part of the defense counsel

---

[43] William Hordern, *A Layman's Guide to Protestant Theology* (New York: Macmillan, 1955), p. 70.

[44] Mark K. Bauman, "John T. Scopes, Leopold and Loeb, and Bishop Warren A. Candler," *Methodist History* 16 (February 1978): 92–100.

[45] Bryan to Ed Howe, June 30, 1925, Grace Bryan Hargraves MSS, Bryan papers.

[46] *New York Times* editorial, July 8, 1925.

[47] Bryan, *Memoirs,* p. 483.

under the sponsorship of the American Civil Liberties Union (ACLU).[48] The WCFA countered by quickly wiring Bryan to guarantee their support of him by passing a resolution which read in part,

> We propose to employ one of the most capable of living attorneys to appear in the courts in behalf of our Association and in the interests of both Christianity and American civilization, demanding a proper consideration of this test case....We name as our attorney for this Trial William Jennings Bryan and pledge him whatever support is needful to secure equity and justice.[49]

A simple court case now took on the aura of a battle, indeed, a "duel to the death," according to Bryan.[50] What were the issues at stake that would give this trial such notoriety? To the defense it was the matter of academic freedom in the light of modern science. To Bryan it was the right of the people, speaking through their legislature, to control the schools which they create and support.[51] Ironically, both sides advocated human rights: one group, minority rights, specifically, the right of an instructor to teach what he wants; the other, the right of the majority to determine what their children would be taught. But to the fundamentalists it went beyond rights. According to Riley, "the battle...was no 'war of words,' it was no 'little scrap over the subject of freedom,' it was no dispute between scientists on the one side and the theologians on the other; it was a contention of false-hood against truth, of faith vs. atheism, of Christianity vs. brutality."[52] Letters and telegrams of support for Bryan came pouring in. The mayors of both New York and Chicago assured the Commoner of their sympathy for his crusade to protect the "plastic minds of the young" from the "seeds of doubt."[53] Norris wrote from Fort Worth, "I repeat what I said to you in Memphis; you are now in the greatest work of your life and giving

---

[48] Initially, the ACLU did not want Darrow. In early strategy meetings most of their leaders claimed that the agnostic was "too radical, a headline hunter, [and with him there] the trial would become a circus." Interestingly, the man who lobbied strongest for Darrow was Scopes himself: "It was going to be a down-in-the-mud fight, and I felt that situation demanded an Indian fighter rather than someone who graduated from the proper military academy" (cited in Larson, *Summer For The Gods,* p. 102).

[49] W. B. Riley, "The World's Christian Fundamentals Association and the Scopes Trial," *Christian Fundamentals in School and Church* 7 (July, August, September 1925): 35.

[50] Levine, *Defender of the Faith,* p. 339.

[51] See Levine, p. 331, and Ray Ginger, *Six Days or Forever? Tennessee v. John Thomas Scopes* (Boston: Beacon Press, 1958), p. 90.

[52] W. B. Riley sermon, Bryan papers.

[53] Cited in Willard B. Gatewood, Jr., ed., *Controversy in the Twenties: Fundamentalism, Modernism, and Evolution* (Nashville: Vanderbilt University Press, 1969), p. 37.

10,000 times more service to the cause of righteousness than a dozen presidents."[54] Yet Bryan stood virtually alone. Where were the other fundamentalist leaders? Bryan had written to them requesting their presence. He wired Straton in New York, asking if he could come and testify; Straton wired back that he would be delighted to come, but for some reason never arrived.[55] Bryan wanted to have Norris (who did provide a court stenographer), J. C. Massee, pastor of Tremont Temple in Boston, and W. B. Riley, but these men planned to be in Seattle to fight liberalism at the Northern Baptist Convention.[56] Princeton conservative J. Gresham Machen politely refused. James M. Gray of Moody Bible Institute declined because of "summer conference work which will keep me on the go until September."[57] Bryan wrote the sensational Presbyterian evangelist Billy Sunday, "I am wondering if you will...come if we need you."[58] Sunday replied, "Thank God for W. J. B. Sorry I cannot be there," and sent a number of anti-evolution statements for use by the prosecution.[59] The only fundamentalist of any note to come was Southern Baptist evangelist T. T. Martin. One can only speculate as to why the others left Bryan to handle the case without them. Allyn C. Russell offered the absurdity that they "probably felt unable to defend their position," when Riley and Straton had been effectively debating evolutionists for some time.[60] It is more likely that either they did not comprehend the gravity of the case or else they felt that their duties were equally important and Bryan was up to the task. It is unfortunate, however, that they did not come; it may account in part for the insistence of Bryan during the trial that no expert testimony be allowed by the defense, since he had none for the prosecution. Much of the trial analysis by some two hundred reporters and journalists centered on the carnival-like atmosphere of Dayton[61] and, in that

---

[54] Cited in Szasz, "Three Fundamentalist Leaders," p. 254.

[55] Ginger, *Six Days or Forever?* p. 101.

[56] Szasz, "Three Fundamentalist Leaders," p. 246, and Russell, *Voices,* p. 184.

[57] Statements found in correspondence with Bryan, Bryan papers.

[58] Billy Sunday papers, microfilm copies at Grace Theological Seminary, Winona Lake, Indiana.

[59] Cited in M. R. Werner, *Bryan* (New York: Harcourt and Brace, 1929), p. 318.

[60] Russell, *Voices,* p. 263, n. 93; for a discussion of Riley's and Straton's evolution debates, see pp. 93–95, and pp. 66–75 respectively.

[61] One of the defense lawyers, Arthur Garfield Hayes, described Dayton as a "revivalist circus. Thither swarmed ballyhoo artists, hot dog venders, lemonade merchants, preachers, professional atheists, college students, Greenwich Village radicals, out-of-town coal miners, I.W.W.'s, Single Taxers, 'libertarians,' revivalists of all shades and sects, hinterland 'soothsayers,' Holy Rollers, an army of newspaper men, scientists, editors and lawyers" (*Let Freedom Ring* [New York: Da Capo Press, 1972], pp. 26–27).

context, interpreted many of Bryan's statements in terms of effect rather than actual content as to consistency of position and perception of basic issues. According to early Bryan biographer J. C. Long, most of the reporters were so biased against Bryan and fundamentalism that their editorials were an unofficial witness for Darrow and the defense. They made it appear as though Bryan and his "outworn" principles were on trial, instead of Scopes.[62] Warren Allem quotes from an editorial in the *New Republic* that journalists

> have schemed and labored to present the court proceedings to American opinion in the guise of a melodrama in which William J. Bryan, the Attorney General of Tennessee, and Judge Raulston are portrayed as reprobates who are conspiring to convict and punish an innocent man, and deprive the jury and the American people of the evidence in the case. What they have actually succeeded in doing is to cheapen not only the trial but the issue by subordinating both of them to the exigencies of theatrical newspaper publicity.[63]

It is this impression of the trial and of Bryan in particular that has endured in the minds of many. Regrettably, however, fundamentalists have evidently not researched the trial very carefully to find out what Bryan actually said, and have settled for not dealing with the trial at all (as in the case of George Dollar, noted earlier) or have merely cited the standard prejudicial sources. Bryan probably should never have agreed to be examined by Darrow. Many of the questions were ridiculous and designed to intimidate. However, upon close examination of Bryan's statements in both the prosecution speeches and the responses to Darrow, one can determine that (1) nearly all of them were perfectly consistent with beliefs he had articulated all during his three–year crusade against evolution. (2) They were legally factual and rationally arguable in a court of law, and more importantly, (3) where they addressed religion, his remarks were in total accord with the consensus of current conservative Protestant scholarship. Let us note some examples.[64]

During the first few days of the trial, Bryan said nothing. When, on the fourth day, defense attorney Dudley Malone quoted Bryan out of context,

---

[62] J. C. Long, *Bryan, the Great Commoner* (New York: D. Appleton, 1928), p. 381. See also, the comments of paleontologist Henry Fairfield Osborn, whose hastily written book just prior to Dayton excoriated the religiously "fanatical" and scientifically "stone-deaf" Bryan as "the man on trial" (cited in Larson, *Summer For The Gods,* p. 113).

[63] Allem, "Backgrounds," p. 30.

[64] All quoted testimony is taken from the court transcript: William Hilleary and Oren Metzger, editors, *World's Most Famous Court Trial: Tennessee Evolution Case* (reprint of 1925 ed., Dayton, TN: Rhea County Historical Society, 1978).

suggesting that he had earlier favored evolution, he broke silence: "At the
proper time I shall be able to show that my position [on evolution] differs
not at all from my position in those days." Did he fulfill that promise on
the following day when delivering his main speech of the trial? After
briefly reflecting on the earlier accusations by the prosecution against him,
Bryan declared that the Tennessee law was clear and absolutely sufficient
and that the court needed no out-of-state expert to tell it what the statute
meant. He restated the issue at hand: "The question is can a minority in
this state come in and compel a teacher to teach that the Bible is not true
and make the parents of these children pay the expenses..."—a position
he had held all along, indeed, his principal objection to the teaching of
evolution in the schools. He rebuked Darwinism, stating that it cannot
be supported by the Bible, and that the Bible itself is a sufficient expert
witness against it. Then, after defending the fundamental doctrines of
Christianity which were being attacked by evolution, Bryan moved for the
exclusion of any "expert" testimony by the defense. It was obvious that
Bryan was suggesting that anything in opposition to the Bible should be
thrown out of court, since there was no higher authority than Scripture.
He was pitting the Bible against evolution. It would be difficult to find
anything in his remarks that was not consistent with earlier writings on the
subject of evolution and his general representation of the fundamentalist
crusade against it. In fact, an actual review of the court transcript reveals
that Bryan was often exuberant, humorous, discerning, and focused during
the trial. It also indicates that he was familiar with Darwin, and understood
evolutionary teachings even better than Darrow. It is not true that Bryan
and his beliefs were crushed at Dayton.[65]

The crucial test of the credibility of Bryan's position came on the
seventh day of the trial, Monday, July 20: the cross-examination of Bryan
by Darrow. This episode most writers on the subject consider to be a disaster,
both for Bryan and for the cause of fundamentalism. Just three years
earlier he had written, "I know of no reason why the Christian should take
upon himself the difficult task of answering all questions and give to the
atheist the easy task of asking them."[66] Yet he believed that in the context
of an open forum and representing the fundamentalist position, it would
be a greater inconsistency not to bring the issues before the public and
he said so frequently during his testimony. One should also consider that
Bryan's insistence that Darrow examine him was based on (1) his desire to

[65] Carol Iannone, "The Truth About *Inherit the Wind*," *First Things* 70 (Fall 1997): 30.
[66] Bryan, *In His Image,* pp. 13–14.

defend the Bible against agnosticism[67] and, most notably, (2) the promise by Judge Raulston that Bryan would be allowed to question Darrow. This is clearly apparent in the court transcript, a fact that Bryan's critics have overlooked:

> Bryan: "If your honor please, I insist that Mr. Darrow can be put on the stand...."
> The Court: "Call anybody you desire. Ask them any questions you wish."

And later in the cross-examination:

> Bryan: "I want him [Darrow] to have all the latitude he wants, for I am going to have some latitude when he gets through."

If the judge had not made this concession, it is doubtful that Bryan would ever have agreed to take the stand.[68] However, once Bryan was there, he should have remembered an old adage that he himself had repeated: any fool could ask questions which the wisest person in the world could not answer. Since many of Darrow's questions were foolish, Bryan would have been better off, perhaps, in not answering them, but he should not be branded an ignoramus for doing so.[69] To Bryan's credit was his constant reference to the Bible. Where it spoke, he spoke; where it was silent, he confessed ignorance. Some of the questions and responses were:

> Darrow: "But do you believe He made them—that He made such a fish and that it was big enough to swallow Jonah?
> Bryan: "Yes, sir. Let me add: one miracle is just as easy to believe as another."
> Darrow: "Just as hard?"
> Bryan: "It is hard to believe for you, but easy for me. A miracle is a thing performed beyond what man can perform. When you get beyond what man can do, you get within the realm of miracles; and it is just as easy to believe the miracle of Jonah as any other miracle in the Bible."
> Darrow: "Perfectly easy to believe that Jonah swallowed the whale?"
> Bryan: "If the Bible said so; the Bible doesn't make as extreme statements as evolutionists do."

---

[67] Bryan's confident response in allowing himself to be cross-examined came out more than once during the trial: "The reason I am answering is not for the benefit of the superior court. It is to keep these gentlemen from saying I was afraid to meet them and let them question me, and I want the Christian world to know that any atheist, agnostic, unbeliever, can question me any time as to my belief in God, and I will answer him" (*World's Most Famous Court Trial*, p. 165).

[68] Bryan had actually prepared a list of questions he would ask Darrow. These may be found in DeCamp, *Monkey Trial*, pp. 430–31.

[69] Smith, *Social and Religious Thought*, pp. 198–99.

Darrow: "Do you believe Joshua made the sun stand still?"
Bryan: "I believe what the Bible says. I suppose you mean that the earth stood still."
Darrow: "I don't know. I am talking about the Bible now."
Bryan: "I accept the Bible absolutely."

Other questions concerned the flood, the exact age of the earth, and existence of ancient civilizations and their philosophies, all of which were designed to make Bryan appear woefully stupid. Darrow's purpose, he admitted later, was to discredit fundamentalism,[70] and to force Bryan into admitting that the Bible cannot be literally interpreted.[71] The two most damaging questions, many believe, were:

"Do you think the earth was made in six days?" and
"Did you ever discover where Cain got his wife?"

While Bryan's answer to the former question was a serious compromise of literalism, it was in harmony with what several conservative theologians had been teaching: "Not six days of twenty-four hours."[72] Even W. B. Riley agreed that the days could be indefinite periods of time.[73] However,

---

[70] Clarence S. Darrow, *The Story of My Life* (reprint of 1932 ed., New York: Scribners, 1960), p. 249.

[71] Literalism for fundamentalists did not mean that every passage of Scripture should be interpreted literally but that the basic hermeneutical approach was the literal mode—the common sense of the passage, Bryan would say. Bryan had a clear understanding of a literal hermeneutic as indicated by his response to an earlier question by Darrow: "You claim that everything in the Bible should be literally interpreted?" Bryan: "I believe everything in the Bible should be accepted as it is given there: some of the Bible is given illustratively. For instance, 'Ye are the salt of the earth.' I would not insist that man was actually salt, or that he had flesh of salt, but it is used in the sense of salt as saving God's people" (*World's Most Famous Court Trial,* p. 147).

[72] See Charles Hodge, *Systematic Theology,* 3 vols. (reprint ed., Grand Rapids: Eerdmans, 1940), 1:571; William G. T. Shedd, *Dogmatic Theology,* 4 vols. (reprint of 1889 ed., Minneapolis: Klock and Klock, 1979), 1:476; A. H. Strong, *Systematic Theology* 3 vols. (Valley Forge, PA: Judson Press, 1907), 2:395.

[73] Editorial in *Christian Fundamentals in School and Church* 6 (October–December 1925): 40. See also, Waggoner, "Historiography," p. 166, note 42, where he states that "Bryan...*never* believed in a literal six-day creation to begin with," and quotes Bryan at length to refute the liberal criticism that most fundamentalists believed in a young earth, i.e., created circa fifth millennium B.C. Another way of accounting for fossils was to posit an indeterminate amount of time between Genesis 1:1 and 1:2. Such a view was so common among fundamentalist leaders as to be almost axiomatic. A. C. Dixon declared, "Now I turn to the Bible and find that between the first and second verses of the first chapter in Genesis, there is enough long ages of deposit in the perfect order of 'the heaven and *the earth*' which God created. And since 'was' may be translated '*became,*' so as to make

Bryan's impression that they were lengthy periods was "not an attempt to argue...against anybody who wanted to believe in literal days."[74] Bryan's reply of ignorance to the second question would not be unusual for a layman; for Bryan and probably for most Christians it simply was not a matter of concern.[75] The issue was certainly not vital to fundamentalism.

When an eye-witness of the trial, H. J. Shelton, was asked if Bryan did an adequate job of defending the fundamentalist position, he replied,

> Bryan did hold his own, so to speak, against the probing questions of Darrow, who did bring up some of the age-old biblical questions having no pat answer. Darrow tried in every way to confuse Bryan by twisting questions... but...Darrow, who was badgering him, [asked]...what this narrator considers many foolish questions that could only be answered in the way that Bryan did respond. The prosecution [Tennessee Attorney General A. T. Stewart] did object many times to Darrow's line of questioning.[76]

What Bryan was seeking to accomplish on the stand he made perfectly clear: "I am simply trying to protect the Word of God against the greatest atheist or agnostic in the United States. [*Prolonged applause.*] I want the papers to know I am not afraid to get on the stand in front of him

---

it read, 'the earth *became* waste and void,' there is an intimation that a great upheaval took place at that remote time.... It was animal life which perished, the traces of which remain as fossils" (*Scriptural Inspiration Versus Scientific Imagination,* pp. 104–05). A twofold benefit of modern creation science, with its emphasis on a universal catastrophic flood, is (1) to provide strong evidence that the earth is actually relatively young and (2) that it is unnecessary to posit an indefinite period of time or "gap" between Genesis 1:1 and 1:2 to account for fossils. See the determinative study of John C. Whitcomb, Jr. and Henry M. Morris, *The Genesis Flood: The Biblical Record and Its Scientific Implications* (Philadelphia: Presbyterian and Reformed, 1961), especially, pp. 92–94; basic to all other arguments is their belief in Bryan's own premise: the verbal inerrancy and absolute authority of Scripture (p. xx). For a refutation of the gap and day age theories respectively, see Weston W. Fields, *Unformed and Unfilled: The Gap Theory* (Phillipsburg, NJ: Presbyterian and Reformed, 1976); and Gerhard Hasel, "The 'Days' of Creation in Genesis 1," *Origins* 21 (1994): 5–38.

[74] Bryan may have had George McCready Price in mind when making this statement. Price advocated a single recent creation of six literal days and a worldwide deluge to account for fossils. He regarded the day-age theory as "the devil's counterfeit" (*The Story of Fossils* [Mountain View, CA: Pacific Press, 1954], p. 39).

[75] The standard biblicist answer to the question is that Cain married his sister. Bryan may not have wanted to answer this way and place himself in the predicament of having to justify incest. For a very plausible moral and genetical response to this issue, see Ken Ham, Andrew Snelling, and Carl Wieland, *The Answers Book* (El Cajon, CA: Master Books, 1991), pp. 177–83.

[76] A taped interview of H. J. Shelton by a professor of Shinn of Statesville, NC, sent to the writer (January 1982).

and let him do his worst."[77] If Bryan's answers made him appear foolish, Darrow's questions and methods of interrogation hardly made him appear any better,[78] but not in the estimation of the liberal press, who flayed Bryan. Russell Owen of the *New York Sun* wrote that Bryan "knew nothing...which one might expect a man...to be familiar with."[79] Joseph Wood Krutch of the *Nation* reported that "under cross-examination the defeated champion provided even [a] sorrier spectacle as he retreated further...into boastful ignorance."[80] Such comments are simply a purulent distortion of the facts.

The intense, and what must have been an exhausting, examination concluded in a shouting match between Bryan and Darrow:

> Bryan: "The only purpose Mr. Darrow has is to slur at the Bible."
> Darrow: "I am exempting you on your fool ideas that no intelligent Christian on earth believes."

According to Jerry Tompkins, Bryan lost the confidence of many people.[81] Undoubtedly, he did with the liberal media, but he did not lose credibility with fundamentalists, as editors of the *Fundamentalist Phenomenon* suggest.[82] In fact, according to Furniss, many who attended the trial later condemned Darrow for his behavior, charging that he "cheapened legal procedure and damaged the liberals' side in the controversy with methods calculated to attract publicity."[83] Evidently Darrow's tactics backfired, according to Winterton C. Curtis. Curtis, a scientist who provided testimony for the defense, related years after the trial that Judge Raulston stopped Bryan's testimony and expunged it, not only because it lacked relevance to the trial, but because popular resentment against Darrow had become so strong that law enforcement officials met secretly with the judge and cautioned against any further examination. "This thing must be stopped. We cannot be responsible for what may happen if it goes on. Someone is

---

[77] *World's Most Famous Court Trial*, p. 164.

[78] Smith, *Social and Religious Thought*, p. 199.

[79] Russell D. Owen, "The Significance of the Scopes Trial," *Current History Magazine* 22 (September 1925): 882.

[80] Cited in Gatewood, *Controversy*, p. 365; for other accounts, see Long, *Bryan*, p. 381. Years later Krutch had still not changed his mind about the trial. To him, "the Bible-belt zealots [including Bryan] were exhibiting themselves as hilarious boobs" ("The Monkey Trial," *Commentary* 43 [May 1967]: 83).

[81] Jerry R. Tompkins, ed., *D-Days at Dayton* (Baton Rouge: Louisiana State University Press, 1965), p. 28.

[82] Falwell, *Fundamentalist Phenomenon*, p. 86; see also, Coletta, *William Jennings Bryan*, p. 267.

[83] Furniss, *Fundamentalist Controversy*, p. 91.

likely to get hurt." That "someone" was Darrow. So the judge put an end to any further testimony from either Bryan or Darrow.[84] This decision, along with Stewart's request to stop the questioning and end the trial, would also help explain why Raulston would not permit Bryan to cross-examine Darrow the next day, a reversal of his earlier promise.

Several fundamentalist leaders defended Bryan. Walter D. Buchanan, pastor of the Broadway Presbyterian Church in New York City, referred to the Great Commoner as "one valiant Knight of God," and called the Dayton trial, "a sad revelation" because "the opposition to the simple faith of our fathers was brought out more boldly...than ever before."[85] Riley took Darrow to task for his "captious and conscienceless" questions: "Imagine a self-respecting attorney putting to such a gentleman as Mr. Bryan the satirical questions..."[86]

The trial must have taken a heavy toll on Bryan. He was not a well man to begin with. After the lengthy and intense interchange with Darrow, he learned that he would not be allowed to question him in court. This had to be a great disappointment to him, and perhaps contributed to his death five days after the trial. Yet during those final days he was a bustle of activity: speaking to large groups of people nearly every day, traveling over two hundred miles, issuing statements to the press, and finally, editing what he considered "the mountain peak of my life's efforts," the last speech he had intended to give in court.[87] It was a composite of all the earlier arguments he had given against evolution. He wrote Norris what the Texas preacher considered his last letter:

> Well, we won our case. It woke up the community if I can judge from letters and telegrams. Am just having my speech (prepared but not delivered) put into pamphlet form. Will send you a copy. I think it is the strongest indictment of evolution I have made. Much obliged to you for your part in getting me into the case. Much obliged too for [L. H.] Evridge [licensed court stenographer sent by Norris to cover the trial]. He is a delightful [man] and very efficient. I

---

[84] Smith, *Social and Religious Thought,* pp. 200–01.

[85] Buchanan, "Significance of the Scopes Trial," p. 889.

[86] Riley, "World's Christian Fundamentals Association and the Scopes Trial," *Christian Fundamentals in School and Church* 7 (October–December 1925): 40. In reviewing fundamentalist literature and in conversing with fundamentalists of the 1920s, David Rausch concluded that "they did not feel a loss of morale or status" (*Zionism Within Early American Fundamentalism 1878–1918* [New York: Edwin Mellon Press, 1979], p. 343, n. 8; see also, pp. 319–20).

[87] Furniss, *Fundamentalist Controversy,* p. 90.

wish you would let me correct my part in the trial before you publish it. Sorry you were not there.

Yours, Bryan[88]

No doubt Bryan was sorry that several of his fundamentalist friends were "not there." Their presence would not only have strengthened the state's position, but bolstered his confidence. From the fundamentalist viewpoint, however, there is every indication that Bryan did give a sincere and responsible "acquittal" of himself at the Scopes trial.

EFFECTS OF BRYAN'S TESTIMONY ON FUNDAMENTALISM AND THE ANTI-EVOLUTION CRUSADE

For the last several decades fundamentalists have generally acquiesced to the biased liberal interpretation of the Scopes trial by conceding to Bryan a Pyrrhic victory; that is, he won the immediate skirmish in upholding the Tennessee law against evolution, but lost the battle for fundamentalism in the public's eye with the news media's negative portrayal of him. Many commentators, both liberals and conservatives, have suggested that the trial was a turning point in fundamentalist fortunes, a "historical watershed; worse still, a rout, fundamentalism's 'Waterloo.'"[89] However, careful examination of the facts indicate that this stereotype is undeserving of both Bryan and the fundamentalist movement. In his masterful evaluation of the trial, Paul Waggoner documents the fact that during the first few years following Dayton (1925–1931), "critical observers did not regard the Scopes trial as a turning point in the fundamentalist controversy."[90] It was not until what he calls the "second phase," running from 1931 to about 1965, that the critical view, or "new consensus" view as he calls it, came into vogue. This view was precipitated by Frederick Allen's satire of the 1920s in which he climaxes the work by virtually lampooning Bryan, and refers to the trial as a travesty of intellectualism.

> It was a savage encounter, and a tragic one for the ex-Secretary of State... he died scarcely a week later. And he was being covered with humiliation. The sort of religious faith which he represented could not take the witness stand and face reason as a prosecutor.... Theoretically, Fundamentalism has won, for the law stood. Yet really Fundamentalism has lost. Legislators might

---

[88] Handwritten, no date. Located in Bryan papers.

[89] Waggoner, "Historiography," p. 155.

[90] Ibid., p. 156.

go on passing antievolution laws...but civilized opinion everywhere had regarded the Dayton trial with amazement and amusement, and the slow drift away from Fundamentalism certainly continued.[91]

Waggoner remarks that "it was not so much the passage of time as it was the popularity of Allen that enshrined Dayton, Tennessee, as the bottomless pit into which fundamentalism stumbled in the summer of 1925."[92] It is this warped image of the trial and Bryan that a number of writers have parroted and have thus perpetuated the negative image indelibly imprinted on the minds of those willing to uncritically accept it.[93]

The trial and even the death of Bryan, far from defeating fundamentalism and its anti-evolutionary crusade, served only to advance them.[94] Fundamentalists considered Bryan a martyr who died in defense of their cause.[95] According to Chattanooga reporter George Fort Milton, his death

---

[91] Frederick Lewis Allen, *Only Yesterday: An Informal History of the 1920's* (reprint of 1931 ed., New York: Harper and Row, 1957), pp. 205–6.

[92] Waggoner, "Historiography," p. 164.

[93] Most notably, those who followed Allen's interpretation were: Gaius Glen Atkins, *Religion in Our Times* (New York: Round Table Press, 1932); Mark Sullivan, *Our Times: The United States, 1900–1925 The Twenties,* 6 vols. (New York: Charles Scribners Sons, 1935), 6:568, 644–5; and a popular history textbook in the 1940s and 50s, William W. Sweet, *The Story of Religion in America* (2nd ed., New York: Harper & Brothers, 1939), p. 572. Sweet concludes that the Scopes trial was "fundamentalism's last stand." Paul Waggoner verifies the impact Frederick Lewis Allen had on altering the perception of the Scopes trial and further traces how various books, beginning in the 1930s, played a role in shaping interpretations of the event in "A Historiographical Essay on the Scopes Trial," an appendix in "New Light on the Scopes Trial" (M.A. thesis, Columbia University, 1957), pp. 158–70, esp. pp. 161–64. Decades later the Allen interpretation persisted in works such as, William Leuchtenburg, *The Perils of Prosperity, 1914–1932* (Chicago: University of Chicago Press, 1958), pp. 217–25; Ray Ginger, *Six Days or Forever?*, pp. 211–12; and, of course, the play and movie *Inherit the Wind.* Interestingly, Waggoner assembles some impressive evidence for the view that *Inherit the Wind* was motivated more by the political McCarthyism of the 1950s than the religious implications of the Scopes trial (cf. "Historiography," pp. 167–68).

[94] Willard Gatewood writes, "To assert, as the liberal *Christian Century* ["Vanishing Fundamentalism," 43 (June 24, 1926): 797–99] did, that fundamentalism was a 'vanishing' phenomenon was as naive as the widely held view that anti-evolution sentiment somehow dissipated in the wake of the Scopes trial" ("From Scopes to Creation Science: The Decline and Revival of the Evolution Controversy," *South Atlantic Quarterly* 83 [Autumn 1984]: 366).

[95] Henry Mencken had quipped, "Heave an egg out a Pullman and you will hit a Fundamentalist almost anywhere in the United States." Roderick Nash comments that, when Bryan's funeral train made its way slowly from the South to Washington, D.C., hundreds of thousands lined the tracks to pay their respects. "Mencken's egg would have hit many a fundamentalist" (*The Nervous Generation: American Thought, 1917–1930* [Chicago: Rand McNally, 1970], pp. 148–49).

was "from an ordeal of faith."[96] To one French observer, Bryan would
have become a martyr even if he had not died. Darrow's ridicule gave the
Great Commoner a "halo in the eyes of millions."[97] With the absence of
his dynamic leadership and prestige, the fundamentalist movement lost a
powerful spokesman but in no wise did this discourage the fundamentalists.[98] In fact, early press reports on the trial served as an impetus for their
continued campaign against evolution. Waggoner states that a number of
journals saw the Dayton trial as a critical fundamentalist triumph. The
Nation and the *New Republic,* both liberal periodicals, expressed alarm
over the "success at Dayton"...[which] "has surprised even [fundamental-
ists] by its completeness."[99] The outcome was a certain "victory for the
fundamentalists."[100] Even H. L. Mencken, perhaps the most caustic critic
of the trial and of fundamentalism in general, warned that "the evil that
men do lives after them. Bryan, in his malice, started something that it
will not be easy to stop."[101] Mencken was right about at least one thing:
the trial was not easy to stop, nor did it stop, fundamentalism.[102] On the
contrary, it re-invigorated the anti-evolution campaign by referring to
Bryan's arguments and the Tennessee case as models for it.[103] This was
especially true in the South, where Bryan's name was highly venerated.
Renewed agitation focused on state legislatures and school boards, and
it was not until 1930 that the crusade was supplanted by other concerns.

---

[96] Cited in Ginger, *Six Days or Forever?* p. 193.

[97] Cited in Gatewood, *Controversy in the Twenties,* p. 427.

[98] Gasper states that, after the trial and the leadership of Bryan, "fundamentalists had
lost their ardor," and fundamentalist "leaders have stated that during this period [the1930s]
despair rather than hope engulfed them." However, Gasper fails to offer any substantial
evidence for this opinion (*Fundamentalist Movement,* pp. 18, 40).

[99] Editorial, "Dayton and After," *Nation* 121 (1925): 153–56. Miriam Allen deFord
wrote that fundamentalist opposition to the theory of evolution [is] more alive and more
dangerous than ever" ("After Dayton: A Fundamentalist Survey," *Nation* 122 [June 2,
1926]: 604). See also, Donald F. Brod, "The Scopes Trial: A Look at Press Coverage After
Forty Years," *Journalism Quarterly* 42 (1965): 219–26.

[100] Nels Anderson, "The Shooting Parson of Texas," *New Republic* 48 (September 1,
1926): 37.

[101] Editorial in the *American Mercury* 6 (October 1925): 160.

[102] Four years after the trial the landmark sociological study of "Middletown" by
Robert and Helen Lynd lent support to the contention that "the mass of the American
people are Fundamentalists" (*Middletown: A Study of Contemporary American Culture*
[New York: Harcourt and Brace, 1929], pp. 315–31, cited in Gatewood, *Controversy in
the Twenties,* p. 37).

[103] Waggoner, "Historiography,"pp. 156–58.

After Bryan's sudden death, the question of succession arose. He had intimated in a letter to his son that the younger's participation in the trial "will give you a standing no one else can have. Every attack from our opponents draws the orthodox Christians more closely to me and you will share in the benefits."[104] Curtis Lee Laws of the *Watchman–Examiner,* one of the few fundamentalist spokesmen who reacted negatively to the trial, wrote that it "ought never to have been made an issue of fundamentalism," and two weeks later: "...the leadership of the fundamentalists is a pretty hard job."[105] W. B. Riley noted that "it will take a number of us [fundamentalist leaders] and that at our best, to fill the place vacated by the fall of this magnificent thinker and leader."[106] WCFA representatives Norris and Riley, along with John Roach Straton and evangelist Mordecai Ham, endeavored to fill the gap by giving innumerable speeches against evolution across the country.

Organizations such as the Bible Crusaders lobbied tirelessly in state assemblies under the direction of T. T. Martin.[107] Their efforts produced anti-evolution legislation in Mississippi (1926) and Arkansas (1928). The Scopes trial proved that an anti-evolution law could be passed and upheld, and pressure on several state assemblies built until 1927, when thirteen states had such bills introduced.[108] In several areas the agitation over evolution was sufficient to cleanse the schools of the "Darwinian heresy" without enacting a specific statute.[109] In Louisiana, for instance, that state's superintendent of schools, in response to Southern Baptist pressure, forbade the teaching of evolution in tax-supported schools.[110] Following the lead of Cameron Morrison, governor of North Carolina, Texas Governor Miriam Ferguson, as head of the state textbook commission, disallowed the use of biology texts mentioning evolution. The California Board of Education was empowered in 1926 to require teachers "to show due respect and consideration [when teaching science] for the fundamental principles of religion, as

---

[104] Cited in Szasz, "Three Fundamentalist Leaders," p. 255.

[105] Editorials in the *Watchman–Examiner* 13 (August 20, 1925): 1071, and (September 3, 1925): 1131.

[106] Riley, "Bryan, The Great Commoner and Christian," 6.

[107] For examples of Martin's labors and speeches, see Ginger, *Six Days,* p. 212; and Gatewood, *Controversy in the Twenties,* p. 237.

[108] Szasz, "Three Fundamentalist Leaders," p. 253; DeCamp, *Monkey Trial,* p. 473. Between 1921 and 1929 thirty-seven anti-evolution bills were introduced into twenty state legislatures (cited in Smith, *Social and Religious Thought,* p. 193).

[109] Gatewood, *Controversy in the Twenties,* p. 289.

[110] For details, see Wallace Hebert, "Louisiana Baptists and the Scopes Trial," *Louisiana Studies* 7 (Winter 1968): 329–46.

presented in the Bible."[111] As late as 1947, the board of education in Wall, South Dakota, eliminated from schools "all books or pages of books which contain...atheistic evolution."[112] Two public school science teachers wrote a detailed article in 1974 showing that

> as a result [of the Scopes trial], the teaching of evolution in the high schools—as judged by the content of the average high school biology textbooks—*declined* [their emphasis]... The impact of the Scopes trial on high school biology textbooks was enormous. It is easy to identify a text published in the decade following 1925. Merely look up the word "evolution" in the index or the glossary; you almost certainly will not find it.[113]

The struggle for anti-evolution legislation in such states as North Carolina (by T. T. Martin), Maine (by Baptist minister Ben C. Buber), and Minnesota (by W. B. Riley) met with failure,[114] but not before Riley and his associates had talked before audiences in two hundred Minnesota towns. He affirmed that nine tenths of the people in the state were in favor of anti-evolution laws, yet a bill was defeated in the state assembly.[115] If Riley was correct, this is an instance where the decision of a few ranking officials outweighed the wishes of the majority, certainly not the first occurrence in America's history!

Writing for the American Historical Association, Howard K. Beale summarized the results of a 1933 questionnaire sent to a cross-sampling of public school teachers throughout the country. He reported that birth control, the non-existence of God, and evolution were subjects not permitted to be discussed in many classrooms. More to the point, he stated that between one third and one half of the teachers polled were afraid "to express acceptance of the theory of evolution."[116] It is evident from this

---

[111] Cited in W. W. Campbell, "Evolution in Education in California," *Science* 56 (April 3, 1925): 367–68.

[112] Cited in Gatewood, "From Scopes to Creation Science," p. 366.

[113] Judith V. Grabiner and Peter D. Miller, "Effects of the Scopes Trial: Was It a Victory for Evolutionists?" *Science* 185 (1974): 832, 833.

[114] For details of the Maine effort, see Gatewood, *Controversy in the Twenties,* p. 311; for North Carolina, by the same author in "Politics and Piety in North Carolina: The Fundamentalist Crusade at High Tide, 1925–1927," *North Carolina Historical Review* 47 (July 1965): 279–90.

[115] Ferenc Szasz implies that a University of Minnesota petition helped kill the bill in 1927. See "William B. Riley and the Fight Against Teaching of Evolution in Minnesota," *Minnesota History* 46 (Spring 1969): 201–16.

[116] Howard K. Beale, *A History of Freedom of Teaching in American Schools* (New York: Octagon Books, 1966), pp. 238, 241. Gatewood adds "that half of all American high school biology teachers shied away from teaching evolution as late as 1942, [attesting] to the enduring impact of the anti-evolution crusade"("From Scopes to Creation Science," p. 366).

response that public and supervisory pressure was sufficiently exerted to prevent the teaching of evolution in many public school classrooms.

One major gain of the fundamentalist crusade was the passage of laws in many states endorsing Bible reading in public schools.[117] By 1931, thirty-five states either required or permitted Bible reading in their schools.[118] This writer can remember attending an Indianapolis public elementary school in the early 1950s where released-time Bible classes at a local church were mandatory. Incentive for such activity can be attributed to the efforts of fundamentalists like Philadelphia pastor Clarence Macartney who spoke to a national meeting of public school superintendents in 1927. He advocated that the schools provide "definite instructions as to the existence of the moral nature of man" in opposition of Darwinian naturalism.[119]

Shortly after the Scopes trial, Swedish fundamentalist Paul W. Rood of Turlock, California, while referring to Bryan as "the Modern Elijah," inaugurated the Bryan Bible League. Nearly a thousand signatures were obtained to oppose "the teaching of evolution in tax supported schools..."[120] This organization, however, was short-lived, much like many local counterparts throughout the country. Spurred on by Bryan's testimony, individual fundamentalist leaders continued their opposition. For them the central issue in the Scopes trial was what Bryan said it was—whether tax-paying parents "shall be made to support...evolution in the schools, while Christianity is ruled out..."[121] Yet five years after the trial the anti-evolution crusade had lost momentum. The subject was not even mentioned in the 1930 WCFA meeting. The silence should not be interpreted as lack of concern, however, but observance of more pressing issues, such as Prohibition and the Depression. Fundamentalists renewed their attacks on the "wets" when the question of repealing the Eighteenth Amendment arose. Attention was also turned to the alleviation of human suffering. Care of the depressed and the displaced superseded court and

---

[117] For an example of this in North Dakota, see Gatewood, *Controversy in the Twenties,* p. 316.

[118] Gatewood, "From Scopes to Creation Science," p. 366.

[119] Harvey Maitland Watts, "Shall We Force Religion into the Schools? II—Which God and Why Schools?" *Forum* 77 (1927): 811–17.

[120] W. B. Riley, "The World's Christian Fundamentals Association and the Scopes Trial," *Christian Fundamentals in School and Church* 7 (October–December 1925): 48.

[121] John Roach Straton, "The Most Sinister Movement in the United States," *American Fundamentalist* 2 (December 26, 1925): 8–9.

classroom struggles.[122] In a wrecked economy many were more concerned with simple survival rather than "survival of the fittest."

Also, a new era of fundamentalism emerged. With the admitted failure to rescue the major denominations from modernism, fundamentalists from both the northern Presbyterians and Baptists began to separate and form their respective groups. In 1929, J. Gresham Machen left Princeton to begin Westminster Theological Seminary and the Orthodox Presbyterian Church, and the General Association of Regular Baptist Churches was organized in 1932 as a sectarian body of fundamentalists to combat liberalism from outside the Northern Baptist Convention. This new direction, from nonconformity to separatism, coupled with the loss of fundamentalism's early champions like Bryan and Straton (d. 1929), contributed to the decline of the anti-evolutionist crusade which Bryan had defended in the Scopes trial. However, such losses did not curtail fundamentalism's overall progress. Joel A. Carpenter has proven conclusively that

> institutional growth in the 1930s of the most vocal and visible evangelicals, the fundamentalists, challenges the widespread notion that popular Protestantism experienced a major decline during that decade. What really transpired was the beginning of a shift of the Protestant mainstream from the older denominations toward the evangelicals.[123]

In other words, what really happened was the numerical and influential diminution of the mainline denominations and the corresponding growth of separatistic fundamentalist Christianity. Carpenter's caveat that fundamentalist leaders "had made themselves look foolish in the anti-evolution crusade," however, is not entirely accurate. It is true that fundamentalists appeared foolish in the eyes of liberal theologians and a cynical press, but they had been biased against fundamentalism long before the Scopes trial. The trial and the anti-evolutionist efforts by fundamentalist leaders only served to further discredit the movement in the eyes of those already opposed to it; but the widespread popular

---

[122] Furniss, *Fundamentalist Controversy,* pp. 178–798.

[123] Joel A. Carpenter, "Fundamentalist Institutions and the Rise of Evangelical Protestantism, 1929–1942," in *Modern American Protestantism and Its World: Fundamentalism and Evangelicalism,* ed. Martin E. Marty (Munich: K. G. Saur, 1993), pp. 57–58, 66–68. See also, Carpenter's "Revive Us Again: Alienation, Hope, and the Resurgence of Fundamentalism, 1930–1950," in *Transforming Faith,* pp. 105–25. Carpenter's views have been further developed in his book, *Revive Us Again: The Reawakening of American Fundamentalism* (New York: Oxford University Press, 1997); see chapter one, wherein he writes, "Loss of the respect of intellectual elites does not necessarily mean loss of popular support, and it may actually enhance a group's appeal in some circles" (p. 15). Evidence indicates that popular support for fundamentalism after the Scopes trial was stronger than ever.

growth of fundamentalism after the trial proves that it was not at all jeopardized, but strengthened. Examples of growth abound. By 1930, there were over fifty Bible schools, and many of these expanded their programs from a two to a three-year program, thus allowing for greater specialization in pastoral studies, missions, Christian education, and music.[124] Fundamentalist schools and churches created publishing concerns, produced informative magazines, and ventured into radio broadcasting. Fundamentalists desiring a liberal arts education could have the choice of going to a fundamentalist college such as Wheaton[125] near Chicago or Bob Jones College in Florida. As a memorial to Bryan and in answer to his wish for a Christian school to be established in the scenic hill country surrounding Dayton, Bryan College was established in 1930. A growing number of summer Bible conferences and Christian camps began springing up after that year. Perhaps the most noticeable and dramatic change was in the area of missions. While liberal denominational mission enterprise waned, mission budgets decreased, and office staffs dwindled, fundamentalist mission programs accelerated. According to findings of the Laymen's Foreign Missions Inquiry of 1932, "fundamentalist-backed missions grew stronger, [were] better financed, and [were] more evangelistically aggressive and more successful in recruiting volunteers than ever before."[126]

Although it is impossible to determine accurately the long term effects of Bryan's involvement in the trial, we need to be reminded that his legacy is significant. He seems generally to be the "forgotten fundamentalist" among those who currently claim that title. One reason may not only be the negativism associated with the Scopes trial, but Bryan's irregular type of fundamentalism. It can be argued that there is a legitimacy to the neglect in that fundamentalism decisively opposes many of Bryan's interests, e.g., a more active centralized government, social progressiveness, and moral

---

[124] William C. Ringenberg, *The Christian College: A History of Protestant Higher Education in America* (Grand Rapids: Eerdmans, 1984), p. 167. Virginia Lieson Brereton reports that, even during the Depression when many institutions had to cut back, Bible schools continued to be founded. At least twenty-nine new schools appeared during the thirties, compared to seventeen during the previous decade (*Training God's Army: The American Bible School, 1880–1940* [Bloomington: Indiana University Press, 1990], p. 84).

[125] Wheaton College was founded in 1857 as a Bible school. Under J. Oliver Buswell, president from 1926 to 1940, the school became a liberal arts college (Carpenter, "Fundamentalist Institutions," pp. 61–62).

[126] Cited in Carpenter, "Fundamentalist Institutions," p. 65. Cf. Beale, *In Pursuit of Purity,* chapter twenty-five, entitled "Fundamentalism's Transdenominational Vitality in the 1930s and 1940s," in which he lists numerous examples of fundamentalism's growth under such headings as Bible Conferences, Bible College Outreach, Radio Ministries, Missionary Agencies, and Publishing Houses (pp. 251–57).

idealism—all liberal planks.[127] Practically speaking, fundamentalists believe that big government is too intrusive, that society is non-redemptive [we must win lost individuals to the gospel out of society], and that good morals only make sin "more respectable." But, aside from the differences, Bryan is relevant to current fundamentalism. His importance lies not in the accomplishment of his political ambitions nor in his goal to force evolution from the public schools; ultimately, he failed in both cases. What he has left us is the reminder of our responsibility to courageously defend what is biblically orthodox and constitutionally just. For instance, his argument of the parents' right to educate their children is reflected in the contemporary Christian day school and home school movements, which have proliferated remarkably since the Scopes trial and especially in the last twenty years. And there is little doubt that most Christian private schools of one kind or another have started over a pastoral and parental reaction to secularism and the resulting breakdown of morals in the public education sector, spawned in part by modern education's endorsement of evolution.

What Bryan has also left us is the most important legacy of all: his unswerving advocacy of an infallible Bible as the final answer to the question of evolution versus creation. While most current fundamentalists interpret the length of creation and the age of the cosmos differently than Bryan, they are in agreement with him that Scripture is the decisive and most effective answer to Darwinism. And so it should be. Propositional verities revealed in the Bible are more effective in answering God's critics than an apologetics for creation which rest on scientific evidences. Such a response will not give credibility to the believer before a cynical Christ-denying world, but it will give him confidence that his arguments are sourced in the final answer of origins—God's Word. Thus his biblical answer of creation against evolution is God's answer. This is infinitely more important than a secular world's credibility rating. Nor should fundamentalists be content with a strategy that seeks "equal time" for

---

[127] Mark A. Noll makes Bryan's evangelical-political activism so distinct from the sectarian fundamentalism that emerged after Bryan that he places them in two "ages"—"The Age of Bryan: and "The Age of Fundamentalism." The major difference, to Noll, is that post-Bryan fundamentalism, with its emphasis on dispensational premillennialism, is pessimistic about cultural progress. The focus is on personal evangelism and piety, not the optimistic socially redemptive themes of Bryan. Noll considers the resulting evangelical neglect of political engagement a "disaster," and new evangelical political activism a welcome change in "The Age of Beginnings" [circa. 1941] ("The Scandal of Evangelical Political Reflection," in *Being Christian Today: An American Conversation,* ed. Richard John Neuhaus and George Weigel [Washington, D.C.: Ethics and Public Policy Center, 1992], pp. 72–83).

creationism in classrooms.[128] This concedes an unwarranted respectability to evolution and compromises absolute truth. Bryan was right in giving no quarter to a demonic philosophy diametrically opposed to goodness and godliness. Evolution is scientifically invalid, but more importantly, it is theologically unacceptable.

CONCLUSION

One reporter who covered the Scopes trial doubted that, as a result of it, "the faith of a single Fundamentalist was shaken, or that a believer in evolution was won over to the acceptance of the literal interpretation of the Bible."[129] Battle lines were already drawn between the evolutionists and the fundamentalists long before the trial. As Waggoner states, "Most of the news reports [about the trial] were simply the convinced reaching the already convinced."[130] If Dayton itself is any indicator of these generalizations, then they certainly have merit. George Rappelyea, the local chemist and self-confessed agnostic who orchestrated the scheme to have Scopes indicted to begin with, wrote the ACLU from New Orleans: "I couldn't stay in Dayton after the trial. I would have been as lonely as the ark of truth on Mt. Sinai." Dayton druggist Frank E. Robinson, reflecting on the trial twenty–five years later, said that folks in the town were "more deeply religious than ever before."[131]

It appears that, in spite of the enormous amount of bad publicity about the trial, fundamentalism was far from being destroyed by Bryan's participation in it. Not only did fundamentalist leaders continue Bryan's cause, but many of their churches grew numerically after the Dayton affair.[132]

---

[128] This was the approach of Nell Seagraves and Jean Sumrall, two San Diego housewives who founded the Creation Research Center in 1970. Beginning in 1962 before the California State Board of Education, they demanded that school textbooks "teach creationism along with evolution as an equally viable theory" (cited in Gatewood, "From Scopes to Creation Science," p. 375). This is also the strategy of the Creation Research Society which appears to have given primacy to scientific rather than religious objections to evolution (ibid., p. 381).

[129] Owen, "Significance of the Scopes Trial," 875.

[130] "Historiography." p. 158. See also, Coletta (*Political Puritan,* p. 278) who writes, "Rather than changing minds, the trial solidified convictions already held."

[131] Cited in Ginger, *Six Days or Forever?* p. 216.

[132] David Rausch mentions that, four years after the trial, Arno C. Gaebelein was speaking at Mark A. Matthews' First Presbyterian Church in Seattle, growing to become the largest Presbyterian church in the world, with a membership of over 9,000. Neither of these fundamentalist leaders was demoralized by the Scopes trial, but continued to speak against evolution. Gaebelein was pleasantly surprised that his anti-evolution remarks in

The so-called "stigma" of Bryanism, therefore, did not prevent people from being led into assemblies pastored by men who were avowedly Bryanist in sentiment.

There is no question that the anti-evolutionists eventually lost the battle to achieve their aims in both school and court. The Tennessee anti-evolution law has been repealed, as has such legislation in all other states where it had been enacted. In 1968, under Chief Justice Earl Warren, the Supreme Court acquiesced to the ACLU's view of free speech in the classroom by overturning an Arkansas law prohibiting the instruction of evolution in public schools. Nine years later, in *Edwards v. Aguillard,* the Court further secularized public education by throwing out Louisiana's "Creationism Act." The Court affirmed that "the Act is facially invalid as violative of the Establishment Clause of the First Amendment, because it lacks a clear secular purpose."[133] Secularization also meant the elimination of sanctioned religious activities. The results have been disastrous to the moral fabric of this nation. Critics of Bryan must now consider if he were not a prophet rather than an obscurantist. To him evolution was symptomatic of the greater disease of modernism which, left unchecked, would produce infidelity and immorality among the youth of America. It must now be wondered not *if,* but *how much,* the "enlightened" educational system of America, which has promulgated evolutionary theories and rejected biblical literalism, has contributed to the advancement of futile secular humanism and the moral dissolution of its students. Bryan said that the teaching of evolution would produce brutishness in our youth and a society bankrupt of godliness and morality.[134] He warned prophetically that "if evolution wins, Christianity goes. Not suddenly, of course, but gradually, for the two cannot stand together."[135] One hardly needs to cite statistics to prove the validity of his claim against American state schools where guns and condoms have replaced prayer and the Bible, and against a western culture, where postmodern relativism appears to reign.

Mathews's church made headlines in the next day's *Post Intelligencer.* The subject was still alive and creating much interest in the papers and was filling the pews of fundamentalist churches by interested hearers (Rausch, *Zionism Within Early American Fundamentalism,* pp. 318–21).

[133] *Edwards v. Aguillard,* 482 U.S. 578 (1987).

[134] Cf. N. I. Seagraves, *The Creation Report* (San Diego: Creation Science Research Center, 1977), p. 17. Seagraves cites a direct correlation between acceptance of evolution and the breakdown of morals in society. Evolution fostered "the moral decay of spiritual values which contributes to the destruction of mental health and...the prevalence of divorce, abortion, and rampant venereal disease."

[135] Cited in Brod, "The Scopes Trial," p. 222.

The teaching of humanistic evolution has left in its wake a cultural climate void of absolutes in a society where questions of truth and falsehood are matters of moral indifference.

The Scopes trial was only a brief episode in the life of William Jennings Bryan, but it is the gross distortion of that event which has left its image of the man on American minds. Darrow and the dramatists and reporters who have taken their cue from him have cheated posterity of knowledge of Bryan, the champion of social justice, moral decency, and life-changing principles founded on Scripture. Bryan's own words from his famous speech "The Prince of Peace" give us an epitaph that best exemplifies that man:

> The human measure of a human life is its income; the divine measure of a life is its outgo, its overflow— its contribution to the welfare of all....If every word spoken in behalf of truth has its influence and every deed done for the right weighs in the final account, it is immaterial to the Christian whether his eyes behold victory or whether he died in the midst of conflict.[136]

Bryan was a Christian statesman and leading fundamentalist who strengthened the movement "in the midst of conflict" by defending an absolutely authoritative Bible at the Scopes trial. It is this man we should remember and his uncompromising scriptural principles we should uphold.

---

[136] Cited in "Thunder in the Pulpit," *Fundamentalist Journal* 6 (June 1987): 58.

Part 4:

Ministry Studies

THE ROLE OF THE HOLY SPIRIT IN PREACHING[1]

David M. Doran

This topic is of vital importance because preaching is the God-ordained means for accomplishing His purposes in this dispensation (1 Cor 1:18–25), and the work of the Holy Spirit is essential to make preaching effective (1 Cor 2:1–5). A defensible statement of the local church's mission might be that it exists to honor God by making and maturing disciples who are becoming like the Lord Jesus Christ. This mission statement contains three components: a doxological aim (to honor God, Eph 1:12; 3:21) expressed in discipleship activity (make and mature disciples, Matt 28:19–20; Eph 4:11–16) which should result in Christlike attributes developed in individual believers so that the church forms a pure bride for the Savior (Eph. 5:25–27).

THE PRIMACY OF PREACHING

Biblical preaching is crucial to the fulfillment of each element of this mission. The Scriptures reveal that the aim of honoring God is supremely accomplished through Christ-centered preaching because it is a method which is foolishness to the world, and God has chosen the foolish things of the world to confound the wise (1 Cor 1:26–31). The preacher is charged with a message that declares that the Creator God who has revealed Himself in His Son and in the Scriptures reigns (Rom 10:14–17; cf. Isa 52:7). That message declares "the glory of God in the face of Christ"[2] (2 Cor 4:6). Such preaching calls for surrender to this great God, and such surrender is a confession that Jesus Christ is Lord (Rom 10:9) which results in the glory of the Father (Phil 2:11). As Piper has rightly observed, "the goal of preaching is the glory of God reflected in the glad submission of the human heart."[3]

The record of Acts is clear that the fulfillment of the Great Commission (making and maturing disciples) is accomplished by the means of preaching, and that this advance is best described as the spread of the Word (4:31; 6:7; 8:4; 8:25; 10:42; 11:1; 11:20; 12:24; 19:20). The strategy employed

---

[1] This article appeared in the 1998 issue of *DBSJ,* vol. 3, pp. 101–21.

[2] Unless otherwise noted all Scripture quotations are from the NASB.

[3] John Piper, *The Supremacy of God in Preaching* (Grand Rapids: Baker, 1990), p. 26.

by the apostles and early church was proclamational. They were devoted to the ministry of the Word (Acts 6:4; 18:5). Modern church growth theories may minimize the role of preaching in reaching unbelievers, but the Scriptures certainly do not.

The Bible is equally clear that preaching is the chief means by which Christlikeness will be formed in God's people. Paul writes, "We proclaim Him, admonishing every man and teaching every man with all wisdom, so that we may present every man complete in Christ" (Col 1:28). It is not insignificant that the gifts of the risen Christ to His church are all speaking gifts—apostles, prophets, evangelists, and pastors and teachers (Eph 4:11). The proper exercise of these gifts[4] is essential "for the equipping of the saints for the work of service, to the building up of the body of Christ; until we all attain to the unity of the faith, and of the knowledge of the Son of God, to a mature man, to the measure of the stature which belongs to the fullness of Christ" (Eph 4:12–13).

THE EMPOWERING WORK OF THE SPIRIT

While the purpose of this article is to examine the nature of the Spirit's role in preaching, it is doubtful that any would dare deny the need for His work. It is clear that the Lord believed that His disciples would need power (Luke 24:49) and that the promise of the Spirit is their access to this power (Acts 1:8). Modern excesses regarding "power" have rightly brought forth strong criticisms, but we cannot allow ourselves to react in such a way as to ignore or minimize the New Testament emphasis on the powerful ministry of the Spirit through the preaching of the Word (1 Cor 2:1–5; 1 Thess 1:5). In fact, Paul's great encouragement to press on in the face of tremendous trials and troubles was that God had given him a "ministry of the Spirit" (2 Cor 3:8, 12). Lloyd-Jones is correct to warn us against being controlled by fear, "You can be so afraid of disorder, so concerned about discipline and decorum and control, that you become guilty of what the Scripture calls 'quenching the Spirit.'"[5]

It is quite possible that some contemporary fundamentalists have allowed wrong views and teachings regarding the nature of the Spirit's work to dull in them a hunger for dynamic ministry through the power of the Spirit. They may have forgotten that the New Testament expectation is that the proclamation of the Word is to be a display of the power of God

---

[4] Eph 2:20 seems to limit the apostolic and prophetic gifts to the founding days of the church.

[5] D. Martyn Lloyd-Jones, *Joy Unspeakable* (Wheaton, IL: Harold Shaw, 1984), p. 18.

(1 Cor 1:17, 18; cf. Rom 1:16), and that the early church experienced this power through the work of the Holy Spirit (Acts 4:31, 33; 1 Thess 1:5). The Apostle Paul was so zealous of having this power in him that he was gladly willing to endure his thorn in the flesh (2 Cor 12:9–10). The clear implication of the New Testament is that we can actually minister without the power of God. Paul could have preached at Corinth in such a way that it was not in demonstration of the Spirit and power (cf. 1 Cor 2:4), or he could have ministered at Thessalonica "in word only" (1 Thess 1:5; cf. 1 Cor 4:19–20).

The crucial questions before us are these: what do we call this work of the Holy Spirit, and how do we obtain or benefit from it? As in any operation of God in the souls of men and among men, these questions are not easily answered. The work of the Spirit seems always to involve an element of mystery for us (cf. John 3:8). The result is considerable confusion about the proper biblical terms and theological framework to discuss the Spirit's work of empowering. The purpose of this article is to examine a popular view that His work is best described as a special endowment with power that comes as a definite experience subsequent to conversion.

POPULAR VIEWS OF THE SPIRIT'S ROLE IN PREACHING

C. H. Spurgeon

Few preachers have enjoyed the power of God upon their ministries to the degree enjoyed by Charles Haddon Spurgeon. The power of the gospel radiated through his preaching and propelled him to an almost unparalleled position as a pastor and evangelist. Spurgeon was abundantly clear about his belief that it was the work of the Spirit that accomplished such great things; he sought to communicate his burden for Spirit-empowered preaching to his students in the most urgent of terms.

> We believe ourselves to be spokesmen for Jesus Christ, appointed to continue His witness upon earth; but upon Him and His testimony the Spirit of God always rested, and if it does not rest upon us, we are evidently not sent forth into the world as He was. At Pentecost the commencement of the great work of converting the world was with flaming tongues and a rushing wind, symbols of the presence of the spirit [*sic*]; if, therefore, we think to succeed without the Spirit, we are not after the Pentecostal order. If we have not the Spirit which Jesus promised, we cannot perform the commission which Jesus gave.[6]

---

[6] C. H. Spurgeon, *Lectures to My Students* (reprint ed.; Grand Rapids: Zondervan, 1979), p. 187.

Even more pointedly, Spurgeon warned, "Unless we have the spirit of the prophets resting upon us, the mantle which we wear is nothing but a rough garment to deceive."[7]

Spurgeon's absolute plea for the necessity of the work of the Spirit is rooted in his belief about the task the preacher faces.

> To us the presence and work of the Holy Spirit are the ground of our confidence as to the wisdom and hopefulness of our life work. If we had *not* believed in the Holy Ghost we should have laid down our ministry long ere this, for "who is sufficient for these things?" Our hope of success, and our strength for continuing in service, lie in our belief that the Spirit of the Lord resteth upon us.[8]

His views of depravity, rooted squarely in the Scriptures and often painted in the most vivid of images, left him no hope in his native abilities. "I shall not attempt to teach a tiger the virtues of vegetarianism; but I shall as hopefully attempt that task as I would try to convince an unregenerate man of the truths revealed by God concerning sin, and righteousness, and judgment to come."[9] Given the impossibility of this task, no wonder his conclusion, "Except the Lord endow us with power from on high, our labor must be in vain, and our hopes must end in disappointment."[10]

It is certain that all would agree with this end assessment, but we must remember that when Spurgeon speaks of having the Spirit rest upon us, he is not merely speaking of being regenerate and indwelt by the Spirit. His comments refer to an experiential work of the Spirit in and upon the preacher.

> Even so we have *felt* the Spirit of God operating upon our hearts, we have known and perceived the power which He wields over human spirits, and we know Him by frequent, conscious, personal contact. By the sensitiveness of our spirit we are as much made conscious of the presence of the Spirit of God as we are made cognizant of the existence of the souls of our fellow-men by their action upon our souls, or as we are certified of the existence of matter by its action upon our senses. We have been raised from the dull sphere of mere mind and matter into the heavenly radiance of the spirit-world; and now, as spiritual men, we discern spiritual things, we feel the forces which are paramount in the spirit-realm, and we know that there is a Holy Ghost, for we feel Him operating upon our spirits. If it were not so, we should certainly have no right to be in the ministry of Christ's church.[11]

---

[7] Ibid.

[8] Ibid., p. 185.

[9] C. H. Spurgeon, *An All-Round Ministry* (reprint of 1900 ed.; Carlisle, PA: Banner of Truth Trust, 1994), p. 322.

[10] Ibid.

[11] Spurgeon, *Lectures,* pp. 185–186.

This experiential element of the Spirit's work, for Spurgeon, is grounded in the new birth, but must be utmost present in those who preach the Word. The absence of the Spirit's presence and power "lies at the root of many useless ministries."[12]

It seems that Spurgeon's was not a finished theology of the Spirit's work that fleshed out all the terms and their respective nuances. He did speak of an "anointing"[13] and an "unction from the holy One"[14] but seemed most at home with the language of filling. The flexibility in his terminology reflects his admitted inability to define precisely this work of the Spirit.

> What is it? I wonder how long we might beat our brains before we could plainly put into words what is meant by *preaching with unction;* yet he who preaches knows its presence, and he who hears soon detects its absence;... Such is the mystery of spiritual anointing; we know, but we cannot tell to others what it is.[15]

The anointing of the Spirit cannot be manufactured but "is in itself priceless, and beyond measure needful if you would edify believers and bring sinners to Jesus."[16]

Whatever the term used, Spurgeon believed that the work of the Holy Spirit on the preacher was direct and sensible, so he could describe his experience as being "distinctly conscious of a power working upon me when I am speaking in the name of the Lord, infinitely transcending any personal power of fluency, and far surpassing any energy derived from excitement."[17] This work can be so profound that

> the divine Spirit will sometimes work upon us so as to bear us completely out of ourselves. From the beginning of the sermon to the end we might at such times say, "Whether in the body or out of the body I cannot tell: God knoweth." Everything has been forgotten but the one all-engrossing subject in hand. If I were forbidden to enter heaven, but were permitted to select my state for all eternity, I should choose to be as I sometimes feel in preaching the gospel. Heaven is foreshadowed in such a state....[18]

---

[12] Ibid., p. 195.

[13] Spurgeon, *An All-Round Ministry,* p. 329.

[14] Spurgeon, *Lectures,* p. 50.

[15] Ibid.

[16] Ibid.

[17] Ibid, p. 192.

[18] Ibid.

We find in Spurgeon the blending of a deep desire for the experience of the Spirit's work with the perspective of practitioner. He does not wrestle with the technical theological matters of this subject. His eye is single: power in the pulpit. We must have this power, and we cannot have it without the Spirit. If we have the Spirit upon us, we know it as we preach and our hearers know it as well. For Spurgeon, this work is an anointing, an unction from on high that is the legacy of Pentecost which ought to be sought fervently.

Reuben A. Torrey

From the rather undefined views of Spurgeon, we move to consider a more dogmatically defined view of the Spirit's work in the life of the believer. R. A. Torrey's views on the work of the Spirit have had considerable impact on the thinking and terminology of fundamentalists.[19] Since Torrey viewed this as the indispensable element of effective ministry, he accordingly preached and wrote much on this subject, which he called the baptism with the Holy Spirit.[20] In his estimation the various expressions in Scripture for the Spirit's work are "practically synonymous" for this work.[21]

Torrey offered a fairly descriptive definition of the baptism with the Spirit as: (1) "a definite experience of which one may and ought to know whether he has received it or not;" (2) "an operation distinct from, and additional to, His regenerating work;" and (3) "always connected with and primarily for the purpose of testimony and service."[22] He viewed the distribution of spiritual gifts as a result of Spirit baptism, but stressed that in spite of diversity of gifts "there will always be power, the very power of God, when one is baptized with the Holy Spirit."[23] That gifts are bestowed with Spirit baptism seems apparent from 1 Corinthians 12:13ff., but Torrey would make the baptism, and therefore the distribution of gifts,

---

[19] E.g., John R. Rice refers repeatedly to the teachings of Torrey as a historical precedent for his own (*The Power of Pentecost* [Murfreesboro, TN: Sword of the Lord, 1949], pp. 155–161).

[20] He was so convinced of its centrality that he could write, "The New Testament has much to say about the necessity for the baptism with the Holy Spirit," yet offer very little textual support for such a claim (see R. A. Torrey, *The Person and Work of the Holy Spirit* [reprint ed.; Springdale, PA: Whitaker House, 1996], p. 215).

[21] Ibid., p. 187. Among the expressions he included in this are "the Holy Ghost fell," "the gift of the Holy Ghost," "received the Holy Ghost," "the Holy Ghost came on them," "the promise of my Father," and "endued with power from on high."

[22] Ibid., pp. 187–198.

[23] Ibid., p. 206.

as generally subsequent to conversion. Additionally, his emphasis on special power bestowed at the baptism seems to be a major distinctive of his position.

That power was the central focal point of Torrey's view of Spirit baptism is obvious from arguments for and illustrations of its necessity. "It is evident then that the baptism with the Holy Spirit is absolutely necessary in every Christian for the service that Christ demands and expects of him."[24] It is equally "evident that the baptism with the Holy Spirit is an absolutely necessary preparation for effective work for Christ along every line of service.... This endowment of power is through the baptism with the Holy Spirit."[25]

It is also plain from human experience and church history that some who have neglected this truth discover their error and are propelled to more fruitful ministries. Torrey observes,

> Religious biographies abound in instances of men who have worked as best they could until one day they were led to see that there was such an experience as the baptism with the Holy Spirit and to seek it and obtain it. From that hour, there came into their service a new power that utterly transformed its character.[26]

This observation presses him to conclude,

> A distinguished theological professor has said that the question, "Have you met God?" ought to be put to every candidate for the ministry. Yes, but we ought to go farther than this and be even more definite. To every candidate for the ministry we should put the question, "Have you been baptized with the Holy Spirit?" and if not, we should say to him as Jesus said to the first preachers of the Gospel, "Sit down until you are endued with power from on high."[27]

Based on these statements it is clear that Torrey believed in a special endowment with the Spirit which was prerequisite to powerful ministry.

David Martyn Lloyd-Jones

Lloyd-Jones used the terms unction, anointing, and baptism in the Spirit as essentially interchangeable. He seemed to tilt toward the terms unction and anointing, but formally defended the position that the baptism in the Spirit

---

[24] Ibid., p. 220.

[25] Ibid., p. 219.

[26] Ibid., p. 207.

[27] Ibid., p. 221.

found in Acts is an empowerment for ministry. For Lloyd-Jones "the real object of 'the baptism with the Holy Spirit' is to enable men to witness for Christ and His salvation with power…it is not given primarily to promote sanctification; it is a baptism of power, or a baptism of fire, a baptism to enable one to witness."[28]

This ministry of the Spirit is essential for effective ministry. With regard to the apostles, Lloyd-Jones makes the following assessment,

> They seem to have all the necessary knowledge, but that knowledge is not sufficient, something further is needed, is indeed essential. The knowledge indeed is vital for you cannot be witnesses without it, but to be effective witnesses you need the power and the unction and the demonstration of the Spirit in addition.[29]

This belief was strengthened by his view of the context of ministry. He found no comfort or hope in human resources.

> Take the situation with which we are confronted today. Look at the task, look at the state of the world, look at the modern mentality. Without believing in and knowing something of the power of the Spirit, it is a heart-breaking task. I certainly could not go on for another day but for this. If I felt that it was all left to us, and our learning and our scholarship and our organizations, I would be of all men most miserable and hopeless. But that is not the case. What we read of in the New Testament is equally possible and open to us today; and it is our only hope.[30]

Whereas Torrey seemed to address this concept more for believers in general, Lloyd-Jones focused on this ministry of the Spirit with particular regard to preachers. His interest in the subject was not disinterested, for he longed for a ministry marked by divine power. He once wrote to his friend Philip Hughes, "Oh! How I long to know exactly what Paul meant in 1 Corinthians 2:1–5 and to experience it in my ministry. I have become tired of all else and when I read of Whitefield I feel that I have never really preached in my life."[31] In another place he wrote, "To me there is nothing more terrible for a preacher, than to be in the pulpit alone, without the conscious smile of God."[32]

How is this work of the Spirit upon the preacher to be defined? Lloyd-Jones uses strong words to describe it:

---

[28] D. Martyn Lloyd-Jones, *Preaching and Preachers* (Grand Rapids: Zondervan, 1971), p. 308.

[29] Ibid., p. 308.

[30] Ibid., p. 315.

[31] Cited in Tony Sargent, *The Sacred Anointing* (Wheaton, IL: Crossway Books, 1994), p. 18.

[32] D. Martyn Lloyd-Jones, *Revival* (reprint ed.; Westchester, IL: Crossway Books, 1987), p. 295.

It is the Spirit falling upon the preacher in a special manner. It is an access of power. It is God giving power, and enabling, through the Spirit, to the preacher in order that he may do this work in a manner that lifts it up beyond the efforts and endeavours of man to a position in which the preacher is being used by the Spirit and becomes a channel through whom the Spirit works.[33]

Lloyd-Jones called this work a "divine afflatus" to describe the dynamic of the Spirit's work in carrying along the preacher. Although he advocated diligent study,[34] he believed that the preacher should not be tied to his preparation so that he may be free to follow the Spirit's leading. Sargent articulates the model involved in Lloyd-Jones' imagery, "Dependent upon the Holy Spirit, he [the preacher] should enter the pulpit and open the Word of God. He should endeavor to unfurl the sails of his mind to the wind of the Spirit and proceed along the course which the Holy Spirit directs."[35]

When the Spirit is at work in the preacher, Lloyd-Jones believes that he knows it.[36] His description of the experience is similar to the one offered by Spurgeon above.

How does one know it? It gives clarity of thought, clarity of speech, ease of utterance, a great sense of authority and confidence as you are preaching, an awareness of a power not your own thrilling through the whole of your being, and an indescribable sense of joy. You are a man "possessed", you are taken hold of, and taken up. I like to put it like this—and I know of nothing on earth that is comparable to this feeling—that when this happens you have a feeling that you are not actually doing the preaching, you are looking on. You are looking on at yourself in amazement as this is happening. It is not your effort; you are just the instrument, the channel, the vehicle: the Spirit is using you, and you are looking on in great enjoyment and astonishment.[37]

Do the people who are listening recognize it?

They sense it at once; they can tell the difference immediately. They are gripped, they become serious, they are convicted, they are moved, they are humbled. Some are convicted of sin, others are lifted up to the heavens, anything may happen to any one of them. They know at once that something quite unusual and exceptional is happening.[38]

---

[33] Lloyd-Jones, *Preaching and Preachers,* p. 305.

[34] "Careful preparation, and the unction of the Holy Spirit, must never be regarded as alternatives but as complementary to each other" (Ibid.).

[35] Sargent, *Sacred Anointing,* p. 36.

[36] D. Martyn Lloyd-Jones, *God the Holy Spirit* (Wheaton, IL: Crossway Books, 1997), p. 252.

[37] Lloyd-Jones, *Preaching and Preachers,* p. 324.

[38] Ibid., pp. 324–325.

An element that contributes to the wonder of this work by the Spirit, in Lloyd-Jones' view, is the sovereignty of its bestowal. He did not subscribe to any mechanistic view of obtaining this anointing. It is in the hands of the sovereign God to bestow as He wills.

> I often say that the most romantic place on earth is the pulpit. I ascend the pulpit stairs Sunday after Sunday: I never know what is going to happen. I confess that sometimes, for various reasons, I come expecting nothing; but suddenly, the power is given. At other times, I think I have a great deal because of my preparation: but, alas, I find there is no power in it. Thank God it is like that. I do my utmost, but He controls the supply and the power, He infuses it.[39]

This does not mean that Lloyd-Jones viewed God's bestowal in any way as arbitrary or capricious.

> There are times when, entirely outside his control, he [the preacher] is given a special authority, special power, an unction which is unusual. And there are good reasons for its bestowal. There are circumstances which he himself is not always aware of, which he only discovers afterwards. Somebody may have come to the congregation who needs a particular message or word, and the preacher, without knowledge on his part, is guided to say something that is just appropriate to that particular state and condition. There is, therefore, this special endowment of power which is called "the anointing". It is something that one should seek and covet, it is something for which one should be constantly praying.[40]

The "givenness" of the Spirit's unction should not keep the preacher from seeking it with full earnestness and faith. Lloyd-Jones concludes his book on preaching with these words,

> What then are we to do about this? There is only one obvious conclusion. Seek Him! Seek Him! What can we do without Him? Seek Him! Seek Him always. But go beyond seeking Him; expect Him. Do you expect anything to happen when you get up to preach in a pulpit? Or do you just say to yourself, "Well, I have prepared my address, I am going to give them this address; some of them will appreciate it and some will not?" Are you expecting it to be the turning point in someone's life? Are you expecting anyone to have a climatic experience? That is what preaching is meant to do…. Seek this power, expect this power, yearn for this power; and when the power comes, yield to Him. Do not resist. Forget all about your sermon if necessary. Let Him loose you, let Him manifest His power in you and through you. I am

---

[39] Sargent, *Sacred Anointing,* p. 59.

[40] Ibid., pp. 97–98.

certain, as I have said several times before, that nothing but a return of this power of the Spirit on our preaching is going to avail us anything.... This "unction", this "anointing", is the supreme thing. Seek it until you have it; be content with nothing less. Go on until you can say, "And my speech and my preaching was not with enticing words of man's wisdom, but in demonstration of the Spirit and of power." He is still able to do "exceeding abundantly above all that we can ask or think."[41]

Stephen and David Olford

A more recent advocate of "anointed preaching" is Stephen Olford, who, along with his son, David, has written a new book on expository preaching which includes a special emphasis on the Spirit's anointing.[42] Their basic premise is straightforward, "We move from the preparation of an expository sermon to the dynamics of incarnational preaching. Only the Holy Spirit can transform a manuscript into a message."[43] The foundation pattern for this operation of the Spirit is the ministry of the Lord Jesus. Even though Jesus enjoyed the ministry of the Spirit prior to His baptism, "there came a crisis in the life of Jesus when He appropriated (by faith and prayer [Luke 3:21–22]) the anointing of the Spirit to fulfill His messianic mission.... As preachers, we likewise *need* this 'sacred anointing.'"[44]

The Olfords, in contrast to Torrey and Lloyd-Jones, distinguish the anointing of the Spirit from the baptism with the Spirit.[45] They believe that Spirit-baptism is "a *one-time* experience (Eph 4:5), and is synonymous with regeneration or new birth."[46] The anointing of the Spirit "represents our *vocation* in Christ...the anointing for preachers (and believers generally) is for *special* Christian service. It is 'the Promise of the Father' (Acts 1:4, 8) and is referred to as *enduement with power* (Luke 24:49).... As the filling suggests an *inward* working of the Spirit, the anointing stresses the *outward* clothing with power."[47]

---

[41] Lloyd-Jones, *Preaching and Preachers,* p. 325.

[42] Stephen F. Olford with David L. Olford, *Anointed Expository Preaching* (Nashville, TN: Broadman & Holman, 1998).

[43] Ibid., p. 214.

[44] Ibid., p. 216.

[45] Interestingly, at one point Olford (p. 227) changes a quote from a biography of D. L. Moody to honor this difference. The quote recounts the famous interaction between Moody and the two women who were praying for Moody to receive power. Olford records it as, "they told him about the definite [anointing] of the Holy Spirit." What they told him about was the baptism of the Holy Spirit!

[46] Olford, *Anointed Expository Preaching,* p. 216. He also makes a distinction between these two, baptism and anointing, and the filling of the Spirit.

[47] Ibid., pp. 216–217.

Tying their understanding of the anointing to the Lord's ministry, the Olfords argue that the anointing has two purposes: "to reach people and to preach the gospel."[48] The anointing gives the preacher a tremendous authority in proclaiming the gospel that can "penetrate the hearts of saint and sinner alike."[49] The pathway to this anointed authority in preaching is holiness, yieldedness, and prayerfulness.[50]

While they do not elaborate very deeply on the effects of the anointing on the preacher, they certainly emphasize its necessity and the urgency with which it should be sought. They conclude their discussion with this appeal,

> We, the authors, can testify to the reality of Moody's experience of the anointing. The difference it makes is the difference between night and day. Fellow preacher, we urge you to proceed no further in your work for the Lord until you have believed the promise (Acts 1:4) and received the power (Acts 1:8), both as an initial act of faith and then as a continual appropriation of faith.[51]

Summary

While others could be added to this survey, these representatives present the essential components of a popular view of the Spirit's ministry, namely that the Spirit's work should be identified as a special baptism or anointing that endows the preacher with divine power. Common among these positions is its experiential nature, i.e., the preacher experiences this enduement. Some articulate this experience as a crisis experience which is as at least as, if not more, definite than one's conversion. For example, Torrey says "there is none of this indefiniteness in the Bible. The Bible is clear as day on this, as on every other point. It sets forth an experience so definite and so real that one may know whether or not he has received the baptism with the Holy Spirit and can answer yes or no to the question, 'Have you received the Holy Ghost?'"[52] This element of a crisis experience of the Spirit seems to be a commonality, yet none would argue for a single experience of the Spirit's baptism/anointing.

Even Lloyd-Jones, who was not governed by a two-stage view of sanctification, advocated a "crisis theology of the Spirit" which he believed

---

[48] Ibid., p. 222.

[49] Ibid., p. 227.

[50] Ibid., p. 218.

[51] Ibid., p. 228.

[52] Torrey, *Person and Work,* pp. 188–189.

was rooted in the book of Acts and substantiated throughout church history.[53] For him, and the others, the crisis experience was an outpouring of the Spirit, experienced in dramatic form initially, but also repeated in the course of ministry and proclamation. Torrey could even argue that we "need repeated refilling with the Holy Spirit" and that "even after one has been baptized with the Holy Spirit, no matter how definite that baptism may be, he needs to be filled again and again with the Spirit."[54]

When the discussion focuses on how this work of the Spirit may be obtained, each offers a unique perspective. The one common requirement identified by all for receiving this special work of the Spirit is prayer.[55] Torrey articulated the most extensive formula for receiving the baptism with the Spirit, a seven-step pathway.[56] Spurgeon offers many helpful observations about obtaining the Spirit's power for ministry, but without the somewhat mechanical nature of Torrey's seven steps.[57] Sargent sees in Lloyd-Jones five requirements for receiving the unction of the Spirit.[58] The variety of answers posed by these teachers reveals that the issue is not as clear as they might suggest.

In conclusion, we may simply say that all agree that this special work of the Spirit is essential to effective ministry, but not all are agreed as to what it is and how we may obtain it. These two issues, terminology and methodology, expose the basic problems in the popular approach to the Spirit's role in preaching.

CRITICISMS OF THE POPULAR VIEW OF THE SPIRIT'S ROLE

The most basic issue relates to defining the Spirit's empowering work, that is, what should this work be properly called? It is my contention that it is improper to describe it in terms of the baptism with the Spirit, anointing, or unction as they are defined biblically. By using these terms in a manner which is not consistent with the biblical usage, this position creates confusion, improperly restricts to a few what God has given to all believers, blurs the distinction between the effects of Spirit baptism and genuine

---

[53] Sargent, *Sacred Anointing,* p. 282.

[54] Torrey, *Person and Work,* p. 229.

[55] Sargent, *Sacred Anointing,* p. 96; Spurgeon, *Lectures,* p. 196; Torrey, *Person and Work,* p. 247; Olford, *Anointed Expository Preaching,* p. 218.

[56] Torrey, *Person and Work,* pp. 232–259.

[57] See Spurgeon, *All-Round Ministry,* pp. 315–339.

[58] Sargent, *Sacred Anointing,* pp. 95–101.

empowering, and dangerously opens the door to fresh communications from God.

Confusing Initial Reception and Subsequent Empowerings

The most significant issue at stake in this discussion is the proper biblical and theological understanding of the believer's initial reception of the Holy Spirit. By virtue of the arguments that Torrey and Lloyd-Jones make regarding the baptism with the Spirit, their position results in confusing usage of terms and the mishandling of several key passages.

Their insistence on equating references to Spirit-baptism, pouring out, filling, anointing, etc., puts them in the position of seeming to contradict themselves. For example, Torrey spends extensive time arguing that the baptism with the Spirit is a repeatable endowment with power, but then turns to suggest that perhaps it would be best to reserve the term "baptism" for the initial reception of the Spirit and use filling for subsequent empowerings.

The question may arise: Should we call these new fillings with the Holy Spirit "fresh baptisms" with the Holy Spirit? To this we would answer that the expression "baptism" is never used in the Scriptures of a second experience, and there is something of the initiatory character in the very thought of baptism. So, if one wishes to be precisely biblical, it would seem to be better not to use the term "baptism" of a second experience but to limit it to the first experience…it would be well to speak of one baptism but many fillings.[59]

This certainly fits well with the terminology of Acts, but it does not seem to be compatible with all the arguments he has made for his own position, namely that the baptism with the Spirit is an enduement with power which may and ought to occur repeatedly.[60] In fact, he is not really consistent with his own counsel, for writing later in the same work, he says, "My *first experience* of being baptized with the Holy Spirit…."[61] Such vacillation severely undercuts their definitions and descriptions of this work of the Holy Spirit.

More significant is the failure to handle adequately the explicit statements of Scripture that tie the baptism with the Spirit to conversion. This

---

[59] Torrey, *Person and Work,* pp. 230–231.

[60] Lloyd-Jones evidences the same confusion. He writes, "the baptism of the Holy Spirit is the initial experience of glory and the reality of and the love of the Father and the Son. Yes, you may have many experiences of that but the first experience, I would suggest, is the baptism of the Holy Spirit" (*God the Holy Spirit,* p. 240). Later in the same work he writes, "The baptism, I suggest, is the initial experience, the filling is an experience that can often be repeated" (p. 243).

[61] Torrey, *Person and Work,* p. 250. Emphasis added.

connection is clearly pointed out by Peter in his sermon on Pentecost. Peter clearly announces the offer of the gospel in these terms: "Repent, and each of you be baptized in the name of the Lord Jesus Christ for the forgiveness of your sins; and *you will receive the gift of the Holy Spirit*" (Acts 2:38, emphasis added). Verse 39 even expands this promise to apply "for you and your children and for all who are far off, *as many as the Lord our God will call to Himself* (emphasis added). Ironically, Torrey uses v. 39 as proof that the baptism with the Spirit is intended for all believers while disconnecting the promise of this verse from the conditions of its fulfillment recorded in v. 38. In other words, he correctly declares that the promise of the Spirit is available to all believers (v. 39), yet ignores the fact that the text says the reception of the Spirit is joined to salvation (v. 38).[62]

Three points are important to buttress my argument regarding its use in Acts. First, verse 33 has already identified the manifestations of Pentecost as the pouring forth of the promise of the Holy Spirit. In light of Acts 1:4–5, which joins the concepts of the promise of the Father and the baptism with the Holy Spirit, it seems clear that Acts 2:33 includes Spirit-baptism. This is what Peter offers to his listeners. Second, Peter explicitly ties the reception of the gift of the Spirit to God's salvific call of people to Himself (Acts 2:39) which is evidenced by repentance and faith in the Lord Jesus Christ (v. 38). Third, the argument made by Torrey and Lloyd-Jones that the disciples were already converted men ignores the entire point of Pentecost being the initial outpouring of the Spirit as promised in Acts 1.[63]

The same observations can be made with regard to Acts 5:32 ("Holy Spirit, whom God has given to those who obey Him"[64]). The evidence is equally, if not more, convincing when one considers the outpouring of the Spirit upon Cornelius and his household. Acts 10:44–45 record that the "Holy Spirit fell upon those who were listening" and that "the gift of the Holy Spirit had been poured out on the Gentiles also." Peter's reflection

---

[62] Ibid., pp. 222–226.

[63] The thrust of their argument is based on the assumption that their opponents equate Spirit baptism with regeneration (cf. Lloyd-Jones, *God the Holy Spirit,* pp. 236–237). To claim that Spirit baptism occurs at the point of conversion is not the same as saying that Spirit baptism is regeneration. Again, they fail to consider the dispensational significance of the day of Pentecost, i.e., many, if not most, dispensationalists believe that the OT saints were regenerate, but they do not believe that they were Spirit-baptized. Cf. John Walvoord, *The Holy Spirit,* 3rd ed. (Grand Rapids: Zondervan, 1958), p. 32; Alva J. McClain, *The Greatness of the Kingdom,* (Winona Lake, IN: BMH Books, 1974), p. 287.

[64] Verse 31 supplies insight into what "obey Him" means—repentance that leads to the forgiveness of sins.

on this event in 11:16–18 joins the promise of Spirit-baptism (v. 16) to the gift received by the disciples at Pentecost[65] after they had exercised faith in the Lord Jesus Christ (v. 17).

Moving outside of Acts, other NT passages seem clear that the reception of the Spirit is at the point of conversion. For example, Titus 3:5–6 ("regeneration and renewing by the Holy Spirit, whom He poured out upon us") uses the language of pouring in connection with the point of conversion.[66] It is quite amazing that both Torrey and Lloyd-Jones would make such strong use of Galatians 3:2 in defense of an experiential reception of the Spirit subsequent to conversion, since the point of Paul's argument is clearly referring to conversion. Paul's question clearly refers to their initial acceptance of the gospel by faith. This is evident from his expression of shock that they are being bewitched away from the gospel (v. 1), and by his direct question in verse 3, "Having begun by the Spirit, are you now being perfected by the flesh?" To dislocate verse 2 from initial conversion destroys Paul's argument. Paul is clearly tying their conversion through faith with the reception of the Holy Spirit.[67]

Restricting to a Few What Belongs to All Believers

Another set of NT texts also makes it difficult to accept the Torrey/Lloyd-Jones position. 1 Corinthians 12:13, 2 Corinthians 1:21, and 1 John 2:20, 27 use their key terms (baptism, anointing, and unction [KJV], respectively) with reference to all believers, not just a select few. In other words, these texts teach that all believers partake of Spirit baptism and have been anointed (received an anointing). Torrey seems to acknowledge this, but his answer is simply to argue that all of the Corinthians had indeed received this special baptism.[68] Lloyd-Jones chooses the same path, "therefore it seems to me that it is more than likely that most members of the early church received the baptism of the Holy Spirit."[69] I suppose that it is impossible to deny their assumption, but it seems to be an overly convenient way of circumventing the problem and reveals a very idealized view of the early churches. It is surprising to find the kind of baptism articulated

---

[65] Acts 10:47 makes this same connection, "who have received the Holy Spirit just as we did."

[66] Paul uses the same verb as Acts 2:17.

[67] Ronald Y. K. Fung, *The Epistle to the Galatians,* NICNT (Grand Rapids: Eerdmans, 1988), p. 130.

[68] Torrey, *Person and Work*, p. 201.

[69] Lloyd-Jones, *Joy Unspeakable,* p. 182.

by Torrey and Lloyd-Jones being argued as universally bestowed upon the carnal Corinthians (or the apostatizing Galatians for that matter).

Opening the Door for Direct
Communication from God

While the other criticisms of the popular view center on the meaning of baptism with the Spirit or anointing, another concern raised by the language used focuses on the tendency to open the way for direct communication from God to the preacher and to his hearers. Because the ministry of the Spirit seems to be viewed as a continuation of the prophetic mold,[70] statements are made which tend in that direction. For example, Spurgeon encouraged his college graduates to leave room for divine assistance:

> I do not see where the opportunity is given to the Spirit of God to help us in preaching, if every jot and tittle is settled beforehand. Do let your trust in God be free to move hand and foot. While you are preaching, believe that God the Holy Spirit can give you, in the self-same hour, what you shall speak; and can make you say what you had not previously thought of; yes, and make this newly-given utterance to be the very arrowhead of the discourse, which shall strike deeper into the heart than anything you had prepared.[71]

Lloyd-Jones, due to the deliberate attention he gave to the subject, is even more open to such assistance from the Holy Spirit. His choice of the word "afflatus" to describe the work of the Spirit in giving unction indicates that he attributed a level of inspiration to the process. One of his chief examples of this work of the Spirit was the ministry of Howell Harris, a Welshman contemporary of Whitefield. Harris explained his preaching practice in these words, "I took no particular texts but discoursed freely as the Lord gave me utterance. As to the subject of my discourse, it was all given unto me in an extraordinary manner without the least premeditation, it was not the fruit of my memory, it was the effect of the immediate strong impulse felt in my soul."[72] It seems that Harris' experience became

---

[70] Spurgeon's comment, "Unless we have the spirit of the prophets resting upon us, the mantle which we wear is nothing but a rough garment to deceive, "shows this linking of the offices (*Lectures to My Students,* p. 187).

[71] *An All-Round Ministry,* pp. 349–350. Jack Deere (*Surprised by the Voice of God* [Grand Rapids: Zondervan, 1996], pp. 89–91) recounts several of Spurgeon's own examples and explanations of this Spirit-directed speech in order to make the case for contemporary prophecy.

[72] Cited in Sargent, *Sacred Anointing,* p. 35. It may be valuable to note that Lloyd-Jones, according to Sargent, appears to have been favorable to the idea of "direct leadings" and "impressions on the mind" by the Holy Spirit which was embraced by both George

somewhat paradigmatic for Lloyd-Jones. Note his comments on Harris's assertion, "I ask a question at this point. Was not this what the New Testament calls prophesying? Was this not the prophesying that we read of in 1 Corinthians 12 and 14? I would venture the opinion that it is. This is a man delivering what is given to him. It is not *revelation* but *inspiration*."[73]

While it is beyond our purpose here, this is what has led some to see Lloyd-Jones as a forerunner of the current prophecy movement.[74] For our purposes, the observation is made to suggest that the hunger for a fresh experience of the Spirit fully compatible to that of the early church seems to lead one invariably to an openness to the same type of communication from the Spirit available to them.

CONCLUSION

The aim of this article was to examine the validity of the popular usage of the language of Spirit baptism and anointing to describe a special endowment with power as a definite post-conversion experience. Since all believers have been Spirit baptized and anointed by God, it is not proper to use these biblical terms in a non-biblical manner. Additionally, the view that spirit baptism is a post-conversion experience does not square with NT teaching on the subject.

Given these criticisms of the popular usage of the phrases "baptism with the Spirit," "anointing/anointed," and "unction of the Spirit," I do not believe that we should perpetuate their usage in our discussions of preaching. Also, it would be best that prayer for preaching should not invoke these ideas (e.g., "anoint your preacher") and discussion of the giftedness or fruitfulness of preachers would be better served without these images (e.g., "he is an anointed preacher"). This does not in any way minimize the desire that so often prompts the unbiblical use of these terms and images. My contention is that one may have a very intense desire for the Spirit's work in preaching without muddying the theological waters through inaccurate use of terms. In fact, the quest toward the noble goal of Spirit-empowered preaching will be aided by the elimination of unneeded confusion and improved concentration on the true access to that power.

Whitefield and Howell Harris. For an interesting, and enlightening, account of Jonathan Edwards' critical response to Whitefield's tendency toward these impulses, see Iain Murray, *Jonathan Edwards* (Carlisle, PA: Banner of Truth Trust, 1987) pp. 240–242.

[73] Cited in Sargent, *Sacred Anointing,* p. 90 (italics added by Sargent).

[74] This seems to be Sargent's conclusion. John Piper, "A Passion for Christ-Exalting Power" (unpublished paper, pp. 8–10) sees Lloyd-Jones clearly in this vein. Deere, *Surprised by the Voice of God*, clearly sees Spurgeon in this light; cf. footnote 70.

REVIVAL AND REVIVALISM:
A HISTORICAL AND DOCTRINAL
EVALUATION[1]

Gerald L. Priest

Iain Murray, in his recent critique of revivalism,[2] laments what he considers a new view of revival that came into vogue during the latter half of the nineteenth century—a view which displaced the old with a distinctly different understanding of the subject. A shift in vocabulary marked the change. He writes,

> Seasons of revival became "revival meetings." Instead of being "surprising" they might now be even announced in advance, and whereas no one in the previous [eighteenth] century had known of ways to secure a revival, a system was now popularized by "revivalists" which came near to guaranteeing results.[3]

Murray relates that critics of revival as well as supporters of it have failed to draw a distinction between professional revivalism and genuine heaven-sent revival. "The two things are treated essentially the same…[they use] the terms interchangeably."[4] For the critics, all revivals can be explained in human terms; for the supporters, revivalism constitutes no real departure from the revivals in America's early history. This has led to a great deal of misunderstanding as to the genuineness of revival and its effects.[5]

Most revisionist historians have failed to see any divine initiative or supernatural activity in the moral transformation of individuals and

---

[1] This article appeared in the Fall 1996 issue of *DBSJ*, vol. 1, pp. 223–252.

[2] *Revival and Revivalism: The Making and Marring of American Evangelicalism 1750–1858* (Edinburgh: Banner of Truth Trust, 1994), p. xix.

[3] Ibid., p. xviii.

[4] Ibid., p. xix.

[5] Examples of the misunderstanding of revival's true nature abound. Two recent works which make little difference between the great awakenings of the past and twentieth century pseudo-revivalism of Pentecostal "latter rain" and new wave or third wave charismatic varieties are: Winkie Pratney, *Revival: Its Principles and Personalities* (Lafayette, LA: Huntington House Publishers, 1994), especially pp. 222–24; and Richard M. Riss, *A Survey of Twentieth Century Revival Movements* (2nd printing of 1988 ed., Peabody, MA: Hendrickson, 1995), especially pp. 7–16. Another somewhat more conservative approach nevertheless fails to discern doctrinal unsoundness in so-called revival movements: Wesley Duewel, *Revival Fire* (Grand Rapids: Zondervan, 1995).

communities. Instead, they have caricatured revival by focusing on the idiosyncratic and aberrational behavior of the credulous in response to dynamic pulpiteers relying on their incredible powers of suggestion.[6] Without admitting the divine origin of genuine revival, historian William McLoughlin criticizes those historians who have treated the subject of revival unfairly.

> Chroniclers, intent upon the colorful or the bizarre, have created a false stereotype. Their real meaning and drama have been lost in exaggerations of their eccentricities. It is a mistake to think that all revivals are orgies of mass hysteria and all revivalists are grim or theatrical prophets. ... If that is all there were to revivals, they might well be dismissed as quaint or picturesque sidelights of American life. But they have been far more than that.[7]

Moreover, fundamentalists have not always been discerning about the differences between revival and revivalism. They have often equated emotional exuberance and numbers of decisions with the work of the Holy Spirit. Their advertisement of and preparation for a revival meeting presumes that revival *will* take place. The approach is: "Since we have promoted it and prayed for it, we *will* have revival." The point of this article is that there is a difference between revival and revivalism, which virtually constitutes a difference of what is genuine from what is false. Many sincere Christians down through the years have longed for

---

[6] For instance, Harry S. Stout portrays George Whitefield as a sensational dramatist who, in marketeering the gospel, became a religious celebrity. To Stout, Whitefield was an actor performing the role of a revivalist on the center stage of colonial American history. Stout virtually rules out the supernatural as an explanation for the evangelistic success of Whitefield and the wonderful awakening which resulted from his preaching (*The Divine Dramatist: George Whitefield and the Rise of Modern Evangelicalism* [Grand Rapids: Eerdmans, 1991], passim; note especially pp. xiii–xxiv). One of the first cultural historians to apply the evolutionary hypothesis to revival was Frederick Morgan Davenport. He advocated that revival was a psychological reversion to primitive animalism. See his *Primitive Traits in Religious Revivals: A Study in Mental and Social Evolution* (New York: Macmillan, 1905), pp. 217, 220, 223–24, 238–39, 297. For a discussion of those suggesting that the use of communications media has "artificially awakened" people, see Leonard I. Sweet, ed., *Communications and Change in American Religious History* (Grand Rapids: Eerdmans, 1993); see especially pp. 11–12, 128–30. These are examples of various attempts to circumvent the divine element in revival.

[7] William G. McLoughlin, *Modern Revivalism: Charles Grandison Finney to Billy Graham* (New York: Ronal Press, 1959), p. v. McLoughlin is a cultural (certainly not a theological) historian who considers periods of revival a necessary therapeutic for the revitalization of society. See his *Revivals, Awakenings, and Reform: An Essay on Religion and Social Change in America, 1607–1977* (Chicago: University of Chicago Press, 1978), pp. 2, 8, 10. Cf. Keith J. Hardman, *The Spiritual Awakeners: American Revivalists from Solomon Stoddard to D. L. Moody* (Chicago: Moody Press, 1983), pp. 19–20.

heaven-sent revival and seen it happen, but often man's work of revivalism has been mistaken for revival or has marred the real thing. The results have been superficial at best. At worst, the cause of Christ and His doctrine have been distorted. It is imperative that we know the difference between revival and revivalism if we are to be scripturally obedient, able to discern what is heaven-sent, and hopeful of God's blessing on our churches.

Three presuppositions underlie this study. First and foremost, only God can produce a revival; it is a divinely sovereign work originating in the good pleasure of the Spirit of God in accordance with the Word of God. Second, revival is simply the intensification of what is normal to biblical Christianity. It can only be extraordinary in degree and extent, not in nature, of what is authentically Christian. As one early commentator on revival explained it, the Holy Spirit produces converts "in more copious measure and in greater power at some times than at others."[8] Third, revival will conform to Christian doctrine as found in the Bible. Revival will therefore be manifested in salvation and sanctification. The test of genuine revival as a work of God will be whether those doctrines, as revealed in Scripture, are clearly evidenced.

If we accept the propositions that true revival is a work originating solely with God, that revival is the activity of God in saving souls and sanctifying Christians, and that only the faithful proclamation of God's Word will produce spiritual fruit, then we must conclude from both scriptural truth and history that there is a great difference between revival and revivalism, as I hope to prove. We will pursue this topic by first of all defining *revival* linguistically and scripturally in order to furnish a theoretical basis of evaluation. Next, we will briefly note practical and theological dissimilarities between revival and revivalism. We will then concentrate on historical and doctrinal differences, using the paradigms of Jonathan Edwards and the Great Awakening, and of Charles G. Finney and new measures revivalism respectively.

DEFINITIONS OF REVIVAL
The Meaning of Revival

Revival is the noun form of the verb "revive," a derivation of the Latin *revivere,* meaning "to live again" or "to return or to restore to consciousness or life."[9] Revival can also be "the restoration of something to its true

---

[8] Joel Hawes in Edward A. Lawrence, *The Life of Joel Hawes* (Hartford, CT: 1871), p. 113, quoted in Murray, *Revival and Revivalism,* p. xiv.

[9] *Webster's Ninth New Collegiate Dictionary,* s.v. "revival," p. 1010.

nature and purpose."[10] Additionally, the term may mean "reform," as in the profound change of social morals or doctrine. It is in this sense we may understand the Protestant Reformation, for example. As we will see, the implication of the term scripturally and historically is that, while revival will result in moral reform, it is essentially a powerful work of the Holy Spirit in saving the lost and sanctifying the saved.[11]

Commenting on the so-called five "harvests" his Northampton (MA) Congregationalist church experienced, Solomon Stoddard (1643–1729) defined revival as "some special seasons wherein God doth in a remarkable manner revive religion among his people."[12] Stoddard's use of the word "revive" would appear to relate revival only to those who have life, i.e., believers, who are in need of reconsecration of life and service to God. Thus revival could be defined as *the awakening of the believer to scriptural obedience*. However, Stoddard's grandson, Jonathan Edwards (1703–1758), considered these harvests as "the conversion of many souls."[13] Revival is therefore more than the rededication of believers; it is also the awakening, or quickening, or impartation of spiritual life to the unregenerate.[14] Thus we may also identify *revival as the conversion*

---

[10] Walter C. Kaiser, *Quest for Renewal* (Chicago: Moody Press, 1986), pp. 14–15.

[11] Murray recognizes that in genuine revival there is "an observable raising of the whole moral tone" of the affected community. In historic revivals, such as the Great Awakening of 1734–41 or the Prayer Meeting Revival of 1857–58, the benefits of God's powerful working are remarkable, e.g., "hunger for the Word of God and Christian literature, importunate prayer, a sense of wonder and profound seriousness" about the things of God; joyful praise; a renewed energy in Christian witness; and the recovery of genuine worship in church and home (*Revival and Revivalism*, p. 348).

[12] From his chapter "The Benefit of the Gospel" in *The Efficacy of the Fear of Hell, to Restrain Men from Sin* (Boston, 1713), quoted by Murray in *Revival and Revivalism*, p. xvii.

[13] Jonathan Edwards, "Faithful Narrative of the Surprising Work of God, in the Conversion of Many Hundred Souls, in Northampton, and the Neighboring Towns and Villages of New Hampshire, in New England; in a Letter to the Rev. Dr. Colman, of Boston" in *The Works of Jonathan Edwards*, revised and corrected by Edward Hickman, 2 vols. (Edinburgh: Banner of Truth Trust, 1974), 1:347 [hereafter cited as *Works*].

[14] Interestingly, in his definition of revival, Russell E. Richey draws a historical difference between a revival and an awakening that I have not sought in this article because of its purely psychological/social (rather than theological) tenor. He states that "when revival in one place helps trigger revival elsewhere, when revival becomes contagious and is communicated to the general society, when revival sustains itself over a prolonged period of time, revival becomes Awakening." To him a "great" awakening depends primarily on a popular communication network to sustain it; both an awakening and a revival are strictly "a social construction" ("Revivalism: In Search of a Definition," *Wesleyan Theological Journal* 28 [Spring–Fall 1993]: 172). Richey's temporal and spatial contrasts do have

of sinners to salvation in Christ. Quite significantly, these two meanings (rededication and regeneration) appear in the scriptural concept of revival.

Descriptions of Scriptural Revival

In the Old Testament, "revival" is a form of covenant rededication, and necessarily includes restoration to divine favor. Israel's spiritual recovery is the focus in Psalm 85, especially verses 4 and 6: "Restore us, O God of our salvation, And cause Thine indignation toward us to cease.... Wilt Thou not Thyself revive us again, That Thy people may rejoice in Thee?"[15] This is a plea frequently repeated by both individuals (cf. Ps 51) and the nation (Ps 80:3). Renewal comes through reform, that is, a return to covenant obedience of Yahweh. One may recognize this with the revivals under (1) Asa of Judah in 2 Chronicles 15 (note, especially v. 12: "And they entered into the covenant to seek the LORD God of their fathers with all their heart and with all their soul"); (2) Jehoash in 2 Kings 11–12 and the destruction of the house of Baal, and repair of God's house; (3) Hezekiah in 2 Kings 18 (particularly vv. 4–6: "He removed the high places and broke down the sacred pillars and cut down the Asherah.... He trusted in the LORD, the God of Israel.... For he clung to the LORD; he did not depart from following Him, but kept His commandments"); and under (4) Josiah in 2 Kings 22–23 (especially 23:3: "And the king stood by the pillar and made a covenant before the LORD, to walk after the LORD, and to keep His commandments and His testimonies and His statutes with all his heart and all his soul, to carry out the words of this covenant that were written in this book. And all the people entered into the covenant"). All of these passages reflect a common theme—repentance: a turning from idolatry and restoration of obedience to Mosaic law and sincere worship of Yahweh as conditions for a return or revival of God's favor. No doubt during these times of renewal many Israelites individually repented and were truly saved.

The Old Testament also speaks of revival as rededication during special events, such as entry into the Promised Land under Joshua (Josh 5); the defeat of the Philistines under Samuel (1 Sam 7); and the rebuilding of the Temple under Zerubbabel, culminating in celebration and worship (Ezra 5–6). A prophetic entreaty for revival can be found in Solomon's prayer at the consecration of the Temple (1 Kings 8, especially vv. 30–40),

---

merit, but his model is a prime example of the failure to make a theological distinction between revival and revivalism.

[15] All Scripture quotations are from the *New American Standard Bible.*

and in Daniel's prayer of confession in chapter 9 (cf. vv. 16–19). Finally, the prophets interject the hope of a millennial renewal of God's wonderful works of judgment and blessing (Hab 3:2) and restoration of His people (Isa 62–66; Zech 2:10).[16] Broadly speaking, all these instances of covenant renewal are revival.

In the New Testament revival is the "awakening" of the church with the conversion of thousands at Pentecost and the inauguration of the church as recorded in Acts 2. One may note several principles of revival from this passage.

(1) The Pentecost revival is a model only for emulation of some, not reduplication of all, of its features. Nowhere in the epistles are Christians commanded to replicate the "signs and wonders" of Pentecost in order to enjoy God's salvific blessings.[17] Nor in the early post-canonical period of church history are believers expected to seek the gift of tongues as part of their spiritual experience.[18]

(2) The Pentecost revival was not in the speaking of tongues, nor the miraculous signs (cf. vv. 2–3), but in the mass conversion of 3,000 people when they accepted Peter's gospel (cf. v. 41) and subsequent devotion to the things of God, namely, doctrine, ordinances, and fellowship (v. 42 ff.).[19]

(3) Since the Pentecost revival was quite obviously a remarkable outpouring of God's blessing in the conversion of so many persons, we may consider certain instances of divine activity as guidelines by which other revivals may be tested as to their scriptural authenticity. To be a genuine work of God, a revival must include a doctrinal preaching of the Word of God that is truthful (vv. 14–36). Second, revival must be an activity of the Spirit of God (v. 33). Third, genuine revival will produce a people of God (vv. 37–47), who will be convicted and who will repent of sin (vv. 37–40); who will be converted (v. 41); who will continue in the faith (vv. 42–46); and who will properly worship God in fellowship one with

---

[16] For a brief but incisive treatment of revival as covenant renewal in the Old Testament, see Roy B. Zuck, ed., *A Biblical Theology of the Old Testament* (Chicago: Moody Press, 1991), pp. 62, 74, 85, 200, 324, 333–35.

[17] Even in the famous χαρίσματα passage of 1 Corinthians 12–14, the gift of tongues is not for everyone (cf. 12:11, 29–30), and therefore cannot be a condition for nor a required evidence of salvation.

[18] The only possible exception to this would be the probability of tongues-speaking among the second century Montanists, but, of course, they were a heretical sect.

[19] It is noteworthy that the tongues-speaking was incidental to the conversion of the lost, and in fact was merely a means to that end in that the mixed multitude could hear the apostles speak "the mighty deeds of God" in their own language (cf. Acts 2:6–11).

another (vv. 46–47). We may confidently assert that these are indications of genuine revival, not only because they are true of Pentecost, but because they are evidences of New Testament Christianity. This supports my contention that revival is essentially nothing more than what is the normal pattern for biblical faith. This in no way minimizes the miraculous element in revival, for salvation is definitely a miracle (cf. Mark 10:26–27). Indeed, true revival emphasizes the supernatural activity of God. Man can no more produce a revival than he can convert a soul; once again, only God can do this.

It is also significant that, according to Acts 4:23–35, revival appears to be the bestowment of power by the Holy Spirit who enables His people to serve Him and persevere in the midst of trials. The Acts 4 revival (a continuation no doubt of the powerful work begun in chapter 2) was accompanied by submission and prayer to a sovereign God (vv. 24–30), wise and bold use of the Word of God (vv. 25–26, 31), and unity and love of the people of God (vv. 32–35). We may use these marks of the first revival in church history as criteria to help us discern what is a truly divine work in subsequent periods.

DISTINCTIONS BETWEEN REVIVAL AND REVIVALISM

Practical and Theological Differences

It is unfortunate that well-meaning Christians often confuse evangelism and revival. They tend to equate the two, calling an evangelistic meeting or campaign a revival.[20] But they are two different things. Evangelism is the proclamation of the gospel, which is every Christian's responsibility. Revival is uniquely a work of God that may or may not take place in an evangelistic meeting.[21] Yet, when revival has occurred in history, it is most

---

[20] An acknowledged authority on revival, Keith J. Hardman, contributes to the problem by viewing as revival mass responses to emotionally-charged messages by ecumenical evangelists and charismatics. Hardman seems enthralled with vast numbers of crusade decisions and pollster results as evidence of evangelical Christian resurgence in the modern world (cf. *Seasons of Refreshing: Evangelism and Revivals in America* [Grand Rapids: Baker, 1994], especially pp. 17, 24–30).

[21] This is difficult for many Christians to accept, but technically speaking, an evangelistic meeting may take place without a single convert. Otherwise, we would have to conclude that missionaries William Carey and Adoniram Judson were not evangelizing for the first six years of their ministries in India and Burma, since they had seen no conversions during that time (cf. Isa 6:8–10). The fact is, they were faithfully giving the gospel, but *God* had not yet given the increase. Neither Carey, Judson, nor any other preacher should be blamed for lack of professions if they are obediently declaring and living according to

often in an evangelistic context.[22] This is understandable since evangelism is the divinely-appointed means of salvation and hence of revival. As the gospel is preached, and several people are truly awakened or converted in a concentrated period and place, one may say that historic revival has taken place. Methodist historian Melvin E. Dieter points out that "the evangelical's acceptance of Christ's final commission to his disciples as a mandate for personal witness and world mission reinforces the urgency that characterizes revival movements."[23] However, should we not question whether it is somewhat presumptuous to advertise an evangelistic meeting as a "revival" when such has not yet occurred?

Since the days of Charles Finney and so-called "new measures" attempts to produce revival, critics have tended to define revival by evangelistic methodology and technique and labeled it revivalism. However, there are serious differences between revival and revivalism. (1) Revival may be considered theocentric; revivalism, anthropocentric. One may note this in the shift of revival emphasis after the Great Awakening from submission to God to pragmatic results, i.e., numbers of decisions. This was due to a move in theology away from the doctrinal content of faith to the subjective experience. This change paved the way for existentialism and rationalism.[24] Michael Horton informs us that the Enlightenment on

---

the gospel of Christ. This reality makes it all the more imperative for us to rely upon the grace of God for the salvation of the lost and revival!

[22] An example of revival occurring in a setting not given to evangelistic preaching per se is the *annus mirabilis* (year of miracles) Prayer Meeting Revival of 1857–58. However, there is evidence to indicate that the gospel was given in sufficient measure to produce large numbers of converts even in that context. See William C. Conant, *Narrative of Remarkable Conversions and Revival Incidents: Including a Review of Revivals* (New York: Derby & Jackson, 1858), pp. 426–35; Hardman, *Seasons of Refreshing,* p. 181; Timothy L. Smith, *Revivalism and Social Reform: American Protestantism on the Eve of the Civil War* (Gloucester, MA: Peter Smith, 1976), pp. 65–66, 69, 77; Frank Grenville Beardsley, *A History of American Revivals,* 2nd ed. (New York: American Tract Society, 1912), pp. 225, 232.

[23] "Revivalism," *Evangelical Dictionary of Theology,* ed. Walter A. Elwell (Grand Rapids: Baker), p. 951.

[24] If one has difficulty seeing how rationalism and pietistic experientialism can accommodate each other, he need look only at the father of modern theology, Friederich Schleiermacher (1768–1834), the product of Moravian pietism and Kantian idealism. In the early American context, one may trace the intrusion of liberal theology, at least in part, to the mixing of Old Calvinism with Enlightenment Rationalism by theological successors to Edwards: Timothy Dwight, Nathaniel Taylor, and Jonathan Edwards the Younger, among others. For a superbly well-written treatment of the liberalization of New England theology, see John D. Hannah, "The Doctrine of Original Sin in Postrevolutionary America," *Bibliotheca Sacra* 134 (July–September 1977): 238–56. To corroborate his

the one hand and Arminianism on the other combined to upgrade man from a totally depraved sinner to a free moral agent. "In the former, people were taught to trust in their reason, and in the latter, their emotions, but in both the individual was enshrined."[25] Bernard A. Weisberger identified the symptomatic cause of the problem as a diluting of orthodox theology: "As theology grew simpler, technique became predominant."[26]

Another difference is that (2) revival comes from God, as a sovereign, undeserved gracious bestowal of renewal; revivalism is the work of man, with emphasis on human ability and agency. Popular nineteenth century preachers as diverse in style as Peter Cartwright (1785–1872) and Lyman Beecher (1775–1863)[27] downplayed this distinction by accentuating man's free will in salvation. Writing of Beecher, Weisberger noted that

> if a literal belief in "inability" meant that the sinner could not really pray properly until he knew he was converted, then a literal belief in "inability" had to give way. Man's utter dependence on God to make him fit for holiness would have to be soft-pedaled, and reliance on study, prayer and penitence would have to be stressed.[28]

Such preachers failed to fully appreciate that revival is a work impossible to initiate by any means other than divine; it comes down from above, often unexpectedly and spontaneously, always sovereignly. Revivalism is a methodology of cause and effect; it is "worked up" and virtually produced by human instrumentality. Man is sovereign in revivalism and the Holy Spirit becomes an agent at man's disposal. A contemporary of Beecher and ardent proponent of genuine revival, Presbyterian minister

---

findings, Hannah cites several original and secondary sources including two outstanding classical works: Frank Hugh Foster, *A Genetic History of New England Theology* (Chicago: University of Chicago Press, 1907), and George Nye Boardman, *A History of New England Theology* (New York: A. D. F. Randolph, 1899).

[25] *Made In America: The Shaping of Modern American Evangelicalism* (Grand Rapids: Baker, 1991), p. 30. See also, William R. Sutton's interpretation of New Haven theology as a means of wedding Enlightenment rationalism with revivalism in America ("Benevolent Calvinism and the Moral Government of God: The Influence of Nathaniel W. Taylor on Revivalism in the Second Great Awakening," *Religion and American Culture* 2 [Winter 1992]: 23–47).

[26] *They Gathered at the River: The Story of the Great Revivalists and Their Impact upon Religion in America* (Boston: Little, Brown, 1958), p. 271.

[27] For examples of Cartwright and Beecher's views on man's ability, see William G. McLoughlin, ed., *The American Evangelicals, 1800–1900: An Anthology* (Gloucester, MA: Peter Smith, 1976), pp. 41–85.

[28] Weisberger, *They Gathered at the River,* p. 83.

Gardiner Spring (1785–1873), astutely cautioned against any facsimile generated by human design.

> With the obvious signs of the times in view, who does not see that this artful foe [Satan] would enjoy his malignant triumph, if he could prejudice the minds of good men against all *revivals of religion?* This he does, not so much by opposing them, as by counterfeiting the genuine coin, and by *getting up* revivals that are spurious and to his liking. Revivals are always spurious when they are *got up* by man's device, and not *brought down* by the Spirit of God.[29]

What I have said thus far should not be construed as a repudiation of human means in revival. It is the use of proper versus improper means that constitutes (3) another difference between revival and revivalism. God has determined the *instrumental* means of spiritual renewal: they are proclamation of the gospel (Rom 10:15–17) and fervent prayer in the Spirit (Jas 5:16). As a result of these legitimate human methods, God may see fit to save souls in an unusually dramatic way which we call revival. In witnessing and preaching, we may expect that a powerful gospel will produce powerful results in saving the lost (Rom 1:16; Acts 4:31–33; 5:42; 6:7). Likewise, importunate supplication may be the means God will use to send revival. History reveals that God has often sent revival in answer to the prayers of His saints who wait upon Him for it. Yet, always, our prayer for revival, as for anything else, should be conditioned by "Thy will be done."[30] The prayer of faith is primarily the prayer that wants God's will to be accomplished and His name to be glorified above all else. Revivalism makes methodology, rather than God alone, the *effectual* cause of spiritual results. Revivalism misplaces reliance—upon a strategy, a formula, or a program, rather than upon the Holy Spirit. However, programs will not produce spiritual results any more than they can replace them. Even prayer and preaching will not compel God to produce revival, but God has chosen to use these scripturally ordained means to bring it about. Therefore, we may, and indeed *should,* pray for the conversion of sinners and sanctification of our brothers and sisters in Christ; we *should* earnestly speak the words of life to a lost world and admonish one another in the faith. Hopefully, God will use such means to send revival.

---

[29] *Personal Reminiscences of the Life and Times of Gardiner Spring,* 2 vols. (New York: Charles Scribner, 1866), 1:217–18.

[30] 1 John 5:14–15; James 5:16–18.

Finally, (4) revival produces genuine scriptural and lasting results, such as continuance in the faith; revivalism produces superficial commitment that soon abates with time and trials. As Gardiner Spring said, "There is one grace you cannot counterfeit...the grace of *perseverance*."[31] The sincere Christian, even in the midst of severe trials and an ungodly environment, will endure to the end.

Revival and revivalism bear something of an analogy to real Christianity and historic Christendom. While the terms are often used synonymously, nevertheless, there is a difference between them. Revival is a divine means of producing distinctly biblical Christians. Revivalism, like Christendom, is practically inclusive, culturally adaptive, and doctrinally heterogeneous. As authentic Christianity exists within the realm of professing Christendom, so genuine spiritual decisions may occur within revivalism.[32]

A Theological Summary

By simple definition, revival is a dramatic movement of God that conforms lives to His will. As Arthur Wallis describes it, revival is more than big meetings or religious enthusiasm. "There is a wealth of difference between missions or campaigns at their best and genuine revival. In the former man takes the initiative,...in the latter the initiative is God's. With the one the organization is human; with the other it is divine."[33] Revival is a doctrinal movement. That is, revival will conform to Christian doctrine as found in the Bible. Thus, revival is biblical salvation and sanctification, not

---

[31] Spring, *Personal Reminiscences*, 1: 51. A common criticism of new measures revivalism was failure of continuance in the faith. A Presbyterian reviewer wrote in 1835, "It is now generally understood that the numerous converts of the new measures have been, in most cases, like the morning cloud and the early dew. In some places, not a half, a fifth, or even a tenth part of them remain" (*The Biblical Repertory and Theological Review* 7 [1835]: 482, 663).

[32] Perhaps one of the better examples of this analogy would be related to the famous "burned over" district of western New York State. Saturating the area in the early 1800s was, in the words of Philip Schaff, a motley sampler of various types of sects: Mormons, spiritualists, Shakers, Millerites, abolitionists, Freemasons, social perfectionists and utopians (e.g., the Oneida communitarians) and, of course, Finneyite revivalism. Yet statistics indicate an unusual degree of religious fervor within legitimate evangelical denominations, such as the Baptists. Cf. Whitney R. Cross, *The Burned-Over District: The Social and Intellectual History of Enthusiastic Religion in Western New York, 1800–1850* (New York: Harper & Row, 1950), p. 10; Weisberger, *They Gathered at the River*, p. 14; and Joshua Bradley, *Accounts of Religious Revivals in Many Parts of the United States from 1815 to 1818* (Albany, NY: G. J. Loomis, 1819), pp. vi–x.

[33] *In the Day of Thy Power: The Scriptural Principles of Revival* (London: Christian Literature Crusade, 1956), p. 20.

merely moral amendment, although godly reformation of behavior will
be the inevitable result of true revival. In summary, then, we may define
revival as *an extraordinarily intensive and usually extensive work of God
in powerfully applying His gospel to people, which results in the salvation
of sinners and renewed obedience of saints.*

A HISTORICAL PARADIGM FOR REVIVAL: JONATHAN EDWARDS AND THE GREAT AWAKENING

At the beginning of the eighteenth century in colonial America certain
factors highlighted the need for revival: institutionalized religion, liberalism in Harvard and latitudinarianism in several churches, pharisaical
self-righteousness and complacency, a largely unregenerate church
membership due to the Half-Way Covenant, and pronounced worldli-
ness among a generally unchurched population.[34] Boston pastor Increase
Mather (1639–1723) lamented toward the end of his life that New England
had become degenerate: "Oh,…what art thou come to at this day? How
are those sins become common in thee that once were not so much as
heard of in this land!"[35] Those sins had been identified and enumerated
at a synod of Congregational pastors over which Mather had presided in
1679. These were a visible decay of godliness, "pride that doth abound,"
a neglect of covenant discipline, pollution of God's name by oaths and
imprecation, Sabbath-breaking, failure of family religion, immoderate
passions, intemperance, promise-breaking, an "inordinate affection unto
the world," opposition to reform, selfishness, and the all-comprehensive
sin of unbelief.[36] Into this spiritually dark scene God sent the marvelous
light of the gospel that resulted in a spiritual awakening of hundreds of
people between 1734 and 1741.

Contextual factors reveal that the Great Awakening was surely a work
of God. First, the revival proceeded in the context of strong doctrinal

---

[34] See A Skevington Wood, *The Inextinguishable Blaze: Spiritual Renewal and
Advance in the Eighteenth Century* (Grand Rapids: Eerdmans, 1960), pp. 53–60; William
Warren Sweet, *Religion in Colonial America* (New York: Cooper Square Publishers, 1965),
pp. 271–73; Joseph Tracy, *The Great Awakening: A History of Religion in the time of
Edwards and Whitefield* (1842; reprint ed., Edinburgh: Banner of Truth Trust, 1976), pp.
1–11; Edwin S. Gaustad, *The Great Awakening in New England* (Gloucester, MA: Peter
Smith, 1965), p. 14.

[35] From J. Gillies, *Historical Collections,* 2:18, quoted in Wood, *The Inextinguishable
Blaze,* p. 54.

[36] Cotton Mather, *Magnalia Christi Americana; or, The Ecclesiastical History of New-
England, From Its First Planting, in the Year 1620, unto the Year of Our Lord 1698,* 2 vols.
(Hartford: Silas Andrus & Son, 1853), 2:320.

preaching of the gracious gospel, against sin, and specifically, as a result of that transforming truth upon "which the church stands or falls"—justification through faith alone in Christ alone by God's grace alone. Jonathan Edwards[37] wrote of the Northampton revival of 1734 that "at its commencement, it appears to have been, to an unusual degree, a silent, powerful, and glorious work of the Spirit of God—the simple effect of truth applied to the conscience, and accompanied by his converting grace."[38] Edwards regarded the Great Awakening as caused, not by appeals to the emotions, but by the truth of God impressed upon the mind by the preaching of the gospel and the agency of the Holy Spirit. It was "the simple effect of a practical attention to truth, on the conscience and the heart"[39] One of Edwards' biographers describes his preaching as stern, "warning the people of their sins and of the great displeasure of God. The sovereignty of God's grace in the salvation of sinners through justification by faith in Jesus Christ was the central theme about which all else revolved. God was present and did a mighty work in their [Northampton's] midst."[40]

Edwards called the revival a "remarkable testimony of God's approbation of the forensic doctrine" of justification by faith alone. This message was prompted by the threat of Arminianism in New England. Its progress had become so manifest as to cause alarm among staunch Calvinists like Edwards.[41] Edwards regarded doctrinal confusion as the chief sore to be healed.[42] The remedy, he believed, was strong preaching on the doctrines of gracious redemption.[43] In addition to forensic justification (God declaring

---

[37] Of the many biographies about Edwards, the finest is Iain H. Murray, *Jonathan Edwards: A New Biography* (Edinburgh: Banner of Truth Trust, 1987). Particularly helpful is Murray's defense of Edwards as primarily a biblical theologian rather than a philosopher (cf. pp. xix–xxxi). His evaluation of Edwards' treatises on the Great Awakening in chapters 12 and 13 is most insightful.

[38] "Memoirs of Jonathan Edwards," ed. Sereno E. Dwight, in *Works,* 1:lxx; cf. Edwards, "Thoughts on the Revival" in *Works,* 1:366, 373, 390, 397.

[39] "Memoirs" in *Works,* 1:lxxi.

[40] Elgin Moyer, *Great Leaders of the Christian Church* (Chicago: Moody Press, 1951), p. 451.

[41] Joseph Tracy, *The Great Awakening: A History of the Revival of Religion in the Time of Edwards and Whitefield*, p. 8.

[42] Gaustad, *The Great Awakening in New England,* p. 22.

[43] Edwards expounded his doctrinal views in such classic statements as the sermon, "Sinners in the Hands of An Angry God" (1741), and treatises, *The Great Christian Doctrine of Original Sin Defended* (1757) and *A Careful and Strict Inquiry into the Prevailing Notions of the Freedom of Will* (1757). Cf. Randall E. Otto, "The Solidarity of Mankind in Jonathan Edwards' Doctrine of Original Sin," *Evangelical Quarterly* 62 (July 1990): 205–21; C. Samuel Storms, "Jonathan Edwards on the Freedom of the Will,"

man righteous in Christ), Edwards preached and defended the traditional Reformed doctrines of original sin, including innate sinful depravity inherited from Adam and the imputation of his guilt to the human race; the necessity of man to sin willfully because of constitutional depravity; the vicarious atonement of Christ; and divine monergism in regeneration. As a result, persons were brought

> to a conviction of their *absolute dependence* on His [God's] sovereign power and grace, and an universal necessity of a mediator. This has been effected by leading them more and more to a sense of their exceeding wickedness and guiltiness in his sight; their pollution, and the insufficiency of their own righteousness; that they can in no wise help themselves, and that God would be wholly just and righteous in rejecting them and all that they do, and in casting them off for ever.[44]

A second contextual factor demonstrating that this early stage of the Great Awakening was a divine work is that what happened took the people by *surprise*. The townspeople did not seek out salvation at first, but were, in Edwards' words, "wrought upon in a very remarkable manner."[45] Edwards' first record of the revival characterized it as a surprising work of God.[46] "The Spirit of God began extraordinarily to set in and wonderfully to work among us; and there were very suddenly, one after another, five or six persons, who were, to all appearances, savingly converted."[47] The awakening was surprising as to the extent of it. Beginning in

---

Trinity Journal 3 (Fall 1982): 131–69; John H. Gerstner, *Jonathan Edwards: A Mini-Theology* (Wheaton: Tyndale House Publishers, 1987), esp. chs. 4–8; and Conrad Cherry, *The Theology of Jonathan Edwards: A Reappraisal* (Bloomington, IN: Indiana University Press, 1990), pp. 90–106.

[44] "Faithful Narrative" in *Works,* 1:351. How foreign is the contemporary gospel of self-esteemism to this biblical message!

[45] Ibid., 1:348.

[46] Edwards record, *A Faithful Narrative of the Surprising Work of God in the Conversion of Many Hundred Souls in Northampton, and Neighboring Towns and Villages* (London, 1737 and Boston, 1738), went through 3 editions and 20 printings by 1739. A hundred years later, Perry Miller stated that it was still a handbook for revivalism in such diverse places as Illinois and Wales (*Jonathan Edwards* [Amherst, MA: Univ. of Massachusetts Press, 1949], p. 137). It was originally a letter to Boston pastor Benjamin Colman, but was revised and published by the great hymn writer Isaac Watts and an associate in London. The American edition included an affirmation by six Hampshire ministers, confirming Edwards' description of the revival. The London edition preface read in part: "Never did we hear or read, since the first ages of Christianity, any event of this kind so surprising as the present Narrative hath set before us."

[47] "Faithful Narrative" in *Works,* 1:348. The revival began in the latter part of December, 1734.

Northampton and Hatfield, the revival moved up and down the Connecticut River, affecting about forty-two towns or parishes in western Massachusetts and Connecticut, from the area of Deerfield (MA) in the north to Middletown (CT) in the south.[48] The effects of it were also astonishing. Individuals from all classes of people were transformed. Edwards stated,

> Presently upon this [the conversion of several people], a great and earnest concern about the great things of religion and the eternal world, became universal in all parts of the town, and among persons of all degrees, and all ages. The noise among the dry bones waxed louder and louder; all other talk but about spiritual and eternal things, was soon thrown by; all the conversation, in all companies and upon all occasions, was upon these things only, unless so much as was necessary for people carrying on their ordinary secular business. Other discourse than of the things of religion would scarcely be tolerated in any company. The minds of the people were wonderfully taken off from the world.... The only thing in their view was to get the Kingdom of heaven, and every one appeared pressing into it. The engagedness of their hearts in this great concern could not be hid, it appeared in their very countenances. It then was a dreadful thing amongst us to lie out of Christ, in danger every day of dropping into hell; and what persons' minds were intent upon, was to escape for their lives, and to fly from wrath to come. All would eagerly lay hold of opportunities for their souls, and were wont very often to meet together in private houses for religious purposes: and such meetings when appointed were greatly thronged. There was scarcely a single person in the town, old or young, left unconcerned about the great things of the eternal world. Those who were wont to be the vainest and loosest,...were now generally subject to great awakenings. And the work of conversion was carried on in a most astonishing manner, and increased more and more: souls did as it were come by flocks to Jesus Christ. From day to day, for many months together, might be seen evident instances of sinners brought out of darkness into marvelous light, and delivered out of an horrible pit, and from the miry clay, and set upon a rock, with a new song of praise to God in their mouths. This work of God, as it was carried on, and the number of true saints multiplied, soon made a glorious alteration in the town, so that in the spring and summer following, anno 1735, the town seemed to be full of the presence of God.[49]

---

[48] Towns Edwards mentioned as being affected by revival were Pascommuck, Northampton, South Hadley, Suffield, Sunderland, Deerfield, Green River, Hatfield, Hill, West Springfield, Long Meadow, Enfield, Westfield, Springfield, Hadley, Northfield, Windsor, East Windsor, Coventry, Lebanon, Durham, Stratford, Ripton, Newhaven, Guilford, Mansfield, Tolland, Hebron, Bolton, Preston, and Woodbury.

[49] "Faithful Narrative" in *Works,* 1:348.

The lives of children and teenagers especially were amazingly altered. Young people were seen and heard speaking of spiritual matters, praying together, as well as with adults. Altogether, about 200 families in Northampton experienced revival in the 1730s. Of 620 communicants, 300 made professions of faith in six months. Fifty of these were above forty years of age; thirty converts were between ten and fourteen years of age. In the spring of 1735, an average of thirty people per week were saved. Almost immediately the new converts quit their sinful practices, dreading their former vices. Backbitings and quarrels stopped. The tavern was left empty, and people generally stayed at home or were in church. Many began reading, praying, meditating, worshipping, and discussing the things of God with great joy. Edwards recorded, "Our public assemblies were then beautiful: the congregation was *alive* in God's service.... Our public *praises* were then greatly enlivened."[50] The effect of changed lives appeared permanent. "I know of no one young person in the town," Edwards reported, "who has returned to former ways of *looseness* and *extravagance* in any respect; but we still remain a *reformed* people, and God has evidently made us a new people." [51] Yet, in 1751, a more mature, reflective Edwards recognized that, even in so great an awakening there were undoubtedly spurious decisions. Shortly after being dismissed from his church for refusing to offer communion to the unregenerate, Edwards wrote a friend to say that the "calamities" that befell Northampton were due in part to the people establishing "certain wrong notions and ways in religion," i.e., resting their conversion on impressions, rather than a "lively spiritual experience." Edwards took the blame: "One thing that has contributed to bring things to such a pass at Northampton was my youth and want of more judgment and experience at the time of that extraordinary awakening about sixteen years ago."[52]

All in all, however, the character of the Connecticut River Valley revival evidenced the divine stamp. For one thing, God's sovereignty and righteousness were exalted. Edwards could write, "I think I have found that no discourses have been more *remarkably blessed,* than those in which the doctrine of God's *absolute sovereignty,* with regard to the salvation of sinners, and his *just liberty,* with regard to answering the prayers...of natural men...have been insisted upon."[53] Also, those "wrought upon" by

---

[50] Ibid.

[51] Ibid., 1:364.

[52] Edwards' letter to Gillespie of Carnock, 1751, quoted in Tracy, *The Great Awakening,* p. 403.

[53] "Faithful Narrative" in *Works,* 1:353.

the Spirit of God were convicted by the justice of God in condemning their "exceedingly vile" sinfulness. Their salvation appeared too good for them; many felt worthy of nothing but judgment.[54] There was no question that God Himself moved upon penitent sinners to produce a definite change and that salvation was wholly of the Lord.[55] Edwards asserted that "conversion is a great and glorious work of God's power, at once changing the heart, and infusing life into the dead soul."[56] Affections once set on the world "are [now] truly spiritual and gracious, [and] do arise from those influences and operations on the heart, which are spiritual, supernatural, and divine."[57] According to him, the instrument of that power was God's Word.

> Persons commonly at...conversion, and afterwards, have had many texts of Scripture brought to their minds, which are exceeding suitable to their circumstances, often come with great power, as the word of God or of *Christ* indeed.... Some are thus convinced of the truth of the *gospel* in general, and that the Scriptures are the word of God: others have their minds more especially fixed on some particular *great doctrine* of the gospel, some particular truths that they are *meditating* on, or *reading* of, in some portion of Scripture.... While God was so remarkably present amongst us by his Spirit, there was no book so delightful as the Bible.[58]

This revival, witnessed by Jonathan Edwards, had every appearance of being a divine work, spiritually, doctrinally, and biblically. It characteristically bore those marks associated with the first revival in church history as recorded in Acts. As a genuine revival, admittedly tainted at times by the extravagances of revivalism,[59] it was nevertheless a prelude

---

[54] Ibid.

[55] In commenting on the Awakening as being solely a work of God, Tracy writes, "It would seem that in every case, the happy change came upon the sinner's mind, instead of being wrought by him. In no case, it seems, did the sinner first form to himself an idea of some volition to be put forth by himself, and then, by direct effort, put it forth, and thus become a convert (*The Great Awakening*, p. 14).

[56] "Faithful Narrative" in *Works*, 1:355.

[57] Edwards, "A Treatise Concerning Religious Affections" in *Works*, 1:264.

[58] "Faithful Narrative" in *Works*, 1:355–57.

[59] James Davenport's antics bear this out. Davenport (1716–1757), great-grandson of New Haven's founder, John Davenport, was an emotionally unstable revivalist who created disorder wherever he preached. He was arrested, pronounced insane, but eventually confessed his errors. See Richard L. Bushman, ed. *The Great Awakening: Documents on the Revival of Religion, 1740–1745* (Williamsburg, VA: Institute of Early American History and Culture, 1969), pp. 45–55.

to the major upsurge of awakening, beginning in 1740, under the preaching of George Whitefield.[60]

A HISTORICAL PARADIGM FOR REVIVALISM: CHARLES G. FINNEY AND THE NEW MEASURES

The First Great Awakening came unexpectedly by God's mercy on a sinful people and in the context of God-centered doctrinal proclamations from Spirit-empowered preachers such as Theodorus Frelinghuysen, Gilbert Tennent, Jonathan Edwards, and George Whitefield. Their messages centered on the holiness of God, condemnation of sin, justification by faith, and the new birth produced solely by the power of God through the instrumentality of His Word. In a profound way, *biblical theology produced genuine revival.* However, toward the end of the eighteenth century, a theological change took place that was to have enormous consequences in the way Americans would come to view revival. Briefly, old line Edwardsian orthodoxy gradually gave way to what some historians have incorrectly called a modified Calvinism, but in actuality was the revival of an old heresy unlike anything John Calvin or Jonathan Edwards would have taught. This "new" New England Theology was an attempt to regain the revival spirit in America but at the expense of the very doctrines God used to produce the Great Awakening in the first place. Centered in Yale College, this theology was, in Stephen Berk's words, an adjustment of "Calvinism to [the] prevailing conditions" of infidelity.[61] A concern for the eradication of Deism from the student body had led president Timothy Dwight (1752–1817) to assume a natural ability in man to accept the gospel. This assumption was based on the faulty assertion that the posterity of Adam are not guilty of his transgression. Each man is solely responsible for his own sin, not Adam's.[62] Dwight advanced the "divine constitution" view of inherent sin, which says that Adam's sin is the "instrumental cause" of man's but not the direct nor the penal cause; man therefore has a

---

[60] Thomas Prince (1687–1758), pastor of Boston's Third (Old South) Church, stated that it "seemed to prepare the way in diverse places for that more extensive revival of religion which in five years after followed" (*An Account of the Revival of Religion in Boston* [reprint ed., Boston: S. T. Armstrong, 1823], p. 7). It was Prince who started the first religious magazine in America, *The Christian History,* in which he reported on local revivals in America and Europe.

[61] *Calvinism Versus Democracy* (New York: Archon Books, 1971), p. 74.

[62] Timothy Dwight, *Theology; Explained and Defended, in a Series of Sermons,* 4 vols. (New Haven: S. Converse, 1825), 1:478.

"propensity" but not an inherent necessity to sin.[63] John Hannah sums up
the unorthodox theological consequences of Dwight's doctrine:

> With Adam's headship merely parental, not causative, all sins are voluntary
> sins and innate depravity is consequently moral [or relative] depravity. With
> the change in the basic nature and condition of man came also a reevaluation
> of the nature of the work of Christ. Since man's liability was in his choices,
> not his nature, the governmental theory of the atonement became an accepted
> explanation of Christ's death. Christ's death was viewed as effecting a virtu-
> ous environment and not as constituting a penal substitution.[64]

Dwight's best pupil and theological successor, Nathaniel William Taylor
(1786–1858), modified his mentor's views to produce a new teaching
known as Taylorism or the New Haven Theology.[65] Taylor said that man's
will is not corrupted by the sin of Adam, that he is not inherently nor
constitutionally depraved but has total freedom of choice for or against
God. Sin, he said, resides in the unrighteous acts, not in the nature, of
man.[66] "He thought that Edwards' doctrine of the will paralyzed revival
preaching and scandalized the average person in democratic, freedom-
loving America."[67] Edwards had taught the inevitable necessity of man's
sin because of imputed natural sinfulness; Dwight had said man was
partially depraved; Taylor now taught that man has "power to the contrary"
not to sin.[68] Taylor was teaching Pelagianism.[69]

---

[63] Dwight, *Theology*, 1:479, and Hannah, "The Doctrine of Original Sin in Postrevolutionary America," p. 246, note 34.

[64] Hannah, "The Doctrine of Original Sin in Postrevolutionary America," p. 247.

[65] Taylor developed his theology (1) as a response to Unitarianism, (2) in opposition to Old School Calvinism represented at Andover Seminary, and (3) as a means of promoting revival. It is the third concern which is of major importance for our study because of its impact on the revivalism of Finney. See James E. Johnson, "Charles G. Finney and a Theology of Revivalism," *Church History* 38 (September 1969): 339.

[66] Nathaniel Taylor, *Concio ad Clerum: A Sermon Delivered in the Chapel of Yale College, September 10, 1828,* cited in Sydney E. Ahlstrom, ed. *Theology in America: The Major Protestant Voices from Puritanism to Neo-Orthodoxy* (Indianapolis: Bobbs-Merrill, 1967), p. 215. See also, Taylor's *Lectures on the Moral Government of God,* ed. Noah Porter, 2 vols. (New York: Austin & Smith, 1859).

[67] Ahlstrom, *Theology in America*, p. 212.

[68] Sidney E. Mead, *Nathaniel William Taylor, 1786–1858, A Connecticut Liberal* (Chicago: University of Chicago Press, 1942), p. 189.

[69] Benjamin B. Warfield (1851–1921), who unrelentingly battled Taylorism as an extreme departure from biblical theology, remarked that "in the teaching of [Taylor]… the downward movement of the New Divinity ran out into a system which turned…upon the Pelagianizing doctrines of…the plenary ability of the sinner to renovate his own soul,

New Haven Theology provided the garden in which Arminianism would prosper, and the Social Gospel would take root and eventually bear the fruit of theological liberalism in America. A biographer of Taylor stated that many of the 768 graduates from Taylor's classes "became the leaders in the great surge of liberal thought that dominated Congregationalism during the next generation."[70] It was Taylorism that provided the impetus for much of nineteenth century revivalism.[71] This theology fit quite well into the new euphoric climate of American independence and man's ability to shape his "manifest destiny." A bold expression of human achievement by a Jacksonian politician prophesied the virtual deification of the American people.

> I believe man can be elevated; man can become more and more endowed with divinity; and as he does he becomes more God-like in his character and capable of governing himself. Let us go on elevating our people, perfecting our institutions, until democracy shall reach such a point of perfection that we can acclaim with truth that the voice of the people is the voice of God.[72]

The New Haven Theology appeared to emulate characteristics of Jacksonian democracy. Self-determination and a romantic belief in self-worth and prosperity displaced the old Puritan view of man's natural moral corruption and absolute dependence on a sovereign God.[73]

A product of Jacksonian democracy and popularizer of New Haven Theology, Charles Grandison Finney (1792–1875)[74] translated Taylorism

---

and self-love or the desire for happiness as the spring of all voluntary action" (*Biblical and Theological Studies* [Philadelphia: Presbyterian and Reformed Publishing, 1952], p. 536).

[70] Mead, *Nathaniel William Taylor,* p. 163.

[71] As one writer put it, referring to an 1831 Finney sermon: "The voice was Finney's, the thinking Taylor's" (Murray, *Revival and Revivalism,* p. 261). Another historian noted that Finney was "Taylor's true successor" (Foster, *A Genetic History of New England Theology,* p. 453).

[72] Quoted in Alice Felt Tyler, *Freedom's Ferment: Phases of American Social History from the Colonial Period to the Outbreak of the Civil War* (reprint ed., New York: Harper & Row, 1962), p. 22. Tyler appears to be quoting Jackson himself, but the origin of the speech is unknown. Dixon Wecter credits the statement to President Andrew Johnson (cf. *The Saga of American Society: A Record of Social Aspiration, 1607–1937* [New York: Charles Scribner's Sons, 1937], p. 100). See also, Jay E. Smith, "The Theology of Charles Finney: A System of Self-Reformation," *Trinity Journal* 13ns (Spring 1992): 64, note 15.

[73] William McLoughlin writes that the generation of settlers to which Finney belonged had "faith in man's ability to solve life's problems by himself, and their growing optimism about the future, made the pessimistic religion which their parents had found strangely satisfying seem singularly unattractive and unreasonable" (*Modern Revivalism,* p. 21).

[74] A critical yet well-balanced biography of Finney is Keith J. Hardman, *Charles Grandison Finney, 1792–1875: Reformer and Revivalist* (Grand Rapids: Baker, 1987).

into a system of revivalism advocating unblushingly that *revival may be and should be generated by human means.* This is a dangerous and false presumption. Such a course replaces principle with pragmatism upon the throne of praxis. The Holy Spirit becomes an agent at man's disposal and revival is reduced to methodology and manipulation calculated to produce moral results. As America's religious Andrew Jackson, Finney spread the democratic gospel of Taylorism along the eastern seaboard and western New York State from 1825 to 1835.[75] This law student turned evangelist would fan the flames of controversy as well as revivalism.

Unquestionably, Finney provided a refreshing alternative to Yankee divines in shoe buckles and powdered wigs. His gospel was a radical switch from the dead Unitarian lecture but also from the Calvinist message of Edwards[76] and Whitefield. Ordained by the Presbyterians, he soon denied their doctrines as contained in the Westminster Confession, and eventually left their denomination. Indeed, he had much in common with the Methodists and helped launch the perfectionist and holiness movements often associated with them. Finney is credited with the conversion of 500,000 people to the gospel, using evangelistic methods still popular today. However, as one examines the gospel Finney preached, he must

---

Lewis A. Drummond's popular biography is another example of the failure to make a difference between revival and revivalism (*A Fresh Look at The Life and Ministry of Charles G. Finney* [Minneapolis: Bethany House Publishers, 1985). With Billy Graham's help (see foreword, p. 6), Drummond portrays Finney as the model revivalist and foremost precursor of modern evangelism. Among the many treatments of Finney's revivalist theology, two excellent discussions are available which include significant influences as well as descriptions of doctrine. These are Jay E. Smith, "The Theology of Charles Finney," and David L. Weddle, *The Law as Gospel: Revival and Reform in the Theology of Charles G. Finney* (Metuchen, NJ: Scarecrow Press, 1985), especially pp. 114–231.

[75] See Sean Michael Lucas, "Charles Finney's Theology of Revival: Moral Depravity," *The Master's Seminary Journal* 6 (Fall 1995): 212–15; Hardman, *Charles Grandison Finney,* p. 151. There is no question among historians that Taylorism played a direct role in "preparing the way theologically for the acceptance of Finney's 'new measures' in the promotion of revivals" (*The Law as Gospel,* p. 147, note 19). Cf. Mead, *Nathaniel William Taylor,* pp. 177–87; McLoughlin, *Modern Revivalism,* pp. 44–46; and especially the treatment of Taylorism by Joseph Haroutunian, *Piety Versus Moralism: The Passing of The New England Theology* (Hamden, CT: Archon Books, 1964), pp. 252–56, 266–80.

[76] It is difficult to take Allen Guelzo seriously when he writes that Finney was only furthering Jonathan Edwards' views of revival ("The Making of a Revivalist: Finney and the Heritage of Jonathan Edwards" 7 *Christian History* [Issue 20, no. 4]: 28–30). John Stanley Mattson, in attempting to draw doctrinal similarities between Edwards and Finney, completely mistakes Edwards' teaching on free will as innate ability. He is correct in saying, however, that "Finney's principal objective was to overthrow the Calvinist emphasis upon inability" ("Charles Grandison Finney and the Emerging Tradition of 'New Measure' Revivalism" [Ph.D. dissertation, University of North Carolina, 1970], pp. 280–81, 291).

consider whether it is not in actuality *another* gospel than what the New Testament teaches. For, as one historian stated, the popular revivalist's "great talent was to make the complicated doctrines of Nathaniel Taylor's 'New Divinity' as clear and as sensible as the multiplication table."[77] Well-intentioned advocates of revival have noted Finney's hard preaching against sin, his impassioned entreaties to the unsaved, and the amazing numerical and moral results generated by his campaigns and have concluded that he is a paragon of evangelism.[78] However, an examination of his theological writings and sermons reveals that his ministry was based on faulty methodology and theology. Any so-called spiritual successes he enjoyed have to be weighed in light of this.

Finney Was a Pragmatist.

Finney asserted that "a revival is the result of the *right* use of the appropriate means."[79] Those means included the adoption of controversial new measures which were calculated to produce conversions. (1) His egalitarian gospel permitted and encouraged women to pray and preach in public. (2) His use of the anxious bench at the front of the meetinghouse

---

[77] Winthrop Hudson, *Religion in America* (New York: Charles Scribner's Sons, 1965), p. 143. Historical scholars are in virtual agreement that Taylorism did play a role in shaping Finney's thought. The disagreement comes in trying to determine the extent of that influence. See Foster, *A Genetic History of New England Theology,* pp. 453, 467; Garth M. Rosell, "Charles Grandison Finney and the Rise of the Benevolence Empire" (Ph.D. dissertation, University of Minnesota, 1971), pp. 100–101; David L. Turner, "A Critique of Charles G. Finney's Theology," (unpublished paper, Baptist Bible College, 1977), pp. 25–36; Smith, "Theology of Charles Finney," pp. 68–69; Johnson, "Charles G. Finney and a Theology of Revivalism," pp. 339–42. After sifting the data, Johnson presents perhaps the most reasonable view: Finney's "theology derived both from the New England group [principally Taylor] and from his own independent reflection," p. 342.

[78] Jerry Falwell's *Fundamentalist Journal* carried articles in the mid 1980s promoting this image of Finney. See Louis Gifford Parkhurst, Jr., "Charles Grandison Finney Preached for a Verdict," 3 (June 1984): 41–43; Charles Grandison Finney, "When to Expect a Revival," 4 (September 1985): 28–29, 31.

[79] This statement was the premise of Finney's controversial *Lectures on Revivals of Religion* (New York: Fleming H. Revell, 1868); see p. 13. Leonard Sweet reminds us that Finney's "penchant for trying on doctrinal garb to suit the climate of the sinner was paralleled by his eagerness to exploit a full range of measures on a trial and error basis, discarding those that failed and devising new ones until he hit upon 'something that will succeed in the salvation of souls'…. The test of the veracity and validity of a measure or message was its performance" ("The View of Man Inherent in New Measures Revivalism," *Church History* 45 [June 1976]: 211, 212). Cf. Johnson, "Charles G. Finney and a Theology of Revivalism," pp. 342–43. For comments on the disrupting effects of Finney's new measures doctrine, see Perry Miller, *The Life of the Mind in America: From the Revolution to the Civil War* (New York: Harcourt, Brace, and World, 1965), pp. 29–33.

was a tactic to pressure sinners to come forward and "pray through" until they found Christ. The assumption was that if a person came to the bench he *would* be converted. (3) Finney's use of publicity and protracted meetings sensationalized evangelism. Again, his philosophy was that revivals could be and should be promoted by any method that worked. (4) Last and perhaps most offensive was Finney's belief that revival was not a miracle, but the right use of proper means. If men followed a prescribed list of moral criteria for revival, it *would* occur.[80] Finney repeatedly argued that results were the infallible proof that what he preached was correct: "The results justify my methods."[81] When critics referred to the impropriety and unscripturalness of his "new measures," he boasted that "when the blessing evidently follows the introduction of the measure itself, the proof is unanswerable that the measure is wise"[82] He convinced his followers that opponents were arguing with God when they questioned him: "It is evident that much fault has been found with measures which have been *pre-eminently and continually* blessed of God for the promotion of revivals. If a measure is *continually or unusually* blessed, let the man who thinks he is wiser than God, call it in question."[83] Such confident optimism intimidated the critics and bolstered Finney's popularity as something of a modern prophet.

Finney Was a Pelagianist.

Like Nathaniel Taylor, Finney denied original sin and man's constitutional depravity because, he said, total depravity is unreasonable.[84] He considered nothing sinful but voluntary action which is contrary to the moral law of God. He wrote, "All sin is actual, and…no other than actual

---

[80] Jay Smith writes, "Salvation no longer requires divine intervention. Moral effort, which can be induced through human engineering and coercion, is all that is necessary. Individuals are in absolute control of their destinies. Thus people are, for all practical purposes, omnipotent in effecting their conversions, creating revivals, and growing holiness" ("Theology of Charles Finney," p. 90).

[81] *Charles G. Finney: An Autobiography* (Old Tappan, NJ: Fleming H. Revell, 1876), p. 83.

[82] *Lectures on Revivals,* p. 211. Jay Smith writes, "Finney's self-confidence and ability had taught him that success was a question of natural ability and determination. Now as a young theologian, his self-confidence and natural talent convinced him that the gospel was also a matter of one's ability and effort" ("Theology of Charles Finney," p. 73).

[83] Ibid., p. 212.

[84] Finney pronounced Jonathan Edwards' *Freedom of the Will* "an injurious monstrosity and misnomer" (*Lectures on Systematic Theology* [Oberlin, OH: James M. Fitch, 1847], p. 30).

transgression can justly be called sin."[85] He left no room for doubt about the matter:

> We deny that the human constitution is morally depraved, 1. Because there is not proof of it. 2. Because it is impossible that sin should be an attribute of the substance of soul or body. It is and must be an attribute of choice or intention and not of substance. 3. To make sin an attribute or quality of substance is contrary to God's definition of sin. "Sin," says the apostle, "is anomia," a "transgression of, or a want of conformity to the moral law."[86]

This self-assured revivalist never tired of inveighing against "thousands of…grave theologians [who] have gravely taught this monstrous dogma [of man's natural depravity]." His blood must have approached the boiling point when he thundered: "There never was a more infamous libel on Jehovah! It would be hard to name another dogma which more violently outrages common sense. It is nonsense—absurd and utter NONSENSE!"[87] To Finney, moral sinfulness consists only in selfishness, a state of voluntary committal of the will to self-gratification. Sin is the bad habit of self-indulgence learned from youth.[88] But such views do violence to the clear teaching of Scripture and are diametrically opposed to what Paul declares in Romans 5:12–21. The Apostle emphatically states that "through one transgression (Adam's sin) there resulted condemnation to all men" (v. 18), and it was through the disobedience of one man (Adam) that "the many were made sinners" (v. 19). As the New England Primer of 1688 put it, "In Adam's fall We sinned all."[89]

---

[85] Ibid., p. 478. Cf. Smith, "Theology of Charles Finney," p. 109, n. 76, and Lucas, "Charles Finney's Theology of Revival," p. 203.

[86] Charles Finney, *Lectures on Systematic Theology,* p. 248 (cf. p. 333).

[87] Charles Finney, "The Excuses of Sinners," sermon in *God's Love for a Sinning World* (Grand Rapids: Kregel Publications, 1966), p. 57. Those who still persist in drawing parallels between Edward's revival and Finney's revivalism should note an irony that perhaps Finney himself did not consider. It is true that both men wrote and preached against Unitarianism. In fact, it was the work of John Taylor (1694–1761), an English Unitarian (*The Scriptural Doctrine of Original Sin Proposed to Free and Candid Examination,* 1740), that prompted Edwards to counter with his work on original sin in 1757. Yet Finney's statement on human nature cited above is remarkably similar to that of Taylor, who represents the Unitarian position: "A representative of moral action is what I can by no means digest. A representative, the guilt of whose conduct shall be imputed to us, and whose sins shall corrupt and debauch our nature, is one of the greatest absurdities in all the system of corrupt religion" (*Original Sin* [London, 1845], pp. 177–78, cited in Foster, *A Genetic History of the New England Theology,* p. 82). These two statements—the one by Finney and the other by Taylor—give us a partial explanation of why New England, inundated with revivalism, could so easily and in a relatively brief period of time succumb to apostasy. Both Taylor the Unitarian and Finney the revivalist were promoting falsehood!

[88] Lucas, "Charles Finney's Theology of Revival," pp. 205–09.

[89] "New England ABC" in *The Annals of America,* 18 vols. (Chicago: Encyclopedia Britannica, 1976), 1:276.

Finney Was a Moralist.

Finney taught that man was an autonomously free moral agent, and is therefore expected to change his own heart from a course of disobedience to God to obedience.[90] According to him, man does not need a new faculty to love and serve God. The Christian receives no new nature, Finney claimed, "but only consecrates to God those [faculties] he had from the commencement of his being."[91] His idea of regeneration is a self-initiated change of natural moral condition, not the supernatural impartation of spiritual life to a spiritually dead person by the Holy Spirit.[92] Finney wrote,

> It is not a change in the substance of soul or body. If it were, sinners could not be required to effect it. Such a change would not constitute a change of moral character. No such change is needed, as the sinner has all the faculties and natural abilities requisite to render perfect obedience to God. All he needs is to be induced to use these powers and attributes as he ought. The words conversion and regeneration do not imply any change of substance but only a change of moral state or of moral character. The terms are not used to express a physical, but a moral change. Regeneration does not express or imply the creation of any new faculties or attributes of nature, nor any change whatever in the constitution of body or mind.[93]

Finney's view of the atonement was likewise influenced by moralism. To him, God was the moral ruler of a universe in which man has the totally free choice to either accept divine regulations on his conduct and be rewarded with salvation or reject them and be cursed. Christ's atonement, therefore, became merely a moral "persuasion" of enlightening man's mind to accept God's rule. In endorsing the governmental view of the atonement, Finney deliberately repudiated the penal substitutionary death of Christ:

---

[90] David L. Weddle writes, "The key to this theology is the unshakable conviction, gained in the study of law,…that conversion is reasoned decision to submit to God's moral government, as an act entirely within the sinner's natural powers" (*The Law as Gospel,* p. 6).

[91] Charles Finney, "Making a New Heart," sermon based on Ezekiel 18:31, reproduced in Revival Theology Resources [document on-line] (Lovejoy, GA: Trumpet of Zion Revival Ministries International, 1995, accessed 12 June 1996); available from http://www.xmission.com/%7Egastown/revival; Internet.

[92] Finney defined regeneration as "a radical change of ultimate intention." It "must consist in a change in the attitude of the will, or a change in its ultimate choice, intention, or preference." But man himself effects this change (*Lectures on Systematic Theology*, p. 223).

[93] Ibid., p. 494.

> In the atonement God has given us the influence of his own example, has exhibited his own love, his own compassion, his own self-denial, his own patience, his own long-suffering, under abuse from enemies.... This is the highest possible moral influence.... The influence of the Atonement, when apprehended by the mind, will accomplish whatever is an object of moral power.... To suppose...that Christ suffered in amount all that was due to the elect, is to suppose that he suffered an eternal punishment multiplied by the whole number of the elect.[94]

The legal mind of the revivalist failed to see that the value of Christ's suffering was not in its amount or quantity but its quality: the provision of a perfectly righteous and obedient substitute who propitiated the wrath of God on behalf of absolutely helpless sinners.

Ironically, the legal-minded Finney rejected the biblical teaching of an essentially judicial act— justification. It was Nathaniel Taylor's aim to overthrow forensic justification, and Finney was the self-appointed agent to carry out the mission.[95] To him, justification by faith is not "a forensic...proceeding," but "a governmental decree or amnesty based upon the infinite love of God.... For sinners to be forensically pronounced just is impossible and absurd."[96] The ground of justification, then, is not the vicarious sacrifice of Christ for the sinner but divine benevolence.[97] It was the sinner's own obedience, not Christ's, that precipitated the divine pronouncement of pardon. Consequently, to Finney, there is no need for the imputation of Christ's righteousness to believers. Indeed, he wrote,

> The doctrine of an imputed righteousness...is founded on a most false and nonsensical assumption.... [Christ's obedience] can never be imputed to us. He was bound to love God with all his heart, and soul, and mind, and strength, and his neighbor as Himself. He did no more than this. He could do no more. It was naturally impossible, then, for Him to obey in our behalf.[98]

---

[94] Finney, *Skeletons on a Course of Theological Lectures by the Rev. Charles G. Finney* (Oberlin, OH: Steele, 1840), pp. 259, 255. Cf. Garth M. Rosell and Richard A. G. Dupuis, eds., *The Memoirs of Charles G. Finney: The Complete Restored Text* (Grand Rapids: Zondervan, 1989), p. 51; Finney, *Lectures on Systematic Theology*, pp. 334–35.

[95] Yet Edwards' preaching of this very doctrine of forensic justification was evidently the divine means of initiating the Great Awakening in New England.

[96] Finney, *Lectures on Systematic Theology*, pp. 382, 401, 395, 384.

[97] Finney, *Lectures on Systematic Theology*, p. 401; Benjamin B. Warfield, *Perfectionism* (Philadelphia: Presbyterian and Reformed Publishing, 1980), pp. 153–55.

[98] Finney, *Lectures on Systematic Theology*, Bethany House Publishers reprint edition (1994), pp. 362–63, cited in Lucas, "Charles Finney's Theology of Revival, pp. 209–10. Cf. Charles G. Finney, "Justification by Faith" in *True and False Repentance: Evangelistic Messages* (Grand Rapids: Kregel Publications, 1966), pp. 54–55, 59, 60..

It is easy to see that, for Finney, the active and passive obedience of Christ did nothing to secure the sinner's righteous standing before God. All that is left is man's own righteousness which God accepts as sufficient. Conversion then is by man's initiative. Finney insisted "that the actual turning, or change, is the sinner's own act."[99] "It is apparent that the change…, effected by the simple volition of the sinner through the influence of motives, is a sufficient change; all that the Bible requires. It is all that is necessary to make a sinner a Christian."[100] In responding to Finney's theology of moral determinism that "all holiness [consists in] the right exercises of our own will or agency," Benjamin B. Warfield wrote, "It is quite clear that what Finney gives us is less a theology than a system of morals. God might be eliminated from it entirely without essentially changing its character. All virtue, all holiness, is made to consist in an ethical determination of will."[101]

Finney Was a Rationalist.

What should be abundantly clear from Finney's own comments is that he refused to accept anything that contradicted his understanding.[102] His conclusions were not based on a careful exegesis of Scripture, but were derived from his own empirical reasoning. For example, in defending his view that God would never command anything beyond our ability, he writes,

> *A gracious* [God-given] *ability to do our duty* is absurd. It is a dictate of reason, of conscience, of common sense, and of our natural sense of justice, that if God require of us the performance of any duty or act, he is bound in justice to give us *power* to obey; i.e., he must give us the faculties and strength to perform the act.[103]

Finney would not accept the Calvinist view that God requires of men what is above their ability for the very purpose of convincing them of

---

[99] *Sermons on Important Subjects* (New York: Taylor, 1836), p. 20.

[100] "Making a New Heart," n.p.

[101] Warfield, *Perfectionism,* p. 193.

[102] A younger contemporary of Finney, Albert Temple Swing, called him "the most rational theologian and evangelist America has ever produced" ("President Finney and an Oberlin Theology," *Bibliotheca Sacra* 57 [1900]: 469). According to Weddle, foundational to Finney's theology was his belief "that God rules by the rational principles of moral law; therefore, any theological statement must satisfy the demands of reason and conscience" (*The Law as Gospel,* p. 113).

[103] *Sermons on Important Subjects,* p. 25. Cf. Smith, "Theology of Charles Finney," p. 83.

their sinfulness, and divesting them of all pride.[104] In reality, Finney's own logical authority preempted the authority of Scripture.[105] Princeton theologian Charles Hodge (1797–1878) assessed accurately Finney's rationalistic approach when he wrote,

> The system of Professor Finney is a remarkable product of relentless logic. It is valuable as a warning. It shows to what extremes the human mind may be carried when abandoned to its own guidance. He begins with certain axioms, or, as he calls them, truths of reason, and from these he draws conclusions which are indeed logical deductions, but which shock the moral sense, and prove nothing but that his premises are false.[106]

Faith in man's autonomous plenary ability to respond to God's moral laws of righteousness was the heart of Finney's revivalism. Atonement was only a government transaction; regeneration is simply a change of attitude.[107] No wonder that Charles Hodge remonstrated that "a very slight modification in the form of statement, would bring the doctrine of Mr. Finney into exact conformity to the doctrine of the modern German school [of rationalism], which makes God but a name for the moral law or order of the universe."[108]

CONCLUSION

Seven years after the beginning of revival in Northampton, Jonathan Edwards had had time to soberly reflect on the subject. He came to the firm conclusion that the Great Awakening, in spite of some emotional outbursts and strident criticisms, was a movement of God. At a Yale commencement in 1741, he preached on 1 John 4:1–7, encouraging the hesitant to support the revival,[109] because it bore what he believed were the scriptural

---

[104] John Calvin, *Institutes of The Christian Religion,* trans. Henry Beveridge (Grand Rapids: Eerdmans, 1966), Bk II:7:8, II:8:3.

[105] Smith, "Theology of Charles Finney," p. 74.

[106] Charles Hodge, *Systematic Theology,* 3 vols. (reprint ed., Grand Rapids: Eerdmans, 1982), 3:8–9.

[107] Hannah, "The Doctrine of Original Sin in Postrevolutionary America," p. 252.

[108] *Biblical Repertory and Princeton Review* 19 (1847): 239.

[109] Edwards was not adverse to promoting revival; in fact, he used every available legitimate means to do so. The problem is not in the promotion but *what* is being promoted. Finney publicized anthropocentric revivalism using questionable and even unscriptural methods; Edwards enthusiastically endorsed what he considered a heaven-sent movement by the use of means in accord with Scripture. Moreover, there is a difference in the *kind* of promotion involved: Finney promoted revival in the sense of producing it; Edwards promoted what he believed God had already initiated.

indications of divine activity. His address was soon after published as *The Distinguishing Marks of a Work of the Spirit of God.* Those marks can still be used as valid criteria for recognizing a God-sent revival. Genuine revival, Edwards said, will

> (1) Produce a greater esteem for Christ (1 John 4:2–3);
> (2) Operate against the interests of Satan's kingdom (1 John 4:4–5);
> (3) Cause a greater regard for the Holy Scriptures, "and establishes them more in their truth and divinity" (1 John 4:6);
> (4) Lead persons to truth, convincing them of those things that are true (1 John 4:6); and
> (5) Be an evidence that the "spirit that is at work among a people…as a spirit of love to God and man…is…the Spirit of God" (1 John 4:7).[110]

An inference that Edwards draws from these scriptural marks of revival is

> that the extraordinary influence that has lately appeared, causing an uncommon concern and engagedness of mind about the things of religion, is undoubtedly, in the general, from the Spirit of God.… And certainly we must throw by all talk of conversion and Christian experience; and not only so, but we must throw by our Bibles, and give up revealed religion; if this be not in general the work of God.[111]

Another inference we may draw from this study is that doctrine determines direction. It has not been my intention to discuss at length the "Finneyan formula," i.e., Finney's measures for generating revival, and I have mentioned only two clearly legitimate means God may use to beget genuine revival: prayer and gospel proclamation. I have centered on the doctrine behind the means in order to demonstrate that the kind of theology a person owns (to borrow a Puritan expression) will determine the kind of methods he will espouse. Edwards was a Calvinist whose regard for God's sovereignty and holiness and man's utter sinfulness appears to have governed his theology and hence his view of revival and his means of promoting it. While Finney gave lip service to divine sovereignty, he was by doctrine and practice an Arminian. His brand of New Haven theology popularized revival and reduced it to a program of social betterment and improved self-esteem. "If," as J. F. Thornbury writes, "Charles G. Finney's evangelism rode the waves of confidence in man's abilities," Edwardsian preachers, like Asahel Nettleton, "clung tenaciously to the rock of the older view that man is totally corrupt and cannot save himself. The symbol of the one type

---

[110] "Distinguishing Marks" in *Works,* 2:269.

[111] Ibid.

of evangelism is the anxious seat, to which men were publicly pressured to repair. The symbol of the other is an inquiry meeting, where trembling sinners were pointed to Christ."[112]

The theological difference between revival and revivalism must be realized but often can be appreciated only by contrast, which has been the attempt of this essay. To summarize this contrast, consider the comment by a new measures revivalist, Horatio Foote: "Man's hope ain't worth a groat [piece of grain] that isn't founded on obedience." This sounds viable until we consider its more biblical counterpart by an advocate of genuine revival, Josephus Brockway: "Man's hope is good for nothing that is not founded on the merits of Christ, and evinced by obedience."[113] Such a seemingly paltry difference is immense when we consider its implications. Finney's rationalism convinced him that man is independently capable of obedience, and the revivalist's desire for converts drove him to preach a pragmatic gospel corrupted by heretical doctrine regarding the gospel of Christ. Such a gospel will not produce genuine revival if Paul's warning in Galatians 1:8–9 has any meaning. If conversions resulted from Finney's meetings, it was not because of, but in spite of, his message. Certainly, Jonathan Edwards had theological inconsistencies, but what concerned him was careful adherence to the orthodox Bible doctrines of Adamically inherited, innate depravity of the human heart; man's total inability to save himself from the effects and punishment of sin; forensic justification and the imputation of Christ's perfect righteousness through faith; gracious redemption on the basis of the vicarious atonement of a sinless Savior; and regeneration of believers by the Holy Spirit. The preaching of *these* doctrines God has used to save souls and bring spiritual awakening.

We may long for and fervently pray for revival, but accompanying heaven-sent petition must be a clarion proclamation of the message of Edwards, delivered in the power of God. In such a holy enterprise, we would not be preaching sensational sermons of self-improvement, but scriptural ultimatums that denounce sin, divest sinners of any pretense of righteousness, demand repentance, and declare the gospel of Christ in clarity and purity. Our motive would not be personal success, but scriptural obedience; our aim, not numbers, but the glory of God. As Doug McLachlan reminds us, "That's why the concern for revival, it's [*sic*] central burden and most impassioned obsession is the restoration of God's

---

[112] J. F. Thornbury, *God Sent Revival: The Story of Asahel Nettleton and The Second Great Awakening* (Grand Rapids: Evangelical Press, 1977), p. 204.

[113] Josephus Brockway (*A Delineation,* n.p., 1827, pp. 57–58), cited in Warfield, *Perfectionism,* p. 28, note 70.

name to the exalted position which it deserves in our lives and culture. In revival there is no room for self-centered motivations, only hunger for divine exaltation!"[114] As we exalt Christ and zealously evangelize with His doctrine, may we not then hope that God would awaken many from darkness to His marvelous light by sending revival to our communities and churches?

---

[114] Douglas R. McLachlan, *Reclaiming Authentic Fundamentalism* (Independence, MO: American Association of Christian Schools, 1993), p. 147.

SCRIPTURE INDEX

416

424

428